The Medvedev Papers

The Medvedev Papers

*Fruitful Meetings Between
Scientists of the World*

*Secrecy of Correspondence
is Guaranteed by Law*

ZHORES A. MEDVEDEV

Translated from the Russian by
VERA RICH

With a foreword by
JOHN ZIMAN, F.R.S.

MACMILLAN
ST MARTINS PRESS

SBN Boards: 333 12520 7
Library of Congress Catalog Card Number: 73-139219

First published 1971 by
MACMILLAN LONDON LTD
London and Basingstoke
Associated companies in New York Toronto
Dublin Melbourne Johannesburg & Madras

Printed in Great Britain by
LOWE AND BRYDONE (PRINTERS) LTD
London

Contents

Secrecy of Correspondence is Guaranteed by Law

Foreword

THE author of this book scarcely needs formal introduction. From the very first page, he speaks to us in his natural voice: spirited, witty, resourceful and ironical. What he has to tell us is devastatingly simple and clear. Turn to his Preface and read on.

When you have finished, however, you will surely wish to know more about him. The basic biographical facts about Zhores Aleksandrovich Medvedev are as follows:

He and his twin brother Roi—now a scholar and historian—were born in Tiflis in 1925. Their father came from Astrakhan, of a modest Russian family of craftsmen and tradesmen, and had recently served in the Red Army: their mother was a professional 'cellist, from a Jewish family of technicians, dentists, music teachers, etc., in Tiflis. In their childhood they lived in Leningrad, where their father taught at the Military-Political Academy and became a Professor of Philosophy at Leningrad University.

By the time he was fourteen Zhores was already interested in biology. Then came those terrible years that scarred every Russian family. In 1938 his father was arrested; he died three years later in some camp in the Far East. Zhores himself served, and was wounded, in the war before entering the Timiryazev Agricultural Academy in Moscow, where he graduated in 1950. He married a fellow student, also a biochemist, and they now have two sons, aged seventeen and thirteen. Until 1963 he worked on the protein and nucleic acid metabolism of plants at the department of Agrochemistry and Biochemistry of the Timiryazev Academy. He then moved to Obninsk, about 110 kilometres from Moscow, to start a laboratory of Molecular Radiobiology, of which he was the head until he was dismissed in 1969. In October 1970, after a period of unemployment, he was appointed as 'Senior Scientist' of the Laboratory of Proteins and Amino Acids of the Research Institute of Physiology and Biochemistry of Farm Animals, at Borovsk, a long and complex bus journey from his home in Obninsk.

A*

For a real scientist, his true biography is his list of publications—his contribution to knowledge and the record of his intellectual progress. I am not qualified to comment on Dr Medvedev's scientific work, but two monographs and a hundred original papers is a good output in twenty years. From this evidence, and especially from the interest shown in his research outside the Soviet Union, it is clear that he has worked with steady concentration as a professional biologist until he is now an expert of international reputation—one of the dozen or so people in the world who can speak with genuine authority on his own specialized topic. As in every field of human activity, there are always higher peaks of influence and fame for those who are luckier or more ruthlessly ambitious, but Medvedev's position in the scientific community is unassailable. He writes from personal experience as a dedicated and successful research worker, with complete mastery of his vocation.

How, then, did he come to write the present work? Like the vast majority of Soviet scientists, he has been abroad only very briefly. His only visit to the West was two weeks in Paris for the International Conference on Isotopes in Scientific Research sponsored by UNESCO, in 1957. There he made his first foreign friends, and was stimulated to learn to speak, write and read a vivid and fluent variant of English. Since that time he has built up, by long letters, picture postcards, and warm hospitality to occasional visitors to Russia, a circle of scientific friends of all nationalities. All this comes out very clearly in this book.

Unfortunately, biochemical genetics is not a comfortable career in the Soviet Union for an honest and sincere scholar. Medvedev had been the pupil of P. M. Zhukovskii, a botanist with genetical and plant breeding interests, who was in charge of the Department of Botany at the Timiryazev Academy and who had been until 1934 a close collaborator and friend of N. I. Vavilov, the prime target of the venom of Lysenko and his supporters. In 1961 Medvedev began to write a history of the great biological-agronomic controversy that had then been going on for nearly thirty years and is still not certainly ended. This work was privately circulated amongst Soviet scientists and played an important part in the defeat of Lysenkoism after 1964; but Medvedev's attempt in 1967 to have it published in the USSR was rebuffed by the authorities.

In the Foreword to *The Rise and Fall of T. D. Lysenko* (published by the Columbia University Press in 1969), Professor I. Michael Lerner explains in detail how a manuscript of this important historical and scientific document came into his hands, and how he took the decision to translate and edit it for publication in English. As he points out:

Full exposure of what happened in the course of Lysenko's rise and fall can do nothing but good for Soviet science, and the Soviet economy. Indeed, as Medvedev attributes patriotic motives to Vavilov, Pryanishnikov and others, so it is obvious that his own manuscript was written out of concern for the welfare of science and the national economy of his fatherland.

But later, in 1969, Medvedev was, as he relates, dismissed from his scientific post. In June 1970, presumably as a result of writing the present book, he was forcibly detained for several weeks in a mental hospital for 'medical examination'. This is, of course, a method by which the Soviet authorities isolate and intimidate nonconformist intellectuals; but the protests of many leading Russian scholars was so vigorous that he was released without harm. The full story has yet to be told of this episode, although many details, comic, heroic and tragic, are now known to outside observers. The psychiatrist who examined him, for example, diagnosed schizophrenia, on the grounds that Medvedev was engaged in two unrelated activities—gerontology and 'publicism'. Academicians Kapitsa and Engelhardt then suggested that the 'psychiatrist' be given a Lenin Prize for discovering a new psycho-pathological entity—the 'Leonardo da Vinci syndrome'. Historically speaking the whole episode is doubly significant, both as a symptom of an attempted revival of Lysenkoism and as a sign of growing self-awareness by the Soviet scientific community. His friends report that Medvedev is by no means cowed, although he is obviously glad now to return to scientific research.

The present work derives from *samizdat*—i.e. a 'self-published' manu-script that has circulated privately in the Soviet Union and which came into the hands of the publishers by the usual unofficial channels. In the present circumstances, it was clearly out of the question to expect it to be published openly in Russia. Was it right to grasp the copyright of the Russian language version, and to publish this English translation, without the explicit permission of the author?

In the first place, this is a risk that is consciously taken by every author of a 'self-published' work. In default of official publication in Russia he circulates his writing as widely as possible by private means; only by translation and open publication abroad can it eventually reach the full audience for which it is intended in his own country. The opinion of experts on these matters is that such publication, when car-ried out in good faith at the implied wish of the author, is not regarded by responsible Soviet intellectuals as a hostile act. In any case, the author's royalties on *The Medvedev Papers*, like those on *The Rise and Fall of T. D. Lysenko*, will be held in trust on behalf of Dr Medvedev—just as the fee due to a British or American scientific author whose book is translated and published in Russia is sometimes made available to him as a courtesy when he visits the Soviet Union.

It is also clear that Medvedev's writing, however critical of the minor absurdities of Soviet bumbledom and some of the major follies of scientific policy in that country, is profoundly patriotic in intention. A significant parallel can be drawn between his work and Daniel Greenberg's exposure of political machinations and corruption in *The Politics of Pure Science*, which raised such an outcry from the American scientific establishment. The point is, surely, that every bureaucratic machine tries to cover up its mistakes and suppress its critics: the responsible and patriotic citizen knows equally well that it is his duty to his country to expose such weaknesses, before follies turn into scandals, and crimes into tyrannies that imperil the nation. By our own standards of judgement, which must surely be shared by most intelligent Russian scientists, the publication of this book can only lead in the long run to a strengthening of Russian scientific activity, with resulting benefits for the Russian people.

The case for the publication of this particular work is even stronger. As Medvedev points out, again and again, science is essentially an international co-operative activity. From the time of Newton and Leibniz, the natural philosopher has addressed himself to all Mankind, and has sought the assent—or constructive criticism—of his learned contemporaries of every nation. This is not some accident of the growth of modern science within the ancient boundaries of Christendom, or a mere infection by 'bourgeois liberal cosmopolitanism'. The universality of the claim of 'truth' for a particular piece of scientific knowledge demands that it should be acceptable to the widest possible community of educated men—that is, to every scholar who is competent to offer an opinion on the matter, whether Protestant or Catholic, communist or capitalist, Red or White, yellow or black or pinko-grey.

Soviet Science is, therefore, merely a section of World Science—or it would not be science at all. It is, in fact, part of British and American Science, and we are parts of it. The gerontologist in California who responds to Medvedev's scientific questions is as much a member of the Russian scientific community as any research assistant in the laboratory at Obninsk. In my own scientific papers on the quantum theory of disordered systems, I have to take just as much account of, say, the work of Professors Lifshits and Bonch-Bruevich in Khar'khov and Moscow as I do of my more immediate colleagues in Cambridge, Manchester and Sheffield. The plight of Soviet Science is our own plight. These men and women are our professional collaborators; to understand their scientific work properly, we need to know, and understand, their personal situation. When we meet Soviet scholars in person, we find that they are people just like ourselves, with the language and mental climate of our science in common; but many of us have been quite baffled by the complexities and frustrations of arranging visits, exchanges, lectures, etc. In the end, the incomprehensibility of some of their institutional attitudes begins to colour our opinion of their scientific achievements, to our loss as well as theirs. Medvedev's lively description of what actually goes on behind the curtains of secrecy and suspicion is extraordinarily valuable for us, not merely as a guide to practical action in such subtle matters as correspondence and personal contacts but as an impression of the atmosphere in which so much of their research actually takes place.

Finally, this book is important as a contribution to the sociology of the scientific community. In the past decade, a few professional scientists and sociologists have come to realize that this is, in itself, a special human group, organized and behaving in its own peculiar way, with its own goals, norms and institutional patterns. If we are to understand what 'Science' is and does, then we must also observe and interpret what scientists actually do, not merely in the privacy of the laboratory or study but in the committee room, lecture theatre and conference hall. Unfortunately, these investigations limit themselves to evidence drawn from the United States and Western Europe, usually ignoring the rich variety of other modes of behaviour and organization in other parts of the world. Of what value are our solemn sociological generalizations about professional recognition, the resolution of controversies, the institutionalization of dissent, etc., when they have not been tested under other skies, on other 'tribes', in very different social and political contexts? Evidence about science in the Soviet Union is limited to the artistic fictions of a novel, or to the meaningless numerical 'facts' of a ponderous OECD survey. Although Medvedev writes in a very personal and direct style, without the trappings of sociological jargon, he has the eye and spirit of the social observer, and gives us an invaluable picture of the workings of the scientific profession in his corner of the globe. The knowledgeable reader may notice occasional errors or misconceptions in his rosy picture of scientific life in Europe and America—

our tax authorities, for example, are not all *that* pliant—but considering his lack of personal experience of Western life it is surprising how well he understands the way we manage our affairs.

To support his proposals for reform, he also states a number of general principles that add up to a coherent philosophy of contemporary science. However much we may feel the self-evidence of such features of modern scientific work as the international division of labour, the importance of rapid communication and the dominance of expensive apparatus, there are few books where these features are emphasized with such force and clarity. Dr Medvedev's analysis of Soviet Science is universal in scope; in many respects to a degree that perhaps he himself does not realize he speaks for the whole scientific community against the uncomprehending and obstructive layman—politician, customs officer, journalist, publisher, cost accountant, government official, army officer, postman or policeman—in every country under the sun. We cannot afford *not* to publish, and read, and publicize his book.

J.M.Z.

Translator's Note

THIS book is translated from two manuscripts of Dr Zhores Medvedev, which were prepared primarily for private circulation among his immediate circle of friends and acquaintances. Accordingly they were not received in precisely that form of finished perfection which one normally associates with a manuscript submitted for press, nor was it possible to consult the author about certain obscurities in the text.

Accordingly, in the course of translation, a number of minor slips have been corrected without note or comment. Certain passages, however, seem to have been based on incomplete or erroneous information—Dr Medvedev, for example, does not seem to have heard of the currency restrictions imposed by Western countries upon their citizens who wish to travel abroad. Such passages have, however, been left as they stand, as further evidence of the difficulties encountered by a Soviet citizen in obtaining or attempting to obtain reliable information about conditions prevailing outside the socialist bloc.

My thanks are due to a number of people who have provided information concerning certain details of current Soviet practice and law, in particular to Mr Peter Reddaway and Dr Ivo Lapenna of the London School of Economics, to Mr Victor Swoboda of the School of Slavonic and East European Studies, London, and to Mr Wolodymyr Mykula, for assistance in deciphering certain near-illegible passages in the text, and to the United Nations Association for providing the standard English versions of a number of UN texts quoted in the course of this work. Thanks are also due to all those who so kindly gave permission for their correspondence with Dr Medvedev to be quoted, in particular Dr Bernard Strehler and the Ciba Foundation for making available the English originals of certain of these letters.

The transliteration of Russian and other Slavonic names used throughout this book generally follows the British Standards specifications for transliteration. For typographical clarity, however, the final apostrophe ('soft sign') is omitted in names such as Gogol and Ryazan. When an accepted English version of a name exists, however, this is used in preference to the strict transliteration—'Beria' rather than 'Beriya', 'Tchaikovsky' rather than 'Chaikovskii'.

V.R.

I

'Fruitful Meetings Between Scientists of the World' Pravda,
11 September 1966

Preface

IT is obvious today that science and technology, and the various forms of art, all unite humanity in a single and interconnected system. As science progresses, the world-wide co-operation of scientists and technologists becomes more and more of a special and distinct intellectual community of friendship, in which, in place of antagonism, there is growing up a mutually advantageous sharing of work, a co-ordination of efforts, a common language for the exchange of information and a solidarity, which are, in many cases, independent of the social and political differences of individual states. This process finds its expression in the creation and development of numerous international scientific and technological societies and associations, in the rapid growth of the number of international congresses, conferences and meetings, in the organization of international institutes and laboratories and combined projects in science and technology. The proportion of 'classified' scientific information in the overall volume of scientific knowledge is continually decreasing.

However, in different countries this historical process of scientific, technological and cultural integration proceeds at different rates, and sometimes runs into definite barriers. Not all the groups of people on our planet are moving with the same enthusiasm and understanding towards this world-wide integration that has irrevocably caught up the world of science. To some people it seems that the free intercourse of peoples of all nations must necessarily be preceded by political unification, the remodelling of all countries on the patterns presented to the world by the USSR or China, the USA or France. The task of the present work is to show the undoubted error of this concept and the loss which is inevitable for countries which put it into practice.

This book consists of three parts. The first part describes some actual incidents which aroused the author's interest in the problem under discussion. Here it is shown how individual efforts in the field of international scientific co-operation may run up against old prejudices and a system of isolation which complicates and impedes natural and necessary links between scientists.

In the second part, a general analysis is given of the immediate economic and political harm done to the country by a policy of restricting the scale and form of international co-operation of scientists and technologists.

In the third part of the book, we consider the legal rules and legislation which, in the USSR and in other countries, govern the foreign travel of citizens, and which in a number of cases preserve an ignorance and violation of the rights of man that are in sharp contrast to the current trends towards the development of the continuity of mankind.

ZH. H. MEDVEDEV

PART I

Some Personal Experiences

A scientist sets out on a course of international co-operation, not under the influence of some directive, but on account of a natural need, a natural necessity connected with his current scientific work, with the more rapid solution of some problem or question in mind. The very structure and burgeoning activity of the world community of scientists involve the individual scientist in scientific co-operation, drawing him like a grain of sand into a whirlwind, into the common vortex of science which did not exist before. And if that grain of sand is held to the ground by some force which stops it entering the general vortex motion, then the whirlwind moves on and the grain of sand is left lying where it lay.

The first section of this work describes the attempts of particular scientists to avoid being excluded from contemporary international science, to enter into a system of intellectual co-operation with colleagues abroad, and to find the same opportunities for work and co-operation which others enjoy. We shall not refrain from showing how these particular attempts, born of international traditions, run into forces and rules which strive to keep the grain in its place, protecting it from the indrawing action of the whirlwind of world science.

I

The Fifth International Congress
of Gerontology

AT the end of March 1960 I received a letter from California in the official envelope of the International Association of Gerontology. At that time few people had heard of gerontology, the special science concerning the processes of ageing in the living world. The letter was written in English and came as a surprise to me. Its text was as follows:

Dear Dr Medvedev,
As President of the Fifth International Congress of Gerontology, it is my great pleasure and privilege to tender you this official invitation to participate in the Congress when it meets in San Francisco next August. All of us believe that your participation will serve to enhance the study of gerontology through the mutual sharing of knowledge and experiences.

Within a short time I shall send you the preliminary program and the enrolment form.

I shall be looking forward to welcoming you personally to San Francisco. In the meantime, if there is anything I can do to facilitate your planning, please feel free to call upon me.

Please be assured of my warm regards and esteem.
Sincerely yours,

LOUIS KUPLAN
President

Louis Kuplan's letter excited me considerably, and for several days I wondered why he was interested in my work in gerontology, which was little known at that time. In 1960 this science had not been developed very far in the USSR, and most of the scientists involved in it were amateur gerontologists who undertook gerontological research in addition to their main work in some other classical field of biology. I myself was such an amateur gerontologist, and my main 'official' work was the study of the biosynthesis of proteins and nucleic acids in plants. During the period from 1952 to 1960, all that I had published in my capacity as a gerontologist was some research on age changes in the protein exchange of plants, and some theoretical papers in which I tried to formulate a new hypothesis of the mechanism of ageing. This hypothesis, which explained the process of cell ageing as being due to the accumulation of errors in the synthesis of proteins and nucleic acids, introduced molecular biology and genetics into the study of the process of ageing, and of course there was an increasing interest at the end of the 1950s in these branches of biology.

All the same, I was puzzled by this letter from Louis Kuplan, who specialized principally in the psychological and sociological aspects of ageing. But some days later I received another letter which dispelled my doubts and aroused a flood of enthusiasm. This time the letter was from Nathan Shock, the well-known American gerontologist, with whom I had been in correspondence for several years and with whom I had exchanged offprints of scientific papers. I saw with amazement from this letter that my colleague was President of the American Gerontological Society. He had been elected to this post, as I learned later, at the beginning of 1960. The gist of Shock's letter, which was longer and more detailed than Kuplan's, was as follows:

Dear Dr Medvedev,

On behalf of the Executive Committee for the Americas, I am pleased to invite you to participate in the Fifth International Congress of Gerontology to be held in San Francisco, California, USA, August 7–12, 1960.

The scientific sessions for the Congress program of the Biological Sciences will be organized under the following general headings: (a) Genetics, (b) Comparative Longevity, (c) Body Composition, (d) Regulatory Systems, (e) Environmental Factors, (f) Cellular Structure, (g) Cellular Physiology and (h) Connective Tissue. . . .

The National Institutes of Health have made a grant to the Gerontological Society which permits us to pay your travel expenses at economy air coach fare from your home to San Francisco and return. We assume that visitors will be able to pay their own living expenses while in the United States. Mr Kuplan has decided to request travel agencies in San Francisco to issue exchange orders to the airline or steamship line which the traveler wishes to use. These exchange orders will be sent to the offices of the lines nearest to the homes of the individuals concerned. . . .

I sincerely hope that you can accept this invitation and will send me at once the name of the line you wish to use and the name of the city of the international airport of embarkation so that I can inform Mr Kuplan.

It is suggested that you make your flight reservations now without waiting for the arrival of the exchange order.

Sincerely yours,

N. W. SHOCK
President, Gerontological Society

Almost simultaneously with Shock's letter there came the rest of details of the congress, the programme of sessions and symposia, registration forms, forms for submitting abstracts of papers and a guide to San Francisco and the neighbouring coast.

Shock's letter was a definite invitation and required rapid decisions. At that time, like most of my colleagues, I could not imagine all the work needed to arrange a journey abroad at short notice. No Soviet scientists had taken part in the previous four International Congresses of Gerontology, and the Soviet Union was not a member of the International Association of Gerontology, since we still did not have a Gerontological Society in our country (it was founded only in 1963). The only public scientific organization for gerontology which we had at that time was the Gerontological Section of the Moscow Society of Naturalists. The bureau of the Section was headed by Professor V. V. Alpatov. I myself was the Academic Secretary.

At the next meeting of the Gerontological Section, my news about the Fifth International Congress of Gerontology was greeted with enthusiasm. Everyone understood how important it was for the development of this science in our country that we should take part in the Congress. The Section adopted a resolution to take part in the activities of the Congress and recommended three of its members for the journey to the USA: Professor V. V. Alpatov, L. V. Komarov and myself. The resolution of the Section was confirmed by the Presidium of the Society and sent, together with copies of the publicity material about the Congress, to the directors of the bodies where the chosen delegates worked. At the same time the Gerontological Section prepared a note addressed to a number of organizations which were interested in this science (the Kiev Institute of Gerontology, which had just been formed, the Khar'kov Centre for the Physiology of Age, the Academy of Medical Sciences, the Department of Science in the Central Committee of the Communist Party of the Soviet Union and others, proposing that they should arrange that Soviet scientists should participate in the work of the Congress as widely as possible. These organizations were also sent photocopies of the publicity material.

Armed with the resolutions of the Gerontological Section and the Presidium of the Society, I went to my own superiors to discuss the practical plans for my making such a journey myself. I should explain that agricultural science, in which I was then working, is not entirely divorced from gerontology. For example, the effect of the age of the parents on the properties and fertility of the offspring; the changes in quality in agricultural produce (such as meat, milk, wool, hides) with the age of the animals—which varies sharply; the regulation of the life span of plants and animals; the sequence of stages of development; the rejuvenation of plants in the fruit-growing industry; the degeneration of forms propagated by vegetative means, and a number of other problems, are matters for intensive study both in gerontology and in general biology. The medical aspects of gerontology form a separate science known as geriatrics.

Professor V. M. Klechkovskii, the head of the Department of Agrochemistry and Biochemistry, which included my small biochemical group, enthusiastically supported my plans and sent a recommendation on the value of the trip to the Rector of our academy. In his turn the Rector quickly prepared an appropriate proposal for the Ministry of Higher and Secondary Education of the USSR. In the Foreign Section of the Ministry the recommendation from the Academy soon received the necessary endorsements, including that of the Minister, and I received permission to write to the USA agreeing to take part in the Congress. I was also permitted to accept the fare for the journey and to thank the Organizing Committee of the Congress for this. About ten days after Shock's letter I sent him a telegram accepting his invitation and informing him that the title of my paper would be 'Ageing at the Molecular Level'.

A week later, at the end of April, I received another letter from Dr Shock, as follows.[1]

Dear Dr Medvedev,
    Your telegram, accepting the invitation to take part in the Fifth International Congress of Gerontology in San Francisco was received this morning. We are all happy that you will have the opportunity of meeting us. Mr Kuplan will send you your travel voucher in the course of the next few weeks.
    I should also like to invite you to act as Honorary Chairman of the Cell Physiology session. Dr Strehler from our laboratory will be in charge from the American side and will deal with all details and preparations.
    I should also like to invite you to visit our laboratories in Baltimore when the Congress in San Francisco is over. If you are able to accept this invitation, then the expenses of this trip will be paid by us on your arrival in Baltimore.
                    Yours sincerely,
                    N. SHOCK (Chief, Gerontology Branch)

[1] This is not the original text; it is a translation of Medvedev's translation—*Translator*.

A few days later came a letter from Dr Bernard Strehler, the American director of the cell physiology section. He notified me of the planned order of work of the session. This plan included several sessions, each with a main theoretical paper by a 'debate-leader' and a subsequent discussion of it. In this discussion one was allowed to make communications about experimental work, but only if it was connected with the subject of the main theoretical speech. My paper came into the 'main' category, and one of the sessions was devoted to the discussion of it. Strehler asked me to send him an abstract of the paper quickly, by 10 May, since at least two months were needed for the publication of the abstracts.

I knew Dr Strehler from his published work as an extremely original researcher who combined his interest in gerontology with work in the field of the biochemistry of plants and who was considered a major specialist in problems of photosynthesis.

I quickly prepared the four copies of the abstract in English which were required and went to the General Post Office so as to get them to Strehler without any delay by express registered airmail. But here I encountered my first difficulty.

'What have you got there?' asked the girl at the international window, turning the package, already stamped and sealed, over and over in her hands.

First of all she looked at the return address. I explained what it was.

'Manuscripts of articles are only accepted from organizations and as laid down in form 103A,' said the girl, giving me back the envelope. 'And it must be handed in unsealed. Private individuals are not allowed to send typewritten material abroad.'

I came back from the post office and went at once to the Academy office that dealt with official correspondence, to ask them to fill out a form 103A for me, or else to send my letter to the USA as official mail. But it turned out that this was impossible. According to regulations, any manuscript material intended for publication must first be provided with a special declaration that it was not of a secret nature and with three signatures of experts, must be reviewed by the Academic Council, approved by the Directors and by the Foreign Section of the Ministry, and finally must obtain a visa from Glavlit,[1] or rather from the Censor.

---

[1] *Glavlit*, the name of the chief organ of censorship in the USSR, originally stood for *Glav*noe upravlenie po delam *lit*eratury i isskustva (Principal director-ate for matters of literature and art)—see the *Small Soviet Encyclopaedia*, Moscow, 1929, vol. 2). But it now denotes the 'Principal directorate for the safeguarding of state and military secrets in the press, attached to the Council of Ministers of the USSR' (Glavnoe upravlenie po okhrane gosudarstvennykh i voennykh tain v pechati pri Sovete Ministrov SSSR) so that the 'lit' part of the erstwhile acronym is now only of traditional significance—*Translator*.

Then, by working backwards, I acquired information about the possibility of sending material abroad, and on the basis of this information how to fill up a form 103A for the post office—signed by the Director and endorsed by the official seal of the organization. This form is filled up in triplicate, two copies of which are handed in at the post office with the letter, while one is endorsed by the post office and kept by the organization as a receipt. Moreover, the Russian text has to be sent to Glavlit, and the English must then be verified as a correct translation. Only after all this can the letter start out on its journey to the addressee.

For all this I had at the most seven days, not counting the six to seven days needed in the post. Naturally it had not even entered Dr Strehler's head that one must ask Soviet authors at least two months in advance, even when it is a matter of barely a page of abstract of a theoretical paper. It would be useless to try to explain to him the difference between myself, and, say, some French author; he simply would not believe there could be such restrictions on sending a mere page of typewritten theoretical text through the post. Abroad it is considered self-evident that it is not a censor but the author himself who decides whether or not his material is secret, and therefore, it is the author and not some commission of experts who bears the responsibility if secret material is published. Moreover this applies only to employees of secret establishments, certainly not to people in agricultural colleges.

Something had to be done. But I found that the next meeting of the Academic Council would not be for another ten days. This clearly would make it impossible to comply with Dr Strehler's request. There were only three possible solutions: firstly, to decline the invitation to take part in the Congress; secondly, to find some short cut to getting a form 103A: thirdly, to get round all these regulations somehow, without breaking the law.

The paragraph of the *Postal Regulations* relating to these restrictions states that it is forbidden to send out manuscripts containing state or military secrets or which may bring political (*sic*) or economic harm to our country. From this point of view, only Glavlit, in the final analysis, can pronounce on the nature of the material. But according to the regulations this refers to typescript and texts prepared for press. A handwritten text can be sent in a private letter without form 103A, but in an ordinary small envelope. This gave me an idea how to comply with Dr Strehler's request without breaking the censorship laws. I would not wait to send him a typescript, nor four copies. I would simply send him a handwritten personal letter in which I would tell him my views on the mechanism of ageing at the molecular level. Then I would appeal to him to edit this into the form of an abstract, pleading that my knowledge of English did not allow me to find the most concise expressions suitable for an abstract. Strehler quickly carried out my request and very soon sent me a copy of the abstract prepared for publication.

In the meantime, after the Minister, Professor V. Elyutin had given his endorsement, the Ministry sent instructions to the Timiryazev Academy for an 'exit dossier' to be prepared for me. At the same time, the Ministry of Health agreed that Soviet scientists should take part in the Congress, and a delegation began to be formed. The head of the delegation was to be the deputy director of the Kiev Institute of Gerontology of the Academy of Medical Sciences of the USSR, the remaining members of the delegation were to be officially treated as tourists. I myself was listed among the delegation, but according to the regulations my 'exit dossier' and everything to do with it were to be dealt with by the department to which the Timiryazev Academy belonged.

An 'exit dossier' for a trip to capitalist (and, in 1960, to all) countries consists, of course, of a series of long forms similar to 'security forms' for those about to work in a secret establishment. These forms include the usual questions on near relatives, any terms of imprisonment, and a description of all the posts which the intending traveller has held in his entire life. In addition, the 'exit dossier' includes a detailed autobiography, copies of the birth certificates of children, a copy of the marriage certificate, medical report, itinerary of the journey indicating the duration and purpose of the visit, and a character reference which constitutes the main document. All the papers are made out in duplicate, and to them must be affixed twelve photographs. The character reference, which must indicate political maturity and moral stability, must be endorsed in triplicate by all one's immediate public and administrative superiors and confirmed at a meeting of the Party Bueau or Party Committee and then at a meeting of the Bureau of the Regional Committee of the Communist Party of the Soviet Union. After this it is endorsed with the Regional Committee seal. All these papers make up the 'exit dossier', which must be forwarded to the Ministry and then to the Central Committee of the Communist Party of the Soviet Union.

My 'exit dossier' went through all these stages very quickly, and towards the end of May I was informed that the Minister of Higher and Secondary Education of the USSR had signed the order for my working visit to the USA for a period of two weeks.

However, my more experienced colleagues assured me that it was far too early for optimism and that the chief hurdle was still ahead. The Ministry's decision, with my 'exit dossier', must be sent for approval to the Central Committee of the Communist Party of the Soviet Union and then be passed on for confirmation by the Section of Science and Higher Education and an 'Exit Commission'. Only the 'Exit Commission' could consider the information about the would-be traveller from his 'file' in the organs of state security. And only after this stage was gone through did the 'exit dossier' go to the Ministry of External Affairs, where a foreign passport was prepared for the traveller and a visa sought for him from the appropriate embassy.

At the beginning of June, the Moscow branch of the Belgian airline SABENA invited me to its office in the Hotel Metropol to settle the details of my flight plan. I had to make a choice between the Polar and Transatlantic routes. The money for the trip had been received from the USA and the Ministry of Higher Education had approved the ticket which bore the same flight dates as those of the rest of the delegation. When I left, the charming young lady assistant from SABENA presented me, as a future passenger, with an elegant SABENA hand-grip.

The date of departure was approaching, and I was working hard at preparing the text of my paper, which was to be delivered in English. During this time, the final programme of the Congress was published and distributed to the participants. This programme allotted me a twenty-minute paper and a summing-up analysis of the discussion at one of the cell physiology sessions.

The programme reached me on 15 June. But two days later I was unexpectedly called to the Ministry, where a bottom-rank employee of the Foreign Section (or rather the Section of International Co-operation) Yu. S. Samokhin, informed me that my trip to the USA had apparently not been approved after all, and that I must notify my foreign colleagues in good time, excusing myself on the grounds of pressure of work or illness or 'family commitments'.

Such a turn of events was quite unexpected and I refused to do as they recommended until I was told why the previous decision had been changed. At first I thought that the entire delegation had had their journey cancelled. But this proved not to be the case, although my colleagues in the Gerontological Section, V. V. Alpatov and L. V. Komarov, had received similar recommendations from their departments (the Foreign Section of the Academy of Sciences of the USSR and the Academy of Medical Sciences of the USSR) and had notified the Organizing Committee of the Congress of their 'illnesses'.

The next day I asked for an interview with the Minister, but was referred to his First Deputy, Professor M. A. Prokof'ev, who was in charge of international relations at the Ministry. The Deputy Minister expressed his regrets, but recommended that I should decline the trip. When I asked for reasons, he became flustered and blamed the employees of the Foreign Section who had delayed sending on my papers to the Central Committee of the CPSU—and according to regulations all dossiers must be received there not later than two months before the proposed date of departure. But this was not quite true, for I happened to know that all the delegation's 'exit dossiers' had already reached the Central Committee of the CPSU. The reason for the refusal, Prokof'ev suggested, should be 'state of health'. I tried to argue and to object, and Prokof'ev was very surprised at this. The discussion began to get heated. I said that I should write the real reason—the fact that the Ministry had refused to approve the trip. Prokof'ev became indignant and accused me of lack of patriotism. According to him, an honourable Soviet citizen would never blame any government department to foreigners. With this we parted, but, as I found out, he at once rang up the Rector of the Timiryazev Academy and recommended that educational measures should be applied to me.

The next day I went to the SABENA office and asked them to cancel my booking and return the money to the Organizing Committee of the Congress. The sum involved was considerable, nearly a thousand dollars. But it turned out that the airline could not do this without instructions direct from the Organizing Committee. And if the Organizing Committee did not cancel the booking at least one month before the flight, then SABENA would retain the money. I therefore had to let Dr Shock know the situation at once. That very day I sent him an express registered airmail letter, saying briefly that the Ministry of Higher Education unfortunately could not approve my trip and that the Organizing Committee should apply for a refund of the money spent on my flight reservation. At the same time I told him that I was continuing my efforts to arrange the trip and that the possibility of my coming had not yet been reduced to zero. (I intended to apply directly to the Central Committee about it.)

Two weeks later, I received the following letter from Dr Shock:

Dear Dr Medvedev,
    I wish to thank you for your letter of June 29. As President of the Gerontological Society, I have written to Prof. Elyutin regarding your attendance at the Fifth International Gerontological Congress.

I have also asked Mr Kuplan, as President of the International Congress, to write to him by air mail.

I have written to Dr Kirk asking him to cancel the arrangements made with CIT (a commercial travel agency) for your ticket and to request a refund to the Gerontological Society. If this is possible, Dr Kirk will arrange to give you a check, payable in dollars, when you arrive in San Francisco. I am sorry that I cannot give you a final promise to do this, since we may encounter difficulties in obtaining a refund from CIT. However, I will do my best and will let you know as soon as possible. I will be staying at the Hotel Whitcomb in San Francisco.

I am also sorry to learn that Dr Komarov is ill and will be unable to attend the Congress.

I certainly hope that all your difficulties will be resolved and that we will see you soon in San Francisco and in Baltimore.

Sincerely yours,

N. W. SHOCK, Ph.D.
Chief, Gerontology Branch

Enclosed in this letter was a copy of the appeal which Dr Shock had sent to the Minister of Higher Education of the USSR. The text of the appeal was as follows.[1]

Dear Professor Elyutin,

The Fifth International Gerontological Congress, which is being held in San Francisco in California from 7 to 12 August 1960 has invited Dr Medvedev (of the Timiryazev Agricultural Academy) to participate in the program. We should like very much to learn of current research on problems of ageing which are taking place in the USSR. We know Dr Medvedev's published work very well, and we should especially like to learn more about his work on the problems of the biosynthesis of proteins in connection with development and ageing. I am writing to you in the hope that you will assist Dr Medvedev to have an opportunity of taking part in the Congress so that we shall be able to learn more of scientific advances in biology which have been made in your country.

Sincerely yours,

N. SHOCK
President, Gerontological Society

Some days later I also received a copy of a telegram sent to the Minister by the President of the Congress, Professor Kuplan.

During this same period a letter came from the Federal Council on Aging in Washington. The author of this letter had not, of course, yet learned of my difficulties, and he wrote as follows:

[1] Translated from Medvedev's Russian text—*Translator.*

Dear Dr Medvedev,

The Federal Council on Aging has been informed that you intend to participate in the Fifth International Gerontological Congress.

The Council extends greetings to you on behalf of the many officials of the United States Government who are engaged in programs and activities devoted to the well-being of older people. The programs and activities are described in the enclosed copy of our 'Report to the President'.

If your plans include a visit to Washington, we would be delighted to have you meet with some of our officials and see some of our work. There may be professional people or program administrators whom you would like to consult, or program operations and laboratories that you would like to observe.

We hope there will be an opportunity for you to be here. If we can be of help in arranging interviews and visits, please write to me regarding your particular interests and your schedule and available time. Should you be interested in certain field establishments outside Washington, we would be pleased to ask them to welcome you.

By direction of the Council.

WARREN T. ROUDEBUSH
Executive Director
Federal Council on Aging

This letter opened up new opportunities for my trip to the USA and I felt that I had no right to slacken in my efforts to help the development of gerontology in our country as much as I could. The only organization which could be of real assistance in less than a month that was left before the opening of the Congress was the Central Committee of the Communist Party of the Soviet Union, and so I naturally turned to them.

I found out that the head of the 'Exit Commission' of the Central Committee of the CPSU was the Secretary of the Central Committee, Comrade M. A. Suslov, and I sent him a detailed memorandum, enclosing copies and translations of the invitations which I had received. In the memorandum I asked Comrade Suslov to look into the situation that had arisen and to come to a decision bearing in mind what was reasonable and in our best interests. I also tried to explain briefly to the Secretary of the Central Committee of CPSU the significance of gerontology and its applied branch, geriatrics, in the struggle to increase the life-span of man. I told him about the achievements of gerontology in the USA, and pointed out how little this science had been developed in the USSR. I also said in my letter that the sum I received from the Gerontological Society would be used to buy from the Congress exhibition trial samples of the large assortment of complex geriatric medicaments and preparations which are produced in the USA and in other

B

countries for it would be a long time before we had facilities for producing such preparations in the USSR. (In the USA strengthening and tonic preparations containing twenty to forty components—hormones, vitamins, salts and stimulants—are widely used. The first such preparation, with eleven components, was not produced and tested in the USSR until 1966.)

The memorandum to the Central Committee of the CPSU was delivered at the window for incoming post in the building of the Central Committee of the CPSU on 9 or 10 June, and I was convinced that in two or three days' time I should be called to the Central Committee. However, it was not until ten days later that they rang me at my work number which I had given on the memorandum. Comrade Filippova, Instructor of the Section of Science and Higher Education, told me to come and see her the following day. Excitedly I went in at Entrance Three of the best known building in Old Square. I was filled with the most optimistic hopes.

I went into a room with the nameplate 'Filippova' (I can't remember her initials) and saw an elderly woman of imposing aspect. And, immediately, without the greeting or the handshake I had expected, there was a sharp question:

'Comrade Medvedev, do you read the papers?'

'Of course I read them,' I replied.

'Obviously you don't read them very well. You ought to know that they're sending U-2 planes over, and dropping spies by parachute. And you've been getting ready to go and visit them!'

'It's not going visiting, it's a congress, and anyway, it's an international congress—not an American one.'

'Well, so it's international, but if this international congress were in West Germany, would you still want to go?'

A conversation begun in this style was no good omen. To all my arguments, Filippova brought out the standard demagogic answers. When I tried to show that if Soviet scientists took part in international congresses it would help raise the prestige of Soviet science, Filippova at once rejected my arguments: 'We don't need the recognition of American pseudo-scientists, we got our sputniks up first. . . .' When I reminded her that the trip was being paid for by the Organizing Committee of the Congress, her reaction was no less swift: 'We don't need charity from American capitalists.' When I asked her why this had happened in my particular case, although a delegation from the USSR was going to take part in the Congress, Filippova beamed: 'Good, so they're going! They'll come back and tell you what went on. They'll bring the materials you're worrying about. The Central Committee knows who needs to be sent. . . .' When I tried to show the need for greater progress in gerontology in the USSR she reacted in just the same manner. 'That's not your worry. When it's necessary we of the Central Committee will worry about it! . . .'

From further conversation it became clear, however, that, although Filippova had on her desk a neat pile of books on physiology and medicine, she was completely uninformed on the questions we were discussing. She knew nothing of the problems of gerontology and had not even read the whole of my memorandum.

As soon as I left Filippova, I wrote a letter of protest to the head of the Science Section of the Central Committee, saying that the explanations I had received were quite unsatisfactory and the instructor was incompetent in the questions she was in charge of. The head of the Section at that time was Professor V. A. Kirillin. As a result of this protest, I was quickly sent for by Comrade Mokhov, the deputy head of the Science Section, who was responsible for Institutes of Higher Education. (Since I worked in an I.H.E., I came within his sphere.)

Comrade Mokhov was more polite than Filippova. All the same, he told me authoritatively that the time for applying for visas had passed, and now only the Secretariat of the Central Committee of the CPSU could intervene; but anyway the matter was too insignificant to be brought to the attention of the Secretariat of the Central Committee. 'Now, if you were a leading scientist like, let's say, Academician Oparin, or if it were a matter of atomic physics, then it might be possible to take the question to the Secretariat of the Central Committee,' said Mokhov. 'But you're not really a leading scientist, are you?' he asked me. Naturally, I could only agree with him. In any case, I was not Academician Oparin, the model for a leading scientist in Comrade Mokhov's opinion.

'But don't get upset,' said Comrade Mokhov as he shook hands. 'I like your enthusiasm. Next time see to all your preparations earlier, and we'll certainly send you. Believe me!'

On 5 August, a small delegation of six flew off to the Congress in San Francisco. I went to the airport to see them off. The delegation consisted of five minor scientists and one young employee of the KGB to keep an eye on them. He was listed as an employee of the Institute of Scientific Information. When they were preparing for the Congress, the Organizing Committee invited five scientists from the USSR whose work was known in the USA. None of them was able to go to the Congress. All those who did go had not been invited in advance. The leader of the delegation travelled at the expense of the Ministry, the four 'tourists' at their own expense, each paying for the trip some 11,000 (old) roubles. Three of them had no connection with serious science, and only one of the delegation read a paper at the Congress on the diseases of women in later life. He was a specialist on the menopause, and was Director of the Tbilisi Institute of Female Physiology and Pathology.

A month later I read in the Academy of Medical Sciences of the USSR the delegation leader's account of the trip. It contained only a formal enumeration of the sessions and papers. The last paragraph of the account was worthy of note. He said: 'All the Soviet scientists behaved themselves with decorum and maintained strict discipline. However, one member of the group, Miss R, did not always react in an adequate manner to the leader's instructions, did not attend the sessions and she was tempted to go on expeditions to the shops. . . .'

2

The Sixth and Seventh International Congresses of Gerontology

THE International Congresses of Gerontology are held every three years. By tradition each new international scientific congress is held in a new country whose achievements in the development of one science or another is recognized by the scientific community of the world. It was decided that the Sixth International Congress of Gerontology should be held in Denmark—in Copenhagen from 11 to 16 August 1963.

Although I was not familiar with the Danish gerontologists (in Scandinavia it is the clinical branches of the science which are pre-eminent), since my paper 'Ageing at the Molecular Level' was published in full in the Proceedings of the Fifth Congress of Gerontology, I was automatically guaranteed an invitation to the Sixth Congress, for the Organizing Committee in the first instance invited to the new congress all the active participants of the last congress.

Since the end of 1962 I had no longer been working at the Timiryazev Agricultural Academy as an amateur gerontologist, but was profession-ally engaged on the study of normal and radiation-induced ageing in the newly formed Institute of Medical Radiology at the Academy of Medical Sciences of the USSR in Obninsk (Kaluga province). I was selected for this institute by open competition for the post of Head of the Laboratory of Molecular Radiobiology. The new institute was conceived as a broad complex of different laboratories, sections and clinics for the study of all aspects of the action of radiation on organisms and the practical applica-tion of radiation in medicine. The irradiation of an organism, in addition to other effects, accelerates the process of ageing, and the elucidation of the molecular mechanisms of this phenomenon was an important task for the newly founded laboratory.

In connection with this I would have especially liked to attend the Sixth Congress of Gerontology. The questions of radiation ageing were a new field for me; no one in the USSR had considered this field before, and at the Sixth Congress a special symposium 'Radiation and Ageing' was planned, in which leading specialists in this field from the USA, England, France and Australia were to take part.

But, my attempt to discuss the possibility of taking part in the Sixth International Congress of Gerontology in Denmark was blighted at the very start. It turned out that the regulations on foreign travel contained the following strict rule: the 'character reference' for a trip abroad could only be given to an employee who had worked in the particular institution for *not less* than a year. Over a shorter period his moral stability and political maturity could not be verified in the manner required.

Two and a half more years went by. In June 1965 I received the following letter.

Dear Professor Medvedev,
On behalf of the International Association of Gerontology I am writing to ask if you will serve as European Chairman of the fourth afternoon Symposium in Biological Sciences of the Seventh International Congress of Gerontology, to be held in Vienna, June 28–July 2, 1966.

This symposium is scheduled for Wednesday, June 29. The subject will be: 'Ageing in tissues, cell populations and cell death.' Your American co-Chairman will be E. Tonna (Upton, N.Y.) and the Introductory Speaker will be B. L. Strehler (Baltimore).

Please let us know at your earliest convenience if you can accept this invitation.
With kind regards.
Sincerely yours,
Prof. Dr F. VERZAR
President, European Biological Research
Committee of the IAG

I shall not hide the fact that I was especially pleased to receive such a letter, particularly since it was signed by Professor Verzar. Verzar's name is very well known to gerontologists. After the death of the founder of gerontology, Professor Lorenchevskii, who also created the International Association of Gerontology, Verzar was chosen as head of this Association. Verzar is a Hungarian, who began his work in gerontology late in life, after winning fame in the fields of physiology and biochemistry. In 1965 Verzar was over eighty, but he was carrying on his active work as a scientist and an administrator. Verzar had founded the first experimental Institute of Gerontology in Europe, in Switzerland, entirely at his own expense.

Not very long before, I had been invited to contribute to a festschrift, *Prospects in Experimental Gerontology*, for Verzar's eightieth birthday.

I was to contribute one of the thirty chapters of the book. Dr Shock was the editor of the book, and it would be prefaced, according to the prospectus, by a biography of Professor Verzar and a description of his institute. At the Vienna Congress of Gerontology it was planned to hold a special session in honour of Professor Verzar and at this session a copy of *Prospects of Experimental Gerontology* would be presented to him as a gift from his colleagues and friends. I knew this plan, which was being prepared by a group of American and European gerontologists, and hence Verzar's letter came as a very agreeable surprise.

In 1960 I had received my invitation four months before the Congress. This time I had a whole year at my disposal, plenty of time for unhurried preparations.

In accordance with existing practice, I sent a short memorandum to the Director of the Institute, telling him that I had received the invitation and attaching a photocopy and translation of the letter. It was the Director's job to advise me how I should reply. Soon afterwards, an assistant to the Director who was responsible for international co-operation informed me that the participation of Soviet scientists in the Vienna gerontological congress was included in the official plan of the Academy of Medical Sciences for 1966, which had been circulated through the usual channels of that Academy. According to this plan, the organization of a tourist group of fifteen people from the medical institutes to go to the Congress was in the hands of the Kiev Institute of Gerontology of the Academy of Medical Sciences. To my enquiry, the Director of the Kiev Institute sent the following letter.

Dear Colleague,
    The tourist group for the trip to Vienna for the 7th International Congress of Gerontology was settled in spring 1965. There are fifteen persons in the group.
    At that time, in answer to our enquiry to the Moscow Society of Gerontologists about suitable candidates for the trip to Vienna, we were given the names of a number of scientists, but unfortunately yours was not among them. It would seem, therefore, that your best plan would be to approach the Section of International Cultural Relations of the Academy of Medical Sciences of the USSR (the Deputy Head is Valentina Georgievna Zakharova) about the invitation you have received and ask to be included as an additional member of this group.

D. F. CHEBOTAREV
Director of the Institute

I did not understand, of course, why I should have been nominated by the Moscow Society of Gerontologists, to which I, as a resident of Kaluga province, did not belong, and why, as a member of the Board of the All-Union Society of Gerontologists, the centre of which was in Kiev, I should not obtain preliminary information about the Congress directly from the Chairman of the Board of this Society, Professor D. F. Chebotarev. Nevertheless, I was grateful to him for his practical advice which I immediately took.

Valentina Zakharova, the personnel supervisor, an energetic woman, received me most courteously in her spacious office in the building of the Presidium of the Academy of Medical Sciences of the USSR. Her large writing desk and numerous shelves were filled with all kinds of foreign publications; on the wall there hung a map of the world showing the widespread links of the Academy of Medical Sciences with other scientific bodies throughout the entire world. In a persuasive and polite manner, she explained to me that over the last few years Soviet scientists had been receiving too many personal invitations from abroad. But since there was a strict limit imposed on the Academy of Medical Sciences and the Ministry of Health from above, restricting the number of man-days—and especially currency-days—available for foreign visits, one could of course only accept official invitations sent by foreign organizations to the President of the Academy of Medical Sciences or to the Ministry of Health. And as my invitation had not been received through official channels the International Co-operation Section unfortunately could not approve me as a candidate.

When I got home I wrote to Verzar, thanking him for his kind invitation. I also told him that I should have been delighted to accept, and that I was extremely interested in the work of the Congress, but since his letter had come too late and the membership of the tourist group was already settled, my trip could not be approved without an official invitation from the organizing committee, sent to the President of the Academy of Medical Sciences or to the Minister of Health of the USSR.

About a month later, I received Verzar's reply. In it he enclosed copies of the official invitations sent by the Organizing Committee and by Verzar himself to the Minister of Health of the USSR and to the President of the Academy of Medical Sciences. In one of the letters sent to the President, Verzar wrote:

Dear Professor Blokhin,
    As President of the European biological section of the International Association of Gerontology and Honorary President of the Seventh International Congress of Gerontology in Vienna (27 June–2 July),

I have invited our esteemed colleague, Zh. A. Medvedev (Institute of Medical Radiology, Obninsk) to read a paper and to be Chairman of the Symposium on Ageing in Tissues which will be held on 29 June 1966.

I am taking the liberty of asking you to make it possible for Dr Medvedev to attend the Congress. We should all be very happy to have a Soviet scientist as Chairman of this Symposium.

A similar letter was sent to the Minister, Professor B. V. Petrovskii.

Another two months went by, but neither the Academy of Medical Sciences nor the Ministry gave any signs of any reaction, at least in my direction. Meanwhile, I received an additional invitation to take part in a special colloquium on the genetic aspects of ageing. This colloquium was being organized by a group of those attending the Congress on the four days immediately before it opened. It was proposed to hold it in a small town not far from Vienna. In addition a letter came from the Organizing Committee in which I was asked, as chairman-elect of one of the symposia, whether they could send me the texts of the papers received for the symposium, so that I could prepare for the discussion and formulate the programme. To this letter were attached the standard instructions for the chairmen of the sessions on the rules for conducting the sessions, and so on.

It was clear that I must let the Organizing Committee and Verzar know the real situation at once, so that in the event of my absence the preparatory work of organization could be carried out by some other scholar who had more freedom to move from country to country.

So, once again, back to the International Co-operation Section of the Academy of Medical Sciences. Zakharova was not there, she was on holiday, on a trip abroad perhaps. One of her colleagues, digging into the post-book, not without difficulty found a record of Verzar's letter. In the post-book was a note that an answer to the letter had been drafted and sent for signature to the President of the Academy of Medical Sciences. And in a special folder she found a copy of the answer. It ran:

Dear Professor Verzar,
Thank you for your letter with the Invitation to Dr Medvedev to read a paper and take part in the Congress of Gerontology in Vienna. The Academy of Medical Sciences is sending a delegation of Soviet scientists to the Congress. Unfortunately, Dr Zh. Medvedev cannot go to Vienna to take part in the Congress since at the present time he is extremely busy with a number of projects.
Sincerely yours, etc.

I went straight away to the International Section of the Ministry of Health to find out the fate of Verzar's second letter. I was worried now, not that the Minister had sent a refusal, but that he had sent a different excuse, illness, for example, or family commitments. But, of course, I was wrong. The bureaucratic machinery functioned properly. The Minister had also answered Verzar's letter and had also regretted 'that Dr Medvedev cannot attend due to extreme over-pressure of work'.

A year and a half later in June 1967, when I met Professor Verzar in Kiev where he had come to attend a Gerontology Symposium at the invitation of the Academy of Medical Sciences and the Ministry of Health, he told me with a twinkle in his eye that it did not surprise him that both the Minister and the President of the Academy of Medical Sciences of the USSR both knew exactly what one of the tens of thousands of employees living in Kaluga province would be doing half a year later in the period from 27 June to 2 July 1966. What amazed him was the exceptional speed with which both these high officials had responded to his letter, and the almost identical wording of their replies.

3

The plan for joint research with Dr Bernard Strehler and the attempt to implement it

NOWADAYS modern science permeates the life of society to such a degree and is so broad and diverse that no single country nor group of countries can provide by itself the whole complex of scientific investigations necessary for the development of society. Any serious scientific problem becomes an international one and is worked on simultaneously by scientists in different countries who each keeps careful track of what the others are doing. Isolation leads only to a senseless loss of time and funds. Between those taking part in such a project bonds arise and co-operation is born, sometimes friendship between those who have never met, often controversy. To attempt to make these personal bonds conform to the framework of some official agreement is impossible and senseless. And if some country restricts and hinders these natural bonds, then it is the first to suffer, creating conditions in which its national science must fall far behind.

Scientists may be divided, irrespective of the power and depth of their thinking and their experimental skill, into two groups; specialists and enthusiasts. The specialist becomes a scientist thanks to his abilities and training, but for him science is a job, and the choice of problems to be investigated is determined by extraneous circumstances: current affairs, the conditions prevailing in the laboratory, the type of organization, top-level decision, and so on. The specialist will with equal skill isolate new bacterial products for antibiotics or death-dealing bacteria for warfare. In the latter case, of course, he will be apprehensive, but only because of the dangerous nature of the work itself. The enthusiast is not dependent on prevailing conditions; he is normally possessed by some definite scientific idea, sometimes from childhood or youth, and, whatever the conditions or circumstances, he strives to work on it and bring it to completion. Often enthusiasm is born in mature scientists too, under the influence of some discovery which they or others have made.

I do not want to create the impression that it is necessary to give special preference to enthusiasts. Science needs both groups, since the working out of fine details, the elaboration of exact methods, the investigation of many branches of science which at first glance seem tedious are absolutely necessary for the development of science and technical progress. Moreover, the enthusiasts include more than a few people who are possessed by erroneous, pseudo-scientific ideas, which do great harm to science. Furthermore, they include egotists and fanatics.

But when a new field of science is created, this is most frequently the task of the enthusiasts. Gerontology as a science was the product of the enthusiasm of a number of scientists who were essentially amateurs in the study of problems of ageing, and whose professional contribution to other fields of biology and medicine were often more significant. Some of the first enthusiasts for gerontology are well known: the microbiologist I. I. Mechnikov; the physiologist, A. A. Bogomolets; the endocrinologist, V. Korenchevskii (who gave the science the name of 'gerontology' and founded the first Gerontology Societies in Europe and the International Association of Gerontology); and the physiologist, A. V. Nagornyi. All these were Russian scientists. Professor V. Korenchevskii, who is known in the West as the 'father of gerontology', was a Professor at St Petersburg University until 1919. He then emigrated to England and worked there until his death in 1958.

One of the most active enthusiasts in gerontology at the present time is the American biochemist Bernard Strehler. Until 1957 he worked away quietly at the biochemistry of plants, and won a wide reputation as the creator of an exceptionally ingenious bioluminescent method of determining energy-rich compounds (the 'macroergs'). In 1957 he found himself involved with the problem of ageing and immediately became a very great authority in the field.

I first read one of Strehler's theoretical works on ageing in 1959. The depth and originality of its approach to the working out of the main problems made a very great impression on me. Previously the majority of scientists in this field, including myself, were involved in trying to find some principal cause or basic mechanism of ageing. Strehler showed convincingly that ageing has many independent mechanisms, that it is a many-channel process. By this he laid the foundations for the linking of different, apparently contradictory, concepts.

My correspondence with Strehler, which began after the Fifth Congress of Gerontology, soon became a regular one. I first met Bernard Strehler in Moscow in August 1961 when he came to the USSR for the Fifth International Biochemical Congress. More than a thousand

Americans took part in this Congress. We quickly became friends. We were both of the same age and shared the same views on many scientific and general problems. Strehler proved to be a man of a broad, progressive outlook; in youth he had had friends among the American Communists, but had changed his outlook somewhat, particularly after the events in Hungary in 1956. Because of these friendships he had been subjected to intensive questioning before a security agency of the American Government.[1]

Strehler began his work on mechanisms of ageing at the Baltimore Gerontology Center, of which Dr Shock was founder and Director. But in 1964, Strehler also established a gerontology laboratory [under Veterans Administration sponsorship]; he was by this time known to many Soviet scientists, since his book *Time, Cells and Aging*, published in the USA in 1962, appeared in Russian translation in Moscow in 1964.

In 1964 I too had finished setting up the laboratory in Obninsk and was endeavouring to direct it to the working out of the molecular mechanisms of ageing. I hope, therefore, that the reader will understand my interest and feelings when I received the following letter from Dr Strehler in the USA.

Dear Dr Medvedev,
    It has been some time since I heard from you. Many things have happened during the last 12 months which bode well for gerontology here in the United States. The Veterans Administration, for example, is setting up a series of satellite laboratories in various locations around the country as a means of stimulating gerontological research. Our new Gerontological Research Building at the National Institutes of Health will be completed about January 1967, and I have recently undertaken to organize a modest-sized lab. as a VA satellite which will cooperate with the scientists in the NIH laboratory.
    Aside from sending you personal greetings and from expressing hope and belief that the more cordial relations among scientists from all parts of the world which have developed during recent years will not be materially altered in the near future, I would like to inquire about the possibility of your spending a year or so in our laboratory either here at the VA Hospital Aging Research Laboratory or in the new NIH Laboratory. I frankly do not know to what extent there are difficulties for you in this regard, and if there are, if they are primarily financial or administrative. If financing your trip, accompanied by your wife and children is a problem, it is possible that some solution

[1] Dr Strehler was never a Communist, but he was sympathetic to various socialistic reforms, and was a close friend of the American liberal, Senator Estes Kefauver, and worked on Kefauver's national staff during the 1956 presidential election—*Translator*.

could be found here and if you can determine that it is administratively feasible for you to join us in a collaborative research effort, I shall use such persuasion and influence as I can muster to help with the expenses involved. I am sure that you would find a visit such as I have in mind a very pleasant and rewarding one which would give you a better insight into the nature of our country and its people and customs and would thus aid in preserving friendly relations. It would also be educational for those Americans who have not yet had the opportunity to meet Russians. . . .

Sincerely,

BERNARD L. STREHLER, PH.D.
Director, Aging Research Laboratory and
Chief, Cellular and Comparative Physiology Section
[Gerontology Center, NIH]

The administration of my institute was very favourably inclined towards this invitation. Only a very short while before, in October 1964 when Mr Khruschchev resigned, important changes took place in biology. The formerly all-supreme 'Michurin biology' or 'Lysenkoism' was under attack in all the newspapers, and in every department resolute measures were being adopted to rebuild Soviet genetics, molecular biology and many other scientific disciplines, in which we had fallen far behind the USA and many European countries during the twenty-five years of Lysenkoism. And among the immediate measures discussed to close this gap, one of the most important points in all the resolutions was to be long-term visits abroad by Soviet scientists to work in foreign laboratories.

Science, unlike industry and economics, can very quickly close any gap that has arisen if a widely co-ordinated programme of experimental and theoretical work is put into operation. And, since the development of science is always mutually beneficial, no country normally hinders widespread scientific exchange, and highly developed countries are always ready to offer other countries the opportunity of direct co-operation. By working, for example, in the USA, and by becoming familiar with modern methods of research and gaining the experience and knowledge which his country needs, a scientist from the USSR, India, Poland or Bulgaria, can at the same time mutually aid the development of the science in his host country and leave there the results of his own research, part of his own intellectual energy. The presence of foreigners, moreover, as experience shows, is a great stimulus to the work of the main staff of the laboratory.

Naturally, since scientific trips abroad were being planned everywhere, the invitation I received could count on a favourable reception from the administration, all the more since the chronicle of scientific exchange in the field of medicine had not recorded a single trip abroad by a Soviet scientist specifically for research in gerontology. The invitation fitted in well, too, with the recent resolution of the Presidium of the Academy of Medical Sciences which planned a broader programme of visits to the USA in connection with questions of genetics and biochemistry.

However, when our institute's proposal on the matter was discussed in the International Section of the Academy of Medical Sciences, the question arose whether the invitation I had received was a unilateral one or whether it proposed an exchange, i.e. that some American gerontologist should come to work in Obninsk or in some other Institute of the Academy of Medical Sciences at the same time. The Academy of Medical Sciences clearly was not disposed to have an American scientist come to our country for protracted work in gerontology.

It was clear to me that Strehler's proposal did not stipulate an obligatory exchange. In most modern laboratories in the USA they plan a certain number of vacancies for foreign scientists coming from different countries. In such cases it is the head of the laboratory who chooses his colleague for joint research, not the 'sending party', as happens in international exchange.

Nevertheless the nature of the invitation still had to be clarified. I sent Strehler a letter, telling him of the initial favourable reaction to his proposal, and asking him to make clear through official channels the nature of the invitation, whether it was an independent one or whether it formed part of some system of exchange of scientists, defined by some formal agreement. I also told him that if I did come, it would be alone and without my family. I knew very well that in such cases it is impossible to take your family abroad. You can only take your family if you are going on a mission that will last more than a year, or if you are a diplomat who always works abroad.

When he received my letter, Strehler took all the necessary steps, but the official invitation was not sent to the President of the Academy of Medical Sciences of the USSR, Professor N. N. Blokhin, until three months later, in March 1965. It should be noted that Professor Blokhin, Head of the Academy of Medical Sciences, was also President of the USSR–USA Society (the Institute of Soviet-American Friendship) which is part of the Union of Foreign Friendship Societies.

The official invitation came [from the Veterans' Administration] on the headed notepaper of the Federal Department of Health, Education, and Welfare of the USA. Its text, which was evidently drafted with the assistance of Dr Strehler, read as follows:

Dear Professor Blokhin,
     It gives us great pleasure to tender hereby an official invitation on behalf of the Veterans' Administration to Dr Zh. A. Medvedev to spend a period of up to a year in a fundamental research inquiry into the genetic basis of the aging process at the Loch Raven Veterans Administration Hospital in Baltimore, Maryland. This hospital is a site of a newly established Aging Research Laboratory (Dr Bernard L. Strehler, Consultant in charge) which is devoted to a fundamental exploration of the sources of aging in human beings and in experimental animals.
     We believe that a collaborative research venture with Dr Medvedev would have a reasonable probability of contributing very important basic information on the nature of the aging process. This problem is the fundamental commitment of this laboratory.
     The theory which Dr Medvedev has suggested as an origin of the decline in function which occurs with aging, namely: the errors accumulated in transcription at the level of ribonucleic acid and protein synthesis is an intriguing one which should receive an early test experimentally.
     We believe that this proposed research offers an excellent opportunity for creative cooperation between scientists of our two countries in the interests of benefits to mankind generally, and that it will, moreover, serve the cause of international understanding and friendship . . . between our peoples.
     If you share our sentiments in the matter of Dr Medvedev's visit we invite discussions from you as to the arrangements. . . . For our part, we are prepared to do what we can to make this visit possible.
                              Sincerely,
                                        JOSEPH H. MCNINCH
                    Chief Medical Director [Veterans' Administration]

A copy of the letter was also sent to me.
     More than two months went by, but I received no indication of the decision about this letter. But at the beginning of June I unexpectedly learned from a very remarkable source that the letter of Dr McNinch had not got lost, but was being studied carefully, perhaps too carefully. One of my colleagues at the Institute was to receive a belated military decoration, in connection with the twentieth anniversary of the victory over Germany. The decoration was presented in Kaluga. At the official banquet in his honour which followed the presentation, one of the guests was the head of the Provincial Directorate of the KGB. Perhaps he had

also received a decoration for the jubilee. Coming up to my colleague, he began to question him about me, with particular reference to my proposed trip to the USA.

In the middle of July I learned that the President of the Academy of Medical Sciences had sent a generally favourable answer to the USA, and soon afterwards our institute received instructions from the International Section of the Academy of Medical Sciences about preparing my 'exit dossier', character reference and medical report for a trip to the USA for six to eight months.

When I returned from leave in September, I received the familiar questionnaire and instructions on the rules for planning my itinerary. The date of departure was set for January 1966. Naturally I let Strehler know at once, since he had been holding his vacancy for a foreign scientist open for almost a year, although he could full well have invited someone else for 1965.

Dr Strehler was delighted to receive my news which, if not definite, was hopeful, and wrote:

> Thank you for your letter of July 2, 1965. I am very happy that progress is being made toward your visit for joint research in our laboratory. I hope that it will occur as you have outlined. . . .
>
> The winters in Baltimore are not severe, but spring, summer and fall are more beautiful times of the year. Dr Daniel Rubenstein will be joining our staff in September. He is a very clever and competent biophysicist who will be working particularly on genetic problems in aging. I am sure that the three of us, plus additional members of the staff, will produce something quite worth while, as the opportunity is presented.
>
> I for one, you may rest assured, will do my best to see that you have a very productive visit, scientifically; and that you will have the maximum opportunity to become acquainted with our country and its people. I believe that this will be equally as beneficial as the research. I hope also, that you will feel free to criticize any aspects of life here in the United States while you are a visitor. This would not be taken as bad manners by most of us and is one way that our people can benefit from contacts with foreigners. . . .

But two months later it seemed to me Dr Strehler was beginning to lose patience. This could be seen from another letter from him, which I did not translate for the higher authorities:

Dear Dr Medvedev,

> I have been waiting eagerly to hear from you concerning the date of your hoped-for arrival in our laboratory, so that we can make specific plans accordingly.

As I was writing the above, I received a call from an official in the Veterans Administration, in which he said that a letter had been received (dated July 7, 1965) from a high official in the Soviet Academy. The letter expressed agreement regarding the desirability of collaborative research here on the genetics of aging, in 1966, and said that a final decision would be made in the future.

Since some $3\frac{1}{2}$ months have passed, you might like to inquire of suitable officials when such a decision will be forthcoming, and, indeed, whether it has been made. If Russian administrative officials have the same characteristics and are as busy as American ones, the appropriate papers may be lying under some other papers on some lower-echelon official's desk. But it usually takes only a single reminder from the directors of organizations to motivate the 'paper-shufflers' into action. . . .

But it was not a matter of paper-shufflers, nor even a matter of the attitude of the Academy of Medical Sciences, which in the preliminary stages, as we have seen, favoured the project. The question of this trip had now been taken up by other departments, whose approval, especially about making a long-term visit to a capitalist country, was obligatory. A copy of Blokhin's letter had been sent to them too, the 'exit dossier' and character reference had to be sent to them as soon as possible, and if they were to say yes or no, they had to make contact with the candidate for a trip abroad.

One day during this period, an affable young man in civilian clothes visited me at the Institute. After a detailed discussion on gerontology, the work we had planned, the history of my acquaintance with Strehler, and so on, he told me very courteously that one of his immediate superiors would like to have a talk with me. I agreed, since I realized that it would be impossible to avoid such a meeting if I really was thinking seriously of going to the USA. After all, doubtless there are special departments to instruct Americans before they visit the USSR.

The meeting with the higher-ranking official soon took place in entirely friendly conditions. Once again there was a detailed discussion of scientific subjects and an exchange of views on current events. It was only right at the very end of our conversation that my interlocutor made me an unexpected proposal about co-operation during my visit to the United States.

I realized at once that my visit to Strehler's laboratory could be considered to be off. On moral grounds, of course, I could not under such conditions avail myself of the offer and invitation of my American friend. But I also realized that this proposal did not relate directly to my trip to the USA but was only a part of some other grand design. I did not, therefore, give a definite refusal at once. It was important for me to find out just what a proposal of this kind really entailed. I did not, however, agree to it, but pointed out that it all depended on what the cooperation involved; if my interlocutor was interested in a deeper understanding of the reasons for the achievements of the USA in biology and gerontology, then I should be delighted to draw up a detailed analysis especially for him when I returned.

At home I carefully thought over the proposal I had been made. It was clear to me that this business had no direct bearing on my trip to the USA, but that the trip had been used as a sort of bait for other purposes. My interlocutor, it was also quite obvious, was employed at the provincial level and had no connection with work in the USA. It goes without saying that if some plans had really arisen in the section dealing with the USA which would involve using the services of scientists, no one would entrust such plans to lowly employees of the internal service. Any business of this kind should be known to the smallest possible number of people.

It was also clear to me that the interest in me shown by the organization represented in these discussions was directly or indirectly connected with their interest in the writer Aleksandr Solzhenitsyn, who was at that time planning to move to Obninsk. Solzhenitsyn's wife, N. A. Reshetovskaya, a physical chemist and biochemist who held the degree of Candidate of Chemical Sciences, had been selected by competitive examination for the post of Senior Assistant in the Laboratory of Chemical Dosimetry in our Institute. Previously she had been working in the Ryazan Agricultural Institute and the Ryazan Polytechnic Institute as a docent in the Chemistry Department. But although the Academic Council of our Institute had selected Reshetovskaya for the post by an impressive majority of the votes (eighteen for, two against) measures were being taken in Moscow to prevent Solzhenitsyn from moving to Obninsk. Furthermore, just at that time in September 1965, three copies of his manuscript novel, *The First Circle*, and a number of his personal papers were confiscated from a friend's flat in Moscow. The editors of *Novyi Mir* had already accepted this novel and announced its forthcoming publication, and it had been lying quietly in the editorial 'files' for some months. But four days after the author took it back from the editors for some revisions, the order came to search the flat of a certain Moscow mathematician, and this caused the manuscript of the novel to fall into new hands. After this, some of the author's friends were summoned to a certain well-known building in the centre of the city, and I was forced to consider that this cup might not pass me by either, since I had played a vigorous part in arranging Reshetovskaya's move to Obninsk, and, from the confiscator's point of view, I was among the possible readers of the 'seized' novel.

In Ryazan, Solzhenitsyn had been unwell; they had lived there in a rather nasty little damp wooden house without any modern conveniences and the local authorities, who were annoyed by Solzhenitsyn's story 'For the Good of the Cause', which told a tale of Ryazan, had for a long time been preventing the author from improving his working conditions in any way.

Obninsk was attractive to the author as a quiet academic town not far from Moscow. He could not live in Moscow itself owing to difficulties with his 'residence permit'. The idea of Solzhenitsyn's family moving to Obninsk arose at the beginning of 1965, after a cordial meeting between the author and his old friend Nikolai Vladimirovich Timofeev-Resovskii, who was in charge of the Section of Radiobiology and Genetics in our Institute. Timofeev-Resovskii, who had a world-wide reputation as a geneticist and biologist, was a man of an exceptionally brilliant scientific talent and broad outlook, while, since the war, Solzhenitsyn had lived through arrest, prison, labour camp, a Convict Research Institute and exile. Chance had decreed that Solzhenitsyn and Timofeev-Resovskii had spent some months together in the same common cell in the Butyrskaya prison in Moscow. There were seventy men in the cell, mainly intelligentsia. Timofeev-Resovskii organized a Scientific and Technical Society in the cell, which met near the window every day after the morning 'rations'. Solzhenitsyn, a physicist and mathematician by training, had graduated from Rostov University not long before the war, and at one of the meetings of this society he gave a talk on advances in the field of atomic energy. After he returned to normal life in 1957 Solzhenitsyn tried to locate Timofeev-Resovskii and find out his sentence, but they did not meet again until 1965, after the head of the prison scientific society had returned from the Urals. He had come to Obninsk in 1964.

In itself, Reshetovskaya's participation in the competitive examination did not depend on these circumstances, and most of the members of the Academic Council did not even know that she was Solzhenitsyn's wife. Only one member of the Examination Commission knew about it, and he had learned of it by chance, from a letter from a former colleague, who had once been a fellow-student of Reshetovskaya's.

The examination for the Institute was a large one, since there were about sixty different vacancies in many different sections and laboratories. A whole new laboratory block had just been opened. In a short space of time, it was necessary to fill seventy new vacancies for scientific workers and almost a hundred posts for engineers, technicians and laboratory assistants. Salaries were specially allotted to the Institute by the State Committee for Science and Technology, and there was an absurd rule that posts must be taken up at once, and all vacancies left unfilled at the end of the year were usually irrevocably abolished. Thus any appropriations not used by the end of the year were cut off, with the result that a rule which had been introduced for the sake of economy actually led to a useless waste of funds.

But taking on new scientific staff to work in an institute in the Kaluga province was an exceptionally complicated business. Moscow was close at hand and was over-populated with scientists of every grade. Institutes had therefore been established in the vicinity of Moscow (there were six in Obninsk) to ease the load on the capital and decentralize science. But in fact the barrier of the 'Moscow residence permit', which once lost, was lost for ever, stopped specialists from coming to Obninsk from Moscow, and the scientists who entered for our competitive examinations came mostly from various other towns, from Siberia, the Urals, Ukraine, Georgia and Central Asia. In 1965 there were a particularly large number of people from Tashkent who wanted to get away from the continual earthquakes. Compared with the general run of scientific talent which the examination brought to Obninsk, Reshetovskaya was clearly first class. It was obvious that she was a fine chemist, she had taken her post-graduate course in the Chemistry Department of Moscow University, she had excellent references for her work and scientific ability, she had been head of a chemistry department for many years, and she was a good teacher, which is of no little importance in a newly formed working group. There were, indeed, no other serious competitors for the post.

After the voting was over, the question of her moving, finding a flat, and so on, came up. And immediately the local authorities began to get worried. The possibility of Solzhenitsyn moving to Obninsk had become a reality, and it was impossible to allot him accommodation since all the housing in the town was departmental property. All this happened in June and July 1965. Until then we had been a quiet and peaceful little town. The Town Committee of the CPSU, the Komsomols and all the other local officials had no cause for alarm. Then suddenly they had to find a flat for Solzhenitsyn and his family. And he, of course, was a figure that many departments, including some high-level ones, had their attention riveted on. In Ryazan, it would seem, a system for keeping Solzhenitsyn under observation had been nicely worked out, and now it all had to be pulled down and built up again elsewhere. In Ryazan, Solzhenitsyn had been something of a lone figure, but in Obninsk he would set up a ferment among the scientists. And Moscow, of course, was twice as close.

I don't know all the details of what went on, but at the end of July, the Academic Secretary of the Institute told me 'as a secret' that Reshetovskaya had been left out of the list of successful candidates which had been sent for confirmation to the Academy of Medical Sciences. It should be noted that successful candidates are officially signed on after the results of the competitive examination have been confirmed by the Presidium and the Personnel Department of the Academy of Medical Sciences. The Director has the right to enrol junior employees as soon as the Academic Council have given a favourable vote.

I quickly let Reshetovskaya know the situation so that she would not give up her job in Ryazan. It so happened that just at this time Solzhenitsyn and Aleksandr. T. Tvardovskii were invited by the Secretary of the Central Committee of the CPSU and Chairman of the Ideological Commission of the Central Committee of the CPSU, Comrade Petr Nilovich Demichev, for a talk on literary matters. While discussing various questions, Solzhenitsyn also told Demichev about the obstacles being put in the way of moving his family to Obninsk. Demichev assured Solzhenitsyn that he would put an end to the illegal persecution, and in his presence put through a call on the direct line to the First Secretary of the Kaluga Provincial Committee of the CPSU and told him very sternly that he must make it as easy as possible for Solzhenitsyn and his wife to move to Obninsk, must have a nice flat allotted to them and must personally see that everything necessary was being done in this matter. The next day the First Secretary of the Kaluga Provincial Committee came to our Institute. He spent two hours in the Director's study, made a quick tour of the Institute and then went off to the Town Committee of the CPSU. The Director of the Institute had his instructions and at once summoned Reshetovskaya from Ryazan, and in the presence of the head of the laboratory in which she was going to work, gave her a most explicit guarantee that the formalities would soon be complete, asked her to choose a flat in a newly built block and urged her to send in her resignation in Ryazan.

But although she did everything she had been advised, the official business of the Institute and the confirmation by the Academy of Medical Sciences were for some reason held up. Soon Moscow wanted all the dossiers of the competitive examination, both junior and senior grades. They were apparently looking for something to find fault with. It is hard to say for certain, but it cannot be ruled out that the Science Section in the Ideological Commission received entirely different instructions. But we were not worried about Reshetovskaya; her personal file submitted to the examination commission was all in order. However, among the sixty other personal files something might well be found out of order. Some references were not in the proper form, some had not had their list of published works officially signed and sealed. These are all very small faults, which no one usually takes any notice of if the scientist is well known and suitable.

Then suddenly came the decision of the Presidium of the Academy of Medical Sciences 'to cancel the results of the *entire* examination', all sixty posts, to change the composition of the examination commission, and to hold the whole examination all over again. At the end of the resolution, and contrary to elementary labour legislation, they stipulated: 'All Staff engaged as a result of the examination are to be dismissed from the posts they are holding.' As we have already seen, the director of an institute has the right to engage junior scientists at once, without confirmation from Moscow. These people had already been engaged by the new institute and had left their old jobs and had moved house; now they were suddenly out of work.

But it was useless to argue—the examination was held all over again. Once more Reshetovskaya was in the list of candidates for election. But at this point a strange event occurred: the manuscript of the novel *The First Circle* was confiscated, although, according to an agreement with *Novyi Mir*, it already belonged to the state. Along with the novel, they also 'arrested' Solzhenitsyn's private papers, including some works which he had written when he was in confinement.

Solzhenitsyn at once let his friends in Obninsk know what had happened, realizing that his wife's chance now of coming to work at the Institute was greatly reduced. Demichev said nothing, although Solzhenitsyn had sent him a letter saying that there had been illegal action in certain quarters.

And, in fact, the Presidium of the Academy of Medical Sciences soon adopted a resolution changing the composition of the Academic Council of our Institute. Seven citizens of Obninsk in the Council were replaced by five people from Moscow. These Moscow men came only once, for the second round of the voting. At later meetings they failed to appear, and so that the Council could go on working, the Obninsk men had to come back and the Muscovites were turned out. But, even with the changed composition of the Commission, Reshetovskaya could still be re-elected if there were a secret ballot. Therefore, following instructions (but no one knew from whom) and moreover contrary to the Regulations for Competitive Examinations, the voting for the post for which Reshetovskaya had applied was put off indefinitely. It should have taken place, and the members of the Council should have been able to demand that it did. But it turned out that the ballot papers had not been prepared and could not be given out to the members of the Council, and without this special type of ballot paper, whatever the outcry, the voting could not take place.

Soon afterwards, in October 1965, a special meeting was called of the Presidium of the Academy of Medical Sciences, with the President, Professor N. N. Blokhin, in the chair. There was only one item on the agenda: should they, or should they not let N. A. Reshetovskaya take part in the repeat of the competitive examination for the vacant post of Senior Scientific Assistant. Summoned to attend the meeting were: the Director and Secretary of the Party Bureau of our Institute, the Chief Academic Secretary and Vice-President of the Academy, the Head of the Personnel Department of the Academy of Medical Sciences and of the Ministry of Health, and the Secretary of the Party Committee of the Academy of Medical Sciences. The whole session was taken down in shorthand and, as was discovered later, a copy of the transcript was sent to the Ideological Commission of the Central Committee of the CPSU. I too was summoned to the meeting because I sent Comrade Demichev a memorandum on the breaches of regulations involved in considering the question of Reshetovskaya's election by competitive examination to the vacant post. When I sent the memorandum to Demichev, I still considered that he had been sincere when he had promised Solzhenitsyn to help eliminate the breaches of law and the special obstacles which were being put in the way of Reshetovskaya's move to Obninsk. This memorandum was a complaint against the arbitrary behaviour permitted by the administration of the Academy of Medical Sciences of the USSR, and I had specially asked Comrade Demichev to deal with the matter himself, or in the Science Section of the Central Committee, and not to pass it on for consideration by the Presidium of the Academy of Medical Sciences. I also asked Demichev's assistant who took the memorandum from me about this. He confidently promised me that he would do as I asked, and would inform his chief of the situation immediately.

But when I arrived at the meeting of the Academy of Medical Sciences, I was astonished to see duplicated copies of my memorandum to Demichev in front of all the members of the Presidium, each of whom told me in his speech that I had not been minding my own business. All the speeches were of the same pattern and all they said was that an employee of an agricultural institute cannot fit into a medical one, even if he is only doing chemistry. It should be said that the head of the laboratory where Reshetovskaya was to have worked, as a Candidate of Physical and Mathematical Sciences, was not invited to the meeting.

In front of the Head of the Personnel Department of the Academy of Medical Sciences, there lay a file with Reshetovskaya's dossier from the examination. First one and then another member of the Commission took it and glanced through it. One important detail leapt to my eye. The personal file always includes a list of scientific works of the examinee. It is customary to support this by offprints of the works themselves for the Examination Commission. But not all journals send offprints to their authors, and therefore the examinee is not always able to attach all the published work to the personal file. When Reshetovskaya prepared her file for the competitive examination, two works on the list were not supported by offprints, as I knew quite well. However, in the file brought to the session, these works were present in the form of photocopies from the Lenin Library. These photocopies had been ordered by the Personnel Department, apparently in the hope that they would find some cause to carp or criticize. As I found out later, all Reshetovskaya's documents were subjected to expert scrutiny.

It must be stressed that the Director of our Institute, Professor G. A. Zedgenidze, did not agree with the Presidium's opinion and refused to exclude Reshetovskaya from taking part in the repeat examination. The legal procedure did not permit any discrimination in Reshetovskaya's case. As a docent and Candidate of Chemical Sciences, as a scientist of fifteen years' standing she had an indisputable right to take part in the examination. And it was the business of the Academic Council to decide this question by secret ballot.

The opponents of this course of action first tried to find some candidate with a stronger claim to the vacant post, and then the Presidium of the Academy of Medical Sciences suddenly altered the staff schedule of the Institute, and cancelled the 'chemical' vacancy, transferring it to the Institute's clinic and making it a 'medical' one. The vacant post for which the examination was held was supported, like a number of others, by funds from the State Committee for Science and Technology allotted specially for the isotope unit. Transferring the post to the clinic meant transferring it at the same time to the funds of the Ministry of Health. According to the regulations existing in 1965, such an inter-ministerial transfer could be effected only by a resolution of the Council of Ministers of the USSR. But this was a special case—perhaps it had been agreed at all levels.

In all these events, I, like Dr Timofeev-Resovskii, played a vigorous part, although Reshetovskaya would not be coming to our department. We had to keep Reshetovskaya and Solzhenitsyn constantly informed of how things were going, writing and phoning to Ryazan, in spite of the envious presence in all these communications of unseen third parties.

And so, against the background of these turbulent events, I had my conversations with the two representatives about putting my proposed trip to the USA into practice, and the Academy of Medical Sciences gave its formal consent to the trip. Of course I understood that these conversations were more closely connected with the history I have just described than with any really serious intention of sending me to the USA for half a year for joint work on the problem of ageing.

A couple of weeks or so after the second meeting, the gentlemen in civilian clothing met me again. Solemnly and weightily they informed me that the higher spheres of their organization were very interested in my trip to the USA which opened up unique opportunities. I replied that before I could decide, I would have to know more about the nature of the possible tasks.

The senior-ranking of the gentlemen, after many general remarks, finally came round to the subject of literature, and became interested in my opinion of the works of Solzhenitsyn, and even asked me outright if I had a copy of the book containing his story 'One Day in the Life of Ivan Denisovich', which he, my interlocutor, had unfortunately not yet read, although he would very much like to. This story, according to him, was very hard to come by. I readily promised to let him have it the next time we met, when he would let me know something about my additional tasks in the United States of America.

These tasks proved to be very interesting and not at all complicated. The basis of the assignment, according to my interlocutor, was that I happened to be the author of an unofficially widely circulated manuscript on the history of the genetic discussion and that this manuscript had been sharply criticised in the press and even at the Plenum of the Central Committee, in 1963.[1] In the opinion of the high-ups, all this anti-Lysenko activity could not have gone unnoticed abroad, particularly since even *Pravda* had criticized me. The organization represented by my interlocutor therefore expected that in the USA I would attract the constant attention of American Intelligence. And if American Intelligence tried to make contact with me, then my orders were not to turn them down but if possible to find out more fully all the means which they used to recruit Soviet scientists in the USA. In the words of my instructor, I was to 'flirt' with American intelligence. . . . It was quite a simple business, therefore, and consisted of not refusing to engage in any conversations which someone or other might start in the USA. Naturally, I said—provided, of course, that I went to the USA— I would be able to carry out such an assignment, and I would give him a detailed account of all cases of non-scientific American bodies taking an interest in me.

After that, the conversation once more took a literary turn, in connection with Solzhenitsyn's story. My interlocutor said that if I had so high an opinion of the writer and his patriotism, then it would be useful if I put my ideas in written form, and then they could be read through by the competent comrades in their organization, and this would help clear up misunderstandings. I replied that the works and personal character of the writer had been widely discussed in the Soviet press and had been considered most favourably even in the international communist publication *Problems of Peace and Socialism*, and my opinion did not differ from the opinion of this journal. We then had a short discussion about the confiscated novel, which I had not read, much to the disappointment, it seemed, of my interlocutors.

Soon there was yet another meeting, which took place after the session I have described of the Academy of Medical Sciences. The interlocutors were the same. They told me that the higher spheres were pleased that I had agreed to carry out the mission. Hence, *since I had agreed to co-operate* (this was particularly emphasized) the higher levels asked me to comply with one formality necessary for a worker carrying out such an assignment. I must make a list of my personal friends and close relatives about whom I might be questioned during my period of 'cultivation' by the Americans, and give a brief note on each of them,

[1] This manuscript was eventually translated into English by I. M. Lerner and published in the United States as *The Rise and Fall of T. D. Lysenko* (Columbia University Press, New York and London, 1969)—*Translator*.

pointing out in particular those who might know state or military secrets. I had two weeks to prepare such a list.

This formality was, of course, unacceptable. I briefly informed Dr Strehler (this was in December 1965) that the arrangements for my visit to his laboratory had run into difficulties, and that such a visit was scarcely possible now for 1966.

By this time the Party Bureau had at last got round to discussing my character reference for the 'exit dossier' for this trip. Knowing very well, however, that even after approval the 'exit dossier' would not get much further forward, I asked the representative of our section in the Party Bureau to tell them that the trip was postponed, owing to the fact that I had to arrange the work in the laboratory, that I had no deputy, or other reasons. On his proposal, the resolution was adopted to postpone the trip.

When some days later my interlocutors had another meeting with me and wanted to know whether my list of business and personal contacts was ready, I told them of the Party Bureau's resolution postponing the trip. My interlocutor tried to convince me that the list was not necessarily connected with this trip, that the Party Bureau's resolution could be changed if they had instructions from above, and so on. At last, losing patience, he began to demand the list sharply and even with threats. But it was useless. His obvious frustration, and his threatening tone only harmed my interlocutor for they revealed his true intention and destroyed all confidence in what he said. For once one of the people involved in a conversation is threatened, then he has a right to defend himself and to make the situation known to anyone who may be able to help him. From the moment when my previously oh-so-polite interlocutor began to put the pressure on, I began to feel free, especially as I had given no formal commitment to keep the conversation confidential.

Bernard Strehler is an intelligent man, and understood my difficulties, it seemed. His friendly letter touched me deeply. He wrote:

Dear Dr Medvedev,
   Thank you for your short letter of December 8. I am sorry to hear that final permission has not yet been granted for your visit to our laboratory. Although there are sometimes delays in getting official approval for new ventures in any government, including my own, I think you must remember that your country has not had a long history of exchange of scientists, particularly individual scientists, with other countries of the West and it is only natural that those responsible for such decisions must consider all relevant factors in deciding what to do in individual cases. . . .

If I were to have an opportunity to visit another country such as yours, on a similar scientific project of potential benefit to both countries, there are several things I would consider. First would be the scientific benefits to all concerned. Second, I would hope that my stay would benefit the cause of world peace. This requires that I respect the hospitality of the country concerned. . . . Certainly I would not visit another land if I believed my visit would harm either my own or the host country in any way.

I respect the love you have for Russia as an expression of certain ideals, just as I hope you respect my love of my own country, which is a positive quality and not based on a negative attitude towards other countries. During the early 1950s, even when I disagreed strongly with some men whom I believed evil, such as Senator McCarthy, and when I was subjected to some unpleasant questioning by government officials, I tried always to tell the truth because I believed this to be a part of the historical right and ideals of my land. There are still many injustices in my country as everywhere, but these do not prevent me from loving America and of hoping that the good things we have to give to the world will some day make life better for all people.

My friend, I hope that my invitation to you will only be of benefit to you and your country. . . . It would grieve me to contribute to any unhappiness in your life. . . .

Please do what is best for you. If for some reason you cannot visit us at this time, I am sure that the day of understanding and friendship between our countries will arrive eventually.

Best wishes for the new year,

BERNARD L. STREHLER

About a year and a half later, in looking through the *Proceedings of the National Academy of Sciences of the USA* (vol. 57, no. 6, 1967), a journal which publishes the most significant and most interesting advances in American research, I was fascinated to read an article by Dr Strehler and two of his colleagues on the success of the experimental work he had invited me to take part in. Dr Strehler was to be congratulated; he had organized and run a really brilliant investigation into the molecular mechanism of ageing. As things stood in Obninsk, or in any other laboratory in the USSR in 1966–7, not only would it have been impossible to carry out such work, it would even be impossible to repeat it, since we lacked a corresponding nomenclature for the equipment and the necessary range of biochemical reagents.

4

The traditional Annual Lecture on the problem of ageing

YET another case from my own experience, and the last which I shall discuss in this book, was even more complicated. Just as a sportsman gradually jumps higher and higher as he proceeds with his training, so in this matter of international co-operation, with each case I came into contact with higher and higher levels which had to decide on these questions.

This story also starts with a letter, and once again it was unexpected. It arrived in the spring of 1965 from an international organization in London for the promotion of international co-operation in medical and chemical research, the famous Ciba Foundation. As one can guess from the name, this organization was founded by the well-known international pharmaceutical firm, Ciba, which produces almost half the medicaments manufactured in Western Europe. The centre of the Ciba Foundation is in London, but the USSR is represented on its Scientific Advisory Panel.

However, when I received this letter I knew very little about the nature of this organization. I only knew the very interesting collections of papers which they had published during the 1950s on the problems of ageing. The letter was sent to me at my former Moscow address, and hence I received it only after much delay.

24 March 1965   41 Portland Place, London

Dear Dr Medvedev,

As you may know, between 1954 and 1959 the Ciba Foundation had a special programme to encourage younger workers to undertake research relevant to the problems of ageing. In 1959 we decided that we had done enough stirring up in this field, but we maintained an interest by continuing to hold one lecture each year on research on ageing. It has become the tradition to hold this particular lecture away from the Ciba Foundation, in conjunction with a meeting of the British Society for Research on Ageing, at some centre in Great Britain where active studies on ageing are in progress. The lecture has been held in Birmingham, Leeds, Liverpool, Oxford and Glasgow, and this year we shall be holding it in Newcastle-on-Tyne.

In 1966 we intend to hold the lecture at Sheffield University, in conjunction with a joint meeting of the British Society for Research on Ageing and the Society for Experimental Biology. This meeting will almost certainly be held from 8–12 September 1966; we have not yet decided just when our lecture would best fit in with the other programme but the whole period should be of great interest to people engaged in active research upon ageing.

I am writing in the hope that you might be willing and able to come to this country in 1966 to give our 10th Annual Lecture on Research on Ageing. The lecture has a small honorarium of £35, and in addition we could provide you with your tourist return air ticket between Moscow and London; take care of your accommodation in this country for 5–7 days, and also cover your travelling expenses between London and Sheffield.

We can give you a free choice of subject, but are presuming that you would talk on some aspect of the molecular biology of ageing. The Ciba Foundation has no book or journal in which your lecture could be published, but the organizers of the BSRA/SEB conference hope that you would permit your lecture to be published with the proceedings of their joint meeting.

It may be helpful to you to see the list of previous lectures in this particular series, and I am enclosing such a list.

I should be grateful for an early reply to this invitation, however provisional it must be in the first instance. I very much hope that you will find it possible to accept, and that we may look forward to seeing you here in September, 1966.

Yours sincerely,

G. E. W. WOLSTENHOLME
O.B.E., F.R.C.P., F.I.BIOL.

A list was attached to the letter of the previous nine lectures, starting with the first, given in London in 1957 by Dr Shock on the subject of 'Age Changes in Physiological Functions in the Total Animal'. In subsequent years, the lectures had been given by scientists from England, France, Holland, Czechoslovakia and Germany.[1] Most of their names were well known to me.

An annual lecture of this kind is a widespread tradition in many branches of science. It seems to have been born in England some two centuries ago. To be proposed to deliver an annual lecture is a great

---

[1] This had not created a precedent of having a speaker from a Communist country, in that Professor H. Ungar, who gave the lecture in 1965 on 'The histology of the intramural coronary branches from birth to age', though born and educated in Prague, was then working at the University of Newcastle-upon-Tyne.

honour which can rarely come twice in a lifetime. This I understood perfectly. I also understood that such invitations are not to be declined. It was necessary to mobilize all my forces, all possible means, to carry out my mission and to go to the highest level. This was a case where a scientist must first decide for himself, and afterwards dutifully try to implement his personal decision. I therefore answered Dr Wolstenholme without delay, accepting the invitation, but leaving some element of uncertainty in my first letter.

> Dear Dr Wolstenholme,
>   Thank you very much for your letter of March 24, 1965, and your honourable and kind invitation to prepare a lecture on molecular aspects of ageing in 1966. I was excited by this invitation and shall do my best to be worthy of your previous lecturers. But I understand that it is a very difficult task because all the lecturers are the best experts in some or another fields of gerontology.
>   Please excuse my significant delay in replying to your letter which was connected with my change of address, the letter was re-sent to me only yesterday.
>   Though I feel that you could probably find a better lecturer than me I accept your invitation because I am sure such perspective will stimulate greatly my work and my thinking on the problem.

It must be said that I was by no means sure that the Ciba Foundation had chosen the right man to give its annual lecture. If it had been a case of the biochemical, physiological, morphological, clinical or other aspects of ageing, I would certainly have suggested to Dr Wolstenholme that he should change his candidate for someone more worthy. But in the narrow field of molecular gerontology, I could only recommend to him, instead of myself, someone from among my foreign colleagues. And this was not because I considered myself to be of so great a stature. It is easy to rank scientists in order of 'magnitude' in the classical sciences, where there are hundreds and thousands of scientists in the country. But molecular gerontology was not yet very advanced in our country; it was poor in personnel, and I simply did not know anyone who was of a high enough standard, even in his knowledge of English, to give a lecture of this kind. It was by no means an easy task for me either, and would require exceptionally concentrated work.

I felt that accepting the invitation of the Ciba Foundation was not only a question of my personal prestige, not only the culminating event of my scientific life, but was also my duty as a citizen. For a short time, on a fairly small sector of the scientific front, I would be a fully-fledged representative of Soviet science. I knew that if I refused, for any reason, the traditional Annual lecture would without doubt be offered to one of my foreign colleagues.

However, the difficulties I had expected in discussing the question of a trip to England did not even come up at first. Obtaining a decision was remarkably simple. As I have described in the previous case, the Academy of Medical Sciences had given a favourable decision about my making a six to eight months' trip to the USA in 1966, and the Foreign Section of the Ministry of Health who had to approve this trip had suggested that I should arrange to include a visit to England. I had accepted this itinerary, by which I should attend the conference in Sheffield on my return from the USA. It was a brilliant prospect and would not need a new 'exit dossier' and foreign passport. This programme strengthened my prospects of making an even more valuable long-term trip to work in Dr Strehler's laboratory, and would give me an opportunity both of an excellent preparation for the lecture itself and for improving my knowledge of English.

Our Institute's recommendation on this matter received a favourable answer from the Deputy Minister of Health of the USSR, A. F. Serenko, and the Head of the International Section of the Academy of Medical Sciences, S. A. Sarkisov; and I was able to write to Dr Wolstenholme definitely, and with the approval of the Section, that I accepted his invitation and was doing all in my power to make the trip possible. And although there was almost a year before the lecture was to take place, I gradually began to prepare the text for it, trying to make it of sufficient interest for the audience I expected to meet in England.

But at the end of 1965, the trip to the USA to work in Dr Strehler's laboratory fell through, as we have already seen. Dr Wolstenholme's letter of 21 December informing me of the final confirmation of the programme of the Symposium reached me almost simultaneously with Strehler's letter expressing his deep regret at the failure of our plans.

Dear Dr Medvedev,

I do not want the year to end without sending you a message of warmest good wishes, and also informing you of the progress of our plans for next September. I am enclosing a copy of the arrangements for the meeting in Sheffield, including your own lecture, and should perhaps say that I shall be inviting a few people to take dinner with you immediately before your lecture on the Tuesday evening.

I hope there continues to be a favourable response from the authorities in your country to your coming to give this important

C

lecture for us. We all look forward very much to this opportunity to meet you and hear about your work.

We send our very best wishes to you for 1966.

Yours sincerely,

G. E. W. WOLSTENHOLME

I read through the programme of the Symposium on the biology of ageing with great interest. It was divided into two parts: scientific papers on set subjects on 5, 6, 7, 8 and 9 September, and the Annual Lecture on the evening of 6 September in the Lecture Theatre of the University. It was to be a public lecture. The individual sessions of the Symposium were devoted to the following problems: molecular and chromosome changes in ageing, metabolic and cellular aspects of the ageing of plants, metabolic and cellular aspects of the ageing of animals, hormone phenomena in ageing and ageing of the whole organism. I was very happy to see that among those taking part there were many of my colleagues who were well known to me from their work, and several friends, including Dr Strehler, who was to read a paper on cellular age changes in man.

However, the failure of the trip to the USA put the proposed trip to England back to square one. I would have to start arranging it all over again, as a separate undertaking and in more complicated circumstances.

My first visit to the Ministry of Health of the USSR showed that the attitude of the Foreign Section towards my trip to England had undergone a sharp change. The Deputy Head of this section, M. A. Akhmetelli, began to talk very vaguely about the fact that the Agreement on Cultural and Scientific Exchange with England had not yet been signed for 1966, and hence it was not clear how many man-days their section would have for official visits in 1966. Naturally, he said, if the plan for man-days in 1966 was not very large, then they would be able to arrange only the most important trips, agreed at the very highest level. Another rank-and-file employee of the same section, who had previously been given the materials from our institute for safe keeping, hunted in his papers but could not find the file with the correspondence about the lecture and the resolutions of the relevant superiors. This file, which he had formerly had in his possession, seemed to have disappeared somewhere. I met the same uncertainty in the Academy of Medical Sciences. Furthermore, it was necessary to start preparing an 'exit dossier' again. The forms for the 'exit dossier' are considered to be strictly accountable papers and are issued by the Foreign Sections of departments only to individuals whose trip has been agreed upon by the department. An institute cannot prepare 'exit dossiers' for capitalist countries on its own initiative.

After waiting a couple of weeks without obtaining any clear-cut decision, nor any official instructions to the institute to prepare an 'exit dossier', I let Dr Wolstenholme know fairly clearly about the uncertainty which had arisen. I told him that the process of getting this kind of trip approved was a multi-staged one and that a first favourable reaction might be changed at various levels on its way to an actual decision. I could not tell him straight out the nature of the difficulties which had arisen, all the more so, because I still did not know exactly what they were. It was necessary to speak in hints.

> The process of arrangements here [I wrote] could be compared to multi-stage chromatography and ion-exchange. Imagine a set of columns with different absorbents and ion-exchangers. A definite substance must pass through all of them. Those molecules which have no (+) or no (−), which are chemically inert have more chances.

Anyone acquainted with chemistry and biochemistry, as Dr Wolstenholme must be, would understand that no compound could pass through a system of both cation and anion exchangers if it had either a positive charge or a negative charge or both types of charges simultaneously on different groups. Only substances which are completely neutral, uncharged, without pluses or minuses, can get through.

> I am not completely certain [I wrote in another letter] that I can by my own efforts ensure my trip to England, nor whether the relevant people will consider the personal invitations which I have received. Taking into account all the existing difficulties, I want to warn you that my trip to England is still problematic. There are two courses open to you to ensure the traditional lecture on ageing: firstly, to invite some other scientist whose personal wish and acceptance is sufficient guarantee of his attending the Symposium in Sheffield, or, secondly, to transfer the discussion of matters relating to this lecture to the official level, which would apparently have to be not lower than that of the Minister of Health. . . .

Again, as in 1960, I did not want to have to take the sins of others upon myself. If the responsible authorities did not reach a favourable decision, then let them conduct the correspondence and let them take the responsibility for the breakdown of this matter. In any event, I would do my duty, the lecture would be written, translated into English and sent to England, whatever the situation. The tenth Annual Lecture on the problem of ageing would take place, whether or not I myself could go to England. With this aim, I began to prepare my first draft of the lecture; it was still too long, but I proposed to cut it later, keeping what was most significant. The lecture could not last more than seventy to eighty minutes.

The programme which I had received earlier was a preliminary one, which had been sent out only so that those attending could fix their plans for going to Sheffield in September, particularly since half of them were from other countries. The programme had not yet been published, and the Ciba Foundation would still be able to ask some other scientist to write the lecture. But, to speak frankly, I was sure that Dr Wolstenholme would choose the second course and would attempt to procure the visit of the lecturer he had already invited by top-level discussions. A short time later, I received confirmation of this. Dr Wolstenholme had drawn up an official letter to the Ministry of Health of the USSR, and had sent copies of his letter to the Director of our Institute and to me. The letter read as follows:

CIBA FOUNDATION
for the Promotion of International Co-operation in Medical and Chemical Research

Trustees
The Rt Hon. Lord Brain, LL.D. D.C.L., F.R.S.
The Rt Hon. Lord Florey, O.M., F.R.S.
The Rt Hon. Sir George Lloyd-Jacobs
The Rt Hon. Lord Todd, F.R.S.

Director
Dr G. E. W. Wolstenholme, O.B.E.

41 Portland Place, London W1

2 February 1966

Copy: Dr Zh. A. Medvedev
Professor B. V. Petrovskii,
Ministry of Health,
Rachmanovskii Str. 3
Moscow,
USSR

Dear Professor Petrovskii,

It is my pleasant duty to write formally, on behalf of the Trustees of the Ciba Foundation, to ask you to give your official approval and assistance to enable a distinguished Russian scientist, Dr Medvedev, to come to England to lecture about his research.

The Ciba Foundation in London is an independent scientific and educational Trust which has been working in the field of international co-operation in medical research for the last sixteen years. We are assisted in this work by eminent scientists in many countries, who serve as our Scientific Advisory Panel. The representatives for the USSR are: Academicians V. A. Engelhardt, A. I. Oparin and M. M. Shemyakin. Any one of these scientists would undoubtedly be willing to give you further information about the activities of the Ciba Foundation.

Some ten years ago, as part of our programme of medical research, we made a special effort to encourage fresh research, internationally, in relation to the problems of ageing. We have held a number of conferences on this subject, and each year we invite a distinguished scientist to visit England and lecture about his own special line of research in relation to ageing processes.

We now wish to invite Dr Zh. A. Medvedev (Chief of the Laboratory of Molecular Radiobiology, Obninsk) to give the Ciba Foundation's 10th Annual Lecture on Ageing Research. We should very much like him to tell us about his work, which we believe to be of international importance, and we should like him to do so in conjunction with a symposium on Ageing Research. This symposium will be held in Sheffield early in September 1966 and is being organized jointly by the Ciba Foundation, the Society for Experimental Biology, and the British Society for Research on Ageing. We hope that Dr Medvedev will come and take part in this 5-day symposium, with his own lecture (on the second day) being the main function of the week. Preliminary letters have been sent to Dr Medvedev and we have ascertained his willingness to prepare a lecture on his special subject for this occasion. We now hope that his visit to England can be given official sanction.

The Ciba Foundation undertake to provide all the necessary travelling expenses, accommodation, and living expenses for Dr Medvedev in connection with this visit to England.

A copy of this letter is being sent to Professor G. A. Zedgenidze (Director of the Institute of Medical Radiobiology of Academy of Medical Sciences in Obninsk).

We should be most grateful for your early, favourable attention to this matter, which we believe will strengthen the mutual respect and co-operation of Soviet and British scientists.

Yours sincerely,

G. E. W. WOLSTENHOLME
O.B.E., F.R.C.P., F.I.BIOL.

Three weeks after receiving this letter, I was summoned by telegram to see the Deputy Head of the Foreign Section of the Ministry of Health, M. A. Akhmetelli. I went in haste to Moscow, almost sure that Dr Wolstenholme's letter had produced the necessary action. By this time I had read up about the wide range of the Ciba Foundation's international activity, and I knew that the USSR received considerable benefits from this organization, particularly in the field of public health.

My hopes, however, were unfounded. Akhmetelli did not receive me in too friendly a manner. He told me that the Minister of Health had decided against my trip to England. Akhmetelli hinted quite clearly that the English had done me too great an honour and that I ought not to be striving so hard to bring it off. When I asked who, in his opinion, was more worthy for such a mission, Akhmetelli was evasive. Akhmetelli also said that it would be rather inconvenient for the Minister to send a refusal to Dr Wolstenholme's letter, and that therefore I should send a plausible refusal to England. If I did not do this, then their Section would hardly be able to do any serious business with me in the future. This was an obvious, although polite, threat, and it was only left for me to tell Akhmetelli my candid opinion of him and his department.

A few days later, the Director of our Institute was summoned to the Ministry. He was advised, in a more official manner, to send a short letter to Dr Wolstenholme, which would save the Minister from having to deal with the problem. I did not learn about this until later, when Dr Wolstenholme sent me a photocopy of this letter and a copy of his own reply to it.

The refusal, written in good English, read:

9 3 1966

Dear Professor Wolstenholme,

I was very pleased to receive your kind letter in which you ask my assistance to enable Dr Zh. Medvedev to come to England to lecture about his research.

I express my regret, but I suppose Dr Zh. Medvedev will not be able to come to England this year because of a great press of work he has to do in his laboratory.

Yours sincerely,

Professor G. A. ZEDGENIDZE
Director of the Institute of Medical Radiology of the
Academy of Medical Sciences of the USSR, Member,
AMS of the USSR

Dr Wolstenholme's reaction was almost instantaneous.

Dear Professor Zedgenidze,

Your letter of 9th March comes as a very great disappointment not only to all of us at the Ciba Foundation, but also to the many people gathering in Sheffield in September who were particularly looking forward to an opportunity of learning at first hand about this work on Molecular Aspects of Ageing.

Dr Medvedev was also invited to the International Congress of Gerontology in Vienna, but had decided, correctly, that the lecture and meeting in Sheffield would give him a better opportunity to have the work discussed by appropriate scientists. It is a very great pity if the work cannot now be heard either in Vienna or Sheffield.

So far as the Ciba Foundation is concerned, this annual lecture has been given by people from the USA, France, Holland, Israel, etc., and it will be a matter of very great regret to us if the USSR is not to appear in this series.

Since Dr Medvedev would have to be in this country for only one week, and, indeed, a visit of 2–3 days would certainly be better than nothing, is it really impossible to spare him from his duties for so short a time, particularly as this is presumably at a time when he might be on vacation?

I should be most grateful if you would reconsider the matter, and hope that there may still be the possibility of a favourable reply.

I am sending copies of this letter to Professor Petrovskii at the Ministry of Health, and also to Academicians Engelhardt, Oparin and Shemyakin who represent the Ciba Foundation in your country.

Yours sincerely,

G. E. W. WOLSTENHOLME
O.B.E., F.R.C.P., F.I.BIOL.

Together with the copy-letters sent to V. A. Engelhardt and the other two academicians, Dr Wolstenholme wrote to each of them asking him to use his influence to obtain a favourable decision about the Ciba Annual Lecture.

Academician Oparin, as might have been expected, completely ignored the request and did not even answer Dr Wolstenholme's letter, but both Engelhardt (the Director of the Institute of Molecular Biology) and Shemyakin (Director of the Institute of the Chemistry of Natural Compounds) actively sought to do what had been asked. I found out about this much later, when Academician Engelhardt's campaign was over and he sent me copies of the correspondence on this matter and told me of the measures which they had taken.

At the end of March, Engelhardt and Shemyakin had prepared a special memorandum to the Ministry of Health of the USSR, and, having obtained an interview with the Minister, they handed it to Professor Petrovskii personally, urging him to take a favourable decision. It was as follows:

Dear Boris Vasil'evich,

Please permit us to turn to you with a request that you take note of the question of granting to the Head of the Laboratory of Molecular Radiobiology of the Institute of Medical Radiology in Obninsk, Dr

Zh. A. Medvedev, the opportunity of taking part, as principal lecturer, in the International Symposium on the Biology of Ageing to be held in England in the autumn of this year.

The Symposium is being held by the scientific organization the Ciba Foundation. We are both members of the Scientific Advisory Panel of this organization, as representatives of the Soviet Union. This Council includes scientists from a great number of countries, since the Ciba Foundation is of an international nature. It is a very solid organization with a high international repute. It undertakes a broad range of scientific and organizational work, it holds many specialized conferences and publishes a large number of monographs and collections of papers. It serves as an active centre of scientific contact between representatives of different branches of medical science with scientists from related fields—chemists, biophysicists, pharmacologists, etc. In particular, one of the fields to which the Ciba Foundation pays special attention is gerontology, in its various aspects. The symposium we are concerned with is the next event of the current year in this line. Preparations for the Symposium began over a year ago, and the organizers nominated as the principal lecturer, to give the Annual Lecture, Zh. A. Medvedev, the author of a number of important papers on problems of the biological principles of ageing.

However, at present, the situation regarding Zh. A. Medvedev's trip to England has taken a considerable turn for the worse.

The Director of the Ciba Foundation, Dr Wolstenholme, has approached us, as members of the Advisory Panel, with the request that, if possible, we should lend our efforts to prevent the breakdown of this long-planned Symposium, since the Annual Lecture is the central point of the whole programme.

In asking you to reconsider this problem, we should like to stress that the Ciba Foundation has always shown great courtesy to Soviet scientists, inviting this one or that to take part in their activities. Our scientists frequently visit the Ciba centre, where there are excellent facilities for scientific work, and avail themselves of the various forms of assistance offered by the Ciba administration. The difficulties which would arise out of a refusal to contribute to the success of this symposium would certainly not be in the interest of the expansion and strengthening of our scientific contacts abroad.

Academician V. A. ENGELHARDT
Academician M. M. SHEMYAKIN

The Minister of Health certainly paid attention to this letter, and turned his attention to the question it raised, but on quite a different plane. I was summoned again, this time by the Head of the Foreign Section of the Ministry of Health (this Section chooses to call itself the External Relations Section in the list of sections), Comrade Novgorodtsev, who advised me in a categorical and high-handed manner to stop all correspondence and activity connected with taking part in the Symposium.

Clearly the trip could be written off as impossible. However, I decided 'no surrender', and I tried to solve the problem one way or another. There was still four months left, quite long enough.

I wrote once again to Dr Wolstenholme, telling him that the Ministry of Health still had not reconsidered their decision. 'Since,' I wrote, 'the programme of the Symposium has already been fixed and since my lecture forms part of that programme, then whatever the circumstances the Ciba Foundation will receive the text of this lecture in English not less than two weeks before the Symposium.' However, I told Dr Wolstenholme, it would clearly be advisable to attempt another try, this time a contact between the Ciba Foundation and the Chairman of the State Committee on Science and Technology, who, being the Deputy Chairman of the Council of Ministers of the USSR, was on a still higher level, and was fully empowered to consider and reconsider any decision of this kind.

I no longer believed in the success of such a contact, but the experiment had to be made, all the more since the Head of the State Committee was Academician V. A. Kirillin, who back in 1960 had been in charge of the Science Section of the Central Committee of the CPSU, and later had been a Vice-President of the Academy of Sciences of the USSR. In 1963, as Vice-President of the Academy of Sciences, he had read my manuscript on the history of the genetic controversy and, so I was told, had been favourable to it.

It was less than two weeks before I received from Dr Wolstenholme a copy of his letter to the State Committee on Science and Technology:

Dear Academician Kirillin,

I have the honour to address you as Head of the State Committee on Science and Technics of the Council of Ministers of the USSR, and would greatly appreciate your kind consideration of the following matter.

In March 1965 I wrote formally, on behalf of the Trustees of the Ciba Foundation, to Dr Zh. A. Medvedev (Chief, Laboratory of Molecular Radiobiology, Institute of Medical Radiology, Obninsk) to invite him to give the 10th in a series of annual lectures on research relevant to the problems of ageing, which are given by people of international importance. . . . The lecture [is to be] part of an international symposium . . . concerned with many aspects of the problem of ageing. Dr Medvedev, from his personal point of view, kindly accepted our invitation. . . .

Dr Wolstenholme then briefly outlined the history of his correspondence with the Minister of Health and the Director of our Institute, and also explained the function and aims of the Ciba Foundation. At the end of his letter, he wrote:

> It is our strong wish to encourage wider recognition of Soviet scientific achievements and, at the same time, to do everything possible to improve official and personal friendship. We greatly hope, therefore, that you would be so courteous as to use your influence to overcome whatever minor obstacles there may be which so far prevent Dr Medvedev from confirming his ability to give our lecture and participate in the international symposium in Sheffield.

Academician Kirillin used his influence, but, like the Minister, in an entirely different way from what Dr Wolstenholme had hoped for. At the end of May, a member of the State Committee for Science and Technology, D. Pronskii, who was Head of the International Section of this committee, forwarded Dr Wolstenhome's letter to the Ministry of Health of the USSR, with a covering letter of his own. In this letter, he stated insistently and in an insulting manner that Zh. A. Medvedev had broken the regulations about 'intercourse with foreign firms' and recommended that these regulations should be explained to Medvedev. Judging from his letter he did not even understand that the Ciba Foundation was not a firm but a scientific organization. Nevertheless, his letter found the necessary response in the Ministry of Health.

In the middle of June, I was summoned by the Head of the Special Section of our Institute, and, on the instructions of the Director, I was made familiar with a letter (of 10 June 1965) which had come to our Institute from the Head of the Foreign Section of the Ministry of Health, Comrade Novgorodtsev, to which was attached a copy of Pronskii's letter to the Ministry of Health. Repeating in part the expressions of Pronskii, Novgorodtsev wrote in his letter that Zh. A. Medvedev had 'broken the regulations about correspondence with foreign firms', that 'he was striving to make this trip by any means, and was involving scholars who had nothing to do with it'. Here he had in mind Engelhardt and Shemyakin. Further, Novgorodtsev expressed his doubt that Medvedev was sufficiently competent in the problems which it was proposed he should raise in his lecture, and he also recommended that the necessary administrative measures should be taken to let Medvedev know that his behaviour, and his position of opposition to the decisions of the Ministry were not acceptable.

It should be noted that Novgorodtsev's letter was sent to the Institute via the Special Section deliberately, for the psychological effect. A copy of this letter from the Ministry of Health was also sent to the Academy of Medical Sciences of the USSR.

Ten days later, via the same route, an enquiry came from the International Section of the Academy of Medical Sciences, signed by a new head of this section, Academician Kovanov of the Academy of Medical Sciences. In this letter, he told the Institute to let him know what concrete measures had been taken by the Party Organization and the Institute authorities about Zh. A. Medvedev, in connection with his breach of the rules on correspondence and contact with foreigners, and a reference to Novgorodtsev's letter on this matter followed.

The Special Section of our Institute demanded an explanatory memorandum from me on this matter. I wrote them one, clearly pointing out the misunderstanding which had arisen both in the Academy of Medical Sciences and the Ministry of Health. I also clearly indicated my opinion on Comrade Novgorodtsev's power to judge my competence in the field of gerontology. So far as I know, my explanatory memorandum was sent to the Academy of Medical Science and the Ministry of Health by the same channels which had brought their letters, but neither an answer nor a 'sorting-out' of the matter followed.

There was now little more than two months until the opening of the Symposium. The lecture was written, and the translation into English almost finished. At the end of July, my old friend Ralph Cooper was arriving for the International Microbiology Congress in Moscow. I was counting on him to help me edit the translation of the text. Dr Cooper and I had worked together in the biochemical laboratory of the Timiryazev Agricultural Academy in 1958–9, when he visited the USSR under a scientific exchange programme. He was at that time a young biochemist who had just finished his postgraduate course at Oxford and had been working for about a year at the Rothamsted experimental station. When he arrived in Moscow, not knowing Russian, he was almost helpless, particularly since our working conditions are so different from those in England. He was at first assigned to the Department of Microbiology, but then he was transferred to our Department of Agrochemistry and Biochemistry. I shared my small study with him, and in the end we used to coach each other in our respective languages. During the year we became good friends, and afterwards we had kept up a constant correspondence. In 1961 Ralph Cooper was a biochemistry lecturer at Hatfield College.

Ralph Cooper was coming to the Microbiology Congress with his son Paul, who was twelve years old. During the Congress Paul was to stay in Obninsk, with us and my sons, the elder of whom, Sasha, could speak a little English.

At the beginning of July, another letter came from Dr Wolstenholme.

Dear Dr Medvedev,

. . . We have received no further news from you or from the Soviet Authorities, and greatly hope that in this interval arrangements are going ahead favourably for your visit to give this important lecture for the Ciba Foundation, and for your participation in the very interesting symposium in Sheffield. I leave for my holidays on 28th July and will be back in England only a day or two before the Sheffield meeting, so that I hope there will be good news before I leave. In any case my office will be in touch with me while I am away.

A room is being held for you at the Ciba Foundation for the nights of 2nd and 3rd September. . . . A room has also been reserved for you in Sheffield . . . for the nights of 4–9th September inclusive. . . .

If the worst comes to the worst, and you are refused permission to come to England—although I cannot imagine what valid reason there could be for this—then we should hope to receive your manuscript, with any slides, in good time so that we could arrange for Dr Strehler to present the lecture for you.

By this time I had already sent the Russian text of the lecture, some forty pages, for the necessary official approval, without which not a single post office in the country would accept it for dispatch. The procedure for such approval was virtually the same as in 1960. Obtaining approval for posting, with the special form 103A, required the preliminary consideration of the text by the Academic Council (with two referees), a certificate of the Commission that it was non-secret, and decisions by a certain department of the Academy of Medical Sciences of the USSR, the International Section of the Academy of Medical Sciences and Glavlit. After permission had been granted for the text to be sent abroad, the English translation had to be considered, and the Institute itself had to verify that this was identical with the Russian text.

The failure of the attempt to get the previous decision about the trip reversed by the State Committee for Science and Technology left me only one possibility of further action—to go to the Central Committee of the CPSU, the final and highest of all departments for all decisions on foreign travel to capitalist countries.

The Secretariat of the CPSU, unlike all other bodies, has the right to send people abroad for short periods, even at short notice. I knew of a case of a footballer who was suddenly required for an international match and was summoned and rushed by air from the resort where he was on holiday, approved by all departments, including the visa section, delivered from Moscow to England, driven straight to the stadium from the airport, and all this within twenty-four hours. He was to play for the Rest of the World against an All-England side. The idea of the match had come up unexpectedly, and no preparations had been made for it. So far as I remember, England won. But this, of course, was a special case: football, sport, the glamour, the prestige! No doubt the Chairman of the Exit Commission watched the match himself in the English stadium or at home on TV. It was not a lecture on gerontology.

A preliminary discussion with some employees of the Central Committee of the CPSU, mainly by telephone, led me at last to the section which had it in its power to be most helpful in the solution of the problems which had arisen. This was the International Section for Capitalist Countries of the CPSU. (There was yet another international section which was responsible for matters connected with socialist countries of the East and West.)

At the very end of June I was received by the First Assistant to Comrade Ponomarev, the Secretary of the Central Committee of the CPSU, who was in charge of this section. Comrade Ponomarev himself was away at this time accompanying the French President, de Gaulle, on his tour of our country. His assistant, Comrade V. S. Shaposhnikov, met me in a most friendly manner, and our conversation lasted more than an hour. He was interested in gerontology, its achievements and the reason why our country was lagging behind in a number of directions in biology. He had made himself thoroughly familiar with my case and the history of the affair of the Annual Lecture. He firmly promised to take all necessary measures to set the matter right and make the visit possible, and, if need be, to interest Comrade Ponomarev in the matter personally. After this visit to the Central Committee of the CPSU, I had the first feeling of confidence that everything would be done and the trip to England would take place.

However, no results were apparent in the course of the next two weeks. When I received Dr Wolstenholme's letter quoted above I once again applied to Comrade Shaposhnikov in writing, and at the same time sent him a photocopy and translation of the letter from England. In a telephone conversation Shaposhnikov said that he was very sorry but he had not yet had time to deal with my case, but he promised once again to do everything possible in the very near future.

At the end of July, my friend Ralph Cooper arrived in Moscow. Naturally I told him about my problems, and, when we had considered the situation carefully, we decided that my best plan would be to send a copy of the English translation of the lecture by him for safety, since the approval to send it by official channels was taking so long. The International Section of the Academy of Medical Sciences had sent the manuscript of the lecture first for review to the Institute of Gerontology in Kiev, and Glavlit, which is not to be hurried, was still to come. Cooper promised that when he got home he would edit the translation from the language point of view, have it retyped if there were a lot of corrections, and deliver it to the Ciba Foundation by mid-August. He would send one copy of the lecture to Dr Strehler. Bernard Strehler was taking part in the Symposium, and I asked him if he would read my lecture in case I could not go myself. I knew from the Biochemistry Congress in Moscow in 1961 that Strehler was a very fine speaker and could carry out this task excellently.

To take advantage of a convenient opportunity such as this for sending the text of a lecture through unofficial channels, was not of course, in the bureaucratic sense, in accordance with the 'rules for intercourse with foreign firms'. But no other way out was left to me. If I could not get the text of the lecture to my English colleagues in good time, I should be to blame in their eyes, I should have defaulted. No reasonable Englishman would ever believe that the procedure for sending a scientific text which I have described above could really exist. He would not believe it, but would think that I had made it all up to cover the fact that I had been unable to write the lecture, although I had already written to England that the lecture was now ready.

The course of subsequent events proved that I had acted correctly. The official procedure (and this only under pressure from me) was as follows. The report from the Institute of Gerontology in Kiev, was received in August. Fortunately, the Kiev experts did not recommend any changes. Glavlit's permission to send the lecture abroad was granted on 4 September, and the text of the lecture was sent to England on 5 September, the day before the session when it was to be delivered. It was received in England on 11 September, when the Symposium was already over.

In 1939, when Nikolai Vavilov was refused permission to go to Scotland for a Genetics Congress of which he had been elected President, he sent the text of his speech unofficially by his Bulgarian friend, Dontcho Kostoff, who was going to the Congress from Leningrad. At that period, Vavilov was risking far more than I was. I regard this as an example for scientists to follow, and in this case I find no moral problem in breaking rules when they have become ridiculous.

In the middle of August, I received from England several leaflets announcing my lecture. These leaflets were being distributed to the science centres, universities and colleges of Great Britain. They announced in large type:

THE 10TH (ANNUAL)
CIBA FOUNDATION LECTURE
ON
RESEARCH ON AGEING
WILL BE GIVEN BY
DR Z. A. MEDVEDEV
(USSR)
SUBJECT:
'MOLECULAR ASPECTS OF AGEING'
on Tuesday, 6 September 1966, at 8.15 pm
in Lecture Theatre no. 1
Chairman: Professor H. N. Robson
Open without fee or ticket to all interested.

It was only not open to the lecturer himself.

At the same time as he sent the leaflets, the Deputy Director of Ciba told me that as a final means of ensuring my trip to England, they, together with the British Society for Cultural Relations with the USSR, had approached the Soviet Embassy in London and asked for their help, and had written to the British Embassy in Moscow, so that, in case the Soviet authorities did request a visa for my visit to England, it could be issued without the delays in correspondence usual in such cases.

Once again, I sent all this material and one of the leaflets to Comrade Shaposhnikov, enclosing a covering letter. There was, however, no answer.

At the end of August, a letter came from Ralph Cooper. He told me that the corrections to the text of the lecture had been completed and that it was now in the hands of Ciba.

The deputy director of Ciba [he wrote], Mr de Reuck, sent a telegram to Bernard Strehler, to confirm that he will be present. He also suggested that I should go to Sheffield as your representative, and, if necessary, give an explanation of your absence. Thus everything necessary has been arranged. . . .[1]

[1] Translated from Medvedev's Russian text—*Translator*.

September drew near, and my hopes of being able to make the trip finally died. Comrade Shaposhnikov was away on leave, and it was now too late to start another round of high-level discussions. I began to be very concerned about the absence of any legal guarantees of so important an aspect of the rights of man and of the scientist, as the freedom to travel abroad and to engage in international co-operation is recognized throughout the world to be. When it was clear to me that the lecture would take place without its author, I decided to send a special explanation to England, making the reason for my absence clear. I prepared this 'explanation' six days before the lecture, and sent it from the International Post Office in Moscow by registered express airmail, requesting an 'advice of delivery' and sending it, for safety, to three people: Dr Wolstenholme, who was by now in Sheffield, the Chairman of the lecture, Professor Robson and Ralph Cooper. I asked them to read this text either before or after the lecture, whenever was more convenient. I was not sure whether or not these letters would get through to England, but as it turned out, only one of them went astray. The other two reached Sheffield on 5 September, and the 'advice of delivery' notes were returned to me.

And so came the day of 6 September, a day which should have been a day of triumph for any scientist. Early in the morning, I set my watch to British time. My lecture was to take place at the evening session. The morning was given over to two sessions on problems of the ageing of plants. I was listed as chairman of one of them. In Obninsk, however, a sterner task awaited me.

In the autumn all city organizations take part for a couple of months in the potato harvest. It just had to happen that the turn of our section, that of Radiobiology and Genetics which comprised four laboratories, to go potato picking came precisely on 6 and 7 September. That morning, with my colleagues from our laboratory, I travelled twenty-five kilometres by bus, out to the state farm. In Sheffield they were just getting ready for the first morning session, someone else was in the Chairman's seat instead of me, while we were carrying baskets and starting to sort the potatoes, moving back and forth along the furrows. The section was assigned to a field of some two hectares. The potatoes had to be collected, sorted into large and small, and the large ones loaded into the backs of the lorries. The small ones went to the farmyard. We finished our working day at around four o'clock. By this time the second morning session in Sheffield was over.

The dinner in Sheffield was at 18.30 British Summer Time. In

Obninsk, I had a few of my friends coming to my home at this time. The dinner in Sheffield did not last long, the lecture followed it. But we in Obninsk had no need to hurry, and we sat over it talking. When by my reckoning my explanation might well be being read in Sheffield, I too read it aloud to my own guests at home.

Dear Colleagues and Friends,

It is a great disappointment for me not to be able to come to your country and to participate personally in the very important and interesting Symposium on the Biology of Ageing and to read the annual Ciba Foundation Lecture on Ageing. The preparation of this lecture occupied all my thoughts, my time and my hopes these last several months, and this work gave me great pleasure and satisfaction. I feel great thanks to Ciba Foundation and especially to Dr G. E. W. Wolstenholme and to the Symposium organizers for this honourable invitation, which, in spite of the failure of the trip itself, gave a great stimulus for my work, gave me a feeling of the importance of this work and I feel myself among you all on this great day of my life, though distance separates me from the Hicks Building of Sheffield University.

Ciba Foundation, the British Society for Cultural Relations with the USSR, my friends here and myself all did our best to arrange the trip to Sheffield but the stupidity of the whole arrangement system here based on the law of counteraction much more than the laws of co-operation was stronger. This almost 15-stage (15-wall) arrangement system from low to top level is the most shameful survival of past distrust in people and I hope very much that this system as any other thing in this world ages and will die in time. And I hope that my own ageing will be a little slower than the ageing of this distrust. This is the most important basis that I shall be able to visit England in the future, and Gerontology is the science which increases this hope very much.

Though I am not in Sheffield now I am duplicating the lecture here. Just at the time when Dr Strehler will be reading this lecture for me in Sheffield I plan to be reading its Russian duplicate in Obninsk for my gerontological friends. And I am sure that all of us who meet for this occasion in Obninsk on September 6 will wish best success to your Symposium and wish it to be an important step in the development of this science, the great task of which unites us all.

Let me thank my friends Dr Ralph Cooper for his valuable help with the translation of the lecture into English and making it available for reading in Sheffield, Dr B. L. Strehler for reading it in Sheffield and for comments and Prof. H. N. Robson for his kind agreement to be chairman of the meeting.

My great thanks also to Dr G. E. W. Wolstenholme for his permanent support, his kindness and his understanding which gave me clear and unforgettable understanding of a real and effective leader of real and effective scientific co-operation.

Thank you all.

Yours sincerely,

ZH. A. MEDVEDEV

Although the 'explanation' was received in England in time, my colleagues decided not to read it in public. Later I learned that they had been worried for my sake. There were newspaper reporters present at the session, and if it had been read in public, the text of the 'explanation' might have received wide press publicity.

On 7 September, the day after the lecture, I received an international telegram from England. It read:

LECTURE SPLENDIDLY PRESENTED AND RECEIVED STOP ALL CONFERENCE DISAPPOINTED YOUR ABSENCE STOP SEND WARMEST REGARDS AND LOOK FORWARD TO A FUTURE MEETING WOLSTENHOLME CIBAFOUND

A few days later a more detailed letter came from Dr Wolstenholme.

Dear Dr Medvedev,

I have just returned from Sheffield and wish to write in fuller detail the news which I have already sent you by telegram.

Dr Strehler told us all that you are one of his two heroes in science, and it was clear from his presentation of your lecture that he felt the greatest admiration and affection towards you. He had spent many hours in making the English of your text more concise and simple, but he did more than just read the text; he frequently repeated the major points and added helpful comments—and occasionally light remarks—so that the fairly large audience of very competent people in medicine and biology enjoyed every minute of it. It was clear from their silent attention and prolonged applause that they appreciated to the full the material of the lecture and the manner of its presentation.

There were many comments afterwards about the way in which you referred to recent work in many countries, analysed the main questions in relation to ageing processes, and indicated the way in which your own research is going. I think that you could not be more pleased at the reaction of this expert audience. A tape recording was made and I understand that Dr Strehler or Dr Woolhouse will endeavour to convey it to you.

Dr Ralph Cooper spoke quietly and movingly at the end of the lecture about your personal qualities, including your kindness to his son. We showed a photograph of you on the screen at this point, but he explained that it was unusual in that you were not smiling.

Your lecture, as carefully edited by Dr Strehler, will be published by the Society for Experimental Biology with the other papers of their admirable symposium.

All this success made it a matter of even greater regret that you could not be present in person. Every member of the symposium and the lecture audience is more impatient than ever to have a visit from you. The obstruction to your coming can have done no one any good and your presence would undoubtedly have been of real value to Russian science in particular and to science in general. We therefore all greatly hope that the time will soon come when you can meet your British scientific friends in this country. I shall always be most pleased to do anything to make this possible.

There was a dinner before the lecture which was attended by the Vice-Chancellor of Sheffield University and Mrs Robson, Professor P. L. Krohn, Professor and Mrs I. Chester Jones, Professor J. Edelman, Dr A. Comfort, G. A. Durnin, Dr R. Cooper, Dr and Mrs Woolhouse, Dr and Mrs Hill, Dr M. A. Sleigh, Dr J. V. G. A. Durnin, Dr B. Strehler and Dr P. J. Thung of Leiden (a former lecturer in the series) and Dr H. B. von Hahn representing Professor Verzar. We all stood and drank your health and I hope you already feel the benefit.

It has been extremely kind of Academicians Engelhardt and Shemyakin and others who have done their best to overcome the difficulties which some petty authorities put in the way of your visit. It is very much to be hoped that all these efforts will not have been wasted and may start an improvement in easier relations between scientists in your great country and those in other parts of the world.

He added, in a later letter of 5 October:

One of the great pleasures of your paper was that your own approach to the problems of ageing was demonstrated to be so intelligent and so advanced. Unfortunately we usually get an impression that the work of your compatriots in medical and biological research is a good way behind research in other parts of the world. Obviously there must be notable exceptions in addition to yourself but the Soviet Union would make a much more obvious contribution—and a more valuable one—to research, in the interests of humanity, if her scientists mixed and discussed freely with their colleagues elsewhere. Your country would so clearly gain, both for its own people and in respect and prestige, if this were accepted. Certainly, we at the Ciba Foundation will continue in our very small way to do all we can to foster and improve such exchanges. . . .

Yours sincerely,

G. E. W. WOLSTENHOLME

At about the same time I received a detailed description of the session from Ralph Cooper. Then came letters from Dr Strehler, Chairman of the Symposium, Professor Woolhouse, Professor Robson, Vice-Chancellor of Sheffield University, and several others who had taken part in the Symposium. Finally, the tape recording of the session arrived safe and sound. According to the tape, the session had lasted for about two hours. I was able and happy to learn from it that Dr Strehler really had made an excellent job of presenting the lecture and had added to it his own experience and talent as a speaker and a scientist.

I also received from the scientific editor of the Scottish publishing house, Oliver & Boyd of Edinburgh, a letter which made me very happy indeed. This company had prepared a somewhat expanded English translation of my book *Protein Biosynthesis and Problems of Heredity, Development and Ageing*, which had been published in Moscow at the end of 1963. Mr Berrill, an editor of the company in Edinburgh, informed me that they had taken steps to synchronize the appearance of the English translation of the book with the opening of the Symposium in Sheffield and were able to make an exhibition of copies of the book for those taking part in the Symposium.

What else can be added to the gerontological history I have described here? Only a couple of days after the end of the Symposium, while I was still taking everything connected with it very much to heart, my attention was caught by a headline in the leader column of *Pravda* of 11 September 1966, reading 'INTERNATIONAL LINKS BETWEEN SCIENTISTS'. I read with great satisfaction:

> Recent months have been exceptionally rich in fruitful meetings between the scientists of the world. . . . The enormous advances made in recent years in all fields of knowledge, have produced a necessity for closer contact between scientists. Extensive scientific co-operation has become one of the necessities of life. . . . At the present time, our possibilities of learning to understand the laws of the development of nature and society are constantly increasing. But this leads to the fact that large-scale problems form part of the agenda affecting the vital interests of all states. . . . A weighty contribution to the treasure house of knowledge has been made by Soviet scientists. In addition they have gained an opportunity of studying the achievements of foreign colleagues, in order to use them in the interests of the further development of Soviet science and technology and the successful building of communism. . . . Soviet scientists visit many countries of the world to deliver lectures, to take part in consultations and joint projects with foreign specialists.

Two months later, I received another letter from Dr Wolstenholme, in which he wrote:

> You will certainly be interested to know that Academician Kirillin, to whom we appealed in vain in connection with your visit, was in

England recently to receive an honorary degree and visited our Prime Minister. On this occasion, Kirillin stressed the necessity of taking effective measures to develop cultural and scientific links between our countries. He has brought nearer the day when you will be able to come here![1]

But I was not sure whether Dr Wolstenholme had taken Academician Kirillin's statement seriously, or whether his last sentence concealed an example of the well-known English sense of humour.

The lecture itself was published in 1967, in the next volume of symposia of the British Society for Experimental Biology. The Ciba Foundation bore the cost of the publication and sent me two hundred offprints of the lecture.

But the principal souvenir which I had of all that had happened was the tape recording of the session, with the introductory speech of Professor Robson, the introductory speech and reading of the lecture by Bernard Strehler and the warm words of Ralph Cooper. And this tape certainly helped me to improve my English pronunciation.

[1] Translated from Medvedev's Russian text—*Translator*.

5

The Darwin Plaque, the Mendel Medal and the Kimber Prize

IN 1959 there were celebrations throughout the whole world in honour of the centenary of the publication in England of Charles Darwin's classic work, *On the Origin of Species*, which was the beginning of the modern era in biology. In connection with the jubilee, the all-German academy of natural sciences, the Deutsche Akademie der Naturforscher Leopoldina, which has its headquarters in the German Democratic Republic, established a special Charles Darwin prize, to take the form of a special rectangular medal-plaque and a diploma of honour. There were to be fifteen prizes, which the Academy awarded to scientists throughout the world whose services to the development of Darwin's evolutionary theory and ideas were the most outstanding. In England a Darwin prize was received by J. B. S. Haldane, one of the classic figures of modern biology and the theory of evolution; in the USA by H. J. Muller, who discovered artificial mutagenesis, that is, the process of reinforcement of natural mutability; and in Austria by E. Tschermak, one of the creators of genetics, who rediscovered at the beginning of this century the laws of heredity first discovered by Mendel and then forgotten.

But the greatest proportion of Darwin prizes were awarded to Soviet scientists. The German academy awarded the Darwin plaque to four Soviet researchers. And they were, indeed, most worthy of it. They were scientists whose names and work were known to biologists throughout the whole world.

The most deserving of them was Professor Sergei Sergeevich Chetverikov, the creator of population genetics, a science which, some forty years before, had combined the Darwinian theory of evolution with genetics, the science of heredity. Chetverikov, who is rightfully considered to be the 'father' of Russian genetics, and who had founded the first school of Soviet geneticists back in the 1920s, was now lying ill and blind in his home in Gor'kii. He had been living there several years in obscurity and poverty, having found peace after the numerous persecutions, dismissals and insults which had begun in 1928 with his arrest and exile to the Urals. 1948, the year of the rout of Soviet genetics, had been especially harsh for him.

The second Soviet scientist to be given this award was Ivan Ivanovich Shmal'gauzen, a brilliant theoretician and outstanding zoologist–evolutionist, the creator of many current concepts of evolutionary thought, the author of some ten books and more than two hundred scientific papers. A member of the Academy of Sciences, one of the creators of the Institute of Evolutionary Morphology and later its director, and head of the Department of Darwinism in the University of Moscow, Shmal'gauzen in 1948 was proclaimed to be a 'Mendelist-Morganist', which did, indeed, correspond to his truly Darwinian views. But after the August 1948 session of the Lenin All-Union Academy of Agricultural Sciences he was dismissed from all his posts and his books were withdrawn from libraries and destroyed. For a long time it was impossible even to cite his name. By 1959 Shmal'gauzen had a modest post as a rank-and-file scientific assistant in the institute he had once founded.

The third Soviet scientist to be awarded a Darwin medal was Nikolai Vladimirovich Timofeev-Resovskii, a pupil and follower of Chetverikov, one of the founders of radiation genetics and the study of microevolution, a talented geneticist, a biophysicist, radiobiologist and zoologist. In 1959 he was working in the Ural branch of the Academy of Sciences, having been released from prison in 1955, together with a group of his colleagues. While in prison he had built up his scientific career for a second time, working up from a prison and camp labourer to being scientific director of a secret 'atomic' radiobiological laboratory.

And finally the fourth scientist to win this prize was Corresponding Member of the Academy of Sciences of the USSR, Nikolai Petrovich Dubinin, an outstanding specialist in the field of radiation and population genetics. In 1948 he was named as the leader of the Morganists and prosecuted. In 1958 he was successful in organizing an Institute of Genetics and Cytology in Novosibirsk, but in one of his speeches Khrushchev brought down on Dubinin a stream of sharp criticisms, and just at the time of the Darwin jubilee Dubinin was dismissed from his post as Director of the Institute on Khrushchev's direct instructions.

The Academie der Naturforscher invited all these scientists to go to Berlin to take part in the Jubilee Session and to receive their prizes.

But 1959, like 1948, was a difficult year for Soviet biology. Right at the end of 1958, by Khrushchev's personal directive the editorial board of the *Botanicheskii Zhurnal* was disbanded on account of its criticism of

Lysenko, and the persecution of its members began once more. Natur-
ally under these conditions none of the Soviet prizewinners could go to
Berlin to receive the award he had won. The question of a trip to the
GDR for any of them was not even seriously considered.

Having received no answer from the Academy of Sciences of the
USSR, the President of the German Academy came to Moscow himself
when the ceremonies were over, bringing the medals and diplomas so
that he could arrange a presentation ceremony at the Embassy of the
GDR in Moscow. But the Academy of Sciences did not agree to this.
A representative of the Foreign Section of the Academy of Sciences
of the USSR received from the President of the German Academy the
medals and diplomas for Timofeev-Resovskii and Chetverikov, did them
up in parcels and sent them to them by mail. Instead of Sergei Chetverikov,
his brother received the parcel with the medal. The classic figure of
Soviet and world science had been buried in Gor'kii not long before the
arrival of the registered parcel which was the recognition of his service
to the international scientific community.

That summer Timofeev-Resovskii was working in Miassovo at an
experimental station of the Ural Branch of the Academy of Sciences.
One of his colleagues happened to see the parcel at the Sverdlovsk
branch, and he put it in his rucksack and brought it out to Miassovo,
where the prizewinner was able to congratulate himself on the recognition he had received by post.

This was the event which for Soviet science marked the celebrations
of the centenary of Darwin's discovery. Four outstanding Soviet
scientists were forcibly deprived of the international honour they had
won, an honour which only the most exceptional scientist can win more
than once in a lifetime.

Nevertheless, no Soviet citizen could have been greatly surprised at
the outcome of this event, which would be extraordinary in any other
country. It was exactly what any of us could have predicted. It was considered natural, natural that is under the system of approval and consideration of trips abroad by citizens which existed in 1959 in the USSR.
This system was completely illegal, with its lack of equal rights of
citizens and elementary trust. The political character of all procedures
up to the end of 1959 was not concealed, and only in 1960 was the
system abolished under which a citizen who was not a Party member
had to obtain not only a mass of various documents, forms and character
references, but also two guarantees from Party members in good standing, certifying his reliability before he could go abroad.

But now five years had passed. In October 1964 Khrushchev resigned, and this coincided with the end of the position under which genetics had been deprived of its rights. The complete domination of Michurin biology came to an end. Of the four Darwin prizewinners, only two witnessed this change; Shmal'gauzen did not survive to see it, he shared Chetverikov's fate. But although only a few geneticists of the classical school were left in the USSR in 1964, each of them became the hero of the day, each of them began to do the work of three. It was necessary to create almost everything anew: laboratories, departments, courses, textbooks and institutes. It was necessary to reconstruct at top speed a great and highly important branch of knowledge and to implement its achievements in agriculture, medicine and education.

Timofeev-Resovskii, a brilliant teacher and propagandist of genetics and one of the world's leading experts in it, now found a wide field of activity opening before him. His energy knew no bounds. At the beginning of 1964 he and a group of his colleagues had moved from the Urals to the Obninsk Institute of Medical Radiology of the Academy of Medical Sciences, and within a short time he had created a large centre for research in the fields of radiation, theoretical and medical genetics. He became the recognized leader of a large school of Soviet biologists. His work went forward at a furious pace, from early morning to late at night. Not a single invitation to give lectures, talks or courses in any provincial college did he fail to accept or to carry out. His lectures and courses were attended by students from Moscow and Leningrad, Kaluga and Novosibirsk, Krasnoyarsk and Erevan. Just outside Moscow at the summer camp of the Moscow Komsomols[1] he held an annual summer school on theoretical biology, where every summer some two hundred to two hundred and fifty young scientists were able to improve the level of their knowledge and scientific thought. I know of no one who gave himself to the task of restoring Soviet biology with such energy and passion. In less than a year, the name of N. V. Timofeev-Resovskii had become one of the most popular among biologists, and not only among biologists.

1965 was a notable year for Soviet science not only on account of the renascence of biology and genetics. It was the centenary of the publication

[1] The *Komsomols* (the All-Union Lenin League of Communist Youth) originally had upper and lower age-limits for membership of 14 and 23. Soon, however, this was extended to permit non-voting ('passive') membership beyond 23 years of age, and under certain conditions a passive member could regain voting rights. In practice membership of the Komsomol normally extends to about 30 years of age—*Translator*.

by the Czech scholar, Gregor Mendel, of his classic work on the laws of heredity, the appearance of which is considered by geneticists to mark the birth of their science. Mendel's discovery is generally considered to be of equal significance to Darwin's, since only after the discovery of the laws of heredity could the theory of evolution become the basis of modern biology. The centenary of Mendel's discovery was a significant date not only in Czechoslovakia. The United Nations had included it in the list of dates which should be marked by celebrations by the whole civilized world, as that of an event affecting the progress of human society. Mendel's name took its place in the list along with those of Copernicus, Leonardo da Vinci, Newton, Galileo and Darwin.

First to celebrate the Mendel jubilee in the Soviet Union was the Moscow Society of Naturalists, the only one of our scientific societies which had not disavowed Mendel during the years of the persecutions of geneticists. In February, on the exact centenary of the day that Mendel's first work on heredity first saw the light, the Moscow Society of Naturalists held a jubilee session at Moscow University at which Timofeev-Resovskii was to deliver a paper on the life and works of Mendel. This he did with his accustomed skill and spirit. Representatives of the Czechoslovak Academy of Sciences and employees of the Czechoslovak Embassy came especially to hear this paper, and it was widely reported in the Czechoslovak press. This was understandable, since after so many years of crude scoffing at the name of Mendel in the USSR, scoffing which deeply wounded the national pride of the Czechs, this session with Timofeev-Resovskii's paper was the first official public recognition of the fact that the shameful period of reviling this great scientist had come to an end.

But naturally the principal international celebrations connected with the jubilee were planned in Brno in Mendel's native land, where he had carried out his research in the little garden of the monastery. Here in Brno, according to a UNESCO resolution, the Czechoslovak Academy of Sciences and the Genetics Section of the International Union of Biological Sciences were to hold an international memorial symposium in honour of Mendel. This was called for August 1965, since large-scale international scientific meetings are customarily held in the summer or at the beginning of the autumn. At the beginning of 1965 special Mendel medals were instituted, which together with diplomas would be awarded by the Czechoslovak Academy of Sciences to twenty outstanding geneticists of the world. Each of the twenty recipients of the Mendel Medal was invited to Czechoslovakia for the ceremonial presentation of the medal and to read a paper at the memorial symposium on questions in the field of work for which the guest was being so highly honoured by the Czechoslovak Academy of Sciences. The papers by the winners of the Mendel Medal would form the first part of the memorial symposium. The second part of the programme was a scientific symposium on mutations; this was planned to take place in Prague, and all the geneticists of the world were invited to come to Czechoslovakia to take part in these sessions and the national celebrations connected with them.

The Mendel Medal of Honour was awarded to a number of Soviet geneticists. A special letter came from the President of the Czechoslovak Academy of Sciences, Professor F. Šorm, inviting them to go to Czechoslovakia to receive it. These Soviet scientists were: B. L. Astaurov, N. P. Dubinin, M. E. Lobashev, N. V. Tsitsin and N. V. Timofeev-Resovskii. Each of Professor Šorm's invitations was sent not only to the scientist personally; a separate copy also went to the Presidium of the Academy of Sciences of the USSR.

The leading scientific centres in our country adopted resolutions to take part in both symposia (in Brno and Prague) and it was expected that about a hundred Soviet scientists would be going to Czechoslovakia. Even a number of recent Lysenkoists, who for many years had bitterly condemned Mendel as a reactionary and obscurantist and had used the word 'Mendelist' as the ultimate in condemnation, decided to try for a trip to the Mendel symposium, although, of course, no one from Czechoslovakia had invited them.

The news that Timofeev-Resovskii had been awarded the Mendel Medal delighted all of us who worked in the laboratory he directed. Our chief, who had received the Spallanzani Medal back in the 1930s, was now the winner of an international scientific prize for the third time. But from the beginning Timofeev-Resovskii had very little faith that he would be allowed to go to Czechoslovakia for this celebration which was so exciting for any geneticist.

And indeed the beginning was not hopeful. The Foreign Section of the Academy of Sciences accepted for the process of approval all the invitations from the Czechoslovak Academy, except that for Timofeev-Resovskii. The Chief Academic Secretary of the Academy of Sciences, Academician N. M. Sisakyan, who until very recently had been a rabid Lysenkoist and an opponent of 'reactionary Mendelism', sent Professor Šorm a letter informing him that Timofeev-Resovskii was working in an institute which fell within the system of the Academy of Medical Sciences of the USSR, and that his invitation must therefore be sent to that body. This was a piece of bureaucratic shuffling, since the Government of the USSR has empowered the Academy of Sciences to establish interdepartmental scientific delegations and to approve visits abroad by any scientists.

The Czechoslovak Academy repeated the invitation and sent the appropriate letter both to the President of the Academy of Medical Sciences and to the Director of our Institute. The Academy of Medical Sciences of the USSR was also preparing to send a small delegation to Czechoslovakia on a tourist basis, and this delegation included several colleagues from our Institute who were to present papers at the symposium on mutations in Prague. It was natural, therefore, that when the Academy of Medical Sciences decided on the composition of this delegation it included both Timofeev-Resovskii and his wife Elena Aleksandrovna, herself a geneticist and the co-author of many of his works.

When the delegations to the Mendel symposia were being formed everyone understood that old sins would be forgotten. All our geneticists had at some time been persecuted, dismissed from their posts and attacked in print. Some of them had been expelled from the Party. Some had been arrested and exiled. No one had 'clean' questionnaires and *curricula vitae* except the Lysenkoists—and their questionnaires were adorned with orders and honours of every kind. If the selection of those to go to Czechoslovakia had been made in the usual way, according to the criteria of biographical questionnaires, there would have been no one to go. There would have been another international scandal. But even Mendel himself, once declared to be a 'reactionary German monk in the service of German racism', had now been rehabilitated as a great son of the fraternal Czech nation and the pride of world science. In the face of this turnabout, if only for the period of the jubilee, the old sins of Mendel's faithful followers should surely have been forgiven.

This 'forgiveness of sins' in Timofeev-Resovskii's case reached our Institute in the form of a little piece of paper, a quarter of a quarto sheet. This tiny little printed form, signed by the Deputy Head of the International Section of the Academy of Medical Sciences, V. G. Zakharova, instructed the Director of the Institute to prepare and send to the Academy of Medical Sciences of the USSR 'exit dossiers' for both Timofeev-Resovskii and Mrs Timofeeva-Resovskaya. A second similar scrap of paper with the same signature was sent to the Health Department, instructing them to carry out a medical examination of the candidates for the trip and provide a written certificate of their state of health. Following this came the questionnaires for the 'exit dossier'.

The approval of trips to the socialist countries of Europe is a somewhat simpler process than for capitalist countries. The would-be traveller has to provide only six photos, not twelve, complete only one and not two 'exit dossiers', and this does not have to include copies of the birth certificates of children nor of the marriage certificate. But a character reference of the same sort is still required, and this must still be witnessed and confirmed at a meeting of the Party Bureau or Party Committee and then by the District Committee of the CPSU, and in small towns by the Town and Provincial Committees of the CPSU. The questionnaires for the 'exit dossier' go to the Foreign Section of the organization concerned and the character reference to the Party Committee, Town Committee, and then to the Provincial Committee. They are then attached to the 'exit dossier', and when it is thus fertilised it can begin to travel further.

Being unused to these matters, Timofeev-Resovskii and his wife toiled for a very long time in filling out the lengthy forms. Every question had to be answered in full. They had to list all close relatives, living or dead, children, parents, brothers, and sisters—both of them had been born into large families—and not just to list them, but to indicate when they were born and died, where they were born and died, where they worked, what they worked at, their latest place of residence and their latest place of employment, for every one of them. They had to state all their own places and dates of work, and for people approaching the age of sixty-five, this ran into quite a long list. They had to list all trips abroad, dates, length of stay, and purpose, and of course both of them had lived nearly twenty years abroad. At last it was all finished, and medical certificates were obtained, according to which both geneticists 'had no deviations from the normal standard'.

After this, Timofeev-Resovskii began preparing two papers, one of which, 'The Genetics of *Drosophila*', was included in the programme of the plenary memorial sessions in Brno, while the other 'The Induction of Mutations' was to be presented in Prague. Both papers were to be delivered in English.

The 'exit dossiers' went off to the Academy of Medical Sciences, and the drafts for the character references to the Party Committee of the Institute. And here the first difficulty arose. The Secretary of the Party Committee, the pharmacologist K. S. Shadurskii, refused to put his signature to it, although the majority of the Party Committee confirmed Timofeev-Resovskii's character reference. Fortunately in June Shadurskii went on leave, and in his absence both the director, who was

Deputy Secretary of the Party Committee and the Chairman of the Local Committee, signed the character reference, and it followed the others to the Town Committee of the CPSU. After making the rounds of the Provincial Committee of the CPSU and some other provincial services, some of the other character references reached the Academy of Medical Sciences, here were united with their 'exit dossiers' and went on their way to the Ministry of Health of the USSR and thence to the International Section of the State Committee for Science and Technology, which sent them on with its 'decision' to the next level up, the Central Committee of the CPSU.

But no one in the Institute yet knew that among all these character references which were converging from various bodies in a single stream towards that big building in the Old Square in Moscow, the most important ones, those of Timofeev-Resovskii and his wife, were not there. These particular character references had never got beyond the Kaluga Provincial Committee to the Academy of Medical Sciences, but they had not been returned to the Institute either. It was only by chance that the workers in the Genetics Section of our Institute discovered that Timofeev-Resovskii's 'exit dossier' had not been sent on to the Ministry of Health and was not being considered for approval.

Just at that time there arrived from Czechoslovakia the printed programmes of the symposia, which were being distributed throughout the world. Timofeev-Resovskii's papers appeared in this programme, and he was also named as the chairman of one of the sessions, for Wednesday 11 August. At the same time a letter came from the Chairman of the Organizing Committee of the symposium, asking Timofeev-Resovskii to give yet another paper, his third, on problems of evolution. He wrote that thanks to the fact that Timofeev-Resovskii was taking part in the symposium they hoped to attract wider international attention to the meeting. At the same time the President of the Czechoslovak Academy of Sciences, Professor Šorm, having had no confirmation from Timofeev-Resovskii that he was definitely coming, nor any definite answers to his enquiries as to which hotel Timofeev-Resovskii preferred and which visits, celebrations and excursions he would be taking part in, once again wrote to the Presidents of the Academy of Medical Sciences and the Academy of Sciences of the USSR and to the Director of our Institute, asking them to assist Timofeev-Resovskii to get to Czechoslovakia, since, in his words, 'this will considerably enhance the scientific interest in the symposium for many scholars'. Shortly after the distribution of the printed programme, Timofeev-Resovskii began to receive letters from his numerous foreign friends expressing their delight that they would be seeing him in the near future at the symposium.

But the matter of getting the exit decision approved was not going forward at all. Hence at the beginning of July 1965 a group of heads of laboratories of our Institute sent a special letter to the Central Committee of the CPSU. This letter was dispatched to the Secretariat of the Central Committee, the Science Section of the Central Committee and the International Section for socialist countries of the Central Committee. This letter explained the role of Timofeev-Resovskii in the renascence of Soviet genetics, the Mendel Prize and the invitations he had received, the interest of the Czechoslovak scientists in his trip, and the facts of the red tape and intolerable confusion in the process of getting his trip to the Mendel celebrations approved. The letter was well documented and it would be impossible to ignore it. In the letter it was pointed out that the approval of the 'exit dossier' had become bogged down in the Kaluga provincial organizations. It was probably for this reason that the letter was redirected from the Science Section of the Central Committee to the Kaluga Provincial Committee of the CPSU. Evidently the Kaluga authorities were asked to sort the matter out. But the sorting out took quite a different form, the form of finding out who the authors of the letters were, and why they were mixing themselves up in the matter.

But the International Section of the Central Committee did not send its letter back to Kaluga. They dealt with the matter themselves, and their attitude seemed to be extremely favourable. The member of this Section responsible for Czechoslovakia firmly assured the representative of our Institute that Timofeev-Resovskii would be going to Czechoslovakia. In theory it was not a complicated business, no visa was needed for a trip to Czechoslovakia, and the Central Committee could arrange a trip to Czechoslovakia within a few hours if it wished. We were all sure that this promise was not simply hot air.

Soon afterwards the largest group going to Czechoslovakia at their own expense as 'scientific tourists' received their necessary identification papers and set off by train for Brno several days before the symposium opened. The delegates from the USSR, mainly academicians from the Academy of Sciences and the Lenin All-Union Academy of Agricultural Sciences, travelled to Czechoslovakia at the expense of their Departments and Academies by Aeroflot about twenty-four hours before the beginning of the sessions. With them at the expense of the Czechoslovak Academy of Sciences flew the guests of honour of the Academy, the winners of the Mendel Medal and the speakers at the Memorial Symposium. Only one of them, Timofeev-Resovskii, was setting off that day with his wife in quite a different direction—to the little station of Miassovo in the Urals, where for many years in succession, right through the difficult time of genetics in our country, he had held every summer, in Mendel's honour, an underground All-Union Symposium on genetics, providing the first scientific school for a large number of young scientists.

In Brno the Soviet and all other winners were presented with the Mendel Medal at a ceremonial meeting in the church where Mendel had worked for so many years as scientist and priest, next to the little plot where he had carried out his experiments on plants. The medal for Timofeev-Resovskii, however, remained in the keeping of the President of the Czechoslovak Academy of Sciences, Professor Šorm. He would not hand it over to the head of the delegation to be presented in the USSR. 'Since you could not arrange for Timofeev-Resovskii's visit here, I cannot give you his medal. Czechoslovakia will present it to the winner on her own territory, in the Czechoslovak Embassy in Moscow, with all due ceremony.'

Several months went by, and it was now December 1965. One frosty day the Assistant Director of the Institute ran into Timofeev-Resovskii's office and told him that on the previous evening a telegram had been telephoned through from the Academy of Medical Sciences in Moscow, and that today at 3.30 p.m. precisely Timofeev-Resovskii was to present himself at the Czechoslovak Embassy to be given the Mendel Medal and the Diploma of Honour of the Czechoslovak Academy of Sciences.

Only three hours remained to the appointed time, and it is 109 kilometres from the Institute to Moscow. The Deputy Director offered practical help. For the journey to Moscow he agreed to provide an old Moskvich car which was now too decrepit to be used for transporting the chiefs of the Institute. Timofeev-Resovskii got ready to go in a twinkling of an eye; he squeezed into the car with some difficulty and I sat down beside him. It was impossible to send him by himself, and there was no one that day from the administration of the Institute who could accompany our prizewinner. But in spite of the shortage of time Nikolai Vladimirovich insisted on first driving several kilometres back to his home in town. After all, he would be moving at diplomatic levels, so he must put on a black suit, a tie and so forth. He could not turn up at a ceremonial reception in laboratory clothes; the Ambassador might be there, representatives of the Academy of Medical Sciences of the USSR, scientists invited by the Embassy and perhaps even a representative of the Czechoslovak Academy.

But the trip proved far from easy. The car would not do more than forty kilometres per hour over the icy roads. The windows of the car would not shut properly; the searing frosty air blew in on us. Seventy kilometres from Moscow, where the Moscow and Kaluga provinces meet, we had to stop. The road was closed by a veterinary barrier. There was foot-and-mouth disease in Kaluga, and only those cars could pass which had a certificate that the wheels had been disinfected. But the disinfection point was ninety kilometres from Moscow, near Balabanovo. We drove back to Balabanovo and got disinfected. But it turned out that the certificate that we had been disinfected had to be obtained at a place 105 kilometres from Moscow, back near Obninsk. We would have to start the journey all over again. But there was no time left for that. We left the car and rushed to the station. Luckily, an electric train came in very soon, and we finished our journey to Moscow in a warm carriage, arriving at the Kiev terminus twenty minutes before we were due at the Embassy. A taxi got us to the Embassy building almost exactly on time. We went into the building, but there was no one in the hallway to meet the prizewinner who had been invited to receive his medal. The receptionist on duty knew nothing about it either. I started making telephone calls. In the end, after several calls, I managed to find out that the Second Secretary of the Embassy of the Czechoslovak Socialist Republic, Jaroslav Nikl, was responsible for the presentation of medals and other prizes. I phoned him, but he was not there. We waited for some twenty minutes and were beginning to think of leaving, when Mr Nikl came in and I was able to inform him by telephone that the Mendel Prizewinner was waiting for him in the hallway. He came down and took us to another building, intended, it would seem, for receptions. We went into an enormous hall used for banquets and meetings. It was in complete disorder. The evening before there had undoubtedly been a large banquet, and it still had not been all cleared away. The air still smelled sharply of stale salad and wine dregs. We quickly went into a small side room, sat down at a table, exchanged a few sentences and at once proceeded to the principal event. Jaroslav Nikl stood up, Timofeev-Resovskii and I did likewise. Then Nikl read out an address by the President of the Czechoslovak Academy of Sciences and presented the winner with his medal and diploma. I offered the winner my warm congratulations and suggested that we toast the occasion in a bottle of wine. Nikl went out, and came back shortly with a

D

bottle of French wine and some glasses. We drank a toast in honour of Mendel, and chatted for half an hour about this and that. Then, after wishing Nikl every success in his work, we left the Embassy. By the evening of the same day, Timofeev-Resovskii was back home again, where we had a proper celebration of this unforgettable event in a scientist's life.

A few days went by, and fate had another surprise in store for Timofeev-Resovskii. At the end of December 1965 a registered airmail letter addressed to him arrived from the USA under the seal of the National Academy of Sciences in Washington. The addressee was away from home at that time, and his wife, Elena Aleksandrova, received the letter and read it to a group of his colleagues to ask their advice. The letter was from Mr Harrison Brown, the Foreign Secretary of the National Academy of Sciences.

In the letter Brown stated that the Council of the National Academy of Sciences had decided to award Timofeev-Resovskii the International Kimber Prize, 'for distinguished contribution to the science of genetics'. The prize had been awarded to Timofeev-Resovskii for his work on the study of mutations. 'The prize,' Brown wrote, 'consists of a gold medal and an honorarium of two thousand dollars. Traditionally, the medal and honorarium are presented annually, at a special prize-giving session of the National Academy by its President.'[1]

This session formed part of the annual Conference of the Academy in Washington in April. Brown also stated that the President of the National Academy of Sciences of the USA, Professor Frederick Seitz, had sent a special letter, on 9 December 1965, to the President of the Academy of Sciences of the USSR, Professor M. V. Keldysh, informing him of the decision of the Council of the National Academy of the USA and asking Keldysh to convey to Timofeev-Resovskii the official invitation of the National Academy to come to the USA on 25–28 April, to take part in the Annual Conference and receive his prize. The expenses of the trip would be borne by the Academy.

Unfortunately, none of us who worked in the Department knew anything about the Kimber Prize, its terms of reference, its character and so on. The Nobel Prizes are known to everyone, but this was the first we had heard of the Kimber Prizes. When the prizewinner himself came home a couple of days later, it turned out that he did not know anything about it either. All the same, of course, both he and we were delighted with this turn of events. In the next few days everyone who worked in

---

[1] Translated from Medvedev's Russian text—*Translator*.

the laboratory tried to find something out about this prize, but this was not so simple. However, when his old friend B. L. Astaurov heard about it, he remembered that during his trip to Brno for the Mendel symposium he had seen an exhibit in the Mendel Museum entitled 'Kimber Prize Winners'.

During the symposium, there had been two large receptions in this museum, and those who had attended the symposium must have had many photographs taken in the halls of the museum, both by the official photographers attached to the symposium and by their colleagues. A search through a number of collections of photographs finally produced a result. In one of them part of the Kimber exhibit could be seen. It was possible to make out a large bas-relief medal with portraits of Darwin, Mendel, Morgan and Bateson, and several photographs of winners of the award. There was a portrait of Curt Stern, a major specialist in the field of human genetics, H. J. Muller, the discoverer of radiation-induced mutagenesis, and G. W. Beadle, creator of the biochemical model of gene function. The character of the prize thus became clear and so did the level of the winners. It is sufficient to note that Muller and Beadle were both Nobel Prize winners as well. It was, therefore, a serious matter, more serious than a routine award in connection with a jubilee.

Airmail from the USA to Moscow normally takes between seven and nine days. Keldysh must have received his letter from the President of the National Academy of the USA, Professor Seitz, in the middle of December. But even by the end of December there still appeared to be no reaction from him. At all events, no reaction had reached Obninsk. We were all sure that Academician Keldysh, who knew Timofeev-Resovskii personally, would have sent him a telegram of congratulations immediately. But mid-January came, and no evidence of Seitz's letter arrived from the office of the President of the Academy of Sciences of the USSR; and all this time the Annual Conference of the National Academy of the USA was drawing closer. Moreover, Timofeev-Resovskii had to answer Brown's letter, and to do this he needed to know the contents of the letter of the President of the Academy. When it became clear that so long a silence on the part of the Academy of Sciences of the USSR might be due simply to the loss of Seitz's letter, Timofeev-Resovskii wrote a personal letter to Academician Keldysh enquiring about the matter. He told Keldysh of the information he had received from Brown and asked him to send a copy of Professor Seitz's letter, if this had ever reached the Academy.

On one of my weekly visits to the Moscow libraries, Nikolai Vladimirovich asked me to deliver this letter to Keldysh at the Presidium of
the Academy of Sciences.

Academician Keldysh's secretary, a venerable lady, sitting outside his
office in the old detached house in Lenin Prospect, opened and read
Timofeev-Resovskii's 'personal' letter there and then, in front of me.
After this she gave it back to me, although I knew very well that Keldysh
was there in his office. Without even looking in the President's registered post-book, she told me that Timofeev-Resovskii's letter should
be taken to the Foreign Section in another building. I attempted to
argue, trying to convince Keldysh's secretary that Timofeev-Resovskii's
letter was by its very nature intended for Keldysh personally, and that
I could not give it to anyone else. I also attempted to convince her that
the letter of the President of the American Academy must surely be
recorded in the post-book of the President of the Academy of Sciences
of the USSR. But all in vain. I moved across to the Foreign Section.

But in the Foreign Section, too, there was no record to be found in
the registered post-book of a letter from the President of the American
Academy dated 9 December 1965, and the secretary to the head of the
section knew nothing of any such letter. She suggested that I apply to
the group dealing with the USA in the section for capitalist countries.
But the official of this group in charge of correspondence knew nothing
of Professor Seitz's letter either. However, he did remember that during
the period from 15 to 20 December, he had been out of town, and
another colleague had replaced him. It proved possible to locate this
deputy. And at last, in the course of discussion, there flashed across his
memory those sentences in Professor Seitz's letter in which he spoke of
the two thousand dollars. According to him, Professor Seitz's letter had
been passed on immediately to the Chief Academic Secretary of the
Academy of Sciences of the USSR, Academician N. M. Sisakyan, who
was to report on it to the President of the Academy of Sciences.

Sisakyan, whom I was lucky enough to catch just as he was arriving
at the Presidium building, also could not recall the letter at once, particularly as his secretary had not recorded the letter as having been
received by the Academy of Sciences. (Why take responsibility in such
a matter?)

But after I had acquainted Sisakyan with the text of Mr Brown's
letter his memory started to clear, and rubbing his brow he said, remembering it, 'Yes, there was such a letter from Seitz, but we sent it on to
N. N. Blokhin at the Academy of Medical Sciences. And we wrote to

Professor Seitz that Timofeev-Resovskii is working for the Academy of Medical Sciences. . . .'

Just at that time I happened to have some business in the International Section of the Academy of Medical Sciences of the USSR, in connection with a possible trip to England to deliver the Annual Ciba Foundation Lecture on Ageing. When I had discussed this, I asked V. G. Zakharova, the Deputy Head of this section, whether her section had received a letter from the Academy of Sciences of the USSR regarding the Kimber Prize. Zakharova seemed somewhat embarrassed at first, but then, learning that I was fully familiar with the matter, she began to question me cautiously about the nature of the prize, why was it awarded to Timofeev-Resovskii and so forth. It became apparent that the President of the Academy of Medical Sciences on receiving Seitz's letter with an accompanying note from Sisakyan, had instructed his International Section to find out the exact status of the prize, establish a list of former winners, and above all to find out who this Kimber was who founded the prize and how he made his fortune.

The source of Kimber's fortune should in principle have been quite irrelevant. Annual prizes of this type derive as a rule from the interest on capital deposited in a bank. $2000 per year for an annual prize meant about $50,000 in the bank.[1] Clearly, Kimber did not belong to the proletariat, but to the propertied class. But, after all, Nobel, the Swedish capitalist, who founded the renowned Nobel Prizes, each of which amounts to $35,000 to $50,000 was no socialist either. He manufactured dynamite and explosives and was the supplier of mines and ammunition for the Russian Tsarist Baltic Fleet. But, of course, it is all to the good that, having no direct heir, he left his capital for the noble purpose of supporting fundamental scientific research, literature and art. Many articles have been written about Nobel and his prizes, but as for Kimber and his prizes, Zakharova could find nothing—neither in Soviet, British nor American encyclopedias. And without this the Academy of Medical Sciences could not even decide to send congratulations to the winner. When she said goodbye, Zakharova asked me earnestly to help her find out something about this prize.

The information, however, could only be obtained from the USA. I wrote to my colleague, Michael Lerner, Professor of Genetics at the University of California, and, after giving him a brief summary of the situation, asked him to send me as soon as possible any information

---

[1] In fact the Kimber Prize is financed by an annual subvention, not by interest on capital—*Translator*.

about the Kimber Prize. I knew that Professor Lerner would certainly clarify everything possible. In corresponding with foreign scientists, one soon begins to learn from the speediness and nature of their replies which of them really are most friendly and willing to help one, and on whom one can rely in any situation. Although Lerner is considerably older than I am and holds a higher position (he is a member of the National Academy of the USA, an Academician by our reckoning) I had always felt him to be a friend. Moreover, Lerner had been born in the Russian colony in Harbin and knows Russian extremely well. He follows Russian scientific literature and fully understands the situation in the USSR. By chance, it happened that Professor Lerner was exactly the man best equipped to answer my question about the Kimber Prize, since he knows Kimber himself, who is also a Californian, very well, and had even advised him on questions of animal genetics. Lerner wrote on 1 February, and his answer came exceptionally quickly. Its gist was as follows:

Dear Dr Medvedev,
Much as it delighted me to know of the award to Timofeev-Resovskii, I was exceedingly distressed to hear of the difficulties he is experiencing in coming here for the presentation. It is hard to know what we can do from this side. I am sure that both Seitz and Brown will do what they can, and only hope that the matter can be straightened out in time.

The Kimber Genetics Award was established by John Kimber, one of the most successful poultry breeders in the USA, a pioneer in the application of modern genetic and statistical methods to animal improvement, who, starting with a backyard flock (some 20 miles from here) built up a multi-million dollar, world-wide business. It was a great privilege for me to be one of the group that formulated the criteria by which winners are chosen. In conformity with Mr Kimber's wishes, it was decided that the gold medal and monetary award ($2,000) for achievement in the science of genetics be based on a person's total contribution rather than upon a single important discovery. I may also say that it gave me great pleasure to serve for the first five years on the selection committee.

The previous winners have been: W. E. Castle, H. J. Muller, Sewall Wright, A. H. Sturtevant, Th. Dobzhansky, T. M. Sonneborn, G. W. Beadle, M. Demerec, J. B. S. Haldane, C. Stern, M. Delbrück and A. D. Hershey. Kimber Farms puts out a leaflet with the biography of each medallist. I am enclosing the first of these and will send you a complete set by air as soon as I obtain one.

I shall not write my congratulations to Timofeev-Resovskii: it is my sincere wish that I shall be able to present them to him in person in Washington.

Yours sincerely,

I. MICHAEL LERNER

The separate airmail packet with the printed material about the Kimber Prize soon arrived: a general description of its status in the 1955 leaflet and a series of leaflets with portraits, biographies and descriptions of the scientific achievements of the prize winners. These leaflets were published by Kimber Farms each year and distributed to scientific bodies and museums in various countries.

The first leaflet contained a large sketch of the Kimber Medal and a description of it. It was cast from pure gold, and weighed almost 400 grammes; it was clearly a work of art. According to the description, the medal was the work of the sculptor, Malvina Hoffman, a pupil of Auguste Rodin. Previously, Hoffman had won great renown for a group of bronzes, a hundred figures, exhibited in the Chicago Museum. In the words of the author of the leaflet, this group was the most remarkable work of sculpture in the history of mankind. The leaflet also described other examples of Hoffman's work. On the Kimber Medal, Hoffman, so the description affirmed,

> has reproduced the likenesses of four of the greatest workers in the field of heredity: 1. Charles Darwin, whose epic studies in the field of evolution prepared the world for the serious study of heredity; 2. Gregor Mendel, who, working largely with peas, established principles which place the science of genetics on a basis similar to that of chemistry; 3. William Bateson, who, working with chickens, first demonstrated Mendelian inheritance in the animal kingdom; 4. Thomas Hunt Morgan, whose work, largely with *Drosophila*, explored the cytological basis of inheritance. . . .

Above this bas-relief group there appeared the words: 'The Kimber Genetics Award of the National Academy of Sciences', and below it was a second inscription: 'For Distinguished Contribution to the Science of Genetics.'

In the description of the Kimber Prize it was noted that it was the only international prize specially for genetics.

There is no need to list here the achievements of the twelve Kimber prize-winning scientists before Timofeev-Resovskii. The names listed in Lerner's letter are known to all geneticists and biologists throughout the world. To a great degree all the developments of genetics in the last thirty to forty years are connected with their work. Only one of them, J. B. S. Haldane, was a European, the rest were Americans. However, two of them, Stern and Delbrück, were émigrés from Germany, and one of them, Dobzhansky, was an émigré from the USSR.

Thus the Kimber Prize was undoubtedly a great honour, and John Kimber himself was an entirely suitable donor from the point of view of the origin of his fortune—exactly the same type of farmer-selectionist-capitalist as Burbank, whom we considered the 'American Michurin'. It was possible to show that Soviet poultry-breeding too had benefited from the achievements of Kimber Farms and its stock had been purchased by the USSR for work on selection.

All these considerations were immediately communicated to the International Section of the Academy of Medical Sciences of the USSR, and thence, it must be presumed, to the President of the Academy of Medical Sciences. But the President of the Academy of Medical Sciences did not hurry with his answer to the USA, although Frederick Seitz had received a preliminary letter from Sisakyan and had sent the President of the Academy of Medical Sciences, N. N. Blokhin, a special very detailed letter. On 17 February Mr Brown of the Foreign Section of the National Academy also sent a letter to Blokhin, a copy of which was dispatched to Obninsk, to let Timofeev-Resovskii know what efforts were being made to solve the problem of this visit to the USA:

Dear President Blokhin,

On 25 January 1966, the President of our Academy, Professor Frederick Seitz, notified you in a special letter of our wish to award the Kimber Prize for genetics to your outstanding scientist N. V. Timofeev-Resovskii. As Professor Seitz stressed by tradition the presentation of this prize takes place in Washington during the Annual Session of the Academy, which this year is on 25, 26 and 27 April.

We feel sure that during his visit to the USA. Professor Timofeev-Resovskii would like to visit his American colleagues and friends in their institutes. So that we may have the opportunity of arranging these visits in advance, we should be pleased to know for how long Timofeev-Resovskii can come to the USA. Since the time to the Annual Session is very short now, we should be grateful if you could let us know your decision by telegram.

The members of the National Academy of Sciences of the USA and particularly the biologists were delighted to learn of the awarding of the Kimber Prize to Timofeev-Resovskii, and will be very pleased to meet him personally. The Kimber Prize, which was founded in 1955 is awarded as an extremely high honour in the field of genetics, and we feel sure that you will share our delight in connection with the award of this prize to a Soviet scientist.[1]

But this cordial letter, like that of Professor Seitz, remained unanswered. Blokhin maintained a complete silence. He did not reply

[1] Translated from Medvedev's Russian text—*Translator.*

either when Timofeev-Resovskii asked him to send a copy of Seitz's letter. Not long before, Nikolai Vladimirovich had sent Mr Brown a letter in which he thanked the National Academy for the high honour they had shown him in awarding him the Kimber Prize. But, as far as a visit to the USA went, all he could do was to express an uncertain hope. But this hope faded with each day. There was no miracle. March went by; April too went by. The Annual Meeting of the National Academy of Sciences with its prize-giving session also went by. At this session, some other prizes of the Academy were presented, in the fields of Physics, Chemistry, Technology and so on, but the Kimber Prize remained unpresented. There was no sound from the Academy of Medical Sciences of the USSR. Not only no congratulations, but not even a simple notification did the winner receive from the official Soviet bodies, and if Mr Brown had not sent his letter of congratulations in December 1965, then Timofeev-Resovskii might have known nothing even by April about the fact that the Kimber Prize had been awarded to him. It seemed as if in certain spheres it had been decided simply to ignore the whole business.

There was only one way to make this plan fail; and that was by publishing a notice about the award of the prize to a Soviet scientist and an article on the first Soviet winner of the Kimber Prize.

In May 1966, three of Timofeev-Resovskii's colleagues, without telling him, of course, wrote a brief news item devoted to the awarding of the Kimber Prize for Genetics to Timofeev-Resovskii. This article described the status of the prize and included a photograph of the medal and portrait of the thirteenth winner. His career in science and main achievements in genetics and related fields were briefly described. The article told of the letters of the President of the National Academy of Sciences of the USA to the Presidents of the Academy of Sciences and the Academy of Medical Sciences of the USSR and of the tradition of presenting the prize at the meeting of the National Academy of the USA in Washington. The article concluded by congratulating the winner in the name of the whole numerous body of Soviet geneticists.

This article was first offered for publication to the Obninsk local paper, *Vpered*. The writers had calculated on local patriotism: look what scientists we have here in Obninsk! But nothing came of it. The editors accepted the article very keenly indeed, but it did not appear in the paper. It was necessary to aim at a scientific journal, although this would delay publication by some months. The choice fell on the journal *Genetika*, only recently founded. The editor-in-chief of the journal

D*

from the time of its inception was the famous botanist, Professor Petr Mikhailovich Zhukovskii, and his deputy was Professor S. I. Alikhanyan.

Zhukovskii had been my first teacher in science and was a true friend. I had started working under him during my first year as a student in 1944, and I remained a pupil of his until I finished my dissertation for my degree of Candidate in 1950, and, although since 1950 we had been working along different lines (I had become a biochemist) and in different towns (Zhukovskii moved to Leningrad where he became head of the All-Union Institute of Plant-Breeding), our scientific contacts continued. Hence I felt sure that when I broached the question of publishing an article on the Kimber Prize he would support my idea with enthusiasm. I did not doubt that the whole editorial board of *Genetika* would also be in favour of doing so. And so it turned out. The article on Timofeev-Resovskii, entitled 'International Kimber Prize for Genetics awarded to Soviet Scientist N. V. Timofeev-Resovskii', went for setting, and as an editorial too. But ahead lay censorship which was outside the control of the editor-in-chief.

Several years ago either Glavlit or a censor had to read all manuscripts and give permission for typesetting. The censor (the 'editor' of Glavlit) read and passed the proofs and then, a third time, read a sample copy, to approve the distribution of the printed edition 'into the light of day'. But then to save time (the production of printed matter was increasing) the censor only read it twice, in proofs and in the sample copy. An article could go for setting if passed by the editor-in-chief or his deputy.

By the end of June proofs of the article with two photographs of the medal and the winner were ready. The photograph of Timofeev-Resovskii was especially successful. It had been taken by one of the best amateur photographers in our Institute. From this portrait the article in the journal would greatly benefit; the reader would see the inspired, weary and resolute face of a scholar who had lived through a great deal. Somehow it harmonized with portraits of the scientists on the medal itself.

But the censor had not even got to the article when something most unusual happened. Also at the end of June Timofeev-Resovskii was suddenly summoned to see the President of the Academy of Medical Sciences of the USSR. The Director of our Institute, Professor G. A. Zedgenidze, was summoned at the same time. It could be assumed that the summons had some connection with the prize. Everyone was waiting for good news.

The next day we heard the details. The President of the Academy of

Medical Sciences received Timofeev-Resovskii very coldly. He informed him officially that in the opinion of the higher authorities the awarding of the prize to Timofeev-Resovskii was a provocation by the Americans. Owing to this they strongly recommended Timofeev-Resovskii to decline the prize. The Academy of Medical Sciences of the USSR did not recognize the prize and would not reply to letters about it. In the words of the President of the Academy of Medical Sciences of the USSR, the award of the prize was not due, in the first instance, to the services of the scientist to genetics, but was due to the fact that before the war he had lived in emigration for many years and had then been in prison in the USSR. It was for this reason, Blokhin considered, that the Americans had chosen Timofeev-Resovskii from among the Soviet geneticists.

Of course the surgeon Blokhin and his instructors had not read the works of Timofeev-Resovskii and could not assess his comparative potential among the other winners and possible candidates for the prize in the USSR. As President of the Academy he was accustomed to measure the stature and significance of a scientist according to his academic title. But to every geneticist in the USSR it was clear that of all the scientists in our country Timofeev-Resovskii was the most worthy to join the ranks of the Kimber Prize winners. He was the author of 250 scientific papers and several monographs, he had a broad outlook, and his scientific work was on the same level as that of Muller, Haldane and Sturtevant. Some of the other Kimber Prize winners were clearly surpassed by him, as regards their general contribution to genetics. Delbrück, the tenth Kimber Prize winner and undoubtedly an outstanding scholar, had been a pupil of Timofeev-Resovskii, and under his influence and in his laboratory had turned from physics to genetics.

It was quite clear that the Americans had *not* selected a Soviet scientist for the prize on the basis of his career. Only the directors of science in our country tried to settle a question on that basis. For some of them, indeed, some points in a questionnaire were of greater significance than the prestige of Soviet science, than law, logic and justice. But what was it about that career which caused Blokhin to adopt so unreasonably rigid a position regarding the prize?

It was a more poignant, dramatic and memorable career than that of anybody I knew, at least among scientists.

A member of the Kaluga nobility in origin, as a youth of seventeen or eighteen, Timofeev-Resovskii had taken part in the Civil War. After the war, while still a student, he began working under Chetverikov on genetics, in the Institute then under the direction of the outstanding biologist N. K. Kol'tsov. Timofeev-Resovskii quickly came to the fore as an excellent experimentalist, and when the Brain Institute in Germany, in 'exchange' for the help they had given in organizing a laboratory in the USSR for the study of Lenin's brain, asked Kol'tsov to help them organize a laboratory of genetics, the young Timofeev-Resovskii was assigned to this mission. At that time no one had even thought of a fortnight's scientific-tourist trip abroad. Scientists went to other countries not on excursions but for serious work, and the length of the trip varied from two to six years. It was agreed that Timofeev-Resovskii's stay should be for the maximum time.

Several years' work in Germany made the young scientist widely known in Europe and America. He published more than fifty papers and monographs, took part in two International Congresses on genetics and in many conferences, including the All-Union Meeting on Genetics and Selection in Leningrad, for which he submitted two works. This meeting was held at the beginning of 1929, the year of the 'Great Divide'. The 'Great Divide' led in particular to a wave of unprecedentedly large-scale repression not only among the peasants in the form of 'de-kulakization', but also among the intelligentsia and 'bourgeois' scientists. Furthermore persons of aristocratic descent were being deported from the capitals in tens of thousands. But although Timofeev-Resovskii submitted two papers for the meeting in Leningrad, which were published in 1930 in the Proceedings, he was not sent the visas for his trip to the USSR. His friends from the Institute of Experimental Biology feared that a trip to the USSR might not turn out very well for Timofeev-Resovskii. His freedom of thought, the sharpness of his remarks, his upright character and his intolerance of any deception were well known. In addition, shortly before the All-Union Meeting, the founder of the first school of genetics in the USSR, Timofeev-Resovskii's older teacher, Chetverikov, had been arrested and sent to the Urals. Of the members of the circle of drosophilist-geneticists which he had founded, 'Drozssor', several had had their homes searched, and one member of the circle, the post-graduate student P. F. Rokitskii, was also deported from Moscow. Several colleagues from Kol'tsov's Institute of Experimental Biology had been arrested.

However, towards the end of Timofeev-Resovskii's assignment in Germany, the situation at home had not improved but had grown worse. The persecution of leading scientists was in full swing. A series of 'open', but obviously rigged, trials of 'bourgeois specialists' inflamed the situation to the limit and heightened suspicion. The press, including the Central press, was full of senseless accusations of genetics and geneticists. Even the poet Dem'yan Bednyi published in *Izvestiya* a satirical poem about geneticists and genes, deriding genetic theories as utter nonsense. In the Communist Academy there were stormy discussions on the reactionary nature of Morgan-Mendelism, which concluded in the rout of the classical geneticists and the victory of the Lamarckians. But what was especially significant for a scientist working abroad was the ban on foreign travel. After 1929 the participation of Soviet scientists in international scientific meetings and symposia practically ceased altogether. Even in the case of the International Congress of Genetics in the USA in 1932, only one person turned up from the USSR, the President of the Lenin All-Union Academy of Agricultural Sciences, Academician Nikolai I. Vavilov. Under these conditions Timofeev-Resovskii decided to prolong his work in Germany, all the more so since he had gathered around himself a large and creative group, unique experimental equipment had been set up, and the experimental and theoretical work of the Genetics Section headed by Nikolai Vladimirovich was admired throughout Europe. Nevertheless he carefully preserved his Soviet citizenship and Soviet passport, hoping that in time the situation at home would improve.

But as we know there was no improvement either in the USSR or in Germany. In Germany the Reichstag fire was staged to serve as an excuse for a campaign of terror against the opponents of National Socialism, while in the USSR the assassination of Kirov was arranged, serving as the start of the widest possible wave of repression. In biology T. D. Lysenko and I. I. Prezent came on the scene with their total denial of genetics and all those scientific truths to which Timofeev-Resovskii had devoted his life. Arrests among geneticists began. In the 'Kirov stream' in 1935 Timofeev-Resovskii's own brother was arrested. A Leningrad Party worker, he was arrested and shot as an 'enemy of the people'. Two years later in Irkutsk a second brother, a zoologist and fur-breeder, was arrested. Yet another brother, who worked in the film industry, and a sister, alarmed by events, denied all connection with Nikolai Vladimirovich and stopped corresponding with him. To have a brother abroad, especially in Germany, was too dangerous. Also arrested were his wife's sisters, his wife's cousins and many other relatives and friends. The International Genetics Congress to be held in Moscow was cancelled.

But the terror was also spreading in Germany; there, too, the political pressure on science was increasing. And Timofeev-Resovskii decided to leave Germany and to take his family with him.

He considered a number of places including the USA. But he felt that the North American way of life was foreign to him, and he did not want to leave Europe. Finally his Russian nature triumphed. Timofeev-Resovskii asked Kol'tsov and Vavilov about the possibilities of returning to the Soviet Union. This was at the end of 1937.

Both Vavilov and Kol'tsov knew only too well what would await the whole family of their colleague and friend immediately they returned to the USSR, but they no longer dared entrust their thoughts and warnings to the state post. Vavilov asked Muller, the American geneticist, who was on his way from Leningrad to the front in Republican Spain, to go to Berlin, and give Timofeev-Resovskii the sternest warning about what awaited him if he returned to his native land. Kol'tsov, the Director of the Institute of Experimental Biology, who had sent Timofeev-Resovskii abroad, took a very risky step to stop his friend and colleague. He went to the Swedish Embassy and sent a letter to him secretly by the diplomatic bag. 'Of all the methods of suicide,' wrote Kol'tsov, 'you have chosen the most agonizing and difficult. And this not only for yourself, but also for your family. . . . If you do decide to come back, though, then book your ticket straight through to Siberia!'

This letter of Kol'tsov's has been preserved; it is in the files of the Kimber Prize winner, in the files which have remained in the hands of a certain organization since the time of Timofeev-Resovskii's arrest in 1945. I learned about this letter not from Timofeev-Resovskii, and even before I first saw him. When the question of Timofeev-Resovskii's move to Obninsk was being considered (this was in 1963), one of the specialist workers in charge of security matters in our institute was assigned to the job of establishing the 'clearance' position of the candidate for the post of head of the section. The specialist went to Moscow to study the file and, overcome by temptation, told a colleague of mine about this letter, commenting on it 'Yes, indeed . . . a romantic story.' He sanctioned the granting of the 'clearance', thus opening the way to our institute to Timofeev-Resovskii. Although ours is an 'open' institute, those selected by the competitive examination to direct large sections are checked along these lines as well and are confirmed by the Bureau of the Town Committee and the Provincial Committee of the CPSU.

So Timofeev-Resovskii remained in Germany. But when in 1939, after concluding a pact of friendship and co-operation with the USSR,

Germany suddenly swooped on Poland and precipitated the Second World War, all persons with Soviet consular passports were interned, just like the citizens of the Western countries who were at war. Leaving Germany was forbidden, and an illegal departure with a family as well was far from simple.

Timofeev-Resovskii's eldest son, a student, joined the underground anti-Nazi organization. In 1943 he was arrested for taking part in a student plot to assassinate Hitler. Being a minor, he was not executed but was sent to Mauthausen concentration camp, where he perished. During the time of the war between Germany and the Soviet Union, Timofeev-Resovskii's department organized the production of false documents and certificates for prisoners-of-war, above all for Russians. He managed to save several Soviet biologists who were among the prisoners-of-war working in German concerns. This was near the end of the war, when a large number of Russians who had escaped from small and poorly guarded establishments, farms and installations were seeking shelter and protection until the Soviet armies arrived.

When the Soviet armies were approaching Berlin Timofeev-Resovskii was invited to move westward into the Anglo-American zone of occupation. But Timofeev-Resovskii refused. He decided to meet his compatriots and preserve the equipment of the department, which was at that time unique.

At first the occupation authorities treated him well. He was even appointed as Director of the whole Kaiser Wilhelm Brain Institute to which the Department of Genetics belonged. But a few weeks after hostilities ceased, emissaries appeared in flocks in the institute, to dismantle and take away all the equipment. Timofeev-Resovskii protested sharply against the incompetent, destructive, chaotic shipment of the unique equipment, which would suffer as a result. As Director of the Institute, he would not carry out some of the obviously stupid directives from the scientific-equipment hunters, who wore the insignia of colonels and lieutenant-colonels.[1] Then one of them, with special plenipotentiary powers, ordered the Director to be shipped from the institute too. He was sent to Moscow, and once in Moscow he was arrested in accordance with the standing orders of the time. An enquiry tried to establish that he was a German spy, using the methods well tried over the years, with no evidence, but using torture and forced

[1] *Author's note:* The titles of colonel, lieutenant-colonel, major, etc., were temporarily bestowed upon the civilian workers sent into Germany to round up equipment.

confessions. The investigation failed to achieve its aim: Timofeev-Resovskii agreed to admit that he was a spy for Chile, but would not agree to being a German one. His sentence of ten years' imprisonment (there were no twenty-five-year sentences at that time) was quite independent of whether he confessed or not.

After the Lubyanka prison Timofeev-Resovskii spent some months in the Butyrka prison in Moscow, in a cell into which seventy-five people were packed, although in Tsarist times it had contained only twenty-five. This was the self-same cell described in Solzhenitsyn's short story 'The Smile of the Buddha'. Solzhenitsyn himself, who became a friend of Timofeev-Resovskii while in this cell, stayed there somewhat longer.

Timofeev-Resovskii organized the Scientific and Technical Society in the cell, with organized lectures. Of the seventeen members of this society, six survived: the founder of the society, the physicist, V. Kogan, A. I. Solzhenitsyn, then a physicist and artillery captain, later to become a writer, the electronics engineers N. A. Semenov and S. S. Karpov, and the chemist Martur.

After the Butyrka prison Timofeev-Resovskii next found himself in a special camp in Northern Kazakhstan. Here once again he organized another scientific society; there was evidently no lack of scientists. The documents which accompanied Timofeev-Resovskii indicated that he was 'to be used only for general labour'. This was a death sentence, the swift and painless forms of which had been temporarily abolished after the war, as part of the victory celebrations. After this regime had been strictly imposed for half a year the future winner of the Kimber Prize had become a certain candidate for the fate described in the most notable speech given at a camp scientific seminar. This speech was entitled 'Non-shameful Death', and its author was a former priest, who died some two weeks after giving the speech.

Timofeev-Resovskii was saved on this occasion by science, atomic physics. Special 'atomic' establishments were being founded even within the MGB system.[1] They began to organize closed institutes like concentration camps, in which imprisoned scientists, including German scientists who were prisoners-of-war, worked from twelve to fourteen hours a day. They needed radiobiologists as well, specialists in the effect of radiation on the organism. In all the camps a search was going on for scientists and specialists to staff the institutes and establishments, which

[1] Ministry of State Security—*Translator*.

were known as 'shady deals'. In Moscow they remembered Timofeev-Resovskii too, a world authority on radiobiology and radiation genetics, all the more so since, even while he was in the Lubyanka prison during his 'investigation', he had on more than one occasion been consulted on the planning of various establishments. And when one of these establishments, founded according to the plans of the scientist under arrest, had been set up in the Urals, an order arrived at the prison camp to send Timofeev-Resovskii to Moscow. He spent two weeks travelling to Moscow in a 'Stolypin-type' prison wagon, in which thirty people were allotted to a six-seater compartment.[1] By the time the train was nearing Moscow there was a lot more room, since a quarter of the passengers had died. People travelled standing up the whole time closely packed together; the seats had been removed.

When Timofeev-Resovskii arrived in Moscow he was unconscious and was taken at once to the Central Prison Hospital of the MGB. The doctors received strict instructions to save the life of this valuable scientist at all costs. The said valuable scientist was suffering from malnutritional dystrophy and avitaminosis.

But doctors, when they wish, can work miracles, and after a few months' treatment Timofeev-Resovskii was back on his feet, cheerful and energetic as ever. Only his sight, which had formerly been developed by the study of all possible mutations in *Drosophila* to an exceptional acuteness, was not restored to its former power. Nikolai Vladimirovich lost his ability to distinguish very fine details. He could no longer look through a microscope, a binocular loupe, nor could he read even with glasses. Reading was an agonising process to him, yet reading was necessary. With a powerful magnifying glass, and a well-lighted page close to his eye he could just about make out a printed text. Finally, after much practice, he could read for many hours each day, which was essential for solving a whole mass of new scientific problems. After moving from hospital to the Ural atomic 'establishment', Timofeev-Resovskii quickly began to transform it into a serious scientific institution. For the first time in two years, moreover, he was able to write to

[1] Petr Aleksandrovich Stolypin (1812–1911), who held the posts of Minister of the Interior and Chairman of the Council of Ministers in Russia during the years of anti-liberal reaction (1906–11), invented a special type of railway coach for the transport of prisoners. This was basically the regular pattern of a corridor train, with the exception that there were no windows on the track sides of the compartments at all, and only slatted windows on the corridor side of the compartments. The doors of the compartments were, of course, kept locked, and the corridors were patrolled by guards. The windows of the corridors were, again, slatted, admitting only sufficient light for the purposes of the guards. Thus the compartments themselves were virtually in complete darkness.

his wife in Germany. After she had said goodbye to him in 1945, Elena Aleksandrovna had heard nothing of her husband for two years. No one had answered her enquiries; the authorities kept silence. And now a letter came. Nikolai Vladimirovich wrote that he was living well, that he was working in a scientific institution and that he had a flat. What he was not able to tell her was that he was still in prison and that his laboratory was behind barbed wire.

But when she received the letter Mrs Timofeeva-Resovskaya quickly made ready for the journey. She packed their baggage, books, prints and even some of the furniture, and with their younger son journeyed to the USSR. The family was reunited, but behind barbed wire. Although no court had ever sentenced Elena Aleksandrovna, she could not leave the atomic 'establishment'.

But Timofeev-Resovskii was not able to work for very long on radiation genetics, even behind barbed wire. The 'August session' of the Lenin All-Union Academy of Agricultural Sciences ended in a complete rout of genetics, and this affected the MGB too. At this session the Lysenkoist I. E. Glushchenko in his pogrom speech remembered Timofeev-Resovskii still existed and called him 'our sworn enemy'. Insulting those in prison was an honourable occupation in Stalin's day, and one to be encouraged. Orders banning genetic research were received by all Ministries. The MGB was not left out of this campaign. Here they knew how to fight the enemies of the Soviet state. Not only was it ordered that all genetic research must stop, but all *Drosophila* flies, the classic subject for laboratory genetics, were ordered to be *destroyed*. According to the instructions they were to be drowned in boiling water. Milliards of these flies live free in nature. They belong to the group of fruit-flies which perform a useful function in eliminating the waste products of plants. In the institutions of the Academy of Sciences and in the Institutes of Higher Education these flies were treated more humanely. It was forbidden to buy food for the flies in the laboratories, but no one was forbidden to open the tanks and let them go free. In his 'establishment' Timofeev-Resovskii began working on a new branch of biology, radiation biogeocenology. Within a short time he had developed a theoretical background, quantitative criteria and fundamental principles of this branch of science, and his group had collected a wide and unique range of experimental material. Unfortunately, a considerable part of his work is buried in the archives of the MGB in the form of reports, while part was used without acknowledgements to the imprisoned authors by their free 'curators'.

Freedom came only after the death of Stalin. But in the first years those who had been released were still not allowed to go to work in Moscow or Leningrad. After 1955, when Timofeev-Resovskii was once again a free citizen of the Soviet Union, he began to form a Biophysics Section in the Ural Branch of the Academy of Sciences. Within a short time this branch became the most productive biological establishment in the Urals and Siberia. Here were published dozens of works, collections of papers and monographs. Not far from Sverdlovsk at the branch's experimental station in the little settlement of Miassovo Timofeev-Resovskii founded an annual summer seminar on genetics and theoretical biology, the first scientific centre for genetics after the ban of 1948. This seminar quickly acquired exceptional popularity. Dozens of people came at their own expense every year, and lived in tents and huts, holding meetings in the fields. I have seen a photograph of several professors sleeping on trestle beds with only a single blanket, and another photo of the famous geneticist, V. P. Efroimson, up to his waist in water because of the heat and with a pointer in his hand giving a lecture on abnormal haemoglobins. His audience were also sitting in the water. This was the highly original Miassovo school of geneticists, which had an enormous effect on the subsequent development of genetics in the USSR.

But the bureaucratic restrictions on scientific work created a new and very delicate problem for the scientist after his release. He had no Soviet scientific degrees nor titles, not even a diploma of graduation from college. In Germany and in Europe in general, lack of a scientific degree does not reflect on the position, work and income of a well-known and mature scientist. If a man has a name in science and has done serious work, no one would demand that he should defend a thesis in order to receive proper documentation as a scientist. Defence of a thesis is for novices, young people; it is a mandate for the beginning of scientific work. If, for example, in England a world-famous scientist, the author of two hundred and fifty papers and some ten monographs, were to be forced to prove his scientific qualifications by the public defence of a thesis, people might think that there was some lunatic, eccentric, humorist or what you will at work.

But the wages-clerks in the scientific establishments in the USSR do not recognize scientific discoveries and papers as proof of a scientist's qualifications. An administrator, even if he is President of an Academy or a Minister, is not free to establish salary levels by such ephemeral indices as scientific achievements. There is an all-State table of ranks and degrees, which begets Candidates and Doctors of Science, scientists who for the sake of money continue to swell the scientific tribe to enormous proportions, and this creates a great difference between scientists with a degree and scientists without a degree, a difference which is completely independent of scientific qualifications. The wages-clerks demand only a Doctor's diploma, or at least a Candidate's diploma, not a bibliography of scientific publications. Without these diplomas, the head of the Biophysics Section of the Ural Branch of the Academy of Sciences of the USSR is only a specialist with the status of a drop-out from higher education.

By 1962 his friends at last managed to convince Timofeev-Resovskii that this system might prevail for a long time yet, and that it would be best for him to defend a thesis. The defence went off brilliantly. The United Council of the Ural Branch of the Academy of Sciences of the USSR unanimously awarded the old scientist the degree of Doctor of Biological Sciences, skipping that of Candidate.

In almost every country the decision of the Academic Council on a degree is final. Surely the universities of Cambridge or Oxford or Harvard, if they had made a decision on the scientific qualifications of a scholar, would not allow this to be reversed by some government commission in London or Washington. Even to think of such a possibility is laughable. But with us it is laughable to think otherwise. A decision of the Academic Council of even Moscow University is only a recommendation, a petition to the special Commission for the Certification of Higher Degrees, which exists in Moscow as an independent and inter-departmental organ. The head of this commission, which we call the CCHD, is the Minister of Higher Education, and the commission consists of panels of experts, plenary sections for the various branches and a Presidium. And, as often happens, those who sit on all these central commissions and sections have all, or almost all, long forgotten the air of the laboratory and the excitement of creative work. Worse still, in 1962 it was the Lysenkoists who ruled there, and Lysenko himself sat in a place of honour beside the ministerial chairman's seat, along with Glushchenko, and many others. The Michurinite, P. Genkel', was head of the 'expert' commission, and his deputy, N. N. Nuzhdin, was also a Lysenkoist. It was indeed a task to get past this mighty barrier. My friend Efroimson 'got through' the CCHD from the defence of his thesis to the award of his degree only after fifteen years. Some sixty reviews of his work were collected, expert commissions sat several times, both regular and joint ones, recommendations from two academies, the

Academy of Medical Sciences of the USSR and the Academy of Sciences of the USSR, were produced, and from two commissions on special problems, but the CCHD was like a lump of granite and refused to come to any decision. But this was a record, perhaps a world record, for red tape in getting a degree approved. When the CCHD received Timofeev-Resovskii's dissertation it seemed as if the CCHD had decided to try and break the record. They had already received some forty-five reviews, including six from Academicians, but the chairman of the expert commission still insisted that his 'Party conscience' would not allow him to confirm the result of the dissertation. So a year went by, and a second. In the spring of 1964 Timofeev-Resovskii and a group of his colleagues came to Obninsk to organize a large laboratory of radiation and experimental genetics and a section of general genetics and radiobiology. My own laboratory became part of that section. In all under Timofeev-Resovskii there were four laboratories, two independent groups and about ten senior and thirty junior scientists. It was a moderate-sized institute. Timofeev-Resovskii was not merely its nominal head, he really did stand at the source of all its activities, cementing the section together by his own energy, his own erudition and his own experimental work. He created a special scientific style, his own school, he established directions and at once made his section stand out from the general chaos of the feverishly growing new scientific complex.

Yet on the payroll of the department the Head of the Section held a very lowly place. He earned only half as much as a junior scientific worker with a Candidate's degree, 98 roubles a month, 10 roubles more than a laboratory assistant. But he did the work of ten men cheerfully with humour and ease. The Director tried by every means to establish a personal pay scale for the Head of the Section that was not dependent on a degree approved by the CCHD. But nothing came of it. Only the Council of Ministers of the USSR can make such a decision.

But now there came a change. In October 1964, the Chairman of the Council of Ministers was replaced. There was also a change of position regarding biology. The CCHD, feeling a wind of change from above, altered its attitude towards Timofeev-Resovskii's thesis. The 'Party conscience' of the chairman of the expert commission also changed. After all, the question of his own scientific qualifications might come up on the agenda. The CCHD, which for so long had broken its own rules and remained deaf to numerous reviews and letters, quickly confirmed Timofeev-Resovskii's dissertation. And when it was confirmed the Chairman of the CCHD, the Minister himself—and this was most unusual—telephoned personally the same day to the Director of our Institute and asked him to give Timofeev-Resovskii his congratulations on being awarded the degree.

It would seem that all problems had been solved; it was possible to go on working quietly, training scientists and creating, yet again, a new scientific centre.

Was Timofeev-Resovskii in debt to his native land? Or was his native land in debt to him? These questions need never have been raised, but Blokhin raised them again by his demand that an honourable and well-deserved international prize be declined. Would the famous 'Pasternak affair' happen all over again, this time in science? Timofeev-Resovskii resolutely refused to comply with the recommendation of the President of the Academy of Medical Sciences of the USSR.

When I came back from a period of leave I made my first task a visit to the editorial office of *Genetika*. I knew that if the censor had had doubts about something, had telephoned someone, tried to make compromise, the article about the award of the prize would not appear in print.

From the faces of the workers in the editorial office, which were somewhat gloomy after I walked in, I knew that things had gone wrong. The Managing Editor immediately guessed what I wanted and attempted to explain the situation in a roundabout manner. 'You know, there is some trouble with the Kimber article.' My heart sank. 'Glavlit would not pass both the photographs.'

'What about the article itself?' I asked, hardly daring to believe in success.

'The article itself was passed and will appear in No. 8; we have the sample copy already!'

To the devil with the photographs, I thought. Nevertheless, putting on a show of indignation, I wanted to know why they had been cut out. The censor, it seemed, had given explanations for his action in both cases. The photograph of the medal had been cut out since they did not want to advertise an American medal. The portrait of the winner was left out since the write-up was so favourable that, if there were a photograph as well, it would appear too good.

Meanwhile in the USA there had been no official publication of the award of the Kimber Prize. There had not even been any comment in the press on the prizewinner's failure to arrive. The American scientists were being careful; they did not want any outcry which could damage the man they were honouring. This was a further proof that the award was not a provocation. It was an act of scientific recognition.

The copy of *Genetika* with the article on the Kimber Prize was sent off without delay to Professor Lerner and to the National Academy. Lerner made a translation into English, and Mr Brown also distributed one among the members of the Academy Council. I learned this later from a letter of Lerner's in which he enclosed a copy of the translation.

On 13 October 1966 Timofeev-Resovskii received a short letter from the President of the National Academy of the USA, Frederick Seitz:

Dear Professor Timofeev-Resovskii,
    We were greatly delighted to read the article in the Soviet journal *Genetika*, noting the fact that the Kimber Prize had been awarded to you by our Academy. We should like once again to invite you to come to the USA, if this is theoretically possible for you. If it is not, then we shall start thinking about other ways of presenting you with your prize.[1]

As might be expected, the prizewinner chose the 'other ways'. Since Elena Aleksandrovna borrowed my Latin-script typewriter to type out her husband's letter, which was written in English, I was able to ask her to let me keep a copy:

Dear Professor Seitz,
    Thank you very much for your kind letter of 13 October 1966, which I received a couple of days ago. The offer of the Kimber award is a very great honour to me. It is an exclusive honour and pleasure to find yourself among the most prominent geneticists, to whom the Kimber award has been already offered. I beg you once more to accept my most sincere thanks to yourself and to the National Academy of Sciences.
    It would indeed be a great pleasure for me to visit again the United States, meet my old friends in your country and make new personal acquaintances. But I am sure, that at least within the next two years it will not be feasible for me. Thus I would be very grateful for your finding other means of transmitting the award and the medal to me; maybe one of such means could be the transmission of the medal through the US Embassy in Moscow and the President of the Soviet Society of Geneticists, Professor B. L. Astaurov (member of the Academy of Sciences of the USSR in Moscow), and the deposition of the award in my name at the Vneshtorg Bank in Moscow.
    With kindest regards.
                                    Yours very sincerely,
                                        N. V. TIMOFEEV-RESOVSKII

[1] Translated from Medvedev's Russian text—*Translator*.

For a long time after this there was no sign of any official correspondence about the transmission of the prize. The winner was in complete ignorance. But since an 'advice of delivery' note which had been sent with his letter to Seitz was returned to Obninsk with Seitz's own signature, the prizewinner was quite unperturbed. And events showed that he was justified in his confidence that matters were well in hand. Five months went by. What discussions went on in official circles during that time is unknown, but the results came to the surface on 30 March 1967. That day the Deputy Head of the International Section of the Academy of Medical Sciences, V. G. Zakharova, was given the urgent task of summoning Timofeev-Resovskii at two o'clock on the afternoon of 31 March to the office of the President of the Academy of Medical Sciences in Moscow. In that office the Vice-President of the National Academy of Sciences of the USA, Professor Kistiakowsky, in the presence of the Foreign Secretary of this Academy, Mr Harrison Brown, and the Vice-President of the Academy of Sciences of the USSR, Professor Kovanov, would present Timofeev-Resovskii with the Kimber Prize.

Zakharova was not able to get through to Obninsk on the telephone so she rang the husband of one of our lady scientists (who lived in Moscow) and asked him to ring Obninsk in the evening, since he had a physicist friend in Obninsk, whose home telephone was directly connected to the Moscow telephone network through the Institute of Energy Physics. He rang this physicist without delay and asked him to ring up his wife on the internal Obninsk exchange. When she heard the news, she rang the Deputy Director for Scientific Affairs of the Institute, and by evening the Deputy Director had told the prizewinner himself about the call from the Academy of Medical Sciences. The news at once became known to many of his colleagues. Without consulting each other, under the influence of a single stimulus, they all began calling up their Moscow colleagues that evening, inviting the Moscow biologists and geneticists to attend the presentation ceremony.

By two o'clock on 31 March, there were some sixty people waiting outside the door of the office of the President of the Academy of Medical Sciences of the USSR. For the International Section the arrival of such a number of scientists was unexpected; the Section had planned a routine presentation. Hence there was no interpreter to translate the speeches of greeting for the audience and for the American scientists; nor were there any bottles of the traditional champagne to drink the health of the winner and the guests. Timofeev-Resovskii at once sent one of his postgraduate students out for a few bottles of champagne. At the last minute Blokhin decided to conduct the ceremony himself. The Americans arrived; there were six of them.

Finally everyone was in his place; only the principals, of course, could sit; the others had to stand around the walls since they had not been expected at the celebration. Blokhin made an opening speech. It was not translated for the American guests. Someone proposed to act as translator, but Blokhin waved him aside: 'No, be quiet, they'll understand!' Then Kistiakowsky read an address from the President of the National Academy of Sciences of the USA, Professor Frederick Seitz, and handed it to the excited winner. He then presented the Diploma and then the gold medal of the Kimber Prize, then a bronze replica of it, and finally a cheque for $2,000.

Timofeev-Resovskii made his speech of reply in English. Those who knew this language understood what he was saying, but those who did not know it also understood; it was easy to do so from the speaker's expressive face. A. A. Prokof'eva-Bel'govskaya gave a warm speech on behalf of Soviet geneticists. A waitress from the buffet opened the bottles of champagne, and the ceremony was over. There had been no plans made for any conversation between Timofeev-Resovskii and the Americans, who were driven away at once. He wanted to give a dinner in their honour next day, but it turned out that they were to fly home next morning.

As we found out later, the delegation of American Academicians had come for official talks with the Academy of Sciences of the USSR on scientific co-operation and to sign an agreement on this question. They had also brought the Kimber Prize along with them. They raised the question of its presentation with the Soviet authorities on their very first day. But, a whole week was needed to obtain permission for the ceremony. The Academy of Medical Sciences at first refused to organize the presentation. The Americans did not want to have to take the medal and prize back with them and insisted on meeting Timofeev-Resovskii. The US embassy, hearing from Kistiakowsky of the problem that had arisen, proposed to invite the winner to receive his prize at a reception in the Embassy. When it became clear to officialdom that a visit to the Embassy presented no insurmountable difficulties for the winner, there was a top-level meeting, to which even the Director of our Institute was summoned. Blokhin still insisted that the prize should be refused but he had no support on this, and there was now no way of preventing the presentation.

But when at last the medal and the prize had reached their rightful owner, when the congratulatory speeches had been made, everyone suddenly understood quite clearly that he was truly worthy of it, that he, perhaps more than all the other medal winners, deserved this particular medal, which was awarded not for a particular piece of work, however outstanding, but for the total contribution, for the entire life's work of a scientist, for uncompromising service to genetics. And everyone understood that one must be proud of such scientists who have raised our science to the level of world attainments, that one must rejoice over such events and mark them in the chronicles of our culture. And this was so obvious that the next day, 1 April, the Central newspaper *Komsomol'skaya Pravda* reported the meeting at the Academy of Medical Sciences on the front page, in large type under the headline 'Principal prize for Genetics goes to a Soviet Scientist'. And the Obninsk paper *Vpered* published an article on the Kimber Prize and its Soviet winner, the self-same article which had been lying dormant in their files for almost a year.

A remarkable article on Timofeev-Resovskii was written by Academician Astaurov and published in *Priroda*, and this time Glavlit did not cut out the photograph of the medal nor the photograph of the winner showing him receiving it.

As for all the mischances and difficulties along the path to this well-deserved recognition, they all found a reasonable explanation. In his letter of reply to the President of the Academy of Sciences of the USA, Timofeev-Resovskii wrote:

> I apologize most sincerely for the fact that I have unwillingly caused you much worry and trouble in connection with the presentation of the Kimber Prize. But I should like to point out that these worries might have been expected, since I was the *thirteenth* in the list of prizewinners.[1]

For the fourteenth winner, of course, things were much easier. It was a woman, the American geneticist Barbara McClintock, who was awarded the Kimber Prize for her outstanding research on plant genetics, which had attracted the attention of biologists of the whole world for nearly forty years and had opened up new lines of enquiry in the study of heredity.

It would seem that this is the place to put a full stop. A Soviet scientist with difficulties had won his rights and had been recognized not only out in the world but at home as well. It would seem that now

---

[1] Translated from Medvedev's Russian text—*Translator*.

neither Zakharova nor the Chairman of the local Party Committee of the Institute would be able to decide whether one should accept invitations of honour from international scientific organizations. But this proved not to be the case. When in September 1967 the Organizing Committee of the Twelfth International Congress of Genetics to be held in Japan in August 1968 invited Timofeev-Resovskii to attend and take part in the work of the symposium and to give a lecture, his path was once again blocked by the 'International Co-operation' Section of the Academy of Medical Sciences of the USSR, which refused the application of our Institute on this question and would not approve the trip, even on a tourist basis. And the special Organizing Committee for the Twelfth Congress on Genetics, set up by the Academy of Sciences of the USSR and the All-Union Society of Geneticists, also proved to be powerless to get this invitation for Timofeev-Resovskii approved.

Where the next Genetic Congress will be held is still unknown at the time of writing. It is being settled in Japan this August.[1] According to tradition, it will be held in five years' time in 1973. Timofeev-Resovskii, who is as old as the century, will be seventy-three. Perhaps by then international co-operation by Soviet scientists will be following a more normal course. Perhaps they will decide in Japan to hold the next Congress on Genetics in Moscow or in Leningrad. And this congress will also be the thirteenth. Let us wish Nikolai Vladimirovich good health and long life. Perhaps the thirteenth winner of the chief prize for genetics will be able to meet his old friends at the Thirteenth Congress —those who have survived. Who knows whether double thirteen may not prove to be lucky.

NOTE ADDED IN SEPTEMBER 1968
As we guessed, Timofeev-Resovskii was not included in the Soviet delegation to the Genetics Congress. However, the question of the next Genetics Congress, the thirteenth, being held in the USSR has still not been decided. The Genetics Congress in Japan opened on 18 August. Straight away at the meeting of the executive committee of the International Genetics Union the question was raised of holding the Congress in Moscow. On 21 September came the invasion of Czechoslovakia by the armies of the Warsaw Pact, and in the atmosphere which this created at the Congress it was impossible to decide the question of holding the next Congress in Moscow. However, since no preparations had been made for discussing the question of holding

[1] Medvedev wrote this earlier in 1968—*Translator*.

it in some other country, no decision has been taken. Discussion of this problem will take place at a later date, and the possibility of holding the Congress in Moscow has still not been ruled out.

POSTSCRIPT WRITTEN IN SEPTEMBER 1969

A year has passed since this account of Timofeev-Resovskii was written. It has been a difficult year, and something should be written about its events, since they were connected with what had gone before.

At the very beginning of 1968 the Academy of Sciences of the USSR began to make ready for its forthcoming elections. The 'birth' of new Academicians and Corresponding Members which takes place once every two to three years is always a difficult affair. 'Academician' and 'Corresponding Member' of any academy of the USSR (the one 'big' academy, the four branch academies, and the fourteen academies of the Union Republics) are not simply titles of honour, as in most countries of the world. In addition to being an honour they also ensure a lifetime's salary, which is paid to the Academician irrespective of whether he is working in the Academy of Sciences or whether he is on a pension. And the pay scales which go with the title are greatest for the 'big' academy, 500 roubles per month for an Academician and 350 for a Corresponding Member. And this is in addition to other benefits (a car, a summer cottage, and so on). The country grudges nothing to deserving scientists, so that they can just keep science moving forward without worrying about the difficulties of life. Since Academicians generally also draw the maximum salary at their places of work, the result is that the monthly pay of an Academician exceeds the monthly pay of members of the Government—Ministers of the USSR and Ministers of the Union Republics.

For every election to the Academy of Sciences the Council of Ministers makes position for several new vacancies, and there are also quite a few vacancies arising from the natural mortality of those elected on earlier occasions. These vacancies are announced for the Academy in *Izvestiya* subject by subject, and throughout every scientific establishment in the USSR the pre-election campaign begins.

In 1968 besides the other new vacancies a new vacancy in the Academy of Sciences of the USSR was announced for genetics. It was not an easy matter to select a worthy candidate for this vacancy. The most outstanding Soviet geneticists, B. L. Astaurov and N. P. Dubinin, were already Academicians, while among the Corresponding Members of the Academy of Sciences—the last step before the Olympian height of Academician—there were only two geneticists, and both of these were

'Michurin biologists'. One of them, N. Nuzhdin, had already been defeated once in a previous election with a great scandal, the other, G. Nikol'skii, had not yet stood for election. The latter was put forward by the Department of General Biology of the Academy of Sciences of the USSR as its candidate as a result of a strange coalition between Dubinin and the supporters of T. D. Lysenko. In order to prevent the election of Nikol'skii, a group of scientists headed by Academician Engelhardt decided to propose Timofeev-Resovskii as a candidate for election, undoubtedly the most outstanding candidate, scientifically speaking, for the vacancy. Timofeev-Resovskii's scientific productivity after 1964 had been very high; in five years he had published more than fifty papers and a monograph, and had supervised the work of more than ten Candidates of Science in his section.

But election as an Academician is a complex process; before a proposed candidate can be included in the list of candidates he is considered by commissions and the Party Committee of the Academy of Sciences, and the names are co-ordinated in the Department of Science of the Central Committee of the CPSU. Finally the names of the actual candidates for the election are announced, and all the Academicians and Corresponding Members who are members of the Party have to vote for the candidates announced. Thus Party control over the election is effected. The elections themselves are secret, but since there is a majority of Party members among the voters, the previously nominated candidate is chosen. Sometimes, of course, there may be a 'breakdown', but the history of the Academy of Sciences in the post-war period records only one such failure, when Nuzhdin stood for election in 1964.

The candidacy of Timofeev-Resovskii was turned down at the very beginning in the preliminary consideration by some commission or other. The principal reason for turning him down was the same old argument that he was an émigré, a traitor to his country, a collaborator with the Nazis. The Michurinites, who abounded in the academy, and Lysenko himself began an active campaign of opposition to Timofeev-Resovskii's election to the academy. A number of rumours and tall stories were put into circulation, even including one that while he was in Germany Timofeev-Resovskii had carried out experiments on Soviet prisoners-of-war in fascist concentration camps. At the Department of Science of the Central Committee of the CPSU a special dossier was compiled from the various denunciations of Timofeev-Resovskii.

In order to counteract this campaign, Academician Engelhardt sent a letter to the President of the Academy of the German Democratic

Republic, Professor Hans Stubbe, who had worked in close contact with Timofeev-Resovskii in Germany, asking him for an account of how Timofeev-Resovskii had behaved during the years of Nazism. Professor Stubbe sent Engelhardt a detailed letter in which he resolutely denied all the falsehoods and gave the names of many other famous German scientists who could confirm that Timofeev-Resovskii had never collaborated with the Nazis, had always been among the intelligentsia who held anti-fascist views, and his German friends had always been afraid that he would suffer for his freedom of expression.

It must be noted that Timofeev-Resovskii himself expressed no interest in his possible election to the Academy of Sciences of the USSR, kept quite apart from the 'pre-election campaign', and all these passions, including the correspondence of Stubbe and Engelhardt, were unknown both to himself and to us his colleagues.

All this might yet have ended quietly with the end of the election campaign, but unfortunately in February 1968 a correspondent of the journal *Ogonek* came to Obninsk to write an article on the young town of science. With him came a photographer, who took many pictures, for *Ogonek* is an illustrated journal. In one of them he had caught Timofeev-Resovskii in the act of lighting a cigarette. And then in the top left-hand corner of the cover of *Ogonek* (No. 14, March 1968), which has a circulation of two million, there was a large coloured photograph of Timofeev-Resovskii with a lighted match and a cigarette. And on p. 31, the caption of the cover photograph read:

> In the Obninsk Institute of Medical Radiology, in charge of many workers in radiation biology and genetics, is the world-famous scholar, one of the pioneers of this science, Nikolai Vladimirovich Timofeev-Resovskii.

The photograph in *Ogonek* started off a new flood of letters, mainly anonymous. In Gorki-Leninskie, at the large experimental station of the Academy of Sciences, where Lysenko is in charge of about a hundred scientists and two hundred workers and service staff, a Party meeting was held at which a special resolution was passed against the publicity given by *Ogonek* to an émigré and Morganist. This resolution was sent to the Central Committee of the CPSU. A certain Miss Glavinich, formerly a post-graduate student of Glushchenko, who had worked with Lysenko in the Institute on vegetative hybridization and had become an 'Academician' in Yugoslavia, sent the Central Committee of the CPSU a letter of protest about scientists being eulogized in the USSR. The file on the Timofeev-Resovskii 'affair' began to grow.

Timofeev-Resovskii did not appear in the list of candidates for election to the Academy of Sciences of the USSR. But neither did Nikol'skii. He repeated the painful experience of Nuzhdin. The Department of General Biology chose him to be an Academician, but the general meeting turned down his candidacy as the result of a stormy discussion. Once again, as in 1964, the vacancy in genetics remained unfilled.

But for Timofeev-Resovskii this was not the end of the matter. The thick dossier in the Science Section could not lie there stagnating. At the end of 1968 it was used in an instruction to provincial propagandists. In this instruction on the education of young scientists Timofeev-Resovskii figured as a negative personality with a shady past who nevertheless had been entrusted with the responsible task of educating young people. The thing for which Nikolai Vladimirovich had always been praised—the creation of a youth circle for discussing problems of music and art—now became an ideological deviation.

The instructional address from the Central Committee was disseminated orally throughout all provinces of the Soviet Union. In Sverdlovsk Timofeev-Resovskii's physicist son Andrei heard of it. In the Kaluga Provincial Committee and in the Obninsk Town Committee they sounded the alarm. The secretary of the Provincial Committee telephoned the President of the Academy of Medical Sciences, Academician V. D. Timakov, requiring him to dismiss Timofeev-Resovskii from the Institute, which was situated within the Kaluga Province. Timakov heeded this request and refused to confirm the Institute's application that Timofeev-Resovskii's term of office should continue until September 1970, that is until his seventieth birthday.

Seventy years of age in the USSR is the age-limit beyond which a scientist cannot be employed in an administrative post. This rule is broken only in special cases by 'outstanding' scholars, Academicians and Corresponding Members. Others must go into retirement on a pension, or into routine posts as scientific workers or consultants, if they want to go on working as scientists after the age of seventy. And this is the right way of things. If they are going to receive a worthy pension then retirement will always occur smoothly and honourably. For Timofeev-Resovskii, it was decided not to wait until he was seventy. He was pensioned off in August 1969, but with the promise that the laboratory which he had created would continue. But this was not done. The scientist who for many years had been the pride of the Institute was not even allowed to keep his permanent pass for unhindered entry into the building where he had once worked. Now every visit has to be agreed by telephone with the Director. His laboratory has been divided among others, like a piece of pie, some of the staff and equipment were given to one laboratory, some to another and some to a third. When he said goodbye to his colleagues at a farewell meeting which was not attended by a single representative of the administration, Timofeev-Resovskii asked them to preserve the scientific traditions of the laboratory, and to carry on the work which had been begun. But these traditions were broken at once.

A scientist's retirement on pension is hard, not only because it breaks off his experimental work. It is also hard in that the pensions for scientists are far lower in relation to their previous salaries than for any other category of worker. This is a penalty for their high salaries in their period of active work. The maximum 'professorial' pension is only 25 to 30 per cent of the salary of a working professor. But to receive this maximum professorial pension, twenty-five years of scientific work are required. Timofeev-Resovskii had completed fifty-one years of scientific work. But for the seven years up to 1925 there were no documents, only scientific papers. The Ministry of Social Security does not recognize those. Then came twenty years and three months of intensive work— abroad. This too is not recognized in the USSR. Work abroad is recognized only when it was in a socialist state. Then came ten years in a prison camp and prison. For eight of these years Timofeev-Resovskii worked as a scientist, but this period cannot count without a special resolution of the Supreme Court, which even nowadays is not easy to obtain. Only the period since 1955 was valid for consideration. The pension was therefore adjusted in proportion to the deficit from the twenty-five years required. But one should not complain; food is cheap now, Timofeev-Resovskii and his wife are not threatened with starvation.

Recently Professor Hans Stubbe sent Academician Engelhardt another letter, in which he asked whether Timofeev-Resovskii had been elected to the Academy of Sciences. Dear Hans Stubbe! Hitler was a worse tyrant than Stalin. That is clear to everyone. It is also clear to everyone that Stalin ought to have liquidated Timofeev-Resovskii. Why Hitler did not do it for the Academy of Sciences is incomprehensible.[1]

---

[1] Nevertheless, Dr Timofeev-Resovskii appears to have been reinstated. In August 1970 *Priroda* (No. 8, 1970) published an article by him, 'The Biosphere and Man' and stated that he was now working at the Institute of Medicobiological Problems of the Ministry of Health of the USSR—*Translator*.

PART II

International Scientific Co-operation— the Facts and their Consequences

The cases which I described in the previous section have a somewhat personal flavour, and it may be objected that they are not typical. But I know dozens of other cases of quite absurd refusals received by scientists who were trying to accept an invitation to go abroad to take part in a scientific meeting, or some joint project. And these are only the cases I have observed myself or have heard of from my closest colleagues. This means that in fact there must be tens of thousands more such cases taken over the whole Union. A rough calculation shows that out of every hundred invitations received by our scientists from scientists, laboratories, institutes, conferences, organizing committees of congresses abroad, at least eighty remain unknown to the administrations of the establishments where the invitees work and are not submitted for approval because there is no hope of their being approved. Of the remaining twenty which are submitted for a decision regarding a trip, not more than one or two ever come off, and the remainder meet with a refusal at some stage or another. Furthermore the invitations which do come off are mainly those received by scientists who are scientific administrators (directors of institutes, their deputies, heads of commissions on specific problems, higher administration workers at the Ministries and sometimes heads of sections and laboratories). As a result, the average age of the Soviet delegation to any international congress is generally some ten to fifteen years greater than the average age of the delegations of many other countries.

But perhaps this should be considered a desirable state of affairs? Perhaps it is the result of a really sound and sensible policy of international scientific co-operation? Perhaps the reason there are so many and so populous international co-operation sections for dozens of departments, committees and academies is to prevent co-operation proliferating beyond bounds, and to set an economic and expedient limit to it, so that the worthwhile may be sorted from the not worthwhile, and that those links between Soviet citizens and foreigners should be selected which are best from the state's point of view? Perhaps other countries also have similar forms of control and planned limitation of scientific contacts, so that scientists are not distracted from creative work in their laboratories, so that their scientific work is not turned into amusement, into international tourism? Perhaps the traditional indirect method of obtaining scientific information without personal contact, but by means of scientific literature, journals, books and technical bulletins is quite sufficient to maintain the necessary high level of scientific research in our country?

To understand this properly we must consider a question which is elementary but extremely important: the question of the scale of international scientific co-operation today, the form it takes, the conditions and principles that apply, and its significance in the development of world science.

I

The methods of exchange of information in world science today

THE fact that any branch of science is now really a world science (world chemistry, world genetics, world physiology and so on) is no longer questioned. It is an indisputable fact. But from this fact it inevitably follows that as a practical policy there must be a differentiation and specialization on a world-wide scale in work on scientific problems. And this specialization is becoming better and better co-ordinated. In other words it has become clear that, if, for instance, complex and expensive projects have been started in the USA or England on the elucidation of the structure of substance X or the working out of the complex synthesis of substance Y, it would not be to anyone's advantage if work on these problems were begun in France or Belgium. It would be more sensible to use the scientific resources of France and Belgium to elucidate the structure of substance C or to work out the synthesis of compound M. At the same time a system of scientific co-operation should guarantee that all four countries could use the results of all the research projects. This is what actually happens. It was especially clearly seen in the study of the structure of proteins. The elucidation of the sequence of aminoacids in proteins, even for one single protein, is a task that takes a well-equipped laboratory several years. There are some fifty to seventy laboratories throughout the world which have undertaken systematic research of this kind. And there are thousands of interesting proteins. Naturally it is to the advantage of these laboratories to agree on a division of labour, rather than to embark independently on the study of one and the same protein compound. In the beginning, when this type of study of the structure of proteins was just starting (about ten to fifteen years ago), there were several cases of duplication of effort. For example, the structure of one and the same form of haemoglobin was being worked out both in Czechoslovakia and in the USA. At the end of five years, when the Americans had completed their work the Czechs had got about half-way. Naturally they stopped their expensive research as soon as it became known that it had been completed in the USA. The situation was the same with the protein of the tobacco-mosaic virus, which was determined independently and almost simultaneously in Germany and in the USA. Nowadays, however, when the number of laboratories working on protein-structure has greatly increased, these laboratories prefer to co-ordinate their work. Co-operation has also benefited their methodological achievements. Due to this, the general flow of world information on the structure of proteins has increased sharply, and the advantage of this for everyone taking part in such work is beyond doubt. A similar situation exists in almost all major scientific investigations.

The front of all sciences is now expanding so rapidly that there is no country, however large, that can support by itself investigations into all the problems which lie at the basis of the development of its economy, industry, agriculture, medicine and so on, especially as these investigations become ever more costly and complicated. A national closed system in any field of science appears stupid and absurd. Such a system still does exist today in certain restricted military fields of science, and this is maintained by various forms of security. By maintaining security in the defence branches of science preventing differentiation in this field, every country in this case offers direct and indirect economic damage to its potential antagonist by forcing it to expend its national resources on working out questions and problems which have already been solved, but under cover of security.

However, in most non-military fields of knowledge, and even in certain indirectly military fields, the closed system of working has given way to a sensible and advantageous differentiation, in which scientific establishments and experimental groups mutually complement one another's work on a world-wide scale. *In these conditions a diverse and effective scientific co-operation has become a necessary form of organization of scientific work.*

In the USSR, especially before the Second World War and in the first years after it, the chief goal was, of course, to create complete economic, technical and scientific independence from the capitalist world. Until 1945 the isolated position of the USSR as the only socialist country and the theoretical possibility of conflict with the entire capitalist world made it essential to keep up an unbroken front of scientific and technical research which was equivalent to what could be achieved by the capitalist world.

But it was never really possible to keep up such an unbroken front of scientific research in a single country, even in one so large as the USSR.

It led to the scattering of effort and the hypertrophy of scientific establishments, while it was necessary to import techniques, apparatus, reagents and scientific discoveries and to hire the services of foreign specialists in order to create and maintain in the USSR an industrial society at the technical level of the present day.

After the formation of a bloc of socialist countries in Europe and Asia the policy of isolation and complete independence at first grew stronger, since the technical and scientific potential of the socialist sector increased, and this created the illusion that autonomous science and technology could expand more quickly. However, the scientific and technical potential of the socialist bloc after the war turned out to be less than in the economically more developed capitalist sector of mankind. As a result, the policy of isolating the USSR and her socialist neighbours from the rest of the world led in many branches of science and technology to a greater and greater lag between the USSR and the level in the rest of the world. It also led to the flowering in the USSR of a number of pseudo-scientific systems which were both extensive and costly, like Lysenkoism, the suppression of quantum-resonance chemistry, the suppression of cybernetics, the concept of 'living matter', the generation of microbes from viruses and a number of others.

The scientific and technological gap between the USSR and the world level gradually increased during the years from 1946 to 1955, and this happened in spite of the free copying and borrowing of any technical achievements from abroad, supported by the refusal of the USSR to take part in international conventions and discussions on patents, licences and priority of inventions. In the USSR all journals, books, sketches of machines, instruments and compounds are received. And they could all be copied and used free of charge, without permission from the countries that hold the patents. This gap became so obvious and self-evident that from 1955 onwards the Soviet Union began to take part, although still in a very limited form, in the traditional forms of international scientific co-operation.

Although previously Soviet citizens returning from abroad had mainly tried to describe all the bad and negative features with which the world of capital was burdened, after 1955 the character of the information they brought back changed sharply. Delegations went abroad who were widely acquainted, often at a high level, with many branches of knowledge. A mass of articles, pamphlets and even books appeared with titles like 'What we saw in the USA', 'What we saw in England' and so forth. The policy of using the attainments of other countries became very popular. Like Columbus we had rediscovered for ourselves the world of foreign science and technology, and we were sternly critical of our own conservatism in many directions. And, although the results of these new trends were very rapid and significant, the level of development of science in the rest of the world and the associated development of forms of international scientific co-operation in the years that followed (1956–1967) greatly outstripped our timid steps in that direction. As a result the lag of the USSR in very many scientific fields and topics is very noticeable even now, and we are still far from becoming part of the general structure of world science, which depends upon international scientific co-operation. The slogan, to 'overtake and outstrip', which is still as senseless as ever, is used in an economically ruinous manner in the sense of doubling, repeating and achieving what has already been achieved, and not as an attempt to take part in the worldwide differentiation and world-wide specialization, which is possible only if co-operation is really free. If the Americans construct some establishment for theoretical research which costs 100 million dollars, instead of sending a few dozen scientists to the USA to work in this establishment and constructing something quite different ourselves, we construct one like it, or one somewhat more powerful but on the same principle, for 500 million roubles which will probably be obsolescent even before it is completed.

What then, in this modern world, are the forms of scientific co-operation which can ensure mutually advantageous differentiation of the scientific efforts of nations and countries? And how do matters stand in this connection in the USSR?

In first place, of course, there is the exchange of printed scientific information, centralized and *individual*, the exchange of scientific works between states, academies, institutes, libraries, laboratories and *individual scientists*. I stress here especially the individual exchange of information between scientists with close interests, since it is precisely this that in the general balance of exchange of information at the present time is becoming more and more important.

In the USSR the predominant feature is and always has been a centralized planned exchange of scientific information between establishments, and scientists obtain their information by reading or copying the materials which reach the libraries. I have in mind current, fresh information published in the journals, since books give a general view of the data after a delay of one and a half to two years. But in most other countries for a number of decades now, the predominant feature has been the individual exchange of information in the form of the exchange of offprints of articles published in the journals and copies of articles sent to press.

Today, when the number of scientific workers in the world is measured in millions, the possibility of useless doubling and repetition of research has increased sharply. In one and the same field of research, even if it is a narrow one, there may be dozens or hundreds of laboratories at work. For example, in our laboratory we are studying the synthesis of haemoglobins in nuclear erythrocytes from the radiobiological point of view. Twenty-five years ago the synthesis of haemoglobins was being undertaken by two, or at the most three, researchers in the whole world. Today the synthesis of various haemoglobins in various animals is being studied in some ninety to a hundred laboratories, and if we add the number of laboratories which are working with haemoglobins generally (structure, anomalous haemoglobins, species variations, evolution of forms, genetics of haemoglobins, etc.) then the number of such laboratories in the world increases to three hundred to three hundred and fifty. A similar situation exists in many fields. And then we admit the synthesis of haemoglobins is only a fairly small part of the overall problem of the synthesis of proteins, which is tens of times larger, since there are thousands of proteins, and it is also necessary to keep up with the work being done in this wider field. On the other hand, it is also necessary to keep up with work on the effect of radiation on the synthesis of proteins. To go back over a path that has already been blazed, to study what has already been studied, to discover the discovered, to verify the verified, would be a useless waste of time and resources. It is uneconomic and useless to use outdated methods, to obtain insufficiently accurate data—all the more so, since the cost of experimental work has sharply increased in all fields of knowledge.

Consequently, if he is to perform useful work, a scientist must be well informed in his own field, must always have an opportunity of obtaining the necessary information about current research throughout the world, and must have all accessible information within his reach. But the volume of information which every scientist needs in this regard is growing with exceptional rapidity. This increases the degree of specialization of scientists and brings it to such peaks of subdivision that it is no longer amenable to organized systems of co-ordination and co-operation planned from above. Inter-state rules can be planned in large-scale branches (metallurgy, coal, medicine, pharmacology, biochemistry, instrumentation, etc.). And this is complicated enough, since there are *thousands* of these branches nowadays. Inter-institute links can be formed for large problems (psychiatry, roentgenology, radiology, oncology, radiobiology, molecular biology, study of the lunar surface, construction of electron microscopes, construction of centrifuges, soil erosion, etc.). Such problems run into tens of thousands. To deal with them institutes have been founded, as a form of organization that can ensure that the fundamental information on a given problem is collected, processed and used. Inter-laboratory links have a still more personal form and deal with subproblems, of which every problem has some-times dozens. (Molecular biology is divided into the molecular biology of viruses, phages, proteins, RNA, DNA, the study of codes, the study of polymer synthesis, etc. Radiobiology is divided into radiobiology of cells, tissues and organisms, quantitative radiobiology, the action of irradiation on longevity, the problem of radiation sensitivity, molecular radiobiology, etc.). In turn each subproblem is divided into topics. Thus molecular radiobiology is divided into the action of radiation on the synthesis of proteins, RNA, DNA, nucleoproteins, ribosomes. Topics are divided into concrete questions, amenable to study by an individual scientist. In the field of molecular radiobiology, for example, this will be the study of the effect of radiation on a given protein, haemoglobin or collagen, or lactate-dehydrogenase or one of the many thousands of others. More than a million such concrete questions are being studied in science and technology today, and the possible number of them is theoretically limitless. Scientific links on a basis of topics and questions under investigation have an individual character and cannot be subjected to All-State planning.

There is not a single library, whether in an institute, academy, branch or city, which can guarantee the scientist that he will obtain complete information about topics and individual experimental questions. By using one library or another for collecting some group of fundamental information, the *creative* worker creates his own complex system of multilateral collection of information, a necessary part of which must be personal contact and constant link with experimental groups working on the most closely related topics and questions, and the constant exchange of offprints. It has been computed that work on the collection and analysis of theoretical information at the level of topics takes up at least half of the creative time for the conscientious scientist. For direc-tors of experimental groups and laboratories this proportion can some-times be even higher. Under such conditions it is becoming ever more and more difficult to keep up the necessary level of knowledge. It has

E*

been carefully calculated that the volume of scientific information is now doubling every ten to fifteen years. In a number of progressive new areas, however, it doubles every two to three years. The number of scientific journals in the world increases every year by four hundred to five hundred titles. G. M. Dobrov in his interesting book *Science of Science* (Kiev, 1966) informs us that in 1964 100,000 scientific periodicals were published in the whole world, and during this year about four million articles were published in them.

In connection with this increasing flow of information, the number of publications which provide abstracts, information and bibliographies is multiplying. But these only help one to find the works required. Reading original papers is still the principal form of theoretical work, and it is still impossible to replace this function.

But now neither an institute, nor even a great city, can accumulate in its bookstacks *complete* scientific information in, say, the field of biology or physics. Even the Lenin Central Scientific State Library in Moscow, which is intended to collect *all* world scientific information, does not have large numbers of journals in many branches of science. I know this from my own experience. For example, in the field of gerontology the Lenin Library does not take such important journals as *Experimental Gerontology, Gerontologia, Geriatrics, Journal of the American Geriatrics Society* and *Advances in Gerontological Research*, and I had to make their acquaintance in other Moscow libraries, such as the Central Medical Library, the Library of Foreign Literature and the Bio-Department of the Academy of Sciences of the USSR. Some of the national gerontological journals (Belgian, Danish, Finnish, Swedish and Austrian) are as a rule not received by a single library in the USSR.

But this concerns Moscow. If we now take such large cities as Kiev, Sverdlovsk, Khar'kov or Gor'kii, the deficit in accessible scientific information in, say, biology is exceptionally large. None of these cities receives, through all channels, more than ten per cent of the scientific information. And this position exists in any other country you like to mention.

When the state system of supplying scientists with complete scientific information on individual concrete topics and questions is so inadequate, the principal role in collection and obtaining information is played by *personal, individual initiative*.

What does this individual initiative consist of, and what does it do to enable, for example, a Dr Brown from the University of Wisconsin, in Madison, USA, or a Dr Campbell at the Institute of Molecular Biology in Edinburgh, to be completely informed?

With a pile of standard request forms on his desk, he runs through the primary specialist current journals and the numerous abstract journals and subject indexes to them which are nowadays printed by computer and which cover the whole of world literature, the bibliographical cards of specific topics which are obtained by the laboratory on subscription from special information centres and other materials, and he then quickly fills out requests for the works which interest him and hands them in at the institute office for forwarding to the authors of the works or the establishments where the work was carried out. All foreign abstract journals, for example, *Chemical Abstracts* or *Biological Abstracts* and other bibliographical publications which process the whole of world literature print the author's address with the abstract as a matter of course. In certain large laboratories, for example in the laboratory of biochemical microbiology of the University of Illinois, a general run-through of journals and handbooks of abstracts and the routine filling out of requests is carried out by a special electronic robot.

As a rule such a request brings the required article to the scientist in his laboratory in the form of a separately printed offprint from the journal. Sometimes a refusal comes back with a note that the supply of offprints has already run out. Laboratories and scientists working on closely connected topics include each other on their 'mailing lists' and send each other articles before and after publication at once, without request forms.

The author of the article in his turn, is almost always able to satisfy the request when he receives it. On the average for every article in a primary journal there are from two hundred to four hundred, and for certain particularly important ones, up to a thousand such requests. Foreign journals therefore prepare, on the author's instruction, for payment, a number of offprints of the article, a hundred, two hundred, five hundred or a thousand copies. Payment for the order is made from the fund which finances the topic in question. (The directors of it hold the cheque-books.) The distribution of offprints is often centralized, and large laboratories send out catalogues of offprints which will be sent on request, free of charge. Here the process is stimulated by the personal interest of the author and the laboratory in the propagation of their work. There are even special envelopes of all sizes with metal clips for mailing offprints.

Thanks to this system a scholar creates for himself in the laboratory or at home a personal, individual stock of original articles on the topic he is working on and related topics, a stock which over the years will grow to many thousands of works. I myself, by adopting this practice, received over the ten years from 1956 to 1966 about six thousand off-prints. In the private stock of offprints of Dr Timofeev-Resovskii there are about twenty-five thousand articles. The stock of offprints of some large laboratories abroad exceeds a hundred thousand titles.

Only by such a system does the scientist avoid the difficult and ineffec-tual abstracting of journals and can read the originals when it is necessary. From this form of scientific work other forms of link between scientists and individual laboratories have now begun, and a more complex interweaving of scientific efforts has arisen.

Now let us turn to the position in this respect of the Soviet scientist, let us say, Candidate of Sciences Sidorov from Sverdlovsk University, or Doctor of Sciences Petrov from the Institute of Physiology in Leningrad.

The Soviet journals he reads and abstracts; those, of course, which he does not subscribe to personally. The fact is that it is generally use-less to request offprints from Soviet authors. Many journals do not run off offprints at all. Those which do print them send the authors not more than twenty-five copies. Previously, some six years ago, this number was fifty, but in 1964 to save paper it was reduced to twenty-five. It is impossible to order an additional quantity of off-prints, whether or not for payment, from any journal, since the type is distri-buted immediately it has been printed. Off-prints in the USSR are pro-duced by breaking up the journal into brochures, and not by a separate printing of each article in the necessary number of copies as is done abroad. Large-format envelopes with clips for sending out offprints are generally not available, and many people stick them together themselves, as necessary.

Foreign journals arrive in most libraries after much delay. The fact of the matter is that in order to save foreign currency most institute and city libraries obtain foreign journals not directly by subscription from abroad but in the form of photo-copy reproductions or photo-offset copies produced in Moscow by the Production Combine of the All-Union Institute of Scientific and Technical Information, who by this practice break the elementary international rules of conduct. About five hundred scientific and technical journals are copied in this manner, and the subscription to them is included in the *Soyuzpechat* catalogues which are distributed free of charge. Thus currency may be saved, to the loss of the foreign publishers, but copies of the journals reach the libraries after six to seven months' delay, and this is a very considerable gap, equal to a term of serious work. But the inter-library service sends to other towns only the journals of the previous year and also duplicates, which they do not have for all publications. Even such universally known and widely read scientific journals which exist especially for rapid publication and which appear weekly, such as *Nature* (London) and *Science* (USA) reach almost all libraries except the central Moscow ones after four to five months' delay in the form of copies from the All-Union Institute of Scientific and Technical Information.

Requesting offprints from journals which reach the scientist's hands after such a delay is by now useless; the author has generally run out of the stock he had. The Soviet abstracting journals, such as *Referativnyi Zhurnal 'Khimiya'*, *Referativnyi Zhurnal 'Biologiya'*, besides working slowly and publishing abstracts after a gap of a year to a year and a half, omit the addresses of the authors of the articles and hence cannot be used for the collection of offprints. Moreover they do not publish quarterly and annual subject-indexes, and hence it is difficult to use them. Due to this, the majority of Soviet researchers do not make extensive collections of offprints from abroad, and this is even more true of the exchange of offprints, since their own supply is so limited.

Furthermore contacts between Soviet scientists and laboratories abroad, even for the collection of available information, have for a long time been artificially hampered by various restrictions, and the inertia of these restrictions is still maintained, especially outside Moscow. Until 1956 offprints of articles (printed matter without a sale price) could be sent abroad only through the Foreign Section of the relevant department. Otherwise the post office returned it to the author, and did not always even do that! At international congresses and conferences, right up to the most recent times, Soviet scientists were often reproached for lack of co-operation in not sending papers when requested. But even after 1956, when the postal service received instructions that offprints of printed works should be sent freely abroad, and privileged rates were even introduced for the exchange of printed works, in most scientific institutes and Institutes of Higher Education, especially on the periphery, the practice was maintained of checking the dispatch of correspondence abroad with the Special Department or administration of the institute. The post, even in Moscow and even today, receives the most contradictory instructions from the International Post Office. Quite recently, at the end of 1967, the International Post Office and the Postal Department in Moscow stopped accepting all correspondence, offprints, letters, etc., if the envelope bore the *business address* of a scientist, except with a special form 103A. But form 103A means the correspondence must be checked before sending by the administration, three copies must be made, and it must bear the signature and official stamp of the director. All this constitutes a psychological barrier and an unnecessary waste of time, and naturally sharply restricts the exchange of information. (In 1968 this rule was relaxed and now applies only to articles posted which do not bear the name of the sender.) As a result the average Soviet laboratory has a supply of current, rapidly accessible information much smaller (perhaps seven to ten times smaller) than the average laboratory in the USA.

The insufficient information available to Soviet specialists leads to an abundance of unnecessary, repeated and duplicated research. In ordinary work in biology, physics or chemistry it is difficult to calculate the loss due to this, but it is almost certainly some ten times greater than the modest saving produced by breaking the publishing conventions. But in the case of losses in patents and inventions due to repeated work, statistical and economic calculations are available. G. M. Dobrov in his book *Science of Science* (1966) quoted the following figures as an example. In England and the USA in 1960 repeated technical work constituted 10 to 20 per cent, and this led to a loss of around 1,000 million dollars. In the USSR in a number of branches of technology the number of repeated inventions rose from 40 per cent in 1946 to 85 per cent in 1961. On the average out of every thousand claims for inventions in the USSR only 240 to 280 do not duplicate former solutions. Dobrov calculated the 'density' of repeated claims and demonstrated that there was a maximum of repetitions in 1936 to 1938 and 1950 to 1955. In these years, as is well known, the terror of contacts with foreign countries also reached a maximum.

Such a position leads not only to economic damage and chronic lagging behind in many branches of science and technology. It sharply intensifies the centripetal tendencies in the organizational structure of the Soviet scientific system. An insuperable tendency is arising to concentrate scientific institutes and laboratories in the region of several large cities, and most of all in the Moscow region. Then come Leningrad, Kiev, Novosibirsk and Riga. In the Moscow region are situated not less than 70 per cent of all the scientifically significant laboratories and institutes in the field of biology, biochemistry, genetics, embryology and biophysics. Around Moscow a series of scientific satellite-towns have been created, Dubna, Pushchino, Obninsk, Chernogolovka, Kryukovo and a number of others. There is nothing similar to this in the USA. The journal *Federation Proceedings* sometimes publishes maps of the distribution of scientific personnel in biology in the various states. The distribution proves to be almost uniform and proportional to the population of the states. Only those states with a good climate and natural conditions, such as California, Florida and Texas, are notably saturated with scientific establishments. New York, too, is naturally saturated with science, but this state is a long way behind California. *The Proceedings of the National Academy of Sciences of the USA* periodically publishes a list of members of the Academy of the USA and their addresses. If we compare this list with the list of Academicians and Corresponding Members of the Academy of Sciences of the USSR, we find a very different picture. Almost 85 per cent of Academicians and Corresponding Members of the Academy of Sciences of the USSR have Moscow addresses. But the distribution of members of the National Academy of the USA over the whole territory of the USA is very uniform, with maxima, once again, in the states of California, New York, Massachusetts, Maryland, Texas, Connecticut and Illinois, where there is also the maximum density of population.

Such is the role of properly organized scientific information, properly organized supply of material to the laboratories, properly organized scientific co-operation, centralized and personal.

The second principal form of exchange of scientific information necessary for every scientist consists of the various international meetings, congresses, conferences, symposia, colloquia and seminars. Are these necessary as a major factor in the development of science? Of course the speed of publication of the results of work in print has, on the average, greatly increased. In the Soviet Union this unfortunately lags behind the world average for time taken, and in certain journals there is a very sharp difference. Here the restriction of the size of journals plays a part. Abroad, the size of individual numbers and volumes of journals is generally not restricted and depends on the number of submissions. Soviet scientific journals have a precisely limited size for each issue and hence a large queue of articles is often formed.

Speaking of the extent and attendance of international meetings of scientists, this has increased very sharply, especially in the last ten years. Significant factors here are not only the increase of the role of such meetings in scientific work but also the improvement in communications, the abolition of passport and visa restrictions in Western Europe and in many other groups of countries. But the principal factor in the growth of the number and diversity of form of scientific meetings is the improvement in the system of international scientific co-operation and the development of specialized international scientific organizations, societies, associations and unions.

To demonstrate the scale of international activity of scientists in this direction we shall quote some figures. The All-Union Institute of Scientific and Technical Information in Moscow (AISTI) has for many years now been publishing a monthly *Bulletin of International Scientific Meetings*, which is virtually a translation of the analogous bulletins issued by UNESCO and a number of other publishers. In this bulletin are published preliminary lists of the international meetings scheduled for the next year or two, which their organizers have registered with UNESCO and other bodies, that is to say, the most important conferences which are free for all who wish to attend. Lists of more narrowly specialist and small meetings are published by other bodies, such as WHO and IAEA.

If we take the AISTI *Bulletin* for the beginning of 1967, which announced the plans for international meetings in 1968, then we can see that every monthly bulletin gives a list of about 150 major meetings (the January issue of the *Bulletin* announced 200 congresses, symposia and conferences, the February issue 121, the March issue 82, the April issue 133, the May issue 152 and so on). In all about 1,600 large international meetings were planned for 1968. If we consider only the international *Congresses*, that is, the principal traditional gatherings of many thousands of scientists, united by their branch of science (and not by a specific problem) and held once every several years for each branch, then in 1968 there are to be around four hundred of them (on genetics, internal combustion engines, purification of metals, timber, geology, sugar cane, concrete, laboratory equipment, the grain trade, jet engines, physiology, photobiology, ophthalmology, sources of energy, neurosurgery, alcohol, transport engineering, corrosion, smelting, cytochemistry and histochemistry, ether oils, endocrinology, zoology, surface-active substances, leprosy, etc.). As a guide, according to the UNESCO data up to a million people take part in scientific congresses and meetings of an international nature every year. And how many more are there of small-scale, special, inter-institute, inter-laboratory symposia and colloquia which are not taken into account in the statistics! According to the UNESCO data in 1964 there were 2,500,000 scientific workers in the world. One in four of them held an academic degree. Thus there were about 650,000 scientists in the world with higher qualifications (for 1964) or about 700,000 for 1968, if we take into account the rate of growth of scientific personnel. Of this number about a quarter belong to the USSR. According to official data (speech of Comrade Brezhnev at the Twenty-third Congress of the CPSU) the number of scientific workers in the USSR in 1966 was 660,000. In 1967 this number increased to 700,000. If one in four of them has an academic degree, then the number of scientific workers with higher qualifications is around 180,000. According to these indices the USSR surpasses the USA by a factor of two. With respect to the number of scientific workers per 100,000 population, the USSR also surpasses the countries of Europe by a factor of two.

Thus, if a million persons per year over the last few years have taken part in international scientific meetings, by proportion the contingent of Soviet scientists should also be a quarter of that number, i.e. 250,000 persons. If we take it that a quarter of the participants in any international conference is made up of citizens of the country where the conference takes place, then, if the international co-operation of Soviet scientists were equal to that of other countries, some 200,000 Soviet citizens would go abroad for this purpose every year.

Let us now look at how the situation really stands in this matter. Unfortunately exact data on the trips abroad of Soviet scientists to take part in international meetings are only available for those organized by the Academy of Sciences of the USSR, which is in a considerably better position than other establishments. This makes the All-Union coefficient quoted below undoubtedly too high. Within the system of the Academy of Sciences of the USSR (including the Academies of Sciences of the Union Republics) there are about 80,000 scientific workers. This constitutes about one-fifth of the total number of scientific workers in open scientific establishments. (The workers in closed establishments go abroad only very exceptionally.) The number of scientific workers with an academic degree within the system of the Academy of Sciences of the USSR is about 20,000 or 25,000. According to the data published in the report of the Chief Academic Secretary of the Academy of Sciences of the USSR, Academician Ya. V. Peive (*Vestnik Akademii Nauk SSSR*, (3), 186–190, 1967) in 1966 3,459 workers from the Academy made trips abroad to countries of all kinds (socialist, capitalist, developing) including cases of scientific tourism. The Academy of Sciences of the USSR received from abroad twice as many, 9,305 foreign scientists. Out of the total number of Soviet scientists making trips abroad, only about half were able to take part in various meetings. Even if we round this figure upwards, this gives us only about 2,000 persons. If we take the figures for the Academy of Sciences of the USSR as being the average for all the other scientific systems of the Union (which in fact they are far from being) then the number of Soviet participants in international congresses abroad clearly did not exceed 15,000 or at the very most 20,000. Much, of course, depends on where the congresses and conferences were to be held. Without a doubt, more than half of this number went to international meetings held in the socialist countries of Eastern Europe.[1]

Thus the figure of 20,000 is only 10 per cent of what would be expected, and we get this only if we equate the Academy of Sciences of the USSR with other establishments. Consequently, in 1966 only one of our scientists out of every 30 or 40 took part in international scientific meetings. Unfortunately, we cannot quote analogous calculations for scientists from England, France and other countries, but it seems to us that the coefficient of participation in this case must be 20 to 30 times greater.

If we take other data from the same speech of Academician Peive, then it is found that to the USA (not less than 50 per cent of the scientific information in the capitalist world originates in the USA) there went 95 scientists from the Academy of Sciences of the USSR and the Academies of Sciences of the Union Republics. 2,183 American scientists came to the USSR through the Academy of Sciences of the USSR, that is twenty times more. 326 Soviet scientists went to England, and 820 English scientists came to the USSR (and there are ten times fewer scientists in England than in the USSR) and so forth.

Anyone who has taken part in any international scientific congress knows very well how small the Soviet delegation normally is. At the International Congress of Gerontology in Vienna there were fifteen scientists from the USSR. But almost two hundred came across the ocean from the USA. At the Third International Congress on Human Genetics in the

[1] According to the data given in the speech of Ya. V. Peive for 1967 (*Vestnik Akademii Nauk SSSR*, (5), 1968), in 1967 a somewhat larger number of workers from the Academy of Sciences of the USSR went abroad—4,522 persons. However, in 1967 the number of foreign scientists who came to the USSR through the Academy of Sciences was about a third of the previous figure—3,590. (Out of the 4,522 persons who went abroad through the Academy of Sciences, 2,362 went to socialist countries, while out of the 3,590 who came to the USSR, 2,900 were citizens of socialist countries—see the additional data in the speech of I. N. Kiselev, *Vestnik Akademii Nauk SSSR* (9), 1968.) Thus the number of scientists who visited our country in 1967 decreased sharply, especially as far as the countries of Western Europe and the USA are concerned. The number of scientists who came to the USSR in 1967 from all the capitalist countries put together was less than the number which came in 1966 from England alone (820)—*Author's note*.

USA in 1966 there were only four papers from the USSR, but none of those who were to read the papers attended. The trip was approved only for one single scientist, Academician N. P. Dubinin, but even he was unable to go. But at this Congress there were sixteen representatives from Sweden, twelve from Israel, fourteen from Holland and so forth. The total list of participants published in the collection of principal speeches of the Congress numbered 920 scientists. At the Fifth International Congress of Biochemistry in Moscow in 1961, 1,200 American biochemists were present. But at the next, the Sixth, Congress of Biochemistry in New York in 1964 about thirty Soviet biochemists took part. And so it is at almost every congress, not to mention the fact that at a very large number of international meetings Soviet science is not represented at all.[1]

However, it is important first of all to determine whether so weak a representation of Soviet scientists at international meetings is a real lack which influences the development of science in our country. Perhaps this is only a sensible way of imposing a rational limitation on unnecessary waste of currency and working time?

International congresses, symposia and conferences, are—although a special one—a means of exchange of scientific information. Of course the development of science would not stop if there were, in general, no congresses and meetings. But the rate of that development would

[1] The best-known international scientific journal published in England, *Nature*, printed on 13 January 1968 (vol. 217, no. 5124, pp. 123–4) a very interesting article by the physicist John Ziman, a Fellow of the Royal Society. The article was entitled 'Letter to an Imaginary Soviet Scientist'. The principal theme of the article, which was written in a kindly tone and with humour, was to demonstrate how strange and incomprehensible English scientists found the cases of non-arrival of Soviet scientists at international conferences, even after their coming has been planned for and agreed. The author of the article draws attention to the very dry and official style of the majority of letters from Soviet scientists, the great delay in replying to letters, the cases when those who come to conferences are by no means the people who were invited and the impossibility of simply inviting a Soviet colleague to come and work in a laboratory. He rightly points out that such a situation damages above all the country which is putting into effect the policy of isolation. In the USSR original copies of *Nature* reach only a few libraries in Moscow. To other parts of the country, on free subscription too, the photo-offset reproduction is sent by the Institute of Information. Naturally Ziman's open letter was not included in this reproduction. However, so that the order of pages should not be destroyed and the reader should not suspect the omission, the Soviet version of the journal had, instead of the Ziman article, various reviews taken from other numbers. In previous times 'undesirable' articles were simply cut out of the journals, and they went into the libraries with holes in them. Present-day technology, as we can see, takes refuge in more refined means of falsification. As for the American journal, *Science*, in almost every number of the 'Soviet-reproduced' version one or two articles are missing—*Author's note*.

certainly slow down. What then is the meaning, purpose and use of international meetings?

Let us pause to consider, first of all, the traditional congresses. The purpose of established, successively numbered congresses for particular branches of science, usually held not more often than once every two to three years, is to present the results of investigations in a given field of knowledge over the previous few years and to elect a new governing body of the international scientific union concerned. At a congress a survey is usually given of the current state of the whole of world science on the given branch of knowledge, and all the principal problems are considered in special sessions and symposia. The materials of each congress which crystallize the given branch of knowledge from a mixture of a colossal number of components of the world-wide system of scientific establishments, with careful study clearly show all the principal and secondary achievements which this branch has attained in the last few years and which it can attain in the near future.

Scientists of one discipline are mingled with numerous other scientists of other disciplines in very odd combinations. Geneticists may, for example, meet in medical, chemical, physical, cosmic, geological and in any other type of establishment, in colleges and schools, universities and private firms. An international congress, once every few years, draws them all, like a magnet, free from the surrounding matter. In his own work, every scientist is of necessity a very narrow specialist. When he comes to a congress he can at once take his bearings in the whole field and the associated branches of science. Probably 80 to 90 per cent of scientists know no more than one foreign language. And if an Englishman who knows French, or a German who knows English, reads the literature in these languages, he still cannot, as a rule, follow the Russian, Japanese, Italian, Spanish or Swedish literature. International congresses with their narrow restriction of working languages and simultaneous translation of all the speeches into the working languages make all the current world information accessible to the participants of the congress. It should be noted that, although before 1917 and even by tradition right up into the 1930s Russian was one of the working languages of almost all the primary congresses, especially in Europe, after 1946, when Russian scientists stopped attending international congresses in any significant numbers, the Russian language disappeared from the programmes of the congresses and was no longer a working language. At almost all international congresses English is the dominant language. It is the main working language, even when international meetings are held in Poland, Czechoslovakia, Romania or Yugoslavia. In particular, the Mendel Memorial Symposium in Brno and the Symposium on Mutations in Prague in 1965, the Gerontology Symposium in Prague in 1967 and the Radiobiology Symposium not far from Prague in September 1967 were conducted exclusively in English. Papers in Russian were not accepted, and there was no simultaneous translation into Russian.

Evidently scientists have some kind of periodic need to bring their own science on to the world scale, to estimate the rate of its development. It is not by chance that, in spite of the greater and greater subdivision of congresses by branches and the ever more narrow specialization of the international associations (there was originally only one committee for International Genetics Congresses, but later another was set up for the independent branch of human genetics; the Association of Microscopy has divided off into an independent branch of electron microscopy, etc.) the scale of the congresses convened by the association is ever increasing. Moreover the very army of scientists is growing. To a branch international congress nowadays there will come not less than two or three thousand people from the whole world, and sometimes considerably more. At the Fifth Biochemical Congress in Moscow there were 5,500 participants, and at the Sixth in New York there were 7,000. 6,000 scientists came to the Microbiology Congress in Moscow in 1966. As many as 9,000 came to a congress on dairying. Even an international congress on what would seem to be a narrow branch, such as electron microscopy, and taking place in a country as remote from Europe and America as Japan drew about 2,000 persons in 1966. Congress programmes are normally distinguished by their extreme diversity. I have before me the programme of the Twelfth International Congress on Genetics which will be held this year in Japan:[1] this includes twenty-six symposia on specific problems, twenty-two thematic general sessions each lasting several days, several plenary meetings, seven exhibitions and some more specialized meetings of leading specialists after the Congress in various cities of Japan.

In addition to its great significance, for organization and information, every international congress stimulates the creative activity of its participants by means of debates, discussions and conversations. There is not only this psychological factor, which cannot be ignored in science. It should be stressed that of all the abundant and diverse means of information which modern science uses in its relations between the individual exponents, *the chief means of critical appraisal of any piece of*

[1] Written in 1968—*Translator.*

work, the demonstration of its strong and weak points, its methodological inadequacies and its position among other investigations in the same field is, even today, verbal, direct and immediate discussion in a circle of understanding colleagues. And this can be most useful, objective and impartial precisely when it is on an international basis.

Modern science has become so diversified and differentiated on the international scale and the number of particular questions being investigated has increased so much that very many scientists simply do not have brothers-in-science in their own country who understand what they are doing. On a given question, sometimes a very important one, a scientist may be the *only* specialist in his country. Such a position is often encountered not only in small countries, where it is simply typical, but even in large states too. I could quote a number of examples in the USSR in the fields of biology and biochemistry.

For example, the problem of post-radiation repair on a suitable subject for this study—yeast—is studied in the USSR only by V. I. Korogodin's experimental group in our Institute. There are a few other such research groups of this kind in five or six countries. At International Congresses of Radiation Biology representatives of these groups normally form a small symposium. The most important question of the biosynthesis of proteins—the study of the sequence of nucleotides in transport RNA—is being investigated by some seven or eight groups in the whole world. Two of these are in the USSR, in Moscow and Novosibirsk. It would seem that even so large a question as the genetics of the process of ageing is being studied in the USSR by only two scientists—G. D. Berdyshev and myself. In the whole world questions of the genetics of ageing enter into the sphere of investigations of about twenty scientists. And naturally in 1966, when at the Gerontology Congress in Vienna there was to be a small four-day symposium before the Congress on the genetics of ageing with some twenty to twenty-five participants and both of us received an invitation, it would have been very far from useless for us to go. And it was we, of course, who lost the most from the fact that we were unable to do so.

A similar situation exists in many other cases, apparently in most other cases. Along with the large questions which are studied by hundreds of specialists even in a single country there are thousands of experimental groups whose work simply cannot receive competent consideration within national frontiers. Moreover the international links of science have become much more complex, since a number of new countries which formerly did not have their own scientists are now engaged on the intensive development of many branches of science. In these countries experimental groups are set up which often have no connection with the industrial and economic interests of the country and which are meaningful only in a system of international differentiation of science.

We all know that in scientific work one successful thought which arises in some five-minute discussion, one critical remark, one piece of advice from a scientific colleague, can determine and change the course of work of a scientist for many years.

Sometimes it seems that in science there are now too many discussions, debates and meetings, and that this is preventing uninterrupted creative experimental work. Sometimes this may even really be true, especially when science is unskilfully directed and conferences and meetings are badly organized. But, in essence, this increase in the balance of discussions is an inescapable consequence of the sharp rise in the cost of experimental work and laboratory equipment. Before paying out an investment of several millions for an experiment, it is necessary to consider very carefully and from all aspects just how far this experiment is really necessary, how far the information obtained as a result of performing it will be really original and definitive and whether anyone else in another laboratory and in another country is doing similar work. Hence the experimental projects proposed by scientists (in countries with special-fund financing of each specific topic there is a precisely calculated balance-sheet) are considered more and more carefully as time goes on. In the USSR where the budgetary financing of structural units (academies, institutes, sections and laboratories) is predominant and not the financing of individual topics, the scientific effectiveness of the funds paid out for experimental work is specifically much lower, precisely because the projects do not receive sufficiently serious professional consideration. In the latter case the project is mainly discussed in connection with administrative matters, never very competently and not with the expert or professional consideration which is given in the case of special-fund financing. Special-fund financing means that the state and private allocations for science do not proceed downwards through the different ranks of the authorities but go into professionally differentiated independent funds which finance topics, in many cases by-passing the administrative hierarchy of the establishment. In the USA there are about 1,800 such funds. A scientist seeks financial support personally and directly from the fund. For example, in gerontology in the USA, according to the material published in *Science* (15 December

1967) not less than 50 per cent of the total number of applications were refused financial support, based on the very careful consideration of the results of previous investigations, world-wide experience and the qualifications of the scientists. In other, more 'expensive' sciences, the proportion is evidently even higher.

Moreover it is clear that, if throughout the world there are diverse international societies and associations with more and more narrowly specialized interests, then the members of these societies who are united by their joint organizational interests must meet from time to time. In addition to the scientific discussions and debates which are very important to the participants, it is also important for them to hold elections and re-elections of the governing bodies, boards, section bureaux, editorial and planning groups, to revise the rules, and so on. The unchangeable tradition of international scientific societies is that the governing bodies must be completely changeable during the period defined by the time between congresses or general conferences. Totalitarian government of societies can easily come to pass if the president once elected remains president until his death. The periodic changing of the whole organization demands a personal knowledge of the candidates and a personal acquaintance with the specialists of the profession in question within the limits of problems and subproblems.

In the world today thousands of international professional societies and associations have been created. Several hundred societies, very large ones and divided on a national and regional basis, have united in their work with UNESCO (see the list published in the book *UNESCO and the Modern World*, published by Mezhdunarodnaya Otnosheniya, Moscow, 1966, Appendix 8, pp. 256–62). However, hundreds of societies are independent of UNESCO. Moreover an enormous number of societies have an international character and an international status, but do not have national divisions, since in many countries there are only a few scientists working on the problem in question, sometimes only one or two. Such societies normally have only one governing body for the entire world. I am very well acquainted with one such society which has its present headquarters in San Juan in Puerto Rico (after the next elections the society will move its home). This is the Society for the Study of Biological Rhythms. In the list of members of this society there are about a hundred scientists. The society collects a world-wide special library of works, mainly offprints, on biorhythms, holds annual international conferences, publishes collections of papers on specific problems, and has, among other things, exerted a very great effect on a number of branches of biology, biochemistry, physiology, etc., having shown by the joint research activity of its members that any process in an organism, starting with respiration and finishing with the activity of the genes, has circadian, seasonal and other rhythms, and that these must now be taken into account in any research into which the time factor enters.

A scientist in the modern world cannot work in isolation. He works as a member of the world fellowship of science, and he must be a full and equal member of this fellowship. Can we imagine a European scientist, fifty to sixty years old, who has never once travelled beyond the limits of his own country, nor ever taken part in an international meeting abroad, nor ever once visited a foreign laboratory, even in neighbouring countries? Of course we cannot imagine it; it would be impossible in England, France or Belgium. But in the USSR this is still true of most scientists. As their desire and right to effective co-operation with the scientists of other countries is restricted, their lives become more and more deprived. But Soviet science—and our own country—is thereby depriving itself of a great deal.

But if we take the whole Soviet group of fifty- to sixty-year-olds their opportunities nowadays are better than those of young people. The maximum number of trips abroad, for example, per hundred persons in a year is apparently that for Academicians, then for Corresponding Members, then for Doctors of Science, then for Candidates of Science and only then come young scientists. Yet, on the whole, international conferences, congresses and meetings in practically all sciences became considerably 'younger' after 1945–50, once the world scientific 'boom' began. There are several reasons why the age of Soviet scientific delegations is so much higher than average. Firstly, this is connected with the preliminary limiting of the number of participants for any international meeting. The preliminary information on congresses and symposia, sent out, for example, by the Ministry of Health, indicates directly, Congress This— ten places; Symposium on That—eight places; Conference on The Other—twelve places, and so on.[1] These figures are indicated for the information of those who really do wish to go and take part in the meeting. And hence, for example, for ten places at some important conference, there will always be ten Academicians and Corresponding Members.

[1] The corresponding letter of instruction of the Academy of Medical Sciences of the USSR on congresses within the public health system for 1969 almost always planned the trip for groups of five persons. This is considerably less then in 1968—*Author's note.*

The second factor restricting the participation of young scientists in international meetings is the high cost of 'Intourist' travel. Most departments now arrange almost all trips through Intourist as tourist trips, with additional days for ordinary sightseeing excursions. Englishmen, Frenchmen, Finns or Swedes can go to a congress in Italy, for example, in their own cars, without any travel agency. If they want to economize, they can camp overnight (hotels in Europe and the USA are very expensive). Most of them obtain their travelling expenses from some appropriate fund. Many are paid by the organizing committee of the congress or symposium. The organizing committee of any congress always establishes a fund to reimburse scientists from distant countries and young scientists. Moreover any congress has a very differentiated system for participation and payment and discussion. The 'student' rate, which even established scientists often use, is very cheap, it provides hostel accommodation instead of a hotel, travel by train or boat instead of by air, and reduced enrolment fees. If a Western scientist pays his expenses for taking part in an international meeting out of his own pocket, then the sum he pays for this will not be liable to income-tax (even if he takes his family). The USSR 'Intourist' which serves the Soviet participants unites them in a single group, without categories of payment and without a student rate for young people. And if, for example, it has already been announced that the cost of the journey to the Genetics Congress in Japan this year will be 700 to 800 roubles, then, of course, this is not for junior scientists and post-graduate students.

It is impossible not to note that the Central Committee of the Komsomols has a special international co-operation programme called 'Sputnik'. Sometimes trips are organized through 'Sputnik' for young scientists. But for the *sake* of science, very rarely! Basically the 'Sputnik' programme, it seems to us, provides fans for the Soviet teams at international matches and contests.

And how many moral traumas are caused by the existing system of organizing international co-operation to scientists whose trips are refused at various stages of the process of approval! How much time is lost in vain! What a sharp reduction there has been in the benefit which our country obtains from taking part in international meetings—and perhaps the overall balance is not always even positive! Those suffer especially who have passed through all the stages but are not included in the group at the last stage because of a lack of places. The international sections of the departments which deal with the sifting out always request more 'exit dossiers' than there are agreed places in the group. Institutes throughout the entire Union propose, let us say, fifty scientists for a trip to some congress, and the International Section, sifting out thirty of them straight away, orders a total of twenty candidates. For thirty to be sifted out at the first stage is unlikely, but this is a very simple example. Due to currency restrictions it is decided, for example, to have a group of ten only, and consequently out of the twenty 'exit dossiers' which have been completed and prepared, only ten will be forwarded to Intourist. But the scientists have been preparing their papers, have sent the abstracts abroad and are included in the programme. They are polishing their weapons and filling their cartridge-pouches like warriors before an attack. They are advancing, but they do not know how many of them will reach the final frontier. Here three of them are 'laid low' by order of the Minister, another four cannot penetrate the barriers of the 'Exit Commission'. Thirteen win past all obstacles, but three of them, all the same, are cut down by the currency budget plan. But the programme of the congress has already been sent out, the times of the papers have been fixed. The whole hall will be sitting and quietly waiting at the appointed time in silence, since it is impossible to bring forward the next paper, it has been announced for a given time and the audiences plan to move from section to section strictly according to the time-table. Most frequently such silent sessions are due to the non-arrival of Soviet scientists. Hundreds of people sit at the meeting with nothing to do, while the speaker himself suffers out these minutes somewhere at home, in Tashkent or in Baku.

Back in 1960, when the Foreign Section of the Ministry of Higher Education was considering the possibility of my taking part in the Fifth Gerontology Congress in the USA, I saw the following picture, which has been engraved in my memory. The delivery of foreign passports was being made to several participants of some congress in Sweden, linguists, it seems. The last to go up to the employee of the Section was a tall Georgian, a professor from Tbilisi, who had come to Moscow especially for the trip. But they did not deliver a passport to him. And the next day, the whole delegation flew off in the morning. What sorrow and bewilderment there was on the face of the Georgian scholar! How persistently he tried to find out the reason for so unexpected a refusal! The employee of the section, weary at last from his questions, took out from the safe the 'exit dossier' of the Tbilisi linguist and showed him on the cover a fat red minus sign. 'You see,' he said, pointing to the minus sign. 'Look there! What can I do?' But who had put the minus sign? Why? Who had been given the right to do so? The Georgian scientist was struck dumb on the spot, and I do not know whether he went home to his own Tbilisi or whether they put him in hospital in Moscow. But when, in a state of total confusion, he had departed from the room of the Foreign Section, the employees sitting there began to smile gaily. One of them was responsible for the minus!

2

Joint international research

CONGRESSES, symposia, conferences and colloquia are the principal means of exchange of information, of the discussion and consideration of research which has been completed, the determination of plans for the future and of the forming of personal contacts and friendships between scientists. But the main form of direct international co-operation is the joint research project, the exchange of scientists for long-term experimental, practical and theoretical work. The opportunity for a scientist to visit some foreign laboratory or another which most closely corresponds to the problems of his projected research for several months or even a year or two is an irreplaceable tradition of the modern (and not only modern) organization of world science.

An active scientific centre, institute or department in, for example, England, the USA, Canada or France may have as many as a third of its posts specially reserved for the work of foreign scientists and research students who come there to work for several months, a year, two years or even longer. In our country there is but one such centre, the International Institute for Nuclear Research at Dubna. A second one, also for physics, is being founded near Serpukhov. But with the current situation in science, practically every really good institute ought to be an international one, unless, of course, it is a top-security establishment.

Institutes with free co-operation are especially productive. There can be no stagnation in them. The Pasteur Institute, which from the moment of its foundation has worked on this principle, has enjoyed world fame for many decades. No less famous is the California Institute of Technology, with its constellation of outstanding scientists, some of whom have received no less than the Nobel Prize (T. H. Morgan and others). The relatively small Cambridge Laboratory of Molecular Biology in England has for many years determined the principal trends of development of this science in the whole world. Five scientists from this laboratory received the Nobel Prize (Singer, Perutz, Crick, Watson and Kendrew). I could quote dozens of other exceptionally fruitful institutes and laboratories in the field of biology, whose publications usually feature scientists from various countries. If we trace the history of the major biological discoveries of the last fifteen years, their international basis is clearly evident. The discovery of the structure of DNA was a joint Anglo-American project; the experimental synthesis of RNA outside the organism was a joint American-French project; the experimental discovery of information RNA a joint Franco-Anglo-American project, the first publication of which was made jointly by six co-authors; the discovery of the polyribosomes a joint American-English project; the systematic elucidation of the genetic code, after the discovery of the first triplet by Nirenberg was carried out in Ochoa's laboratory by an experimental group which, as well as Americans, included a Brazilian, an Indian and an Argentinian. It would be possible, of course, to quote a multitude of similar examples for other sciences and branches.

Research carried out internationally by the formation of free groups to deal with specific problems possesses great economic advantages and intellectual potentialities.

We have already stressed that present-day research is extremely expensive. The exceptionally high cost of work in physics, astronomy, aviation, rocketry and similar fields is known to all. The major projects here are estimated in hundreds of millions of dollars, and a 'moon-shot' at more than a thousand million. A modern large telescope, even an optical one, runs into hundreds of millions of dollars. And the radio-telescope installations near Serpukhov extend for almost a kilometre. The development of a new aircraft requires many years and hundreds of millions of dollars. Synchrotrons and similar devices intended for theoretical research, which are often a quarter of a kilometre in diameter, also run into hundreds of millions of roubles or dollars. It is obvious that it is simply not within the power of most countries to set up experimental systems of this kind. Not to mention the countries of Asia and Africa (the entire state budget of Indonesia for a year is considerably less than the cost of a single 'soft landing' on the moon) it should be noted that even for the economically developed and relatively large countries of Western Europe, many of the modern research projects undertaken in the USA and the USSR are unattainable, and that inter-state All-European funds are being established for their support.

But in biology too, the high cost and complexity of research is increasing. It has been calculated that the technical cost of a single medical

Ph.D. in the USA[1] in the field of biology per year is about 50,000 dollars (the cost of the group working with him is taken into account here). Certain apparatus, without which work in modern biochemistry is unthinkable, for example, an analytical centrifuge, an aminoacid analyser, etc., cost tens of thousands of dollars each. A modern analytical centrifuge with ultraviolet optics, of Soviet manufacture, costs not less than 100,000 roubles.[2] The cost is the same for a block of thirty flats. In such a situation the establishment of well-equipped laboratories and institutes is a great task and a very expensive one. Under these conditions many countries carry out a considerable part of the research needed for various projects at foreign bases, on the principle of reciprocity for some other problems. Thus there is created a gradual national specialization and differentiation. It is economically and creatively justified not only in physics or cosmology but also in biology. If in some experiment it is necessary to use neutron irradiation, analytical centrifuging or ultraviolet microcytospectrophotometry, it is by no means always reasonable to construct a nuclear reactor, buy an ultra-centrifuge or instal an ultraviolet microcytospectrophotometer. It is simpler and cheaper to send a colleague to work for a month, two months or a year at some other institute where all these methods are already in operation—maybe in another country. Yet this is by no means always done, and often identical exceptionally expensive items of equipment are purchased by a number of neighbouring institutes and used in each of them to about a tenth of their capacity. When plans were being made for our Institute of Medical Radiology, it was decided to build a nuclear reactor on its site to carry out irradiations. The plans had already been drawn up, with an additional allocation of several million roubles. In another, chemical, institute being founded across the road from us, the Karpov Institute of the Radiochemical Profile, a nuclear reactor, an even more powerful one, was also being built. By chance one of the rank-and-file workers of the State Committee on Science and Technology noticed how close the institutes were together, and managed to get the construction of a reactor in our institute cancelled. This worker did not receive any decoration, although he saved the budget many millions of roubles. And in the Ministry of Health they were very

[1] A medical Ph.D. in the USA is the equivalent of our Candidate of Sciences and also of a Doctor, since in the USA one qualifies as a Doctor straight after being a post-graduate student, and a mature scholar does not have to defend a thesis a second time—*Author's note*.

[2] The current value of the rouble is slightly more than that of the American dollar—*Translator*.

unhappy about this, they wanted to have their own reactor, which would have been more convenient than having to take samples over to the neighbours for irradiation.

Not only apparatus, but even the reagents for the research often have four- and five-figure prices, even for a small beakerful—and especially 'labelled' radioactive organic compounds with a high specific activity, salts and substances of especial purity and many biological preparations and enzymes. From the international catalogues it can be seen that a pack containing a milligramme of tritiated thimidine with very high specific activity costs £1,000 sterling, more than a new car. This is just for a few experiments with a few rats, not more, and research with tritiated thimidine can be found in any cytological journal. In 1966-7, when work was begun in the USA using *l*-asparaginase for the treatment of leucoses, the amount of enzyme required for the treatment of a single patient cost $50,000-$100,000.

In recent years there have arisen a number of international organizations especially for the encouragement and support of international research and of international scientific co-operation. In the first place, of course, there is the United Nations Educational, Scientific and Cultural Organization (UNESCO).[1] The whole world is covered by the World Health Organization (WHO), the International Agency for the Peaceful Uses of Atomic Energy (IAEA) and others. There exists a number of private independent organizations for the support of international co-operation in different sciences (Ciba Foundation, the Rockefeller Foundation, the Joseph P. Kennedy Foundation for research into congenital defects, etc.). An enormous role in international co-operation in research is played by associations of scientific societies. They frequently organize international courses for study and the

---

[1] UNESCO, the United Nations Educational, Scientific and Cultural Organization, was set up at the Inaugural Conference in London in November 1945. 44 countries took part in the Conference. Since 1946 UNESCO has been one of the principal specialized establishments of the UN. In the first years of the existence of UNESCO, the Soviet Union was critical of its activity and refused to join the organization. Only in 1954, after the death of Stalin, did the USSR and also the Ukrainian SSR and the Byelorussian SSR recognize the UNESCO charter and become members of the organization. At that time there were 64 countries in UNESCO. At present [1968], 120 countries take part in the work of UNESCO. UNESCO is the most all-embracing and authoritative organization for international scientific and cultural co-operation between nations and states. With UNESCO are associated many international associations, organizations, unions, alliances, federations, councils, committees and clubs (243 international scientific, social, religious, tourist, literary, women's, educational, youth organizations, etc., with their own constitutions.) The central administrative building of UNESCO is in Paris. In the USSR there is a government commission for UNESCO affairs—*Author's note.*

improvement of qualifications and set up research groups. All these organizations have, taken together, thousands of grants which maintain inter-state exchange of young scientists for long-term research.

To explain why the participation of Soviet researchers in all these programmes is so slight, reference is usually made to currency saving. But this argument is absolutely unfounded. The annual outlay of currency of a state as large as the USSR is very great, and the proportion spent on international scientific co-operation, on paying for the foreign travel of scientists, cannot be so great a proportion of the total sum that it could affect our economic interests. On the contrary, really effective and widespread scientific co-operation would result in the creation of a great saving of currency, since a well-qualified body of scientists and experts would be created who would know foreign technical and scientific achievements from their own experience and would be able to guarantee really economic and maximally rational outlay of the state currency and gold reserves. Moreover, better relations with the world would guarantee the formation of additional resources for the sale of Soviet goods, for the improvement of their quality, and so on. Proper scientific co-operation is constructed on principles of reciprocity, and its currency balance for the USSR could and should be positive. We have already seen that in 1966, twenty times more scientists came to the USSR from the USA through the Academy of Sciences of the USSR than went to the USA from the USSR. Consequently in the Academy of Sciences of the USSR alone there are large potential currency dollar reserves which simply have not been used and which thus are lost to the state. And the same position exists in the exchange programme with England, France and Japan.

To speak seriously now, it must be recognized that a very great quantity of currency is expended by our country to no purpose whatsoever, precisely because of the lack of freedom of scientific co-operation and the artificial restriction of joint research. In addition to the numerous purchases in currency made abroad to an enormous sum, which are the fruit of economic and planned calculations of an All-State character,[1] large sums of currency are lost in buying scientific equipment for research when it is not really needed and without proper thought. This

[1] Such as the currency and gold purchase of wheat in Canada in 1963–5, the purchase of wheat in Australia and New Zealand, in the Federal German Republic and the USA, the purchase of macaroni in Italy, butter in Denmark, meat in the Argentine, cellulose in Finland, etc. All these are traditional goods of Russian and Soviet export, but in the period in question they became import products to be paid for in currency and gold—*Author's note.*

F

happens precisely because the state tries to raise the level of scientific research by buying equipment from abroad, thus compensating by a considerably more expensive method for the limitation of the scientific work of Soviet specialists abroad. In seventeen years of working in scientific establishments, how much expensive and super-expensive imported 'currency' equipment have I seen which is obsolescent and useless due to the lack of spare parts, ready for scrapping or unnecessary since there are exactly equivalent home-produced types! And how many unused currency reserves there still are in our country! One big sturgeon can compensate for fairly prolonged research of a scientist abroad. But the USSR, which once had almost unlimited reserves of these most expensive and unique fish, has so sharply reduced the stock of them, due to pollution of rivers of the Caspian basin, that now she takes only second place, after Iran, in the world trade figures for the catching of sturgeon and the export of black (sturgeon) caviar, although Iran borders on only a small portion of the Caspian Sea and has only small rivers for spawning. Questions of currency policy will be considered in the special section on 'currency barriers' where we shall see that it is not currency saving which restricts international exchange in the field of science at all. But here we should like to stress that even those currency investments which the USSR makes in the form of grants to scientists of the IAEA, WHO, UNESCO and other departments of the UN as part of our currency payments to these organizations are not used completely and are lost for Soviet science. The overwhelming number of invitations of Soviet scientists to congresses, symposia, laboratories and courses with all expenses paid by those issuing the invitation, which is the usual scientific tradition, are not made use of. Those issuing the invitation bear the expense, but by investing in the foreigner's knowledge and experience, they retain the fruit of his labour. In 1966 not one single such invitation from the USA was put into effect.

If one studies the problem of international scientific co-operation seriously it is evident that its restriction is mainly a loss to the country which imposes the restriction. By excluding itself from the valuable widespread circulation of knowledge and experience, by isolating itself from world science, this country creates for itself conditions of stagnation in many branches of knowledge. And in science any lag means direct and indirect economic damage. The lag, of course, is not uniform. Some fields which come under the special attention of the state and receive considerable subsidies, can, of course, even outstrip the world level. We all know the outstanding achievements of the USSR in the study of space, aircraft construction, the construction of an atomic icebreaker, atomic power-stations, mathematics, metallurgy, construction of hydroelectric plants, high voltage electric power lines, etc. But in a number of fields which cannot be planned from above, which are broken up between thousands of independent groups with free choice of problems, even today the USSR lags considerably behind the world level, precisely because its mutual relations with world science are insufficiently developed, due to the isolation of Soviet scientists from direct contacts with the best foreign centres.

In 1960 when I began to make a serious study of the damage which the monopoly of 'Michurin biology', or more correctly Lysenkoism, had brought to Soviet science, I decided as a biochemist to make a comparison of some comparative indices of Soviet and American biochemistry.

It was not possible to speak about genetics, it simply did not exist in our country as a serious branch of study, but according to the official declarations biochemistry was in its beginning stage. This was the time just before the International Biochemistry Congress in Moscow, which was to be held in August 1961. I selected a number of indices of the achievements of 1960, sometimes the second half of 1960, for objective comparison: the number of members of the biochemical society (professional biochemists), the number of biochemical publications, the number of scientific journals on biochemistry, the number of laboratories (according to addresses in publications), the range of biochemical reagents (according to the commercial catalogues), the percentage of research carried out with the aid of isotopes, the range of radioactive organic compounds and their specific activity, the speed of publication of papers after they had been prepared for press, the number of new enzymes discovered, the number of decoded aminoacid sequences in proteins and peptides, the number of projects using the ultracentrifuge.

All these comparisons were, of course, carried out without absolute precision, which would have been possible to achieve only with the help of a group of colleagues and then not very rapidly. Simply from scanning the current journals and review journals I recorded in a special order the indices I have mentioned. After collecting the statistically reliable values for part of 1960, they were extrapolated for the whole year. I had intended to publish this work in the form of an article, but the picture was too detrimental to the USSR, and I had to give up the project of drawing it up in a definitive form.

In 1960 our lag behind American biochemistry was very considerable. The listed membership of the biochemical society (in the USA one had existed for many years, in the USSR one was founded only in 1959) was approximately the same, around the level of 2,300 persons in both countries. In the speed of publication of papers, we lagged behind the USA by a factor of three to four; in the USA some three to four months elapsed between the submission of papers to a journal and their appearance, while for us it was up to a year or eighteen months. In this connection we also had a considerable lag in the number of publications per year per professional biochemist (a factor of about two and a half). The total volume of biochemical publications (taking the number of journals into account) was three to four times greater in the USA (they collect papers from all over the world), or, using the data of the abstract journals, five times greater, since many Americans publish their research in European journals. In the use of the ultracentrifuge we were some ten times behind. The list of names of commercial biochemical preparations in the USSR runs into dozens of names, but in the USA into thousands. Biochemical preparations in the USSR go into the ordinary chemical catalogues, but in the USA special catalogues of biochemical preparations have been issued for many years. No new enzymes were described in the USSR, no aminoacid sequences in proteins were determined, while in the USA these branches of biochemistry were going through a period of intensive accumulation of material. There was also a considerable lag in the list of radioactive compounds and principally in their specific activity.

And, while Soviet biochemistry made undoubted advances in its development up to 1967, the gap in the general level evidently did not diminish, or diminished only by an inconsiderable amount. It is sufficient to say that in the principal direction of advance of these years, the deciphering of the genetic code, the determination of the quaternary and tertiary structure of proteins, and in the study of the sequence of aminoacids in proteins and nucleotides in nucleic acids, that is in work requiring first-class equipment, we were even further behind our American colleagues. Not one of the 64 codons of the genetic code was experimentally deciphered in the USSR. We were not able to undertake such work technically, but, worst of all, we were not willing to send Soviet researchers to take part in this kind of research, even when it was being carried out, as it often was, on an international basis.

Certain Soviet biochemists who have had the chance in the last few years of prolonged research abroad are today especially outstanding for the high level of research which they are now carrying out within the scientific framework of their native country. And if these chances were not a special privilege of the few, if it had been decided at last to stimulate free scientific exchange, then we should long ago have had a first-class and modern biology, long ago our agriculture would have been saved from the destructive elements of pseudoscientific propaganda, long ago we would have been ahead in the level of our natural sciences, at all events in Europe. I am sure that if the question of the introduction of *free* scientific exchange with other countries could be decided by ballot, then an impressive majority of scientists would vote for a free, wide-ranging effective form of international co-operation to enable Soviet science really to blossom as part of the world-wide scientific front.

3

Training abroad

THE possibility of a proportion of young people receiving their training abroad in universities, colleges and research courses must be part of a programme of free scientific exchange. This will arise spontaneously once the existing barriers to trips abroad by Soviet citizens come down. We shall discuss these barriers in the next chapter on legal aspects of the matter.

The USSR has achieved very considerable successes in the development of education, especially higher education. Nevertheless in a number of respects this education is incomplete. Firstly it does not give a knowledge of foreign languages, at all events of the spoken language. Lack of knowledge or only slight knowledge of a foreign language under modern conditions is a sign that a specialist is scientifically not fully qualified. A second serious lack in education in the USSR, both at the secondary and higher levels, is its Union-wide universal standardization, a phenomenon which is impossible in the countries of Western Europe and America. All schoolchildren in the USSR work to the same standard, with one and the same programme of studies and from the same textbooks. The same is true of the Institutes of Higher Education. All the hundred agricultural IHEs in the country have the same programme of studies, with slight variations for the Zootechnical, Vegetable Crops and Agronomy Faculties. Such a system, while possessing a number of advantages from the administrative point of view, contains at the same time many hidden hazards. Unavoidable faults in study programmes and textbooks at once become Union-wide. This is especially apparent in biology and chemistry. Study programmes in the biological sciences, which began to change in the direction of 'Michurin biology' as early as 1937 and were completely altered along the lines of pseudoscientific Lysenkoism after 1948, destroyed and warped biological thinking in several generations of the *whole* of Soviet youth, causing an enormous loss to the country. In the period between 1950 and 1960 there was a similar defect in the university chemistry curriculum which was reflected in the economy of the entire country. Obviously similar examples on a smaller scale could be cited from other sciences. I shall not speak here of the humanities, which are always hurling themselves from one extreme to the other and always throughout the Union. Training abroad, even on a reciprocal basis, even for two to three per cent of the youth, would create compensating phenomena similar to heterozygosity, and would increase the vitality of the total reserves of knowledge of our intelligentsia.

For those who are not acquainted with genetics and who do not know the concept of 'heterozygosity', which illustrates our argument so well, I must give a short explanation. All the features of an organism are determined by a double complex of genes, one from the mother and the other from the father. There are tens of thousands of these genes. And if a gene from the mother is defective, then it is very unlikely that the same gene from the father will also be defective. The father does have defective genes too but these do not coincide with those from the mother. This creates heterozygosity, in which the insufficiencies of the genes of one of the parents are compensated by the normal genes of the other. The maternal set of genes may bear dozens of lethal mutations, but these will not produce death, since they are compensated by the normal genes of the father, and, on the other hand, the lethal genes of the father, since they do not coincide with those of the mother will likewise not be apparent in the phenotype. But as soon as two lethal identical genes coincide in the father and mother their offspring perishes. This coincidence begins most frequently with homozygosity, with inbreeding, that is, with the crossing of closely related individuals, with the crossing of brothers and sisters in several generations. But the single set is especially unstable when there is no paired determination of features and there is no possibility of compensating for the defects which are bound to arise somewhere or other. Now it is on the single principle, or at best on the homozygosity principle that we plan our system of education over the whole country for each special subject. In this case, so genetics decrees, there will arise pure strains, but their vitality and stability will be very low.

As far as a full research course abroad is concerned, this is restricted not only by the limitations on foreign travel, especially long-term trips, but also by the fact that foreign academic degrees are not recognized by the Soviet system of certification of scientific personnel. The Commission for the Certification of Higher Degrees requires a new defence or a new certification, while not a single foreign academic degree can be converted into the Soviet degree of Doctor of Science.

4

Scientists' trips abroad

CHARLES DARWIN began his scientific career as a naturalist when he made his round-the-world voyage in the *Beagle*, and he was travelling for scientific purposes for five years. During this voyage he accumulated the fund of knowledge which led him to the law of natural selection, which explains the origin in nature of adaptation and variation of species. And if Darwin had not completed such a voyage, if in England it had been necessary to obtain for it such a complicated system of permissions which stand before a Soviet naturalist in an insurmountable wall, he would not have become the founder of modern biology.

D. N. Pryanishnikov could not have given such great benefits to Russian agriculture if in his time, still before the Revolution, he had not travelled the length and breadth of Europe carrying out investigations in various laboratories, observing and studying agriculture. He recognizes this himself in his book *My Memoirs* (posthumously published, Sel'khozgiz, 1957), which gives a practical description of the author's foreign travels and their role in his formation as a scientist.

And how would it have been possible for N. I. Vavilov to solve his vast problem of strain rejuvenation of agricultural crops if he had been forbidden to travel abroad? In that case we would not have had our world-wide collection of cultivated plants, and Soviet selection could not have been carried out effectively and on an industrial basis in all the climatic zones of the USSR. In 1934 Vavilov was actually forbidden to travel abroad, and this undoubtedly did our science a great deal of harm.

And who can estimate how much science was benefited by I. I. Mechinkov, who had the opportunity of long-term work at the Pasteur Institute in Paris?

Examples of this kind can be quoted in great numbers.

In Japan, in the USA and in many other countries, a scientist is obliged to make an extensive trip abroad at least once every few years. This is considered to be a means of increasing his qualifications and horizon. Most professors in the USA enjoy a sabbatical year every five or six years, especially for travelling and work outside their own university, on full salary and with travelling expenses paid.

In 1962 at the meeting of the Moscow Society of Naturalists, I got to know Dr Chester Bliss, a biometrician from Connecticut, USA, who was to deliver two lectures on biometry to the Moscow biologists. Bliss is considered to be a very great authority in this field. In 1936–7 when he was still a young scientist he was invited to the USSR for two years to start up biometric investigations and experimental work in the Lenin All-Union Academy of Agricultural Sciences; he worked in Leningrad and knew Vavilov well.

In 1962 Dr Bliss was in the USSR *en route* from India to Switzerland and England while on his trip round the world during his sabbatical year. He spent ten days in the USSR, after visiting New Zealand, Australia, the Philippines, Japan, Taiwan, Hong Kong, Thailand, Turkey, Egypt, the Lebanon and India. And he still was intending to visit ten countries in Europe. And in the course of his trip he was giving lectures on biometry, having consultations on the methods of experimental work and agitating for the formation of national biometric scientific societies.

I went with Bliss to several Moscow agricultural institutes so that he could learn about the method of the design of agricultural experiments in the USSR and the development of biometrical research. We also visited the department of experimental methodology in the Timiryazev Academy. Dr Bliss was astounded by the design of experimental work on strain testing methods in the USSR, from the point of view of methodology and statistical processing of results. Even in Turkey and India, he said, he had not encountered such out-of-date archaic methods. They had remained with us from pre-Revolutionary times. Scientific biometry had not been seriously developed in the USSR at all. Evidently it was in the hands of the Lysenkoists, who were then the rulers of agricultural science, and who after 1948 had succeeded in having the teaching of higher mathematics abolished in agricultural institutes, a course of study which was previously obligatory in all Institutes of Higher Education.

But if it had not been Professor Bliss but our own experimental scientists who had been able to travel freely about the world and get to know the achievements of other countries, then certainly so stagnant a situation would not have lasted in our country right up until 1962.

The insufficient contact of Soviet science with the rest of the world affects not only the general level of education, the knowledge of languages and general culture. It is also reflected in the converse effect of the socialist world on the economics and politics of other countries, especially the developing countries. The Americans have taken this fact thoroughly into account; with their 'Peace Corps' programme they try to win these countries to American culture and science. We, however, by ignoring the individual influence of our citizens, rely much more, but in a vain hope, on press and radio.

When I was working at the Timiryazev Agricultural Academy up to 1962, I often had occasion to note that the USSR cannot carry out many of its obligations to IAEA and UNESCO under the programme of providing other countries with experts on agriculture and the peaceful uses of atomic energy for international courses of study, etc. A considerable proportion of the requests to send experts and advisers to Pakistan, Brazil, Iraq and the African countries are not fulfilled, since it is not possible to find the combination of all the necessary qualities, political reliability in the stupid sense in which it is understood in our country, moral stability, a good knowledge of the subject, an easy command of the language (especially French, Spanish, etc.) and a willingness to volunteer. And the task of these experts includes consultations on the creation of experimental research stations, land development installations, purchase of equipment, surveying of territory, and so on.

And, in the final result, the failure to carry out these programmes is in some degree reflected in our economy too, since the amount of Soviet equipment purchased by other countries is decreased.

5
The problem of the 'brain drain'

OUR newspapers love to write about the problem of the 'brain drain', especially from Europe to the USA, as if hinting that this is an essential defect of the free interstate movement of scientists and free exit from the country.

It must be pointed out that the problem of the 'brain drain' really does exist and really is connected in part with free travel. But covering the state frontier in many layers of barbed wire is none too economic a means of reducing the possibility of such a 'drain'. Every country undoubtedly loses by the emigration abroad of qualified specialists and scientists. But in any system it is always necessary to take into account the overall balance of profit and loss. And if the profit from free co-operation is greater than the damage which arises due to certain losses of trained specialists changing their citizenship, then cases of emigration should not cause any great disquiet. First of all it is necessary to look into the causes of this emigration and reduce their effect.

I know of only one fairly clear example where free movement not only was not balanced by the gains from co-operation but really was an impoverishment to the country. This was in the German Democratic Republic before the building of the famous Berlin wall. The conflict between the state's interests and those of democracy was solved here to the advantage of the state's interests, and the road was closed by which this illegal 'drain' of specialists and ordinary members of the population had taken place. But it was not closed until more than two million people, among whom there were very many specialists and scientists—the finest forces of science—had crossed over from the German Democratic Republic to the Federal German Republic through West Berlin. A reverse migration did also take place, but on a considerably smaller scale. But this was a special case, this was migration within the limits of one nation artificially divided into three parts (the Federal German Republic, the German Democratic Republic and West Berlin). The one-way character of the migration in this case is natural, since the

Federal German Republic is four times as large, and in 1945–6 more than twelve million Germans from East Germany and East Prussia were displaced from the lands which became part of the USSR and Poland, mainly going to the Federal German Republic. Millions of families, millions of friends and colleagues and dozens of organizations were divided between the FGR and the GDR. And since the FGR is four times larger, it now exerts a greater force of attraction by all these ties of family, friendship and the rest; the economic level of the FGR is higher, the pay of scientists is higher. Moreover, from the FGR scientists can travel freely to other countries, while from the GDR they can only go east. Hence it is impossible for there to be a balance in such a case. Several nations, formerly one but now divided geographically, economically and socially, born of dangerous experiments by the great powers, have now become sources of unrest for the entire world. Such are China, from which Taiwan has been separated, Korea, Vietnam and Germany.

In the rest of the world there are two main flows of the 'brain drain'; from Europe to the USA, and from the developing countries of Africa and Asia to Europe. Every year hundreds and thousands of specialists and scientists from all the countries of Europe move to the USA, attracted by better working conditions and higher pay. According to UN data, published for instance in the *Morning Star* (6 March 1967) in the course of the two years 1963 and 1964 5,000 specialists went to the USA from Great Britain, and 15,523 in all from Europe. Over the fifteen years from 1949 to 1964, 85,000 engineers, scientists and doctors went to the USA from Europe. Of the forty-three Nobel Prize winners now working in the USA, sixteen are Europeans who were awarded their prizes while working in European countries. The minimum loss, according to the UN calculations is that of France; it seems that French patriotism is greatest. A large number of specialists go to the USA from Canada and South America. The reverse migration of scientists from the USA to Europe is considerably less marked; generally due to former Europeans returning home because they have been unable to adapt to conditions in America. However, every year many thousands of American scientists go to Europe for temporary work, under arrangements for joint research groups. To some degree this evidently compensates for the loss to European science, but, of course, not completely. It should be noted that in the last three years emigration from England and from Europe in general to the USA has been sharply curtailed. This is principally connected with US aggression in Vietnam, with a war which is very unpopular in Europe and with the militarization of the USA. Moreover, a number of measures have been taken for the improvement of the working conditions of European scientists. According to the data given in the article 'World Economics and International Relations' (No. 9, pp. 111–16, 1967) the question of the curtailment of emigration from England was entrusted to a special parliamentary commission. This commission came to the conclusion that a considerable role in the migration of scientists from England to the USA is played by the higher salaries of American scientists for the same qualifications. In England, the salaries of scientists vary from £800 to £3,000 a year ($2,000 to $7,500 at the rate of exchange before devaluation). In the USA they vary from $5,250 to $18,000 a year, i.e. they are almost double. In order to diminish this factor, the pay of all scientists in England was raised by 30 per cent.

Recently a new law on immigration came into force in the USA which should reduce immigration from Europe, and consequently the European 'brain drain', considerably. But the American press predicts that the new immigration rule will entail a loss to Asia and Africa in this respect.

As we know from history, the USA is a country almost entirely created by European emigration. The principal role in the creation of the American nation was played by emigration from England, then from Germany and later from Ireland, Italy, Russia, France and so on. Emigration from Asia and Africa had no great significance—I have in mind free emigration, and not the slave-trade which used to flourish in the USA.

The previous immigration law which was adopted in 1920 and which remained in force until 1965, limiting immigration from the Eastern Hemisphere to 150,000 persons per year, had quotas for nations which were relatively proportional to the number of persons of a given national origin in the population of the USA. Thus, for example, the British, who had a maximum proportion in the American population, had practically unrestricted opportunities of settling in the USA and becoming citizens. After them came the Germans, the Irish, and so on. Indians, however, or Pakistanis, of whom there were only a few in the USA, had under the old law a very restricted limit for entry into the USA (for permanent residence, of course, not as tourists). The limits for immigration from certain countries of Africa and Asia did not exceed a hundred persons per year. At the same time, 65,000 could enter from Britain, 25,000 from Germany and 18,000 from Ireland. 70 per cent of the immigration quotas were allotted to these three countries (see *Science*, vol. 159, No. 3812, 1968).

The new law revised the national quotas and increased the total limit of immigration from the Eastern Hemisphere to 170,000 persons a year (and 120,000 from other countries in the Americas). But under the new law there are categories of preference for relatives. The total number of immigrant specialists from all countries coming outside the preference categories and under conditions of free employment has a limit of 10 per cent, i.e. 17,000 a year. From each individual country no more than 20,000 persons can come each year under all four categories of immigration. The new immigration rule has sharply reduced the possibility of a drain of specialists from Europe, but it increases the drain from the developing countries, which is a cause of great anxiety to the governments of those countries. Previously a very large number of specialists from these countries settled in Europe, especially those who had received their higher education there. The specialists who migrated from Europe to the USA were mainly ones who had received their education in their native countries. Many capable young people from Asia and Africa go to Europe and America to obtain an education which they cannot obtain in their own countries. After many years of study in universities, colleges and as post-graduate students, many of them, almost 70 or even 80 per cent, do not return to their own countries; they marry and settle in the countries which gave them their education, and find work there. This flow is partly compensated by specialists and teachers from Europe and the USA going to the developing countries under various programmes. According to UN data about 70 per cent of the professorial and teaching staff of the universities of Central Africa is made up of foreigners.

Although only a minority of the young people who go to Europe from the developing countries come back when they have got an education, these countries cannot, of course, restrict their citizens from going abroad to study. In this case they would lose still more. But gradually these countries are developing their own centres for higher education and scientific work, and this is reducing the acuteness of the problem.

It must be stressed that the international scientific differentiation on a world-wide scale which is now taking place at a breakneck speed naturally creates a mutual movement of scientists. Because of the increasing costs of many projects, the 'small countries', both in Europe and in other parts of the world, do not have the resources to maintain very many projects, so they specialize. Hence those scientists whose type of work is 'phased out' in these countries sometimes prefer to go to another country rather than to qualify again in some other branch. Belgium, Switzerland and apparently other small countries of Europe have stopped research on modern supersonic aircraft construction. This research became too much for their budgets. Hence specialists in this branch of technology had to migrate to the USA, the FGR, France or Britain which were continuing and developing this kind of research. Serious programmes of space research are now being carried out only in the USA and the USSR, and it is natural that enthusiasts for this subject will try to attach themselves to these projects. The majority of them, of course, go to the USA where there are fewer security restrictions on such investigations. In the era when space research was based on the use of small rockets, small telescopes and less expensive technology, scientists and technicians in this field were more dispersed throughout the world.

Many countries do not in any way consider their citizens who have gone abroad to have 'betrayed their country', and often are proud of the achievements of their compatriots abroad. This is conducive to the maintenance of contacts which are in general useful for the homeland. India keeps a special state list of Indians living and working abroad and often turns to them for help in various scientific and technological projects. It would clearly be interesting to study the problem of Russian scientists abroad. An especially large number of outstanding Russian scientists left their country in 1918–29; in 1918–22 many scientists were often simply expelled or persecuted as 'bourgeois specialists'. The second generation of this emigration is also rich in talent, and one may very often encounter Russian surnames in publications of foreign works. A considerable proportion of these scientists did not cease to think of themselves as Russians and did not lose interest in their native land. And I am sure that under corresponding conditions of free co-operation we should yet witness a certain migration back to Russia, especially from Western Europe.

The cases given above of the migration of scientists, excluding the special cases of divided Germany and emigration from Russia during the civil war, are all migration within a single capitalist social system. Within the socialist system settling in another country is very rare, almost negligible, and occurs only when two young people from different countries who have met on a joint study course set up house together.

A special case is that of the migration of scientists between the two world systems, the socialist and the capitalist. This takes place at an extremely minimal level. And this is not only because scientific exchange itself between these systems is negligible; not only because measures are taken to hinder people from not returning by stopping them travelling with their families, including employees of the security organs in delegations and keeping up an expensive multi-layered and continuous system of frontier defence around an enormous territory. I do not doubt that if they abolished all these measures, which are economically very burdensome, and introduced unrestricted travel, the overall number of cases of non-return would be extremely low, although they would increase in proportion to the increase in the total number of journeys. We should not lose our valuable scientists, but the total exchange of useful scientific information which Soviet scientists possess would increase considerably.

The Soviet Union is a great country with greater potentialities than the USA, let alone the countries of Europe. The scale of problems, so important for science, is at a maximum in our country. We have developed our own ideology, which has greatly increased the patriotic tendencies of the people and their national pride. These are all important moral factors which guarantee stability. So large and rich a country in conditions of greater democratization would inevitably become not a source of a 'brain drain' but a centre of attraction. The development of modern science and the formation of a single world scientific system create problems mainly for the scientists of small nations and states. The large states gain from it, and this is an inevitable process. It is especially sharply reflected in the question of the language of science. Once in the remote past there was one language of science— Latin. Then came the national disintegration of the scientific language. Now once again the small languages are dying as languages of science. They are ceasing to be even the means of expression of national scientific achievements. Greeks, Swedes, Romanians, Norwegians and Danes hardly ever publish their scientific papers in their national languages. They turn mainly to English, sometimes to French or German. The majority of scientific journals in these countries are published in English or in German. The same process is taking place in the USSR. Here Russian is displacing all the dozens of other national languages in the scientific literature. The scientific journals in Africa and Asia appear in English or in French. Thus an internationalization of the scientists of small countries is taking place. According to UNESCO data the world scientific output at the present time is divided by languages as follows: 60 per cent of world scientific information appears in English, 11 per cent in Russian, 8 per cent in German, 9 per cent in French, 3 per cent in Japanese, 2 per cent in Spanish, 2 per cent in Italian. All the other languages of the world account for only about 5 per cent of scientific information. Naturally the scientists of other countries no longer study these languages.

As we have seen, the Russian language ranks second in the world as a source of scientific information, and the strengthening of the connections between Soviet science and the rest of the world will only help to increase the amount of national scientific information published in Russian.

6

The development of international scientific and cultural co-operation leads to the formation of an intellectual community

THE world in which we live is very unstable. It is in a state of constant preparedness for global war. It maintains some reserve of stability, not on account of rational discussion of problems but as a result of a balance of nuclear rocket forces of annihilation. Strike forces are compensated in the group of world powers by retaliation forces, and under the cover of this unstable guarantee the economic development of the human community takes place, science flourishes, education is improved, culture blossoms and the question of improving man's biological nature itself is arising.

It would seem that in a rationally organized multinational human community, every nation and every country must obtain from the existence of other countries and other nations an enormous direct and indirect advantage, and this will be the greater the higher the technical, scientific, cultural and economic levels of the other countries. After all, each country in isolation cannot maintain the rate of technical and scientific progress which is typical for humanity as a whole. Even great states, like the USSR and the USA, cannot do so. Each country must obtain a large part of what it needs for material, technical and cultural progress, in the form of inventions, patents, ideas and the results of scientific research from abroad. Great discoveries and outstanding inventions are the property and product of almost every large nation.

I have never been in the USA and cannot judge how strongly the development of that country has depended on the Old World in the last few decades. But judging from what I know from history, it is clear that the USA is in essence a product of Europe; it is in the intellectual sense a very viable hybrid of British, Italian, Irish, German, Russian and European emigration in general.

As for the Soviet Union, however, it is clear to all that in spite of foreign intervention during the Civil War and the German aggression of 1941–5, which brought incalculable harm to us in the economic,

human, agricultural, technical and scientific fields, in the course of all
the fifty years of our development we have obtained and borrowed a
very great deal from the remaining,capitalist world, though chiefly in
the fields of culture, music, the cinema and literature, not to mention
the spheres of fashion, living conditions, and so on. If during these years
the USSR had developed in complete isolation, then its scientific, technical and cultural progress would have undoubtedly been slower,
although our native science made an enormous jump forward in that
period.

All the same, if we analyse the problem seriously, it is clear that the
means by which we used and implemented the achievements of other
nations and countries were not perfect, and this slowed down the rate of
our development, lowered the level of our economy and especially the
level of quality of our goods, the technical standards of our production
and technology. We know well that the greatly increased rate of our
industrialization was due to a technical reconstruction of the conditions
existing in old Russia, which thrust the USSR up to the general
European level. A considerable part of industrialization in many
branches took place not because we invented new methods and models,
but because we imported foreign technology and industrial equipment,
which were at that time in advance of ours. There were, of course, some
original solutions of our own, especially in military technology, but in
industry as a whole they could not constitute the majority. This was
simply impossible. As far as *rates* were concerned, they were maintained
first and foremost by the growth of the working class at the expense of
the peasantry, and the increase in the 'additional cost of labour', i.e. at
the expense of the standard of living of workers and employees. Being
the only socialist country in the world, we did not enter into the various
bourgeois conventions on patents, licences, etc., and could have complete freedom to borrow and use foreign inventions without paying any
compensation to the countries who owned the patents. During that
period we mainly put raw materials on to the world market, and hence
the fact that we were not a party to agreements on licences did not
trouble us. Our industrial goods hardly went abroad at all. Obviously in
the prewar years this method of industrialization was extremely rapid
and cheap for the USSR.

But in the post-war era, when the industry of the capitalist countries
was going through a period of reconstruction and technical revolution,
and when a bloc of socialist countries with a common economic policy
was being formed, the continuation of the old methods of borrowing

instead of co-operation ceased to guarantee the rise in the economy to the necessary level. By 1955 our country, in relation to the qualitative indices of industrial production, of automobiles, locomotives, instruments, agricultural technology, products of light industry, automation and many other things, was far behind the USA and the countries of Western Europe. We were also behind in the productivity of labour. Many important goods, such as computers, we then did not produce at all.

During the time when the USSR was pursuing a policy of rigid isolation from the capitalist countries (up to 1955) this gap was not very noticeable, or rather it was hushed up in every possible way. Many of us will remember the campaign against grovelling before the West, which quenched any discussion of the technical and scientific achievements of the Western World—and not only quenched them but nipped them in the bud. And at this time, when all our propaganda tried to show that all basic inventions and discoveries had been made in Russia or in the Soviet Union, in the industries of the main capitalist countries a fantastic amount of reconstruction and introduction of original inventions and constructions was taking place. The catalogued names of goods and technical means increased tenfold in a short time. Under the stimulus of cybernetics, forbidden in the USSR, programmed automation of industry was being introduced in the West. The complexity of instruments also increased very sharply.

What was going on in our country during this period is excellently described in V. D. Dudintsev's novel, *Not by Bread Alone*, the action of which is set in these very years. In our country, people were afraid even to quote foreign literature in scientific papers. Western melodies were excluded from music programmes on the radio, the width of trousers increased and home-bred pseudo-scientists such as T. D. Lysenko, I. I. Prezent, G. M. Bosh'yan, O. B. Lepeshinskaya and others, who announced the creation of special anti-Western sciences, were encouraged.

But when, as 1955 approached, the atmosphere cleared somewhat, when the first steps began to be taken in the establishment of scientific contacts, correspondence with other countries was permitted, and the first delegations of scientists and employees of the ministries and government departments made journeys abroad, when those running the state, like Peter I in the past, began to go abroad and see what it was like, our scientific and technological lag became clear. The slogan of using the scientific and technical experience of other countries was proclaimed.

But the ways of using this experience, except for some excursions abroad, remained in essence the same as before. These were the ways of borrowing, of manufacture according to existing models, and not the inclusion of the USSR and the countries of the socialist bloc in a normal system of free scientific and technical co-operation, unimaginable without the free movement of citizens of the USSR about the world and the participation in international conventions on patents, licences and inventions.

But, as it turned out, the practice of copying in the new conditions did not guarantee progress but only a permanent lag. The rates of technical progress in the world increased so rapidly, methods of construction and instruments changed so fast, that the process of copying turned into the copying of the obsolescent and the obsolete. Furthermore the time taken for introducing what had been copied into production increased, since the catalogues of instruments were large and their complexity increased sharply. I will give only a single example from a field close to me, but it is typical of many cases.

The development of many fields of chemistry and biochemistry and also a number of scientific and technological defence applications were held back after the war because of the absence in the USSR of especially high-speed analytical centrifuges in which substances are separated according to their molecular weights. Simple centrifuges precipitate large particles of a substance—for biochemists and biologists, whole cells. Analytical centrifuges can precipitate molecules from solution. The gravitational acceleration in such centrifuges reaches 400,000 g and more, and the instrument is exceptionally accurate. Analytical centrifuges were developed back in the 1930s in Sweden, but by 1946–7 the best improved models were made only in the USA, the famous 'Spinco'. America understood the importance of the centrifuge in technical development, and therefore Harry Truman placed an embargo on the sale to socialist countries of all forms of centrifuge with an acceleration of more than 40,000 g, putting them in the category of strategic supplies. (All the same, it was, of course, possible to get them through neutral countries, since they were not military devices and were sold freely on the world market.)

In about 1947 the instrument industry in the USSR was given the task of starting production of the analytical centrifuge. But this is not a simple piece of apparatus, it contains thousands of parts and components of the finest precision, since it operates at colossal speeds. Moreover, during the time of revolution of the rotor the cuvette with the substance must be photographed for the absorption and refraction of light, which permits the rate of precipitation of the substance to be recorded optically. The working parts of the centrifuge rotate in conditions of high vacuum. In 1947 such centrifuges were large-scale instruments with numerous independent sub-units. They were used not only for separation, but also for the determination of the molecular weights of substances, principally of polymers.

To invent from the beginning the whole of such a machine was too long a task, and hence special contruction bureaux were founded and began to work on making a copy. As a basis for copying they chose not the American instrument but a German variant, which was simpler, but technically less perfect. Copies were made of both the preparative and analytic versions (the UCP and the UCA). This all took many years, since the copying of a complex instrument is no easy business; it was necessary to reproduce the quality of the metal, to ensure the same precision of manufacture, and to set up production, that is, build a factory. And here too they needed special machines for manufacture, and to acquire the means of production without licences was much harder than acquiring the end-product, the instrument.

It took twelve years before actual production of such centrifuges could be started in the factory which had been built in Frunze, and by 1960 the UCP-1 and UCA-1 models could be offered on the internal market for laboratory technology. However, there were not many who were keen to buy this model since after twelve years it was hopelessly out of date. During this time the American and German firms, which had amalgamated, had replaced several models to satisfy the demands of science which had arisen in the meantime. Not only was the UCA-1 obsolescent technically, it could not solve the new problems confronting science. The class of substances which were accessible to study in visible light had been dealt with, and science had gone on to the study of substances in the ultraviolet part of the spectrum. They had begun to produce centrifuges with ultraviolet quartz optical systems. Speeds had been increased. The Soviet UCA-1 gave an acceleration of 280,000 g; the new 'Spinco-Beckman' models gave 600,000 g and more. The scale of these models and the number of sub-units had been reduced. The UCA-1 was a compressed air device, it required special foundations and could only be set up in the basements of buildings. By 1960 the American model had long been an electric device, required no foundations and could be set up on any floor of the building. It was very reliable and hence did not need a special engineer to operate it.

There were many other advantages of a technical and scientific character. Moreover, the embargo on the sale of analytical centrifuges had by now been raised. Accordingly everyone wanted to have a 'Spinco', and no one bought the UCA-1. The 'Spincos' already installed in a number of institutes were working full out, and biochemists came long distances to work on them.

But a plan is a plan. The factory in Frunze had produced the UCA-1 in large numbers. The construction bureau rushed through new more up-to-date models, and the old UCA-1s piled up in the factory depot. They did not know what to do with them. When the factory went over to the production of a new model, say the UCA-4 or 5, they decided to give away the old ones from the depot to establishments free of charge, just to get rid of them. It so happened in 1964 that by an oversight of the service engineer, who was tempted by the free gift of an instrument, our Institute acquired such a UCA-1 and then a UCP-1 as well. Until then, for four whole years, they had been lying in the depot, spoiling. To set them up we needed engineers, four basement rooms, foundations and all the rest of it. Yet there would still be no one to work on them. The Institute has an analytical centrifuge of Hungarian manufacture and two preparative 'Spincos'. And to think of how much work the Kirgiz workmen and engineers had wasted on the production of useless centrifuges of this type. Such is the price of copying.

But this was still not the worst case. Who is there that does not remember how the production of maize was copied from America. In America it is grown only in the moist and warm 'maize belt', but in our country they tried to extend it almost up to the tundra.

Moreover, the method of copying very rapidly comes into conflict with the needs of foreign trade. Instruments and techniques copied without licence cannot be sold on the external market for foreign currency.

All the same, the doctrine of 'use foreign experience and achievements' did, of course, give definite positive results. It did not guarantee advance, but it did stimulate a certain progress. The development of our economy after 1955, when excursion trips abroad began, became more rapid and its results more tangible.

It was not until 1966 that our country put an end to the practice of copying and entered into the international convention on patents, licences and inventions. We went over to buying the rights to the production of certain articles of world standard and to the use of inventions, and to the similar sale of our own patents. However, according to what I have been told by those employed in the State Plan and Licences

Committee systems, we had a debit balance in 1966 and 1967. Very few Soviet patents were sold. With time, one must suppose, the situation must change.

However, having embarked on this sensible course of international mutually advantageous and sincere agreements—the only right one in present-day conditions—we must now reorganize and normalize the system of international scientific and technical co-operation and intellectual co-operation generally. This is the only way we can raise the mass of our specialists to the present-day level. While reforming the law about scientific and technical relations between states we must also introduce firm legal safeguards enabling Soviet scientists to have personal relations with citizens of other countries. We must introduce legal standards where administrative tyranny still holds sway. We should thus take a very important step in the development of socialist society in its transformation from a semi-closed to an open system.

In a final result, as I have already noted, the existence of other nations and countries of any political, economic and cultural nature benefits any other country. It is only fanatical extremist regimes, whether capitalist or communist in their principles, that can do harm to the world-wide co-operation of nations and states. Under such extremist regimes there is aggression, the desire for world domination and the subjugation of other countries in conflict and not in fruitful co-operation. We all know examples of such sharp conflicts and antagonisms both between capitalist countries and between socialist ones. At the same time there can be both sharp enmity and sincerest friendship between socialist and capitalist countries. Recent history provides us with an abundance of examples. The conflict between Hitler's Germany and France and Britain, the conflict between Stalin and Tito and the war between the USSR and Finland were all replaced by good friendship without changing the social principles of any of these countries. The very sharp conflict between China and the USSR followed upon a period of the most faithful and unbroken friendship. We know of bitter strife within the limits of countries with a single nation. The conflict of the two Germanies, the two Koreas, the two Vietnams. The Arab countries are constantly quarrelling and making peace among themselves. Sharper racial conflicts are often superimposed upon social conflicts. The short war between Israel and the neighbouring Arab countries was not an unexpected event. But the world was shaken when a fierce, but happily brief, war flared up between two peace-loving nations, India and Pakistan. China and the USSR are always hurling accusations of treachery at each other, but they are both aiding the struggle in Vietnam. In Vietnam, Soviet and Chinese arms are being used to fight against the Americans, but in Geneva, the USSR and the USA in conditions of complete mutual understanding are reaching agreement on the proposed pact on the non-proliferation of nuclear weapons in which they give simultaneous guarantees to the non-nuclear powers against nuclear aggression, clearly hinting that China is not a party to the pact. In Vietnam, the USSR and China are helping a friendly power together. But in India the USSR is helping the Indian people in their struggle against Chinese aggression by sending modern arms to India. Cuba is receiving enormous economic aid from the USSR and is always railing against the Soviet Union. Nasser has imprisoned all the communists in Syria and the United Arab Republic and has banned the Communist Party. King Hussein did the same some time ago, but the USSR is arming these countries against Israel, in which 90 per cent of the economy and agriculture is run on co-operative principles, a country where the 'workers' party' and the communist parties (there are two) operate in conditions of complete legality. Everything in the world is confused. The government in too many countries is carried out incompetently, sometimes as in Rhodesia and the United Arab Republic in violation of the law. What is, and always has been, dangerous for the world is not so much the differences in economic systems but the character of the concentration of power in a country; either it is totalitarian and dictatorial, concentrating power in the hands of one or a few, or else it has wise and democratic forms. Only in the latter case can the government of a country be carried out scientifically, and its relationships with the rest of the world and neighbouring countries be on a mutually advantageous basis. A totalitarian regime, as we know now to our great sorrow, is possible and is very dangerous even in countries with a socialist economy. Not only the rigid dictatorship of Stalin with its personality cult is fresh in everyone's memories; in the countries of Eastern Europe there were the regimes of Rakosi, Klement Gottwald and Yugov. And at the present time before everyone's eyes Enver Hoxha and Mao Tse-tung have established in their countries, a one-man dictatorship resting on brute force and not on the law.

Then too we see other examples when a recently aggressive country has suffered a severe defeat and then embarked on a course of friendly co-operation with its neighbours, on a course of economic and scientific co-operation, on a course of free intercourse with the rest of the world and has demonstrated a vigorous rise in science and its economy and culture. I have Japan and Italy particularly in mind. The rate of industrial and economic growth in these countries in the last decade attained a world maximum (10 to 11 per cent) higher than the USSR. No aggression, no conquests gave Italy and Japan such results, which they are now getting by sensibly organized peaceful co-operation with other countries. And if only these countries had not fallen into the sphere of American influence, which promotes militarization, then their economic prosperity would undoubtedly be even higher. It is no coincidence, for example, that the highest standard of living in Europe and in the world has been achieved in a neutral country, Sweden.

In the USA, according to information published in *Science* at the end of 1967 (vol. 158, No. 3806) the special fund and state allocations for science in 1968 not only were not being increased, as they had been every year in the past, but were being cut down in almost all forms of scientific research. According to the evidence of this journal, which published the allocation figures for all subdivisions of science, this was connected with the expenditure on the Vietnam war. This war had already consumed so much of the wealth of the USA that if it had been saved it could have made the whole of Vietnam the richest country in the world and thus have wiped out all cause for enmity between North and South. For the primary cause of social conflict is inequality in the distribution of the national product.

Examples of such paradoxes, which do not correspond to dogmas and are simply absurd and irrational situations, can be numbered in tens, and even hundreds, throughout the world. They arise within any kind of social system, any economic structures or any ideological principles. They arise when the state displays the common human vices, ambition, egoism, avarice, cruelty, self-love, vanity, the cult of power, intolerance, incompetence, megalomania, emotionalism, mistrust, pride, and so on. When these qualities or these vices become inherent in social, national and political groups, situations arise which are dangerous for nations, and, under modern conditions, dangerous for the whole of mankind, especially when at the head of a country there is a psychologically abnormal individual or a criminal. And, alas, history shows us such cases, and not very ancient history either!

There is only one social group of people in the world which, not only on account of its position in society but simply on account of the humane qualities inevitably inherent in it, on account of its selection of people for these qualities and on account of the character of its daily activity, is connected in a world-wide mutually dependent, mutually advantageous, mutually respecting system in friendship independent of national frontiers, constantly sharing among itself all possible help and interested to the utmost in the progress of mankind, of which it is the standard-bearer and motive force. This group consists of the scholars, the scientists, the intelligentsia, in the sense of the scientific, technical and culturally creative intelligentsia, and not simply that class of people who have had a secondary or higher education.

This group has been continuously increasing in numbers in recent years, and today in the economically developed countries its growth is limited primarily by biological factors, by the fact that the percentage of the human population suitable for scientific work, or intellectual activity generally, is limited, and that only limited numbers of people occur with any particular talent.

Scientists, technical specialists and those active in culture, have already created with their innumerable international organizations a special world-wide society, a system which develops according to the principle of mutual interest in the progress of each part. Mutual co-operation even within this system is not yet perfect, of course—it runs into barriers —but all the same, inter-state and international relations among scientists and those who are culturally active are the wisest and most trustworthy. And the wisdom and trustworthiness of these relations increase as the scale of international co-operation increases. I am concerned with average indices, general trends and not individual cases, individual breaches of the rules, for among scientists it is not rare to meet, as we know from the case of Lysenkoism, pseudoscientists possessed by megalomania and striving to impose their influence on the whole world. Likewise in America, I believe that the former Secretary for Defence of the USA, McNamara, was a qualified mathematician. But, if we take the American corporate scientific body as a whole, it constitutes the principal opponent to the war in Vietnam, while the universities and colleges are centres of the movement of the intelligentsia for peace. The student youth throughout the whole world today is most active in the struggle for democracy.

It seems to us that the expansion of mutual relations and mutual co-operation in this section of humanity is leading us towards the creation of a truly intellectual and moral society. In such a society any aspect of public activity is considered on the principle of the maximum benefit for the whole of humanity and the whole world. Such a society will not be created by revolution or military *coup d'état*. It will arise as a result of gradual development of both the socialist and the capitalist system. Following the world-wide scientific and technical differentiation which already actually exists, there must inevitably come a slow industrial and economic world-wide differentiation.

We have already said a great deal about the effect of scientific and technical progress in the capitalist countries on the development of technology and science in our country. The converse scientific and technical effect has been weak. But the social and political effect of socialist society on the capitalist world is undoubted. It has stimulated the modernization of social relationships in the USA, France, Britain and other countries; it has intensified the activity of those who are working to raise the standard of living, and, as a final result, has reduced the level of exploitation and improved the character of the distribution of the national income. And if the rigid regime of Stalin had not greatly weakened this effect, the drawing together of the two systems not only towards coexistence but also towards co-operation would have undoubtedly been greater.

Today the highest level of co-operation and mutual aid between the two basic world systems takes place in science. The growth of the influence of science on all spheres of the life of society and the increase in the army of scientists is undoubtedly strengthening the mutual co-operation of nations and states.

Consequently the activity of the progressive elements of society must be concentrated on the struggle against those forces and regulations which in some countries are directed at limiting the free co-operation of scientists and those active in culture. We must struggle against any trend towards the narrow 'nationalization' of science turning it to the service of narrow and selfish interests of various political groups and to militarization. After all even cinema gangsters like Fantomas depend on scientific progress and the latest gangsterish technological improvements. We must make laws that will guarantee useful international co-operation so that those trends of development can take place on which mankind rests its main hopes.

Is all well in this respect in our country? Does the USSR have a firm legal basis of international co-operation? Do we have constitutional rights to such co-operation? How does the USSR regulate trips abroad by its citizens? By law or by privilege, on rational principles or by arbitrary administrative decisions? What developments in this field of human activity have taken place in the last few years in our country and in the whole world?

We shall try to give answers to all these questions in the next section.

PART III

Civil Rights and Legislation on Travel Abroad and State Frontiers

When we spoke earlier of 'national' frontiers, we had in mind that international scientific and technical co-operation affects not only relations between states but also international relations within federative states like the USSR, Yugoslavia, Czechoslovakia and India, where it promotes the trend towards integration between the nations in the state. In the present section we shall be concerned chiefly with links between states arising from citizens travelling from one country to another.

The international co-operation of scientists is only a special case of an international link between citizens of different countries. This co-operation is therefore naturally covered by the same general legislation which regulates the rights of all citizens of a given country in this respect. If the rights of citizens are repressed, then the opportunities of scientists are also diminished. In different countries the political structure and effective legislation react variously on the international integration of science and on the urge of scientists to extend the individual rights of man. In the words of the President of the International Association of Scientific Workers, affiliated to the World Peace Council, C. F. Powell (World of Science, no. 1, 1967, p. 3).

In many countries of the world, old and new, the military regimes existing there are hostile to the formation within the country of an effective scientific community and the development of independent thinking connected with it. In these countries scientists do not have the right of going to international conferences.

Therefore the question of modern trends in the development of international scientific co-operation cannot of course be considered without touching upon and discussing the more general and more important question of international links between citizens in general, of the rights of people to international travel, of the rights of man as man, and the duties of man as man, that is, the actions of man which arise from his feeling of responsibility to all mankind and to the destiny of the whole world, and not only to his own nation and his own country.

There is a considerable and serious theory concerning the rights of man.

On the basis of this theory, laws are conceived and formulated. If all citizens are equal under the law, then we have a system of equality. If different categories of people are divided by the law into special groups with different rights, then we have a system of privileges. Systems of privileges exist in almost all countries, even the most democratic. For example, in the USA, a person who has not lived in the USA for ten years or more (and who was born outside the USA) does not possess American citizenship and does not enjoy the protection of all the articles of the law. A person of American citizenship who has lived almost all his life in the USA but who was born abroad cannot stand as a candidate as President of the United States. In every country persons who are minors enjoy fewer rights, cannot take part in elections, and so on. For the privilege of voting belongs only to those of a certain age. There is a broad system of different limitations of rights and privileges in our country, too. For example, a collective-farm worker without an internal passport has considerably fewer rights even of movement and settlement within his own country and of employment than a 'passport-bearing' citizen. Persons whose passport has a 'Moscow permit' have the privileges of employment and residence in Moscow compared with all other citizens of the USSR. After the rehabilitation of the Germans of the Volga they were allowed to settle in any part of the USSR (in rural localities) except the territory of the former Volga German Republic, etc. The number of groups of citizens with limited rights in the USSR up to 1953 was very large. Gradually, as our country developed, the position in this respect was normalized and the limits of equality were extended. The individual rights of citizens were generally increased. This is true, too, of the right of foreign travel and international co-operation. Up to 1955 such rights were completely lacking to citizens of the USSR, and all trips abroad were of an official character. No one at that time, in effect, had even realized that such a right was worth fighting for.

But the right of foreign travel, the external appearance of which now exists and is confirmed by hundreds of thousands of purely tourist journeys abroad by citizens of the USSR every year, has, in fact, not yet become a legally established right, equal for all Soviet citizens. The possibility of travelling abroad was first seen in 1955 in the form of privilege rights for certain classes of the population and then proceeded to develop as a new special privilege, to some extent of the nature of an incentive.

During the era of the personality cult, trips abroad by citizens of the USSR were of an exclusively official nature and were predominantly journeys by diplomats, trade representatives, foreign correspondents, not to mention employees of the MGB. They were thus connected with carrying *out general state functions and were not in any way privileges. In the main, Soviet citizens were afraid of foreign travel, for an affirmative answer to the question of having been abroad on any questionnaire was considered as a serious reason for mistrust.*

Nowadays this attitude to this point in a questionnaire is rare. Many of the former privileges of certain classes of citizens have also vanished. But there is still no general legal basis for foreign travel for Soviet citizens. Trips abroad have become not a legal right but merely the result of the state institutions. The range of official questions dealt with by means of official trips abroad has widened. Foreign tourism has become a form of incentive in one's work. Making a tourist trip abroad has become not the personal private business of the individual as it is in other countries, but one of the functions of the establishment, its trade union and Party organizations. And making such a trip and availing oneself of the privilege of foreign travel has become hedged round with highly complicated procedures and depends on a multiplicity of factors. All sorts of things are taken into account: the candidate's work for the community, his Party status, membership of a trade union, relationship with his wife, 'moral make-up', political maturity, the 'fifth' point of the questionnaire,[1] past biography, origins, number of children, existence of relatives abroad, age and sex, state of health, whether he has been abroad before, his academic rank and level of education, attitude to alcohol, attitude to women and seductresses, the job he holds, his knowledge of foreign languages, and sometimes even his outward appearance.

Undivorced persons have an advantage over divorcees, married persons over single, persons with children over persons without children, those with many children over those with few children, those wishing to travel alone over those wishing to travel with husband or wife, and even more so with their family. Legally it is much more difficult for a collective farm worker to go abroad (never mind if he can afford it) than for a worker, while it is more difficult for a worker than for an intellectual. It is easier for a Russian to go than for a Kazakh or a Jew, easier for a Jew than for a Tatar, while it is easier for a Kazan' Tatar than for a Crimean Tatar. For a German citizen of the USSR it is hardest of all to go to Germany, and for a Jewish citizen of the USSR it is hardest of all to go to Israel. To go to Bulgaria is easier than to go to Poland, to go to Poland easier than to Czechoslovakia (before August 1968) and Czechoslovakia easier than the

---

[1] All Soviet questionnaires begin with the following five questions: Surname, given name, patronymic, date of birth, nationality. The 'fifth point' is thus nationality, the Soviet Union being a multi-national state. As is explained below, the nationality of Soviet citizens can affect their chances of permission to travel abroad—*Translator.*

GDR. To go to a socialist country is ten times easier than to a capitalist one. But even the capitalist ones are not all the same; it is easier to go to France than to Italy, easier to go to Italy than to Britain, easier to Britain than the FGR and easier to go to the FGR than the USA. To go to Yugoslavia is just as difficult as to a capitalist country. And all this is independent of the purely material differences which exist everywhere. It is always easier for someone with a high salary to make a trip abroad than for someone with a low salary, and this difference is more pronounced in the USSR, since a candidate for a trip has to give a written guarantee several months in advance that he will be able to pay a certain sum for his tour, and only after this can the question, for example, of going to a certain congress begin to be raised at high administrative levels which are not directly connected with Intourist (to whom the money has to be paid).

But all the same, these discriminatory conditions are not legal ones, they are all arbitrary, they are established in practice and not by law, they are connected with the procedure of approval and not with the legislation.

But perhaps such a practice has always existed everywhere? Perhaps it is the ordinary and natural state of affairs to be found in any country? Perhaps, according to the science of it, right and law do not come into the picture?

For an answer to these questions we must look at the right of citizens to make journeys abroad in other countries and at other periods of history.

G

I

The Universal Declaration of Human Rights, adopted by the General Assembly of the United Nations, and its bearing on the problem of international co-operation

ON 10 December 1948 the General Assembly of the United Nations Organization adopted the famous Universal Declaration of Human Rights, a significant document of the epoch. The current year, 1968, has been proclaimed Human Rights Year by the United Nations to mark the twentieth anniversary of this Declaration.

However, in the USSR the text of the Universal Declaration of Human Rights is known to very few people, since the Russian language version of this Declaration has *never* been published in the Soviet general press. Its text was published only in a special low-circulation collection of documents on international law, and discussed in specialized journals on law and international law. Only in 1963 were certain Soviet readers able to read the text of the Declaration in the Paris journal *Courier* published by UNESCO, the Russian version of which reaches certain Soviet libraries in limited numbers. The December issue of this journal was devoted in full to the fifteenth anniversary of the Declaration.

The Universal Declaration of Human Rights adopted almost twenty years ago, today possesses a great spiritual force, especially in the struggle against every kind of restriction of the rights and freedoms of man which hinder the development of the human personality in all directions. We shall not analyse all the paragraphs of this document, however, but shall turn our attention only to what is directly relevant to the present question.

Article 13 of the Declaration reads:

(1) Everyone has the right to freedom of movement and residence within the borders of each state.
(2) Everyone has the right to leave any country, including his own, and to return to his country.

The Declaration of Human Rights was adopted at the session of the

General Assembly of the United Nations by a majority that was rare at that time. Only the USSR, the Ukrainian SSR, the Byelorussian SSR and five countries, called in our press 'countries of national democracy', *abstained* from voting on the Declaration.

The Soviet Union was represented at this Session of the United Nations by the Minister of Foreign Affairs, Andrei Vyshinsky, who was formerly the chief inquisitor of the Stalinist tyranny, the Procurator General of the USSR during the era of massive repressions, organizer of rigged trials in 1933 and 1938, perpetrator of the destruction of thousands and thousands of Soviet people, a man who distorted and broke all the elementary rules of law and justice.

Instead of the Universal Declaration of Human Rights, adopted by the General Assembly of the United Nations, the Soviet papers of the time printed a very long speech of Vyshinsky's containing criticisms of the 'draft' Declaration (Central press, 12 December 1948). These criticisms were of a hypocritical and casuistical character. Vyshinsky simply needed an excuse not to vote for the Declaration, and he thought up 'amendments' which were clearly not acceptable to the majority of delegates. To the general declarations and proposals on the rights of man which the draft contained, Vyshinsky demanded the addition of compulsory specifications, stating in what conditions they could be implemented and in what conditions not. The declaration on the general and universal rights of man would thus be transformed in nature into a tendentious 'Instruction', which could be treated by any government in a very arbitrary manner and which would chiefly serve the interests of the governing classes and not the masses of the inhabitants of this planet. For example, to the general proposition of the Declaration on the right of man to freedom of expression regardless of frontiers, Vyshinsky demanded the addition of a compulsory stipulation as to which opinions could be expressed unhindered ('progressive' and 'democratic') and which ones must not be expressed at all ('reactionary', 'racist', 'fascist'). Reasonable objections were raised against Vyshinsky, that the concepts of 'reactionary', 'racist' and so on, were very contradictory and diverse, especially in state propaganda. Every political activist is sure that it is his ideas which are progressive! At the same time, truly progressive ideas are quite often suppressed as being reactionary. And these objections were completely justified. We all remember that just at that time, in 1948 in the USSR, the ideas of classical genetics were declared to be racist and reactionary, the question of classical genetics had become reactionary in our country, the question of cybernetics and even of the theory of relativity had become reactionary in our country. We can also remember that just at that time, in 1948 in the USSR, Marshal Tito was declared to be a fascist, and the state structure in Yugoslavia was declared to be fascist, although by all objective criteria it was socialist. On the other hand, just at that very time in the 'free and democratic' American state McCarthyism was beginning to flourish, and special committees on Un-American activities were beginning to persecute true democrats. Under these conditions it was quite evident that the objections to Vyshinsky from the majority of delegations were entirely well-founded.

Voting on the Declaration first took place paragraph by paragraph and point by point. The delegation of the USSR and also the delegations of the Ukrainian and Byelorussian SSRs at this stage of the voting voted 'yes' to some paragraphs, 'no' to others and abstained from the rest. The newspapers of the period do not give definite information on this matter, and I do not know what was the attitude of the USSR to the paragraph of the Declaration which we have quoted. I assume that it was negative, or else an abstention, since a positive attitude to this paragraph would have been in complete opposition to the policy and practice of the Stalinist government of the country at that time.

But in spite of Vyshinsky's opposition, the Declaration of Human Rights was adopted by the General Assembly of the United Nations, and in accordance with the Constitution of the United Nations, which was recognized by the Soviet Union, it became a document binding upon all members of the United Nations. The Declaration could not be vetoed. If the propositions of the Declaration were not to be observed and were to be ignored in some country or other, it would be necessary first of all to conceal the text of the Declaration from the citizens of that country and to conceal the contents of the document. This method was adopted in the USSR, whose inhabitants were given practically no information about the contents of the Declaration, except some negative statements. It should be noted that foreign broadcasts in the Russian language were at that time totally jammed, and hence even that source of information was closed.[1]

[1] In modern textbooks on international law for Soviet faculties of jurisprudence and international affairs it is no longer possible to get away with ignoring the Universal Declaration of Human Rights completely. However, the text of the Declaration is not given, and there is only a short and arbitrary discussion of it. The proposal on freedom of movement and freedom to leave one's country and to return to it, of course, is not given and is not discussed, any more than the proposals on free choice of place of residence within one's own country, free expression of ideas, freedom of the press, freedom of creativity and others. Nowhere in the textbooks is it stated that the USSR abstained from voting on the Declaration. Sometimes, for example in the textbook *Course of International*

The unfavourable attitude of the Soviet delegation to the Declaration of Human Rights could have been foreseen. Only a year before the session of the General Assembly, when they were only just beginning to work out the draft Declaration, the Presidium of the Supreme Soviet of the USSR adopted a decree on 16 December 1947, 'On the intercourse of state departments and officials with the state departments and officials of foreign countries' (see *Vedomosti Verkhovnogo Soveta SSSR*, no. 5, 1948) which utterly restricted all possibilities of contact between Soviet citizens and citizens of other countries whether personal or by correspondence. By 'officials' the decree understood all persons in the state service, that is employees of state departments or establishments. The decree of the Supreme Soviet prohibited all those working in such departments or establishments to have any contact with foreigners or free correspondence with the citizens of foreign states. According to the decree, contact and correspondence could be carried out only through the Ministry of Foreign Affairs of the USSR and the Ministries of Foreign Affairs of the Union Republics and their sections in the corresponding branch ministries. These sections had to be informed of all applications, questions, letters and requests from foreign citizens 'irrespective of the nature of the matters discussed'. The decree was extended, as was especially noted, to foreigners living in or visiting the USSR for work, but was not extended to cover requests of foreigners dealing with routine matters of everyday life. A long list of names was then given of enterprises which were entitled to deal with foreigners on major matters without having to apply for approval to the Ministries of Foreign Affairs of the USSR or the Union Republics. This list included laundries, hairdressers, baths, telegraph and post offices, shops, newspaper kiosks, cafés, shoemakers and a number of other similar establishments. Similar decrees were soon published by the Presidia of the

---

Law, p. 268 (Mezhdunarodnye Otnosheniya, Moscow, 1966) the authors flout the truth and write the exact opposite: 'Due to the continuing struggle of the Soviet Union which took an active part in the drafting of the Declaration, the fundamental principles of social and economic law were confirmed in it.' In fact the Declaration was adopted and drafted in a satisfactory form not due to, but in spite of, the attitude of the delegation of the USSR.

The Soviet Union has associated itself with the United Nations Human Rights Year programme for 1968. Let us hope that in connection with the Twentieth Anniversary of the Declaration it will be at last published and discussed in the Soviet general press.

Note added in February 1969: This, alas, did not occur. Even twenty years after the voting in the United Nations, the Universal Declaration of Human Rights is still too democratic for the existing legal conditions in the USSR— *Author's note.*

Supreme Soviets of all the Union Republics, and all the subordinate bodies of the Republics were issued with appropriate directives. (For the Russian Soviet Federative Socialist Republic see: *Chronological Collection of Laws, Decrees of the Presidium of the Supreme Soviet of the RSFSR and Council of Ministers of the RSFSR*, Gosyurizdat, 1958.) Officially these decrees have not been repealed, and they provide penal and administrative disciplinary sanctions for any breach of their provisions.

Thus not only the right to leave one's country, but even the elementary right to any form of direct or indirect contact with foreigners became prohibited after this decree was issued. In the USSR a dread grew up, or rather, became intensified, of any contact with foreigners. Any meeting, any conversation with a foreigner, any letter from abroad, if it reached the addressee, had to be reported to the appropriate level of the official apparatus. Some remnants of this fear remain even now; they still have not been blown right away, although the practical enforcement of the aforesaid decrees is impossible. The amount and number of contacts, letters and journeys to and from foreign countries have increased so much that one cannot cope with all of them with only the help of the Ministries of Foreign Affairs. The systems of control, of course, have also increased, but a large number of contacts with foreigners now take place apparently unrecorded, especially during the trips of Soviet citizens abroad.

However there is still no legal foundation for making trips abroad, and the arranging of such a trip, not only for business purposes but even simply for tourist or educational ones is primarily an administrative question to be solved in an arbitrary manner by a long hierarchy of clerks who set their course not by the law but by subjective criteria. All these procedures of approving journeys out of and into the country exist at the present time not to implement and protect civil rights in accordance with some legal standards, but to choose, to select, to sift out, to separate from the multitude of applicants the most 'worthy', the most reliable, to settle the questions of foreign travel not from the point of view of human rights but from the point of view of the interests of the state, interests which are interpreted, of course, from a bureaucratic point of view. Here we come up against the extremely pertinent question of the rights of the individual in a socialist society, his theoretical and actual rights, and we shall best begin our analysis of this question with a consideration of the passport regime, with that document which certifies a person as belonging to the citizen body.

2

The Soviet citizen and his passport, internal and external

In most countries of the world there is no passport system to certify the identity of a citizen and his right to live at a particular place in the country, confirmed by a passport registration in the local department of the militia or police. In other words, in most countries there is no passport in the sense of 'residence permit', and the very concept of passport is interpreted only as a *foreign passport*, a document to protect a citizen travelling outside his own country, with blank pages for entry and exit visas from the officials of other countries. For a citizen of such countries to hold a passport means that he is given the right to leave his country for a certain period of time.

In the USSR, as in old Russia, the passport system has a double function, internal and foreign, each of which is represented by a different passport. The internal passport is a 'residence permit' and a certificate of the identity of a citizen of the USSR, required when he performs certain definite functions, such as cashing a postal order, commencing work, paying a fine, and so on. However, the internal passport does not fulfil this function for all citizens of the USSR, but only for residents of towns and urban settlements. On the last page of every passport there are extracts from the Passport Regulations confirmed by the Council of Ministers of the USSR on 21 October 1953.[1] Article 1 of these regulations reads: 'Citizens of the USSR of 16 years of age and upwards living

[1] It should be noted that the extracts in every passport give only a small part of the *Passport Regulations* confirmed by the Council of Ministers of the USSR in 1953. These *Regulations* have never been published in full and are secret. They are not to be found in a single collection of Resolutions of the Council of Ministers of the USSR, nor in *Vedomosti Verkhovnogo Soveta* (*Gazette of the Supreme Soviet*) nor in *Byulleten Soveta Ministrov SSSR* (*Bulletin of the Council of Ministers of the USSR*) nor in any other publication. Thus the facts of our daily life, the life of every citizen of the USSR, are regulated by a secret resolution. The fact that the Passport Regulations belong to the class of secret documents has also meant that the passport system as a whole has ceased to be an object of study and investigation by specialists in the field of law. In addition to the resolutions of 1953, further resolutions were later adopted which intensify the passport system and the system of permits, especially in the large towns—*Author's note.*

in towns, regional centres, settlements of urban type . . . are obliged to have a passport.' Residents of rural settlements, of course, do not have passports, instead of a passport they are issued with a collective farm booklet or some other document of local significance. The document which certifies the identity of a peasant is not a legal document and residence permit like a passport. With such a document one cannot register in a town or be accepted to work in government establishments of factories. It is not even possible to move to another locality of rural type without special permission.

This division of the population of the country into town-dwelling 'passport-holding' citizens, and rural 'passportless' citizens has a long history in Russia, and its origins are connected with the serfdom laws, from the time when most of the population of Russia was made up of serf peasants who did not have freedom of movement, while in the towns lived free men, the bourgeoisie, nobles and other urban classes. The abolition of serfdom in 1861 did not alter the passport differentiation of the population and the privileges of town-dwellers. By this means the towns, which had a fairly low density of population, were saved from swamping by people from the country. And the same well-tried method was used after the triumph of socialism in our country, to keep the collective farm workers in their place, to avert their massive flight to the towns, to forestall their moving from a poor collective farm to a rich one, from one village to another, and so on.

It should be stressed that the October Revolution abolished the passports system which had divided the peasants from the town-dwellers. For a long time this was considered to be one of the most important achievements of the Revolution, making the law equal for peasants and the town-dwellers; while the old passport system was criticized as a survival of serfdom. However, in 1932, by a Resolution of the Central Executive Committee and the Council of People's Commissars of the USSR of 27 December, the passport system was reborn in our country in a form that was the same in principle as before, that is, with the introduction of passports only for town-dwellers. This decision was connected with collectivization in the villages. Moreover, a famine had started in many rural regions of the country. The starving rural population was streaming into the towns. Passports imposed a strict barrier on the flight of the starving population from the villages and collective farms.

Thus the denial of a passport in such a system means a definite infringement of the rights of a man, a means of forcing him to work in a definite place and to do work of a definite type (peasant work). But even a town-dweller's possession of a passport, which gives him more rights to work and employment in establishments and enterprises, also primarily serves, not the interests of the individual but the interests of the government. It guarantees governmental control over the movement of passport-holders and the places of their permanent and temporary residence. The passport differentiates the citizens of the country by nationality, which is indicated in it, and by certain other indices. According to the extracts printed on the last page of the passport, a person visiting any locality for more than three days must take his passport to the militia within twenty-four hours for a temporary or permanent permit (Article 37). If this is not done, the militia must fine the offender. For repeated breach of the permit rules the guilty parties will be treated as criminally responsible (Article 38). The same article places criminal responsibility on persons who reside without a passport where by the regulations they must have a passport.

It is quite evident that under such a system a passport, in addition to its function of identifying the individual, is a typical police surveillance document, which allows various restrictions to be imposed on citizens with the aid of the militia. The principal one is the refusal of a permit, without which a man cannot settle in a given town, region, or province for permanent or temporary work.

In the Lenin Museum in Moscow, I once saw the Imperial Russian passport of Lenin himself, issued, I think, by the Pskov police department. This passport was far simpler in its system of entries than the modern passport of a town-dweller in the USSR.

In general, the possession of a passport as a means of identification has definite advantages for a man in his daily life, because of the frequent need to identify himself. In countries without internal passports, such as the USA, this function is performed by other documents, such as birth certificate, driving licence, etc. As for the other functions of passports— the separation of town and country dwellers, control of movement, militia permits, etc., these, from the point of view of civil rights are, of course, incompatible with a democratic society and ought to be abolished.

However, a general analysis of the passport system in the USSR is outside the scope of the present investigation. Here we are concerned primarily with the question of foreign passports, traditionally the embodiment throughout the world of the right to foreign travel. Early on, the Soviet foreign passport was lauded by V. V. Mayakovskii:

G*

Like a wolf, all bureaucracy I'd gnaw away.
To mandates no honour, no never.
To the devils and all their dams go on your way
Bits of paper! But this one, however . . .

I shall take from my trouserlegs wide
In duplicate this priceless burden.
Read then, and envy, a citizen I
Am of the Soviet Union.

Mayakovskii wrote those proud lines on the Soviet foreign passport in 1929, when there was still no internal passport. And that year he was deprived of his right to obtain this passport. This was due not only to the introduction in 1929 of special restrictions on Soviet citizens travelling abroad but to reasons of a personal nature as well. This is how Aleksandr Gladkov describes the event in his still unpublished book *Meetings with Pasternak*:

> I asked G.O. [Vinokura] to comment on a phrase that was strange to me, which B.L. [Pasternak] had recently used, that 'Brik's flat was, in effect, a department of the Moscow militia . . .' G.O. smiled and was silent, but then, remarking that this was only his personal opinion and so forth, he began to speak about the friendship of Brik and his wife with the famous Yan Agranov, a high-ranking member of the Cheka who was especially concerned with literary matters.
>
> At first Agranov was in charge of the Special Section in the GPU and NKVD but afterwards he became a Deputy People's Commissar and perished in 1937. Agranov and his wife often visited Brik. G.O. himself met him there. Under his powerful protection Mayakovskii very easily received permission to travel abroad, but when Mayakovskii fell in love in Paris with Tat'yana Yakovleva and proposed to her, and had to go back again to Paris in autumn 1929, they did not give him a visa. It is possible that Brik and his wife were afraid of Mayakovskii marrying an émigrée and probable that they informed Agranov about it. For the first time in his life Mayakovskii was refused a visa, and this made a terrifying impression on him. With his integrity he could not understand nor reconcile himself to the fact that they did not trust him, Mayakovskii. Thus began the internal drama which led to his suicide . . .[1]

As we have seen, the Soviet Union restored the old Russian passport system in 1932, with a number of additional complications. For some time after the October Revolution the old system of issuing foreign passports was preserved, at all events, legally. However, the system by which

[1] The same version of the reasons for Mayakovskii's suicide is given in greater detail in the sketch 'The Love of a Poet' (*Ogonek*, 1968)—*Author's note*.

citizens of the USSR obtained foreign passports was then radically changed, and made more restrictive.

We know that in pre-Revolutionary Russia obtaining a passport presented no difficulties. Lenin, already a known revolutionary, frequently went abroad quite legally on the foreign passport which had been issued to him. Many party conferences and meetings of the Russian Social Democratic Workers' Party, the Bolsheviks, Mensheviks, Socialist Revolutionaries, the Bund and other illegal organizations aimed at the overthrow of Tsarism were held with a full quorum abroad, in England, Switzerland and other countries, and most of those taking part in these meetings obtained their foreign passports quite legally through the town authorities. And this was natural since there existed a well-known, accepted legal and generally accessible system for Russian citizens to obtain foreign passports and arrange journeys abroad. The historical development of this legal and state system is well described in the *Encyclopaedic Dictionary* published by F. A. Brockhaus and I. A. Efron in St Petersburg at the end of the last century. This system did not change at all until 1917. Volume 44 of this *Dictionary* (1897) contains two detailed articles on 'Passport and Foreign Passport'. It is appropriate to quote a few extracts from the latter article:

> In pre-Petrine Muscovy, travelling abroad was complicated by the fact that no one was permitted to pass through the frontier posts of the various regions without a travelling certificate from the local voivode, and in the voivodeships frontier control of the frontier posts was especially vigilant. . . .
>
> Not only did Peter I not hinder Russians from travelling abroad, he encouraged them in every way. . . .
>
> Paul I, wanting to preserve Russian society from revolutionary ideas forbade young people to travel abroad to study. The Emperor Nicolas I, finding that the young people who had received an education abroad sometimes returned to Russia with very false ideas about it, not knowing its true needs, laws, rules, attitudes, and not infrequently even the language, passed a Law on 18 February 1831 that young people from ten to eighteen years of age must be brought up in Russia, on pain of losing the right to enter the government service. According to the same Decree, the absence of a nobleman abroad must not exceed five years and that of a commoner three years, after which he would be considered to have 'abandoned the fatherland'.
>
> . . . In 1851, these periods were shortened to two years and one year respectively.

The article in the *Encyclopaedic Dictionary* describes the procedure for obtaining a foreign passport, usual at the end of the nineteenth century, as follows:

Foreign passports are issued by the chief officials of the 'territory', governors of provinces or towns. Persons seeking the issue of a foreign passport must furnish a police certificate that there are no legal obstacles to their going abroad. The police can refuse to furnish such a certificate only if legal proceedings are brought against a person either by private individuals or government bodies and persons. The police certificate may be replaced by a guarantee from reliable persons. . . .

The permitted length of stay abroad for all Russians is five years . . . Those who go abroad without obtaining a valid passport will be subject on their return to a financial penalty not exceeding three times the fee for a passport and in addition must pay for the time of their stay abroad. . . .

According to rules of that time, to obtain a passport one had to pay a fee of fifty kopeks and, in addition, for each half-year abroad there was a special tax of ten roubles. For journeys to Jerusalem and other holy places there were special reduced rates.

This system worked simply and effectively. My uncle, who lived in Tiflis before the October Revolution, decided when he was eighteen years old to go to Switzerland to train in the electrotype industry, and he says that it took him about three hours to obtain a foreign passport and have it put in order.

After the October Revolution, in spite of the more complicated international situation and the enormous number of secret service and sabotage trips into and out of the USSR by the numerous counter-revolutionary and conspiratorial elements of the time, the actual procedure for getting a foreign passport was very simple. Only the fee for the approval of a trip was increased, since it was mainly the well-to-do part of the population (those with commercial interests, 'NEP-men'[1] etc.) who tended to make these trips. A barrier to trips abroad did exist, but it was purely an ideological one, such trips simply were not encouraged. During that era there were also a great number of trips of scientists to various international conferences and meetings. In particular, at the Berlin Congress on Genetics in 1927, the Soviet Union was represented by a very numerous delegation. This included N. K. Kol'tsov, S. S. Chetverikov, G. D. Karpechenko, N. I. Vavilov, A. S. Serebrovskii and many other Soviet scientists. Long-term trips by

[1] The New Economic Policy (Novaya Ekonomicheskaya Politika), introduced in 1921, was an attempt to save the Soviet economy by a partial return to capitalism. A certain amount of private trade, etc., was permitted under the NEP, and the term 'NEP-man' now has the overtones of 'profiteer', referring to those who took advantage of the NEP concessions to line their own pockets at the expense of the common good.

young scientists abroad for educational purposes and to work in various laboratories, mainly in Europe, were a regular feature up to 1929.

Such a position was natural. Lenin and his advisers, many of whom had received an education abroad and had spent a considerable time as émigrés, while maintaining a close connection with their homeland, were psychologically unable to close down the freedom of movement of citizens, the freedom of travel abroad, and even the freedom to emigrate abroad. Being men of a European education, when they came to power they simply could not imagine the possibility of a socialist state isolated from the rest of the world. They envisaged such a state as being connected by every possible link to the proletariat and peoples of other countries. They understood that a socialist fatherland should unite its citizens by ideas, enthusiasm, grand projects, potential achievements, education, and a rise in the level of culture, and not by barbed wire along all the frontier posts. Banishment abroad was at that period the supreme measure of punishment specified in the Penal Code and frequently applied to dangerous political offenders and even saboteurs.

This position underwent a fundamental change in 1929, and this was, of course, no chance occurrence. This was not a matter of personal reasons only, not only due to the fact that Stalin had overcome all opposition and assumed exclusive power in the country. (Stalin knew no foreign languages, had never lived abroad as an émigré and in short was not an educated man.) In 1929, of course, a very widespread wave of repression began. We look back with pain at the years 1937 and 1938. Much is spoken about them, since in those years the repression engulfed thousands of Party and military leaders known throughout the country, hundreds of thousands of Party members, communists, heads of establishments, of the Soviet apparatus, people who had risen through the building of socialism and the October Revolution. But it is impossible to forget that there was a no less powerful and stern wave of repression in 1929–30; this did not, however, seize upon Party workers and the Soviet apparatus but upon other classes of the population. It swept from its path four classes of citizens of our country: 1. The more prosperous groups of peasants—the 'kulaks' and 'kulak-sympathizers'—and here the score ran into hundreds of thousands. 2. The exploiter elements in the towns, the 'NEP-man', who had hitherto been encouraged. This group, which had been stirred into life by Lenin's New Economic Policy, had in its hands a considerable proportion of retail trade, restaurants and cafés, and the production of everyday necessities. It possessed considerable financial resources and contacts with abroad.

The score here ran into tens of thousands. 3. Former members of the aristocracy, tens of thousands of whom were deported from Leningrad and Moscow; and 4. 'Bourgeois specialists', and, in effect, the old Russian intelligentsia. It was in 1929 that the first show trials, staged for the public, were organized against groups of scientists and technical specialists.

In addition to these classes which consisted of certain professional and social strata, former members of other parties, the socialist revolutionaries, the cadets, etc., were subjected to repression.

It was these repressions, and not any threat from without, which provided arguments for the abolition of almost all opportunities for citizens of the USSR to travel abroad, except for those involved in trade and diplomatic links. A country in which so massive a wave of repressions was being planned and carried out could not remain open. And since these repressions did not cease until the very death of Stalin, but simply passed through periods of maximum intensity and temporary lulls, this isolation of the Soviet people from any public opinion from abroad, this iron curtain which cut off any flow of information to or fro, especially information about the repression, depriving the victims of tyranny from the possibility of escaping from the doom prepared for them and of the possibility of appealing to public opinion, became the basis of State policy. Links with foreign countries were maintained only at the highest level and became the absolute monopoly of the Central Committee of the All-Union Communist Party (Bolsheviks) and the Council of People's Commissars. An ordinary contact, a mere conversation with a foreigner, could become grounds for arrest or denunciation. A characteristic xenophobia grew up.

During the Second World War this isolation inevitably decreased. The country needed allies in the rest of the world. The former enmity to all could only have led to the destruction of the state. For a short time military friendships with a number of countries and the duties of an ally healed the mentality of our society. Millions of Soviet soldiers and officers went into Europe with the army, to Poland, Hungary, Germany, Czechoslovakia, Bulgaria, Yugoslavia, Austria and China, and in a brotherly manner shared the burdens of war and the joy of liberation from fascism with the people everywhere. And these events did not vanish without a trace, in spite of the sharp change of course in 1946.

And when, after the death of Stalin and the execution of his closest associates in the repressions, Beria, Avakumov and a number of others, a partial state of law and order slowly began to arise in our country,

there also inevitably arose the question of widening the practice of trips
abroad by citizens of the USSR and visits to the USSR by citizens of
foreign countries—and not only for purely official business purposes,
but also on their private business and simply for tourism. International
economic and political systems had arisen, and a country which had
kept its inhabitants isolated from the outside world could not make its
doctrines attractive and could not play an important role in the development of the world society.

The first 'ordinary tourists' to and from the USSR occurred in 1956
after the Twentieth Congress of the CPSU. At first Soviet citizens were
able to visit a number of countries of the Socialist bloc, but in the same
year small groups of Soviet tourists also visited Western Europe. A
tourist cruise by steamer around Europe was introduced. The first
steamers with Soviet tourists caused a sensation everywhere in Europe.
Every time they docked a press conference was held for foreign journalists. Among the tourists there were many Soviet journalists and writers
who systematically gave reports to the Soviet press. Tass informed the
Soviet citizens at home about every event on the journey of the steamers
around Europe. After the voyages detailed descriptions appeared in the
journals and then in book form about what the travellers had seen in
Europe. The voyage of the *Chelyuskin* through the Arctic ice was not in
its time followed so closely in the USSR as was the journey of a group
of Soviet citizens aboard a comfortable steamer through the placid
waters of the Mediterranean.

But with time we grew accustomed to these trips, they became a
commonplace. The number of tourists began to be measured in tens of
thousands, and then in hundreds of thousands per year. There was a
sharp increase in the number of foreigners coming to the USSR.
Numerous friendship societies with foreign countries were founded. The
policy of 'peaceful co-existence' with other political systems became
popular. This was a healthy and, in itself, revolutionary process, and
was welcomed by almost all Soviet citizens.

It might have seemed that, with the widening of the practice of
journeys abroad, their legal basis should also have been formulated and
that some general principles for preparing and obtaining foreign passports and exit visas should have been laid down. But unfortunately this
was not done, and in the arranging of a journey abroad the main factor
became not the law but a principle of selection by a humiliating procedure of checking and examining a person. In form, this procedure is
practically identical with that which is necessary to obtain a pass for

secret work. Even the questionnaires to be filled out are the same in both cases. However, obtaining a 'pass' is simpler and quicker. The growth of scientific and ordinary tourism has been accompanied by the growth of the various sections and establishments which arrange it. Every kind of Board, Section, Sector of International Co-operation, External Relations, International Connections, etc., has multiplied in unprecedented numbers, and, it appears, has eaten up no small proportion of the benefit which the country has received from international co-operation. Thousands of highly-paid clerks were needed to check papers and questionnaires, to approve matters according to special instructions which were often not published for general information.

In the old days the procedure for getting foreign and internal passports was described in general encyclopaedias. Nowadays, even the special legal encyclopaedias do not given any clear information about it. In searching for information on this question, I looked through all the calendars of laws and decrees on open access in the Lenin Central State Library, but I found no clear indications on the legal basis of foreign travel by Soviet citizens and the procedure for getting a foreign passport. It is interesting to note that even the internal passport system, one of the basic facts of our life, is completely closed to scientific examination and even its legal aspects are not discussed in Soviet publications. Apparently the question of passports falls within the list of subjects forbidden by Glavlit. In the subject catalogue and in the subject index of the principal library of the country, which categorizes both books and articles (in the Russian language) into roughly 60,000 subjects, the word *Pasport* does not appear. *Paslen* (solanum family), *Paslenovye* (solanaceae), *pasmo* (a disease of flax), *pasoka* (sap extruded from cut on plant due to root-pressure), are followed by *passazhirskie topki* (passenger stoves), *passazhirskie vagony* (passenger coaches) and a mass of other passenger articles. Between *pasoka* and *passazhirskie topki*, *pasport* should come alphabetically, and with it should come the bibliographical cards of articles or books discussing this subject. But it was not there. *Pasport* was not there; 'the hammer-and-sickled Soviet passport' was not in the catalogues. Only after long searches in a special subject-catalogue of works on statehood and law and their associated sciences, among the collection of more than a million catalogued works I at last found a section on 'Documents on certification of identity' (Code Fa 322.41). But in this section there was only a single bibliographical card, indicating the presence in the holdings of the Lenin State Library of only one small

booklet on this subject, published in Voronezh in 1932, under the title
How to Replace a Lost Document.

Having been unable to settle the problem of finding out legal bases
for the practice of issuing foreign passports prevailing in the USSR, I
decided to consult the Institute of Statehood and Law of the Academy
of Sciences of the USSR on this question. I felt that this Institute, which
is situated in an old-fashioned detached house in Moscow (10 Frunze
Street), ought to have some information about the problem on its
shelves.

I walked along the corridors, and, having checked with the notice
board, asked to speak to someone about the question which interested
me. In the Sector concerned with the legal aspects of international
co-operation my questions completely stumped the two employees
working there. They could not understand why any legal basis was
necessary for the issue of foreign passports. They are issued to those who
need them! Nor could I obtain any logical and comprehensible explanation in the Sector of Problems of Socialist Jurisprudence. What I
needed was some document setting out the legal first principles, but no
one in that Sector knew of the existence of such a thing, not even the
Director, who was hurrying off to a session of the Supreme Court. I
went to the Sector of Civil Law, and then to the search room for practical legal investigation. In this room success awaited me. One of those
working there remembered that in the Institute there is an office with
records of legal Acts and bibliographical and other information. There,
he thought, I might be able to find something on the problem which
interested me. The information room of the records office was entirely
filled with bibliographical filing drawers. After long searching, the
elderly woman in charge of the records of Acts told me that the rules
for issuing foreign passports to citizens of the USSR are controlled by
a Resolution of the Council of Ministers of the USSR, published in
1959, in No. 12 of the weekly *Collection of Resolutions of the Government
of the USSR*, pp. 325–9. In the same office I soon found the required
issue of the *Collection* and the appropriate resolution but unfortunately,
I did not find in it either the legal preambles or the standard procedure
for granting foreign passports.

In the resolution it was simply laid down what types of foreign passports there are (diplomatic, government service, ordinary citizen's
foreign passport and 'residence permit'). It was then stated that foreign
passports are issued by the Ministry of Foreign Affairs and the Ministry
of Internal Affairs of the USSR and the corresponding Ministries of the

Union Republics. And finally it was then stipulated which categories of persons are issued with diplomatic and government service passports. On the subject of to whom and under what conditions ordinary citizen's foreign passports may be issued the resolution is completely silent. Tourists, according to this resolution, must be issued with government service passports. Tourism is thus transferred from a personal to a governmental basis. At the end of the resolution it was stated:

> Instructions on the adoption of this resolution are being issued by (a) the Ministry of Foreign Affairs of the USSR under the agreement with the Ministry of Internal Affairs and the Committee of State Security (KGB); and (b) the Ministry of Internal Affairs under the agreement with the Ministry of Foreign Affairs of the USSR, the KGB and the Ministry of Defence.

It was clear that everything that I wanted to know would be set out in these instructions. I had only to turn to them to find the answers to my questions at last. But the records office of legal Acts could no longer help me. They explained to me that such instructions are of 'top secret' documents. The Institute of Law only records Acts which have legislative force, that is, which are published in the open press.

It is impossible to read instructions marked 'secret', or, if you have read them, to quote them. Here we are brought to a halt by what is called a 'state secret'. And it is precisely this secret which takes the problem beyond the law, beyond the limits of legal knowledge. The law can be applied only when it is known and published in an accessible form.

But although the practice which ought to be governed by law is controlled by secret instructions, the essence of these instructions cannot remain a secret. For these instructions are applied in approving thousands of trips abroad, they dictate a procedure known to thousands and hundreds of thousands of people. From the nature of this procedure and from the system of approval it is possible to postulate clearly the sense of the secret instructions, it is possible to guess at the content of its paragraphs. Given a specified procedure, a student can carry out an operation or produce a reaction. But an experienced chemist can reconstruct the procedure by observing the reaction. It may not correspond exactly with what is laid down in the textbook, but the essence of it will be the same in both cases. I am not an experienced specialist in legal problems and though I have a clear empirical picture of the reactions which these 'instructions' produce, to generalize the empirical data into a sophisticated theoretical form is fairly complicated. So I must apologise to the reader for possible omissions and errors in the next section.

3

How a trip abroad from the USSR is arranged

THIS subject must from the outset be divided into two on the same principle on which all questions touching on the world outside our country are divided into two.

(A) TO CAPITALIST COUNTRIES

In the first part of this work we have already dealt in general outline with the problem of arranging private journeys abroad to capitalist countries. Practically the same type of arrangements are necessary for purely official business journeys, i.e. when a citizen of the USSR is sent abroad on the initiative or instructions of Higher Departments of the State. But such cases fall outside the framework of the present book, outside the framework of the legal question. When it is a case not of the personal desire of the individual, not his own initiative even of a business or scientific nature, but of a citizen being *sent or dispatched* abroad on state service, in an embassy, in a trade delegation, as a correspondent, a guide at an exhibition, an engineer on some project, an expert to the UN, a delegate to international conferences and meetings, then the state organs are completely entitled to arrange any check on the traveller, or rather envoy; they are entitled to study him from all aspects, starting with the character of his great-grandmother and ending with his sexual inclinations. A one-party state is entitled to send abroad on state business Party members only. The state pays the salary of specialists working abroad, and these salaries are not low, and it is natural that the state should consider whether this outlay is being justified in the best possible manner. The same applies to those journeys of scientists which are undertaken under special inter-state agreements. If the state found it necessary to send abroad an engineer on car brakes to study this matter, then a specialist on women's diseases would not be justified in feeling hurt that he had not gone but that an efficient engineer had. We can criticize the small scale of this type of agreement, the absence of links in many branches of science, the poor organization of international co-operation, and the second part of this book was, in effect, devoted to this. But this aspect of international travel has no direct bearing on the question of civil rights. Nor are we interested, in the present instance, in the numerous journeys abroad of footballers, basket-ball and hockey players and other sports teams, theatrical companies, ensembles, etc. If the Ministry of Culture wants to send the Georgian Ensemble and not the Buryat-Mongolian Opera to France in a given year, that is the Ministry's business.

In the present section, we shall confine the question to those cases, numerous enough, when a trip abroad is planned to be carried out because of an *individual* desire and an individual decision, either in response to an invitation to work abroad, or to a conference or congress ('scientific tourism'), or for educational purposes, or simply for a holiday ('ordinary tourism') or as a guest, or on one's private affairs. In short, we are concerned here with all the cases when the citizen himself bears the expenses of this trip or these expenses are borne by those inviting him and the USSR has no outlay connected with the journey, but simply receives the direct or indirect benefit.

All these cases differ very much in complexity. A 'short stay' trip as a tourist is easier than a long one. A trip to a conference is easier than a long-term stay in a laboratory. A trip as part of a group is easier than on one's own. A trip to visit a brother is easier than to visit a friend, and so on. However, none of these differences in complexity have any legal basis, they are subjective and arise from the subjective attitude of the workers in the apparatus, who are responsible for carrying out the various stages of the overall, almost universal, system. Hence we shall begin with the simplest case. A citizen of the USSR, let us say of middle age and employed as a senior scientist, with a salary of 300 roubles per month, passing the notice board sees a paper pinned to it with the following text: 'Tourist places are available for a trip to Italy for the— Congress. Cost 400 roubles. Length of the trip, 13 days. The Director.'

Such trips come under the heading of 'scientific tourism'. The members of the group attend the congress for four to five days, and then the representatives of Intourist in Italy take them about the country, showing them places of interest. Sometimes the announcement takes the following form: 'In the Central Committee of the Trade Union of Medical Workers there are the following tourist places for trips abroad in 1967. To Socialist Countries. ... To Capitalist countries: France 10 places, Italy 8 places, Belgium 12 places . . . Cost of the trip 450 roubles. Length of trip, 14 days.'

In this case it is a matter of a purely tourist trip. Such tourism is treated as leave. A scientific-tourist trip is not considered as leave and one does not lose one's right to one's regular leave. But from the point of view of arranging an 'exit dossier' there is no difference between a scientific-tourist and a tourist trip; both of them finally pass through the foreign section of the Ministry, although they are planned differently: the scientific-tourist trip by the administration and the simple tourist trip by the Trade Union organization.

Our senior scientist, let us say of a medical institution, has seen one of these notices.

The engineers, physicians, even the junior scientists pass by such a notice unperturbed. 450 roubles for two weeks is too high a price for them; for some of them it is three months', and for some even six months', pay. Of course, it would be possible to go to Italy more cheaply without the Intourist service, by train and not by aeroplane, and to live there student class. Or as a touring motorist, driving a car. But this is an individual form of tourism. For trips to capitalist countries this is not yet practised by Intourist. One can send Soviet citizens abroad with a far quieter mind in delegations, where one can keep an eye on them. The English, French and other Europeans, do not need to go on tourist trips or even to congresses herded together in groups. Individual and motor tourism accounts for some 80 to 90 per cent. If money is short, they camp out or stay in student hostels at minimum cost. In most cases they do not use tourist agencies. But Soviet citizens can only work through Intourist and its agents, and the market principle prevails. The demand (the number of applicants) always exceeds the supply (number of places allowed in the group) and hence every tourist man-day can be sold for a maximum price. Hence the middle-income bracket pass by advertisements for foreign tours.

But high-ranking scientists are not so calm about it, and soon a number of applications are received by the local committee (or by the Director's office if a trip to a congress with an additional tourist 'makeweight' is planned). But the institute has a limit, for example, seven persons and no more. They are informed of this figure by the Ministry of Health. Nor has the Ministry dreamed this figure up out of thin air. The Ministry also have an annual limit on tourist trips abroad which some special service sends them from the Council of Ministers of the USSR. Let us suppose that the Ministry is allowed 20,000 currency man-days per year, of which 15,000 are for socialist countries and 5,000 are for capitalist countries. 5,000 is not a large number, it is possible to send 500 persons abroad per year for an average of ten days each. First of all they calculate the minimum requirements for scientific-tourist groups to take part in congresses and other meetings, and a little is allotted also for ordinary tourism. In accordance with the plan, the Ministry decides to send a group of twenty people to Italy in a given year. In seven or eight establishments of appropriate type the order goes out for thirty-five to forty candidates, with a surplus to allow for subsequent sifting out. If only twenty 'exit dossiers' were ordered, after the sifting out there would be less than the number required, say twelve or thirteen people. This would be fine for the Ministry, they would save currency! But it would not be good for Intourist. The overheads per tourist would increase, but the cost of the trip would remain the same. They would have to 'order' guides abroad for a party of twelve, not twenty, and a leader and an 'observer' and a motor bus and so on. And if the Ministry did not provide a group which would bring Intourist some profit (groups of less than ten people mean a loss for Intourist) then Intourist would refuse to act and the trip would break down. Hence the Ministry reaches a preliminary agreement with Intourist for a group of a given size and must make up the losses if they occur. For this a reserve of 'exit dossiers' is necessary, it guarantees both Intourist and the Ministry against financial loss. And if at the last minute many of this 'reserve' still have to be excluded from the group, this should not upset anyone, as they will not have to pay for it!

Let us return, however, to the scene of action. The limit from the Ministry (taking the reserve into account) for a certain large establishment is seven people, or rather seven 'exit dossiers', and there are thirteen applications as a result of the advertisement. And these are all from heads of laboratories and sections or senior scientists.

If it is a case of simple tourism, not connected with any congress or symposium, they will not refuse anyone straight away. In the case of scientific tourism, speakers naturally have an advantage, i.e. those whose papers form part of the programme of the meeting. All the candidates who have expressed a desire to go to Italy are given whole booklets of papers for the 'exit dossier' to fill out. The personnel section receives instructions to prepare for each candidate the main document—the *character reference*. This is prepared in a special form and certain details must be mentioned, such as political maturity, moral stability, family circumstances and other such data. In the 'exit dossier' is a large questionnaire with twenty-five questions which include the traditional list of all close relatives, and not merely by name, but giving the dates of their birth and death, place of birth and death, where they worked or work, home address and degree of kinship. This is a considerable task for those with a large family or those who were born into a large family. Furthermore, when filling out the questionnaire, one must list every place of employment during one's whole life and all the jobs one held in these places, answer the question as to whether one was oneself—or one's close relatives were—taken prisoner or interned during the Second World War, indicate the number of scientific papers or inventions, place of study, and much other information about prizes, elective posts, etc. And all this has to be done in duplicate. Then one has to provide two copies of a detailed autobiography, twelve photographs, two copies of the birth certificates of children and a copy of one's marriage certificate. And this, of course, is not because one is travelling with one's family. It is simply that the higher authorities must have proof that the candidate proposing to make a tourist trip is a respectable father of a family, that is, a man bound to his fatherland not only by love of his country but also by family ties. Into the 'exit dossier' also goes a health certificate in a special form and made out from careful observation (X-ray, cardiogram, blood-pressure, general and cerebral, neuropathological, analysis of blood and urine). In the medical certificate for young people, they put 'good general health', for middle-aged and elderly people 'no deviations from standard', for middle-aged and elderly people always have something wrong with them, high blood-pressure, emphysema, weaker sight or hearing, or heart trouble, but all this falls within the standard for their age. The most important thing is to make sure that the tourist will not die in the next ten days due to change of climate! But the certificate is issued four to five months before departure, and no one examines the travellers just before they leave!

The questionnaires and all the copies and certificates are filled out and handed in separately. But according to instructions, the *character reference* is not put into the candidate's hands. The future tourist is not even supposed to see it; in practice, of course, this is not so. A draft of the character reference is drawn up by his immediate superior, and it passes through the personnel section to the Party Committee or Party Bureau. Until 1959 in addition to the character reference for non-Party members it was necessary to have two guarantees from Party members of long standing. And woe to the members of the CPSU if those whom they recommended committed some offence abroad! Reprimand was inevitable and they might even be expelled from the Party for lack of foresight. After 1958 this practice of 'making scapegoats' ceased to apply.

How they assess the character references in the Party Committee (or Bureau) I will not undertake to describe, for non-Party members are not invited to these sessions. Here the initial selection takes place. Now it is necessary to forward seven dossiers to the Ministry, and there are thirteen candidates. But they still do not cut it down to seven at the Party Committee stage. There must be a reserve for sifting out by the Regional Committee or Town Committee and Provincial Committee. At the Party Bureau stage, therefore, they drop only two, who are clearly not suitable for foreign tourism. One of them has a third wife, he has no moral stability! The other one has no self-control regarding alcohol. Eleven character references are endorsed, 'approved at the session of the Party Bureau of ——' with the date, and they are forwarded to the Regional Committee (if the town is divided into 'districts'), or to the Town Committee (if it is a small town). In the District Committee of the CPSU (or in the Town Committee) the character references are once again considered by the Bureau, which passes ten. These ten are endorsed 'Approved by the Bureau of the District Committee ——' with the date, and signed by the First Secretary, who affixes the District Committee's seal. One of the 'tourists' comes to grief here; they have remembered his low political activity and his refusal to work on election propaganda for the People's Judges. Only in Moscow is the District Committee the final authority; for there the District Committees have the status of Provincial Committees; in other parts of the USSR the character references proceed to the Provincial Committee in the provincial centre. They have to be considered by the Bureau of the Provincial Committee and pass through its 'Exit Commission'. In this commission there are representatives of the KGB, and here the tourists' 'files' are considered. The 'files' on a citizen of the USSR are at provincial headquarters of the KGB, only in Moscow are there sections of the KGB at district level. And in these 'files' are concealed all the secret faults and shortcomings of the candidate, everything which has been written about him by informers and intelligence-men during the whole of his life. The KGB does not open its 'files' to elected Party workers. It only gives a special certificate, objecting or approving the citizen as a tourist abroad. But, by its very nature, only negative information goes into the 'files'. Intelligence-men do not waste time in recording the creditable events in people's lives. I have been told of a case, some years back, of a well-known scientist who was appointed to work at UNESCO in Paris. All the work and political records of the candidate were favourable and he had already been selected in the Central

Committee of the CPSU. But the KGB did not decide to give its 'all clear'. Then the Central Committee demanded to see the whole 'file' (only the Central Committee can inspect the complete 'files'). And there it all was, denunciations going right back to 1927. And even a photograph of the candidate with Bukharin and Zinov'ev in Leningrad. Bukharin was talking to the scientist and smiling upon him favourably. The question of the appointment to UNESCO had to be specially considered once more by the Secretariat of the Central Committee of the CPSU, but the decision was favourable. Bukharin at that time had not yet become an international spy.

After the character references have been checked and approved, they finally go to the Department in Moscow in charge of approving tourist trips. Foreign passports for citizens of the Russian SFSR to go to capitalist countries are issued only in Moscow, even in the case of a resident of the Crimea who is to visit neighbouring Turkey. And the character references do not leave the Regional Committee all together, but in sequence, one after the other.

When the time comes the Ministry sends a notification that for the ten 'exit dossiers' previously received from the institute, eight approved character references have come from the District Committee. Two of them did not get through the filter of the District Committee, but there is no information why, and no one even asks. Those who have been stopped guess at it. One of them, during his childhood, lived in temporarily occupied territory, the other has been corresponding too freely with foreigners. No one knew about this in the institute but the 'files' reflected it all. Or maybe it is the other way round, the man is of such integrity and honour that he has been entrusted with important secrets and his 'immunity' has not yet run out, he is still 'hot'. It is considered that people who know secrets should not be sent abroad (except for classified workers, of course). For different secrets the 'cooling down' time differs. In biology it is three years, while in technology it is seven years. After this time it is assumed that any secret loses its value. For this reason it is rare nowadays that anyone in an open establishment willingly agrees to read a paper marked 'secret' or 'top secret'. You read it, you sign for it, and straight away you fall into this category of unreliability.

And so there were thirteen applicants, but only eight character references came back to be put together with the questionnaires. There is generally no solidarity in the group, no one will protest on behalf of the others. The eight who have passed are glad that they have been found worthy, and that is all. It is just the same as in a lottery. They take their winnings gladly, although it is at the expense of their fellow-citizens. And anyway, everyone knows that the number of places is less than the number of candidates, and the selection is still not over.

In the foreign section of the Ministry 'exit dossiers' for the trip are being collected from many institutes in different parts of the country. According to the plan, a group of ten persons is being formed, but twenty-seven 'exit dossiers' have arrived from various places. But of course the process of approving the tourists is still not over. In the foreign section they put aside only one dossier, that of a candidate who has recently come back from abroad, and the rest go on further. In the category of scientific tourism all dossiers may reach the Central Committee of the CPSU only by way of the State Committee on Science and Technology of the Council of Ministers of the USSR. Its business is to co-ordinate the work. Of course, it may happen that two different authorities are preparing delegations of tourists for the same occasion, and in this case they must be combined into a single group.

The principal decision is taken in the Central Committee of the CPSU in a special 'Exit Commission'. Dossiers for scientific tourism still have to pass the Section of Science and Higher Education of the Central Committee of the CPSU. Without the decision of the 'Exit Commission', the Ministry of Foreign Affairs of the USSR cannot deliver a foreign passport into the hands of the candidate tourist. But the preparation of passports is normally done earlier, on the request of the foreign sections of the departments, who send to the Ministry of Foreign Affairs of the USSR one copy of a special certificate on the 'exit dossier' and photographs. The fact is that the 'exit dossier' is sent to the 'Exit Commission' of the Central Committee not less than two months before the planned departure. It is impossible to hurry the 'Exit Commission'. It has to deal with thousands of dossiers from the whole Union and with everything from simple tourism to delegates to the UN. But according to international agreements, a 'visa' for a capitalist country must be requested not less than four weeks before departure. But to request a visa it is necessary to submit a passport at the Embassy. In other countries, when a citizen has obtained his passport, he takes it himself to the embassy or consulate, or else gets an agent of the tourist company to do it for him. But in the USSR, a foreign passport is delivered to the citizen only on the eve of his departure, and all the business with the embassies is carried out by the state service. Hence visas are often requested in advance, before there is a decision of the 'Exit Commission' of the Central Committee. By then all the candidate tourists have received an advance notice 'Have your 450 roubles ready at such-and-such a time'. Recently a written guarantee to pay the required sum at the required moment has been required from candidates together with the 'exit dossier'. They are also warned of the possible time of the call to Moscow so that they can all be ready. The tension among the candidates starts to increase. No one yet knows whether he will get past the final authority, but of course everyone has to get ready for the trip all the same. In the case of scientific tourism this preparation is especially serious, one's paper has to be translated into a foreign language, and approved by Glavlit. The candidates read literature about the country, renew their wardrobes, and spend their time, money and energies on getting ready. But all the time none of them knows for certain whether he will be called to Moscow or not. And if the call does not come, this is taken most painfully, for it is a sign that one has been found wanting.

Now the agreement with Intourist comes into force. Although twenty-six dossiers have been sent to the 'Exit Commission', Intourist, as agreed, is preparing for a group of twenty people. They have ordered twenty tickets there and back, twenty places in the hotels and excursions. Intourist cannot wait till the last day either. So six persons will have to be refused even if they have been approved in the 'Exit Commission' of the Central Committee. And now the day has come. About ten to twelve days before the planned departure (and sometimes only three to four days), the Ministry is told the names of those who have been approved by the Central Committee. There are twenty-three of them. Why the three did not get through no one asks. Three dossiers are discarded at random in the Ministry, or perhaps only two, and the remaining candidates are called 'to come to Moscow at such-and-such a time, bringing everything ready for departure and to pay for the tour'. It is necessary to keep one or two in reserve, a visa may be refused, things may go wrong in the interview in the Central Committee, and finally the candidate himself may have to refuse for financial reasons. This is especially frequent in the case of long-distance trips to Japan, the USA or South America. This costs from 800 to 1,400 roubles, a large enough sum to make the hands of a candidate who has negotiated all these reefs shake at the last minute.

When they are called, the candidates go to Moscow. All the decisions are there, and the final stage begins at top speed. But this is if all goes well. Sometimes, especially in the summer when there are many trips and few workers in the 'Exit Commission' because it is holiday time, the decision is delayed. The candidates are called before the decisions have come. They learn about them in the last day or two, and sometimes departure is delayed. In 1966 the tourists who were to go to Japan for a Congress on electron microscopy were three days late at the Congress because of this. They had already paid their money to Intourist, and every day they assembled on Revolution Square outside the Metropol' Hotel, where Intourist has its offices, with their suitcases, and waited several hours for the 'decisions', and then dispersed to their own hotels. And the Congress in Japan had already begun, and some of them were to have read papers on the first two days. At last the 'decisions' came, they all received passports and a special flight of Aeroflot flew them to Tokyo. Three days were lost, the date of return was not changed, but Intourist, of course, did not refund any of the money. After all, the delay was not Intourist's fault, and they still had to pay the Japanese contractors the agreed sum.

The foreign passport is delivered into one's hands only after the decision of the Central Committee, and even if this is taken well in advance, this passport is rarely delivered more than one or two days before departure, for, of course, someone with a passport and visas could go off on his own, earlier than intended. The frontier guards would not be able to stop him. This is why one is furnished with a passport only at the very last moment, and one's internal passport is taken in at the same time as a 'pledge' that on one's return the foreign passport will be surrendered at once.

But this is not the final phase. There is still one more obligatory one, which as a rule takes place in the final twenty-four hours. This is an interview in the Central Committee. There is a special panel of instructors in the Foreign (International) Section of the Central Committee of the CPSU. Working down the list, they have a talk with everyone who is leaving for a capitalist country (some years back it was for socialist countries, too). It is necessary for them to have a personal impression of everyone who is going. First of all, in the reception room of the international section of the Central Committee, every tourist and non-tourist is given a special booklet marked 'secret'. It contains recommendations and rules of conduct for the Soviet citizen abroad. The candidate for a tourist trip signs that he has read it and proceeds into an office for the interview. The instructor of the International Section may have done the job a thousand times, he puts standard questions and gives various words of advice and opinions, some of a sexual nature, and warns that it is not permitted to visit nocturnal establishments. This is often embarrassing to the candidates, who are normally serious people.

And moreover, according to their character references, they are all 'morally stable'. Many of them are going abroad not for the first time and have already endured an interview of this type, for they are repeated before every trip. But generally no one argues; why tempt fate, especially when you have already paid your money! For, of course, your interlocutor can cancel your trip right at the very last moment. There have been cases when a passport has been withdrawn from a tourist even at the airport or at the railway station. This made an inauspicious impression! The interview is a necessary ritual of any trip. But there are exceptions. I know of one. A colleague, a biochemist working in Vladivostok, was a member of a group which was going as scientific tourists to the Biochemistry Congress in Japan in 1967. While on a business trip to Moscow, he agreed with the leader of the delegation that the leader would get his foreign passport for him and that my colleague would join the delegation at Vladivostok when they transferred from the aircraft to the steamer. He left the leader of the group the money to pay Intourist. If the leader of a delegation has the confidence of the foreign section of the Academy of Sciences of the USSR he can carry out all financial and other business for all members of the delegation. But my colleague forgot about the interview in the Central Committee. And on the very eve of the departure the summons came to him in Vladivostok 'to come to Moscow for an interview'. His passport was already made out, the decision had been given for him, but he had not undergone the interview. He had been abroad on a previous occasion, he knew what the 'interview' was like, and he did not want to fly from Vladivostok to Moscow and back again to Vladivostok at his own expense, just for this. He telephoned the foreign department of the Academy of Sciences of the USSR and said that he was withdrawing from the trip to Japan. Imagine his surprise when the leader of the delegation arrived at Vladivostok *en route* to Japan not with his money back but with a foreign passport with all the visas! Obviously the ludicrous nature of the situation was clear to everyone, and this helped them to make an exception to the rules.

But let us return to our group. And to the scientist who saw an advertisement for a tourist trip. He has been lucky, he has got through all the checks, all the commissions, he has been found honourable and worthy. The 450 roubles, which seemed a great sum to him, seem very little now that he is in the aeroplane. He understands that even if the tourist himself pays the cost of the tour, the state suffers a material loss. In tourist somehow manages to make ends meet. But who pays the hundreds of clerks in the preliminary stages? The trip lasts twelve days, but how many days were spent on arranging it, how many people sat in commissions, committees, bureaux, deciding whether candidate tourists are worthy? How much time was spent by personnel officers and experts studying and checking questionnaires and documents? On discussions and interviews? On the work of doctors? And all this for 450 roubles! It seems that he is travelling at his own expense, but in fact it is at the expense of the state which has paid with open hand this whole army of checkers and approvers out of the state budget.

But everything described here concerns the simplest case of organized tourism. If it is a matter of individual tourism—and for a trip to capitalist countries—the whole thing becomes quite impossible. Intourist simply does not have an individual service for Soviet citizens. There are only rare exceptions, and every one of these requires a special decision of the highest authority. Of course, it is true that the poet Evgenii Evtushenko travels freely around Europe, America and other countries. He even has a permanent foreign passport (as Mayakovskii did once), and he goes with it himself to foreign embassies to get visas. When he visited the US Embassy for a visa, there was a broadcast about it on American radio as something sensational. But this is not an example of democracy. There has simply been a special decision exempting Evtushenko from the general rule, and making him a screen for the lack of rights of other writers. And he, gratefully receiving this act of mercy, this privilege, tries sincerely to show that any Soviet citizen can freely give recitals in any country.

In most cases they refuse to approve all individual trips in response to invitations received from colleagues, friends and society organizations abroad, even when these invitations include the cost of the trip being paid by those sending the invitations. Only old pensioners who have close relatives abroad can sometimes, after many months delay, obtain permission to go abroad 'as guests', through the Department of Visas and Registration of the Provincial Headquarters of the militia. But even in this case a character reference is required and other papers, too, for a specially approved summons from abroad. Previously these cases, too, were refused, but after a series of international petitions and recommendations, the USSR began to allow meetings of relatives in the direct line and marriages with foreigners, which were formerly categorically forbidden. Now a daughter who is a citizen of the USSR can sometimes visit her mother living in France. This, of course, is a great achievement, but it does not concern general civil rights and falls outside the framework of this investigation.

The typical system that I have just described of approving trips which are made from *a personal desire* to go abroad is so arranged that all the basic decisions are taken by the Party organs at different levels. The organs of Soviet power and Government departments have this significance: each ordinary tourist trip becomes a matter of state and a tourist receives a government service passport. The tourist does not go abroad, he is *sent*, he is directed on a tourist trip, to him is entrusted the difficult mission of tourism.

We understand that in any European country it would be an absolutely ludicrous situation if every ordinary tourist trip abroad had to be organized and approved by a special department like the Ministry of Health or of the Coal Board, or by some Committee on the Press. The consideration of the question of such trips by committees of the ruling party would be ludicrous. If a tourist decides to make use of the services of a tourist agency, then it does everything for him. The very question of a passport is one of law, and hence falls outside the competence of specialized departments and Party apparatus. Its refusal can be sanctioned only by a court as interpreter of the law.

But our system does not presuppose an equal legal basis for everyone. The state does not guarantee a *right*, the same for everyone, but makes a plan for trips in 'currency man-days' and thus creates a system under which people compete to be selected for privileges.

In such a system of organizing international tourism, and with the exceptionally inflated staff of all the sections and authorities concerned with international co-operation, the conditions have been created for corruption and abuses, a system of bribery in kind, and the custom of bringing back expensive 'presents' from abroad for the clerks in these departments in gratitude for their goodwill. And the clerks generally stress their own important role in the selection of candidates.

In all civilized countries the refusal of the state organs to grant a foreign passport on the application of a citizen is an extraordinary event and must be confirmed by the decision of a court. The court considers how far the refusal to grant the passport is *legal*. We all remember from the papers of the Stalinist era how in 1950 the government of the USA refused to issue a foreign passport to the famous Negro communist singer, Paul Robeson, for a trip to the USSR and a tour of Europe. For several years, so the papers wrote, Paul Robeson had been deprived of his civil rights. Finally the singer appealed to the Supreme Court of the United States. This court declared by a majority of one, that the decision of the US Government was unconstitutional, and Paul Robeson was given his foreign passport. He came to Moscow, and his 'victory' was marked here with great celebrations.

In the USSR there is no law which allows such rights to citizens. And not only is there no legal basis, there is not even the possibility of a court considering such disputes, or cases of refusal. The Supreme Court of the USSR and the Supreme Courts of the Union Republics only consider disputes connected with settling in another country to join part of a family or with relatives in the direct line (for example daughters and mothers). In this case the refusal can be considered by the court, since there exists an international legal agreement on such matters. But all other cases of refusals to issue passports and visas are not open to appeal to the court. Decisions of the Party Bureau, decisions of the Town Committee, the Provincial Committee, the Ministry, the 'Exit Commission', the KGB, etc., are not open to appeal. The Ministry of Foreign Affairs of the USSR does not usually deal with citizens on matters of going abroad and obtaining passports. Even supposing that in the case of some particular invitation to Britain the Embassy of the USSR in Britain decided that it would be a good thing to accept, but the secretary of the Party Bureau of the establishment thought otherwise, the Embassy would have to give way. It is not the Embassy's business to worry about the rights of its citizens.

But that is how the matter stands for trips of Soviet citizens to the capitalist countries of Europe, Asia, Africa, America and to Australia. For trips to Socialist countries the matter is somewhat different—or rather, to some of them. The fact is that, if capitalist countries fall into a general category, with socialist countries there are as many special cases as there are countries. Trips to China, North Korea and Albania are especially complicated. But this is due to rules existing in those countries themselves. Yugoslavia, which has an open frontier with its neighbours, ranks with the capitalist countries. There are also differences between the remaining countries, but these are less, and hence we shall consider the question of these countries together.

(B) TO THE SOCIALIST COUNTRIES OF EASTERN EUROPE
Tourism to the socialist countries of Eastern Europe (Czechoslovakia, Poland, Romania, Hungary, Bulgaria and the GDR) is still the main form of international tourism for citizens of the USSR. These countries account for more than 90 per cent of all our trips abroad. Of course, this is not due only to the serious restriction of tourism to capitalist countries, entirely natural factors also play a part; closeness, relative

cheapness, that is the accessibility of tourism to a greater range of the population, a common social structure and Slavonic unity with some of these countries. Travel to each of these countries from the USSR has its own history and particular character, controlled by bilateral agreements. For example, before the building of the Berlin wall, the GDR, for the purpose of travel from the USSR, was put in the same category as the capitalist countries. This was because a citizen who went to the socialist German Republic could relatively easily visit capitalist West Berlin as well. After the events of autumn 1956, tourism to Hungary stopped for a long time. Tourism to Yugoslavia, which first of all went through a period of increase, has in recent years been subject to restriction from our side. About three years ago Yugoslavia opened her frontiers for free entry to foreigners from the West, for transit to Greece, and reduced her frontier posts, abolished the total frontier control which is typical of other socialist countries, and allowed the free movement of her own citizens across the frontier into neighbouring countries. This at once put Yugoslavia, for the purposes of Soviet citizens visiting it, into the same category as the capitalist countries. Socialist countries remote from the USSR, such as Cuba, also belong to this category for Soviet tourists, for to get there one has to cross many capitalist countries.

All this goes to show that the principal factor in the approval of tourist trips by Soviet citizens to another socialist country is not the nature of its social structure, not its degree of friendship with the USSR, but simply how far it is isolated from the capitalist countries.

Since the countries of Eastern Europe are the dominant factor in the balance of Soviet tourism, tourism in the other direction of citizens of these countries to the USSR is the intensive dominant factor in the total number of tourists visiting our country.

The economics of international tourism are very simple. Commercially speaking, it is to the advantage of any country to be the object of foreign tourism. It is a comparatively easy source of influx of foreign currency, and entails no great capital outlay. The country sells its natural beauty, its landscapes, places of interest, health resorts and cultural monuments. For many countries the influx of tourists from abroad brings in the same profit as international trade, and for certain countries tourism is the main item of trade. On the other hand, if the number of its own citizens travelling abroad is greater than the number of foreigners visiting a given country, then we have an unfavourable situation for that country. For countries lacking in natural beauty, good climate, open spaces, ancient history, architectural monuments, etc., and at the same time industrially developed, with a high standard of living of the population, a negative tourist balance is inevitable. For example, the number of British people making tourist trips to Europe each year (to Italy, France, Spain, etc.) is 6 million, twice as great as the number of tourists visiting Britain for tourist purposes each year. About 17 million people visit Spain each year, while the number of Spaniards leaving the country for tourist purposes, can hardly exceed 1 million per year.

For a long time it was easier for citizens of Eastern Europe to come to the USSR than for tourism in the other direction both economically and from the point of view of organizing the trip, and hence their tourist balance was negative, i.e. unfavourable. And since the balance of trade for many of these countries was also negative, it was natural that they began to put a definite pressure on the USSR to stimulate and facilitate tourism by Soviet citizens. This pressure, which was exerted through all possible channels, bore fruit, and in 1965 real measures were adopted in this direction. We have in mind the signing by the Soviet Union of agreements with a number of socialist countries of Eastern Europe on travel without visas for citizens including not only tourism but even simply trips on one's private affairs, by-passing the state tourist organizations. The corresponding Protocol signed between Czechoslovakia and the Soviet Union on 17 September 1965 stipulated that citizens of one of the signatory countries, travelling on their private business on the invitation of relatives, friends and acquaintances, may leave the country, enter it and stay within the territory of the other signatory without visas within the limits of time laid down in the invitation, but not exceeding ninety days, and also proceed without visas to a third country, with which both signatories have agreements on travel without visas on one's private affairs. These agreements permit a relatively free exchange of currency (but not exceeding 15 roubles per person per day), and enable Soviet citizens to make individual trips abroad, a form of tourism and holiday not practised previously. These types of agreements are significant as a matter of principle. They legally recognize the *right* of any Soviet citizen *freely* to visit a neighbouring country when he has cause to do so. The recognition in the agreements of these rights is undoubtedly a significant achievement of democratic trends. Thanks to this kind of agreement, a situation has arisen in which any citizen of the USSR who obtains an invitation of a personal nature can go, for example to Czechoslovakia, simply as a guest, freely, without a foreign passport and visas, taking his internal documents which attest his Soviet citizenship.

His internal passport, collective farm 'book', or identity certificate will be recognized by the Czechoslovak frontier service as permitting free entry into the Czechoslovak Socialist Republic. Without such a personal invitation a citizen of the USSR can go to Czechoslovakia (and to Bulgaria, etc.) with a group organized by Intourist.

However, when they signed this type of agreement, the countries concerned had quite different attitudes to it. The governments of our socialist neighbours welcomed these agreements enthusiastically, and took all possible steps to see that the citizens of their countries knew all the details of the agreements and made use of them. The population was very widely informed about these agreements in the press. The day after the Protocol was signed in the Ministry of Foreign Affairs of the USSR, the Central Czechoslovak paper, *Rude Pravo* of 18 September 1965, published a telephone dispatch from its Moscow correspondent on the signing of the Agreement in a prominent place in the first column. The paper gave the details of the agreement with bold headlines and described it as a new step in the development of friendly links between countries.

The Soviet organs of information treated this agreement quite differently. They simply concealed it from the population. The Soviet Central papers (*Pravda, Izvestiya, Trud*, etc.) in their issues of 17, 18, 19 and 20 September, and subsequently, did not say a single word about the signing in Moscow of such important documents. At the same time, however, diplomatic events on an immeasurably smaller scale (reception of ambassadors and envoys, dinner in honour of —, lunch in honour of —, talks with the Brazilian trade delegate, etc.) were treated at considerable length in the diplomatic chronicle in these same newspapers. Nor were these agreements published in the general Soviet press at a later date. They were not even reported by the Soviet special journals concerned with international diplomacy, not even in the sections which give a chronicle of diplomatic life. Only in one special small-circulation scientific diplomatic booklet (B. V. Klimenko, *The Right of Passage Through Foreign Territory*, 1967) on page 4, is there a brief mention of such agreements. It apparently got into the book by an oversight of the censor. Hence even now practically no one in the USSR knows about these agreements and makes use of the freedoms which exist.

But even these 'freedoms' are very relative. While recognizing in words and recording in the text of Protocols the legal right of Soviet citizens to travel freely without visas to certain neighbouring socialist countries, the Soviet signatory has left these rights to be put into effect by the organs of the militia, who in their turn have created a procedure for this purpose which in practice totally denies the existence of any such *rights* and creates all the conditions for arbitrary rule. According to this procedure, it turns out that to have an internal passport and an invitation, which the Czechoslovak frontier service accepts as sufficient for entry and passage into Czechoslovakia, is not, however, accepted for *exit* and passage from the USSR by the frontier service of our country. The Soviet frontier service lets through only those citizens who have the special 'exit' certificates issued in exchange for their passports by the Provincial Headquarters of the militia. But these certificates are issued by the militia not simply in exchange for passports, but after a special procedure, which in the first stages does not differ from the approval procedure for capitalist countries. There is a difference only at the highest stages in that the final decision is given not by the 'Exit Commission' of the Central Committee of the CPSU but by 'Exit Commissions' of the Provincial Committees of the Party. To obtain a permit one must first fill out just as complicated a questionnaire, and most of all have a character reference from one's place of employment (in addition, autobiography, health certificate, invitation, statement of purpose of journey). Unlike the case of a trip to capitalist countries, copies of one's marriage certificate and the birth certificates of one's children are not required, if one is not planning to take members of one's family. The questionnaires and other materials have to be made out in one copy. From the time of delivery of the documents to the Provincial Department of Visas and Registration to receiving an exit certificate, two months or more may elapse. I do not know any statistics on favourable and unfavourable decisions, since the practice of 'private' visits is still too limited. I can only tell you that in doubtful cases the higher authorities still concern themselves in the process. One of my acquaintances, a writer of progressive views, was arranging a trip to Poland in the summer of 1967. It took several months to arrange, and in this case the final decision was obtained in the 'Exit Commission' of the Central Committee of the CPSU. The Foreign Section of the Union of Writers, which has the right to make the final decision on questions of travel to Poland, Czechoslovakia, Bulgaria and Hungary, in this writer's case decided to pass on the question for consideration by higher spheres. And it was decided favourably. But in the case of another writer who wanted to avail himself of a series of invitations from Czechoslovakia in the summer of 1967, a negative decision was received. He had a letter from the Foreign Section of the Union of Writers in which it was stated that 'your trip to Czechoslovakia has been found to be inadvisable'.

Thus we can see that the 'free' way of travelling to the socialist countries of Eastern Europe without visas is actually hampered because a series of internal decisions has to be obtained from the establishment where the citizen works (in the form of a character reference), from the militia, the Provincial 'Exit Commission', the Department of Visas and Registration and from other unknown supplementary authorities who are concerned with certain ideological aspects of behaviour. As far as scientific tourism to these countries is concerned, that is, tourist trips arranged through Intourist by scientists to attend various symposia and conferences and paid for entirely by the scientists themselves, these are still arranged and decided through the Ministry and department and are rigidly limited in quantity and quality. There are still no free trips without visas for scientists going to scientific meetings, say in Czechoslovakia or Bulgaria, even in the holiday period. And refusals in this sphere are commonplace, although juridically, in view of the inter-state agreements on free exchange without visas, they are illegal. Illegal, too, are all the other procedures for obtaining a permit for a private trip in response to an invitation. For, if these inter-state agreements apply equally to all full citizens of both countries, then the means of approval should be based on the rights of citizens and not on the decision of various levels of authority, and on obtaining a character reference, etc. The militia, like the police in Old Russia, should in this case only watch to see that the permission to go abroad is not made use of by those under investigation, under trial, deprived of their rights by sentence of a court, recidivists, and so on. A medical certificate, of course, is also necessary to stop people with psychological illnesses, or infectious illnesses (open forms of tuberculosis, etc.), from going abroad, unless they are invited by friends or for treatment in clinics. The existing restrictions on trips to the socialist countries of Eastern Europe, although they are not so serious as the restrictions on travel to capitalist and neutral countries, nevertheless considerably weaken the trend to develop links of friendship and business among the various socialist countries and deflect the integration of the small socialist countries of Eastern Europe away from the East and towards the West. Western Europe, knowing no international restrictions on the movement of its citizens, exerts through its massive tourism and business visits an enormous effect on the socialist countries bordering on the USSR, inevitably introducing into them all kinds of Western European culture as well as ideology.

The contact of people is a mighty force, and to illustrate how little it is used by our country, which concentrates on high level contacts, we shall quote here some actual figures.

The 'Political' Section of Intourist of the USSR publishes a monthly hectographed journal for internal use in the Intourist system, *The Bulletin of Tourist Information*. This *Bulletin* is distributed to the various departments of Intourist and to certain libraries. In particular it can be found in the Lenin State Library in Moscow. This small journal publishes a wide range of statistical material dealing with trends of international tourism throughout the world. For example, in no. 4, 1967, figures are given for the distribution of foreigners visiting Czechoslovakia in 1966. In 1966 there went to Czechoslovakia: 907,334 citizens of Poland, 872,601 citizens of Hungary, 832,332 from the GDR, 284,455 citizens of Austria, 223,311 citizens of Federal Germany and 49,588 citizens of the Soviet Union. Hard on the heels of the USSR comes Bulgaria (40,901 persons). But the population of Bulgaria (8 million) is only one-twentieth of even the European part of the USSR. Bulgaria has no common frontier with Czechoslovakia, and to go to Czechoslovakia from Bulgaria it is necessary to cross two countries, Romania and Hungary. The journey from Bulgaria to Czechoslovakia is considerably more expensive than from the USSR, and, of course, the standard of living of Soviet citizens is on the average higher than that of the citizens of Bulgaria. I shall not speak of the technical and economic links, which are far more numerous between the USSR and the Czechoslovak Socialist Republic than between the Czechoslovak Socialist Republic and Bulgaria. Yet in numbers of tourists Bulgaria is overtaking us in absolute figures. As for Czechoslovakia's closer neighbours, the USSR, as we can see, lags a long way behind. The number of Poles visiting Czechoslovakia is practically equal to the total number of Soviet citizens going abroad in 1966 to all the countries of the world. Tourism to Czechoslovakia from more distant capitalist countries is close to the level of tourism from the USSR. In 1966, 37,872 persons came to the Czechoslovak Socialist Republic from France.

The figures for trips by citizens of the USSR to Hungary in 1966 are somewhat higher (see *Bulletin of Tourist Information*, no. 7, 1967). But all the same the number of visits from the USSR to Hungary was six times less than from Czechoslovakia, half as many as from Poland or from Bulgaria, and less than from Austria.

Now it is quite obvious that if each year a country, such as Czechoslovakia, receives more than half a million Western citizens from

Austria and Federal Germany alone and one-tenth of that number of Soviet citizens, then the effect of these countries on the population of Czechoslovakia will be greater than the effect of the Soviet Union, while tourism in the reverse direction of Czechs and Slovaks to Austria and the Federal Republic of Germany will be greater than reverse tourism to the USSR. This is what we actually find in real life, and the number of citizens of Czechoslovakia who visited Federal Germany and Austria in 1966 was also ten times greater than the number of these citizens visiting the USSR. After this is there any cause to wonder at the growth of 'pro-Western' sentiments in Czechoslovakia and the gradual 'loosening' of its links with our country? In the present conditions in which economics, technology, science and culture depend on the creative activity of an enormous number of people and individual contacts have an increasing role, the friendship of nations can no longer be based on the friendship of the leaders of parties and governments. We do not need invisible friendship but visible friendship between nations.

4

How to arrange a trip to the USSR from other countries

OUR survey would not be objective if we passed over this question in silence. Although far more citizens of capitalist countries come to the USSR than go from the USSR to these countries, in certain socialist countries of Eastern Europe the balance with the USSR is almost equal. And this balance, as we have seen, is at a very low level, much lower than the corresponding balance between foreign states both socialist and capitalist. This might make one think that in any country coming to the USSR is governed by certain restrictions on departure, or that our country imposes certain restrictions on entry for the citizens of other states. Perhaps it is as complicated for a citizen of Czechoslovakia to arrange his trip to the Soviet Union as for a citizen of the Soviet Union to Czechoslovakia. Perhaps the same is true for the French, the Germans, the British and the inhabitants of many other states. We have in mind here only procedural, legal, visa and passport barriers, and not currency barriers. The question of the currency barriers to entry into our country and exit from it will be dealt with separately in the next section.

The answer to the question raised above can only be a negative one. For a trip to the USSR from the socialist countries of Eastern Europe on business and in response to personal invitations, all formalities have been reduced to a minimum since 1965, and indeed somewhat earlier. The legal formalities take not more than one day, and there is no procedure of exchanging one's internal document for a special exit certificate at all. Citizens of Czechoslovakia, Bulgaria and a number of other countries can travel to the USSR on the same identity certificate which is effective for internal purposes. No character references are required for exit approval for Czechoslovak or Bulgarian citizens going on a trip to the USSR, and the inhabitants of these countries can visit ours during their holidays without informing their superiors where they work, let alone the Department. The same is true of trips made through the state tourist agencies. Limits on the number of tourist visits from abroad, by agreement with other agencies, are set only by our country, and this is due to shortages of hotels, camping facilities and tourist routes. Which of us who has travelled on business around his native country does not know of the sad practice of suddenly turning Soviet citizens out of hotels if foreigners arrive who must be put up somewhere. The Soviet citizen in a good hotel is given his room number only after he has signed a written confirmation that he is ready to vacate it at once if required by the administration. There are no special restrictions on visits to our country by invitation, since in that case it is those who send the invitation who have the trouble of finding accommodation for the visitor. The invitation, however, must be made out in a special form, signed by the town administration and by the militia, and to obtain these signatures the person issuing the invitation must have some extra living space— usually an apartment with all the amenities.

At the end of 1967 I received an invitation from Czechoslovakia to take part in the celebrations of the sesquicentenary of the Moravian Museum in Brno. This museum has a section in honour of Mendel, who lived and worked as Superior of the monastery in Brno. Having had painful experience of failure to get travel approved through the Department, I decided this time to plan my trip as a private visit, all the more so, since the museum had a hostel. The Director of the Museum, Dr Orel, sent me a personal invitation, and I decided on this occasion to take a two-week holiday and make a trip to Czechoslovakia on the basis of the 1965 Agreement between our countries. However, the approval arrangements, which were begun three months before the sesquicentenary, were still not completed by the time the celebrations began in spring 1968, and the trip was off. Dr Orel was distressed at my failure, and in March I received a letter from him which I feel can be quoted here as evidence of the system of leaving the country which exists in Czechoslovakia.

Brno, 20 March, 1968

Dear Dr Medvedev,
    I was most distressed to learn that you will be unable to come to Czechoslovakia on the date of the sesquicentenary of the Moravian Museum. However, I hope that you will be able to come to our country in the near future, and I will renew your personal invitation and include an invitation confirmed by our authorities for a two-week visit in May or the summer of this year.
    Every citizen in our country has a passport with permanent permission to go to any socialist country. To go to the USSR it is necessary to have the permission of the Soviet authorities which can be

obtained within ten days, and this is all that is required for the trip. The same passport is also valid for trips to capitalist countries with the difference that in that case to obtain a visa it is necessary to have an invitation (of any kind).

I hope to see you soon.

With best wishes,

Yours sincerely,

V. OREL

For citizens of capitalist countries to come to the USSR, conditions are especially advantageous; this is because of our wish to obtain foreign convertible currency. Especially great advantages have been established for Finland. For a Finn to come to the USSR is much easier than for a Bulgarian. The balance of trade of the USSR with Finland is adverse. We spend greater sums in buying from that country than we earn by selling. Hence by opening our frontier in one direction for Finns to come in, we are trying to decrease the trade deficit and increase the balance of Finnish currency compared with Soviet.

Since there are no internal passports in Finland, the permitted free entry without visas of Finns into the regions of Leningrad, Vyborg, Petrozavodsk and into Estonia allows Finns to enter the USSR through the Finnish-Soviet frontier generally speaking without any documents. The number of the car, the number of passengers in the coach, and so on, are recorded. Instructions are issued to the inhabitants of Leningrad at their places of work to be on the watch so that people do not come to Leningrad in the guise of Finns, but who speak English, German and other languages, and to report suspects. Certain Finns come from Helsinki to the USSR on account of the 'dry' laws in Finland; they come into Leningrad or Vyborg simply to sit in restaurants with their friends.

But trips from the USSR to Finland are controlled by the rules that apply to capitalist countries. There are certain privileges only for inhabitants of the Baltic republics for short group trips (so as not to leave the Finnish steamers unemployed which have brought tourists from Finland to these republics). These privileges consist in being able to get the visits approved (with the necessary character references) within the Union Republics and not in Moscow.[1] But this 'indulgence' was introduced only after Finland had committed herself not to grant the 'right of political asylum' to citizens of the USSR, and she now extradites under guard visitors from the USSR who do not want to go back home

---

[1] But the limits on the total number of trips of Soviet citizens to Finland are very small. The Estonian SSR can send only 750 to 800 persons per year— *Author's note.*

to their own country. In this respect, Finland has adopted the practice previously established among the socialist countries.

It is well known that in Western Europe there exists a long-established completely free inter-state movement of citizens without any passports or visas. Citizens of one country are generally free to take up employment in the business enterprises of another. These traditions are many centuries old, they have been interrupted only during the various wars which have ravaged Europe. Emerich de Vattel in his classic work, *The Law of Nations*, first published in 1758 (the latest edition of this book in Russian translation came out in 1960) wrote that in Europe the right of free entry into any country and the right of free exit from it are extended to all. As examples of countries which to their own detriment and for incomprehensible reasons deny this right, de Vattel quoted Japan and China. In the eighteenth century he had no examples geographically closer at hand.

However, to go to the USSR from the countries of Western Europe it is necessary to obtain a passport. (By passport, in those countries, they mean only a foreign passport.) Not contenting myself with the information on the procedures for obtaining such passports given in the most recent editions of the *Encyclopaedia Britannica* and *Encyclopaedia Americana*, I discussed this matter with a number of colleagues when the opportunity arose. As a result of a complex study of the question, I have been able to establish that for a citizen of England, France or the USA to obtain a foreign passport is an elementary process, not as a rule requiring character references from one's Department nor decisions of Party or trade union, nor generally speaking, the permission of one's employers. The passport is issued by special services and departments of the Ministries of Foreign Affairs through tourist or passport agencies, and also by any embassy or consulate abroad. When he has got his passport the citizen normally need not tell his superior about it, especially if he plans to go abroad during his holidays. A passport is issued not for a single trip but for several years and is not surrendered on return. It can always be used again, since a passport automatically guarantees an exit visa. A passport issued to a husband may also be valid for trips with his family, no additional documents being needed for his wife and children.

In the USA according to the information in the *Encyclopaedia Americana*, a citizen who is going abroad has to notify the State Department what countries he is planning to visit. (At the present time Americans are forbidden to visit Cuba, the Chinese People's Republic, North Korea and North Vietnam.) The time an American spends abroad should not, according to the rules, exceed two years, after which it can be officially extended. For the British, French, Italians and other Europeans, this kind of restriction is considered as undemocratic, and they are not obliged to tell anyone their itinerary.

It should be pointed out that even the socialist countries of Eastern Europe (apart from the GDR), which formerly followed the USSR in imposing restrictions on their citizens going to the countries of Western Europe, in recent years have lifted many of these restrictions. Yugoslavia has established for her citizens complete freedom of entry and exit to and from neighbouring countries, and nowadays thousands of Yugoslav citizens in the border regions go to work in a neighbouring country, in Austria, Italy or Greece, returning home at the weekend. This only aids the prosperity of the country and its citizens by creating better opportunities of economic co-operation.

Of course, in other countries, too, certain restrictions are possible and do exist, and these are sometimes connected with political motives. By no means all countries are equivalent in the code of laws which govern this aspect of community life. We know that in a number of countries today the activity of the communist parties is forbidden (Indonesia, Portugal and certain South American and Arab States). More than once our newspapers have reported cases where a foreign passport has been refused to citizens of the USA. For a long time Paul Robeson could not obtain such a passport, nor could Winston, a leader of the American communists, and certain other progressive activists. Most of them finally achieved this through the Supreme Court of the United States. And although the Supreme Court in these cases normally gave a favourable decision, this undoubtedly occurred, according to the evidence of our press, under the pressure of world opinion. Serious restrictions on leaving the country, are being imposed at the present time by the Greek military junta on a number of progressive activists.

However, even for communists in the world at large, coming from the capitalist world to the socialist to take part in various meetings is, with certain exceptions, generally no problem. Soviet biologists, physiologists, geneticists, orientalists or agronomists have never enjoyed such freedom of contact with their foreign colleagues even for purposes and aims completely supported by the Soviet government as the communists of most countries in Western Europe and the world enjoy in their contact with their Soviet colleagues, for the purpose of changing and sometimes overthrowing their own governments. It is easy to assess this by the representation at the international meetings of the communist parties held in Moscow. Back in 1957, during the World Conference of Communist Parties in Moscow, to which leaders and members of the Central Committees of more than seventy Communist Parties came and then, with a few exceptions, lawfully dispersed home to their own countries, every Soviet citizen could clearly see that the exit and entry of even the most extreme opponents of the existing regimes presented no problem in most capitalist countries. To tell the truth, as far as I remember my own impressions at that time, I was not greatly astonished at the representation at the Conference. I understood that communists are resolute and determined people, especially in those countries where they are in opposition, and that they would get to Moscow even if it were by secret paths through neighbouring countries. As far as I remember, the greatest danger of this kind was that of the Portuguese communists and the delegation from Venezuela or some other South American Republic. All the other delegations, from the most imperialist countries, came and went by regular flights on international airlines, direct from their own capitals, where their sympathizers sent them off in style and then welcomed them home again, clearly directing the attention of the press to their leaders' trip to Moscow.

And then, later, in 1960, the new World Conference of Communist Parties had no difficulties over the non-arrival of any party. On that occasion delegates of the communists of around a hundred countries gathered in Moscow. To the Twenty-Third Congress of the CPSU in March and April 1966, delegates came from the Communist Parties of ninety countries. Almost a hundred Communist and Workers' Parties sent their delegations to the celebrations of the Fiftieth Anniversary of the Great October Revolution. And yet very few of these Parties constitute the ruling Party in their own countries. The majority are in sharp opposition, and they came to Moscow to a Conference where documents are signed which hold their own governments up to shame and call for the rapid removal of these governments. In the speeches published in the Moscow press the delegates of the Communist Party of, for example, France, demanded most sharply that an end should be put to the dictatorship of de Gaulle, a regime of personal power, and the delegates of the USA denounced the bloody crimes of American imperialism. And then they all went home by direct flights, to come back to the USSR next year for a conference, a festival, or simply a holiday in a state villa on the Black Sea coast.

I do not think that the governments of France, Italy, the USA or Australia were particularly pleased at the activities for which the representatives of the Communist Parties of these countries gathered in Moscow. And perhaps they would be glad to stop them! But, frankly speaking, they simply cannot do this legally. They have no real means of stopping the departure of a citizen of their country abroad, and this is not only due to the fact that the boundaries of these countries do not have an unbroken and impenetrable frontier guarded by technical and military means; nor because it is in effect an open frontier; but simply because the departure of a citizen of the country abroad is a right guaranteed by law and as such comes under the protection of the court whose decision is more powerful than the decision of the government. The Supreme Court, even in the USSR, in questions of the interpretation of laws and the rights of citizens takes priority over the government, but since there is no law stipulating the right of free exit of citizens of the USSR, since the Constitution takes no account of this possibility, any real interference by the court in the restrictions imposed by the government organs is, practically speaking, impossible. If a similar situation existed in the majority of countries, then no representative meetings of Communist Parties could ever gather in Moscow, there to dig the grave of bourgeois democracy.

5

Currency barriers to international co-operation

THERE is a very widespread opinion that at the bottom of all the principal difficulties of foreign travel for citizens of the USSR is the problem of currency—a shortage of the currency which must inevitably be spent in trips by Soviet citizens to capitalist countries. And it must be said that a currency barrier really does exist. But this barrier is to a great degree artificially created. It was invented precisely as a barrier, isolating the USSR from the rest of the world during the period of the abolition of the New Economic Policy, in 1929–30, after the campaign conducted by the OGPU withdrawing gold and foreign currency from the population, after the abolition of any real gold-backed guarantee of the Soviet monetary units (*chervontsy*). The *chervontsy* [10 rouble notes] which had served in 1923 as the basis for the currency reform, and had put an end to the inflationary disasters and economic anarchy, ended their life during the era of our history when the Leninist course of development of the economy, agriculture, culture and science came to an end, in the era of the 'great change', which was accompanied by unprecedentedly massive acts of violence, both in the towns and in the villages, liquidation of the 'kulaks' as a class, liquidation of the petty and middle bourgeoisie of the towns, repressions among the old intelligentsia and purging of the Party itself from all opposition and generally free-thinking elements in the beginning of Stalin's stern dictatorship or the era of the 'personality cult'.

But first of all it is necessary to consider what this currency barrier actually consists of and how it works.

In its classical form, international tourism has always been connected with currency problems, leading to the profit of one country and the loss to another. Let us take some typical examples; France and Italy, which are traditional and deservedly attractive countries for foreign tourism, have as a result an enormous gain in foreign currency and a positive tourist balance. Britain and the USA, which are less attractive to tourists (Britain as a highly industrialized country, the USA on account of its distance from Europe and the high cost of living for travellers, especially for touring motorists) have an adverse tourist balance and large annual losses of foreign currency, which 'sails away' abroad together with the American and English tourists who are availing themselves of the freedom of exit. From an economic point of view, these countries would have an interest in a certain restriction of the departure of their citizens abroad, in the introduction of limits in some degree similar to the limits of man currency-days which Soviet departments receive. However, the conflict between civil rights and the economy in this case is resolved in these countries in favour of civil rights, if we ignore propaganda appeals to the citizens of these countries to restrict their spending abroad. But maybe for the USSR, a country which has not reached the economic level of the USA and England, it is really more correct to resolve this question not from the point of view of civil rights but from the point of view of the economy? This is the very important question of principle of the entire problem analysed in this work, and a great deal depends on its answer. If the abolition of the system of discrimination and restriction of international links for the citizens of our country, the simplification of the difficulties connected with going abroad, will as a final result be to the economic detriment of our country, will worsen the life of our people when everything is taken into account, then evidently the questions raised in our work should be put off to be reconsidered in some ten or fifteen years' time, when the prosperity of our people will have increased immeasurably and international tourism and travel will have become a *necessity* of life, a necessity to be satisfied only after the other basic necessities of society and its members have been satisfied. As we shall see in one of the following sections, in most countries of Europe, a holiday abroad has already become a necessity for the broad mass of citizens.

However, in passing on to consider the currency problems of international tourism in the USSR, it must be noted that here every aspect of these problems turns out to be quite different and to have an entirely different basis.

In the ordinary conventional form in which the currency problem of international tourism applies in Britain, the USA, Belgium, the Federal German Republic and other industrial countries with a high economic level of the population but an adverse tourist balance, the currency problem does not even arise for the USSR. With its wealth of natural resources, territory, forests, lakes, seas, hunting, fishing, variety of climatic zones, mountains, mighty rivers, traditions of culture, monuments

of antiquity and art, and its intermediate position on the way between West and East, *the tourist balance of the USSR past, present and
in the future for ever and ever, can only be positive.* If the business were
organized in the *normal* way more people would always come to us from
Europe and Asia than the number of citizens of our country who
would go abroad as tourists if the frontier were completely open. This
is elementary, and requires no special proof. It is clear to everyone.

But perhaps by restricting the exit of our own citizens and encouraging
the visits of foreigners, we are aiming at an even greater economic
advantage? Unfortunately this is by no means true. Tourism, like every
serious business of an international nature, can never be quite spon-
taneous. It must be organized. It needs routes, car camping sites, hotels,
guide-books, literature, guides, interpreters, restaurants, it needs a
special expert tourist service. Even the most apparently 'wild' international motor touring cannot escape from control and organization,
especially at the present time when a considerable part of the territory
of any country is closed to entry, not only by foreigners, but even by its
own citizens. A tourist should know, therefore, even if he is running
'wild' which road he may follow and which not, where he can take photographs, and where not, where he is permitted to camp for the night, and
so on. All this service is provided by specialized tourist firms, and
independently of whether the tourist has bought his tour as a package or
not, he must pay for individual forms of the service. Hence, without
tourist firms and agencies, international tourism could not continue on
its present scale, it would break down into chaos and vagrancy. There
are now more than ten thousand of these firms, large and small; in Italy
alone there are more than a thousand. And in the USSR there is one
such firm, very large and diversified, Intourist, which holds a complete
monopoly in international tourism in our country.

Thus we come to the very important question of the reasons for the
development of tourism by our Soviet citizens which began in 1956. At
that time it became clear that tourism in the modern world is a most
important article for attracting foreign currency, it is a branch of industry
which we were obliged to develop—all the more so, since greater and
greater numbers of people from abroad wanted to come and visit us. It
was clear that for the USSR too, tourism from outside was exceptionally
advantageous to the economy. The whole world had started to travel,
and we could no longer keep our frontier closed to widespread tourism
from other countries without serious loss of prestige. It was necessary
to abolish the external political and financial barrier to foreigners coming

to the USSR, not on business, not by invitation, but at their own desire. The external financial barrier, about which I shall have more to say, further consisted of the incredibly high cost of a trip to the USSR for a foreigner, created by the absolutely arbitrary rate of exchange of the rouble up to 1956. But developing tourism from abroad to the USSR would only be possible on a basis of reciprocity, on the basis of business agreements with foreign tourist firms. Here there must be a principle of reciprocity. This is a strict international rule. The same principle exists for example, in the setting up of international airlines. If Aeroflot wants to establish an international through-route to India, Pakistan and Japan (it is cheaper and quicker for Europeans to fly to Asia via the USSR) which will be exceptionally advantageous for it, it can only do so by making agreements with the airline companies of these countries, by which half the flights must be operated by the aircraft of these countries. In other words half the profits from running these routes, a large part of which lies over the USSR, must go to the foreign partners of Aeroflot. No one will co-operate with Aeroflot on any other conditions.

The same situation exists in international tourism. Foreign tourist firms will serve their citizens in organizing tourist trips to the USSR and will allow Intourist to have representatives and branches within their own countries only if Intourist guarantees that they shall serve Soviet tourists in these countries. For example, Intourist serves Czechoslovak tourists in the USSR but grants the Czechoslovak firm, Čedok (also a monopoly), the right to serve Soviet tourists in the Czechoslovak Socialist Republic. Čedok guarantees Intourist its earnings from Czechoslovak tourists only if Intourist guarantees Čedok the earnings from Soviet tourists. The same kind of agreements are necessary with firms in capitalist countries. Here, of course, it is not necessary to make any exchange of tourists in equivalent numbers, so many there, and exactly the same number in return. This is impossible in most cases for a number of reasons. But if we were to cut out entirely or substantially reduce organized visits of citizens of the USSR as tourists to countries with which such agreements exist we should be unable to avoid reducing the amount of reverse tourism. Thus we can collect foreign currency as a result of external tourism only if some part of it, evidently not less than half, goes back again in the form of Soviet tourism to those countries. I will not vouch for the accuracy of the proportion of 'sharing' of earnings, it may be different when different countries are partners. *But it is quite clear that the USSR can increase its currency earnings, can expand the influx of foreign currency through this channel, not by reducing the number of trips* of Soviet citizens abroad, with a simultaneous increase in the number of visits of foreign citizens to the USSR, but only by increasing the total number of exchange journeys, with the inevitable positive balance in its favour.

We see, then, that to explain the restrictions limiting the number of Soviet citizens going abroad especially to countries with freely convertible currency, as a necessity to save currency spent on paying foreign firms for the trip (in exchange, of course, for payment for the trip by the tourists themselves in roubles) is a mere excuse. *In practical terms, we are arbitrarily limiting reciprocal tourism and for completely different, evidently prejudiced political considerations, and are depriving our country of a most important and very considerable source of earning foreign currency.*

In the course of the last fifteen years, with the steady expansion of technological and economic links with other states, with the increasing amount of purchases of the means of production and necessities from abroad, and, which is most unusual, the basic food products (wheat, butter, meat, temperate climate fruits) which are bought in large quantities in the capitalist countries, the Soviet Union's need for foreign currency has constantly been increasing. It is possible to quote many examples of unreasonable waste of currency, not only in the national economy, but also in science. An enormous amount of equipment purchased from abroad is lying about in establishments and institutes without proper use and technical servicing, or else is not used due to the lack of spare parts. But this is a completely different problem. Even with the most sensible and rigid economy of the currency and gold reserves of the country, with a careful analysis of the advisability of various purchases from abroad, it is still quite evident that scientific and technological integration in the modern world means that the USSR must spend more and more of its currency reserves every year. Therefore, a supply of currency must be ensured by all possible means. The experience of many countries shows that tourism is an important item in the currency balance. Even so economically developed a country as France relies on foreign tourism for *half* of all her foreign currency earnings. As for small countries, such as Jordan, Portugal or Norway, or even large ones which are not very industrialized but are geographically attractive, in some years foreign tourism accounts for some 80 to 90 per cent of all their currency earnings. The number of tourists from abroad going to Norway in 1967 was almost equal to the number of inhabitants of the country, and was twice as great as the number of foreign tourists visiting the USSR (according to the data of the *Bulletin of Tourist Information*).

It is natural that sooner or later the Soviet Union would have to abolish the very expensive and burdensome isolation of the country from the outside world, which had been created under Stalin. The isolation of the USSR from the outside world was in no way connected with any threat from without, initially as we have noted it was created in 1929 to 1930. Up to 1929, travelling abroad for citizens of the USSR was not limited by a system of political and legal prohibitions. Tourism to the USSR was relatively flourishing, and at that time throughout the world tourism was limited to the upper bourgeois classes of society. Only rich people spent their holidays in travelling abroad. We all remember the psychology of international tourism of that time by the children's rhyme:

> Mr Twister was a minister,
> Mr Twister was a millionaire,
> He owned factories, houses, steamers,
> He went round the world for a change of air.

In the Soviet Union the top prize in the lottery at that time was not a car but a round-the-world trip.

In 1929 this situation changed sharply. Since travelling abroad at that time was of interest only to the more prosperous classes of society, which just then were being abolished, the liquidation of the right to go abroad, with simultaneous restriction of the entry of various Mr Twisters from abroad, passed unnoticed. At the same time a very strict system of selection of candidates for government trips abroad was introduced. This system followed upon the speech of Sergo Ordzhonikidze of 3 July 1930, at the Sixteenth Congress of the All-Union Communist Party (Bolsheviks). Ordzhonikidze in his speech to the Congress dealt very sharply with the question of the large number of workers on trade and diplomatic missions abroad who did not return; he pointed out that the number of 'non-returners', almost a quarter of whom were members of the Party, was growing yearly, from 26 persons in 1927 to 43 in the first half of 1930 alone (see stenographic transcript of the Sixteenth Congress of the All-Union Communist Party (Bolsheviks) Gosizdat, 1930). These figures appalled the Congress. From the Presidium and from the auditorium Ordzhonikidze's speech was interrupted by comments. 'We must send abroad only workers from the factory bench!' shrieked Comrade Zemlyachka, and the system of selecting candidates for working abroad was revoked.

The isolation continually increased with the years, just as the 'personality cult' increased. And this isolation was especially detrimental from an economic point of view. The losses were not only of an indirect nature (not taking advantage of opportunities of earning) but direct as well. The isolation of so enormous a state from the outside world was an incredibly expensive business. No state has ever borne so great an economic burden as the Soviet Union did and even today still does, in protecting its population from the outside world with a total guard of its frontiers and technical means of protecting the 'ether' from foreign broadcasts, postal 'customs', censorship and a mass of other means and devices. And one of the principal means of isolation, which also entails a great loss to the exchequer, was Stalin's invention of the 'currency barrier', which worked in both directions. When Khrushchev was faced with currency problems he first of all tried to change the nature of the 'currency barrier' by turning it into a 'currency valve' which could be entered from without but not from within. But the 'valve' system did not prove effective. From this time there began a slow and at first experimental *reciprocal* tourism. But this process is still in its very early stages, and it is not as yet growing steadily.

What was Stalin's 'currency barrier' and how did it work? I am no financial expert or economist, but I hope that the facts and information which I shall give below represent the real situation, past and present. I shall not consider the pre-war period, but shall examine the situation created by the monetary reform of 1947. Before the war the USSR was the only socialist country in the world, and hence the measures of isolation, which were of course economically very detrimental and politically harmful, nevertheless had some psychological foundation and were based on certain real prejudices. After the war, when the USSR became the centre of a group of socialist countries, the centre of world politics, one of the founders of the United Nations, and one of the Big Five great powers, the psychological foundation of international isolation disappeared.

In 1947, when the long overdue monetary reform was carried out, a rigid but absolutely unreal gold standard was established for the Soviet rouble. One gramme of gold cost, on the official rate of exchange, four roubles. Accordingly, one dollar was equivalent to four roubles. At the same time, even the official sale of gold objects to the population in the state trade (rings, brooches, watch-cases, etc.) estimated one gramme of gold at 70 to 80 roubles, twenty times higher than the official gold standard. The rate of exchange with other hard currencies was determined in relation to the dollar. The rates of exchange for the currencies of the People's Democracies were somewhat better, but still sharply biased in favour of the rouble.

At the same time the purchasing power of the dollar and the four roubles which corresponded to it according to the rate of exchange naturally differed sharply in favour of the dollar. Since no one within the USSR could buy anything for a dollar no one noticed this difference, but it really did exist. This rate of exchange was very actively used for the counter-propaganda journals *British Unionist* and *America* which at that time were still freely circulating in Moscow (their publication ceased in 1949). They often compared prices in roubles, dollars and pounds and showed that various articles in the USA and England were many times cheaper than in the USSR.

As far as international trade was concerned, this highly unreal rate of exchange of the rouble against foreign currencies created a special situation. It was impossible to make any calculations in roubles. As a result of this there at once appeared two Soviet currencies, ordinary roubles, and gold (non-currency) roubles. Accordingly on all export-import goods, there appeared two prices, in roubles and in non-currency roubles. Any item, X (flour, cloth, a suit, petroleum, paper, etc.) could cost a certain number of units, for example, 1,200 ordinary roubles or 95 gold non-currency roubles. The first price was for the internal market, the second for the international market. But the gold, non-currency roubles, were entirely symbolic, they were not represented by any special monetary token. But in such a situation a foreigner who came to the USSR when he changed his dollars or pounds into roubles obtained not the symbolic gold roubles, but ordinary rouble notes with which Soviet citizens pay for goods in shops. It was a remarkable picture. If the foreigner had wanted to buy some items of Soviet manufacture back home in his own country, he might pay for it, say, a hundred dollars. But if he wanted to make the same purchase when he came to the USSR, he would have to pay some ten to fifteen times more for it. In other countries goods are always cheaper where they are manufactured, but in this case the situation was entirely the reverse and to a very considerable degree.

As a result of this system a trip to the USSR for tourists and businessmen was several times dearer than to any other country. A visit to the USSR was possible for a foreigner, but he would have to be a very rich man. At the same time it was impossible to hold any serious international meeting, conference or congress in the USSR. A trip to our country was out of the question for scientists. And if the Academy of Sciences or some other body had decided to hold some meeting on an international basis then it would have been necessary for the USSR to pay all the expenses of the foreigners invited. International co-operation became very unprofitable for the country. Nowadays international congresses and conferences held in the USSR by international associations bring the Soviet Union large currency earnings and the journeys of foreign scientists to the USSR are arranged through Intourist. But for many years after 1947 enormous sums of money had to be planned for and allocated to the bodies concerned to pay for foreigners who came to the various conferences which were sometimes held in the USSR to maintain prestige. The arbitrary rate of exchange of the rouble aroused constant criticism from foreigners, but nevertheless it existed and acted as a *currency barrier* hindering any considerable ingress of foreign citizens, let alone tourists, into the USSR. This barrier kept foreigners outside the frontiers of the USSR better than any 'iron curtain'.

But there was also a 'currency barrier' in the opposite direction. It seriously hindered Soviet citizens from going abroad, but for an entirely different reason. Foreigners considered the existing rate of exchange of the rouble as extortionate. Nevertheless a citizen of the USSR was forced to change his roubles into dollars or pounds at the official rate when he had to go abroad. But this operation was greatly to the disadvantage of our State. In exchange for four paper roubles, the citizen of the USSR should have received from the Ministry of Finance through the State Bank of the USSR, one real dollar. A two weeks' travelling allowance which in the USSR would have negligible real value was turned into a sum with enormous purchasing power, being multiplied by ten to twenty times after the roubles were changed into foreign currency, and naturally the State Bank of the USSR did not want to sell foreign currency to Soviet citizens at so low a price, although it was the rate of exchange that it itself had set. This led to the strictest limitation of all such operations and to an outcry of the need of saving currency—and perhaps even to some understanding on the part of our financial experts! However expensive and unprofitable it was for a foreign citizen to visit the USSR, it was just as expensive for the Soviet Union to have a Soviet citizen go abroad. But for the citizen himself it was very, very advantageous, and interest in getting official short-term postings abroad rapidly increased. Thus it is evident that the 'currency barrier', which was economically damaging to the interests of the State, was created specially to put a brake on the exchange of tourists and citizens. In international trade the arbitrary rate of exchange of the rouble gave our country absolutely no advantages or profit at all. All the same it was necessary to calculate all prices for goods bought in gold or in dollars, and no one sold us anything for roubles. Moreover, the artificial rate of exchange led to the complete undermining of trust in the rouble on the international market. Indeed in 1950, when Mao Tse-tung signed an agreement in Moscow for credit for China, he asked for this credit in dollars, although the matter concerned the delivery of Soviet goods on credit. China was granted a very modest credit of 300 million dollars, although we did not have many of them. But to obtain even a multi-million credit in roubles was of no advantage to China, for it would have had to be repaid in Chinese goods whose value was calculated on the official rate of exchange. By setting the value of our rouble too high we suffered incalculable economic losses, and firmly isolated Soviet society by means of currency. Moreover Stalin considered that there was enough gold in the country to purchase the goods abroad that the state needed. All the same the country's gold reserves, the size of which is normally secret, could not have been considerable at that time. The war demanded great expenditure of currency. Large quantities of gold were consumed in purchasing arms from the USA and Britain. During the war the USA doubled its gold reserves, principally on account of the gold received from the Soviet Union.

But such a situation could not go on for ever. It was impossible to deprive the country of simple and easily accessible currency earnings just to satisfy political considerations, all the more since the country was continually needing more and more currency. When, after the death of Stalin, it became apparent that we were lagging behind many countries in the technology of many different branches of industry, a course of technological reconstruction was undertaken, and the leading technological achievements of other countries were introduced into the Soviet economy. It was necessary to buy from abroad a number of installations and plants for chemical technology, synthetic textiles, light industry, etc., machine parts and instruments and even large consignments of consumer goods. Tourism, being the most rapid and simple means of obtaining foreign currency, at once attracted attention.

However, not a single tourist firm was willing to make contracts with Intourist on the basis of this unfair rate of exchange of the rouble. Consequently, as was to be expected, the Soviet side carried out an unofficial devaluation of the rouble with respect to foreign currencies. In 1956 the State Bank of the USSR adopted a special 'tourist rate of exchange' of the rouble. In *Izvestiya*, which periodically prints a table of the rate of exchange of the rouble with the main currencies of the world, the old rate still held good, four roubles to a dollar, but for foreign citizens coming to the USSR the State Bank changed one dollar into ten roubles. A similar tourist rate of exchange was established for the other 'hard' foreign currencies. A somewhat smaller devaluation of the rouble against the currencies of the socialist countries was also introduced. But the reverse exchange of roubles into foreign currency for Soviet citizens going abroad remained as before, although it was decided to change considerably smaller sums for Soviet tourists and those on official missions. Thus the higher authorities tried to create a 'valve' system encouraging entry but not exit.

If before there existed a double position of the rouble against foreign currencies, now, with the introduction of the 'tourist rate of exchange', it became a triple one. The 'tourist rate of exchange' did not, however, correspond exactly with international prices, it was not completely fair. The exchange of currency according to this rate of exchange could only take place through Intourist, a foreigner who merely went to the State Bank of the USSR to change his dollars would still receive four roubles for a dollar. Complete confusion arose. If, for example, a foreigner bought a trip to the USSR from a tourist firm in his own country, let us say, for dollars, then one dinner would, by this calculation, cost roughly one dollar. But he could only get this for coupons in special Intourist restaurants. The same dinner, at the 'tourist' rate of exchange, after he had changed some of his dollars in the USSR (supposing there were no Intourist restaurant near at hand, and he needed one) would now cost him three dollars. But if he had no time to change his money at the 'tourist rate', and was getting ever hungrier, and only the State Bank or one of its branches were handy where dollars are changed according to the rate published in *Izvestiya*, then the self-same dinner would cost seven and a half dollars, a phenomenal sum in any European country (we are speaking here of an ordinary, everyday dinner). Such a system could not, of course, continue for very long. An official and considerable devaluation of the rouble was necessary. But for reasons of prestige it was decided not to do this, since devaluation is always taken to mean economic insolvency. Finally in 1961 a solution occurred to some financial genius. He devised the idea of carrying out devaluation under the disguise of revaluing the rouble. Khrushchev rapidly grasped the value of the proposal and carried out a new currency reform, all the more willingly since this provided an opportunity of a gradual slight increase in the prices of certain goods. The mechanism of the reform was simple. The rouble was devalued two-and-a-half times, that is, to approximately the tourist rate. But at the same time the rouble was revalued internally, all old roubles were replaced by new roubles in the ratio of one new to ten old, and all prices fell to a tenth. Before, one dollar was equivalent to four roubles and one gramme of gold also cost four roubles. Now one dollar on the official rate of exchange was equivalent to 90 kopeks but a gramme of gold also cost 90 kopeks. The newspapers rightly commented on the increase in the gold 'content' of the rouble, previously one rouble had been equivalent to 0.25 grammes of gold, but from 1961 one rouble was equivalent to 1.1 grammes of gold. But no one paid any special attention to the fact that this was a completely different rouble, and that the wages of all citizens of the USSR had been reduced to a tenth. This revaluation also had another purpose. After the symbolic strengthening of the gold reserves, one-tenth of the amount of paper money would be needed in circulation. In spite of the 10 to 1 change of money value there was a new issue of banknotes by the State Bank of the USSR, starting with the ten-rouble note. But for less than ten roubles, the monetary symbols were still treasury notes not backed by gold. The same had been the case before the monetary reform, except that the new ten roubles corresponded to the old hundred roubles. The old fifty, thirty and ten roubles, which were formerly banknotes of the State Bank, became treasury notes.

But on the whole this whole reform was economically very useful and necessary, and it exerted and still exerts a favourable influence on the economics of the country. The devaluation of Soviet money in relation to foreign currency was also useful. It simplified tourism to the USSR, and, what is still more important, it lowered the currency barrier for Soviet citizens going abroad. Each individual person, going abroad on an official mission or as a tourist, received for the same sum in roubles a much smaller sum of foreign currency and for him the price of the trip increased. But for the same total sum of currency almost twice as many Soviet citizens could go abroad.

But the new rate of exchange turned out not to be quite fair and did not truly represent the comparative purchasing power of various currencies. One need only add that in 1964, when the state had had to expend large sums of gold to buy wheat in Canada, Australia, New Zealand, the USA and the Federal German Republic to avoid a famine after the failure of the harvest in 1963, it began to buy gold and gold objects from the population at special purchasing centres. The price for the purchased gold was around four to five roubles per gramme, that is, 400 per cent above the official rate of exchange.

The 'currency barrier' had decreased, but it still remained and was once again two-way. A trip to the USSR for foreign citizens was still too expensive for pleasure, especially for the middle ranks of society. At the same time energetic measures were being taken in all countries to encourage international tourism. But the currency earnings of Intourist remained low, and the 'plans' for accumulating currency remained unfulfilled year after year. It became evident that a new devaluation of the rouble against foreign currencies was inevitable, since the former double position of the rouble (simple roubles and non-currency, 'gold' roubles) had been preserved.

At the beginning of 1965 this devaluation was carried out, but once again a 'tourist rate of exchange' was unofficially introduced at the same time. The same device of the 'valve' was used to attract foreign tourists to the USSR without an equivalent increase of Soviet tourism abroad. The new devaluation was effected by putting into circulation a special form of currency called 'certificates'. In Moscow and in other large towns and resort towns accessible to foreign tourists, there were special shops and kiosks of the Berezka firm and the Department of External Trade and Consignment in which goods of Soviet and imported manufacture were sold for foreign hard currency (dollars, pounds, West German marks, guilders, kroner, etc.) and for certificates of the Department of External Trade and Dispatch and cheques of the External Trading Bank of the USSR at very reduced 'privileged' prices. The old foreign trade emporia of the New Economic Policy had returned in strength. (In Ukraine 'Berezka' [birch] operates under the name 'Kashtan' [chestnut].) In Moscow there is a two-storey departmental Berezka store, a foreign currency grocery store, more than ten large specialized shops and foreign currency restaurants in hotels, and three night bars in the Ukraina, Natsional and Metropol.

The point of this new arrangement was that the prices in these shops were a third to a fifth of that in normal trade for ordinary Soviet citizens, and the quality and range of goods and the quality of service was much better. Now a foreigner coming to the USSR need not exchange his money at the official detrimental rate of exchange, but can spend it without changing it at all, making use of the privileged prices, which in a number of cases are even lower than those which, due to various duties, exist in his own country. Nowadays certain items can generally only be bought in Moscow for foreign currency and the 'certificates' of the Department of External Trade and Consignment. This applies even to such traditional Russian goods as black and red caviar.

After 1965 life for foreigners in the USSR became three or four times cheaper than it had been before, and this undoubtedly stimulated foreign tourism to the USSR. The new Berezka shops made a trip to the USSR even more advantageous. Caviar can be bought in Moscow four or five times cheaper than in London, cameras are likewise two or three times cheaper, even Scotch whisky is half as dear in Moscow as it is in Scotland, where the prices of alcohol are very high due to special duties which apply only within Great Britain.

But the Berezka firms and the Department of External Trade and Consignment, which opened up all this trade into the USSR, also performed another very important function, which helped to save currency: they brought back to the USSR part of the salaries in foreign currency of citizens of the USSR working abroad.

At the present time many thousands of Soviet citizens work abroad carrying out various projects under agreement. Thousands of people, engineers, excavators, concrete-experts, and other workers are labouring on construction of the Aswan dam in the United Arab Republic. Hundreds of specialists and workers are building a metallurgical complex in India. Hundreds and thousands of technological specialists are working in Iraq, Syria, Burma, Algeria and in the African countries. Many Soviet experts have particular posts in UNESCO, IAEA, in the UN and in various other international organizations. Hundreds of correspondents, persons on business missions and trainees are working in various countries. Diplomats, workers in foreign trade missions, in airlines and sailors with international shipping lines all receive their pay in foreign currency. Previously all this currency was spent abroad in acquiring various goods and came home in the form of suitcases full of various foreign objects. There was a rule by which any foreign currency left unspent had all to be handed over, without compensation, when one returned home. Accordingly everyone tried to have no foreign currency left.

Now the position has changed. It was decided to let these 'workers abroad' have their currency and bring it back to the USSR. Instead of being surrendered, it is changed into certificates in the USSR or in the embassies, or else is used without changing it in the foreign currency shops. Goods are sold in the USSR for these certificates at international prices, or often even lower, which makes it more advantageous to buy the goods at home than to bring them back, say, from Belgium or the USA, and pay excess baggage.

Moreover, under this system of using foreign currency, the Soviet 'workers abroad' do not have to pay customs duty, which is very high for certain goods (for example, cars). They can also buy goods which they could not formerly have bought because it was impossible to bring them home (furniture) or even flats (the price of a square metre of space is some three or four times cheaper in foreign currency than in roubles).

From the economic point of view, this trade, of course, brings certain advantages, at all events it increases the state's currency earnings. But from the moral point of view, its closed character and the unusually low prices of goods in short supply do harm of an ideological nature. The inflation of the prices for many goods in normal trade and the imperfect nature of the Soviet currency system is becoming evident to everyone who is familiar with certificate trading. Moreover the very existence of 'smart' closed shops arouses resentment in those who cannot go to those shops. And information on foreign-currency-certificate trading is gradually becoming known to a wide circle of people. In the hotels handouts from Berezka and the Department of External Trade and Consignment and its Information Bulletins lie on the tables, addressed to foreigners (in English, German and other languages) and also to Soviet 'workers abroad' (in Russian). In many of these handouts prices are quoted in certificate roubles or dollars. A Volga automobile costs 1,130 certificate roubles (on the ordinary market it costs 5,600 roubles), a Moskvich automobile costs 880 certificate roubles (one would have to pay 4,500 ordinary roubles), a suit which would cost 130 roubles through the normal trade network sells for a fifth of the price in certificates, a Bologna waterproof costs 7 certificate roubles and 60 ordinary ones (this difference is made much use of by foreign students for speculation purposes), radios, television sets, cameras and so on all sell at a third to a quarter of the cost in certificates. In Moscow there are now more than twenty such shops and kiosks. The advertising handouts for goods are produced in a Western format, polite, informative and attractively got up.

I have in front of me one of the attractive illustrated Bulletins of the Department of External Trade and Consignment, no. 14. I read:

> The Department of External Trade and Consignment wishes to draw to the notice of all Soviet 'workers abroad' that at the Berezka furniture store in Moscow (20, 1812 Street) there is a large selection of foreign and Russian furniture, including items from Czechoslovakia, the German Democratic Republic, Bulgaria, Poland, Hungary and Finland. In addition to furniture from these countries, at present the shop has fairly large quantities of English beds, divan beds and armchairs, from the English firm Slumberland. This firm is especially well-known for its beds, which are comfortable and long-lasting. . . .

It then goes on to give a detailed description of the construction of the beds and their prices. Addresses of Berezka furniture stores in other towns are also given.

And then, in large type, comes the slogan:

GET CERTIFICATES OF THE DEPARTMENT OF EXTERNAL TRADE AND CONSIGNMENT.
With these certificates you can buy the goods you want at keen prices in shops that have been especially opened in the USSR and are especially well supplied.
USE THE SERVICES OF OUR FIRM.
IT IS CONVENIENT AND PROFITABLE.

These advertisements are distributed through the embassies and Intourist and are issued to those going abroad, in vast quantities, for the most diverse goods, groceries, electrical equipment, television sets, clothing, etc., etc.

But the 'workers abroad' are not equal in the face of this trade, nor are all foreign currencies of equal value. The 'information bulletins' advertising all kinds of transistors, tape-recorders and automobiles state:

'*These are sold for certificates without distinguishing bands.*' What does this mean?

Certificates without bands are issued for freely convertible (hard) currencies, dollars, pounds, guilders, francs, etc. The currencies of economically less developed countries (United Arab Republic, Iceland, Finland, India, etc.) with a capitalist economy are changed for certificates with a *yellow* band. Certificates with such bands cannot be used in most shops of the Department of Foreign Trade and Dispatch. Certificates with a *blue* band are given in exchange for the currencies of the European socialist countries, Polish zloty, Czechoslovak crowns, etc. The blue band is the poorest, with it you can go to only two shops and even there you have to stand in a queue and can only buy articles of clothing. For yellow certificates you can also buy technical goods, but of Soviet manufacture only, and not imported ones.

The certificate-currency shops keep the blinds of their windows down—why should ordinary citizens see such tempting goods, which anywhere else they would have to queue for all night, or wait for on a list for many weeks, or never even encounter at all? On the big glass windows of the shops are blinds with the name, Berezka, and notices in foreign languages. At the doors there are commissionaires. The commissionaire casts a well-trained eye over anyone who comes to the door.

Foreigners he recognises at once and throws wide the doors in a most affable manner. But Soviet citizens get a very different reception.

'You there! Have you any currency?'

'No.'

'Then move along there. Don't block the doorway!' And he bars the way unceremoniously.

'You've got certificates? Show them! With a yellow band! . . . No yellows and blues here, only plain ones. Yellows must go to Trade Union Street!'

You go to such a shop on Lenin Prospect near the Moskva Departmental store taking a dime from your son's collection. You are asked the standard question: 'Have you any currency?' Without wasting any words you show the guard a dime instead of a pass and he throws wide the doors in a most affable manner. There are no queues, only pleasant and courteous salesmen and a full range of all goods. It is mainly the wives of 'workers abroad' and foreigners who are shopping there.

Thus a way to attract foreigners unilaterally without a new devaluation of the rouble was found. It is not hard to calculate that after the introduction in the USSR of legal foreign-currency state trading at reduced prices, the purchasing power of foreign convertible currencies has risen nine to ten times since 1947. And this is calculated in respect of Soviet currency, without taking into account certain falls in prices in the period 1948 to 1953, which were reflected equally in the purchasing power of both Russian and foreign currencies.

Thus the currency barrier has been practically abolished for foreigners but this barrier remains for Soviet citizens, it is preserved in spite of its obvious economic harm, in spite of the fact that it puts 'workers abroad' in a privileged economic position in comparison with the rest of the population. Recently however, these privileges have been reduced, but not by the normal means of putting the currency exchange in order, but by the introduction of a 'currency quitrent'. Now all 'workers abroad' who receive their pay by agreement with foreign firms, through international organizations, or from organizations which have invited them, etc., do not have the right to keep more than eight to eleven dollars per day, excluding accommodation. The rest must be surrendered without compensation either to the embassy or on their return. And if they do not surrender it, they have to pay a fine of ten times the sum in Soviet roubles.

All this exceptionally complex system, it seems to me, has got itself into a blind alley and requires other solutions. The most sensible of them would be to lower the artificially raised prices on many goods and to halve the present value of the rouble (taking into account that the prices of foodstuffs in the USSR are at the average European level, but that certain forms of services, transport, communications, flats, are lower than the European and American levels). It would be reasonable and politically very valuable to make Soviet money into a hard world currency, freely convertible into any other basic currency. Today it is forbidden to take the Soviet rouble abroad, and all Soviet external trade is based on the state reserves of gold and foreign currency. We are feeding an enormous quantity of gold into the world market, thus strengthening the financial system of capitalism. It is not difficult to calculate that if, over the last five years alone, Soviet gold had not been flowing onto the capitalist market, the dollar would not have kept its value in the recent financial crisis. The devaluation of the dollar was inevitable after the gold reserve of the USA fell to 10,000 million dollars. It had fallen from 18,000 million dollars to 11,000 million, and then the fall in the gold reserve ceased. But how much of the 11,000 million was former Soviet gold? According to an article in the *US News and World Report*, published in New York, which was reprinted in *Za Rubezhom* (23–29 February 1968), in 1965, 500 million dollars of Soviet gold came on to the London gold market for sale to capitalist countries, almost a quarter of all the gold going into the reserves of the capitalist countries in that year. In 1963 and 1964 still more Soviet gold was sold on the London market, gold which Khrushchev was feverishly pouring into the capitalist world to hide with purchased grain the painful results of his adventures in agriculture. At the end of 1963 in just a few days, 400 metric tons of Soviet gold were sold in London (see article 'Gold Movements in the World', *Za Rubezhom*, no. 6, 1966). But the annual sale of gold on the London market is 730 metric tons and this is three-quarters of the world sale of gold. In all, over the five years from 1961 to 1965 the USSR sold about 2,500 metric tons of gold on the international capitalist market. In 1966 the USSR did not sell gold on the world market, evidently there was not much left in the gold reserves of the country, the size of which nobody knows. But from the fact that in 1966 certain treasures from the former Tsarist treasury in the Armoury and the Hermitage were sold, one may conclude that these reserves are not bottomless in spite of energetic output. (According to the estimates of Western experts the mean annual output of gold of the USSR equals 200 metric tons.)

The economic advantages to an industrially developed country of making its currency convertible are very great. In this case not only gold. but also its own currency, backed by goods, can be used for purchases abroad. At present the USSR purchases abroad only with gold and foreign currency, and this sharply restricts our international opportunities, forces us to opt out of many international projects, increases our debts in international payments (even our dues to the United Nations), sharply reduces the number of trips Soviet citizens can make abroad and our opportunities of helping other countries, and, in general, our political and economic activities on an international scale. In order to have a convertible currency it is not necessary for it to be all backed by gold reserves, but only, say, a quarter or less of the mass of money in circulation. The total volume of all the world operations per year for a gold reserve of 10,000 million dollars may amount to tens of thousands of millions of dollars. The USA operates on the world market with its own dollars, which it also uses within the country. They operate in tens of thousands of millions of dollars. I repeat that I am not a financial expert and I may be talking nonsense. But it is very strange to me, that we, a gold-producing, economically developed, great country also *mainly operate on the world market in dollars*—and partly in English pounds—in dollars of American origin. Old, poor Russia under the Tsars had its own world currency with a smaller gold reserve, or at all events a smaller output of gold. The USSR procures American and English currency for its own economy in every way it can. And all this is due to the artificially created currency barrier, to the unreal rate of exchange of the rouble, at which no country with a hard currency will agree to exchange roubles.

The United States, which has expended an enormous amount of its currency abroad for political and economic aims necessary to it, and which has permitted the adventurist 'escalation' of the war in Vietnam, as a result has increased the expenditure of its currency to such considerable amounts, that even in that country with its exceptionally developed economy, financial difficulties have arisen. Over many years the USA has poured out tens of thousands of millions of dollars abroad in maintaining military bases, armies in Europe and Asia, military aid, etc. The war in Vietnam alone takes about 20,000 million dollars per year, of which several thousand million go abroad, not in the form of equipment but as paper currency. As a result, the USA now finds itself in a difficult position and is taking measures to limit the flow of its currency abroad, including a 25 per cent reduction in the funds for financing scientists abroad, and a special tax on foreign tourism which increases the cost of a trip to Europe (see *Science*, vol. 159, no. 3819, page 1080, 1968). But in the USA this situation has arisen due to an excess of America's own currency, US dollars, in world circulation. But is it really not strange, that the USSR which bases its international co-operation and the tourism of its citizens to capitalist countries on the convertible currency which they receive, should also due to this have to follow the USA by introducing still more new restrictions on foreign travel in addition to those which formerly existed? Even in Comecon (Council for the Mutual Economic Aid of the Socialist Countries) all prices and balancing calculations are carried out in dollars, at all events up to the end of 1968. A certain economist of Comecon has of course said: 'I don't know what we would do without the freely convertible capitalist currencies. The basis of prices would disappear.'

The Soviet currency undoubtedly ought to take its rightful place in the economic and political life of the modern world, but for this it is necessary first of all to abolish the 'currency barrier'.

6

The state frontier

WHOEVER loves the sea, the sea-coast, whoever loves boating or yachting, aqualung diving, marine hunting, fishing, beaches, even he who does not love all this but simply lives close to the sea coast, every such person, if he thinks about it, can see the fundamental difference between the Soviet sea coasts and the shores of other countries. Although very few people have seen in reality the life of the shore zones around the Mediterranean, they will certainly have seen coastal landscapes and shores in Italian, Greek, French, English or American films, on postcards and in illustrated journals.

I myself have often been to the Black Sea coast, in regions where in summer millions of people gather, packed together on the beaches and in the water. I have seen the Baltic Sea and the Gulf of Finland. And I have always been astonished at the emptiness of the sea. I have always wondered why the sea even in quiet, calm weather was not gay with hundreds and thousands of boats, with the white wings of yachts and skiffs, little launches and motorboats. The seaside resorts of other countries always appear to me in films and postcards full to overflowing with people making sea trips in boats and yachts, and with amateur fishermen. Every morning hundreds and thousands of fishing smacks and boats set off for the fishing-grounds hidden by the horizon. Why, I have thought, is hardly anyone in the USSR attracted to sea-boating sports? Why, even in Yalta, is there no yacht club, no boat station, no base for little individual craft? The whole seascape is essentially empty, with only a few launches and steamers on set routes. Only sometimes, right inshore, does a 'pedalo' from a sanatorium go plopping along.

It was only quite recently that I realized that all this is due to the fact that along the sea coasts, at a distance of twelve miles from the shore, there runs an invisible *state frontier*. Beyond this frontier any free individual boating excursion is forbidden along all the coasts of the Soviet Union, which run for many thousands of kilometres.

But other countries have a frontier along the sea, sometimes only three miles from the shore. Why can people use the territorial waters and beyond in those countries, why does no one turn them back, forbid them to take out boats and yachts, forbid them to take sea trips, to enjoy a rest afloat, to go out fishing alone? Thousands of boats, sailing craft, and yachts large and small, are seen in the roadsteads near every European seaside resort and harbour, a whole swarm of small launches. Safe moorings are provided for them. Seaside boating sports and recreations are exceptionally popular throughout the whole world, increasing in scale continually. Even the dangerous, unquiet and stormy coasts of England are full to overflowing with a fleet of individual sailing and motor boats. Of small sailing craft and yachts of various classes alone, there are in England, according to the data published in *Angliya* (no. 33, 1967) more than 200,000. And to that one must add all the motorboats. As for Japan and China, the number of boats and junks in their coastal waters are numbered in millions.

But the Black Sea is empty. The inexhaustible masses of healing sea air are wasted in vain. It is in the sea air the curative properties of the Crimean coast lie. It is the principal and best health resort for lung diseases in Europe. Due to a number of causes the air directly above sea-water has fundamental curative properties. The Crimea is arid, and when the dry air from the land flows out over the sea, that is, at the very edge of the sea, before it has become saturated with water, before it has become moist, under the action of the sun and sea-water, it acquires a special complex of ions, which stimulates both the unhealthy and healthy organisms. The dry, strongly ionized, pure air right above the sea-water is the principal healing power of the Crimea. Sitting on the sea-shore one benefits from this air, too, now and then, but only when the wind blows from the sea. And when it reaches the shore, it is moister and mixed with dust from the beach.

But the sea, the healing sea, is inaccessible; far on the horizon the coastguard vessels are steaming, vigilantly watching the smoothness of the sea. The doctors in rest homes and sanatoria take water from the sea and in their physiotherapy cubicles pulmonary cases, throat cases and bronchitics breathe it in atomized form. This is called sea-water inhalation. For this purpose there is a special device, an inhaler. All this, of course, is necessary especially in winter, when you cannot go out in a boat, or in stormy weather.

But on a peaceful summer day, how many hundreds of thousands of people could enjoy the sea in its clearest, most active, most intense and enjoyable form? Every year half a million invalids and a million and a half people in good health go to the Crimea; and almost ten million people along the length of the Black Sea coast.

But on the Baltic things are even stricter. For foreign lands, Finland and Sweden, are close at hand. Dozens of kilometres of shoreline, of the most beautiful beach on the northern part of the Baltic coast, where it is only about a hundred miles to Finland, are wound around with coils of barbed wire, and there is no access to the sea. Every day a roller goes along the shore trampling down the sand and earth so that all traces of fugitives can be seen. But of course, before the Baltic republics voluntarily joined the Soviet Union there was none of this on this coast. Fishing settlements used to flourish here which have now withered away to nothing, the sea fed tens of thousands of people, and gave rest and recreation to hundreds of thousands.

And now only rare small boats appear on the sea, each one by permission of the frontier posts who communicate the fact of the boat's departure to the patrol vessels. There, at a distance of twelve miles from the spring-tide low-water-mark, is the boundary, the sea frontier, at set distances apart are the armed high-speed large frontier protection launches. They watch the whole boundary zone with radar and keep each other informed about all boats and vessels close to the shore. The wireless-operator of one launch taps out to another: 'In square 57 an old man is fishing with rod and line . . . I have him under observation . . . if he moves into square 77 please inform.' From the other launch they send periodical reports on the movements of the lone fisherman. As soon as he gets more than a kilometre from shore they signal to him, and if he does not react and goes on heading out to sea, a launch goes over to him and escorts him back to the frontier post.

With such a system of surveillance of the sea, every little fish becomes more precious than gold. Therefore they do not allow many boats along the coast. Only a few local people manage to get permission for a boat; these are generally harbour employees, scientists, employees of the militia, the most active members of the Party and Soviet organizations and those employed in sanatoria and rest homes. I do not know whether to obtain permission for a boat they fill up some sort of 'exit dossier', but from the experience of one of my friends, a biochemist, who works a few kilometres from Yalta, I know that it is by no means a simple matter. It took him three years to obtain permission for a boat. But now he has the boat, he is hardly ever able to use it. Every time he wishes to go out in the boat, he has to give advance notification by telephone to the Yalta frontier post, telling them in which zones he will be fishing. It is impossible to go more than a kilometre from the shore. It is impossible to fish in the evening or at night. He has to notify the frontier post of the surnames and given names of everyone who is going out in the boat with him. After going for a sail, it is not enough to draw the boat up to a safe place on shore, or to leave it at anchor if the weather forecast were good; it has to be taken to a special 'pound' sealed off by barbed wire, with padlocked gates and an armed guard. The boat, too, has to be padlocked. And this is not because the owner himself is afraid the boat might be stolen. These are the rules for the security of boats all along the coast, so that no one can use a boat to escape across the frontier and flee to Turkey. Of course, a boat is not a very light object, it must weigh 80 to 100 kilogrammes, no one could carry it away on his own. But even fishing boats which weigh up to a ton also have to be hauled up each day by hand or by rope into the protected zone, and the fishermen of the Black Sea and the Baltic Coast have to tax their strength with this after a hard day's fishing. And then they have to launch them again. Even a small private yacht cannot be left in the roadsteads. A yacht has a large keel, and it cannot be beached, but a sail is a dangerous object, for in a yacht, even a small one, you will not come to grief on the high seas; yachts are seagoing vessels, every year groups of enthusiastic yachtsmen sail right across the Atlantic. In the USSR there are many yacht clubs, but only on lakes and reservoirs. There are none on the sea, except on gulfs which penetrate deep into dry land. Only responsible workers who come to Government sanatoria or state holiday villas can experience the delights of a sea trip in a yacht—and, of course, international sportsmen, training in this field of sport. But for them there are two or three bases at certain places far from the crowded resorts, and which have no open access.

Is there anywhere in the world, any other such country which treats its sea coast and watering places in this way? Are there any reasonable grounds which can justify depriving millions of people of the right to find pleasure and health in sea-water and the sea-air and to indulge in marine boating sports? Is it possible to understand the economic principles of spurning the richest production of the sea, and using of its shore zone for the rest and recreation industry, for health, sport and individual fishing?

It is necessary first and foremost to draw a strict distinction between the military and boundary protection of the sea and land frontiers. An ignorant person thinks that all these complicated restrictions on the use of the rich resources of the sea have some significance in the defence plans of the country. But in fact this is not so at all. The whole system of boundary restrictions is not intrinsically connected with the military protection of the frontiers and military reconnaissance. The defence of the frontier from possible invasion and the service which watches out for military movements on the other side of the frontier is undertaken by completely different kinds of armed forces, which come under the Ministry of Defence and which are directed by the Army General Staff. The frontier service until very recently came under the KGB, and its task is limited to blocking ways of individual and group violation of the frontier and to catching spies and deviationists sent in by other countries.

If one is to believe films and detective novels, spies frequently choose the water route. The spy comes close inshore in a submarine, and then swims the last few kilometres underwater with an aqualung and then lands on the slipway of the most populous beach in Sochi.

Maybe it is really so. But maybe the spy comes in quite freely as a tourist. And, instead of his going home, someone else goes on the same passport. Maybe agents get into our country through the open Finnish frontier, or maybe they drop from a parachute and a following wind takes them some twenty kilometres inside the USSR. With the present scale of inter-state tourist travel it is no problem for an intelligence agent to penetrate any country. No sensible foreign agent would risk getting through the barbed wire somewhere on the Turkish frontier or crossing the Baltic or the Black Sea in a rubber dinghy. Statistics show that most real frontier violations are committed by teenagers who have quarrelled with their parents or who are carried away by the romance of travel. Sometimes they are committed by smugglers. At one time, on the Soviet-Iranian frontier quite a number of repatriated Armenians were caught. They came in the first years after the war in tens of thousands from various countries, actively called home to their native land. But when, in 1949, Beria began to carry out a wide purge in their ranks, arresting those who were discontented or critical, a large number of them decided to flee to the country whither they had fled before from the Turkish butchery. Hence the Iranian frontier has been reinforced by a complicated system of electric wires and barbed wire, with posts every few dozen metres which keep watch over the inside zone, and not the zone outside at all. Sometimes kinsfolk try to visit each other; some villages and *kishlaks* are cut in two by the frontier. There are very many such cases in Central Asia, in the Caucasus and in Moldavia.

Of course, all these are undesirable breaches of orders and rules.

People who commit them ought to be fined just as those who travel without a ticket are fined. But from the point of view of logic and commonsense, to try to combat these phenomena, to keep an army of half a million frontier guards for this purpose, and equip them with all the resources of modern technology, to feed half a million dogs, which eat more meat than three million men, to plough up millions of metres of no-man's-land and take out of use tens of thousands of square metres of the broad boundary zone is possible only if one has lost all sense of reason. In suburban electric trains there are inspectors who check the tickets. And this is right. On one trip, there are no inspectors, while on another trip the inspectors come on board. If someone travels without a ticket, he knows that it is possible to do so, that, according to the theory of probability, he risks a fine on one trip out of seven or eight, if not less frequently. But the risk is there, and this induces those who might have broken the rule to take a ticket. But, even with this probability of being fined, people do break the rule. In order to have 100 per cent certainty that no one was travelling without a ticket, it would be necessary to have a hundred times as many inspectors on the railway as there are at present. It would be necessary to check the tickets over every stage of the entire route. But then, at certain times, there would be more inspectors than passengers on the railway, and the railway would suffer enormous losses. But our frontier service operates precisely on this principle of a total, round-the-clock guard, with a probability of keeping *everyone* back. And, of course, there are ten times as many boundary guards in the USSR as there are potential and actual violations of the frontier—and a thousand times more than the number of dangerous violations. And on the sea frontier, this relationship is even more strongly weighted towards unprofitability. And all this without taking into account the indirect damage of frontier restrictions on sea and on dry land.

There will always be a few who are thirsty for adventure. The famous Leningrad physicist, Gamow, at the beginning of the 1930s tried to cross the Black Sea in a boat, in order to escape to America to do some work or other there. The patrols caught him. But then he managed all the same to carry out his plan, by not returning from some international conference. He became famous in the USA and is known to biologists by the fact that he was the first to work on the theoretical problem of the genetic code in 1954. But cases of such flights can only be exceptionally rare, even with a completely open frontier.

But it is absurd that just on account of the possible adventurous spirit of a few persons tens of thousands of others should be involved in guarding the coastal regions, and that millions of people should be kept away from the use of the sea. It is simply an uneconomic approach to the use of the riches with which fate, history and geography have endowed our country, whose coast is washed by three oceans and fourteen seas.

As far as the dry-land frontiers are concerned, the regime which surrounds our country is excessively expensive. In former times, when the USSR was a lone country, surrounded by enemies, total defence of the frontiers might have had some kind of justification. But, in fact, before the war the frontier service was never so numerous and diversified as it is today. The Soviet-Polish frontier is guarded today with incomparably more care than in 1940, when Hitler's million-strong army was standing on the Polish frontier. The Soviet-Finnish frontier at the present time is guarded in a zone almost 150 kilometres in depth. Even in the period before the Soviet-Finnish war, even on the Karelian isthmus, there was no such system of defence. The state simply did not have the resources to maintain such an expensive defence of its frontiers. Now we are richer. And, although there is really no military threat to us from Bulgaria and Poland, although it is clear that Finland is not going to attack the Soviet Union, we have created complex lines of blockade and defence, reaching back dozens of kilometres into our own territory.

It is impossible to dispute the fact that boundary defence is necessary. The customs service is also necessary. The defence of unquiet boundaries is especially necessary. Today, the most unquiet boundary is the Chinese. The Chinese make hundreds of provocations every month. But in the case of the difficult, 2,000-kilometre mountain frontier with peaceful Afghanistan, we are simply wasting large quantities of our forces and resources without cause. And a particularly high expense to our country is the frontier with the friendly socialist countries to the west, with Bulgaria, Romania, Hungary, Czechoslovakia and Poland.

We are not yet ready to open our frontier both ways, even with friendly countries. But we shall have to make ready for it. We cannot avoid this historical event. The control posts will remain on the roads, and so will the control units who will detain and fine anyone trying to violate the frontier, but the time when an attempt to cross the frontier without the permission of the government was punished by incarceration in a prison-camp for six or seven years and was accompanied by the risk of being shot on the spot will have receded into the past. The right to shoot people violating the frontier, even before they have revealed

I*

their identity, if distance does not allow them to be detained by other means (the frontier is close, and the guard with the gun is a long way off) ought, of course, to be abolished. No other country in the world treats crossing the frontier as so serious a crime. Even in China, with its fierce terror and nationalism, there is no frontier defence in our sense of the word. Hong Kong, a British colony and a country open to the whole world is connected with mainland China only by a bridge across the strait.[1] And, until recently, this bridge was not guarded by the frontier guard. Across it to Hong Kong tens of thousands of Chinese fled from the persecution of the Red Guards in 1966-7. Only recently have the Chinese set up a guard here, but this is in the form of control posts, which do not stop anyone crossing the frontier in connection with their business activities.

Violation of the frontier is, by the nature of the action, not a crime but a breach of certain rules. After all, a man may blunder into the frontier, when gathering mushrooms or berries, or by getting lost on a walking tour or out hunting—especially in Karelia which is a favourite spot for anglers and hunters. Here the frontier zone is so wide that you could lose a whole European state in the forbidden zone. The boundary posts start 150 kilometres from the frontier. In this forbidden zone there are a mass of pretty little lakes and rivers, plenty of game and fish. The only people who have permission to come here (with a special pass) for hunting and fishing are the most active types of classified personnel. Once the Minister of Agriculture of the USSR brought the President of the German Academy of Agricultural Sciences here on a hunting trip, and they killed some ten head of deer. But for ordinary mortals entry into this forbidden zone is forbidden, and they can, indeed, be shot, especially at night. Not long ago, in connection with the jubilee of the boundary service, they showed a newsreel in Obninsk about the protection of the boundary. The central incident was the killing of someone who infringed the frontier. An unknown man was running towards the frontier. The zone was close to him, and the soldier who saw him was some distance away. The soldier called out, 'Halt!' The man did not stop. Then a burst of machine-gun fire cut him down close to the frontier. As the film proceeded it turned out that the man was a spy, films and weapons were found on the body. But this was after the killing.

---

[1] Medvedev seems to have confused the lack of restrictions between the island of Hong Kong and the British territory of Kowloon on the mainland with the frontier between Kowloon and China—which is very strictly guarded—*Translator*.

It could have been that he was not a secret agent, but simply a psychologically disturbed person or a drunkard who was not responsible for his actions.

Sometimes, of course, the use of arms is justified. This is when the military intelligence nature of the violation is established. We know of one such case, the shooting down by rocket of the U-2 aircraft which was overflying the Sverdlovsk region. On that occasion, the American intelligence agent, Powers, was taken prisoner. But in accidental cases, even when the frontier is violated by an aircraft, shooting at it is not permissible. In the same year as the U-2 was shot down (1960), an unknown aircraft violated the Bulgarian frontier in a mist. The Bulgarians opened fire on it and brought it down. But it turned out that this was a peaceful passenger aircraft which had gone somewhat off course and was making for Turkey. About sixty innocent passengers and the members of the crew were killed. The whole world condemned this act as unjustified brutality, as barbaric. Bulgaria agreed to pay compensation. And cases of going off course are not rare nowadays, especially in mist. In a BBC news broadcast in English on 29 August 1967, I happened to hear of the following case. The Czechoslovak boundary guard opened fire on a family of four who were crossing the frontier with Austria. The head of the family, the father, was killed when he had already reached Austrian soil. One of the children was wounded. And how many victims have fallen on the Berlin wall. The captains of Soviet ships on international routes have instructions to shoot if any of the ship's company or crew try to swim ashore to a foreign coast.

When going to foreign ports most of the crew of many vessels are not allowed to go ashore. Only those are allowed ashore who have been approved for journeys to a capitalist country. But sometimes a steamer is sent on an international voyage unexpectedly, and there are many 'unapproved' persons on board. Do captains of vessels of other countries have similar instructions? I feel sure that they do not.

The first decree setting up the boundary control department and its functions, signed by Lenin and adopted by the all-Russian Central Executive Committee on 28 May 1918, did not contain any mention of the possibility of using arms to detain those violating the frontier. Yet that was not a peaceful time and, in fact, a great number of deviationists and conspirators were making their way across the frontier. The next statute on the state frontier, adopted in 1927, sharply increased the defence system. But it still was not too fierce. Then new statutes on boundary protection were adopted, always stricter and stricter. In the pre-war years this was, to some extent, justified. But the strictest and most thorough statute was adopted in 1960. The Decree of the Presidium of the Supreme Soviet of the USSR on the new statute on the state frontier of the USSR was published in *Vedomosti Verkhovnogo Soveta SSSR*, no. 34 (1018) 13 August 1960. This detailed statute, which is in the main just and well founded, contains, however, two serious defects, which should be changed in the future. *Firstly*, the statute does not indicate the depth of the frontier area. In the decree of 1918 it was stated precisely that 'the boundary zone extends seven versts inward into the Republic'. The new statute which introduces a whole number of restrictions on the entry of citizens into the boundary zone and the use of it, does not indicate nor set a limit to the breadth of this zone. This permits the zone to be extended arbitrarily, sometimes up to hundreds of kilometres, as in Karelia. But it is quite obvious that a hundred-kilometre boundary zone is absolutely ludicrous and wasteful. *Secondly*, article 39 of the new statute gives the right to '*use arms against those violating the frontier of the USSR on land, on water, and in the air, when it would be impossible to detain them by other means*'. In the preamble to this article it is pointed out that on the sea pursuit and the use of arms may be extended beyond the territorial waters of the USSR, if it has not proved possible to detain the offender in the territorial waters.

This article is illegal and unjust. It is like giving jealous spouses permission to kill each other on the mere suspicion of unfaithfulness. If in Tsarist Russia there had been such a code concerning the frontier, how many members of the Russian Social Democratic Workers' Party would have perished in the boundary zones, and how many communists and progressive people would have been killed if other countries introduced the custom of shooting at people who violated the frontier! It is amazing that our state ethics tend to encourage people to violate frontiers provided they are violating the frontiers of another state. We are delighted to write about Lenin's agents of *Iskra*,[1] who illegally crossed the Russian frontier and brought in literature. We pay tribute to the valour of Lenin, who was smuggled across the frontier by locomotive in 1917 into Finland, which was then almost independent. We do not consider the crossing of a frontier to be *always* a criminal offence. We consider it a crime only when it is a matter of crossing the Soviet frontier, even if it is the frontier with a neighbouring friendly socialist state.

[1] *Iskra* (*The Spark*) was the first Russian illegal Marxist newspaper. It was founded by Lenin in 1900 and was first produced in Leipzig, then successively in Munich, London and Geneva. Copies were smuggled into Russia and illegally distributed—*Translator*.

Consequently, article 39 of the statute on the frontier is dictated not by scientific logic but by *jealousy*. The statistics, which cannot be unknown to the authorities, show that 99 per cent of those who violate the frontier (according to the unofficial data of a writer who specializes in the subject of the frontier and often visits posts to collect material) are not military agents, spies or malefactors. They are people with a grudge, sometimes ill, sometimes stubborn and opinionated, often simply romantics, mostly local inhabitants and about half of them are immature teenagers. No one abroad needs them, and in most cases they return quickly if they do manage to get abroad. In other cases, they are returned by the frontier guards of the other country, after an initial sorting out, as in the case of Ostap Bender,[1] who crossed the Romanian frontier. Our frontier is too extensive, millions and millions of people live close to it and are subject to restrictions even for a mere stroll in the woods to pick mushrooms and berries. And we must also consider how to relieve them of this constant threat.

There is another 'violator' of the frontier about which I should like to say a few words: radio waves in the 9–25 metre bands. Foreign radio sets generally have a range of wavelengths starting at 9 or 11 metres—sometimes at 13. This is quite understandable, since this short-wave range is the daytime one. Long-distance transmissions can be heard in the daytime only at wavelengths of 20 metres or less. Longer waves cannot be transmitted for great distances by day, there is too much solar noise. From 25 metres upwards short-wave transmissions are received only in the evening and at night. But the range of up to 20 metres operates poorly at night. Our radio industry is fully aware of the advantage of radio sets with a range below 20 metres and is obliged to manufacture them for export. These export model radios can be bought in Moscow, too, but only for currency or 'plain' certificates. For the internal market since the war (until 1941 there was no such rule) radio sets are produced which start at 25 metres. Wavelengths of 9 to 25 metres are *forbidden*. A radio mechanic who manufactured a set with this wave-band for financial gain in his workshop would be liable to criminal prosecution if discovered.

Accordingly, during the day it is impossible to listen in to short wave foreign broadcasts on Soviet sets. What is permitted to the citizens of every other country is not allowed to Soviet man.

[1] Ostap Bender is a fictitious character created by the humorists Il'f and Petrov in their novels, *The Twelve Chairs* (1928) and *The Golden Calf* (1931). He is a typical example of the 'NEP-man', a shrewd, likeable crook—*Translator*.

The reason for this 'prohibition' is simple. It is connected with the formerly flourishing practice of jamming foreign broadcasts. Nowadays jamming is maintained not on all stations but only on those which are not state services but belong to some other organization. (In 1964 the USSR entered into the convention on international broadcasting and now has no right to jam the *state* radio stations of other countries.) Jamming in the 9 to 25 metre wave-band is very difficult. These transmissions are propagated over long distances and are reflected from the ionosphere several times. Consequently, they strike any point of the USSR from above at an acute angle. The network of stations to jam these wavelengths would have to be too dense. The budget of the country could not stand such a network of jamming stations. The jamming stations which do exist are far from cheap. When the jamming campaign was in full swing, between 1956 and 1960, it absorbed considerably more money than broadcasting, since the wave-bands of the jamming stations were many more, and each wave-band needed not one, but a network of stations across the whole Union.

And, once again, we provide the only example in the world. Hitler introduced the jamming of broadcasts during the war. At that time we proceeded in a simpler and cheaper manner. All radio sets were collected from the population, and there were very strict penalties for owning a radio set. Maybe during a war this measure was justified. But after the war, Hitler's discovery was used by only one country, and for twenty-three years this one has been going on sending a wild, senseless, neuropathological caterwauling concert into the ether on a number of wavelengths. What instrument was invented to do this, I do not know. I should like to see it! And when, turning the knob of my radio I chance upon this noisy devil's sabbath, it seems to be a microphone near which a siren has been turned on and an iron barrel, packed with empty tin cans and bottles is being spun round. And what do intelligent beings on other planets think if they happen to pick up this terrible whistling and clanking, alternating with croaking, which the first socialist country in the world sends out into the ether?[1]

---

[1] This section was written in February 1968. It must be pointed out that since 21 August 1968, the jamming of all foreign state broadcasts in Russian, Ukrainian and other languages of the peoples of the USSR has been reintroduced with great intensity. It even includes the 9, 13 and 16 metre wavebands, since many radio amateurs have constructed sets with these wavelengths for themselves and foreign sets have become a commonplace for citizens of the USSR. The jamming of foreign radio stations was reintroduced to try to stop information on events in Czechoslovakia from getting into the USSR—*Author's note.*

7

Present trends in the international integration of mankind

IN spite of the diversity of political regimes in society today and the differences in national traditions and customs, in spite of wide gaps between the economic levels of countries, the inequality of distribution of poverty and riches over the globe, in the face of racial prejudices, the integration of mankind is undoubtedly taking place with ever-increasing speed and is the principal trend today—a social, political, economic and biological integration. The sharp conflicts and contradictions which arise here and there as a manifestation of political and nationalist extremism and of remnants of imperialism and colonialism cannot prevent, but can only delay, this process. Nor is integration hindered by the growth in the number of independent self-determining states, mainly in Africa and Asia; on the contrary it makes cultural and economic integration less painful and non-violent.

Cultural and economic integration of mankind has already been taking place through the whole extent of recorded history, but it is in the last two decades that it has become exceptionally rapid, due to the scientific and technological revolution and the growth of means of communication and means of exchange of information of a scientific, political, economic and ideological nature.

In past millenia, centuries and decades the process of integration often took the ugly and cruel form of military and colonial conquest, of the striving of individual political systems and forms of civilization and religion for world domination. The wars of conquest of Alexander of Macedon, of the Roman Empire and of the Mongolian lords in ancient times, of Napoleon in the last century, of Hitlerite Germany and the Japanese militarists within living memory, were all piratical, ugly, egoistical and cruel attempts to unify mankind by forced means by subjugating all other nations to a single political system. Happily all these attempts in extreme form came to grief. Some of them, if we consider the consequences as a whole, brought some benefit to mankind (the spread of Greek and Roman culture), while others brought incalculable harm (the Mongolian yoke, Fascism).

The most noble and scientifically well-founded attempts to unify mankind on an ideological and economic basis were the teachings of the utopian socialists and Marx in the last century. As a result of this there arose the idea of 'world revolution'. But this, too, proved unattainable. To build socialism at once over the whole heterogeneous world was impossible. But the individual countries in which the proletarian revolution had taken place came into inevitable conflict with the capitalist states and this reduced the stability of the world. Only one country was able to stand its ground in this conflict—the Soviet Union. But military intervention and other forms of struggle against the Soviet Union drove Russia to create a military-proletarian dictatorship and even to introduce a reign of terror based not on law but on force. The need to create a militarily strong and powerful state led not to the reduction of 'surplus value' but to its growth. The centralization gradually continued until it became the dictatorship of a single personality—Stalin. This was not inevitable, but it did not happen by chance. When the democratic rights of citizens were curtailed, the power of the punitive organs were hypertrophied until they transgressed the law. The phenomenon of Stalin's tyranny was one way in which the new formation of society developed. But capitalism, too, eroded by crises and contradictions, gave birth to yet another harsher form of tyranny and arbitrary rule, the dictatorships of Mussolini and Hitler, fascism and national socialism. A world war became inevitable, since the world was being ruled not by the sum total of its scientific intellect, not by wisdom and common sense, but by pathological, psychologically sick tyrants, maniacs who hoped for super-monarchical power. Luckily science at that time had still not invented atomic weapons, thermonuclear bombs and intercontinental missiles, and the war which came did not become a form of suicide of the whole of civilized humanity, nor put back its development by centuries.

But common sense and the basis of reason found in the United Nations Organization, a means of peaceful co-operation of nations and their integration on the basis of certain universal principles among which the Universal Declaration of Human Rights does not take the last place, has not triumphed throughout the whole world. Tyranny as a form of rule of countries has not vanished and is still a danger to the fate of the world. Besides the small personal dictatorships and monarchies, which are no great danger to mankind as a whole in Africa, South America and Asia, together with local foci of blind nationalism, we have become witnesses

of an ugly chauvinist dictatorship in China, a fanatically anomalous
tyranny armed with atomic and thermonuclear weapons. Most regret-
tably this new and very dangerous tyranny has arisen just next door to
our country and on the basis of a socialist system. And its expansionist
tendencies which have been inflamed by crises about the imperialist
danger, are in reality directed against the Soviet Far East and Siberia.
Another thing causes intense disquiet. The richest and most powerful
country in the world, the USA, despite its manifest democratic freedoms and traditions, is committing an evident act of international piracy
and from senseless obstinacy and considerations of prestige and influence is waging a hopeless and most dangerous war in Vietnam, it is in
effect, taking part in a civil war. In this war, as in the Chinese 'cultural
revolution', there is no common sense nor real thought or concern for
the future of humanity. The Vietnam war which the USA is waging is a
result of faulty decisions by the leaders of the country, who have too
much and too arbitrary power in their hands. We can see that neither
socialism nor bourgeois democracy is able to prevent the appearance of
political dictatorship, even under a parliamentary and presidential
system. Any dictatorship is egocentric and acts subjectively and therefore often wrongly, and this in the modern world can lead to the suicide
of mankind. An individual brain, even if it is the brain of the 'great
pilot' may act on the basis of the comparison of thirty or forty variables
and upon a very vague estimate of the consequences of the decisions
taken. Nowadays to make an optimum decision it is necessary to compare
and estimate thousands and tens of thousands of factors and a considerable time in advance, too. There are about two hundred independent
states in the world. In these conditions, political dictatorship, and
especially military dictatorship, is outdated as a form of ruling society,
and is in unacceptable contradiction to the technological and scientific
development of the modern world. They must gradually be replaced by
particular forms of the scientific organization of ruling society, based on
a profound intellectual analysis of the prospects of the world and sub-
ordination *to the principal force of peaceful progress*—to the science of
government—not only in the narrow sense of scientific socialism, but in
the wide sense of the whole sum of forces determining the progress of
our knowledge.

For the Soviet Union, which is now among the great powers, between
the extreme and dangerous forms of Chinese regimented totalitarian
'socialism'—'Mao-ism'—and American militarized imperialist 'democracy', there has arisen a favourable opportunity for a reasonable and

scientifically based internal and external policy which will be a real support for progress and a model for many other countries. I am picking out the position of our country among the great powers for purely practical reasons. Among the two hundred states in our world there are undoubtedly some in which better solutions have been found to the conflict between the individual strivings of people and the functions of society, between power and democracy, between social structure and productive forces, between the prosperity of the family and the wealth of society, than the various solutions in the USSR, China, the USA, Great Britain, France, Germany or India. But the experiences of small countries which are inevitably dependent on and belong to some bloc or group are poorly suited to propagation and imitation. It seems to me that the best way to strengthen the position of the USSR in the modern world even more is to demonstrate that we know how to make a reasonable and multilateral analysis of internal and external events, to criticize freely our own shortcomings, past and present, and to open up completely free opportunities of historical and social analysis of those events and causes which led in the past to the sombre times of Stalinist lawlessness and arbitrary rule, the ignoring of the rights of the individual and the absence of democratic standards. We need to show that we put into the government of the country people who are really wise and sensitive to their responsibility for the fate of the entire world, really the best people in the nation. This could be done chiefly by introducing greater freedom of the press and restricting the censorship, which would lead to a free discussion of the personal, political and administrative attributes of candidates for government posts, to a system of democratic elections and to the objective appraisal of all aspects and consequences of taking any decision. At present, although possibly to a lesser degree than under Stalin and Khrushchev, the structure of the organs of power in our country is such that it protects them from criticism and influence from below. But in a rationally constructed society the structure of the organs of power must in the first place protect the people and the individual representatives of the people from abuse by the organs of power, from acts of lawlessness, from excessive exploitation and from arbitrary rule.

With such an abundance of unpleasant features and selfish attitudes which have become apparent over several decades, both in the capitalist and the socialist world, one can only assume that in the immediate future neither of these systems has any real opportunity of dominating the world. The conflict which has arisen between the USSR and China shows that there is no truth in the notion that the total abolition of capitalist economics would lead to the disappearance of interstate antagonism, the arms race and the risk of war. Perhaps 'co-existence' consisting of peaceful competition between different social and political systems is not a temporary product of the balance of forces of annihilation but is the only possible course of development for heterogeneous humanity—heterogeneous in all respects. *And if we acknowledge that the political heterogeneity of society and the social, economic and ideological differences of countries and nations are inevitable, then the principal force capable of leading the world towards peaceful and gradual cultural, political and economic integration will be mutually advantageous scientific, technological and cultural co-operation and freedom of contact of the peoples of different countries, freedom of travel, freedom of exchange of information.*

In the course of the last two decades science and technology have created massive means of communication and contact between peoples, which have united the whole world into a single information system. World-wide radio and television, the development of national broadcasting to other countries, the propagation of newspapers and journals, the rapid growth of international tourism and international trade have created a mutual understanding and mutual influence of nations and countries as an observed fact. The citizen of almost any country who is sufficiently intelligent can now form his view of the world from international information, and can make his own selection from the information which he receives from various sources. If there is not enough information from his own country, he can borrow from other sources. This leads to a society which is ideologically and politically heterogeneous and makes the governments of countries tolerant of different points of view in the population. This kind of tolerance does not always appear without friction, and in the events in our own country, for example, we can see attempts to preserve abnormally monolithic ideology and opinions by far from the best means. But the general trend is under way in our country too.

Modern technology has created forms of production which can exist and develop only if there is world-wide co-operation and national specialization. And this specialization has become reality. Specialization arising because natural resources are not uniformly distributed has existed for a long time. The industry of the whole of Western Europe depends on supplies of petroleum from the Near East or from still more distant countries, on supplies of rubber from the tropics, on uranium, diamonds, gold and a mass of other products and raw materials. In recent years this kind of interdependence has spread from raw materials to the most complicated technological developments. Many technological projects are so expensive and complicated that it takes the efforts of several countries to bring them into being. Even the production of aircraft and automobiles has been internationalized. The firm of Fiat was late in constructing an automobile factory for the USSR as contracted, since certain parts of the complex were obtained by the Italians themselves from the USA, and the USA did not want to provide them for the USSR. Nowhere in the whole of Europe are these parts made, since it is considered more sensible to obtain them from the USA. Often not only production but planning as well is internationalized, no single country has the whole complex of scientists and engineers necessary for it. The production of computers, large ships, metallurgical and chemical equipment, not to mention rockets and other military supplies is now international in scope. Similarly such a great shipbuilding power as the USA will order super-tankers from Japan. Now only simple, mass-produced goods, like pens and pencils can be produced in each country independently, and even then there is rivalry between firms. It is not by chance that the Common Market has grown up in Europe, nor is it by chance that other European countries want to join it. Nor was Comecon (The Council for Mutual Economic Aid)[1] formed by chance, which has worked out schemes for specialization within the group of socialist countries. Unfortunately, the degree of co-operation within Comecon is still considerably less than in the Common Market, not to speak of the degree of integration of science and manpower. Perhaps it is this very limitation of free interaction of intellectual forces within the group of European socialist countries which acts as a brake on maximum integration.

But besides information (radio, television, the press), industry, science and economics, an enormous role in the integration of mankind is played by the growth of international human relations, international tourism. This tourism reflects many aspects of international co-operation and is creating a completely new atmosphere in relations between nations.

The principal difference which has arisen in the world in the course of the last twenty years consists of a sudden jump in the prosperity of the industrially developed countries of Europe, America, and to a lesser

---

[1] The name of the organization is very unfortunate. 'Aid' means something episodic and altruistic. It would be better to call it the 'Council for Economic Co-operation'—*Author's note.*

degree Asia. Corresponding to this, there has also been a rise in the prosperity of the masses of the population of these countries. In the course of twenty years the world has become several times richer. There has been a sharp growth in the productivity and intensity of labour, but at the same time the working day has become shorter. The amount of free time for rest and recreation enjoyed by the masses of the population has considerably increased. Between 1946 and 1966 the mean life-span of people in Europe and in other developed countries has increased by fifteen years, and, consequently the number of elderly and old people has also increased, and their proportion in the total bulk of the population has become considerable. And, of course, they are mainly pensioners, people who have a very great deal of free time. As far as the increase in prosperity is concerned, mankind has done as much in the last twenty years as was done in the previous two hundred. Accordingly, the range of interests of people has also changed. International tourism, which until recently was an expensive luxury for the upper levels of society, has become massive in the last few years and is now a necessity, a fashion, a habit, a commonplace and ordinary affair. And not only for a holiday, for his summer leave, but simply for a 'week-end', for Saturday and Sunday, an employee or a worker can get in his car and drive to a neighbouring country, from France into Italy or Switzerland, from England to France, etc. It has been calculated that the average length of stay of foreigners in Italy is two to three days, that is, it is basically a matter of short visits and not of long tours around the country. A great movement of people to and fro has begun in the world, and this has undoubtedly aided the stabilization and development of the trend towards peace far more than any general manifesto of any organization. And if our country really wants peace and security, then we must become an effective part of this evolutionary process, casting off old prejudices and disregarding possible individual complications. We must learn to think in terms of free contact with other nations, and free the organs that govern the state from feelings of jealousy in their attitude about the interests of the Soviet people concerning the political, economic and social problems of other countries, their life and their people. We can see only one side of this trend, the effect of processes of integration on the ideology of Soviet society. But at the same time the integration which is taking place is an exceptionally many-sided process and is very beneficial for the life of every nation. Small countries of course, feel this especially. For them integration is absolutely vital. And we are witnesses of the fact that the isolationist tendencies which prevail in the

USSR are driving our socialist friends in Eastern Europe into the general integration of Europe. We have already noted that tourism in Yugoslavia, Hungary, Poland, Czechoslovakia and Romania from the capitalist countries is many times greater than from the Soviet Union. Likewise, citizens of these countries go more frequently and more easily to their capitalist neighbours than to the USSR. Even little Austria, which has no seaside resorts, no diversity of nature or open spaces, with its eight million inhabitants has considerably outstripped the Soviet Union as an object of tourism from Czechoslovakia, Hungary, Poland and Romania. And this is understandable, since tourism develops reciprocally. Forces of attraction and sympathy, uncontrollable from above, are arising, since no tourist is isolated from the population of the country which he visits. The drawing together of states today in the era of massive tourism depends more on the drawing together and friendship of people than on the friendship of their leaders. Interest in one country or another largely depends upon knowledge—that is upon the amount of knowledge about that country both directly based on reciprocal tourism, and indirectly due to information obtained about that country from books, newspapers, journals, the cinema, imported goods and radio, etc. Our people know almost nothing about Indonesia, Australia or New Zealand, and hence the events in these countries do not greatly excite us. The amount of our knowledge about a great number of other, far closer countries is amazingly small, since direct information about them is also exceptionally small. The chief source of information about foreign countries for the Soviet people has been in recent years the tendentious journal *Za Rubezhom*, which prints carefully selected translations from the foreign press. The dry reports on international tourism are witness of how far the USSR is behind the world-wide trends towards integration, and how much our relative isolation from the rest of the world is becoming intensified.

1967 was proclaimed International Tourism Year. Our country, too, associated itself with this resolution of the general assembly of the UN. In connection with this, in 1967 it became customary to study and survey the results of touristic activity of various countries. It is interesting to quote a series of figures. In 1965 throughout the whole world according to UNESCO data, 115 million visits of foreign tourists were recorded, and in 1966, 128 million. (This figure does not include unrecorded international journeys, for example, from Norway or Finland to Sweden.) The expenditure of tourists in 1966 amounted to 13,000 million dollars. In comparison with 1958, eight years before, the increase in the number of tourists in the world was 239 per cent, which made it the most rapidly expanding branch of the economy in the entire world. (See *Bulletin of Tourist Information*, no. 3, 1967 and *Unesco Courier*, no. 12, 1966.) These figures refer strictly to tourism and do not take into account international business trips. One can estimate how high the total figures for international travel of people may be from the fact that in 1965 the airlines alone conveyed 180 million international passengers.

The *Unesco Courier* (no. 12, 1966) states that in Western Europe international tourism now accounts on the average for 8 per cent of family expenditure. Over the last ten years the number of times foreigners crossed the frontiers in cars has increased: into Spain by 6 times, into Denmark 6.5 times, into Yugoslavia 30 times, and so on. In 1965, 6 million persons went abroad from Britain, 3 million from Italy, and around 7 million from France. In 1965, $2\frac{1}{2}$ million citizens of the USA crossed the Atlantic to visit Europe. Europe became the chief object of tourism in the world. In 1950, 16 million international tourists were recorded in Europe; in 1963, 66 million; and in 1966, 99 million. And these are only partial figures. The *Unesco Courier* recognizes that in Europe it is possible to record only 45 per cent of the international journeys of citizens, since the free movement of citizens without visas and the number of touring motorists who camp without using the services of tourist firms make it difficult to record the number of foreigners in each country.

In the total balance of international tourism, Africa accounts for about 1 per cent, Asia and Australia 2 per cent, the Near and Middle East 2.6 per cent.

Some countries enjoy especial popularity as an object for tourism. First place in the whole world is held by Spain; in 1965, 17 million foreigners visited Spain, and the net profit from tourism was more than a thousand million dollars. In second place in 1965 was Italy, visited by 15 to 16 million foreign tourists. Italy's income from tourism in 1965 was also more than a thousand million dollars. The *Bulletin of Tourist Information* (no. 7, 1967) states in a note on Italian tourist statistics that in 1966, 26 million foreigners in all visited Italy for tourist and business purposes. The breakdown of the foreigners who visited Italy by nations is interesting: 5,500,000 Germans from the Federal Republic, 4,600,000 French, 2,622,000 Austrians, 565,000 Danes, 1,006,000 Belgians, about 3,000,000 British, 1,705,000 Americans (from the USA), etc. In bottom place in the published list came Pakistan. From this distant country 14,000 persons came to Italy. The Soviet Union was outside the list, included among the other countries the number of visits from which did not exceed 10,000. Even the tiny countries of Europe have incomparably outstripped the Soviet Union according to the published information. From Norway 206,000 persons visited Italy, from Ireland 88,000, from Finland 111,000, from Luxembourg 112,000. Among the socialist countries the one with the highest number of tourist trips to Italy in 1966 was of course Yugoslavia, 1,200,000 of whose citizens visited Italy.

Yugoslavia is the first of the socialist countries which has acknowledged the right to travel freely and to guarantee this right by appropriate measures.[1] As a result of this, in 1966 Yugoslavia overtook Britain in the number of visits to it by tourists. In 1966 3,600,000 foreign tourists visited Yugoslavia, three times more than visited the Soviet Union. Britain in 1966 was visited by 3,100,000 persons from abroad. Breaking this down for the European nations the first place as regards the number of visits to Britain is held by the French, and the last place by the Poles. In all, 13,000 of them visited Britain. Here, too, the Soviet Union fell outside the list (less than 10,000) thus lagging behind Poland.

Unfortunately Soviet tourist statistics carefully conceal the breakdown by countries of Soviet tourists going abroad. Nor do they reveal the figures of foreigners coming to the USSR broken down by nationality. In our country, only the total figures are published, which unless they are split up into countries cannot be objectively checked and analysed.

In 1965, according to the total figures, 1,260,000 foreigners visited the USSR. In the same year, even little Norway was visited by 3,500,000 foreigners (see *Bulletin of Tourist Information*, no. 6, 1967).

[1] *Added in October 1968:* The first country in the Warsaw Pact which legally implemented the right of free entry and exit for its citizens and freedom of international tourism was Czechoslovakia. As a result of this it became theoretically possible for Germans in the GDR to emigrate via Czechoslovakia and also for Poles, Hungarians and the citizens of other countries to do so. In order to prevent this it became necessary to consider Czechoslovakia as a capitalist country when settling questions of tourism. The problem which arose was one of those which the other countries of the Warsaw Pact tried to solve by rendering 'brotherly' aid to Czechoslovakia, introducing into Czechoslovakia an army half a million strong and damming its boundary with the German Federal Republic and Austria. It must be noted, however, that, in fact, the result of the establishment in Czechoslovakia of a democratic system of international relations, was not emigration, but the return of Czechs and Slovaks who had left their country in the past. Tens of thousands of citizens, mainly the intelligentsia, returned home from abroad. After Czechoslovakia had been rendered friendly Soviet aid these people once again began to emigrate from the country. After August 1968 about 70,000 persons left Czechoslovakia.

The mass-circulation tourist journal, *Tourist* published in the USSR popularizes internal tourism only. Even in the International Tourism Year this journal contained hardly a single article on international travel by Soviet citizens. Only in one number (no. 5) was there a dry article by V. Babkin, the head of the Information Section of Intourist, on international travel. Babkin recognized, in a somewhat strange way, that international tourism throughout the world has become massive. 'Fear of revolution,' he writes, 'the successes of the Socialist countries and the pressure of the workers' movement have forced the bourgeoisie to make a partial compromise on conditions of labour and social security. This phenomenon has revealed itself, in particular, in the democratization of the social status of tourists in the capitalist countries.' (*Tourist*, no. 5, p. 30.)

Apropos of this, Babkin should make a comparative analysis of the social status of international tourists from the USSR, especially those who go to capitalist countries (the cost of tours to these countries is very high). I am certain that the percentage of workers and peasants among Soviet international tourists is less than among international tourists from Britain or the Federal German Republic.

According to Babkin's data, in 1966, 1,280,000 Soviet citizens went abroad (on business and tourist trips). Although this figure is very low by modern European standards, I have some doubts about it. The statistics which the *Bulletin of Tourist Information* quotes in notes on the foreign tourist bulletins show that the totals given by Babkin are exaggerated. Moreover, no less than 80 per cent of Soviet tourism is to five countries: Bulgaria, Hungary, Poland, Romania and Czechoslovakia.

Moreover Soviet tourism abroad is marked by a considerably lower degree of contact with the population. About 95 per cent of it is group tourism and not the individual kind. Groups and delegations of Soviet tourists have strictly regimented programmes, while, according to the UNESCO data, it is individual and family tourism which predominates in other countries. In 1965, this constituted 90 per cent of all tourism 75 per cent of tourists travelled around Europe in their own cars. For this reason international tourism is much cheaper for foreigners than for Soviet citizens. In 1967, 1,800,000 British and Irish visited France. 56 per cent of them did not stay in hotels but on car camping sites (*Bulletin of Tourist Information*, no. 1, 1968). In Japan, special cheap hotels have been opened for young international tourists, where they can get a night's lodging, breakfast and dinner for a dollar and a half per day. The number of foreign tourists in Bulgaria in 1967 reached 2 million persons, that is, it considerably exceeded foreign tourism to the USSR. Yet in Bulgaria the whole population totals only 8 million. Little Austria in 1966 was visited by almost 7 million foreign tourists, while the number of Soviet tourists was too low to be included in the break-down by countries of foreign tourists published by Austria. Finland has 3 million inhabitants; 1 million of them go each year to Sweden alone, while 57% of these go to Sweden for rest and recreation.

It is interesting to note that the richest country of all, the USA, is in a difficult position because of the rapid and vigorous development of inter-national tourism. A trip across the Atlantic does not rank as cheap (about 500 dollars return by air). It is easier for the richer Americans to make this trip than for Europeans. Consequently, every year many more Americans visit Europe than Europeans visit the USA. In 1966, 2,975,000 Americans made trips across the sea (to Europe, Asia and Africa) while 1,360,000 persons visited the USA from overseas. Ameri-cans spent 4,000 million dollars abroad. (*Bulletin of Tourist Information*, no. 9, 1967.) With the threat of inflation of the dollar, which has arisen because of the colossal American expenditure on the war in Vietnam, on military aid to other countries and on keeping up its overseas bases, this expenditure by tourists constituted a financial problem. In 1968 the Government of the USA proposed a special tax on the spending of dollars abroad, and this, it is forecast, should reduce tourism from the USA by one-third in 1968. At the same time, the USA has accumulated considerable excesses of the currency of certain countries (Ceylon, Burma, Yugoslavia, Poland, Tunisia, the United Arab Republic, India, Pakistan, the Congo, Guinea and Israel) and American tourism to these countries will be especially encouraged (see *Science*, vol. 159, no. 3819, p. 1080, 1968).

It would be possible to quote analogous figures, data, comparisons and so forth. They clearly show that international co-operation of people at all levels has become a necessity in modern society. A universal desire has arisen to compare, to study, to observe the life of other nations and social systems. The diversity of countries, of race, politics, culture and history has become a factor not of repulsion but of attraction, developing mutual interest to the same degree as does the diversity of natural resources and natural wealth.

The international exchange of children between families for long periods of time has grown enormously. This helps them to get an excellent knowledge of foreign languages and the ways of other countries while they are still children, and, is, all in all, an excellent means of education. The whole of Europe is covered by a network of special 'youth hostels' which charge practically nothing, in which all facilities operate on a communal basis. These hostels make international and internal tourism for school children a favourite form of summer holiday, and it is undoubtedly a more progressive, useful and pleasant form of holiday than the fenced-off summer camps for Soviet school children.

At the other end of the age scale, tourism has become especially popular. 'Travelling societies' for pensioners have grown up, in which they live in 'trailers' on wheels and move from one country to another. This has greatly increased the vitality of elderly people, who formerly suffered from loneliness and boredom.

As a gerontologist, I have seen our Soviet homes for the aged. They are a wretched, miserable sight. And here my professional purpose coincides with my sociological purpose set out in this study. International co-operation, international tourism, and the freedom of movement are not only useful for science, for technology and for the development of society and the integration of mankind. They are also, it appears, beneficial simply for health, and form a good way of solving certain important questions of gerontology, that science with which my interest in the problems considered in the present work began.

NOTE ADDED IN MAY 1969

In 1969, at long last, the *Bulletin of Tourist Information* (no. 2, p. 1, 1969) published some data on the number of tourists going from and coming to the USSR, broken down by countries. These data were given in the form of tables of the total figures for 1966–8. No commentaries on the tables were published in the *Bulletin*. Since we have already given some comparisons on the materials for 1965–7, it will be interesting to analyse the total figures for 1968.

According to Intourist data, in 1968, 1,686,160 foreign tourists came to the USSR (1,083,292 from socialist countries and 592,868 from capitalist countries). 1,499,963 persons went abroad from the USSR on tourist trips, of whom 804,329 went to socialist countries and 695,635 went to capitalist countries.

The total amount of international tourism to and from the USSR in comparison with other European countries is, as usual, negligible, and the Soviet Union takes the bottom place in Europe as far as tourist indices are concerned. For example, in 1968, 4 million foreigners visited Hungary, twice as many as visited the USSR (*Bulletin of Tourist*

Information, no. 1, 1969). But even these figures, minimal for a European country, which Intourist published, evoke serious doubts on careful consideration of the table. For example, let us consider the section of Soviet tourism to capitalist countries. We noted earlier that this form of tourism is especially difficult for Soviet citizens. The figure 695,635, however, does not seem small, especially when one takes into account the complications of arranging and getting approval for such trips. Is this figure reliable? A simple glance at the breakdown of tourists by country shows that it is unreliable. And this is so from many points of view.

In the table, this figure is totalled up from the data of Soviet tourism to the sixteen main countries from a tourist point of view (Austria, Belgium, Canada, Denmark, the Federal German Republic, Finland, France, Great Britain, India, Italy, Japan, the Netherlands, Norway, Sweden, Switzerland and the USA). All the rest are given under the heading 'other countries'. In 1968, the sixteen main tourist countries had 397,251 visits from the USSR, and the 'other countries' had 298,384 visits. In 1967, according to the same table, the 'other countries' received an even larger share of Soviet tourism—347,120 visits. What are these 'other capitalist countries' which receive almost half of Soviet tourism? In Europe, they are Greece, Iceland, Spain, Portugal, Luxembourg, Monaco, San Marino. But there is almost no Soviet tourism to Greece, due to the fascist regime. Spain and Portugal have no diplomatic relations with the USSR, and hence trips by Soviet citizens to these countries must be calculated in single figures. The mini-states, like San Marino and Monaco are visited mainly by gamblers. In America 'other countries' means the South American states. To go to these countries costs almost 400 roubles more than to go to the USA, and we do not have diplomatic relations with all of them. If, according to Intourist, about 3,000 persons went to the USA in 1968 (this is the lowest figure for the group of capitalist countries given in the table) then not more than this number could have gone to South America. We are left with Africa and the Near and Far East. Soviet tourism to the Arab countries is undoubtedly minimal, owing to the tense political situation there, while, apparently, not a single Soviet tourist went to Indonesia. We need not even discuss the Philippines, Thailand, etc. So we are left with 'Black Africa', and to it must go almost half of Soviet tourism to capitalist countries. But Africa constitutes 1 per cent in the total balance of world tourism. It can hardly form more than 1 per cent for Soviet tourism too. It is impossible, of course, to suppose that in 1967–8

600,000 Soviet tourists visited Asia and Africa. This is far greater than the total number of Soviet tourists visiting Western Europe—the main world centre of international tourism—in two years. The arbitrary nature of the total figure for 'other countries' is also confirmed by the figure for reverse tourism to the USSR. From the sixteen main capitalist countries named above, 592,868 tourists came to the USSR in 1968. From the 'other countries' only 92,915 persons came. In the 'other countries' there is too great a discrepancy between the number of Soviet tourists-visiting these countries and the number of their own citizens who come from these countries. Tourism with the 'other countries' gives the Soviet Union large currency losses, all the more so since we have hardly any surpluses of their currencies. Tourism with the main capitalist countries guarantees a profit. Yet the loss-bringing tourism with the 'other countries' continues from year to year. Can we believe in this? Have not these figures on the 'other countries' been introduced arbitrarily, to raise the total figures, to make the numbers coming to and going from the USSR apparently balance?

There is also great doubt about the unduly high figures for Soviet tourism to Japan. The table shows a figure for the number of Soviet tourists going to Japan which is considerably greater than the number of Soviet tourists going, for example, to Italy or France. But the cost of a trip to Japan is twice that of a trip to France. Only a little more than half as many tourists come to the USSR from Japan, and thus tourism to Japan also involves the USSR in a currency loss.

Another question also remains unclear when the tables are analysed. On many trips, especially in the case of sea tourism (cruises), one person visits some six to ten countries. In adding up the data on Soviet tourists to different countries, Intourist does not introduce any corrections to the total figures to take this into account. Instead of the number of Soviet tourists, it gives, in effect, the number of visits of Soviet citizens to different countries. It is also not known whether the figures given per country are tourism figures, or whether these are the total figures for all visits to a given country not only for tourist purposes but also on business including sailors of the mercantile marine, the builders of the Aswan dam, and so on.

Finland occupies a special position in the group of capitalist countries, as far as tourism is concerned. In 1967, 327,980 tourists came to the USSR from Finland, almost half the total number of tourists from all the capitalist countries. In 1968, tourism from Finland fell to 192,025 persons which was almost one-third of the total tourism from capitalist countries and 50 per cent of all European tourism to the USSR. Yet less than 1 per cent of the total population of Western Europe lives in Finland. The fact that little Finland accounts for almost half the tourism to the USSR from the 'currency' countries is clear evidence of the slight extent to which we make use of the tourist possibilities of our own country and the great role that the facilitated entry of Finns 'without visa' into the USSR is playing. However, since visits from Finland are restricted to the Leningrad zone and Estonia, and normally are short one-day or two-day trips, their economic significance cannot be very great.

For economic comparisons and, in general, for the correct conclusions to be drawn, Intourist must publish not arbitrary figures of 'visits' but data on the cost and earnings of international tourism to the USSR.

Over the group of socialist countries in 1968, first place for Soviet tourists was held by Poland (216,509 persons) and second place by Bulgaria (125,553 persons).

CONCLUSION

What the author would like to say to certain organizations which control the international co-operation of Soviet citizens

I

To Intourist

THE name of your monopoly firm for international tourism into and out of the USSR is preserved, I feel, from the time when no Soviet tourists went abroad.[1] There were only foreign tourists coming to the USSR, and even these in very sparse numbers. Nowadays, in addition to your former functions, you have to serve Soviet tourists as well. But for some reason you do this in a very strange manner. As, for some reason, I could find no Intourist office in my own provincial centre, I went to Moscow and visited the Intourist central office to find out what foreign trip they could offer me in the autumn of 1967 for two weeks' leave I had still due to me. I imagined the position of any Mexican or Swede who was faced with such a problem of having a fortnight's holiday abroad. There would be dozens of tourist firms at his service. He would only have to go there, and in half an hour he would come out with a complete programme and tickets for all the proposed itinerary. But I am not a Mexican or a Swede, and hence I was faced with the modest problem of finding out from Intourist the possibilities of my going, in September 1967, to just one country—Czechoslovakia. This was before the removal of Novotny and the internal upheavals there.

The Intourist central office, which is situated in the monumental building of the former US embassy, opposite the Natsional Hotel, delighted me with its explicit organization and structure of sections. On the doors of the rooms were impressive signs: 'Directorate for Sweden', 'Conference Section', 'Directorate for Soviet Tourism to the Countries of Africa and Asia', 'Directorate for Small Countries', 'Directorate for Soviet Tourism to Czechoslovakia, Hungary and Poland'. I went in at the last of these doors. The room was furnished with several tables, and there were posters on the walls advertising the beauty of the countries concerned. Above the table on the right hung a poster with a view of a seaside resort in Bulgaria, above the table on the left a panorama of Prague. A girl was sitting here to deal with the tourism of Soviet citizens

[1] Intourist is an acronym for '*I*nostrannyi *turist*' (foreign tourist)—*Translator*.

to Czechoslovakia. According to the statistics, 150 Soviet tourists go to Czechoslovakia every day, and nearly 500 to Bulgaria, but there were no prospective clients in the room. I went over to the table where the clerk for Czechoslovakia worked and put my request to her. She could not understand me at first, and when she did understand me, she gazed at me as if, at the very least, I had tumbled out of the moon or Mars.

'Excuse me, citizen, but don't you even know that Intourist does not deal directly with individual citizens? We only deal with organizations, Ministries and the provincial trade union committees. We don't do business with private persons.'

'All the same,' I began to argue, 'I know that people come to this country from abroad mainly as individual tourists!'

'Yes, but they're foreigners. In our country, one has to get approval. Go to the Section of Foreign Tourism for Soviet Citizens of the Moscow Council of Trade Unions, and they'll explain it to you there. But it will be useless, anyway, now, this year's quota for Czechoslovakia is full.'

I went to the Regional Council of Moscow Trade Unions on Belinskaya Street. The small room, where three inspectors of foreign tourism for Soviet citizens sat, was not encumbered by the presence of clients, although here, it would seem, the threads of international tourism converge for all the many millions in Moscow. Here I put my request once again. And once again the reaction was negative: 'We don't approve individual tourists, only groups on application from the Departments. Only Departments can consider "exit dossiers". You must apply to your own establishment about questions of tourism,' the inspector explained to me.

And so it became clear to me that there are no agencies or firms in the Soviet Union to serve Soviet citizens over foreign tourism, similar to the tourist firms which serve the citizens of all other civilized and uncivilized countries. International tourism in the USSR is still one of the forms of activity of state institutions, factories, institutes and Ministries. They are the intermediaries between Intourist and the individual citizen who wishes to travel. Is this normal? Of course not! In effect, this structure of foreign tourism destroys its chief quality, the feeling of rest, of a break in one's routine duties and one's regular habits. For even abroad a man is surrounded by his colleagues, and the group leader keeps a careful eye on him. No one who chooses to take a foreign trip as his holiday during his leave period can be quite sure that this will be possible, that the trip will not be cancelled, that all stages of approval

K

will be successfully negotiated, that in the end it will not all come to nothing, as a result of some prohibition that cannot be questioned.

It seems to me that Intourist ought to treat Soviet citizens as humanely as it treats foreigners. It is necessary to give the firm a new name such as International Tourist and give it the function of *arranging and approving* individual tourists and groups, freeing other Soviet establishments from this duty. And, of course, the process of approval should be simplified, especially in the case of repeated trips. This is not only rational, but economic. Nowadays the approval of tourist groups occupies thousands of establishments, hundreds of departments. An army of officials have to check no less than a million and a half 'exit dossiers' and 'autobiographies' every year, carefully analysing all the answers to all the questions, giving some of them special consideration. And the tourist does not know what significance all these humiliating questions and answers have. Who, for example, can foresee the significance to the answer to Question 17: 'Were you or any of your relatives taken prisoner or interned during the Second World War? State who, where, when, and under what circumstances liberated?'

Sitting in the various Foreign Sections, these clerks work with no criteria, and in most cases there is nothing much for them to do. If they transferred all these red-tape bundles of papers from the budgetary departments to a tourist agency which worked on a business basis and on the principle of profitability, then the procedure of approval would soon be simplified and the clerks would soon have their work cut out. The number of unproductive workers in the country would be reduced by millions of man-days which are wasted on approving questionnaires, references, character references, etc., and on checking them; and they would be able to be used for some more worthwhile purpose.

If we do all this in the next few years, then perhaps the Soviet Union will soon overtake Bulgaria or Finland as far as international tourism is concerned.

2

To the All-Union Geographical Society

Your society has a very rich tradition and for many years has enjoyed well-earned fame. In your modest house in Demidov Lane in St Petersburg the famous Russian travellers N. M. Prjevalsky, N. N. Miklukho-Maklai, G. Grumm-Grzhimailo, V. Semenov-Tyan-Shan'skii, Langsdorf and Yu. M. Shokal'skii presented reports on their expeditions. For almost ten years the President of the Society was Nikolai I. Vavilov, a burning enthusiast for botanic-geographical expeditions.

But the flourishing of the Geographical Society all seems to have taken place at the end of the last century. There was some increase in activity noticeable at the end of the 1920s and beginning of the 1930s, but then a depression occurred in dry-land geography expeditions, which has not been entirely wiped out even today. From 1934 onwards and right up to his arrest in August 1940, even the former President of the Geographical Society, Nikolai Vavilov, could not obtain permission for a single one of the foreign expeditions which he wanted to organize. At the International Geographical Congress in Warsaw in 1934 there were only two representatives from the USSR.

But even today serious journeys of Soviet scientists to the countries of the world are a rarity. It is easier for a Soviet geographer, botanist, zoologist, ethnographer, entomologist or plant-breeder to get to Antarctica or the North Pole than on an expedition to Australia, South America, Africa, India or Pakistan. Marine expeditions on special ships came to have a clear predominance over dry-land expeditions.

How many orientalists have never seen the countries which they study? How many Africanists have never been to Africa? How many Americanists have never been to America? The majority! And how many teachers of geography are there in the USSR who have never seen a foreign country? Also the majority.

Somehow it has come about that we learn about foreign countries from the descriptions of journalists and writers rather than from geographers and explorers. For instance, during the years of Soviet rule, there has not been a single serious geographical expedition to Australia, and only recently did we learn about this country from the travel note-books of the writer Daniil Granin, who spent some time there (*A Month Upside Down*, Lenizdat, 1966). Before his trip to Australia, Granin went to the Australian Department in the Institute of Anthropology and Ethnography of the Academy of Sciences of the USSR in Leningrad to find out all that he could about the country from the experts in the Acad-emy. The episode of this visit has stuck in my mind more vividly than anything else in the book.

In the Institute, Granin met the experts on Australia. They showed him dozens of books, albums, maps, and their own articles and works on Australia. But all these works had been written at second hand. Granin then speaks of the Australianists:

They smiled in a somewhat wry manner. None of them, it turned out, had ever been to Australia. All their lives they had studied Australia from afar, like astronomers. They knew everything about Australia. They knew its colours, its people. its scents, legends, songs and paintings. The accuracy of their knowledge I could check only after I returned from Australia. I went then to the Institute to tell them about my trip and did not notice how I began listening to their tales instead.

On that first occasion, Vladimir Rafailovich took me into the museum. In an empty, half-dark room behind glass sat some dusty aborigines among their boomerangs, axes and spear-throwers. The collection had been compiled by Miklukho-Maklai and then by Yashchenko. From the time when Yashchenko visited Australia, sixty years before, the museum had received nothing special new to replenish it. No expeditions were sent out. Vladimir Rafailovich is one of our Australianists who studies Aborigine life in all its details: he could go to the Aborigines and become indistinguishable from one of them. But sitting on Vasil'evskii Island you will not become a Miklukho-Maklai. When I listened to him, I felt that he would even be willing to sail on a raft, like Thor Heyerdahl, to get to his beloved Australia. How many possible Miklukho-Maklais, enthusiasts, cour-ageous, selfless would-be travellers are forced to pass their whole lives in these rooms, filled with the bookshelves? (*A Month Upside-Down*, p. 17.)

A large part of our information on present-day—or rather recent—South America, Africa and Asia, on the life of the nations who inhabit these continents, has been gained over the last fifteen years from the books of the Czech engineers and travellers Jiři Hanzelka and Miroslav Zikmund.

Now geography is, of course, an especially complex science. Without geographical investigations modern botany could not develop, nor could zoology. Within the USSR there are not more than 1 per cent of all the animal and plant species which inhabit our planet. But it is only the gates of zoological parks and botanical gardens which are freely open to our zoologists and botanists. Pedology, plant-breeding, ethnography and anthropology cannot develop without international expeditions. Even genetics nowadays requires extensive expedition research, and Soviet genetico-geographical research has contributed hardly a single grain to the compilation of maps of the world distribution of a number of hereditary diseases, one of the major achievements of human genetics of the last decade, except for that which was carried out within the USSR. There was very little done even of this, and many maps of this kind do not include our country.

My first teacher, Professor P. M. Zhukovskii, who in 1951 became Director of the All-Union Institute of Plant-Breeding, tried to revive Vavilov's tradition of expeditions. As part of the scientific work of the Institute an expedition to South America was needed to find the wild species of potatoes which grow there in abundant diversity in their native land. The Institute needed immune species for cross-breeding. He went on pressing for permission for the expedition for several years. A trip was planned for a group of colleagues headed by the Director. But, in the end permission came through for only one person—the Director of the Institute. Even the chief specialist on potatoes, who formerly under Vavilov's direction had found many new species of potatoes in South America, could not get permission for an expedition in 1966. Zhukovskii at first wanted to turn down the trip, but afterwards he decided to go. Many years before, on another expedition to Asia Minor, he had also roamed about on his own for two years. 'The expedition from our country consisted of one man,' he wrote, in the foreword to his book *The Agriculture of Turkey*. He had to repeat this sentence in 1956, with the difference that he was now seventy years old, and it was not easy for him to do useful work alone, to collect plants, pack them and dispatch them, particularly in the tropics. But even on this expedition a great deal was done. How much more would have been done if the whole of the designated group, including young people, could have gone on the expedition?

And how many hazardous journeys have been made in the last few years by foreign single-handed sailors, enthusiasts who have sailed around the world in little boats and yachts. Not long ago we heard of two such Soviet daredevils who sailed more than a thousand kilometres in the Arctic Ocean. But why is it only the Arctic Ocean that is open to Soviet sailing enthusiasts?

Geography is a science which cannot develop without the romance of travel, without boldness and without enthusiasts for adventure, without the risk of uncharted roads. It is possible nowadays to forecast that it will be Soviet explorers who are first on Venus. But in the study of our own planet we are lagging behind. And it is not the fear of difficulties which is to blame. For many people it is easier to cross the mountains of Tienshan, to carve a way through the tropical jungles, to cross the Sahara and sail across the Pacific than to overcome the barriers of questionnaires, 'Exit Commissions' and plans of 'currency man-days'.

3

To the Ideological Commission of the Central Committee of the CPSU

THE Ideological Commission of the Central Committee of the CPSU controls both science and the press in our country, and hence the present book obviously cannot avoid this Commission on its undoubtedly difficult road towards publication—all the more so, since we have been so rash as to touch upon questions of ideology in it. Instead of speaking of the implacable conflict of ideologies, we have spoken of certain trends towards integration (although integration may also occur as a result of conflict). Hence I should like once again to make clear my position, my purpose and the questions which arose in the work on this book. Wait, pause a little, before declaring it an 'ideological deviation', 'anti-Soviet', and 'Anti-Party'. Back in 1963 another one of my books, a scientific monograph on the synthesis of proteins, was sent from the press to your Commission, for special consideration by your editors, when the former Deputy Chairman of the Commission, Comrade Snastin, also found it to be an example of an 'ideological deviation', simply because several pages of the book were devoted to a criticism of T. D. Lysenko, more correctly to a criticism of his concept of heredity. The same charge was repeated by the former secretary of the Moscow City Committee of the CPSU, Comrade N. G. Egorychev in his speech to the June Ideological Plenum of the Central Committee of the CPSU in 1963. The book was at once withdrawn from all shops and the offending pages were cut out and replaced by neutral text. But after a few more years it became clear that Lysenko really was a pseudo-scientist, an eyewash-peddler, and that his 'materialistic' biology was so much bluff.

And how many similar stories could one tell about chemistry, physics and the legal sciences! *Short Course in the History of the All-Union Communist Party (Bolsheviks)* which was once the summit of Marxist thought is now under a ban. Former 'enemies of the people' have been rehabilitated, and their accusers feel very awkward. The history of the last fifteen years teaches us *not to make hasty decisions*, even if they seem to be beyond doubt.

The very concept of an 'ideological deviation' which in recent years has very often been used as an accusation and even in judicial deliberations, is very subjective and undefined. Scientifically speaking, it is senseless and absurd. If ideology is a science, if communism is a science, if Marxism-Leninism is a science, then any criticism of any proposition in these sciences is also a science and not a 'deviation'. In any science, if it is not a collection of empty dogmas, certain propositions are continually going out of date and need to be replaced, new ideas, new propositions are always appearing in connection with new circumstances, new conditions, new relationships. 'Deviation' according to this concept, literally means an act of sabotage or wrecking within the opposition camp by means of spies smuggled in or enlisted on the spot. Consequently if our ideological opponents, for example, the British Labour Party or the Chinese Maoists, publish critical statements about certain aspects of life in the USSR, for example, the Labour Party about the dominance of censorship and the absence of freedom of the Press, or the Chinese on the weakness of censorship in the USSR and its inability to prevent the appearance in the press of revisionist articles, then this is not really a deviation. This is criticism from outside. But if the same sentiments begin to be expressed by Soviet citizens, this is generally called deviation, more correctly 'ideological deviation', and the Soviet citizens who get such thoughts in their heads are considered to be ideological agents of the Western or Eastern powers. If the Soviet citizen expresses critical thoughts in the pages of the foreign press, then this is considered to be even worse, an act of 'ideological treason' or even a crime.

There is no foundation for this approach in common sense, let alone scientific logic. It is based only on the principle of *infallibility*, a principle which can be only a dogma of religion and absolute power. Since a complex state system and political and economic realities cannot normally exist unless there is criticism and self-criticism, unless errors and deficiencies are analysed and the results of work are considered, it becomes necessary to limit the boundaries of permissible criticism. We must determine which forms of criticism are 'ideological deviations' and which are not, which can be considered as useful self-criticism aiding the development of society along the path to its ultimate aim, the building of communism. These limits are set, as I see it, by the Ideological Commission and to some extent by the censorship (apart from its tasks of preventing the leakage of military secrets).

As a scientist accustomed to analyse facts it is quite clear to me that there are *no explicit criteria for demarcating the permissible forms of criticism*. We can all see that what it was possible and even laudable to do some years back (for example, to abuse the personality cult and unmask Stalin's errors and crimes, to praise 'Michurin biology', the Councils of National Economy, to publish literary works about labour camps, to praise life in Yugoslavia) is now impossible and is now treated as an 'ideological deviation'. The censorship in 1968 would not pass for publication many of the works of 1960–2 if they were written now and not then. Solzhenitsyn's *One Day in the Life of Ivan Denisovich* was published in 1962 as a result of a unanimous vote of the Presidium of the Central Committee of the CPSU and was received enthusiastically by readers and critics, but now this work is quietly being withdrawn from the public libraries. But the instructions upon which the censorship changes the face of the press and the direction of criticism are top secret. How then is it possible to learn the difference between normal criticism and 'ideological deviation' at any given moment?

The criteria of demarcation are worked out, of course, by those who determine the nature of the instructions for the censorship and the directives for the editors-in-chief of publishing concerns. But who are they? I think that I will not be wrong if I assume that these directives are worked out in the Politburo of the Central Committee of the CPSU, in the organ of political direction, to which we all turn with maximum trust. Nevertheless I do not consider that this kind of determination of the permissible boundaries of criticism is scientifically sound. If the ideology of society in its broad sense is a science and not merely a weapon of political power, then the organ of power, whether state or political, should not regulate the permissible limits of discussion. It should merely keep watch to see that discussion, criticism and analysis take place by lawful means. If the organ of power itself takes part in the discussion and uses force and breaks its own laws, which it established, roughly meddling in the constitutional rights of those taking part in the discussion, in that case it turns ideology not into a science, but into a pseudo-science, dogma, a collection of subjective rules.

If it is recognized that 'ideological deviation' is not a phantom, but is something real, then from the point of view of strict scientific logic, it cannot be the expression of certain propositions which contradict those which are official, or current, or predominant at a given moment or even those which are shared by the majority, nor propositions which agree with those which are recognized as correct in another country, but only be a breach of the law in disseminating some proposition or other, and the use of illegal means by one side of the discussion or the other.

K*

If a critic of some scientific proposition breaks the law in an argument, if, for example, he hits his opponent over the head with a club or makes deliberate slanderous accusations about him, then he commits a crime, a *deviation*. If, on the other hand, the defender of some scientific theory hits his critic over the head or stops his mouth for him, then this action can be considered as a crime, a deviation.

Passing now to the field of ideology, we find the same relationship between polemics and 'ideological deviation'. The side in an argument which starts to break the law thereby adopts the method of deviation. And if a government which at a particular moment in time adopts a particular point of view uses illegal measures in its polemics against those who hold different views; encroaches upon the secrecy of correspondence, arbitrarily extends the legal functions of the censorship, dismisses people from work, prosecutes them, breaking the standards of legal procedure, commits slander, restricts civil rights, and so on, then this means of ideological warfare is an ideological deviation from the ideology of communism as a whole. The Marxist communist ideology is something international and universal, it extends in time into the past and future, it develops and becomes more complex with the inevitable increase of exchange of information. The chief aim of communism, as a political system, in the works of Karl Marx, consists of 'destroying all attitudes under which a man can be humiliated, oppressed or outcast'.

The international character of the communist ideology and Marxism makes the restriction of any scientific discussion in this field by internal organizations absurd. No science can be built on the principle on which the ideological system in our country is built, with the restrictions in our country on propagating certain ideas. The normal development of the political, economic and philosophical sciences, literature, sociology, and so on, must be free. The truth is tested by time. Restriction of the freedom of discussion leads to most undesirable consequences. Here the following analogy is very appropriate. The advancing course of knowledge can be compared to the flow of a river. It receives from its watershed a great number of individual streams and rivulets, and becomes ever deeper and finally flows out into the general sea of knowledge. If a dam is put in the river with a gap in it which does not allow the passage through it of the whole bulk of water, then part of the water will be held back, and will overflow the limits of the ordinary bed of the stream, forming a lake, filling all the available lowland of the valley. This water cannot disappear entirely, since it is produced by perpetual circulation. It overflows, finds an outlet, forming a number of new small rivers, flowing out into the valley. If the gap in the dam is too small, the rise of water in the valley may quickly reach such a level that it floods over the countryside and returns to the old bed. It can even wash the dam away. But if the dam is strong and the gap is not too small, the excess of water will only gradually bog up the valley.

Human creativity is of its nature diverse. It requires a free channel. If a dam stands in its way, then part of its creative energy, the production of the intellect and talent of people will be lost, and will not reach the eternal sea of knowledge of all mankind. A discovery is hidden with its author, never seeing the light of day, an outstanding novel perishes without being read by anyone, and all mankind is potentially the loser.

Formerly, during the time of the 'personality cult', this excess water which could not get through the narrow gap in the dam was not able to flow over into the valley. They imprisoned it in underground reservoirs, they boiled it away in enormous vats. The valley remained dry. Then, for a certain period the gap in the dam was considerably widened and almost all the force of the stream was able to pass through it. And then, again, it began to close. And streams flowed forth on all sides— '*samizdat*' streams. The people living in the valley became richer and bolder, they began to make small channels for the surplus water and used it to irrigate their land. The products of creativity which did not pass through the dam into the main river bed were now not completely lost. From neighbouring valleys someone cut tunnels through the watershed, and part of the surplus water began to flow out that way; since you do not need it, let it flow down into the general sea of knowledge by other channels, which were not theirs. Thus the situation was created which we see now. The official channels of the press are very narrow, there are only a few publishing houses, and they are not able to cope with the output of the creative intelligentsia. Furthermore, censorship and editorial caution bar the way for many works and writings. And there are many other barriers. But just as the earth still oozes forth the water which it feeds to the rivers, so do people do creative work, and do not always think according to the current political situation. If the product of their creativity, a story, a song, a novel or a scientific work on history or sociology, a publicist sketch or a picture which possesses a high artistic quality, an innovation or the force of truth is stopped by the dam of various obstacles, it will no longer simply be lost. And again this is the result not just of less fear of the consequences than formerly, but of the greater prosperity of the people whose amount of free time has sharply increased. It is not only the state power which now controls the means of manifolding copies; these means now belong to a great mass of the population, especially the intelligentsia. There are hundreds of thousands of scientists, the technological and academic intelligentsia are numbered in millions and journalists in tens of thousands. And a very great number of these have typewriters, cameras and tape-recorders. And they have the free time to copy out one work or another. Even if a half per cent of this mass of people is ready to put aside a little time to have some work or another, this will enable it to be manifolded in thousands of copies. This is the famous 'samizdat' which is a phenomenon of the modern world.

Of course, the distribution of literary works in manuscript is in itself no new phenomenon; it is as old as the world. It also flourished in Tsarist Russia. How many of Pushkin's poems circulated only in manuscript! Lermontov's famous poem on Pushkin's death was manifolded by the 'samizdat' of the day, by copying out by hand. I have seen in the collection of one amateur the famous work of Lev Tolstoi *The Kreutzer Sonata* in a 'samizdat' variant, accurately copied out by hand and bound up in book form. *The Kreutzer Sonata* was originally forbidden by the Tsarist censorship and for a long time could not be printed.

Nevertheless, 'samizdat' today has many peculiar features. It arose relatively recently not as some hidden, secret affair, as previously, limited to a small 'edition' for a very narrow circle of people and used predominantly for the propagation of poems, often anonymous ones. In Stalin's time there was practically no 'samizdat', it was all nipped in the bud. The only things that flourished were political anecdotes propagated by word of mouth, and this developed especially in the first few years of the 'Khrushchev decade'. The modern 'samizdat', the tide of which began to rise in the last years of that decade as a reaction to the restraints being introduced on literary, historical, sociological and, in part, scientific (biological and agricultural) creative activity, became very apparent in the work of the ideological plenum in June 1963, and at once revealed itself not as a hidden but as a powerful force.

What is held back by the dam which has been erected is spontaneously manifolded by the intelligentsia, not only poems and small literary works, shorthand records of speeches, etc., but also large-scale works of a historical, sociological and literary character. 'Samizdat' has caught up in its stream stories and novels of considerable length, extensive cycles of songs, and sometimes, in rare cases, translations of foreign authors. Even large-scale works are rapidly manifolded in hundreds and thousands of copies and, once they are on the conveyer belt, so to speak, tens and sometimes hundreds of thousands of people read them, without a break, over many years, until the photocopy paper is torn completely to rags. The process is a sort of chain reaction.

But the process has its own laws, determined by the interest of the reading masses, people who think and think seriously. Practically none of the great quantity of anti-Soviet works, sometimes in Russian, which are sent to us from other countries is manifolded by our intelligentsia. The reason for this is not only the strong tradition of caution towards foreign anti-Soviet propaganda, nor the far stricter laws relating to such literature, but, first and foremost, because this sort of literature is very poor and feeble and shows very little knowledge of our internal problems. I personally have seen several such works, and they did not arouse any interest in me whatsoever, except for books describing the events in Hungary in October 1956. I must say, straight away, that the books which I read did not fall into my hands via the NTS[1] or any other illegal means, but by an entirely respectable and approved means. There exists a very odd but, in general, useful tradition that the most important books, even if they are anti-Soviet, which are published in the West are also printed in the USSR, but in a very small, private edition, and are then sent out, according to special lists, to responsible workers of the Party and state apparatus. It is considered that these workers are strong enough in their ideals for such books to be useful to them, and not dangerous. These books have no sale price, and all the copies are numbered. Generally between 1,000 and 2,000 of them are produced, but sometimes the edition is less, sometimes only 25 to 30 copies, just for the use of the Politburo. A large proportion of the copies are sent out by the lists without any obligation on returning them, and the books obtained in this way are sometimes kept in one's personal library at home. But if such a book disappears from its owner and is found in free circulation, then they establish the culprit who has failed in his vigilance by the number, and, it must be supposed, he will have to pay the penalty for it. I myself am not on any such list, but sometimes it has been possible to read such books in the libraries of workers whose names are on the list and who have now retired or died.

The Soviet intelligentsia likewise have not manifolded nor shown any special interest in the literary works of Tarsis, Sinyavskii and Daniel', which have been widely published abroad and have even penetrated into our country through certain channels. I have not had occasion to

---

[1] (Narodnaya Trudovaya Soyuz)—the 'National Labour Union', a Russian émigré organization, see below p. 463—*Translator*.

read them, and I shall not suggest any reasons for the absence of interest in these works. It is certainly not a matter of literary talent. I am absolutely sure that even a brilliantly talented detective-story, the most remarkably outstanding novel on the reign of Ivan the Terrible, or a work of genius on solid state physics would not be taken up by a massive 'samizdat' if the official press had turned it down. These works can be read, too, in the manuscripts prepared by the authors, but no active interest is taken. 'Samizdat' takes up only those works which appeal to the thinking part of our society as an ideological weapon, which, while being talented, are also a force within the state and have the courage of new forms and approaches and a depth of thought, and which evoke a response in the soul of man by their undoubted truth. When a man feels that the work which he has read must certainly be read by others, that it changes something for the better, that it will call the guilty to account and reveal the roots of an evil which is felt by all, then the reader will want to help the author, and will want to use his work and his voice and his pocket in preserving and propagating the work which he has read. 'Samizdat' is a better estimate of the worth of a book than the official literary criticism. I feel sure that if from 1963 to 1967 all book-publishing activity in the country had stopped and that nothing scientific or artistic written in those years had been published, there would have been no important changes in the 'samizdat' catalogue. What appears today in hundreds of thousands of copies on the shelves of bookshops from presses such as Mysl', Progress, Sovetskaya Literatura, Molodaya Gvardiya and Kolos is all entirely useful literature, but it is hardly likely, if this flow had been stopped, that it would have been sent on its way with the aid of people's own typewriters and cameras.

When, at the end of 1962, Khrushchev began to introduce additional censorship restrictions, which were sharply intensified in 1963 (so as not to spoil the picture of the ten-year jubilee of the 'new course') he undoubtedly did not foresee that a phenomenon such as 'samizdat' would arise. The government was not ready for 'samizdat', and there were no laws permitting them to punish this form of activity of the Soviet people. Nor could there be any logical or judicial base for such laws, since all this activity of the population lies in the sphere of personal, private life. It would be just as absurd to punish people for other activities apart from their work, 'hobbies', collecting stamps or matchbox labels, fishing or playing chess.

It is impossible to impute guilt to the authors of works manifolded in this way. In the final analysis an author always has the right to show his work before publication to a number of people. If the author has no official agreement with a publishing house, if he has not done the work as an assignment that is part of his job, in working hours paid for by the state, then it remains his own personal property, the right to which is guaranteed by the Constitution. And as his own undoubted property, the author can show the manuscript to any other person, can make a gift of it, send it through the post, deposit it for safe-keeping, change it, revise it in accordance with people's observations or without them and also destroy it or bequeath it. He can also manifold it by legal means on his own account, send it to editors or colleagues for comments and observations, to possible readers to study their reactions, hold readings and verbal discussions. All this is entirely legal, it is not a criminal activity, even, if it turns out that the work contains serious 'ideological' errors. It is because of this that it is necessary to check the manuscript carefully while still in manuscript, in order to correct possible defects.

As a result, an entirely legal activity by the author and the duty of the readers as patriotic citizens sometimes lead to the manifolding of works, especially in cases when the reader feels from his experience of life that the work he has read will not 'get through' in the official press. Every one of us knows just what this official press is.

But how inoffensive is the work which is turned down by the press? How harmless is the manuscript forbidden by the censor? How powerless the idea propagated by the ancient method of hand-written copies? Here we come to a special and also new phenomenon. We have no right to avoid an analysis of it, since it is connected with all the questions which have been considered in this work. This is the phenomenon of international co-operation in the production of works of spiritual and material value, the outflow of the water held back by the dam into other valleys through the tunnels hewn out by international communications. The chain reaction of ordinary lawful copying of some literary or polemic work, for example, and its propagation through personal channels, among individual groups of enthusiasts, if it continues for a long time and does not die down, having exhausted its energy and satisfied only a narrow circle of people, may also spread across the state frontier. The international movement of people is now so considerable that to avoid the outflow across the frontier of information that has been freely propagated by personal means is as difficult as to keep a virus within national boundaries. Moreover one must admit that there is probably some kind of ideological and political paying agency employed by foreign intelligence and publishing houses, or in émigré organizations and among diplomatic representatives. The propagation of works by 'samizdat' may come into contact with a secret agent of this sort at some level. And, finally, we have all recently been witnesses of the fact that certain young people, like Galanskov and Ginzburg who recently were convicted, have been active in collecting 'samizdat' works, making them into collections of the type of the journal *Phoenix* and the *White Book* and sending them abroad, without concealing their activity. For the sending abroad, *per se*, of a non-classified manuscript cannot be ranked as a criminal offence. Accordingly, Galanskov and Ginzburg were not tried for sending manuscripts abroad, but on other charges, which were not very clearly proved by the court and the investigation (connection with the NTS and currency operations).

But once it has got abroad, the manuscript of a Soviet author may find a publisher there; it may be manifolded and translated into various languages not by individual methods but by modern industrial means. 'Samizdat' is transformed into 'tamizdat'.[1] Then, by means of radio, and, if the opportunity arises, sometimes, although rarely, by post, it returns to its native land, where it is read or heard by hundreds of thousands or millions of people. This turn of affairs has begun to cause serious disquiet to those spheres in the Soviet Union in charge of the control of the press. When cases of this kind could be counted in single figures, it was possible to ignore them. (Boris Pasternak's novel *Doctor Zhivago* which drew the attention of the world to the hidden reserves of Russian literature went abroad by a different, legal, way, with the permission of the press which were contemplating publishing the novel in the USSR.) But in 1966–7 there began a massive 'outflow' from the USSR of works which had accumulated behind the 'dam' of the censorship. A great impression was made abroad by Evgeniya Ginzburg's book *The Steep Path* which was published in many countries and which describes life in women's prisons, camps and deportation settlements during the Stalinist tyranny and the courage and will of the Soviet patriots and communists who had been unjustly convicted. This book, based on real facts and on the author's experience, is a reportage book, written with talent, which had circulated in the USSR for two years by 'samizdat'

---

[1] 'Samizdat' means 'self-published', from the Russian *sam*—self, and is now a well-recognized name for the phenomenon described. 'Tamizdat' from *tam*—there—is apparently Medvedev's own coining, to describe the publication abroad of a work which can circulate in the Soviet Union only in 'samizdat' form—*Translator*.

after it had been refused publication in a number of the literary journals. During that time it was read by many thousands of people, and finally it fell into the hands of a certain Italian who published it in Italy in Russian and Italian, in an enormous edition, and arranged for its translation into many other languages. The same fate befell Lidiya Chukovskaya's story 'Sofia Petrovna', which was published in England, stories by Shalamov, some brief stories by Solzhenitsyn, the famous letter of Solzhenitsyn to the Fourth Congress of Soviet Writers, the letter of the poet Andrei Voznesenskii to the Editor of *Pravda*, Galina Serebryakhova's story of the Stalinist camps, collective letters of groups of Soviet writers on various subjects and a great quantity of other materials and works. Recently the foreign radio announced that Solzhenitsyn's story *Cancer Ward* and his novel *The First Circle* were being published in the USA. *Cancer Ward* was discussed for some years in literary circles, and was even set in type for publication in *Novyi Mir*, but it never came out in the USSR. As for *The First Circle*, an agreement on its publication was concluded with the author back in 1964, but then the novel was confiscated. 'Samizdat' took these works abroad, and now they have become a matter of 'business' for Western publishers.[1]

In almost all cases, the Western presses publish the works of Soviet authors without contracts, without the consent of the author and without the consent of the USSR. And the Soviet authors have no protection against this robbery. It can happen that what gets abroad is an unrevised version of the work, incomplete and preliminary. The author still wants to work on it and to take people's comments into account. The translation of the book is done not as a work of quality, since the press which gets hold of the manuscript is some gutter press or anti-Soviet émigré house which dresses the book up with its own cheap commentaries and notes. The author, if he learns about the possible publication of the book, protests and sends letters forbidding it, but all in vain. 'Business', commercial gain and the speculative approach are triumphant. Soviet authors are robbed, exploited and violated, since they have no defence against such robbery and piracy. Almost all countries protect the authors' rights of their citizens abroad, by associating themselves with the special international conventions on authors' rights and copyright. So far the Soviet Union has refused to associate itself with these conventions (the Berne Convention and the Universal Copyright Convention which

[1] The novel *Cancer Ward* and the novel *The First Circle* were published in the USA, England, Germany, France and Italy in the autumn of 1968—*Author's note.*

came into force in 1955 and which was worked out by a special commission of UNESCO). Many times it has been proposed that our country should associate itself with these Conventions, but the Soviet Union has always refused to do so. But if our country did not refuse to enter into this agreement, then maybe the robbery which Soviet authors suffer would be reduced. The presses over there, at least some of them, would be perturbed by feelings of remorse. But now nothing perturbs them. It does not perturb them, because the USSR also, and certainly on a much wider scale, inflicts the same robbery on foreign authors and presses. Just as in the past, when we refused to participate in the conventions on patents and licences and thought it more advantageous to borrow foreign inventions for ourselves, without paying the foreign inventors and patent-holders the sums due to them, so in the book-publishing business we consider it permissible to print for ourselves translations of literary and scientific works by foreign authors, and simply to reproduce these works untranslated, without paying royalties to the authors of these works and without asking permission either of the presses with whom the authors have a contract, or of the authors themselves.

The Universal Copyright Convention, which protects the interests of authors and the publishers who have contractual agreements with them, states that an author has an unconditional right to royalties earned, not only on the edition of his book published by the publisher with whom he has the primary agreement, but also on translations of this work put out by publishers in other languages. In this case, the presses who have the primary contract and sell the translation rights receive the appropriate financial compensation. It is clear, of course, that if a book first appears in the German language, and then a massive edition of it comes out in English, that this will decrease the earnings of the German edition. Many people who know both German and English may prefer to buy the English version. If there were no English version, they would buy the German one. The Convention has a universal application. But the Soviet Union which inevitably produces a mass of translations from other languages (without this the life of a developed civilized society would be simply impossible) in order to save currency refuses as a rule to pay royalties to foreign authors and to pay for reproduction and translation licences. Only sometimes are 'progressive authors' paid royalties at the request of Soviet establishments and social organizations, but only if the author comes to the USSR. And since Soviet publishing houses can publish foreign authors both in translation and in the original (with massive editions 'for those studying foreign languages'), since these

translations and reproductions are not infrequently exported and compete with the originals in certain markets (in the socialist countries and
in Africa) coming on to those markets at very low prices, and since all
this is done as contraband, without the permission of the authors and
the foreign presses, then the foreign presses, by way of counter-
measures avail themselves of any Soviet publications and the works of
Soviet authors without taking account of the interests of the Soviet
authors or the Soviet presses. A Soviet author, supposing his work,
which is not being published in the USSR, has been manifolded by
'samizdat' and sent abroad, can avoid its being used for anti-Soviet purposes, its publication in Russian by émigré circles, its use in Russian-
language transmissions on foreign radio and for other forms of political
speculation to the harm of our country, in only one way. He must conclude an official contract with a reputable foreign publishing firm. In
this case, even a Soviet author is protected by the international conventions and the laws on authors' rights. He has complete control over
all forms of his work, and can forbid its use for anti-Soviet purposes,
protect it from distortions, translation into other languages, publication
in Russian by the gutter press, filming and other actions which would
injure his feeling of patriotism and cause harm to our country. In the
complicated situation of today, the practice of Soviet authors concluding
direct contracts with foreign presses is a lesser evil than the uncontrolled
publication abroad of works that have not been published in the USSR.
It should also be said that the press agency, Novosti, which has the
status of a firm in the USSR and not of a state agency, not infrequently
sells foreign firms the right to translate the works of Soviet authors
which for one reason or another have not been published in their own
country. But private individuals, apart from a very few exceptions, are
generally held back from making direct contracts with foreign publishers, even if the danger of political speculation with their works
abroad is a very real one. The reason for this is the traditional caution
in contact with foreign organs of the press and the absence of normal
channels for business discussions of this kind of problem with foreign
publishers. As a result, the author who would be able to protect himself,
his work and his country with the aid of international legal rules, becomes
the object of arbitrary action and exploitation.

It is clear from all this that the abolition of 'samizdat' as an undoubtedly abnormal phenomenon in a cultured state is possible in only
two ways: by granting permission for Soviet authors to make contracts
with foreign publishing houses, or for the Soviet Union to associate

itself with the international conventions on publication and authorship. Some short-sighted people propose another course, that of persecuting authors whose works are circulated unofficially, the readers of such works and those who decide to copy manuscripts which have not been published by the official press, and of confiscating the manuscripts themselves. But, under present conditions, this method can only have the reverse effect. This can well be seen from the history of Solzhenitsyn's most recent works. As soon as the author began to suffer persecution, as soon as his personal papers and manuscripts of his novel *The First Circle* were confiscated in a private flat by the organs of the KGB, these self-same works of Solzhenitsyn began to circulate by 'samizdat' in vast numbers. There was already a contract with *Novyi Mir* for the novel *The First Circle* and it therefore could not circulate or be read by anyone without the permission of the editors, but once the manuscript was confiscated and it was 'banned' it began to circulate and to be manifolded, and thousands of people read it.

It is not the imposition of fear and repression, but the honest international co-operation of countries and peoples, within the framework of international law, which is the real way out of the situation our country has got into by restricting the freedom of creativity. Creativity in all its forms and aspects is the chief wealth of mankind, the chief force of the development of society, and our main hope and strongest guarantee of a better future.

Obninsk, July 1967 *to May* 1968

Notes and comments, October 1968 *to June* 1969

II

*Secrecy of Correspondence is
Guaranteed by Law*

The government of any country or any party always and no doubt for the best motives would always like to know as accurately as possible the thoughts and feelings of its citizens and their attitude to various events. In a democratic society, when there is real freedom of speech and of the press, all necessary information of this kind may easily be obtained from newspapers, magazines, books, political pamphlets and leaflets, from radio and television broadcasts, from meetings and rallies. All these means of information exist precisely for the purpose of expressing different opinions. Contradictory views are inevitable in a heterogeneous society. The scientific analysis of such data is generally carried out by special institutes which study public opinion.

The fact that it is precisely the freedom of the press which is the real criterion of a free, democratic society is stressed with the greatest clarity by the founder of scientific communism, Karl Marx, in his articles on censorship and the freedom of the press.

The free press is the bright eye of the spirit of the people, the incarnate faith of the people in itself, the speaking bonds which unite the individual with the state and with the whole world; it is an incarnate culture, which reflects the material struggle in the spiritual one. . . . The free press is the creed of the people revealed to itself, and a frank confession, of course, is a saving grace. It is a spiritual mirror in which the people sees itself, and self-knowledge is the first condition of wisdom. . . .[1]

In societies with an undemocratic regime, freedom of the press and freedom of discussion have throughout human history been subjected to numerous restrictions. In these conditions, as Marx likewise stressed, the media of mass information, in their comment on current events always reflect the opinion of the government.

[1] Karl Marx, 'Debate on the Freedom of the Press' in Karl Marx and Friedrich Engels, Collected Works, 2nd Russian edition (Moscow, 1955), vol. i, p. 65— Author's note. All subsequent references are to the Russian edition—Translator.

A censored press has only a demoralizing effect. The supreme vice— hypocrisy—is inseparable from it. The government hears only its own voice. It knows that it hears only its own voice but nevertheless it keeps up the self-deception that it hears the voice of the people, and demands from the people that they too should keep up this self-deception.

The expression of critical viewpoints and opinions and freedom of discussion are still possible under these conditions, but they can occur only in confidential discussion, in the private conversations of friends and in the private correspondence of citizens. Correspondence is also, in essence, a private conversation between friends, separated by some distance between them. It is natural, therefore, that if the governments of countries in which there is only a censored press *want to know all the shades of opinion of society, they must find secret means of controlling all forms of confidential exchange of information. They must create an army of secret informers, set up a system of bugging telephone calls and conversations in one's home and introduce a secret check on the private correspondence of citizens. Sometimes such a practice is adopted nowadays. 'The Land of Total Espionage', this was the title of an article I read in the journal* Za Rubezhom *on the system of surveillance in the USA.*[1] *Modern science and age-old practice have created an extensive arsenal of effective means to this end.*

But public opinion is always opposed to the secret surveillance of the inhabitants of a country. And the Soviet Union used to be a pioneer in this respect. The extremely democratic Soviet Constitution, adopted in 1936, not only laid down the basic democratic rights of citizens as regards the freedom of the press, conscience and assembly, but also established in Article 128 the principle that the secrecy of correspondence is guaranteed by law. *In connection with this, the Criminal Code of the RSFSR and the codes of the other Soviet Republics stipulate that violation of the secrecy of correspondence by individual persons and state departments is liable to prosecution under the law (Criminal Code of the RSFSR, Article 135, Izdatel'stvo Yuridicheskoi Literatury, Moscow, 1968).*

This view of the secrecy of correspondence was later included in the Universal Declaration of Human Rights, adopted by the General Assembly of the United Nations in 1948. In 1966 the same principle was written into the International Covenant on Civil and Political Rights, also adopted by the General Assembly of the United Nations.

'No one shall be subjected to arbitrary or unlawful interference of his privacy, family, home or correspondence, nor to unlawful attacks on his

[1] No. 42, 1968. It was an extract from the book by Omar Garrison, *Spy Government* (New York, 1967)—*Author's note.*

honour or reputation. Everyone has the right to the protection of the law against such interference or attacks', proclaims Article 17 of this Covenant, in the formulation of which the Soviet Union made a considerable contribution.

In the history of the USSR, as we know, there was a period when the government was forced to break the principle of the secrecy of correspondence. This was during the Second World War, from 1941 to 1945, when 'military censorship' of correspondence was introduced throughout the entire country. This measure, the positive value of which was extremely doubtful, diverted some tens of thousands of 'military censors' away from useful work, led to the destruction of large numbers of letters and stopped people from sending news to each other. But, theoretically, 'military censorship' was one form of military tactics of combating the enemy. It prevented the spread of panic and military secrets. Military censorship was open, and obligatory for all. The state did not conceal its existence and abolished it as soon as the war was over. After the war, the principle of observing the secrecy of correspondence once again assumed its previous constitutional force in the USSR.

The preservation of the secrecy of correspondence by the postal service is something which does not admit of doubt in any civilized country—even a country which has censorship of the press. The opening of personal letters and the secret perusal of them by some organization nowadays seems so immoral, unworthy and disgraceful that it is as hard to believe that such a thing is being carried out systematically as to believe in the possibility of the church deliberately breaking the secrecy of the confessional.

The principal law of the post is its absolute honesty. How this law is observed in today's complicated and contradictory world is the subject of the present work.

I

First complications with the post

THIS work is devoted principally to international correspondence, since it is here that the question of observing the secrecy of correspondence has always been most important. For a scientist, international correspondence is a necessary element in his research, a kind of link with world science. I began writing to people abroad in 1955. Just at this time, the Soviet Union abandoned its fruitless struggle against 'cosmopolitanism' in science and turned its scientists' attention to the need to make a serious study of the achievements of science and technology abroad.

Most of my international correspondence at this time consisted of the exchange of offprints of scientific works with colleagues, and sometimes brief letters and postcards connected with this exchange. Gradually a constant personal correspondence grew up with certain biochemists and gerontologists in other countries, and this dealt not only with strictly scientific matters. At that time foreign scientists also took a great interest in the life and work of their Soviet colleagues. Over several years I sent out and received more than a thousand packets of printed matter, letters and postcards, and the post operated irreproachably in every case. Gradually I became inspired with complete confidence in the post and I encouraged many of my colleagues to take advantage of international exchange of information.

Perhaps one day, in some research on the post, statistical data will be published on the international links of Soviet citizens. The curve of the growth in the number of international letters will start to go up in 1954 and will rise for many years. This process will first of all be concentrated in Moscow and the other capital cities, and then will be taken up by the provinces too. People came to believe in the integrity and reliability of the post, and this was the main thing. Old suspicions, of course, were overcome only with difficulty and I met and still meet a few people who do not write a letter abroad, not even in answer to a letter they have received. Only time and happy experience can cure this disease.

The first remarkable incident in my experience with the post occurred only in 1960 after many years of correspondence. One of my biochemical correspondents sent from England an emotional letter written by hand in inconceivably difficult handwriting. After a long time spent in deciphering it, I understood that the Englishman was upset by the fact that his Russian colleagues had not come to some joint conference in London; none of the delegation had come. Rooms had been reserved for them in hotels at the expense of the Organizing Committee, their papers had been included in the programme, people had gone to meet them at the airport. But no one had turned up, and nobody had even let them know beforehand. It was this last fact which upset the Britisher most of all. 'They could at least have sent a telegram or a letter,' he complained.

I had no personal connection with this conference, and I did not know why my compatriots had not gone to London. But I did know that shortly before this conference, a certain Golub, a junior scientist from Sverdlovsk, who was in Holland with a delegation of Soviet scientists, went to the police and sought asylum just before they were due to return home, and then gave some scandalous interviews on the radio.[1] Because of this, some unnecessary precautions might have been introduced concerning the trips of other scientific delegations.

I expressed my sympathy with my English colleague, but said that whoever was to blame in the breakdown of the trip of the Soviet scientists to the conference, it was not, of course, the scientists themselves, and one should not be upset about their behaviour. I sent this letter to England by airmail. From subsequent correspondence with my colleague, however, it became clear that he had not received that particular letter. I sent him a copy, and let him know by postcard that it had been sent. But the copy-letter did not reach him either. I could not follow up the fate of these letters at that time; I had not yet learned how to do so.

The second remarkable loss of my letters occurred in 1961. The British journal *Nature* published a theoretical schematic model of the synthesis of protein. As a result of this model, I had some new ideas, which I set out on two pages and sent to the Editor. This journal always contains a section of 'Letters to the Editor' which publishes brief experimental and theoretical scientific communications which require rapid

---

[1] After about a year, Golub and others, having grown disillusioned with Holland, asked for permission to return to the USSR. Permission was granted, but when they came back to the USSR, they were arrested, put on trial, and condemned to seven years' confinement in strict regime camps—*Author's note.*

publication. In each issue of the journal, which appears weekly, some thirty to fifty such brief communications are published. I knew, of course, that the sending abroad of the works of Soviet authors entailed a great number of stages and formalities, confirming that there were no state secrets in the article. But I assumed that this rule must apply only to experimental articles. A comment, so I thought, does not need so complicated and long-drawn-out a procedure, since it is, of its very nature, an immediate and personal reaction to some other publication.

After sending my note to *Nature*, I did not receive the usual acknowledgement of receipt of the manuscript. Then I sent it a second time in a letter with an acknowledgement of receipt. But this acknowledgement did not come back. I asked the Editor by postcard about the fate of my article, but received an immediate reply that the Editor had not received the article. I did not attempt to send the note a third time.

But, for the rest, the post operated irreproachably, and the two little clouds did not veil the blue sky. From 1961 to 1967 the postal sky was cloudless for me. Sometimes, very rarely, it happened that some letter or other was lost in the post, but when I sent a copy it reached the addressee, and that was enough for me. In the opposite direction, all letters and printed matter also reached me quite safely. During the whole of this time, there was only one case when important material sent to me was lost, but this was finally resolved satisfactorily for both sides.

My colleague, Professor J., sent me by registered book post from the USA a series of published articles and with them three manuscripts which had not yet appeared in print. Professor J. was working on the history of biology. In a separate covering letter, Professor J. asked me for my critical comments on these articles. I received the packet, but I found in it only the offprints of the published articles—no manuscripts. I quickly wrote to the International Post Office in Moscow, requesting a search for the lost manuscripts. I pointed out that they had to be returned to the author with comments. Of course, I was not sure that the manuscripts had been removed by the postal or customs service of the USSR. It was just as likely that the post in the USA could have done this, if the rules for sending manuscripts abroad were as complicated in the USA as in the USSR. But when, two weeks later, I received in an official envelope from the International Post Office the manuscripts which had disappeared, my confidence in the postal authorities of both countries was restored. The envelope also contained an accompanying letter as follows:

INTERNATIONAL POST OFFICE
14 January 1966
Our ref. 10/8/K

Obninsk
Kaluga Province
Institute of Medical Radiology
To Zh. A. Medvedev

In reply to your letter of 27/12/1965, I am writing to inform you that on taking out your correspondence from the packet received from the USA, the enclosure fell out and it was not possible to determine from which envelope it had fallen out. Consequently, the enclosure was held at the International Post Office until claimed by the addressee.

Enclosed herewith three articles (61 pages).

V. DANIN
(Head of the operational department)

The envelope was equipped with a special metal clip, which would stop the enclosures from simply 'falling out'. But since, in accordance with international conventions, printed matter may be subjected to examination by the customs, the taking out and examination of envelopes containing printed works is common practice. According to the rules of the Universal Postal Union, printed matter may be sent at a lower privileged rate. But this rate is allowed only when the book or article is sent in an open unsealed envelope, easily accessible for inspection. If the sender seals the envelope up firmly, then he must send it at the letter rate which is considerably higher.

At the end of 1967 and the beginning of 1968, losses of letters became somewhat more frequent. I had failed to receive two letters from Dr R. in England, in which he had given me a detailed account of certain events relating to my lecture *in absentia* in Sheffield on the problem of ageing and also some general questions of the laws of copyright. Dr R. was so discouraged by the loss of his long handwritten letters, of which he had no copies, that in the future he would not discuss any matters by letter at all. Our correspondence which had not been interrupted since Dr R.'s year in Moscow, in 1958–9, when he was working with me in the biochemistry laboratory of the Timiryazev Agricultural Academy, practically ceased after the loss of these letters. The lost letters had not been registered, but nevertheless I asked the Central Bureau of Claims of the International Post Office about their fate. In reply, I received a letter from E. Malkov, Deputy Director of the International Post Office

(Ref. b/n-vkh 1243/3) in which he said that to make any check as per my claim 'unfortunately would not be possible, since unregistered mail is not recorded along its route in post office documents'.

In February 1968 it also became clear that I had failed to receive two letters sent to me from the USA by the aforesaid Professor J. These letters, fortunately, were registered, and it was possible to study their fate. To my enquiry, the same E. Malkov sent me the following answer immediately:

6 March 1968
Ref. b/n vkh 442/3

To Comrade Zh. A. Medvedev,
To your claim of 3 March 1968, I have to inform you that all correspondence arriving at the International Post Office is dispatched as addressed in good time. As far as the receipt of registered letters is concerned, it is necessary for you to indicate the postal number of the letter and the exact date of their dispatch from the USA.

I knew the dates of the letters from Professor J.'s postcard, but naturally I did not have the numbers. I sent my colleague a postcard and two weeks later I received an airmail postcard from him, saying that he was sending me, under separate cover, by registered airmail, photocopies of the postal receipts for the two letters previously lost. But I did not receive these photocopies either.

This, in essence, was the limit of the definite losses of correspondence in this period. Theoretically they do not, of course, prove the violation of the secrecy of correspondence by some censor. All these losses amounted to much less than one per cent of the total bulk of my correspondence for the period which had elapsed, and this value lies within the confidence limit. The loss of letters, even registered ones, is to some extent an ordinary occurrence for any postal service and is provided for in the conventions and agreements of the Universal Postal Union. It is for this very reason that provision is made in the conventions for compensation for the sender or addressee for the loss of a registered letter, except in the cases of loss of mail due to *force majeure* (storm, fire, air crash, etc.). For countries which are members of the Universal Postal Union, the compensation for the loss of a registered letter is very high (25 gold francs per letter). So that the fluctuations of the rates of exchange of currency should not affect the scale of compensation the convention specifically stipulates that each franc must correspond to 322 milligrammes of gold of 0.900 purity. The Soviet Union is a member of the Universal Postal Union, and the most recent statutes of the Union were ratified by a Decree of the Presidium of the Supreme Soviet of the USSR on 27 February 1959. Accordingly the statutes of the Postal service of the USSR provide for high compensation for the loss of an international registered letter, 7 roubles 35 kopeks, almost fifteen times higher than is paid for the loss in the post of an internal registered letter. Since all this is so strictly controlled, it is evident that the post considers it possible that letters will be lost due to some chance causes and therefore undertakes serious obligations to compensate sender and addressee.

But all the same I could not consider the loss of letters in my correspondence as rare chances. There was a definite trend to be felt in them. Somewhere in the depths of my consciousness a thought arose: could there not be within the postal service some secret censorship making a spot-check on certain letters? The possibility of a complete check I thought very unlikely, of course.

Since correspondence with foreign colleagues was inevitable, I decided to make myself more familiar with the details of the rules governing the operation of the post in this respect. I carefully looked through the *Postal Regulations of the USSR* and the *Statutes of the Postal Service of the USSR* and also the textbooks for communications engineers and postal employees. The hypothesis of the possibility of even a spot-check censorship had to be discarded. The postal rules of the USSR strictly forbade the opening and reading of any letters, even in order to preserve official secrets. Those letters which are incorrectly addressed and so cannot be delivered and which cannot be returned to the sender because there is no return address, are, according to the Act, kept for a certain time and then destroyed unopened, even if opening in this case might help to establish the required address.

The post is allowed to 'withdraw' and check the letters only of those people undergoing trial or legal investigation, and for such an action it is necessary to have previous permission from the court or the procurator. This is done for purposes of investigation and to stop criminals from communicating with each other. However, even in this case letters to a person on trial must be delivered so that he does not know that his correspondence is being secretly checked. The contents of the correspondence is also kept secret in this case. The legislator considers, quite correctly, that if a person under investigation suspects that his correspondence is being checked, then he will conduct it in such a way as to cheat and confuse the investigation. In this case, it is the investigator himself who reads the correspondence and not postal employees. This has nothing in common with censorship.

The post is thus beyond suspicion. But besides the post there is another independent service, the State Customs Control, in the path of international correspondence. This has special rights and plenary powers, and these are quite legal and justified in the modern world which is flooded with contraband. There are customs services in every country. In the Soviet Union the customs regulations contain long lists of goods, materials and printed works which it is forbidden to import or export, but letters which are in the nature of personal correspondence do not come under the control of the customs and must, according to the regulations, be allowed through without let or hindrance. The customs are not allowed complete rights of unsealing letters, but they can unseal and check letters which from their external appearance evoke some suspicion that something illegal is enclosed in them, for example, explosives or poisons. In this case, according to the *Customs Code of the USSR* confirmed by the Council of Ministers of the USSR, and the *Regulations on the Material Responsibility of the Postal Service for the Loss of International Postal Communications*, any act of confiscation of mail by the customs must be 'confirmed accordingly by the Customs and Communications Department'. The sender or addressee is informed of the confiscation, and in this case alone he has no right to consider the mail as 'lost' and to demand compensation for its loss.

If the customs have no grounds for destroying mail or confiscating it, but identify some piece of mail as breaking the customs regulations of the USSR, they return it to the sender with the appropriate explanation. One of my colleagues who tried to send a manuscript of a book abroad, quickly had it returned with an explanation that manuscripts can be sent abroad only if accompanied by a form 103. I twice came up against a similar regulation myself. In 1961 I sent two colleagues a small booklet of the themes of the speeches of a conference on gerontology held by the Moscow Society of Naturalists. Both packages quickly came back to me with the explanation that according to the customs regulations only books with some indication of the retail price on them could be accepted for dispatch abroad. Books which do not have a price on them are considered to have been printed for internal use in some organization and cannot be sent abroad. This fact, with the growth of international links of scientific establishments, has led to the situation that nowadays publications of this kind almost always have a retail price on them.

A study of the postal and customs regulations thus assured me that my correspondence was completely safe. The post was a true friend, helping me and other Soviet citizens to set international co-operation going. It was an instrument of mutual understanding and peace. It was a reliable custodian of our thoughts and discussions, and it did all this at a very low cost, since the postal rates in the USSR are lower than in other countries.

2

The question of the return address

THE curve of the increase of international correspondence of Soviet citizens, and in particular of Soviet scientists, as we have noted, has been rising steadily since 1954. This curve also reflects the increase of scientific information freely obtained by exchange from abroad. This process has been extremely useful to the whole of Soviet science, and it is impossible to value its effect too highly. However, at the beginning of 1967 a complicated postal obstacle arose in the path of this international activity of Soviet scientists, so useful in all respects, which markedly reduced the exchange of scientific information. This incomprehensible and harmful obstacle was the problem of the *return address*, a problem to which no one had paid any attention before.

In 1967 employees of scientific establishments, and also, evidently in other establishments in the USSR, unexpectedly began to have their mail, ordinary letters, printed papers and even standard postcard requests for offprints returned to them by the International Post Office in Moscow and the provincial post offices. In the office of our large institute this returned mail, with the stamps already cancelled in Obninsk, began to pile up. Stuck on each item was a label from the International Post Office or the Kaluga Post Office with the following message: '*To the sender: Returned for approval as per form* 103M.' Registered letters simply were not accepted for posting. The girls in the post office had a quick look at the return address and then handed back the letter with the words: 'Letters with a business return address are accepted only with form 103M.' If the sender, who had already sealed up the envelope, began to explain to the clerk that the letter did not contain material for publication (form 103M was previously required for manuscripts sent out for publication and passed by Glavlit) but was of the nature of a personal or business letter, they generally replied 'Put your home address on it as the return address, not your business address.'

The sender was generally worried at the idea of following this advice, since he would remember the old directives, which had never been changed, according to which scientists should not put their *home address* but only the institute address on their international correspondence. Some years ago, for some reason or other, it was considered undesirable to let people abroad know the home addresses of scientists. Moreover, putting one's home address as the return   address on scientific correspondence, for example when requesting or sending an offprint, seemed very absurd. To put after one's name not the number of one's flat and house but the name of the laboratory and institute seemed obvious practice in such correspondence, since this at once gives an indication of the degree of one's professional similarity of interest and the common nature of one's research problems; it shows that the sender is an active scientist and not a retired one or an amateur collecting offprints. A scientific address is simply the tradition in scientists' correspondence, it is the scientist's *right*; and to deprive him of it is simply a humiliation. Almost all scientists' correspondence is always carried on from their business addresses.

Now, without a form 103M this became impossible, and the flow of letters and other mail dried up at once, since filling up a form 103M for every case proved a burdensome business. Form 103M is made out in triplicate and must be signed by the director of the establishment and ratified by the official seal. This form gives the exact address of the sender and the nature of the enclosures. In addition, to get a form 103M completed, the sender has to submit the letter to the office of the institute, open and with a copy, for checking. The director of the establishment bears the responsibility for the contents in this case, and hence he or some special assistants read the letter which is to be sent and ask the writer what he means and why he has written it. Previously a scientist had been able to write to a colleague by hand, but now he had to type the letter, taking a copy. For letters in the Russian alphabet this was not difficult, but roman alphabet typewriters were still not very widespread. Previously a scientist writing a letter in English or French was not very shy about grammatical errors—the main thing was to be understood—but now he had to have a flawless knowledge of the foreign language. Taken over the whole institute, this all added up to a good deal of work, and in the administrative offices they had to appoint special experts on international correspondence. Furthermore many establishments, including our institute, while approving all personal correspondence as business correspondence, made the authors of the letters bear all the cost of the correspondence.

The fact that establishments undertook the dispatch of all the correspondence of their employees could have been a progressive beginning. Some of my foreign colleagues and Soviet scientists who have worked in foreign laboratories have said that abroad it is common practice to dispatch employees' mail through the office or library. This enables employees to avoid the postal expenses of scientific correspondence and especially the dispatch of offprints. Each published paper brings in two to four hundred requests for offprints, and postal rates are higher abroad than in the USSR. But this procedure does not, of course, imply that the establishment censors letters. Moreover, it is introduced voluntarily *by the establishment itself and not by the post*.

For the post it obviously makes not the slightest difference who dispatches the letter—the scientist himself or his institute by means of some clerk, nor what is put as the return address, his home or business address. All that is important to the post is that the letter should be prepaid at the appropriate rate and should have some addresses on it.

But the new order which Soviet citizens encountered in 1967 was established by the post. This was its principal absurdity. The post has no right to meddle in the procedure of preparing a letter, and the return address for an ordinary letter generally has no significance in principle. According to the communications statutes of the USSR, a prepaid letter dropped into the post box is accepted for dispatch even if there is no return address on it, but only the address of the recipient to whom it is to be delivered. By a century-old tradition, the return address is only relevant when the letter has to be returned if the addressee cannot be found. Indeed the return address is written principally not for the post at all, but to tell the addressee where to send his answer. The sender thus puts the address which he considers to be more suitable, and this is his indisputable right. This is one of the elements of the confidential nature of correspondence; it is the reason for *poste restante* and subscribers' letter-boxes—a person wants to receive different kinds of correspondence at different addresses, and almost all the world takes this into account. The post has no right to impose any special conditions about the return address, especially for sending back *ordinary* letters or postcards dropped into a post box and prepaid with stamps and bearing a comprehensible forward address. In this case it is normally not necessary to look at the return address, for the post need only to look at it as a last resort if the addressee has moved away or cannot be found. Moreover, under the new order, letters which had been collected from the post boxes and cancelled were being returned to senders everywhere, and coming back after a few days or even a week. This made a very poor impression on the senders.

The total amount of correspondence undoubtedly began to fall, and accordingly the influx of information from abroad also began to decrease. This process continued for almost a year and a half.

I do not know whether anyone protested against so ludicrous and un-natural a situation, which infringed civil rights and undoubtedly damaged Soviet science.

For myself, I submitted some of my letters with form 103M, but more often I put as the return address my own personal subscriber's post office box at the Obninsk post office. The post office box was not, of course, a professional address, but all the same it did not create the same moral difficulties in scientific correspondence which arose through having to put a home address. At the same time I was excused the humiliating enquiries concerning my letters—why did I write this and not that, who was Professor D. to whom I was sending the letter and Doctor M., whom I had mentioned in a critical tone, and so on.

On one occasion, I posted in Moscow some ordinary printed matter packages, containing offprints of an article in English, which I was send-ing to a number of colleagues. The article was on the molecular theory of ageing, and on the cover of the offprint the business address of the author followed the name, as is always done both in Soviet and in foreign journals. From force of old habit, I put on the envelope as re-turn address my professional address, and not my home one. There were very pretty stamps stuck on the envelopes, and I dropped them in the big post box for printed matter in post office K-9, in the building of the Ministry of Communications of the USSR. All the envelopes, as is required for the dispatch of printed matter, were open.

Within six days all the packages came back to me with the stamps cancelled and labelled 'for approval on form 103M'. The clear absurdity of the post office's action was obvious. For if I had simply put no return address at all, the packages would have been sent abroad without any trouble. By sending the packages back to me, the post involved me in considerable financial loss, since each package was stamped at the airmail rate.

The Soviet legislature creates many difficulties for Soviet citizens attempting to obtain a decision on some particular question of law. It is usually impossible to bring a 'personal indictment'. But when the matter concerns the financial loss which some service, in this case the law, im-poses on citizens, then it is impossible to avoid considering the matter.

And the post knows this. The action of the post in illegally returning correspondence which has already been posted and accepted implied such arbitrary behaviour, involving financial loss, that I quickly wrote a detailed protest to the Minister of Communications of the USSR, and sent it to him together with the collection of returned envelopes. In my letter (of 14 June 1968) I pointed out that throughout the world scientists conduct their correspondence putting their professional address on it, and the post has no right to meddle in it. I argued that to require a form 103M for material which had already been published in the Soviet Union or abroad was absurd, since printed matter according to the basic postal regulations can be sent abroad quite freely. I also argued that the return address is mainly the concern of the sender, it is the address at which it is convenient to receive an answer—and no more than that. The post has no right to impose any such humiliating conditions on Soviet scientists. Its duty is to guarantee *communications*, not to control correspondence. For the postal clerk to ask the question, 'What sort of letter are you posting, a personal one or a business one?' was, I thought, a breach of the secrecy of correspondence.

About two months later, I received an answer to this letter. The Deputy Head of the Chief Postal Control of the Ministry of Communications, Comrade V. Matsnev, in his letter of 8 August 1968 (ref. GUPS-303) officially informed me that the post offices in Moscow had been given instructions to accept letters from citizens with their business address as the return address without a form 103M. But if the surname of the sender did not appear in the return address but only the name of the establishment, the letter must be considered as a business letter and sent with a form.

The next time that I was posting registered mail in Moscow, the post office girl, remembering our former *contretemps*, looked at the return address and said with relief: 'Now I can accept these letters. We have received written instructions. We have received written permission to approve such letters in the usual way . . . it's very odd that we were not allowed to do this earlier, but all the instructions were verbal, and we were fined for mistakes or lost our bonuses. But now we have clear written instructions.'

The problem of the return address had been solved, it would seem. But the very fact that it arose and existed for a year and a half inevitably forces one to think a great deal about it. Why did it arise? The answer to this question can still only be a hypothesis. Twice when I asked clerks at the international post office why they refused to accept letters without form 103M, they replied, 'But why don't you fill up the form? Your letter will get there several days earlier with a form. . . .' It can therefore be assumed that a letter with a form 103M and an ordinary letter are at some point processed through different channels. The capacity of these channels and the quantity of relevant correspondence must correspond. The expansion of international correspondence had caused some break-down of the equilibrium. The channel for free correspondence could no longer cope with the flow of letters, while the channel for checked business correspondence was not fully loaded. So the post tried to balance the flow by artificial and illegal means.

This hypothesis does not necessarily assume censorship of free corre-spondence. The difference may also arise at the customs stage. Business letters and printed matter packages with form 103M do not need to be submitted to customs inspection, for they have been reliably checked by the administration. Form 103M absolves the post of responsibility for the contents of the mail. By imposing the function of checking even part of the mail on the establishments, the post tries to 'unload' itself some-what. But by sending letters back the post went so far in this direction that it began to involve its clients in financial loss. This was a dangerous course. It must be assumed that in deciding to dispatch letters with a professional return address, the Ministry of Communications is still try-ing to find a way of lightening its work. And, in fact, the directors of the various establishments began to issue special instructions requiring that employees should have their correspondence approved through the administrative office. Bureaucratic measures were imposed on the bureaucratic organs. But the post, as a service department, once against turned a friendly face to its regular clients.

3

A strange paradox of the Moscow International Post Office

IN 1967 I undertook to help one of my Moscow friends in solving a problem which was very important for him, and which, besides everything else, entailed a fairly heavy international correspondence. For a long time he would not undertake this, for he had not had enough experience of international correspondence. Moreover, the old suspicions about the attitudes of the post and the possible disappearance of letters were still alive in him, and these prejudices were not unfounded. But they were based on experience of long ago, and with some difficulty I convinced him that times had changed and that the post could now be trusted. My friend agreed with my plan, but on the condition that we should duplicate all the correspondence. He would write and address letters in Russian, and a few days later I would prepare a translation of the letter into English and send it to the same address, attaching to the letter an accompanying text, setting out my own point of view. This correspondence went on for more than a year and was quite successful. The problem under consideration was partially solved to my friend's complete satisfaction. I should like to point out, in passing, that the problem was not scientific, but rather one of law. In this case, however, it was something else that was important. We decided to duplicate the correspondence for two reasons: firstly to make it easier for the recipient to read the letter—the presence of a translation with the Russian text did actually prove useful—and secondly to increase the chances of 'getting through'. We assumed, that if in some unknown establishment letters passed through a secret censorship, a letter written in Russian and a letter in English must go through different sections of this establishment. Now the average intellectual level of the controllers who can read English must be higher than those who know only Russian. To decipher a foreign language in different handwritings requires some education. But people who have studied foreign languages must have less fear for their position and will as a rule have fewer prejudices. This, by our hypothesis, should give the 'English' letters a better chance of getting through. It proved in practice that our hypothesis was itself a prejudice, since neither Russian nor English letters were lost in this correspondence. Nevertheless our method allowed us to make a quite unexpected discovery of quite another kind.

Usually my friend and I sent the duplicated letters to one and the same person, and in all we have seven main correspondents in different countries (France, the Federal German Republic, the USA, Sweden, England, Italy and Denmark). These correspondents sometimes replied to us by different letters at different times, but sometimes by one and the same letter, sending the answer to both addresses simultaneously, the original to my friend and a copy to me.

As the correspondence progressed, the situation which came to light became more and more interesting. One day, when I looked in my own post office box in the Obninsk city post office, I found a letter from Hamburg which contained some information of great benefit to my friend. The letter had been dispatched by airmail from Hamburg on 27 April 1967 and arrived in Obninsk, according to the post mark, on 2 May, five days later. This was very good going, especially when one remembers that airmail to Obninsk from Europe comes by way of Moscow, and from Moscow onwards it comes by ordinary mail since Obninsk is not served by airmail. Even the internal post from Moscow reaches Obninsk only on the second or third day. The letter which I received from Hamburg was a copy of the letter which had been sent to my friend at his home address in Moscow. On 5 May I was in Moscow, and I went to see him to discuss this letter, but I was very surprised to learn that he had not received the original. Three days later it had still not come, and we decided that it had been lost. Then unexpectedly it arrived. The Moscow postmark bore the date, 11 May. The Hamburg postmark was the same as on my copy, 27 April; and the fact that it was cancelled with a special slogan indicated that the letters were posted at the same time and from the same post office in Hamburg. A difference in the time of arrival of two letters posted at the same time could, of course, occur just by chance. The second letter could have accidentally been sorted into the ordinary mail and come to Moscow by the surface route. But on 12 July 1967 I received a similar copy-letter posted in Paris on 6 July at 20.30 hours from the Eighth Arrondissement. (French postmarks show the time to the nearest half-hour.) The original, sent by the same post, was not postmarked in Moscow until 17 July. Both letters came by airmail. And finally a copy-letter posted to me from the USA by airmail on 11 January 1968 and received in Obninsk,

Kaluga province, on 20 January beat the original, posted the same day from a New York post office, by eight days. I still have all these pairs of envelopes, as very interesting philatelic souvenirs. They were the beginning of my collection of this kind of postal paradox.

But my friend was not to be fooled. This strange phenomenon, in my opinion, could mean only one thing—that his mail was being held up somewhere for inspection, while Zh. A. Medvedev's came through without any hitch. We carefully kept all the correspondence on the problem under consideration, including envelopes and receipts. We collected up all the envelopes for 1967 (sixteen of my friend's and nineteen of mine) and carefully inspected all the postmarks of posting and receipt. The picture was most striking. Letters to my friend's Moscow home address came from the various countries of Europe and from the USA in eleven to eighteen days, and they were all sent by airmail. But letters from these countries sent to my business address or post office box in Obninsk took six to nine days. Although these letters were sent at different times and were not identical in text or sometimes even in language, the difference in the time of delivery could not, taken as a whole, permit any doubts. The result did not allow any other explanation than the one I have given above. And, since my friend had his old suspicions, when he was sure that his correspondence was being checked, he stopped his international correspondence once again. Luckily the main aspect of our problem had been solved, and this somewhat softened the unpleasant nature of the discovery we had made.

However, some months later it became clear that the explanation which had seemed indisputable was wrong and did not prove selective censorship of my friend's mail. New and interesting facts revealed that this paradox was of far greater complexity.

At the beginning of 1968 I was greatly disturbed by the loss of several registered letters from the USA. I could not rule out the possibility that they could have been lost not on the USA–Moscow leg but *en route* from Moscow to Obninsk by way of Kaluga. Ordinary mail from Moscow to Obninsk does not have to go to the provincial centre, since Obninsk is closer to Moscow and is on the Moscow–Kiev railway line. Kaluga is situated some way to the side of this line and the direct trains to Kiev which bring the mail to Obninsk do not pass through Kaluga. But international mail for Obninsk is sometimes sent through Kaluga. Apparently the international post office sometimes puts all the mail for Kaluga province into one sack. The intermediate post offices do not, of course, stamp letters, and it is difficult to establish whether a letter went

to Kaluga first. But sometimes this is indicated by special stamps report-
ing damage to the envelope or package *en route*. This stamp 'received
by the Kaluga Post Office in a damaged condition' occasionally appears
on the envelope. Sometimes Kaluga happens to put the ordinary round
stamp on during sorting.

So as to guarantee my correspondence against loss, I decided to rent
a post office box in Moscow as well. It is not easy to get a box in Moscow,
they only have them in the large post offices, and they have generally
been held by the same subscriber for a very long time. But by chance I
was able to rent a post office box in a new post office in the centre of the
city, where these boxes had only just been installed. Using these subscribers' boxes is much more convenient than *poste restante*, and the
cost for one is very cheap, only two roubles a year. Thus I now had two
personal post office boxes, one in Obninsk and one in Moscow. After
this I informed my regular correspondents of my additional Moscow
address and asked those of them who had been affected by the loss of
letters to send important letters in two copies, the original to Obninsk
and the copy to Moscow, or *vice versa*. The chance that two letters
sent to different addresses would both be lost at once was reduced almost
to zero.

I was greatly surprised to find that a letter sent by airmail from the
USA reached Obninsk several days before the copy posted at the same
time arrived in Moscow. In my collection there are four pairs of envelopes posted to me at the same time and from the same place and sent
to me in Moscow and at Obninsk by airmail. These are their dates of
reaching their destination:

Date of posting in the USA	Date of arrival in Obninsk	Date of arrival in Moscow
25/3/1968	31/3	7/4
20/1/1969	28/1	5/2
19/2/1969	3/3	17/3
18/3/1969	24/3	2/4

All these letters came from the same person in California. They
reached Obninsk on the average twice as quickly as Moscow (6, 8, 12
and 6 days to Obninsk and 13, 16, 28 and 14 days to Moscow).

Besides these pairs of identical letters, during 1968–9 I received at the
Moscow address a number of letters both from the USA and from
Europe, without copies being sent at the same time to Obninsk. But the

same people on other occasions wrote to me from the same addresses to Obninsk. If we group together the letters and postcards from the same addresses and sent to Obninsk and Moscow, we obtain the following picture. I have not made a special choice for the Moscow post, I did not receive any other letters in the Moscow box except those given below. My Obninsk mail was bigger, and in the table I give the times for letters from the same addresses sent in the same month.

TABLE I

TIME TAKEN BY LETTERS FROM THE SAME SENDER TO REACH
OBNINSK AND MOSCOW

| Type of letter | Delivery time in days | |
	to Obninsk	to Moscow
Ordinary mail from England[1]	8	15
Registered airmail from USA	7	12
Airmail from USA	7	15
Registered airmail from USA	9	17
Airmail from USA	8	15
Registered airmail from USA	7	7
Airmail from USA	16	19
Registered airmail from USA	9	21
Airmail from USA	7	12
Airmail postcard from USA	6	18
Airmail postcard from USA	6	12
Airmail from France	5	13

The seventh letter, with its unusually delayed delivery time for Obninsk, came in December 1968, when due to New Year greetings the volume of mail was greatly increased and the delivery of letters delayed.

The delaying of my Moscow mail was quite evident. There was no reason to think that airmail letters from other countries take different times to reach Moscow according to their eventual address in the USSR. There is only one international post office in the USSR, and it is in Moscow; this determines the further fate of letters for various points of the USSR. Two letters arrive from the USA at this post office simultaneously, but the one that has to go on to Obninsk is delivered

[1] Medvedev seems unaware that all first-class mail from Britain to Russia goes by air—*Translator.*

especially quickly. Yet a letter to a Moscow address from this Moscow international post office arrives seven to ten days later. Yet all internal Moscow mail is delivered within Moscow very rapidly on the same or the following day. This includes my personal mail to the same post office box. So, not only in my friend's case, but in my own case too, the Moscow post office was behaving suspiciously. But in Kaluga and in Obninsk they know me, they trust me, and therefore they do not check my correspondence. This explanation is strange, but logical.

But one can also make another more likely supposition. One can also suppose that there was no selective censorship of my mail nor of my friend's mail but simply that all the Moscow international mail was processed very slowly, due to the very large bulk of correspondence for Moscow. Letters from abroad for Kaluga province, however, are very few and hence it does not take much time to deal with them. The Moscow section of the international post office (or the international section of the Moscow post office) is in a chronic condition of being unable to cope with the sorting of the abundant mail for Moscow, and letters lie in a queue for a long time, while the mail for Kaluga is dealt with in Moscow or in Kaluga at normal speed. I checked this assumption in several ways.

Firstly I compared my own Moscow mail of 1960–2 (I was then living and working in Moscow) with the Moscow mail of 1968–9. My idea was this. If it were a question of slow processing due to 'overloading', then the earlier speeds would be greater, since the bulk of correspondence with foreigners in 1960 was less than in 1968 and especially less than in the first half of 1968 (the events in Czechoslovakia had an adverse effect on the flow of letters into the Soviet Union).

In my files I hunted out some old envelopes from letters which I had received in Moscow in 1960–2 and some postcards from the same period. There were three ordinary letters from England, which took 7, 11 and 8 days, an air-letter from West Germany which took 9 days, five air-letters and two air-postcards from the USA which took respectively, 10, 13, 9, 8, 8, 3 and 11 days. Three days was the record and has never been broken once until now by any of the letters from Europe and the USA which I have seen. The date on the postmark of the place of posting does not raise any doubts, it coincides with the date put on the postcard by the sender. But maybe there was a mistake on the postmark for the date received.

Although the number of envelopes which I had kept from old letters was not very large, the figures on the average were better than the present-day ones. And simply from memory I can say that in 1956–62 I would receive airmail letters in Moscow from the USA within seven to nine days.

The second method of checking this assumption consisted of determining the time of delivery of letters to other addressees in Moscow and in Obninsk, where possible using those who carried on only scientific correspondence. Up to the present time, I have recorded the delivery times of airmail to Moscow for about eighty letters from the USA and Western Europe to fourteen or fifteen scientists at their business addresses, and twenty-five letters of the same kind to five addressees in Obninsk. The Moscow and Obninsk addressees worked in different establishments in different regions of the town and were served by different postal departments. These data showed clearly that international airmail is delivered to the inhabitants of Obninsk much more quickly than to the inhabitants of Moscow—by a week, on the average. But, in the case of the Moscow post, besides the usual 12 to 16 day periods, there were occasional 6 to 7 day periods, which showed what the Moscow post could do if it tried.

In one case I was given the delivery times of air-letters from France to the home address of a Moscow scientist. All these letters were from the same person, with whom the scientist was in constant personal correspondence. In all in 1969 nineteen letters were sent from France to Moscow (there is a direct air link three or four times a week) taking the following number of days: 15, 13, 12, 19, 20, 16, 17, 11, 12, 16, 17, 16, 21, 16, 20, 25, 21, 17, 10.

In my own correspondence for 1969 I found nine letters from various people in France. Their delivery times from France to Obninsk were as follows: 5, 4, 5, 6, 6, 7, 9, 5, 5 days.

Thirdly and finally, it might be supposed that mail to Obninsk is for some reason especially quick. To other towns of the Soviet Union international mail might take just as long to be delivered as to Moscow. While I do not have very many data for studying the question from this point of view, the little I do know does not confirm that mail to Obninsk is exceptional. In the summer of 1969, when I was in the Crimea, I made a survey over several colleagues of the delivery times of international airmail to them. These varied from six to nine days (one letter from Argentina took fourteen days). My colleague from Ul'yanovsk, who has for many years had an extensive international correspondence, at my request gave me additional data on delivery times of air-letters to him from the USA and Western Europe in the period 1967–9. The average time for the letters to reach Ul'yanovsk was also seven to nine days. It might be supposed that when the Ministry of Communications becomes acquainted with the results of these investigations, it will carry out its own extensive analysis of the 'Moscow paradox' and will take the necessary measures for a better service to Moscow addressees. Whether they do this by increasing the number of employees or by raising the level of automation and mechanization of some process or other does not concern the citizens of Moscow. But they have the right to demand that Moscow, which is undoubtedly better provided with food supplies and consumer goods than other cities in the country, should not suffer from so clear and insulting a discrimination as regards international correspondence.

It is interesting to note, on the other hand, that in the reverse direction letters going abroad from Moscow reach their addressees quicker than those from Obninsk and other cities, as would be expected by normal reasoning. A letter sent from Moscow to the USA gets there two or three days earlier than a letter sent to the USA from Obninsk or from Yalta. This I have long established with complete certainty from letters written in answer to mine. An experienced addressee always writes in his letter of reply, 'Your letter of (such and such a date) was received yesterday . . .' In addition this is confirmed by a large collection of 'advice of delivery' receipts returned to me from the USA and from Western Europe. On these 'advice' notes there are the dates of posting, receipt by the addressee and return. From Moscow to the USA an airletter takes on the average six to eight days—sometimes only five days —a speed which is completely acceptable.

Why international letters are processed considerably more quickly on the 'way out' from Moscow than on the 'way in' is not known for certain. Maybe there are far fewer letters going out. But maybe (once again foolish suspicions force their way into one's head) it is easier to check Russian letters than foreign ones. The Ministry of Communications should answer this question.

4

Another strange paradox of the international post

ONE of my friends whom I approached on the question of the time of delivery of letters drew my attention to an airmail letter which he had received from London. This letter reached him in seven days. 'Almost up to pre-Revolutionary speed!' he exclaimed with delight. My friend was close on eighty years of age and he could remember how the old Russian post worked.

This exclamation really made me think. For, of course, in those days there was no airmail in Russia or Europe. Letters from London travelled to Russia by railway or sea. The express railway journey across the whole of Europe took at least seventy-two hours to reach Moscow. Today the regular direct air service from London takes four hours. From New York to Moscow there are four flights a week and the flight takes eleven to twelve hours.

Nevertheless it was necessary to check my friend's assertion, for an old man's memory is not too reliable a source of information. The very same day I went specially to see another colleague, who besides having scientific interests was a very keen philatelist. He collected Russian stamps, especially Russian 'Zemskie' stamps, and also old stamped envelopes. He had a special box of international mail envelopes. There were not many of them, about thirty. I carefully copied down the time of posting and receipt as shown by the postmarks. I obtained the following picture which I am quoting in full to give greater authenticity to the extraordinary speed which few correspondents nowadays would otherwise believe. In considering the data of the table, one must take into account that in Russia the dates on the postmarks are given in the 'old style' which was twelve days behind European dates until 1900 and thirteen days behind in the period between 1900 and 1917. Only the October Revolution put an end to this difference.

Especially remarkable was the exceptional uniformity of the figures. The sender clearly could know exactly when his letter would be received, and this is sometimes very important.

TABLE 2

DELIVERY TIME OF INTERNATIONAL MAIL TO AND FROM RUSSIA IN THE PERIOD 1875–1914

Points of posting and receipt	Postmark of posting	Postmark of receipt (old style)	Delivery time
Manchester–Kovno province	14/5/1900	5/5	4 days
Manchester–Dinaburg (Baltic)	5/6/1885	28/5	4 days
Hambledon (England)–St Petersburg	6/9/1904	27/8	4 days
Rye (England)–St Petersburg	30/7/1905	21/7	4 days
London–Mozzheika (Baltic)	25/7/1898	15/7	3 days
Liverpool–Riga	16/8/1897	8/8	4 days
London–St Petersburg	24/8/1897	16/8	4 days
Wittersham (England)–St Petersburg	24/8/1905	14/8	3 days
London–St Petersburg	20/8/1903	9/8	3 days
Maidenhead (England)–St Petersburg	25/7/1904	15/7	3 days
Finsbury (England)–St Petersburg	21/12/1903	12/12	3 days
London–St Petersburg	15/7/1904	9/7	7 days
Geneva–St Petersburg	17/2/1880	9/2	4 days
Berne–Essentuki	22/7/1913	15/2	6 days
Berlin–St Petersburg	9/2/1908	31/1	5 days
Berlin–Kuntsevo	16/7/1912	6/7	3 days
Stockholm–Moscow	26/6/1906	17/6	4 days
Brussels–Moscow	17/8/1890	10/8	5 days
	(old style)	*(new style)*	
St Petersburg–London	2/2/1879	18/2	4 days
Riga–London	24/8/1913	8/9	3 days
St Petersburg–London	18/3/1913	3/4	4 days

When I told my friends about this, most of them did not believe me. Three days from England to St Petersburg without any airmail seemed quite impossible. In February 1970, however, there was a long article in the *Literaturnaya Gazeta* (No. 6, 4 February) which pointed out that in old Russia the internal post was delivered much faster than today. The delivery times of letters from Moscow to St Petersburg, from Moscow to Kaluga, and so on, were two or three times faster than today. The article sharply criticized the Ministry of Communications for this.

For comparison with pre-Revolutionary times, the authors of the article quoted the delivery times of Lev Tolstoi's letters according to the stamps on the envelopes which are kept in the Tolstoi collection.

This course suggested an interesting idea to me: the classic authors of Russian literature also kept up an international correspondence, and in the archives their envelopes are undoubtedly preserved. But it turned out that these data can be obtained without studying the archives. In complete collected works the last volumes usually contain the correspondence of classic authors, giving the dates of the letters. From the notes and from the letters in reply it is easy to establish the delivery times of the post at that era. Here are a few examples. Anton Pavlovich Chekhov wrote from Nice (South of France) a letter to his brother in Russia on 7 October 1897 (letter No. 2012, vol. 17 *Collected Works*). The answer to this letter from his brother Aleksandr Chekhov is dated 11 October 1897 (see note to letter No. 2012). On 22 November 1897 Chekhov wrote from Nice a letter to Sobolevskii in Russia. Sobolevskii's reply to this letter is dated 25 November (see letter No. 2048 and note on it[1] vol. 17).

Even the New Year international mail at that time was not held up due to overloading. A New Year letter from Anton Chekhov in Nice to his brother in Russia is dated 28 December 1897. Aleksandr Chekhov's answer to it is dated 1 January 1898 (see letter No. 2085). It was not only letters that travelled as fast as this between France and Russia but also the proofs of Chekhov's stories. Of course not all Chekhov's correspondents answered his letters as soon as they received them, and often the dates on the answers differ from the date on the letter received by five, six or seven days. But the minimum times of three to four days indicates the efficiency of the post.

This picture is confirmed by the correspondence of Turgenev, who lived for a long time abroad, and of Gor'kii and other writers. Even the letters of Lenin, sent from France and Switzerland by ordinary mail, reached his family in Simbirsk with the same speed, although the Tsarist government had good grounds to subject the correspondence of V. I. Ul'yanov to censorship.

Even at the beginning of the twenties Sergei Esenin's letters from the USA (where he was in 1922) reached the USSR in twenty to twenty-five days by seamail, which today takes letters and printed matter from the USA in forty to fifty days.

Above we considered the 'Moscow paradox' for *airmail* material from the USA and from Europe. If we recall these data, it becomes apparent

that present-day airmail delivers letters *more slowly* than ordinary mail
in pre-Revolutionary times, and *much more slowly* when it is a matter of
letters addressed to Moscow. But what about ordinary surface mail from
abroad to the USSR? Surely the delay in delivering letters by railway is
even more marked?

I shall quote some figures for 1969 from envelopes in my collection
of letters to different addressees in Moscow, Leningrad and Obninsk.

TABLE 3

DELIVERY TIMES OF INTERNATIONAL ORDINARY MAIL FROM
WESTERN EUROPE TO THE USSR IN 1969 (IN DAYS)

England–Moscow	15, 13, 13, 17, 9, 14, 12, 20, 10, 18, 21, 16
England–Obninsk	5, 7, 6, 5, 7, 8, 6, 8, 7, 7, 8, 8
France–Moscow	11, 11, 14, 10, 16, 17, 16, 10
France–Obninsk	5, 6, 12, 7, 8
West Germany–Obninsk	22, 16, 11, 12, 18, 18
France–Leningrad	7, 13, 13, 16, 9
Italy–Obninsk	12, 19, 11
Spain–Moscow	41, 36, 34, 40, 29, 27, 29

The sharp difference in speed of the Moscow mail from that of
Obninsk is maintained, as would be expected, with the ordinary mail.
Moreover, there is almost no difference in sending a letter from France
by ordinary mail or airmail. In both cases it goes extremely slowly. This
shows yet again that the delay is due to some *non-transport period* in the
process of delivery. *Literaturnaya Gazeta* criticized the post for the fact
that in comparison with Old Russia, the *non-transport* processing of
letters of the internal mail had increased by one to two days. But the
non-transport processing of letters of the international mail in Moscow
has increased on the average by ten days! From the Socialist countries of
Eastern Europe a letter reaches both Moscow and Obninsk fairly
swiftly, in four or five days. But in 1969 the non-transport processing of
letters from Czechoslovakia suddenly became much slower, they began
to take fifteen to twenty days. This was astonishingly slow. One does
not know what to compare it to. The letters of Belinskii and Herzen at
the beginning of the nineteenth century, before the first railway line had
been laid in Europe, moved much more swiftly. Balzac in France received letters from his bride in Ukraine more swiftly as well. In the
Selected Works of Spinoza (Russian edition, Gospolitizdat, 1957) there

is published an extensive correspondence between Spinoza and his colleagues in the years 1660 to 1680. From Germany to England Spinoza's letters to Oldenburg sometimes took four or five days, and to Holland three days. I have not yet been able to obtain access to Lomonosov's correspondence from St Petersburg with his colleagues in Western Europe. If I happen to be in the archives of the Academy of Sciences, perhaps I shall find some precise data on this. But it was not exceptional for Lomonosov to receive information more rapidly from the European centres of science than it is received by mail by a modern scientist at the Moscow State University.

5

Does the nature of international airmail affect its delivery time

EVERYONE who sends and receives international correspondence cannot help being concerned about the time it takes to travel. If he sends a letter or simply a request for an offprint of a published article he inevitably makes an estimate in his mind of when he can expect an answer. He knows from experience the delivery times of airmail and ordinary mail which we have quoted above, although very few people have undertaken a statistical calculation of these times. I myself began to make a systematic record of the delivery times of letters and printed matter a very long time ago, back in the 1950s. When I requested an offprint of a scientific paper, I always put the date of sending the request on my bibliographic record card for this paper, and when the paper arrived I noted on the card that the offprint had come and added the date. Thus from my own personal catalogue I could always know which works I had received in the original and which not. I began recording the arrival times of letters only in 1967. Then I had already turned my attention to the phenomena described above. I have already mentioned that sceptics suspected that the principal cause of delay of international mail was censorship. The censorship of printed matter packages is legal and is practised by many countries. It is provided for in the international postal regulations. But the censorship of letters cannot be—it is absolutely illegal. But sceptics do not always believe that the law is strictly observed. For example, it is easy to explain the 'Moscow paradox' by censorship, but to prove it is very difficult; and personally I was not inclined to believe that letters were censored. At all events the thought of the possibility of censorship never had any influence on the content of my letters. One of my friends, with whom I shared my doubts, went so far as to laugh at me: 'You are like Rabinovich in the anecdote'— another accursed riddle. (The lover put out the light each time, and Rabinovich could not consider that his wife's guilt was conclusively proved.)

One of the sources of my doubts was the fact that in my personal correspondence which, as we have seen, was delivered fairly quickly in Obninsk, there was no visible relation between the type of mail and its delivery time. Registered letters for the USA took on the average the same number of days *en route* as simple postcards requesting offprints and even as the regular airmail return of 'advice of delivery' slips, which do not contain any meaningful text. There would clearly be nothing for the censor to do with these slips. Consequently their delivery should not be delayed. To illustrate this fact I shall quote some figures. In 1968–9 the registered air-letters which I received from the USA at my Obninsk post office box had the following delivery times, in days: 7, 6, 6, 6, 10, 9, 5, 6, 5, 7, 7, 8, 10, 7, 7, 10 . . . The average delivery times taken over thirty letters was 7.2 days. The airmail 'advice of delivery' notes for my letters came back after the following rate in days: 6, 7, 8, 5, 10, 7, 7, 8, 5, 9, 7, 6, 9, 9, 10, 9, 10—average speed 7.6 days. A few letters and 'advice' notes came very slowly, taking from 23 to 31 days. But according to statistical method, such data which show so great a deviation are not taken into account in the calculation of the average, but are attributed to the action of chance factors. In our case it might be due to airmail getting put in with ordinary mail.

I shall quote some other average figures without giving all the initial data. These figures are characteristic of my mail in 1968–9:

Postcard requests for offprints by airmail from the USA were delivered to me in an average time of 7.5 days (reckoned over 70 postcards), and from European countries in 6.2 days.

'*Advice of delivery*' *notes from Western Europe* by airmail were delivered in 6.4 days.

Airmail postcards with text from the USA reached my business address in 6.8 days, and my post office box in 6.2 days.

Airmail from the USA (*not registered*)—to my business address 8.1 days, and to the post office box 6.8 days.

Airmail from Europe (mainly from England and France) to the Institute 6.0 days, to the post office box 6.5 days. For registered mail, 7.1 days and 5.8 days respectively.

Printed matter airmail was delivered on the average in 7.8 days (from the USA).

Speed records. Once I received a letter from New York in 4 days. From England two air-letters out of twenty-five came in 4 days. From the USA the post three times delivered letters in 5 days from New York State, and four times from other states. One printed matter envelope containing an offprint came from the USA in 4 days. One 'advice' note came from France in 4 days, and two from the USA came in 5 days. One request for an offprint from the USA came in 4 days and two in 5 days.

Four to five days from the USA to Obninsk seems absolutely incompatible with censorship. But a sceptic could find matter for doubt here, too. For printed matter, he will say, is obligatorily subjected to a legal customs inspection and checking, but its average speed of delivery by airmail is about the same as for letters. Moreover, he will say, in the absence of too great a bulk of correspondence, the censor who is on the transmission line for Obninsk mail will not hold the letters up very long. To open them, read them through and seal them up again does not take very much time. If a photocopy is necessary, that is a fast process, too. Even if each letter is held up for twenty-four hours, this will not introduce noticeable changes in the overall picture, since there is so large a number of variable factors affecting international mail, and since there are not daily flights and hence such a delay will not be revealed by mathematical processing. The absence of any difference in the delivery of letters with a complicated text and simple 'advice of delivery' forms the sceptic will say indicates nothing. Maybe, according to instructions, the censor has to process all correspondence in turn, as on a conveyor belt, not passing the 'advice' forms through. On an 'advice' form the recipient, in addition to his signature, can insert a couple of sentences in fine handwriting. Finally, the sceptic may agree on a compromise deduction that censorship is not total but is of a selective nature. According to some criteria or other the censor chooses certain letters out of all the mail and works on them. In this case the letters which fall into his hands take 10 to 13 days *en route* to Obninsk, and the others are delivered to the addressee in 5 to 8 days. It is not excluded that the censor has a list of surnames of people whom it is necessary to check but that neither Zh. A. Medvedev nor his friends are on that list, in view of their undoubted loyalty and their reluctance to receive in letters from abroad narcotics, explosives or even stamps, which also fall into the category of objects which it is prohibited to send through the post.

The only argument of the sceptic which has any foundation, is that there is acknowledged to be censorship or customs inspection of printed matter, yet it comes at the same speed. The 'customs inspection' of printed matter is, of course, censorship, and consists of checking of the contents of the text. But this is a legal censorship, which does not violate the secrecy of personal correspondence. The fact that the censorship of printed matter exists no one who systematically receives scientific and other literature from abroad can doubt. Besides the special numerical stamps which the controller puts on the printed matter itself and on the envelope, it is evident from the very package. If the package is sealed up by the sender in a large envelope with unmistakable signs of containing printed matter, the control opens it fairly roughly. It has to be sent on to the addressee in the USSR open. If it is in a padded envelope then he rips it in several places with a knife to check that there are no forbidden enclosures in the padding between the double walls of the envelope. The customs are not embarrassed by these signs of their attention to the mail since they consider that they are legal. But letters reach the addressees without any sign of being opened. Although the censorship of printed matter does not violate the secrecy of correspondence, nevertheless some special aspects of this censorship must be considered, since any censorship, open or secret, must have certain common features. For if it is found that it is impossible to obtain certain information in the form of printed works, then the authorities in charge of checking would hardly be happy to know that this information can penetrate in the form of personal letters. Approaching the problem of the secrecy of correspondence from this new angle, we pose the problem in the following form: let us consider what foreign information they are trying to protect us from and which it is impossible for us to obtain with the aid of the post and to read? Who is protecting us in this way and how is this all done? After this it will be easier for us to continue our discussion on how the secrecy of private correspondence is guaranteed by law.

6

The system of checking printed matter sent through the post

JUST like any other country, the USSR receives an enormous amount of printed matter of various types through the post. Without such a flow of external information, the life of a developed, cultured and industrial society would now be impossible. But since almost any state in the modern world has enemies and ill-wishers, this flow of information may contain harmful matter as well as what the state intelligence organs consider to be beneficial. They therefore try to filter this out by some means or other, and this is a usual practice for which the law makes provision. In the USSR such functions are officially imposed upon the customs control, and, apparently, as we shall see later, on a special organization known by the name of Glavlit. Why it has this name and what it signifies I do not know, but doubtless it would be possible to find out from the resolutions of the government in the twenties, when Glavlit was set up as a temporary measure as a temporary replacement of the censorship. The resolution on the functions and status of Glavlit was published at that time.

Open and legal censorship was, of course, abolished by the February Revolution of 1917. This was a very important event in the history of Russia. For the first time since 1790, our country had a free press. (Before 1790, of course, there had been the 'free press' created by Empress Catherine II. But after this, when A. N. Radyshev published *A Journey from St Petersburg to Moscow* with a private press, the tsarist autocracy was forced to increase the censorship.) The abolition of the censorship facilitated the intensive development of the Socialist and Bolshevik press and the further development of the revolution. Censorship in the hands of an autocracy and in the hands of any anti-democratic regime is a powerful weapon for the suppression of all forms of freedom. The essence of this censorship was expressed most clearly by Karl Marx:

Censorship does not annihilate the struggle, it makes it one-sided, it transforms it from an open struggle into a struggle between a principle without power and a power without principle. The true censorship, which is rooted in the very existence of the freedom of the press, is *criticism*. It is the judge which freedom of the press engenders within itself. Censorship is criticism as a government monopoly. But will not criticism lose its intelligent character when it becomes not open but secret, not theoretical but practical, when it acts not as a sharp knife of the intellect but as the blunt scissors of arbitrary rule?[1]

Censorship, by Marx's definition, is a 'quack, driving the rash inwards, so that he does not see it, without any concern that it can infect the more delicate internal parts of the body'.[2]

Lenin himself was no less energetic an opponent of censorship. His burning words are well-known:

> Until there is freedom of assembly, and freedom of the press, until that time the shameful Russian inquisition will not disappear, which hounds down faiths and ideas and doctrines which are not officially supported by the state. Down with the censorship! . . . Against its demands, the conscientious proletariat will fight to the last drop of its blood.[3]

'Censorship—what an abominable word,' said Lunacharskii, the first Soviet People's Commissar of Culture.

In the first years after the October Revolution there was actually no opportunity for censorship, since the bourgeois and Menshevik and other similar organs of the press were closed. During the period of the New Economic Policy, however, a purely temporary control of the press was introduced, in the form of Glavlit at the centre and the local Oblits and Gorlits. The function of this organization with respect to the internal press does not fall within the scope of the present investigation. And we would gladly pass over the other functions of Glavlit, had we not come to the conclusion that it is clear that Glavlit voluntarily assists the customs organs in dealing with international correspondence and in particular with the exchange of printed matter. Such co-operation between the customs and Glavlit is quite natural, since it is, of course, difficult for the customs officials to *read* the texts, particularly the foreign ones. Glavlit, however, has considerably more experience and opportunities in this matter.

We have deduced the co-operation of the postal and customs organs

[1] Marx and Engels, *Collected Works*, vol. 1, pp. 59–60.
[2] ibid., p. 64.
[3] Lenin, *Complete Collected Works*, vol. 7, p. 125.

with Glavlit in dealing with international correspondence from comparatively simple evidence, by analysing certain marks which are made on packets and printed matter arriving from abroad, and also by analysing the nature of the information which does not get through the defensive net.

We are in no way disputing the right of a sovereign state to control the flow of printed matter across the frontier. This right is recognized in the international postal conventions and by international law. Customs control is an entirely legal matter and the list of goods which fall into the prohibited category is an internal matter for any country. Some countries forbid the import and sending into the country of pornographic literature, other countries stop books of a militarist character. Egypt certainly does not let in Israeli literature. China lets in nothing at all. About three years ago I read an article in the American journal *Science* on the working of the New York postal customs. The article criticized the censorship by the customs of printed matter coming from the USSR. In one year, so the article said, the New York central customs confiscated about a million items of post containing printed matter of a propagandist nature.

Since it is legal to inspect printed matter, the international postal regulations provide that packages of this type must be open and easily accessible to inspection. For this purpose, many types of packets and envelopes are manufactured abroad with clips, laces, pins, tacky flaps, and so on, for sending through the international mail, books, newspapers, journals and offprints of articles. These wrappers bear the legends, 'Printed matter', 'Book post', etc. Likewise the USSR man does not seal up packages containing printed matter sent abroad, but simply fastens them with a string.

Why do we consider that Glavlit is also involved in the business of checking international correspondence containing printed works?

A long time ago, when I had just started to carry on an exchange of offprints and to collect by this simple and effective means the scientific literature needed for my work, I noticed the large numbers stamped on every packet containing an offprint. These numbers, generally violet in colour, with figures some 10 mm. high and 5 mm. wide, were almost always below and to the right of the address to which the package was sent. Sometimes they were on their side or even upside-down. For many years these stamped figures did not interest me, just as the postmark does not interest the person who receives the letter. But around 1960 I noticed that these number stamps had disappeared from packages arriving from socialist countries: Poland, Hungary and Bulgaria, etc.

But on envelopes containing offprints arriving from capitalist countries, they have been retained until the present time.

On the offprints themselves, generally to the right of and above the title, there were also numbers put on with a violet stamp. But these numbers were of quite a different kind. The figures were smaller in size (4 mm. high and 2 mm. wide for each symbol) and moreover these figures were preceded by a special double angle, thus: ≪345 ≪448 ≪101. These figures unexpectedly disappeared in 1960 from all offprints, socialist and capitalist alike. But they remained on books and journals coming from capitalist countries. On journals they were usually on the cover, in the top right-hand corner, and on books they came above the title, in the top right-hand corner of the title-page. I also encountered the same symbols on journals in the libraries. But these figures, too, for a long time did not interest me. I began thinking seriously about their significance only in 1967, when I came up against the phenomenon of the loss of printed works.

I have already noted that until 1967, letters to me and from me were lost only extremely rarely. But printed works were lost even more rarely, at all events I did not notice the loss of them. However, in 1967, my friend in the USA by way of book exchange (he was interested in obtaining literature from the USSR on the history of natural science) took out a subscription for me through the American Association for the Advancement of Science to the journal *Science* published by this association. This journal is a weekly and is considered to be one of the most interesting ones. As I received the journal regularly, I noticed that some of the numbers did not reach me. I made enquiries of the publishers, but they assured me that all the numbers had been sent. Nevertheless, I was missing ten issues for 1967. (In 1968, 12 numbers out of 52 were lost). The international post office did not answer my enquiry on this matter. Sadly, I turned to the Ministry of Communications, but received no answer from there either.

In addition to *Science*, in 1967 two packets containing works of creative literature in a cheap 'pocket' edition and two works on the Israeli-Arab conflict sent to me from the USA were also lost.

All these strange losses of literature, which certainly did not contain any anti-Soviet propaganda, made me do some serious thinking. Had the customs extended their range of confiscations? And why were these confiscations not accompanied by some statement, informing the addressee of the reasons for confiscation, as is required by law? The irritation due to this obvious but incomprehensible arbitrary behaviour on the part of some service along the route of international correspondence made me consider the unexplained figures on packets and printed matter. I decided that they had some bearing on this matter. At the beginning of 1968, I began a more thorough study of this aspect of the operation of the post. I was driven to this by the disappearance *en route* to me of an issue of *Science* in which there appeared an important article on achievements in the struggle against leucosis. I had been told of the publication of this article in the course of correspondence, as an example of an original biochemical-genetic solution of the problem. The same number of the journal was confiscated *en route* to the Lenin State Library and other libraries as well. Since at that time we were starting work in our laboratory on this same anti-leucosis factor, I sought this journal through a certain Academician, and when I read the article I discovered that the issue of the journal had been confiscated *en route* to its subscribers because of some trifling sociological remarks. I could guess how much other extremely useful scientific information was lost to Soviet science by this practice, and I found this alarming.

I began by examining the large numerical stamps. The big envelopes manufactured abroad for offprints are very convenient for keeping various papers in. Therefore I had at home and in the laboratory a whole collection of such envelopes from offprints which had been sent to me over a number of years. They had contained literature in the English language, but came from different countries, the USA, England, France, West Germany, etc. I noted down on a large sheet of paper all the numbers on them indicating the country from which the offprint was sent and the date of sending and receipt (from the postmarks). The highest of the numbers which occurred in my mail was 139.

The first question which I asked myself was: *Who puts on these numbers, and where?*

In all, I processed about four hundred envelopes with numbers. If one puts them in numerical order and indicates by dots the number of envelopes with each number, one gets the following picture:

```
 1   . .
 2   . .
 4   . . . . . . . . . . . .
 5   .
 6   . . . . . .
 9   . .
10   . . . . . . . . . . . . . . . .
12   . . .
```

13 . . . .
14 . . . .
15 . . . .
18 . . . .
19 . . . .
22 . . . .
23 .
24 .
26 . . . .
27 . . . .
28 . . . .
30 .
32 . . . .
34 . .
35 .
36 . . . .
37 . . . .
43 . . .
44 .
45 .
47 . . . .
48 . . . .

and so on up to

138 . .
139 .

Out of the possible numbers below 140, only 61 actually occurred, the rest (3, 7, 8, 11, 16, 17, etc.) were not on this list. Between 115 and 133 there was not a single number. Furthermore, some numbers were over-loaded (10, 22, 27, 28, 54, 57, 75, etc.) and others were underloaded (1, 2, 5, 23, 24, etc.).

The first deduction which I made was that identical numbers encountered on different packets and at different times were physically produced by the same stamp. This was easily visible from the fine details of the figures.

The second deduction was that the numbers were put on in Moscow. Packages which from time to time arrived at my old Moscow address and then were sent on to me by hand had precisely the same numbers. Moreover, other addressees in Moscow received offprints with these very numbers on the envelopes. I checked this in more than fifty cases. Among the 'Moscow' numbers there was not a single one which did not occur in the Obninsk mail as well.

These numbers were not directly related to the addressees—this was my third deduction.

Of the other deductions, the following should be noted: *The numbers were not directly related to countries nor to the dates of posting or receipt.* Packages from Sweden and the USA could have identical numbers and these could be almost any of those listed above. Packages arriving on one and the same day could have different numbers. The meaning of these numbers still remained elusive, since without some explanation of the nature of their differentiation, no one could understand their significance.

I tried to differentiate them according to different indices: firstly by language. Sometimes I was sent works in German as well as English. Five packages which had contained works in the German language had the numbers 8, 83 and 141. Not one of these numbers had occurred previously in the English group of numbers. Works from West Germany in the English language went under numbers also encountered on packages from the USA, England, New Zealand, etc. *Differentiation by language was therefore not excluded.* In order to check this, I collected in various places about forty envelopes in which printed matter in various languages had come to Moscow and Obninsk. *Differentiation by language was perfectly evident.* German works took the numbers 8 ., 61 . . ., 59 . . ., 141 . and 62 . . . . Printed matter in French had on the packages the numbers 5 . ., 20 . ., 45 ., 51 ., 58 . The first four numbers do not occur in the English literature group. The Swedish, Danish and Finnish numbers 60, 73 and 137 are not found in the English group. Japanese works go under the numbers 17 and 70, a Yugoslavian offprint had the number 116 on the package, and an Italian one 63. None of these numbers occur on packages with literature from these same countries in English.

Consequently, all these numbers are put on by groups of employees differentiated by language. Let us call these groups 'sections'. There is an extremely large English section, a German section, a French, a Japanese and a Scandinavian section, and so on.

Then I tried to establish how the numbers are differentiated in the very large English section. For this I made separate lists of the numbers on packages with offprints of biological, chemical, medical and physical literature, on book catalogues, advertisements for instruments and other laboratory technical material, on wrappers from *Science* and two gerontology journals which I received regularly. My conclusion was as follows: *There is no differentiation of the numbers whatsoever according to the branches of science.* There is no difference in the character of the numbers when one compares offprints with advertisements and catalogues. Books come in packages with the same numbers as offprints, books on the humanities and works of creative literature have numbers which are also found on packages with offprints on biochemistry. *However, packages with journals have their own special journal numbers.*

Over two years, for example, I recorded for *Science* the following numbers on the outside of the packages: 10, 19, 26, 28, 35, 69, 102, 105, 112, 130, 134, 137. Some of these numbers also occurred on packages containing offprints (10, 19, 26, 28) but these numbers as a rule occurred very rarely, only once or twice on the packages of *Science.* Usually the numbers 102, 105, 112, 130 and 134 were put on these packets, and these numbers never occurred in the offprint group. This differentiation was quite explicit, the number 130 was the principal one, and occurred on the *Science* packages 43 times, that is, in 50 per cent of all cases. The number 102 was put on 21 times, 134 six times and 112 five times. Evidently, in the 'English section' there was a 'journals section', or rather a '*sector of periodical literature*' and a sector of '*non-periodical literature*' (books, offprints, advertisements). The non-periodical numbers were sometimes put on journals when their packages went by mistake to the other section.

This deduction about the two English-language sections was confirmed by the numbers on the packages containing the gerontology journals. For these, over two years, I noted the following numbers: 41 . . , 64 . . . . . ., 92 . ., 94 . . ., 100 ., 102 . . . None of these numbers was encountered in the group of offprints. In Moscow I was able to get hold of the envelopes and wrappers of journals and newspapers received at a particular publishing house in 1969. These were mainly publications in the humanities and newspapers of a general kind, such as *The Times.* Among the Anglo-American Accessions, I listed the following numbers on the outsides of the packages: 41, 24, 35, 64, 80, 92, 48, 104, 112. Except for 24, 48 and 104, I had found none of them in the group of offprints, advertisements and books. But these three 'non-periodical' numbers occurred only once each. The others were found five to seven times or more. The 'gerontology' and 'humanities' journal numbers 102 and 112 also occurred for *Science.*

The division of periodical and non-periodical literature, of course, is a rational one. Offprints and books are individual items, they arrive in no kind of order, as with letters it is impossible to group them, one has to look through each one. But journals come in bulk, dozens of the same issue together. Newspapers can come in hundreds and thousands of the same issue. There is no sense in reading and checking them haphazardly, it is sufficient to check a single copy, and according to it to decide the fate of all the other copies of this date. All these facts permit one to postulate that *the differentiation of the numbers on the packets according to language and type of literature reflects the differentiation of the employees of some organization or other. Every employee has his own personal number,* and, although not very strictly so, he is appointed to deal with particular classes of literature (for example, No. 130 for *Science*).

The personal number stamp eliminates the lack of personal responsibility of the employees in checking the packages. If on examination it is found that an offprint of some anti-Soviet article or a prohibited book has got through, then it is at once seen who is guilty, No. 10 or No. 137. A similar system is used in industry, too, where checkers and inspectors each have their own personal number. On books and other publications in the 'production note' the special complicated number of the Glavlit editor concerned is always to be found (T-03201, T-05239, BF-34036, etc.).[1] In books of the twenties and the beginning of the thirties, the employees of Glavlit were not restrained from indicating where they worked as well as their number, and they put their signature stamp in the following form: 'Authoriz. Glavl. B-23035', or 'Leningr. City Lit. No. 20245', or 'Leningrad Prov. Lit. No. 56918', etc. In these five-figure numbers are combined the number of the employee and, apparently, the number of the publication on the Glavlit list.

Thus the numbers on the outsides of the packages result from the activity of a particular set of controllers. There are about 140 of them and they are divided into sections according to the working language, and into sectors within the sections according to the groups of periodical and non-periodical literature. Since these controllers put their own personal numbers on the envelopes and the outsides of the packages, it must be supposed that they are part of the staff for the customs postal checking of mail. They belong to a body which checks printed matter only, since on packets containing chemical reagents and specimens of materials arriving from abroad there are various other marks of customs inspection, but no similar numbers.

[1] A production note occurs on the last page of all Soviet books. It states the names of the authors, the title of the book, the language of the book, the publishing house, the general editor of the series (if applicable), and 'technical editor' of the book and the proof corrector; also the date it was passed for press, the paper size, the size of the edition and the Glavlit editor's number. In the case of a book in a language other than Russian, this note is both in Russian and in the language of the book—*Translator*.

M

Let us now turn to the other numbers preceded by a double angle. They are put on the title-pages of books and journals. They are not present on offprints after 1960. These 'title' numbers have many features in common with the large numbers on the packets, but they are apparently more important. They are also put on by employees, but of some other service. The same number may occur on many different packets, for example 130 on the packets of *Science*. But the same journal may have *different* 'title' numbers (118, 185, etc.). The outside packet numbers also occur on packets from socialist countries. The 'title' numbers are only put on journals and books arriving from the capitalist countries.

What is on the outside of the envelope governs its being sent to the addressee. If a check mark is to have any significance for the postal service itself, it is put on the outside of the packet. A mark put directly on the book or journal has significance for the recipient or for the fate of the book itself, independent of the postal packing. Since this number is not merely a number but is put after a double angle, it indicates personal responsibility and some *sign*. On foreign pre-war publications and on old foreign journals I found similar numbers put in a single angle and in a circle. This confirms the guess that we are dealing here with some special sign.

In order to explain the nature and significance of these numerical 'title' symbols, we carried out the same work on them as in the previous case, analysing the differentiation of these symbols, with respect to many factors. Here the number of cases which we used in our processing was much larger, since besides our private library and the holdings of the Institute, we were able to note down these signs on the journals and the books of colleagues, in libraries and at exhibitions of foreign books.

First of all we noted that these signs were put on in the USSR, mainly, if not exclusively, in Moscow. Some of the rules derived from the analysis of the data are discussed below in systematic order.

Rule 1. There are 500 'title' numbers with double angles which appear on books and journals. Before 1960, when these numbers also appeared on offprints of individual articles, there were also 500 of them.

Rule 2. Each identical number is put on by one and the same physical stamp at different times and on different publications.

This argues in favour of the numbers being *personal ones* and indicates that literature has been checked by a particular employee. The material from which the stamps are made is remarkable for its excellent hardness, which permits them to be used for many years. On various publications one often finds, for example, No. 303. But this very productive number has a defect in the zero, in the lower part of which there is a characteristic snag in the form of a comma ≪303. This characteristic number I observed on several issues of *Science* and journals on gerontology in my own library, received in 1966–8, on four books which I received (one from Japan and three from the USA), on a number of medical and other journals in libraries, on books on linguistics, one of which was published in 1958. I found this number on two offprints sent to me in 1956–7. I saw the same distinctive zero with its tail on a Canadian textbook received by a library in 1947! The numbers 340 and 343 have characteristic features of the figures. On No. 340's stamp, figure 4 is too close to the zero, and the zero is of incorrect form. In No. 343 the first figure touches the second, and the second the third. These unique numbers I found on old offprints from the USA (1959), on a book on haemopoesis which came from England (1968), and on various publications in libraries over a number of years.

This rule has been checked over many cases.

Rule 3. There is a clear, although not absolute, specialization of numbers with respect to the languages of the publications.

Absolute specialization is not necessary, since the employee wielding stamp No. 100 may know two languages, German and English, or French and Italian. But since most of them undoubtedly have command of only one foreign language, there must be differentiation by language.

Out of the 500 numbers, about 120 different numbers (from 4 to 498), belong to the English language, about 30 to German and 20 to French. Practically all journals in Finnish are checked by No. 168. The same number also takes in Norwegian. Journals in Japanese are checked by four numbers (83, 120, 149, 460), and so on. There is no need to give all the data on which this rule is based, it takes up a lot of space and is constantly growing. The differentiation by language is absolutely clearly defined, although, for example, in the German language group only 24 numbers are solely for German, and five take in both German and English literature. Three French numbers also know English. The Italian number, No. 124, also knows Spanish.

Rule 4. There is a fairly clear, but not absolute, differentiation into journal and book numbers, that is on the principle of checking periodical and non-periodical literature in different 'sections'.

'Title' number stamps are distributed between 1 and 500. But 90 per cent of all numbers on the journals (checked over hundreds of examples) lie between 100 and 300. *Book* numbers in 80 per cent of the cases are numbers up to 100 or between 300 and 500. Differentiation by languages is subordinate to this main differentiation. On the offprints received before 1960 there were only 'book' numbers. I made a list of the numbers from fifty offprints from 1955 to 1958 and noticed that they all lay between 1 and 100 or 300 and 500 (050, 405, 343, 437, 328, 411, 077, 340, etc.).

Rule 5. There is no specialization of the 'title' numbers by country of publication when journals from different countries are published in one language, for example, English.

The same numbers can appear on English language works published in England, USA, Austria, Holland and Japan.

Rule 6. Neither in the group of journals nor in the group of books is there any clear differentiation of numbers according to the branches of science. An employee of the English section with, for example, No. 130 reads through and stamps with equal effect technical, biological, medical and other scientific journals, and also historical, linguistic, political and bibliographic journals. When I have been in libraries I have noted down, over the course of almost two years, the 'title' numbers of different journals on open access in the Lenin State Library (LSL), the All-Union State Library of Foreign Literature (ASLFL), the Central Medical Library (CML) and others. The following picture was obtained of the differentiation according to branches of science, the frequency of the numbers being recorded by full points:

TABLE 4

DISTRIBUTION OF 'TITLE' NUMBERS ACCORDING TO BRANCHES OF
SCIENCE IN THE GROUP OF ENGLISH-LANGUAGE JOURNALS

Technical	Medical-biological	Humanities	Bibliographical
		4 .	
			49 .
63 .			
101 .			
	105 .		
	106	106 ...	

Technical	Medical-biological	Humanities	Bibliographical
110 ...	110		
	....		
118 .			
	125	125 ..	
126 ...	126	126 ...	126 ......
	.....		
	127 .		
	129 .		
130	130	130	130 ....
....	....	....	....
	....	....	.....
	....		
	.....		

and so on up to the highest number, 498.

The most 'loaded' numbers were the same in all branches of science. These were 130, 145, 147, 160, 179 and 185. Numbers above 300 occurred as isolated units, except for 303, with its defective zero. He got top marks for the group of journals. He simply must be some genius of the checking service.

In the group of journals, we processed about twenty technical journals, seventy medical-biological ones, fifty on the humanities and twenty-eight bibliographical lists of journal titles, different volumes and issues of each journal. In the group of books we noted down numbers from roughly 500 different publications in different languages. In the group of natural sciences and publications on the humanities there were very many numbers the same, and No. 303 held top place for productivity in both groups. Numbers are the same for different special subjects far more often than for different languages. Reference books and encyclopaedias were checked by the same group of numbers.

Rule 7. The same issues of the same journal found in different libraries and in personal use generally have the same 'title' number. For example, issue No. 3864 of *Science* which I have at home, and the copies in the LSL, ASLFL and the Biological Section of the Academy of Sciences of the USSR have the same number, 470, which is a rare one for *Science*, while issue No. 3865 in all four holdings has the 'title' number 185. The same issue of the *Gerontologist* in my home and in the CML have the same 'title' numbers with a double angle, 179, 184 and 303. This is because the journals come to the subscribers in the USSR in bulk, with many copies of the same issue in one sack. If this is not so, then they are first of all sorted somewhere by title, and then one employee checks the number and puts his stamp on the whole lot.

Rule 8. Although there is no specialization according to the branches of science, a particular journal does not fall to any one of the 200 employees with numbers between 100 and 300, but to a small group of employees consisting of 3 to 5 persons.

This is still not a very explicit differentiation of the journal checkers with 'title' numbers. If, for example, we put *Science* in date order, and then write down the consecutive 'title' numbers we obtain the following picture: 112, 112, 112, 112, 130, 130, 130, 407, 407, 303, 303, 436, 436, 185, 185, 175, 303, 303, 470, 185, 185, 185, 185, 185, 185, 185, 185, 185, 185, 185, 185, 158, 158, 158, 156, 156, 156, 185, 185, 185, 185, 185, 185, 185, etc. It is quite clear that the numbers go in groups, two months are checked by one person, then six months by another, and so on. The same rule is observed for other journals. *Brain Research* in date order has title numbers: 130, 303, 303, 130, 130, 160, 130, 160, 160, 160, 160. The *Journal of the Canadian Medical Association* is checked by the following numbers: 147, 147, 147, 147, 147, 130, 130, 130, 184, 184, 184, 184, etc. The rule has been checked for thirty journals on biology and the humanities.

It is possible that this differentiation is connected with the rooms in which the employees of the journals department sit. According to the lists certain journals are delivered to one room, others to another, and the number of tables in the rooms determines the number of numbers in the group connected with a given journal. We can offer no other explanation.

Hypothesis 1. On the permissive and prohibitive significance of the 'title' number stamps.

Journals arrive in the USSR from abroad in bulk. *Science* and *Nature* evidently at a rate of 200 to 300 copies of each issue, though each copy is packed separately and bears the address of the subscriber. The sack with the journals of a given issue falls, let us say, to No. 185, and he naturally does not leaf through each copy. He knows that they are all the same, and therefore he only needs to look through carefully the top copy of the pile of journals, and then to throw the whole pile on to the conveyor belt taking them away for sorting by addresses. But the stamp 185 appears on *every* copy. Why does No. 185 do all this work himself, for stamping the title-pages also takes time? Evidently, as we have already suggested, these stamps have some significance for the addressees, mainly libraries, or for some subsequent stage of movement of a particular package. A further suggestion, which we put forward much earlier, is that the number with the double angle is a permissive symbol. The journal or the book with such a symbol continues further. It is possible that the employee of this checking service has two types of stamps, one double-angled permissive stamp, and another of a different shape which is a *prohibitive* stamp. Publications with prohibitive stamps have not reached me, naturally, since they presumably go into the special holdings of libraries or are simply destroyed.

But once I happened to see a symbol, which evidently had such a prohibitive significance.

In 1968 it was absolutely necessary for me to read an article in *Science* which dealt with a method that was very important for our current experiment. I knew about this article from my correspondence, but the issue of the journal with this article had not reached me. I went into the library in Moscow, but it turned out that this number of the journal had not reached the Moscow Central Libraries either. On application to the Director of the Lenin State Library, I received the explanation that this issue of the journal had gone into the 'special holdings', and to read it it was necessary to have a special application from the governing body and special section of the Institute. But I did not want to be concerned with the special holding and acted otherwise.

My subscription to *Science* was arranged on a book exchange basis and was not registered with Soyuzpechat. In the USSR it is also possible to subscribe to this journal through Soyuzpechat, but the subscriber will not receive the original, but a photo-offset reproduction, which arrives after six or seven months' delay, has various omissions, is on poor paper and is considerably dearer. But within special limits subscriptions in the USSR for the original editions of foreign journals are permitted for Academicians of the Academy of Sciences of the USSR. And if the Academician takes out his subscription through the appropriate Section, then he should receive all issues and the customs ought not to make any confiscations.

One of the Academicians whom I knew (now deceased) had such a 'permitted' subscription to *Science*, and I asked him to let me look through the copies for 1968. The complete set of the journal stood in his office in his Institute. I quickly found the issue I needed, and at once I noticed that instead of the triangle which I knew so well on the cover of the journal, in the top right-hand corner there was a strange *double hexagon* with the number 185, the usual one for *Science,* inside it. This hexagon was very reminiscent of the formula for a chemical

compound of the aromatic series: ⟨⟨185⟩⟩

Similar hexagons appeared on some other issues of the journal, and when I got home I ascertained that these were the very issues which I had not received in 1968, and which were not listed in the open access catalogue of the Lenin State Library.

It was natural to assume that the hexagon was a *prohibitive sign of the censorship.* This was confirmed by the Academician, who said that he could not, according to the rules, give permission for the issues of *Science* with this symbol (he called it a 'nut') to be taken out of the Institute.

It would not have been right to expose the Academician, who was at risk because of an ordinary American journal, to any penalty, and I read through the necessary article in his office. But I remembered the 'nut', and I kept watch on occasion to see whether I might meet it again somewhere. Once I caught sight of it on the cover of a French political journal on the desk of an employee of one of the Central newspapers, and another time on the American journal *Newsweek.*

Quite recently a colleague told me that since 1964 many foreign journals in the library of his Institute had been taken out of the 'special holdings' into open access, after many years of being kept hidden. As it was easy to ascertain, they had gone into the 'special holdings' due to critical articles on T. D. Lysenko and 'Michurin biology'. My colleague had noticed that on the title-pages of these journals there were not the usual numbered triangles but hexagons, cancelled by some kind of paint. Evidently the 'declassification' of publications requires the removal of the prohibitive 'nut' by some plenipotentiary or responsible worker.

These few facts are enough for one to assume that each of the 500 employees of the checking service has two forms of numbered personal stamps, one angular *permissive* stamp, and the other a hexagonal *prohibitive* stamp. On some publications he puts the angle ('I permit'), and on others the hexagon ('I prohibit'). And the form of the stamps has evidently been chosen with the profound sense, as to the emblem. In the double angle the number stands in an open access, the double angle seems to be thrusting it away: 'Go freely, serve people.' In the double hexagon the number is closed in, shut up on all sides, walled in by a double grille. A book with such a symbol is sentenced to imprisonment in 'special holdings'.

But there are publications which do not even go into 'special holdings', but suffer destruction. To sentence a book to such a fate, there must be yet another special symbol. This I have never seen. By analogy may one

assume that it is something reminiscent of a gallows ⌐ ০

Hypothesis 2. How publications with prohibitive symbols are delivered to the addressees.

The prohibitive 'nut' on printed matter clearly means that the work in question cannot be received by a private individual and must be confiscated. But such literature does go to the addresses of establishments who are allowed to subscribe to it, and to libraries, that is, to safes, 'special holdings' and closed reading rooms. If the editor of some newspaper or journal is allowed to receive specialist newspapers and journals from abroad, then the post must deliver these newspapers and journals to the editor even if they have 'nuts'.

But newspapers and journals from capitalist countries are sent to the USSR in open packages. The sender does not know in advance whether the publication will get an angle or a 'nut'. In such a case can the ordinary post be entrusted to send publications with 'nuts' to the addressees? For then they could be read by employees of the post office, van drivers, postmen and employees of the establishments. It would of course be impossible to allow such a situation, for a publication with a 'nut' is obviously classified material. Evidently they are taken on to the various towns by some 'special postal service'. We shall leave this question without an answer, and only note the following detail which gives one food for thought.

On letters and packages reaching the addressee by ordinary mail there is a postmark with the date and town of posting and the postmark of delivery—the local post which serves the addressee. In Moscow these are different, G-9, A-8, K-9, etc., for the city sorting communications centres. In Obninsk it is the town communications centre. But once I was given a batch of envelopes from international mail packages, among which were many envelopes with the characteristic trademarks of foreign journals and newspapers such as *The Times, Der Stern, Die Zeit*, etc. On these envelopes there was the red stamp of the International Post Office. There was no other delivery post office stamp on them. I concluded that the Moscow organizations which receive this mail send responsible employees with letters of authorization direct to the International Post Office for it, and that there they receive against a receipt publications with a 'nut' and put them in a locked briefcase. But what do the employees of provincial establishments do? Do they get periodic business trips to Moscow? Evidently not, but it is most probable that they have to go for this mail to the post offices in the provincial centres. How many working days are lost to the state by this parallel system of special self-delivery of correspondence with a 'nut' no one, of course, has calculated.

CERTAIN PHENOMENA FALLING OUTSIDE THE GENERAL RULES

1. *Not all scientific journals coming from capitalist countries have All-Union 'title' number symbols.*

I receive two gerontology journals from the USA: the *Gerontologist* and the *Journal of Gerontology*. Each of these comes out once a quarter; the first is more popular, and the second more academic. On the issues of the first journal (I have a complete set from 1961) there are always 'title' numbers with a double angle, on the second there are no numbers, only the large numbers on the packages. This phenomenon is also to be found in the libraries. In the All-Union State Library of Foreign Literature there are no number stamps on European and American scientific abstracting journals, nor on some chemical and medical ones. In the Central Medical Library almost half the sets of journals have no ordinary numbers of the All-Union service with double angles, but only some special large 'title' numbers from 1 to 20, differentiated by language (4, 11, 17 are English, 6 and 3 are French, 19 is German, etc.). These same numbers appear on many foreign journals in the main library of the Academy of Medical Sciences of the USSR. It is easy to establish that on journals of a more general nature—general medical journals, popular medical journals, journals on psychology, social medicine, etc. (such as *The Lancet, British Journal of Psychiatry, California Medicine*) there are the All-Union stamps with the double angle. Evidently they pass through the main checking system. The specialized medical journals (*Acta gastro-enterologica belgica, Urologia, Cancer*, etc.) have more local 'title' numbers, put on, apparently, by some department of the Ministry of Health.

In the libraries of the Institutes of the Academy of Sciences of the USSR, a number of highly scientific journals (*Chromosoma, Anatomical Record*, etc.) also have no angular stamps. Nor do they have the 'title' numbers of the medical type. But they do have numerical signs on the back cover, differentiated by language.

Nor are there 'permissive' title numbers on publications of the United Nations and the specialized agencies such as UNESCO, WHO and IAAE.

It is possible that as a result of the increase in periodical literature coming into the USSR from abroad (the number of journals in the world doubles every ten years) the 500 persons of the angle/hexagon checking line can no longer cope with the flow of literature. They are faced with the same problem that faces aeronauts in a balloon. One can try to inflate the balloon more when there is danger of falling. But one can also gradually begin to throw out ballast. The chiefs of the organization have reached a statesmanlike solution to the problem. First they threw out the ballast of publications from the socialist countries, where, of course, the press is already censored. Then they threw out the checking of offprints from scientific journals, of which there were too many. Later they began on the unnecessary ballast of certain highly scientific journals. And the balloon continued its flight at the former altitude.

2. *Creative and children's literature coming from capitalist countries to private addresses, does not, as a rule, have 'title' check stamps.*

This phenomenon is very interesting and is little understood. But it does exist. Among the publications which I personally received from England and the USA in 1964–8, twelve works of creative literature (novels, plays, critical works), eight children's books and two works on sociology, there were no number stamps on the title-pages. On all the scientific books from the USA and England there were stamps. Certain of my colleagues in Moscow and Obninsk found the same picture.

Perhaps creative and sociological literature is not generally checked? This is hardly likely, since the percentage of 'losses' and disappearances in the category is extremely great. In my own case it was about 50 per cent. Moreover, I was able to check that, for example, the American, British and West German creative literature in the holdings of the Lenin State Library had the ordinary book angular 'title' numbers. In the book exhibitions of the All-Union State Library of foreign literature, the creative literature also has the permissive numbers.

Why, then, do these books come into private hands without numbers? This must be a result of a complex combination of factors. On a scientific book, the employee responsible puts his permissive triangle with confidence. He forbids a political work or a James Bond espionage novel to be sent on further with equal confidence, stamping his 'nut' on it. Maybe there is even a special list of forbidden books, where he can look them up. But then there falls into his hands a novel of H. G. Wells, a play by Shaw or the children's book, *Alice in Wonderland*. Or even a detective novel by Agatha Christie. There are no grounds for prohibiting these books from being received. But it is also impossible to read them through carefully. The daily norm of pages to be checked would not be fulfilled. Scientific literature only has to be glanced through—it is all incomprehensible anyway. So the wielder of the two stamps vacillates. If you don't let *Alice in Wonderland* through, the sender and addressee will start to protest, especially as the package is registered. But if you let it through with your own number, that is dangerous, for the book will circulate. For suppose in several years' time it turns out that *Alice* and Agatha are not to be read, your personal number will show that you did not foresee this. It is impossible to send a book to a library without a number—they will send it back as 'unclear'. But it can be sent on to an individual recipient without triangle or hexagon; he will not be worried on this account.

3. *Journals and newspapers of communist parties coming from capitalist countries to libraries and for open sale do not have 'permissive' numbers.*

The communist press of England, the USA, France and other countries (*Morning Star, L'Humanité, Worker*, etc.) do not have number stamps. These stamps undoubtedly have a censorship significance, and to put them on communist publications would naturally be anomalous. But this literature, of course, is also very carefully checked and is put on sale with large gaps, and individual subscriptions to communist newspapers from capitalist countries are not allowed. For the articles published in these newspapers do not always correspond to the interests of Soviet policy, and they give more detailed information about certain events which are often not reported in the Russian press due to lack of space.

For example, during the events in Czechoslovakia in August and September 1968, the sale in Moscow of all communist publications from Western Europe was stopped. Nor were they available on open access in libraries. At the end of September, *L'Humanité* began to appear again, and after some time the other journals too, but with difficulties from time to time.

Sometimes the editions of these papers are held back because of over-cautiousness beyond all permissible bounds. For example, the British communist newspaper, *Morning Star*, of 4 December 1969 was with-drawn from sale and did not even get into the Lenin State Library periodicals room simply because on the second page a short letter from a reader was published, commenting unfavourably on the expulsion of Aleksandr Solzhenitsyn from the Union of Soviet Writers. The issue of the paper of 10 December 1969, in which there was a letter from another reader approving the expulsion and entering into polemics with the first reader on this question, was sold in Moscow and got into the libraries.

When the British or Italian communist newspapers are confiscated in the USSR because they make and print both Soviet and Chinese versions of border incidents, it is, of course, stupid; but it is understandable from the point of view of censorship—the censorship must have some instructions on so important a question of state. But to confiscate the whole edition of the *Morning Star*, of which at least 20,000 copies come into the USSR every day and sell at 8 kopeks a copy, because of a little letter to the editor from a private individual expressing his personal opinion about a decision of the Ryazan branch of the Union of Writers is not only extremely stupid, but it is also a loss for the state, which pays an annual subscription to this paper in foreign currency.

A FURTHER HYPOTHESIS

In conclusion to this part, it is, of course, relevant to ask who is responsible for these angular and hexagonal permissive and prohibitive signs which appear on the title-pages of books coming from abroad. What is this organization which numbers 500 responsible employees, who know a great number of foreign languages, and presumably at least as many less responsible employees of the service staff? A thousand persons implies an enormous building or a number of smaller buildings, not less than three or four hundred rooms. Earlier we assumed that the large numbers on the outer wrappings of packages were put in by the postal customs service. In that service there are 140 persons who know various languages and they check all the packages containing offprints or journals coming from all countries. If the customs confiscates something, then, by law, by the very Code, they must inform one of it. Customs statements on confiscation are known to many, especially to philatelists who carry on a contraband exchange of stamps. The customs have no right to make any such mark on the contents of packages, or to put their own stamp on any articles.

The Code does not provide for the stamping of books and journals by the customs service. The customs could confiscate literature too, if a book falling into their hands happened to be on a list of prohibited books. But current journals and newspapers cannot yet be on such lists. The customs officer examines and checks, he makes holes in padded envelopes, he can even open them up without constraint, if they are glued down, but he is not in a position to read books and journals. *The customs service could not put special symbols on journals forbidding libraries and the directors of Institutes to issue these journals to readers.* The power of the customs over scientific publications cannot stretch to such omnipotence.

In the USSR there is only one organization which has the necessary plenipotentiary control of the press. This is Glavlit. Everyone knows that Glavlit controls publications inside the USSR. But perhaps there is an International Section in Glavlit. It is well known, too, that the post office has instructions to transmit abroad only those manuscripts and printed materials which have a Glavlit visa. One can only send through the post for publication abroad material which has been 'approved' with a form 103M. But perhaps only 'approved' material from abroad can get on to the library shelves and into private hands? And the angular or hexagonal stamps—are they symbols of Glavlit?

In order to be able to discuss this question with greater certainty it is necessary to touch upon yet another important problem of the international postal service, the problem of the confiscation of printed matter *en route* from sender to addressee.

7

Confiscation and alteration of printed matter from abroad

A SOVEREIGN state, as we have already noted, has the right to protect itself by legal means against the penetration of undesirable literature from abroad. Enmity between states, alas, is still a very common phenomenon, and it will find its first reflection in the press. Complicated political, economic and military conflicts between states arise as a result of many diverse causes of an ideological, territorial, historical, racial, religious and sociological character. But since military clashes in the era of atomic, hydrogen and rocket arms have become too dangerous for the entire world, instead of 'hot' war, there is the 'cold' war, an important arm of which is the press. The press has become a weapon, and every country creates its own means of defence against hostile propaganda, the chief of which is the confiscation of hostile press propaganda by the customs organs. The right of customs confiscation is extended to literature coming from abroad through the post and this kind of action is provided for in the international postal agreements, and there is a familiar standard procedure.

In many cases the control of press propaganda from abroad is not only legal but beneficial, since it tends to reduce the amount of hostile propaganda and reduce the scale of the 'cold war'. For if the weapons of the 'cold war' do not reach their target, their production will decrease.

At the same time, there is no doubt that any defence must have reasonable limits. The protection of a country against harmful propaganda must not isolate it. Too strict a filtering of press information brings a country perceptible harm—economic, scientific and cultural—and makes it lag behind world progress. The censorship of printed works coming from abroad is a highly delicate matter, and it should be in the hands not of secret controllers of no great competence, but of those who actually need this literature. The balance between benefit and harm in all 'restrictions' is very unstable, and any extension of the range of confiscations, any hard and fast ruling and bureaucracy in this field soon lead to a situation in which this balance in the control of the flow of literature and especially scientific literature, swings over towards harm.

In the present study we cannot, of course, make any final judgements, since the bulk of our information in this field is hermetically sealed off from general objective study. *However, we should at once state that any interference by the censorship and customs services in the international exchange of scientific information is necessarily harmful and absolutely wrong.*

But the media of mass information are one thing: they are for unlimited circulation (newspapers, mass-circulation journals, leaflets, etc.) and can be designated as 'propaganda'. Scientific literature, not in only the natural sciences, but philosophy, economics, politics, statistics, etc., is quite another matter. There should be *no* barriers in the path of these journals. But even to the media of mass information they should be applied reasonably and legally. In the case of the USSR, it should be concerned with the confiscation by the customs organs of specially anti-Soviet literature sent unsolicited and in bulk to various addresses. But if some citizen, in the course of his exchange of literature with a colleague, sends from abroad an ordinary newspaper or journal, *Die Stern* or *Der Spiegel*, the *Saturday Evening Post* or *Life*, or such universally famous newspapers as *The Times*, the *New York Times*, or the *Observer*, there should be no grounds for confiscating these publications which are sent to a citizen of the USSR for his private study.

The state has a right to prohibit the import of such international foreign publications for open sale, and this has long been the practice in the USSR. But it should not take away the right of any citizen of the USSR to read these publications, if he wishes to do so to increase his knowledge of some problem. Any person has an absolute right to obtain the maximum amount of information on any event in the world which interests him. But the Soviet press, even the Central papers, have for a long time provided only a very small volume of daily publication of information about world events. TASS sends out to all the newspapers *the same* information, very limited in quantity. Any Central newspaper publishes daily only a twentieth or a thirtieth of the information about events outside the USSR that any leading newspaper in the USA, England or France gives about events taking place outside those countries. Even the Western Communist daily newspapers, *Unità*, *L'Humanité* and the *Morning Star*, print much more daily news than *Izvestiya* or *Pravda* (*Unità* and *L'Humanité* four to five times, the *Morning Star* twice as much) and in England there are only about 15,000 members of the Communist Party. Realising that the Central newspapers due to lack of paper are quite inadequate as sources of current information and can create a false impression, TASS prepares for responsible workers a special 'closed circulation' newspaper bulletin, known as *White TASS*, which appears every day and runs to a hundred to two hundred pages. This *White TASS* is intended for those responsible workers who do not know foreign languages and cannot read the foreign newspapers. But if some citizen of the USSR knows a foreign language and wants, for example, to know all the details about some outstanding event in the history of world civilization, such as the first flights of man to the moon and the landings on the lunar surface, then he has an absolute right to do so. But it is impossible to do so from the Soviet press, as the Central newspapers reported these events extremely stingily in brief notes upon page three, as something not particularly interesting or important. The Chinese press told its readers nothing at all about the flights to the moon; not even a tiny note on these events occurred in the Chinese papers. But if a citizen of the USSR is interested in the details, and decides that he will order from England or Belgium through a friend or colleague, a selection of newspapers or weeklies covering the period of the moonflight, or that he will read these newspapers in some library, then he has an *absolute right* to receive and read them, as confirmed by declarations and conventions on human rights. No censorship has the right to interfere. And this does not apply only to events in space.

Today this right of citizens of the USSR is being violated, and these violations are performed by the postal customs service and by Glavlit. By restricting the right to receive information, these organs are doing great harm to the development of society, by restricting its cultural resources and its political maturity. The censorship behaves like a nursemaid who decides, even when a person is no longer a baby in arms, to spoonfeed him with semolina pudding and a bottle of warm milk and will not let him go out into the road. But an organization reared with no contact with the outside environment, will not have enough immunity, its defence mechanisms will not develop, its means of resisting harmful influences will be stunted. Adaptation to the outside environment remains at the lowest level. Even ideological workers in their own counterpropaganda lack the necessary strength in the struggle and competition of ideas. These workers are many, but they are weakened and numbed, shut in by the solicitous cowl of the censorship.

Censorship of the mail closes the way to hundreds and thousands of publications of *normal* types, not only to personal individual addresses but also to state public and scientific libraries. The fact that in the science room in the main Lenin State Central Library in which only scientists work, and in the current periodicals room, it is impossible to read the old established world-famous British newspaper *The Times*, or any British newspapers at all, except the communist *Morning Star*, and then not in the form of a complete set, is intolerable in a modern, civilized country, particularly in so great a state as the USSR.

When the postal customs service decides the fate not of mass-circulation but of scientific literature, when it confiscates or retains scientific journals and monographs, when it devalues subscriptions or tells libraries what can and cannot be included in catalogues and general holdings, this practice seems to me the highest degree of civil service idiocy and bureaucratic stupidity—it is absolutely arbitrary behaviour. The actions of the censorship not only cause political, ideological and cultural damage to society, they also slow down the scientific, technical and industrial development. This damage must not be exaggerated but it must not be ignored. One of my American colleagues, who had learned that a scientific journal with an article to which he wished to draw my attention had not been received by me and had not been received by the main Moscow libraries, although other issues of this journal were there, exclaimed in a letter with sincere amazement, 'It is impossible to understand how so extremely widespread a censorship can be at all profitable.'

But maybe I am exaggerating it, and it has not been like this for a long time. Maybe all this happened long in the past, and nowadays there are enough well-marked paths through the censorship and customs frontier? Maybe the censorship no longer hits you on the head with a hammer to kill a mosquito which has settled there?

Let us turn, however, to the facts which are at our disposal, to the facts of 1967–9, which relate mainly to science. I shall begin by considering the fate in the USSR of one of the most famous general science journals, the American and international journal *Science*, which we have mentioned several times before. This journal has been published by the American Association for the Advancement of Science since 1848, that is for more than 120 years. Like the similar British journal, *Nature*, it comes out weekly, fifty-two issues per year. For this reason it is chosen by the scientific intelligentsia for the rapid publication of the most important research in various fields of natural sciences, in biology, chemistry, physics, geology, etc. In this journal the works of Soviet authors are rarely published (in *Nature* they appear more frequently).

Science, like the British *Nature*, is not a popular science journal. It publishes original papers, written in strictly professional language and intended for specialists. It differs in this respect from the Soviet journals, *Priroda* (Nature), and *Nauka i Zhizn* (Science and Life) which are sometimes compared to *Nature* and *Science*. In fact there is no equivalent to *Science* and *Nature* in the USSR, not only as regards the academic level, but also in social significance. *Science* and *Nature* are not only professional scientific journals, they are also organs expressing the political, economic, social and sociological views of the scientists of the USA and Great Britain. They are democratic mouthpieces of the scientific intelligentsia, their own kind of scientists' newspapers. According to a UNESCO survey, *Science* and *Nature* hold first place in the list of most widely-read professional scientific journals. No serious scientist in any country can get by without scanning and reading these journals. About one-quarter of all scientists read only these journals regularly, and this evidently ensures that they get the minimum scientific information they need.

As regards politics, *Science* always takes the most progressive position in the USA. In its sections of 'News and Views' and 'Letters to the Editor', and also in the weekly leading articles, *Science* calls attention to all important world events, often opening a discussion and trying in this way to have an effect on the ideas of the community. In this respect, *Science* is often in opposition to the policy of the Government of the USA on many questions, especially on the question of the Vietnam war. This is recognized by the Soviet press. Comparatively recently, in *Novyi Mir* (No. 8, pp. 219–25, 1968) an article was published by D. Sukharev, entitled 'Pure Science and Dirty War' which was devoted to analysing the attitude of *Science* to the American Government's Vietnam policy. The author of the article analyses the material from *Science* at the end of 1967 and beginning of 1968. He gives high praise and sympathy to the journal's bold attitude, which gave scientists the opportunity of expressing their opposition to President Johnson's policy. In the *Novyi Mir* article there was a detailed analysis of the material published in *Science*, on the anti-war action of scientists, on their refusal to carry out research at the demand of the military department even when generously financed. 'The discussion of this problem,' write Sukharev, 'which had already begun in the spring issues of the journal' (he is writing of 1967) 'would in no way lead to the delight of the state administration, who were accustomed to think that scientists were there to do what they were paid for.' Besides analysing the anti-war attitudes of American scientists, and their critical action in their address to the Government, and telling of the solidarity of British scientists, Sukharev quotes, in particular, material from Nos. 3799, 3791, 3816 and 3868 of the journal. I do not know in what book holdings Sukharev read these issues of *Science,* but they are not in open holdings of the Lenin State Library. Nor did I receive them on my exchange subscription. Not until six months after these numbers appeared did their 'surrogates' get into the libraries, i.e. the photo-offset reproduction of the journal prepared by the All-Union Institute of Scientific and Technical Information (AISTI). These 'copies' of *Science* undergo complicated surgery before reproduction, as a result of which some articles in the original do not get into the 'copy'. In the copies of these issues, it is the articles on sociological and political themes that have been removed. They have been cut out by 'the blunt scissors of arbitrary rule', although they contained nothing anti-Soviet, but on the contrary, the point of view on political events expressed in the articles was closer to the Soviet point of view than to the attitude of the American authorities. Evidently the censorship on the AISTI has instructions not to leave any political articles in *Science*; either they have no time to investigate political shades of opinion, or else they do not wish to show that American scientists are at least allowed to discuss in the press what Soviet scientists in their press can mention only in the form of an old political joke about a critic of President Eisenhower. (This joke is known in a number of variants. One of them goes: An American, boasting of the freedom of speech in his country, said to a Russian colleague, 'Why, I can go out on to the square and shout "Down with President Eisenhower!" and nothing will happen to me.' To which the Russian replied: 'But just think, I can go out on to the square and shout, "Down with President Eisenhower!" and they will *praise* me!')

I have already mentioned that as a subscriber to *Science* I did not receive a number of issues in 1967. But I noticed this only at the end of the year when I was sorting the copies into date order. In 1968 I was more observant. In the first half of the year, I failed to receive numbers 3816, 3817, 3820, 3821, 3827, 3832, 3834, 3841 and 3842. As a regular reader of the journal, I naturally wanted to look through *all* the issues, and hence I tried to read the missing issues in the Lenin State Library. But to my enormous surprise, I could not find these very issues either in the catalogue of the library or in the current periodicals room. All the other numbers of the journal were there. I went to the All-Union State Library of Foreign Literature, but there, too, all the numbers I have mentioned, except one, were absent. The AISTI reproductions of these numbers had not arrived yet either.

The fact that these missing numbers corresponded led me to think that they had been withdrawn for some reason by the censorship. But this method seemed strange to me. In former times, I remembered, if there was some undesirable article in *Science* or *Nature*, for example on Lysenko or the fate of Vavilov (there were many such articles in the period 1948–54), then these articles were carefully cut out by the censorship. Sometimes other articles were affected but not many. They also blacked out the title on the contents with Indian ink (but in the annual index of articles in the last issue of a volume, the censor did not think to black out the titles, and this made it possible, if one wished, to discover the character of the articles which were cut out). In former Stalinist times I also happened to see other journals with pages or parts of pages cut out. The censorship cut out what did not please it, but the rest of the scientific contents of the journal was retained for use. The approach was crude, but commonsensical. The censorship at that time was not reluctant to show its hand. Later on there were no more such cut-up journals, and I thought that this was the end of the censorship of foreign scientific journals. The cause of peaceful co-existence and scientific co-operation had put an end to the old barbaric practice. Then suddenly I discovered that this was far from being the case, that the censorship was now not only removing certain notes with the aid of the scissors but even depriving the reader of the whole journal with all its positive scientific content, just so as not to show its censor's face. The readers might not notice the loss of some issues, and perhaps would not try to find out why the volumes were incomplete. But this proposition still seemed hard to believe, perhaps the journals really were lost on their journey, or had not been sent to the subscriber due to an oversight of the publisher. This latter possibility had to be checked first of all. In September 1968 I wrote to the editor of *Science* saying that as a subscriber to *Science* I was very distressed at the loss of certain issues in 1967 and in 1968, and that I should like to know whether all the issues were sent to European subscribers and whether there had been complaints from other subscribers. I did not say which issues of the journal had not been received at this stage, so as not to alarm the publishers with a long list. My letter was sent by registered airmail with an 'advice of delivery' note. Knowing that letters are sometimes lost, I sent a copy of the letter the next day, in the same manner, from the Moscow Post Office. Both letters were addressed to the editor of the journal, Professor Adelson.

However, at the due time I received neither an answer nor the 'advice of delivery' note. Once again, I sent such a letter, but dispatched the copy to one of my colleagues in Washington, asking him to forward it to the editor. Just as with the earlier difficulty over the note sent to *Nature*, it might be supposed that the customs would check correspondence with a journal for prohibited enclosures more carefully. This supposition evidently turned out to be justified. The letter to the editor was lost again, but the copy-letter to my colleague reached him and went on to the editor. This I could judge from the returned 'advice of delivery' note. Soon an answer came, signed by the Managing Editor Dr Robert Orme:

> I am sorry that you have been unable to receive certain issues of *Science*, but I cannot explain this. Copies of the journal are sent out immediately to all subscribers, but it is possible that there is some irregularity in loading the ships in New York. If you would send us a list of the missing copies for 1967 and 1968, then we shall be pleased to send you replacements. If you do not want these back numbers, however, then we will extend your subscription gratis for three months to compensate you for the lost copies.

Dr Orme nobly took the responsibility upon himself. I wrote briefly to thank him for his kindness and told him the numbers of the journal which I would like to receive for 1967 and 1968. Subsequently I received by registered post four of the issues that were previously lost (Nos. 3789, 3791, 3816 and 3817). Perhaps the other issues were sent but were lost. However, I could not exploit the editor's kindness any further.

Why No. 3789 was lost in the first place, I do not know, evidently by chance, due to *force majeure*, since it did not contain any political or sociological articles. But No. 3791 was undoubtedly withdrawn because it contained an article entitled 'Developer of Russia's Bomb', with a portrait of Academician I. V. Kurchatov. This article subsequently did not go into the AISTI-reproduced surrogate variant of the journal for Soviet subscribers. At the same time the censors of the All-Union Institute of Scientific and Technical Information removed from the reproduction of this number one of the letters to the editor (criticizing chemical and bacteriological weapons) the editor's leading article criticizing the Budgeting Commission for Science of the United States Congress and a couple of notes. The titles of the omitted articles were cut out of the contents as well.

But the removal of the article on Kurchatov from the journal and the holding back of the copies sent through the post only proves that the censors do not read the articles in the journals *seriously*. In the pursuit of productivity they waste no time deciding on the fate of publications according to certain superficial indications. Perhaps these are merely instructions forbidding the publication of material on the Russian bomb. In reality, however, the article 'Developer of Russia's Bomb' (pp. 912–13) is a review of the book *I. V. Kurchatov* published in the USSR, and written by Kurchatov's close friend and colleague I. V. Golovin. This book was published by the Atomizdat publishing house in 1967. Since the book on Kurchatov was the first account published in our country on the history of the development of atomic weapons in the USSR and the role played in this by Academician Kurchatov, it was natural that this did not go unnoticed in the USA. *Science* published the review which was very favourable and recommended the translation of the book into English. The editors obtained a photograph of Kurchatov from the TASS photographic archives, and under the photograph they noted: 'Courtesy Sovphoto'.

Science No. 3816 was also withdrawn without any serious grounds. If one compares the original of the journal with the AISTI photocopy surrogate received by the libraries half a year later, then it can be seen that what has been withdrawn from the Soviet reproduction is a brief editorial leading article on the work of the American Association for the Advancement of Science, an article which contains no criticism addressed at the science of socialist countries; and pages 750–7 are also missing. These contained an account of the Meeting of the Association and a biography of its new President. In the reproduced copy there was also a strange empty space on page 723, right in the middle of a review of two books by American authors. On comparison with the original, one finds that *two paragraphs* are missing from the review, in which the opinions of Freud and Bertrand Russell on psychoanalysis are expressed. In these paragraphs the term 'scientific materialism' is used, and this evidently alarmed the censor. But the author of the article did not use it in a pejorative sense.

And, finally, the last of the forbidden issues of *Science* which reached me, No. 3817: from the AISTI reproduction were removed two letters to the editor (on the necessity of birth control and on the harmful effects of smoking), a leading article discussing an interesting moral problem (on the contradiction between human rights regarding matters of confidence and the publication in medical articles of research with descriptions of the illness of particular patients), and also four articles from the section 'News and Comment'. In one of these articles there was a photograph of the presentation of a medal to Professor Kistiakowsky. The medal was being presented by President Johnson. Here, too, was printed an extract from President Johnson's speech at this ceremony. The other three articles withdrawn were also devoted to internal questions of American science.

It should be noted that these deletions were not made to save paper, on the grounds that the articles were of no interest to Soviet readers. Deletions in reproduction are concealed whenever possible, and this entails more work. It is necessary to cut out and paste up a new contents, so that the titles of the articles removed do not give away the censor's action. But it is impossible to change the order of the pages in the journal, for in bibliographical notes, authors must, as a rule, cite the pages of the article cited. Therefore, in order to hide the deletion, the layout man replaces them by completely useless advertisements from other issues of the journal. If a sizeable portion of the text is withdrawn, then the wounds in the journal are left open; but so that the subscriber does not send the issue back as defective, below the journal's English contents list appears the sentence in Russian 'Certain pages are not included in this issue.'

In fairness I should add that deletions of this kind are not only made in reproductions for Soviet subscribers of those issues which do not reach the libraries and individual subscribers of the original publication. Something is cut out by the AISTI censorship in the reproduction of almost every issue of *Science*. This censorship acts independently and more ferociously than that in the postal channels. Evidently Glavlit considers such a reproduction as an internal publication which is distributed by Soyuzpechat. Hence the regulations for the internal press are applied to it. Or perhaps it is simply done so that the castration department set up in the AISTI should not have slack periods but should be kept working at a regular rate. This latter supposition is far more likely, since the majority of omissions are inexplicable and senseless, they simply mutilate the usual appearance of the journal. Most frequently of all they remove and replace by advertisements the editorial leading articles and the Letters to the Editor. If one compares and considers the original and the copy, not selectively but in order as they follow in the library, one finds the following picture. From No. 3793 they deleted in reproduction two Letters to the Editor and a discussion of the new books on Mendel published for the centenary of the discovery of the laws of heredity (pp. 1119–20) and an editorial article on the politics of admitting students to the various departments (p. 1126). From No. 3794 they took out pages 1282–5 containing an article on the events in an American college in Oregon and information on a discussion in the National Scientific Foundation (NSF). In No. 3795 they again cut out the leading article on the Conference of the American Association for the Advancement of Science. In No. 3796 they cut out in reproduction the Letters to the Editor, the leading article and pages 1533–42 with a number of interesting articles on the relationship of science and politics. In No. 3797 they cut out the leading article on the problems of Negro students (pp. 99–100). In No. 3798 the censors cut out a factual article on the 1968 science budget in the USA (pp. 230–3) and a critical article entitled 'Money for research. Prospects for next year are gloomy'. Perhaps the censor decided that these 'gloomy' figures, expressed in thousands of millions of dollars, should not be communicated to Soviet scientists who, generally speaking, do not know their science budget and cannot discuss it openly. In No. 3799 they cut out the leading article on Westin's book *Privacy and Freedom* with a criticism of the surveillance system and also a detailed article on the Federal budget for science (pp. 357–60), etc.

The list of these omissions in almost every number may be continued both backwards to 1966 and 1965 and forward to 1968 and 1969, the numbers for which are now being prepared for reproduction by the AISTI (in 1969 the reproduction of journals by AISTI was very delayed, as much as nine or ten months). Almost all the cuts in 1969 were due to the discussion by the journal of internal scientific problems and international problems connected with American politics. (They cut out all articles campaigning for the abolition of the draft in the USA, on the principles of the preparation of offprints of articles, on disagreements between President Nixon and scientific associations about the appointment of leading scientific administrators, on university freedom, etc.)

But the activity of the censorship in cleaning up the AISTI-reproduced journals has no direct bearing on the theme of the present work and we shall not go very deeply into it. We shall only point out that in the USSR about five hundred foreign journals are thus republished in the language of the original. This is done to save currency and avoid paying subscriptions to the original for a whole number of scientific libraries. In the lists of the AISTI copies distributed by Soyuzpechat are almost all the most important scientific journals of the USA, England, France and West Germany. But unfortunately the copies are delayed by five to seven months, and therefore most scientific establishments, especially outside Moscow, learn about scientific work in corresponding disciplines only after half a year's delay—a full research cycle. Thus AISTI worsens the chronic lag of Soviet science behind the general world level and increases the number of projects that are duplicated. Even the physics Institutes, where the technical work is extremely costly, only get the AISTI copies if they are outside Moscow. I believe that the losses from this practice greatly outweigh the saving of currency by the press committee.

Returning to the work of the post, I must admit that I was very depressed when I found that issues of *Science* had been confiscated. The senselessness of these actions was all too evident. Somewhere there sit ill-educated clerks like censor No. 303 with his defective zero, and they hurriedly check everything from English grammar and *Science* to monographs on gerontology. For if in my personal library alone there are some ten publications stamped by No. 303, how much literature must one censor deal with in a day? And in this haste the censor decides where he should put a double angle and where the prohibitive hexagon, isolating Soviet scientists from such publications. Does the Soviet Government, I thought, really trust this nameless group of numbered clerks, these five hundred people cowed by instructions, more than their army of almost a million Soviet scientists? Surely this practice has simply remained unchanged from the old Stalinist times.

In order to draw attention somehow to this stupid arbitrary behaviour of the postal customs censorship that is so harmful to Soviet science, I wrote two letters. One of them was addressed to the International Post Office, the other to the Director of the Lenin State Library. In the first, I drew the attention of the postal department to the fact that the practice of confiscating scientific journals *en route* to the subscribers (I quoted *Science* as an example) was illegal and harmful to scientific work. I stated which numbers of the journal I had not received and asked them to explain the reasons for their confiscation, to state who had taken this decision, and, if possible, to return to me the literature which had been retained. To the Director of the Lenin State Library, I wrote as a regular reader of *Science* and *Nature* deploring the fact that the volumes were incomplete, and indicating the series of numbers of the journal which had not gone into the science periodicals room.

No answer came from the International Post Office, although not long before, the Presidium of the Supreme Soviet of the USSR had published a Decree about Departments and Establishments paying attention to the claims and complaints of citizens. This decree set a period of a month as the limit for replying to claims and complaints, and threatened bureaucrats who did not reply to claims with various penalties.

From the Lenin Library an answer did come, after a long delay. The temporary Executive Head of the section dealing with unbroken runs, O. D'yakonova, stated in a letter (Ref. No. 25/946) of 24 December 1968 that all issues of *Science* were in the holdings of the library. However, she wrote,

> the issues of the journal which you mention, Nos. 3821, 3827, 3832, 3834, 3841, 3842, 3846 were received by the library at the proper time but they are not kept in the current periodicals room but in the holdings of Section 13. The two copies of *Nature* (London) which you mention are also kept there. The library does not decide the question of where periodical publications are to be kept, and hence cannot at will transfer a journal from one holding to another.

On my next visit to the library, I asked the periodicals room attendant whether I could obtain these issues from Holding 13. The answer was negative. Holding 13 was a closed holding, a 'special holding', and people could only get in there with special permissions and applications from establishments, that is, only if they had a 'pass' similar to that necessary for a visit to a top-security Institute. Foreign journals and our own military installations were classified in the same manner.

Since there was no answer from the International Post Office, and the lost journals had not been returned to me, either, I wrote to them again, pointing out that the loss of journals was still going on. In addition I wrote a complaint to the Ministry of Communications. In this complaint I did not dispute the right of the customs to make confiscations, but I recalled that according to the law and the Customs Code of the USSR (confirmed by a Decree of the Presidium of the Supreme Soviet of the USSR of 5 May 1964) the customs must inform the interested party of the confiscation and state the reason for the confiscation and the nature of the breach of the customs rules. (When an order for confiscation is presented, an objection may be made within two weeks to the Chief Customs Control or to the People's Court. If no objection is made, the decision on confiscation stands only after the period for objections having expired.) I drew the attention of the Minister of Communications of the USSR to the fact that the periodic losses of journals and books were not accompanied by any statements or reports from the customs, and in this case it was impossible to decide whether they were connected with the confiscation, or if it was simply a theft, which should be prosecuted as a crime.

I received no answers to these new letters. But the losses of *Science* did not decrease, either for me, or in the libraries. In 1969, three issues out of fifty-two were lost. Many issues came very late, and not in order (for example, I received the January issue in June) but the editors themselves had given due warning of this possibility, informing subscribers in Europe that due to the two-month dockers' strike in New York harbour (December 1968 to January 1969) there might be some irregularities in the delivery of the magazine to subscribers.

In the letter from the Lenin Library, we note the sentence that the library does not decide the question of where periodical publications are kept, and does not have the right to transfer journals at will from one holding to another. Who then decides this question? Undoubtedly the power of the hexagonal stamp governs the State Library. In the unbroken runs section they divide angles from hexagons, and only publications with angles are sent into the open holdings. Hexagons go into Holding 13, the special holding, and are buried there for a long time. The article on account of which a hexagon was put on has long since lost its topical nature, but the library nevertheless cannot transfer journals at will from one holding to another.

It is only fair to point out that the State Libraries on the whole actually benefit from the action of the censorship, since a considerable proportion of the printed works confiscated by the customs and the International Section of Glavlit is sent to the special holdings of libraries, and sometimes even to open access. One of my colleagues from Leningrad, who had been on a long business trip to the USA, decided shortly before he returned to send most of the books which he had bought or had been given in the USA home by sea mail. He wanted to reduce the weight of his luggage, since sending books by sea mail was much cheaper than paying to take them as excess baggage when he flew home.

Unfortunately he miscalculated. More than half his books which he sent by mail failed to arrive. Great was his surprise when after some time he came across a book in the library, which he found from a list he had kept was one of those labelled lost, and most of them proved to be in the holdings of the library. They bore his signature, but his attempts to get them back were unsuccessful. The books were now considered to be the property of the library.

This piracy is a common occurrence and extends to all kinds of publications. Many paperback and ordinary editions of works of creative literature in various languages in the holdings of the Lenin State Library and the All-Union State Library of Foreign Literature find their way into both closed and open holdings as a result of customs 'confiscations'. The currency reserves of the libraries are very limited, and the State Committee on the Press does not recommend that they be spent on *belles-lettres*. But this does not only affect *belles-lettres*. My colleague sent copies of his book, *Genetics, Evolution and Society* from the USA to six Moscow geneticists. Three of them, including the author of the present work, received their copies safe and sound. The other three did not receive them. One of them, Professor A., received a hard wrapper with his address, but there was no book inside. Although Professor A. put in a claim to the International Post Office and sent the packing back to them, the book was not returned. But some time later, I spotted this very book in the new accessions display in the Lenin State Library. It had been checked by Censor 455, who had also checked the copy which reached me. Since books are checked haphazardly, this was evidence that the book in the Lenin State Library was one of the same batch of gifts. But for sending Professor A. the empty box someone in the censorship received a reprimand. According to the rules, the box and packing should, no doubt, have been destroyed.

It is interesting to note yet another case, indirectly connected with this question. Professor M. bequeathed his scientific library as a gift to the library of one of the Institutes of Higher Education. In it there were many foreign books, brought back from his trips abroad. There were no censor's angles on his books, and the library refused at first to take them, considering that they did not have the right to put in their holdings books which had not been 'passed'. Later the problem was dealt with by calling in an employee who looked through the books and stamped them.

Another rather curious case of the extremely disgraceful behaviour of the censorship occurred in my laboratory practice in 1963. At the request of the laboratory, the Institute obtained a set of additional rotors and spare parts for the American 'Spinco' centrifuge from the USA. The case from the USA was delivered at the Institute warehouse, but according to the instructions, it could only be unpacked in the presence of representatives of 'Machine and Instrument Foreign Trade' or 'Medical Imports', who would check that everything was there as ordered and make sure that it had not been damaged *en route*.

After everything had been checked, the representative of 'Medical Imports' carefully collected up all the packing paper and asked for it to be taken out into the yard and burned. I did not want to do this at first, as the case with the equipment still had to be carried from the warehouse into the laboratory, and the shock-absorbent packing could do no harm. The representative, however, steadfastly explained that these were the strict instructions of Glavlit. All packing waste-paper from capitalist countries must be burned, since it often contains foreign newspapers and journals. And he was, of course, quite right, although he was not sufficiently observant. In the box with the small parts, which the representative did not unpack, I actually found later waste fragments of Californian newspapers and journals from about 1962. But they were cut up so fine that it was obvious that they had gone into the packing as a shock-absorber and not as propaganda.

8

Secrets of the 'Black Office'

THE 'Black Office' is an historical term. As the *Encyclopaedic Dictionary* published by Brockhaus and Efron states (vol. 45, St Petersburg, 1898) it is an establishment in which private letters are checked. The name comes from the special section of the French post, founded by King Louis XIII and Cardinal Richelieu in the seventeenth century for opening and checking correspondence. This Section was like a prison, and the clerks were not discharged from it until the end of their life. If anyone did depart thence, it was only to the Bastille. The reading of the people's letters was especially dear to the next king, Louis XIV. The French Revolution abolished the 'Black Office', but later Napoleon restored it and extended its duties.

The violation of the secrecy of correspondence has as ancient a history as correspondence itself. The ancient Roman post gained some experience in this respect, which may be the reason why the violation of the secrecy of correspondence has acquired the name 'perlustration' throughout the world, from the Latin *perlustro*—I look through. I should add that some facts on the history of perlustration I learned when preparing the present work, only after many of the events which I have described had happened. These events, in effect, had aroused my interest in the historical analogues. Even the word 'perlustration' I met for the first time in 1969. At first I did not understand it very well, and looked it up in the *Big Soviet Encyclopaedia* (vol. 32, 1955), where I read the following:

> Perlustration is the secret opening by the state organs of correspondence sent through the post. Perlustration first arose in ancient times and was widely practised in Western Europe from the Middle Ages onwards. In France in the reign of Louis XIII a special organ, the 'Black Office', was set up for this purpose. In Russia, perlustration was widely employed in the eighteenth century. Under Catherine II it became an important means of political investigation. In the eighteenth and nineteenth centuries the correspondence of many eminent Russian progressive activists and writers was subjected to

perlustration (A. I. Radyshchev, A. S. Pushkin, etc.). In the USSR, secrecy of correspondence is guaranteed by law. (Constitution of the USSR, Art. 28.)

The Brockhaus and Efron *Encyclopaedic Dictionary*, published at the end of the last century, gives considerably more detailed information on this question in the articles on 'Perlustration' and 'Secrecy of Correspondence'. In Russia, according to this encyclopaedia, the censorship of letters was first introduced by Peter I. He ordered that there should be an 'expert' for this purpose in the post office. But Peter I instructed them to open and read only letters from hostile Sweden. By these means he discovered two conspiracies and established the secret links between the enemy and the Tsarevich Alexis.

In 1779 Catherine II ordered that the secretly opened correspondence of the diplomatic representatives of foreign states should be delivered by the post office to her. But the letters of Catherine II herself to Western liberals such as Voltaire were opened and read in France. Alexander I [1812–25] established a special 'Black Office' and entrusted it with the checking not only of international correspondence, but also selected internal correspondence, the personal letters of high officials and courtiers.

But the *Encyclopaedic Dictionary*, which gives a critical account of this activity of the Russian tsars of the past, states that from the reign of Alexander II [1855–81], the activity of the 'Black Office' apparently ceased. On 24 February 1868, Alexander II promulgated the imperial order forbidding the opening and reading of the letters even of persons under investigation, or under open supervision by the police. This, according to the order, was necessary 'in view of the impossibility of permitting the examination of personal correspondence without the clear violation of society's trust in the post office and telegraph, undermining the main purpose of these establishments'.

But Alexander III [1881–94] restored to the legal authorities the right to seize and secretly to read the correspondence of persons under investigation.

For the contemporaries Pushkin and Gogol, the perlustration of letters was evidently no secret. The opening and reading of letters by the Provincial Post Master is clearly indicated by Gogol in *The Government Inspector*:

> In one ear what I hear is, 'Eh, don't break the seal! You'll perish like a fowl!' and in the other, some sort of demon whispers, 'Break it! Break it! Break it!' And when I press the seal, fire runs through all my

veins, and once it's unsealed, a frost, Lord, what a frost. And my hands tremble and everything grows hazy.

After the February Revolution of 1917, and then again after the October Revolution, several articles appeared on the activity of the 'Black Office' in Russia. The most detailed and competent elucidation of this question is to be found in the pamphlet by S. Maiskii, *The Black Office* from the memoirs of a former censor, Byloe Publishing House, Petrograd, 1922. This pamphlet is in the Lenin State Library (catalogue number W $\frac{262}{475}$).

For ten years before the Revolution Maiskii worked on the censorship of foreign newspapers and journals in the St Petersburg Post Office. In this censorship there was also a secret 'Black Office' which undertook the reading of letters. The official name of the 'Black Office' was the 'Secret Dispatch Office'. According to Maiskii's account all foreign printed matter packets without exception were delivered by lift up a special tunnel for inspection in the newspaper and journal censorship department of the St Petersburg Post Office. Maiskii does not describe what the checking consisted of, but he tells us that

the censors of foreign newspapers and journals were mostly very respectable people all with higher education, and, as well as the censorship, where they were required only in the morning or, when their turn came round as duty-officer in the evening, they also worked in other establishments in the Ministry of Foreign Affairs, in the University or as grammar school teachers. . . . There were also famous linguists and polyglots among them who could read some 15 to 20 languages, and one who could read 26 languages.

A concealed 'built-in' door led from the newspaper and journal censorship into the 'Black Office', and only the employees of the 'Black Office' had keys to that door.

To the 'Black Office' from the Post Office Dispatch Department all out-of-town and foreign correspondence went up in a special lift, and secret clerks decided from the addresses and handwriting whether it was necessary to read each letter or not. Fifteen years ago, due to the increase in the bulk of the post, the selection of letters for reading was transferred to the Dispatch Department of the Post Office and was carried out by special secret clerks. Each day some two to three thousand letters were selected for reading.

Maiskii explained the principles of the selection of letters for reading. The main mass of letters were of no interest to the Ministry of Internal Affairs and the Police Department, and there would be no sense in

N

studying them. Hence it was important to know how to select the interesting letters. In the first place they opened diplomatic letters, letters of political émigrés and the correspondence of people specially listed by the Police Department. Against each name on this list were instructions—'especially strict observation', 'exact copy', 'photograph' or even 'to be produced in the original'. In addition to this, the 'Black Office' also read the letters of high dignitaries, personnel of the Tsar's court, Ministers, Governors, Heads of Administration, etc. In this way many abuses were discovered, for example, the case of the Minister of Transport who arranged for a strategic railway to be laid not in the direction shown in the plans but across his wife's estates.

The principle of selecting letters for reading according to their external appearance and handwriting (if the name of the sender was not indicated) was very simple.

The difference between men's and women's handwriting, between children's and adults' [points out the former censor] is clear to all. Just as clear is the difference between a peasant's writing and an intellectual's. Moreover, an aristocrat writes in a different hand from a bureaucrat, his handwriting is generally nervous, large and angular. The bureaucrat's writing is confident and sharp. The literary man writes in a tiny, clear hand, the business man in copperplate, revolutionaries in an unformed, almost schoolboy hand, and anarchists are distinguished by the coarseness and clumsiness of their handwriting, which resembles that of an uneducated person.

The letters were generally opened with a small bone knife which was inserted into a suitable flap for opening the letter (top, bottom or side). Steam was also used. For this there was a special metal vessel from which a thin stream of boiling water was poured through a small hole. Holding the letter in his left hand, the reader directed the stream towards the place which had been opened by the knife, and the steam made the work quicker and easier. In the St Petersburg 'Black Office' one man worked only at opening letters, he could open a thousand letters in two hours. Reading the letters occupied four people, two made copies and one took photographs. Together with the other experts (on seals, etc.) twelve people in all worked in this section. There was also a 'Black Office' in Moscow, but it was smaller, seven people worked there. In Warsaw the 'Black Office' had five employees, in Odessa also five, in Kiev four, in Khar'kov, Tiflis, Tomsk, Vilna and other large cities the Black Office had only two employees.

Letters sealed with wax required great attention, but in this matter the Russian 'Black Office' had achieved perfection, and was far ahead of other European countries. In the time of Catherine II, the process of opening letters with a seal was complicated. The crux of the matter was that it was necessary to make a new seal with which to seal the envelope after reading. A beeswax mould was made from the old wax seal. This was used to make a plaster form. From this a lead negative was prepared, and this was used to make the new seal. In the 1870s, a new method was invented in Russia using a silver powder and amalgam but this had a number of disadvantages. In about 1907, a talented clerk invented a special device for making imitation seals out of metal, very quickly. When Stolypin reported this to the Tsar, this clerk was awarded the Order of St Vladimir 'for useful and practical discoveries'.

As a result of technical improvements in the 'Black Office' there were seals which were identical with the seals of all the diplomatic representations and missions and copies of the personal seals of high dignitaries.

The only thing that took up a great deal of time was envelopes sewn on sewing machines.

Not without pride does Maiskii say ' "Black Offices" exist everywhere, but justice requires one to say that nowhere in the world did a "Black Office" work so cleanly as in Russia and especially in St Petersburg.'

Of the high dignitaries, so Maiskii tells us, only Count Ignat'ev knew how to save himself from the attentions of the 'Black Office'. Being Ambassador to Turkey, he knew of the practice of reading letters in European countries and guessed at the methods of selection. In future, therefore, he always sent his letters by ordinary, unregistered mail, in cheap envelopes which had been lying next to pickled herring and soap. He would ask his valet to address the envelopes, and the letters were not sent to his dignitary friends but usually to their hall-porters. And his letters got through safely.

There were some strange episodes in the working of the 'Black Office'. On several occasions letters were sent on in a hurry without enclosures. Once some papers from the Spanish Embassy were enclosed in an envelope from a letter to the Dutch Ambassador. But even this did not betray the existence of the Russian 'Black Office'. From further correspondence it appeared that suspicion always fell on the Austrian 'Black Office', since the mail to Russia went through Austria. And the Austrian 'Black Office' was well known to the embassies for its rough handling of mail.

Diplomats' letters were read so quickly that no one could suspect censorship. If the postbag was taken from the Embassy to catch the evening train, then it went by the evening train; within an hour or so all the mail in the bag had been read. The embassy diplomatic couriers had, for the most part, been bribed and themselves brought the mail to an appointed place for reading.

The information obtained by the 'Black Office' was reported according to its nature, to the Ministry of Internal Affairs, the Head of the Police Department or even the Chief of the General Staff. Selected material was reported daily to the Tsar. A special employee presented Nicholas II with a sealed envelope containing excerpts and summaries from the letters, typed out according to subject. When the Tsar received the packet he dropped all other business and buried himself in reading it. Catherine II, Alexander I, Nicholas I and Alexander II, according to Maiskii, always read the reports from the 'Black Office' eagerly, but Alexander III refused to read other people's letters, saying that he did not need to.

Under the monarchical regimes in Europe in the last century and the beginning of this one, when there was bitter international conflict, the violation of the secrecy of correspondence was evidently very frequent and did not cause any great surprise to society at that time, in spite of the fact that the principle of observing secrecy of correspondence was officially recognized in the conventions drawn up in 1874 by the World Postal Union. Even the British post which has always prided itself on its respect for the law was not irreproachable. This can be seen very well from the correspondence of Karl Marx and Friedrich Engels, who were living in England as émigrés. Marx lived in London and Engels in Manchester, and the intensive correspondence between them occupies several volumes of the *Works*.

In England at that time letters were stuck down and then sealed with sealing-wax. Letters took no more than a day to go from London to Manchester, the post in England being famous for its fast delivery. But in that one day, according to the correspondence of the founders of scientific communism, their letters could be read and sometimes suffered rude damage. Their letters from abroad, especially from Prussia, were often lost completely, and hence their most important letters to their homeland were always sent by hand when someone happened to be going. Even in the correspondence between London and Manchester they had to have recourse to various means to deceive the British post. Engels sent his most important letters not to Marx's home address but to a friend who then delivered the letters to Marx. I shall now quote certain remarks of Marx and Engels in their letters which are evidence of how seriously they had to take into account the fact that their letters were being read. The number of such quotations could easily be multiplied tenfold.

Your packet for *Revolution* and *Tribune* was opened and they did not even bother to stick it up again.[1]

(Marx to Engels, 3 March 1852)

I am sending back the envelope of your letter, received today; there was evidently an unsuccessful attempt to open it.[2]

(Engels to Marx, 24 September 1852)

Someone undoubtedly did try to open the envelope of the previous letter which you sent back to me. But clearly it was done blunderingly and without result.[3]

(Marx to Engels, 28 September 1852)

Your letter to me today has been opened, judging from the fact that not all four corners of the envelope were properly stuck down.[4]

(Engels to Marx, 27 October 1852)

Dear Engels,
We must take steps concerning our correspondence. Beyond a doubt, in Derby's Ministry we have a 'partner' who reads our letters. I cannot, therefore, write anything at all to you which I think it is undesirable at the present moment to be notified to the Prussian Government.[5]

(Marx to Engels, 25 October 1852)

Engels advised Marx to send his letters in business envelopes and provided him with the necessary materials.

Put a business seal on them [he wrote back to Marx]. Your old Wedemayer coat-of-arms and clumsy S will not do at all. Use on your letters to Manchester some other sixpenny seal. From time to time send Schneider less important registered letters so as to lead these fine fellows into error and make them think we have given up sending letters by conspiratorial means because we have not the addresses. You need have no doubt that the people whose addresses you receive together with this letter will deliver these letters wherever necessary.[6]

(Engels to Marx, 28 October 1852)

---

[1] *Works*, vol. xxviii, p. 28.
[2] ibid., p. 122.
[3] ibid., p. 126.

[4] ibid., p. 137.
[5] ibid., p. 134.
[6] ibid., p. 147.

If you have to write to me on important matters, do so to the address, Mr A. Johnson, Esq., Bank of England, Department of Bullion.[1]

(Marx to Engels, 28 October 1852)

In England, banknotes were generally sent in letters. But, being convinced that their letters were being opened, Engels and Marx decided not to send money in letters, since they were afraid that they would be stolen by the censor. At that time, Marx constantly needed financial assistance from Engels who was doing commercial work in his father's factory. Hence these classic writers on political economy worked out a simple means to protect the money which was sent. Engels tore the banknotes (for £5, £10 or £20) in half. One half he sent straight to Marx and the other half to one of their friends, whose name Engels told Marx only in the next letter. Marx would go straight to the friend, obtain the incomplete half of the banknote and then exchange it at the bank. The correspondence of the friends is therefore enlivened with such paragraphs as this:

Dear Marx,
You have probably already received the £5 note, half of which I sent yesterday direct to you and half in an envelope addressed to Lupus.[2]

(Engels to Marx, 2 March 1852)

Lupus was the pseudonym of Wilhelm Wolf.

Dear Marx,
. . . I am sending you the first half of a £10 note. . . . The second half will follow either today by the second post or tomorrow.[3]

(Engels to Marx, 21 May 1852)

Dear Marx,
I am enclosing half of a £20 note, P/E 90 138. I shall send the second half by a later post, since I have no other address.[4]

(Engels to Marx, 1 June 1853)

These examples could be continued further. They relate to the British post. It is good that the letters at least were not lost. As for the Prussian post, it not only opened and confiscated Marx's letters (for example, when Marx was taking the cure at Carlsbad in 1875, see *Works*, vol. 34) but in a number of cases, they even falsified these letters, forging Marx's signature (see note 242, vol. 28, p. 594). One of these forged 'Marx

[1] ibid., p. 146.   [2] ibid., p. 25.   [3] ibid., p. 59.   [4] ibid., p. 211.

letters' figured in the 'Cologne Process' ('Exposure of the Cologne Process of the Communists', *Works*, vol. 28, pp. 475–7).

As the evidence of the former censor, Maiskii, shows, in Old Russia printed matter coming from abroad was subjected to censorship. Evidently, some of it was confiscated. But since the censorship was strictly secret, no special marks were put on books and journals. There are no numbered stamps on foreign books and journals printed before the Revolution. In an exhibition at the Lenin State Library, I saw the very first edition of Karl Marx's *Das Kapital* in German, which was received by the Library of the Rumyantsevskii Museum (this was the name of the Lenin Library before the Revolution) back in 1867. There are no marks of censorship nor seals of the 'special holding'. There are no similar restricting symbols on the books, *The Position of the Working Class in England* by Engels (1845) or Marx's *Critique of Political Economy* (1859).

But once I did encounter traces of the tsarist censorship. In an old German encyclopaedia the article on 'Finland' was completely obliterated by Indian ink. This country, formerly independent, had become part of the Russian empire, and the censorship would not admit the German treatment of its history.

After the Revolution, a more careful checking of *scientific* publications coming from abroad began in about 1926. The first numbered stamps began to appear on title-pages at that time. The figures were larger than

nowadays, each enclosed in a circle How many censors there

were at that time and how they were distributed with respect to languages and other criteria, I have not, of course, been able to calculate. In the small selection of numbers of stamps I have noted down in the course of a rapid search in the All-Union State Library of Foreign Literature, the highest number is 31. In 1931 the checking service for foreign publications was reorganized and enlarged. The numbers in circles were abolished and replaced by numbers more like the present ones, in an angle. However, the angle was still not a double one, and the figures were twice as big and thick <71. The stamps were legible, clear and easily visible. These numbers are encountered on foreign scientific publications right up to the beginning of the war. In all the small selection which I noted down there are the following numbers: 1, 9, 28, 33, 40, 71, 73, 84, 94, 142, 174, 175.

Small faint numbers of the modern type in a double angle appeared in about 1947, that is, at the time when the struggle against all kinds of cosmopolitanism was most bitter. There were many of them at once—500, and this number has been maintained up to the present time, although the bulk of literature coming into the USSR from abroad has increased since then at least ten times. Instead of increasing the number of employees, the censorship has sensibly decided to give up many forms of checking. First of all, the triangle numbers stopped appearing on printed works from the socialist countries, then on offprints of articles sent from all countries, then on certain strictly specialized scientific journals. Furthermore, apparently, the productivity of labour has increased due to various useful discoveries and inventions applicable to this task.

The censorship of printed works from abroad was thus completely restored and considerably extended after the Revolution. *But was the 'Black Office' for the checking of private correspondence restored at the same time?* To give a definite answer to this cardinal question in the history of the Russian post is difficult, since there are too few facts for analysis. Maiskii's publication, and a number of other publications on the 'Black Office' which came out in 1919–22 say that the Old Russian 'Black Office' ceased to exist immediately after the February Revolution of 1917. Did a need arise at a later date to restore the censorship of private letters?

For legal purposes, some such offices equipped for the secret opening of certain letters must exist in the big post offices, since the law of the USSR permits the correspondence of persons under investigation to be examined. And during the period of the Stalinist repression the number of such persons ran into millions. Although crime statistics are not unfortunately published at the present time, some tens of thousands of people are put on trial each year on criminal charges. To check their correspondence in the course of investigation something like the 'Black Office' is necessary. Moreover, much of an investigation is concealed, for it begins with the discovery of the crime and not with the arrest of the criminal. At the beginning of an investigation there may be many suspects, whose correspondence may be secretly examined or impounded at the sanction of the Procurator. The criminal code of the USSR, however (Arts. 2 and 74 of the criminal code of the RSFSR) does not allow the contents of correspondence to be divulged nor the very fact that correspondence is being checked to be betrayed. The letters must be read secretly and must be delivered to the addressees.

The *Encyclopaedic Dictionary of Legal Knowledge* (Sovetskaya Entsiklopediya Publishing House, 1965) explains the concept of secrecy of correspondence thus:

The Soviet state guarantees the maintenance of secrecy of all forms of postal, telegraphic and also radio and telephonic correspondence of citizens. Exceptions from this rule are permitted only in cases when knowledge of the correspondence is necessary for the purpose of the detection of crimes or the discovery of a criminal—but only by the investigatory organs and authorized by a special order sanctioned by the Procurator.

Since in order to check the letters of persons under investigation and those suspected of crimes it is necessary that such letters be first picked out from the total flow of correspondence and since, for example, at any given moment there may be not less than a hundred, and perhaps even a thousand such persons in Moscow, the post offices must have some kind of additional secret sorting, with a list of persons whose correspondence is to be picked out. It is impossible to transfer this task to the postal department, since the correspondence of criminals may be sent to accommodation addresses, *poste restante*, post office boxes, etc.

But letters may also be picked out from a list authorized by the City Procurator in large sorting offices, in the big railway post offices, and so on. It is also clear that to open letters and packets without leaving a trace, to copy them, remove the seals from valuable letters and so on, is a task for a professional, and that it needs practice and experience. It must also be secret and be carried out in buildings properly equipped and sheltered from the curious eyes even of other post office workers. And, of course, this is similar to the 'Black Offices'. Yet it is something quite different.

The 'Black Office' earned its grim name not for its activity in checking the post of persons who had committed a crime or who were suspected of having committed a crime. It was so called by society because its activity was in itself criminal, it constantly broke the law, and its arbitrary actions took place with the permission of the executive power.

A 'Black Office', as we have seen from Maiskii's description, is able to censor any correspondence, and its activity is limited only by the numbers of personnel. The twelve men in the St Petersburg Post Office could check no more than three thousand letters per day. This was their limit, their norm, their daily work, their ceiling. For the censorship of these three thousand letters no sanction of the court or Procurator was required. The members of the 'Black Office' could read any letter taken from the flow of post. The Old Russian post, as is known from the statistics, dealt with about 600 million letters a year. If we make a rough estimate of the capacity of the 'Black Office' of Moscow and the

N*

other cities, then at least 20,000 letters passed through the censorship every day. This makes about six million per year, which is one per cent of all correspondence. And no one was immune from this censorship. It was purely piratical, and hence the people hung the pirate's black flag on it.

When they overthrew autocracy, the people abolished these piratical organs too; they made an end of the 'Black Office', of total surveillance of the citizens of Russia. And there were no grounds for thinking that anything similar might be born again in a law-abiding state.

There are, indeed, many doubters and sceptics on this matter, who maintain that besides the legal checking of the correspondence of persons who are under investigation, there is also a selective censorship of the correspondence in general, and especially of international correspondence.

These suspicions are most frequently founded on two fairly common phenomena: firstly, that letters are quite often lost, as many people who conduct international correspondence are aware; secondly, that letters containing prohibited enclosures (stamps, short articles) are returned to the sender, even though their nature can only be determined by opening the letter which is being sent as personal correspondence.

But the loss of letters, even if fairly frequent, is not a conclusive proof of censorship. Even when legal checking is sanctioned by the Procurator, the law does not allow the letters to be *destroyed*. Even the Old Russian 'Black Office' did not attempt to destroy letters, and considered its professional duty to consist 'purely' of reading them. The unduly high percentage of losses of letters which I have observed in the international correspondence of certain people I know may be due to various causes. It may be due to the untrustworthiness of certain post office employees who steal letters with pretty foreign stamps (such instances are well known, and the post office has a special rubber stamp 'letter received with damaged stamps', to exonerate the Soviet postal workers from suspicion); it may be due to *force majeure*, or to more serious thefts of the mail when valuables are enclosed in it. It is permitted to send money from abroad in letters, and therefore professional criminals may be interested in the post. In one English film I saw how gangsters stole a whole railway postal van.

When registered letters are lost the sender can put in a claim, and the post is obliged to make an investigation and to inform him of the result. They will also pay him compensation. It is hard to believe that the post would wish to bear the expense of deliberately destroying letters. In my files there are two interesting documents which show how the post explains the loss of letters which sometimes occurs. One of these letters refers to international mail, the other to internal. The people who passed these documents on to me agreed to have them cited in this investigation. I shall begin with the loss of a registered letter from Moscow to Ryazan. This is the answer which was given to Comrade L. B. Ternovskii's claim:

Ministry of Communications of the USSR
Sverdlovsk Communications Branch of the Moscow Post Office
No. 564/c   6 January 1970

Moscow M 452
Balaklava Prospekt No. 4
Block 6, Apt 431
To your request for a search for registered letter No. 997/2 with receipt sent from Moscow K 9 on 18 November 1969 to A. I. Solzhenitsyn, Flat 11, Yablochkov Prospekt, Ryazan 12, I have to inform you that the letter was forwarded as designated, but that the letter was not received at the designated point. Unfortunately, it has not proved possible to establish the location of the loss of the letter or the person responsible.

I offer you my apologies for the loss of the letter. On the basis of the law on financial responsibility, you will be sent compensation to the sum of 50 kopeks plus 14 kopeks postage. Total 64 kopeks.
                                                           SOROKIN
                        Head of the Sverdlovsk Communications Branch,
                                                Moscow Post Office

The second document is much like the first.

To the Ministry of Communications of the USSR
Claim:
On 9 February 1969 at the Moscow Postal Department K 9, a registered letter (Receipt No. 198) was posted by me, with an 'advice of delivery' note to the Union of Czechoslovak Writers. This letter has so far not been delivered, as I see, (1) from the fact that the 'advice of delivery' note has not been returned to me: (2) from a telegram sent by the Union of Czechoslovak Writers on 20 February and just received by me.

I would not draw attention to this occurrence were it not that, since April 1968, I have observed and definitely established *many instances of the interception* of my correspondence, letters, printed papers and telegrams, both in the internal and international mail.

I consider that this has gone beyond the limit.

I demand that an investigation of this occurrence (Moscow K 9, Receipt 198/9/2/69) be made in the Ministry of Communications and that

—it should be established and explained to me precisely why and
for what motives my letter was intercepted;
—the guilty party should be punished;
—the letter itself should be delivered as addressed.

If all this is not carried out by the Ministry of Communications I
shall collect all the cases known to me of the interception of my correspondence over the last year, document them and make a complaint
to the President of the Council of Ministers of the USSR concerning
the *theft of mail* in the Ministry of Communications.

For it is impossible to call it anything else.

A. I. SOLZHENITSYN

Three months and two weeks later came the following reply:

International Post Office, No. 198/679/3, 7 June 1969
To Comrade A. I. Solzhenitsyn,
Yablochkov Prospekt 1, Flat 11
Ryazan 12

In answer to your claim of 22 February, addressed to the Ministry
of Communications of the USSR, I am writing to inform you that
the registered letter No. 198 of 9 February 1969 from Moscow,
addressed to the Union of Czechoslovak Writers was forwarded from
the International Post Office as directed in good time.

However, according to the information received from the postal
service of the Czechoslovak Socialist Republic, it has not proved possible to establish the further fate of this communication, and they
have agreed to pay compensation to the sender. On this question you
can apply to the Head of the Ryazan Post Office.

Yours faithfully,
for the Head of the International Post Office

B. YASTREBOV

Puzzling losses of letters have also occurred, as has already been
noted, in my own personal international correspondence. This phenomenon is strange and inexplicable, even if we admit the reality of the
'Black Office'. From what we have seen of the past, 'Black Offices' do
not have powers to confiscate letters, since this would entail admitting
their existence, which they cannot reveal without compromising their
illegal power. In Russia, according to the author of the pamphlet on the
'Black Office', they were very interested in the identity of the author of
an anonymous book, published in England, on the scandalous secrets of
the Russian Imperial Court. With the aid of the 'Black Office' they
were able to establish that the author of the book was a baron close to
the Tsar. The Minister of Internal Affairs reported the matter to

Nicholas II. Nicholas II took this into account, but he did not dismiss the baron staight away for fear of revealing the source of the information he had received. The secrecy of the 'Black Office' was more important than the secrets of the tsarist court.

The second source of suspicion about the secrecy of correspondence arises from philatelists who carry out an international exchange of stamps. According to the customs rules it is forbidden to send postage stamps inside envelopes (used stamps, foreign and Soviet stamps, etc.). The international exchange of stamps is considered to be a state monopoly.

But philatelists often break this rule, sending stamps in ordinary envelopes disguised as private letters. In most cases these letters actually do get abroad, and the exchange of stamps with foreigners flourishes. But sometimes (in about one case in twenty or thirty) the philatelist has his letter sent back to him. The letter has been opened and there are no stamps, but in their place there is a declaration that the contents have been confiscated as contraband. The sender is reminded that he has broken the customs rules.

These confiscations seem to imply that a fairly small percentage of international letters is selected and checked by the customs. But this does not violate the secrecy of correspondence since the contents of personal letters do not concern the customs. The customs has no right to open *letters* unless it suspects there are forbidden enclosures, but maybe there is some device which can establish the presence of stamps within the envelope, for example, by the fluorescence of inks under the action of soft x-rays or by the relief of a letter ironed out by a special rolling press. Technically it is possible, and the customs has the right to use any technical means to detect contraband. But the customs and the 'Black Office' are two very different things.

Besides these two things which support the suspicion that the secrecy of correspondence is being violated, I know of several fragmentary facts which in certain circumstances could also be construed to the disadvantage of the post. But they could be explained in other ways, and to use them as a conclusive proof in a court of law that post is violating the law on secrecy of correspondence would be extremely difficult.

In my personal internal and international correspondence until very recently I treated the post with complete confidence. I did not rule out the possibility of selected checking of a small number of international letters, but this did not alarm me. On the whole the post maintained all my links with foreign colleagues and friends, and the rare complication did not lead to any misunderstandings. I began to notice some strangenesses in the behaviour of the international post only in the second half of 1968, that is almost at the same time that Solzhenitsyn noted that the theft of his mail began.

9

The 'Black Office' shows its face in the post today

THE customs postal laws in the USSR are very complicated and the regulations about what may or may not be sent through the post can be interpreted in various ways. The powers of the customs organs are also very far from being clearly defined. According to the postal regulation, an international *letter* may weigh up to 2 kilos. That is, a letter may be a fairly big packet, containing together with a personal message some enclosure or other, a book, manuscript, materials, etc. A printed matter package differs from a 'letter' in not containing an enclosure in the nature of a personal message. All items sent through the post which do not contain personal messages are sent at a greatly reduced rate, and this, from the point of view of the post, constitutes the chief difference between 'letters' and 'printed matter'. Since it is cheaper to send enclosures as 'printed matter' it is rare that a sender combines a letter with, for example, a book in a single package. He sends the personal letter separately and the book as printed matter. According to international postal regulations, the only items of post subject to customs inspection are those which have a customs declaration stuck on when they are posted. Registered or ordinary printed matter packages are checked by the post office clerk on posting, and after that should be forwarded unhindered, if the clerk did not consider it necessary to supply them with a customs declaration. Ordinary standard letters, enclosed in a standard envelope and weighing up to 20 grams generally do not have to go to the customs. The customs is a completely different establishment, having its own staff. *The post of the USSR, like the post of any other country, in accepting a letter which has all the outward signs of a personal message, gives a complete and unconditional guarantee of delivering it to the addressee, observing absolute secrecy of correspondence.*

Unfortunately, the principle of secrecy of correspondence has been violated very often in history, and for this reason there is a deep-seated suspicion that one cannot trust the post. And I would be deceiving the reader if I pretended that I have always trusted that the principle of absolute secrecy of correspondence was always observed. I was concerned only in the principle of the *obligation to deliver mail*. There is nothing secret in my correspondence, and I would be quite ready to leave my letters unsealed if the post would accept them open. Unfortunately, the post accepts letters only in a sealed form, being concerned lest the letter drop out in transit.

History relates that a certain ancient Roman philosopher always sent his letters open. The post in those days was slow, and knowing human nature, he considered that the courier from mere curiosity or boredom with the journey would open and read the letters he was carrying. So that the package would not be damaged the ancient philosopher always sent his mail open. This attitude was not unlike my own. I had no secrets from the post, and I certainly wanted my letters to reach the addressee. Therefore I often sent them registered and with 'advice of delivery' notes. I did not doubt that if there were some checking of correspondence it was selective. I felt sure that it would be quite impossible to check the entire international mail of the USSR; this would entail a very large staff of censors, and it would contradict the principle of keeping such an unconstitutional practice a very dark secret. But since letters, even registered ones, had sometimes been lost in puzzling circumstances, I would sometimes send a copy of the letter as well to make sure that the message was delivered. It was very unlikely that two letters of the same type would be lost if the control of correspondence was selective. Having worked out these rules empirically, I maintained my scientific and personal correspondence with friends abroad without mishap; and through thirteen years of correspondence (from 1955 to 1968) I had no cause for any serious worry about the fate of my letters.

When writing to regular correspondents, I usually adopted a very useful rule, borrowed from experienced people, of numbering consecutive letters. Each of my letters to a regular addressee, in addition to the date, had a number indicating its place in the sequence. Normally the sender judges the prompt delivery of the letter from the answer. But in the case of regular correspondence, by no means every letter, of its nature, requires an answer. There may be one answer to a whole series of letters. In this case, the numbering of letters is very useful. If, for example, letter 13 is lost, then when the addressee, who has received No. 12, finds that the next is not No. 13 but No. 14, he knows that letter 13 must have been lost and he will inform one of it. I also assumed that the numbering of the letters in sequence would have a definite psychological effect on the supposed censor, since the loss of such a letter would at once be apparent both to the addressee and the sender. More important letters I always sent not only by registered airmail with an 'advice of delivery' but with an 'express' or 'special delivery' label, for which the post charges an additional 18 kopeks. The next day I would send an additional message to the addressee by picture postcard, informing him that the letter had been posted. Such an airmail picture postcard does not have a return address on it, the signature on it is illegible, but the addressee can of course tell from the message from whom it has come. The text of the postcard is usually very simple, and the main point of it is to inform the addressee that a letter has been sent to him. Such a postcard may, for example, read as follows:

Dear Dr L.,
    In the registered letter which I sent to you by airmail yesterday, I forgot to mention that your letter of 12 May reached me very swiftly, and that my delay in answering was not due to the post, but to the fact that I was away for a week.

All these precautions, which only add to the post's income, arose gradually as an inevitable reaction to the loss even of registered letters. Such losses, although rare, were nevertheless a reality which one had to take into account.

In the first chapter I have already noted that in the first half of 1968 the losses of letters became for some reason frequent. This phenomenon continued into the second half of 1968. In the middle of August 1968, in my correspondence with Professor L., an American geneticist whom I had known since 1962, it became clear that my July letter to him, No. 34, had not been received. The letter was a short one, only about one page in English, but it was important since the questions in it required discussion. The contents of the letter were not connected with genetics and were different from my usual correspondence with Professor L. At that time I was making a serious study of the possible sociological consequences of the international integration of scientific research. I had given Professor L. a brief outline of my interest in this topic, and I wanted to know what works on this topic published in the USA I ought to read. Professor L. was also interested in the sociological aspects of science, and especially in questions of co-operation in research carried out in the USSR and the USA.

I sent Professor L. a copy of letter No. 34, again sending it by airmail with an 'advice of delivery' note and an 'express' label. But, the advice note (also an airmail one) did not come back, and Professor L. informed me by postcard (in reply to my postcard) that he had not received letter No. 34.

In October 1968, I had to send two successive letters to Mr T., the director of a scientific publishing house in New York. This publishing house proposed to publish one of my scientific works in an English translation, and in my letters I simply gave Mr T. a short list of colleagues in the USA and in Europe to whom my publishers should send a copy of the book on publication with my compliments as a present from the author. Both letters were sent to New York by registered airmail and with 'advice of delivery' notes, but bearing in mind the recent unhappy fate of letter No. 34 to Professor L., I sent copies of these letters to New York three and four days later. It was important to me that they should reach the addressee at the appointed time, and hence I did not wait for information about the fate of the originals which had been posted earlier. When the time came, none of the four advice notes came back, and in reply to the postcard which accompanied the letters, Mr T. told me that he had not received my letters with the list of colleagues.

At the same time I sent a letter to a gerontological colleague of mine, Dr W., in London, a very punctual correspondent who over the course of several years had always answered my letters immediately. Dr W., who took a great interest in gerontology, was the head of a scientific organization especially created to develop international co-operation between scientists working in medical chemistry. When he was away, a deputy or secretary answered the letters. My letter to Dr W. was on a similar topic to that of letter No. 34 to Professor L. Since communications with Professor L. had been 'impaired', and were perhaps due to some failure by the post in the USA, I tried to obtain the answer I needed from my English colleague who was extremely knowledgeable in that very field.

The 'advice of delivery' for the letter to England came back after two weeks, with a London postmark but without Dr W.'s signature—only an incomprehensible squiggle. But no answer to the letter followed. Although the 'advice of delivery' note had the proper address of sender and addressee, it was not the advice note which I had filled up when posting the letter. The advice note which came back had been filled up by someone who had mixed up the Latin and Russian alphabets, and I was ashamed that anyone in London should read so illiterate a mixture of English and Russian. Even the name of the addressee was written in a mixture of English and Russian letters. The origin of this strange advice note remained unsolved, since from further correspondence with Dr W. it was clear that he had not received that particular letter.

These happenings in the post puzzled me extremely. They were quite new phenomena, which would not fit into any of my previous theories about the workings of the post, nor into any of the hypotheses about the checking of letters. All other correspondence at this period, with the exception of the loss of certain letters to *Science* which I have already mentioned, went on normally. The offprints of articles which I had requested arrived punctually, my offprints were safely delivered to their addresses. Just at this period, an intensive correspondence was going on with the Plenum Press in America which had decided to translate my book, *Molecular-Genetic Mechanisms of Development*, into English. (This book had been published in Russian by the Medgiz press in Moscow in August 1968.) The agreement on the translation of the book had been concluded not with me personally, but with the Mezhdunarodnaya Kniga association, and I had received instructions from this external trade organization that I must conduct all correspondence with the American publishers through them. However, this was too complicated, and after one occasion when I had had to wait in the Permit Bureau of the Ministry of External Trade on Smolensk Square for two hours, and then, after not issuing me with a permit they sent a courier of Mezhdunarodnaya Kniga to me at the front door, so that he could take from me the package, already stamped, containing the originals of the diagrams, I washed my hands of this important organization and began to write to the Plenum Press direct. This correspondence consisted of corrections and additions to the Russian text, original drawings and English captions for the diagrams, and other such material. Although all this was intended for publication and did not come under the heading of 'personal correspondence', none of the numerous letters of this series was lost.

At the beginning of November 1968 I put in a claim to the International Post Office for all the letters lost in August, September and October, attaching the receipts for them. But this time the Central Bureau of Claims of this Post Office, which formerly had answered claims fairly rapidly, preserved a complete silence.

In the middle of December a new reason for international correspondence arose, somewhat outside the exchange of biochemical and genetic information. Listening to the radio one evening, I picked up a Russian language broadcast from London of an interesting statement by Academician Andrei Sakharov, devoted to the question of intellectual freedom and the danger of atomic war. I had read Sakharov's paper in manuscript at the beginning of 1968; it had been circulating among scholars in Moscow for some time. The fact of its publication abroad was new to me. Sakharov, one of the most famous Soviet physicists, a Hero of Socialist Labour (two or three times) had in 1963–4 played a very energetic part in the fight against the dominance of Lysenkoism in biology, and at that time I had had two conversations with him. Naturally, I started listening attentively to the broadcast from London. The BBC did not transmit Sakharov's paper in its entirety, and in their version I hoped that they would cut out the part of the paper where Sakharov gives high praise to the manuscript of a book by my brother, Roi Medvedev, on the history and genesis of Stalinism and expresses his regret that this remarkable book, 'written from a Socialist, Marxist point of view' has not yet been published. But unfortunately the BBC announcer particularly emphasized just this part of Sakharov's paper. The next day Sakharov's paper was broadcast once again, and not only from London. They also began to broadcast it from West Germany and the USA. From these broadcasts I learned that Sakharov's paper had been published in various countries, and translated into many languages.[1]

The publication of Sakharov's paper, loudly hailed abroad as the 'Sakharov manifesto', was a painful event for him personally, although the contents of the paper were profoundly patriotic. (And in fact, Sakharov was immediately dismissed from working in a strategically important top security establishment, whereby, of course, the establishment suffered more than he did.) But in addition to Sakharov's fate, what worried me was the fate of my brother's book, since this book was still not finished, and it had now attracted international attention due to Sakharov's paper. Sakharov himself had read a preliminary draft in manuscript, and just at this time, at the end of 1968, Roi was beginning a new revision and expansion of the manuscript, intending after this to submit it to the Central Committee of the CPSU for consideration and determination of its further fate. As a member of the Party, my brother could not offer the manuscript of such a book to any of the Soviet publishing houses before it had been considered by the Central Committee. Hence the broadcasting of information about this comprehensive work of about 1,400 typewritten pages in December 1968 was somewhat premature. Nevertheless it had happened.

I came to a swift decision, and without even consulting my brother

[1] Andrei D. Sakharov, *Thoughts on Progress, Peaceful Co-existence and Intellectual Freedom* (Foreign Affairs Publishing Co., London, 1968)—*Translator*.

I decided to write to three colleagues, asking them to keep me up-to-date on comment appearing in the foreign press on Sakharov's paper, especially on any references to my brother's book. My colleagues were biologists, but with a range of interests wider than biology, and they were friends who had helped me for many years to prevent the piratical publication abroad of my manuscript on the history of the genetic discussion, which had been circulating widely in the USSR since 1962 and had even got abroad. In 1967, a special commission of representatives of three Academies and the Science Section of the CPSU (headed by the Vice-President of the Academy of Medical Sciences of the USSR, N. N. Blokhin) unanimously recommended that the final version of my book should be published by the Nauka publishing house, but the implementation of this decision was delayed. At the beginning of 1968, it became known to me that the publication of an old version of this book in Russian had been announced in an anti-Soviet journal, and, in order to frustrate this, I approved a plan to have this work published in English translation by a serious scientific publishing house. All this activity, which began in February 1968, entailed an intensive correspondence to various addresses, and not one of the several dozen letters sent and received by me on this matter were lost.

All these explanations are necessary to present more clearly the question of the content of letters and their fate in postal channels.

I sent the letter asking for details of comments on Sakharov's paper and whether my brother's work was mentioned to Professor L., the Head of a Department of Genetics who had often helped me on many matters. He had played an important part in clearing up the trouble which had arisen over presenting the Kimber Prize for genetics to Professor Timofeev-Resovskii, head of the section to which my laboratory belonged. Professor L.'s father was a Russian, and although he himself had never lived in the USSR, he knew Russian extremely well and maintained wide and friendly links with Soviet geneticists. But I also decided to send two other scientists a copy of my letter to Professor L. so that they could also help me in obtaining the necessary information. One of them, Professor C., was a well-known English gerontologist, who in addition to gerontology was interested in sociological problems; the third, Professor J., was a specialist in the history of biology. I knew all three not only from correspondence. Professor J. had visited the USSR in 1962 and in 1965, Professor C. had taken part in the conference on Problems of Ageing in Kiev in 1967, and I had seen Professor L. at the Mendel Symposium in Czechoslovakia in 1965. All three of them knew Russian and therefore my letter was written in Russian. Moreover, all three of my correspondents knew each other from their published work, since they were all interested in genetics.

I sent the one letter to three addresses as a means of ensuring safe delivery. The fact that the letter could be read by the censorship did not worry me. After the series of losses of letters at the end of 1968, and in the absence of any answer from the Claims Bureau, I was now certain, not only that censorship of letters existed but also that it had increased very sharply. The theme of my letter was too specific to hope that it could pass easily through the censorship barrier. Therefore I sent three identical letters to different addresses, supposing that they could not all get into the batch for checking. I did not exclude the possibility that Professor L. might be on a list for special checking, all the more so, since my letter No. 34 to him had twice been lost. There had been earlier cases of loss of letters in my correspondence with Professor J., but the British gerontologist, C., could not possibly have got on any censor's list. Therefore, so I supposed, if my letters to Professors L. and J. were lost, I could always ask Professor C. to send them copies of my letter from England. Such was my plan to get through the supposed censorship. But this was still not all. If all the letters were sent simultaneously by the same post, they might all get into the same bag for one and the same censor. This must be avoided. It was necessary to send the letters by different posts on different days. But this was not all. Let us assume, I thought, that the sorters have on their lists for selecting for censorship not the name of Professor L., but the name of the sender, Zh. A. Medvedev. In that case, all the letters of Zh. A. Medvedev sent by different posts will still end up in the hands of one and the same censor. Therefore, besides the main letters sent to these three addressees by 'extra' class (express airmail, with airmail 'advice of delivery' notes), I made another set of copies which I intended to send a few days later by ordinary registered airmail. On the registered letters the addresses were typed, on the ordinary letters they were written by hand in slipshod handwriting. The return addresses on them were not all put in the same way. On two letters I gave my Moscow post office box without the sender's name, and the third letter was in a New Year's Greetings envelope with no return address at all, only the recipient's address. Thus six letters with identical contents were to be sent. The time, too, was more propitious, since it was before the New Year. There is a sharp rise in the number of international letters at this time, probably by twenty or thirty times, and if the censorship on ordinary days deals with a definite load, then when the flow of letters suddenly becomes many times greater, such a secret establishment will hardly be able to mobilize temporary assistants from outside. This is not a potato-picking detail! There will inevitably have to be an increase in the percentage that gets through without careful checking.

After planning the operation so carefully, I did not, of course, doubt its success. Naturally, in addition I also sent each of the addressees a New Year's Greetings postcard in which among other things I mentioned at the end that I had sent a detailed letter on 17 *December*. The registered letter to Professor L. was sent on 17 December 1968 from Postal Department K-9 in the building of the Ministry of Communications, the letter to Professor C. on the morning of 18 December from the Main Post Office, and the letter to Professor J. on the evening of 18 December from Postal Department G-19. The unregistered air-letters with the copies were posted between 20 and 24 December, only one of them being sent from Moscow. The second one was posted in Obninsk and the third in Leningrad, where one of my friends was going on a business trip. This provided different launching of the letters towards the many-faced censorship.

But the first ten days of January went by, and not one of the 'advice of delivery' notes had returned. From all three addressees postcards had come in reply. They thanked me for my New Year Greetings but told me that they had not received my letter of 17 December. I was not worried about this, since I allowed for the New Year mail to be slowed down due to overloading.

But on 13 January 1969 I received an answer from Professor C. to quite a different letter, discussing certain gerontological questions which I had sent him on 27 December, that is ten days after the copy-letter which had been sent to him 'extra class'. In his reply Professor C. told me once again that he had not received my letter of 17 December and expressed his bewilderment at this.

By the middle of January it was clear to me that I had evidently underestimated the powers of the censorship, and that all six letters were 'lost'. Very annoyed at this piracy, I prepared yet another copy of the letter to Professor C. and took it direct to the International Post Office in Moscow. From here letters go straight abroad. Again, I sent it as an express air-letter with 'advice of delivery', and with this letter I handed in a statement for the Head of the Central Claims Bureau of the International Post Office. The Claims Bureau is in the same building, and one of its representatives is always on duty in the post office hall itself. In the claim I pointed out the possible loss of the letter sent to Professor C. on 18 December and informed him that my newly posted registered letter No. such and such was a copy of that letter. I asked him to keep track of it, so that this copy would not be lost.

With this statement, attached to the letter I had posted, I put the International Post Office in a difficult position. On my side, everything was strictly according to the law. When I asked the representative of the Central Claims Bureau straight out whether there was censorship of mail in the USSR and whether private letters were opened, she denied the presence of any such censorship completely. I showed her the letter I had ready and asked her to check if it was all correct. Moreover I proposed that she should read the letter through before it was sealed up. But she naturally refused to take on this censor's function. After this, between my letter and Professor C., there was only a direct aeroplane from Moscow to London, and the British post which has the best reputation in the world.

Twenty-four days went by, however, and not a single 'advice of delivery' note came back. The fate of all my previous December letters remained unclear.

On 11 February 1969, after a meeting of the Academic Council of the Institute, the Head of the 'First Section' (previously such sections were called 'Special Sections') came to me, and invited me to come to the Section for a little conversation.

He affably offered me a chair and then turned to me with the question: 'Have you received a copy of a letter from Comrade Aslanov, Head of the International Post Office?'

'No, I haven't,' I replied.

'That's impossible!' My interlocutor was greatly surprised. 'I've had Comrade Aslanov's letter since 30 January, and it says on it "Copy to Zh. A. Medvedev, Post Office Box 25, Obninsk, Kaluga Province".'

'I don't know,' I shrugged, 'but I can assure you that I have received no copy.'

Then, after a little delay, the Head of the First Section took out of his safe a large envelope, and from that he drew out three envelopes which I recognized. I saw at once that two of them were my registered letters to Professors L. and J., and the third was my letter to Professor C., which I had recently posted at the International Post Office. The stamps had been cancelled and the envelopes were unsealed.

Further conversation revealed that the Head of the First Section was well acquainted with the contents of the letter and even wanted to know a number of additional details about the matters discussed in it. I, of course, quickly cut short all attempts to discuss my private correspondence. Then my interlocutor pressed the point that I had broken the instructions on correspondence which require that all letters are sent abroad only with a form 103M. I explained to him that I could not observe this instruction since it was unknown to me. The instruction was shown to me, but from the introductory part it followed that this only applied to those doing classified work, which I was not. Nevertheless the Head of the First Section asked me to prepare for him an explanatory account of my activities and to preserve strict silence on the subject of our conversation. I promised to do as he asked, but on condition that he would observe the same secrecy, and that neither the fact of the return of my letters, let alone their contents, would be made the subject of publicity. Since my interlocutor very soon broke his promise, I naturally became free to break mine.

The next day I took my explanatory account to the First Section. In it I explained that the intercepted letters had been of a purely personal nature, that they were not connected with my work at the Institute of Medical Radiology and were devoted to questions which had nothing to do with medicine. They did not contain any enclosures forbidden by the customs rules of the USSR. 'The fact,' I wrote, 'that the letters were returned not to the sender but to the Special Section, that they had been opened and read by many people, is a crime as laid down by the Criminal Code of the RSFSR, a breach of constitutional guarantees, and a breach of the Postal Regulations of the USSR.'

I demanded the swift return of these letters to me. In addition, I wrote a sharp protest about these arbitrary acts to the Ministry of Communications of the USSR.

To get a little ahead of my story, it must be said that on 21 February 1969 I actually did receive via my post office box a letter from Comrade Aslanov, sent from the International Post Office in Moscow. It was a 'registered business' letter, but, according to the postmarks, it had taken a very strange path before it reached my post office box. It had been sent from the International Post Office to my address in Obninsk on 3 February. But for some reason or other it had gone to Kaluga, not Obninsk, although Kaluga is 100 kilometres further from Moscow and off the main railway line. The 'Kaluga-Province' postmark was dated 5 February. By some mistake in Moscow the letter must have been put into the sack with the Kaluga mail. But then the letter was held up in Kaluga for some reason. It turned up in Obninsk only on 21 February, as the Obninsk postmark testified. Where the letter had been lying for sixteen days remains unknown. Evidently it had been sent from the International Post Office with a batch of international mail, and had got into the 'special delivery' at the Kaluga Post Office. There in any case it was read and put aside in bewilderment; to send to the sender copies of letters opened by the secret censorship seemed to the Kaluga experts the height of irresponsibility. But when I stated in writing in my explanatory account that I had received no copy of Aslanov's letter, Aslanov was informed about it, and this excited anxiety about the fate of the copy of his letter. Checking its course from the registration, Aslanov set it moving further, although judging from my explanatory account, he saw that I was already acquainted with its contents.

In Comrade Aslanov's letter there were no instructions as to its secrecy, it came to me through the ordinary postal channels, and hence I consider that I can quote it here in its entirety.

International Post Office, Ministry of Communications of the USSR
  30 January 1969, No. 30
To the Head of the First Section, Institute of Medical Radiology, Academy of Medical Sciences of the USSR, Obninsk, Kaluga Province
Copy to Zh. A. Medvedev
Post Office Box 25
Obninsk
Kaluga Province
  In our letter No. 0401 of 31 December 1968, the International Post Office sent you three letters sent abroad by an employee of your Institute, Dr Medvedev.
  Comrade Medvedev has approached the International Post Office with a request that a letter be resent to London on his behalf.
  Since the International Post Office does not undertake the service of resending correspondence, we are sending you the letter of Comrade Medvedev asking you to explain to him the proper way of sending a letter abroad.
Enclosure.   B. ASLANOV
                    Head of the International Post Office of the
                    Ministry of Communications of the USSR

Thus I became the possessor of a very interesting document. It told me a great deal. From the discussion with the Head of the First Section, during which I protested vigorously about the breach of the law on the secrecy of correspondence, I learned from him that my letters had been opened 'by chance' by the customs on suspicion that there were stamps enclosed in them. But, although there were no stamps, since the outsides of the letters were damaged on account of having been opened it was impossible to send them on, and so they had been returned to the Institute. There was no censorship; it was the carelessness of the customs which was to blame. The letters had been read, however, when they were returned to the Director of the Institute, V. P. Baluda, since he has the right to read business correspondence, sent with a form 103M. The fact that they were not business letters was apparent only too late, and the 'secrecy of correspondence' was violated by accident, due to a misunderstanding. But once it was violated, the contents of the letters seemed suspicious to Director Baluda and he decided to take measures to investigate it.

Thus, in preparing to summon me for interview in the Special Section, the organizers of this affair thought up a suitable version to hide the 'Black Office', the secrecy of which must not come to the surface. But they had overlooked my powers of observation and the carelessness of the Head of the First Section who showed me the correspondence which had been returned. There was no damage to the envelopes, they had been opened very carefully, only the top flap had been unglued, and it would have been no trouble at all to the 'customs' to seal the letters up and send it on, once they saw there were no stamps in them.

But in Aslanov's new letter about sending on the copy to London, it was impossible to stick to the version about the customs and contraband stamps. It was necessary to make the clearly foolish assertion that 'The International Post Office does not undertake the service of resending correspondence'—as if it were not all the same to the post whether the sender puts in a sealed envelope the original of a letter or a copy. The post should only be concerned that the address is correct, and that there are enough stamps on it. And I had paid for the stamps at the maximum rate possible.

There were other interesting details in this affair. My registered letters of the first series were sent on 17 and 18 December. They came back to the Institute on 31 December, and they were returned, as emerged from the conversation in the Special Section, not by post but by courier against a receipt from the Head of this Section. Aslanov's second letter had the name and address of the Head of the First Section typed at the top. How was his name known to the International Post Office? The second time the letter to Professor C. also lay about somewhere for two weeks before it came back to the same address, although it was only a copy. What happened to the non-registered, ordinary air-letters? They apparently were simply destroyed.

The main mistake of the censorship in these matters was that they, of course, decided that the Institute of Medical Radiology in Obninsk was a closed classified establishment. They were apparently led into error by the word 'radiology'; it was difficult to imagine that work on radiation was not secret. Maybe they were also led to believe in the classified status of the Institute by the fact that the rest of the Institute mail always went with a form 103M. If these assumptions had been correct, then as an employee of a secret establishment I would have broken the well-known instructions to those doing classified work about conducting correspondence with foreigners. The return of my letters to the Special Section by the censorship would have been considered as a denunciation of these breaches. What the penalties with which these instructions threatened me were, whether relating to my job or criminal ones, I do not know; perhaps when Aslanov signed his letter he already saw me locked up in an interrogation cell.

But fortunately our Institute is completely open and even has international status. Foreigners come to visit us, not only on excursions but to work in our laboratories. True, this is very rare. Since there was no 'criminal element' in my postal operations, my extracurricular activities were not subject to encroachment by various 'Special Sections'. But the employees of the 'Black Office' had not learned this. I could imagine their surprise when, after having fired such a volley of his own letters back at Medvedev, within a few days they found in the mail they were investigating copies of the same letters to Professor L., sent to the USA in unusual form.

10

The revenge of the 'Black Office'

THE hypocritical cynicism with which my letters were opened and sent to the 'First Section' shocked me very much. I paid the post at the highest rate for the services, and it not only destroyed my letters, which showed its inadequacy, not only used them to denounce me to the security organization, but also tried to do me obvious harm in my job. The same day, when I came back home after my conversation with Comrade Shevaldin, I made two more copies of my letter to Professor L., and on the evening of 13 February I went into Moscow to send them off from the Main Post Office. I had an original plan.

In the post office there are two stands where they sell fancy envelopes and postcards of all types. Some enthusiasts collect not only postage stamps but envelopes as well, and the USSR post now prints envelopes with various portraits, emblems, pictures, etc., leaving only a small space for the address. Other countries do not issue these decorated envelopes, since they hamper the rapid sorting of letters. When I arrived at the post office, I soon found what I was looking for. At the end of 1967, the Ministry of Communications of the USSR issued a special envelope in honour of the fiftieth anniversary of the organs of State Security and a special inset with the same emblem in case the citizens of the USSR wanted to send good wishes to each other on so notable and joyful a date. To the amazement of the post office this idea came into only a few people's heads, and the envelopes with the emblems of the organs of State Security did not sell very fast. This emblem in a cinnamon colour showed a shield and sword. On the hilt of the sword there was a red star, and on the shield was written in white letters '50 years VChK-KGB' (the dash between these abbreviations symbolized, of course, several other names: OGPU, NKVD, MGB). The sword was slashing down at some plant with berries, evidently poisonous.

As well as these envelopes and insets, the USSR post also issued a special jubilee stamp for this date. I bought some of these envelopes and stamps. Then I put copies of the letters into the envelopes, stuck on the necessary amount of stamps with the pictured emblems. In an accompanying note on an inset I wrote to each of the addressees (Professors L. and C.) that this was a copy of the letter which had been lost several times. Now I was sending it in a special envelope and with special stamps issued in honour of the fiftieth anniversary of the organs of State Security. 'I would think,' I wrote, 'that a letter sent in such an envelope will at last come under the protection of the law on the preservation of the secrecy of correspondence. If it is lost this time, too, and does not reach you, this will mean that the KGB, now celebrating its golden jubilee, has made the post into its censorship department to check the thoughts and actions of Soviet citizens.'

Having posted the letters, next day I quietly got on with the current work in the laboratory. Several days went by. On 19 February, during the day, when I was just getting ready to leave my office for the lunch break, the telephone suddenly rang. The Director's secretary told me that I must come and see the Director of the Institute, and that the Director's private car had been sent for me. (The administrative block and the clinics, due to some badly thought out plan, had been built several kilometres away from the experimental sector, and hence hundreds of employees of the experimental sector could only get in contact with the administration, accounts department and other services by means of a thirty-minute trip on an overcrowded bus.) A few minutes later the well-known Volga drew up at entrance No. 2 of the laboratory block, and for the first time in my six years' employment at the Institute, I made the trip from the experimental sector to the administrative block in comfort. Why the Director had sent for me I had not the slightest idea, but the honour shown me for the first time and the unusual affability and courtesy created the best possible expectations. Not long beforehand, I had put in a request for approval of my making a trip to Czechoslovakia in March 1969 on the invitation of the Director of the Mendel Museum in Brno, and I thought that perhaps a favourable decision had been made on this matter.

The Director's secretary, who was generally supercilious and somewhat rude even in her dealings with elderly professors, sprang to her feet when I appeared, and, in a pleasant and smiling manner, opened a massive door, upholstered with expensive leather, which led into the long office of the Director of the Institute, an office like that of a Minister. When I went in, I felt at once that I had got into a 'trap'. The Director of the Institute, who had only just come back on duty after a long illness, was gloomy and official, and at the long conference table there sat a group of people, the composition of which boded no good. The Director sternly told me to be seated. On my right sat V. P. Baluda, the Deputy Director of the Experimental Sector. He was also, at that time, secretary of the Party organization. Beyond Baluda sat Professor K. S. Shadurskii, Head of the Pharmacology Section and a member of the Bureau of the Town Committee of the CPSU. Still further along sat the Head of the First Section, A. M. Shevaldin. Opposite me sat a man I did not know, obviously not a scientist, but evidently a personage of position, since only he had a folder with papers open in front of him.

'We invited you here,' said the Director of the Institute, G. A. Zedgenidze, after a short period of silence, 'to have a serious talk with you about some of your actions, and in particular about your strange correspondence with foreigners.'

Excusing myself, I interrupted him immediately and explained that I never wrote private personal letters in working hours and did not send them from the Institute office. Therefore there was no reason why I should have to discuss the matter with the administration of the Institute. I, in my turn, was interrupted by the unknown man sitting opposite me: 'Yes, but the customs organs, suspecting that there were stamps in your letters, opened them by chance, and we have learned of the contents of your letters and cannot let it pass without taking some action.'

'You have been writing to capitalists, you know,' came the voice of the Head of the First Section, 'and they could take your letters and publish them in bourgeois newspapers.'

'Excuse me,' I said, turning to the unknown personage and trying to keep calm, 'but who are you and why do you read letters that were not written to you at all, when, according to the Penal Code, you can get six months' forced labour for doing so?'

'Before you is Comrade Kopylov, a worker in the Town Committee of the Party,' the Director replied for him.

At that point the telephone rang. The Director, excusing himself, picked up the receiver and then went into the reception office to speak on another extension, so that we should not all learn the contents of his conversation. While he was out of the room, everyone was silent, waiting for him, and I remembered who this Kopylov was. The shortish man, with a professionally mordant face, sitting opposite me, held the post in Obninsk of Head of the Ideological Section of the Town Committee of the CPSU. I knew several stories about his vigorous ideological activity on the 'normalization' of the position among scientists and intelligentsia in Obninsk. As a result of his activity, the Obninsk team of the 'Merry and Bright Club'[1] had quietly come to an end, which in the past had won fame for our town by a television victory over a team from Dubna. The traditional weekly *Scientists' Day* had quietly died, since, after the removal of the head of the House of Culture who had been sympathetic to the organizers of the *Day*, all invitations to take part in the *Scientists' Day* had now to be confirmed by the Bureau of the Town Committee of the CPSU. Even the Central Lecture Bureau of the Moscow House of Littérateurs had received, on the initiative of the Obninsk Town Committee, a serious reprimand that they had given a permit to the well-known writer V. A. Kaverin, to lecture in Obninsk, and this lecture had made a very poor impression on the workers of the Town Committee. But Kopylov had received his greatest fame from the 'personal proceedings' he started against the editor of the local paper, M. Lokhvitskii, who was a capable journalist. While he held this post, Lokhvitskii made the local paper really interesting. Lokhvitskii's son, a student in the ninth grade, had written an essay on Aleksandr Pushkin and his time in which, inspired by some incomprehensible whim, he had said something like 'The means of dealing with heterodox thinkers and literary men in Pushkin's time were the same as today. There were denunciations, libels and secret shadowing. But then it was all simpler, one could challenge one's opponent to a duel. . . .'

Kopylov's wife, who worked as a teacher in that school, heard the staff discussing this sentence, and told her husband about it all. Kopylov at once began an ideological investigation, summoning the teachers who had not promptly reported this anti-Soviet essay. The father of the lad was held responsible for the incorrect ideological upbringing of his son, and he was held to be in sympathy with certain 'liberal' physicists. On the formal grounds of 'loss of Party vigilance' he was removed from membership of the Plenum of the Town Committee of the CPSU, expelled from the Party and dismissed from his job. He had to leave Obninsk. The rest of the staff at the school stopped speaking to Mrs Kopylova, and she was transferred to another school. Thus the person sitting opposite me had a professional love of 'personal proceedings'. He had challenged me to a political duel and had invited his seconds.

The Director soon returned, but just then his deputy from the

---

[1] The 'Merry and Bright Club' (*Klub veselykh i naryadnykh*) is a television game in which teams from different towns compete partly in general knowledge tests, and partly in tests of dexterity and skill—*Translator*.

Chemical Sector came into the office with two doctors and informed us that according to the graph, Zedgenidze would have to go now for his next medical treatment; they could not interrupt the regimen, particularly as the Party meeting was coming soon. Since the Director really had only just recovered from a compound fracture of the leg, Kopylov had to agree to the loss of one of his seconds. Zedgenidze went away, thus avoiding an interesting interview. Kopylov took over the meeting himself. First of all he tried in every possible way to discuss the contents of my letters, to elucidate in detail who were the three Professors, L., C. and J., where and how I had got to know them, where they had learned Russian and so on. But since the discussion along these lines did not give the 'Commission' the material necessary for a report and kept running aground on my references to the articles of the most democratic Soviet constitution, the interview was unexpectedly given a quite different, general political, turn.

'What do you think of the events in Czechoslovakia?' Kopylov asked suddenly.

'A lot of different things have happened there,' I replied. 'I am in favour of some, I disapprove of others.'

'Don't try to be naïve. We are interested in your attitude to the international action of the socialist countries in introducing the united armies of the Warsaw Pact to help the Czechoslovak people.'

'I do not think that I am bound to discuss my opinion on this matter in public since I do not know enough about it,' I replied.

Kopylov then energetically began to develop his thesis, which had already been published several times in the newspaper *Vpered*. The essence of this was that the head of a scientific collective must be not only a scientific head but an ideological and political one as well. (As a result of the implementation of this thesis in Obninsk several heads of laboratories had already been dismissed or demoted.) After this, in his capacity now as official representative of the Town Committee, he asked me to explain my attitude to the 'International Action' of the socialist countries in giving brotherly help to the peoples of Czechoslovakia.

I then replied that I did not force my views upon anyone, but that I was not afraid to state them to those who were really interested in them. If my interlocutors were very keen to know, then I could confirm that I considered that help was necessary for the people of Czechoslovakia, but that I did not approve of the form which that help took. The introduction of an army without warning into the territory of a sovereign state, I considered to be a very risky mistake.

o

Of course, this at once gave the 'Commission' rich food for discussion.

'You disapprove of the policy of the Party and Government!'

'You don't understand that it was an international duty!'

'You are not interested in the fate of the Czechoslovak people, who were being threatened by Neo-Nazi Germany,' and so on.

When this theme was exhausted (and there were quite a few points yet on the sheet of paper lying in front of Kopylov), Professor Shadurskii suddenly went back to the subject of the former genetic discussion, calling to mind my unpublished work on this discussion which had at some time come into his hands. 'It must be acknowledged, of course,' the pharmacologist stated, 'that this is a cheap and lying work, it intentionally paints things in exaggerated colours, trying to destroy confidence in the Soviet structure of society.'

I reminded Shadurskii that at the time he had felt differently about this work, he had defended it and twice borrowed it from me to read, once for himself and once for his son who was a student.

The discussion went on to the refusal of permission for this work to be published in the USSR, and the possibility of its coming out in translation in the USA. Judging from it all, the 'Commission' was not only in session on account of my letters which had recently been intercepted. I explained my position in the matter. It came to this, that if rough and unfinished drafts of some works, whether scientific, polemic or literary, are distributed spontaneously and independently of the author and frequently get abroad by various channels, then the author's rights regarding the illegal use of those works ought to be protected by the state, which should participate in the international conventions on the protection of authors' rights. Hence Soviet authors, when threatened with the 'piratical' publication of unauthorized manuscripts by various members of the gutter and anti-Soviet press, who live on contraband speculations in other people's works, must use individual means of protection, the only ones available. The most usual protection is to conclude a legal contract with a serious publishing house. Such a contract automatically deprives all other publishers of the possibility of publishing the work by contraband means. I was also threatened by provocation on the part of an anti-Soviet journal, which had got hold of some old version of the work, possibly with a number of distortions, and the Academy of Sciences Press to whom I had submitted the work back in 1965 and which had more than fifty favourable opinions and the decision of a special commission recommending publication, had done nothing to protect my rights and had refused to conclude a contract. Hence I was forced to agree with the arguments of my friends abroad who proposed that I should take some serious measures to counteract the provocation being prepared by this anti-Soviet journal. Accordingly, I had lifted my veto of many years' standing on the publication of a scientific version of this work abroad.

This approach to the problem once again evoked a stormy reaction from my interlocutors, who considered that in any situation having international aspects, it was always necessary to turn for help to the state and Party organs and not to take one's own initiative.

Time went by, and now the session must be concluded, but they still had not put to me many of the questions that had been prepared. Kopylov cut short the discussion on rights, looked at his list, and began to put new questions:

'What is the basis of your relationship with the author Solzhenitsyn?...

'Are you personally acquainted with Pavel Litvinov? With Ginsburg and Galanskov? . . .

'What is your attitude to Pavlinchuk? . . .

'What sociological and political journals do you subscribe to? . . .

'Do you take part in political seminars? . . .

'Why have you brought your son up so badly?' etc.

The only things that the 'Commission' were not interested in was my scientific work in the Institute and the work of the laboratory.

The conversation went on for almost three hours, but the director did not come back from his treatment.

Next day, work in the laboratory went on as usual. We were giving injections of uridine labelled by radioactive tritium to a group of animals, so as to study the synthesis of the ribonucleic acids in the nuclei of control and irradiated animals and were preparing to take blood samples from them. But then I was called once again to the telephone.

'Comrade Medvedev,' said the Director's secretary, 'please do not leave the laboratory. A messenger from the Director's office is coming to see you.'

A few minutes later, the Director's Volga drew up at the laboratory block again. The girl who brought various instructions to the departments normally came by the bus. This time, she had some extra important business, and they sent her in the Director's car.

Seeing me in the laboratory, she choked with relief.

'Zhores Aleksandrovich, you are requested to make yourself familiar with the Director's instructions and to sign that you have received them,' she said, opening a folder.

The instructions were brief. On the basis of certain paragraphs of the rules on competitive examinations, and some instruction of the Ministry of Health on the regulation of the numbers of laboratory staff, 'Zh. A. Medvedev' was 'to be relieved of his duties as head of the laboratory of molecular radiobiology'. The personnel and equipment of the laboratory of molecular radiobiology were to be 'transferred to the laboratory of radiation genetics'.

The instructions were completely unexpected and illegal. Although I signed that *I had received* the instructions, the courier refused to leave the sheet of instructions with me, although this was stipulated in the rules. I began insisting that a copy should be shown at least to the Head of the laboratory of genetics, to whom I suddenly had to hand over, without her consent, my 'personnel' and to surrender all my equipment. But the girl courier said that she had definitely been asked to bring the instructions back. The instructions were dated 19 February, that is, they had been drawn up immediately after the session of the 'Commission'. Evidently the formulation of the instructions had not completely satisfied the Code of Labour Law and it had afterwards been proposed to amend it somewhat.

After the 'Commission' I had assumed that they might demote me in position, making me a Senior Assistant. I was prepared, too, that they might hold a competitive examination and might try not to choose me for another term of office, giving me a bad character reference in the political sense. For more than a year a 'purge' had been going on in Obninsk to free the scientific establishments of 'politically immature' scientists, and already before my case, some fifteen scientists in various institutes had been dismissed, although they had not been carrying on an international correspondence. My friend, the physicist Valerii Pavlinchuk, had been dismissed from the Institute of High-Energy Physics at the end of 1967 for reading unpublished manuscripts. But he had been dismissed more humanely by withdrawing his 'pass for classified work'. Understanding, however, that it is hard to live without work, they did not simply put him out on the street, but transferred him to the post of a book-keeper in the housing department. The administration reckoned that a theoretical physicist would be up to the duties of a book-keeper. They dealt just as humanely with another friend of mine who was head of the laboratory of radiation dosimetry in the Institute of Physical Chemistry. He had also lost his 'pass' because of his favourable opinions of Solzhenitsyn's works, his participation in the organization of a speech by Kaverin and for taking an active part in Pavlinchuk's funeral (he died in the summer of 1968 of inflammation of the lungs, complicated by nephritis). But he, too, was not simply put out on to the street, he was transferred to the post of sanitation engineer in the commercial housing section. Not unjustifiably, the administration thought that a Candidate of Technical Sciences would be able to cope with problems of drainage and waterpipes. But the laboratory he had created was not closed down; they appointed a new temporary head. And this was right. For the laboratory had been founded many years ago for a definite purpose and not from personal but from state funds.

But my laboratory, according to the instructions, was just to be closed down, although it had only recently been created, and it had not yet been able to produce enough to justify the large government expenditure involved in equipping it. And the laboratory and the problems it investigated had been planned in the structure of the Institute long before I had begun to work on it; the theme of the laboratory formed part of a scheme described in the State Plan for the National Economy. The decision to dissolve the laboratory was stupid; it would not harm Zhores Medvedev, but it would damage the cause for which an enormous radiological and radiobiological complex had been set up in Obninsk. Even without a new competitive examination, it would have been possible to find in the Institute a temporary head, and a new head could then have been chosen by examination. On the balance sheet of the Institute the equipment of the laboratory was estimated at several hundreds of thousands of roubles. But all Kopylov needed for his work was a telephone and a writing desk.

The formulation of the instruction was incomprehensible to me. Everything in it contradicted the labour laws. For dismissal there needed to be some cause. A scientist could be dismissed if he had not been chosen in the competitive examination, but no examination for my post had been announced and the term of the previous one had not yet expired. He could be dismissed 'due to cutting down of staff', but there were not normally any staff cuts in February, and besides the Institute was not yet fully completed, and the staff was increasing from year to year. He could be dismissed due to loss of his 'pass', but only in classified establishments doing secret work. Dismissal from work on political or religious grounds is not permitted by the Code of Labour Laws (CLL), since this goes against the international conventions on labour, which the USSR has ratified. The Soviet laws, in order to prevent arbitrary action, permit the dismissal of employees only in accordance with some definite statute of the CLL and in conditions specified in the code.

They have all these codes of laws in the personnel department. But the instructions about me were signed on 19 February, apparently immediately after I had left the Director's office. There had been no time for them to consult the CLL. Why they were in such a hurry remains unknown. Perhaps someone, somewhere, had to be informed by 19 February that measures had been taken and Medvedev had been dismissed. Perhaps even in the 'Black Office' or in some brighter associated office. The personnel section could sort out the necessary articles of the law afterwards. So it turned out. I was still busy making an inventory and transferring equipment to the laboratory of genetics, and had not managed to get to the personnel department to find out the exact reason for my dismissal, when I received by post from the personnel section of the Institute a package valued at 10 roubles and sealed with sealing-wax.

In it they sent me my 'Labour Book', not waiting for me to go and get it for myself when I had finished up my work. In the section in the labour book dealing with my work in Obninsk, after certain expressions of gratitude 'for conscientious work' came the inscription '*Dismissed for incompatibility with his duties*' (Institute Instruction No. 71 of 19/2/1968).

In the library I took out the CLL and found in it this convenient and all-embracing statute. However, none of the criteria for the application of this statute applied to my case. But even if they had applied, my dismissal would have been illegal. The fact is, that a question of 'compatibility with duties' in scientific establishments when the appointment is by competitive examination, can only be decided by the Academic Council. The law was logical. Once a scientist is selected for a post by competitive examination and thereby judged worthy by the Academic Council, then his inadequacy also should be judged by the Academic Council. Since the Director of the Institute does not have the right to engage scientists without a competitive examination and the decision of the Academic Council, he likewise does not have the right to dismiss them without a competitive examination and decision of the Academic Council, except, of course, when an employee leaves 'at his own request'. I had been chosen for the post of head of the laboratory by the Academic Council, and chosen unanimously. This choice was confirmed by a special decision of the Presidium of the Academy of Medical Sciences.

For my dismissal to be legal it would require a new decision by the Academic Council and a new decision by the Presidium of the AMS. Only these collegiate bodies have the legal right to determine the 'compatibility with his duties' of the head of a laboratory. This closed the way to arbitrary behaviour and guaranteed the interests of the state which allotted considerable funds for financing various projects. It created stability and good order and insured the budgetary appropriations against losses due to arbitrary behaviour, egoism and personal conflict. The legislator knew that the scientific needs of the country depended primarily on scientists and not on the employees of the Town Committee or Party Commissions. Scientists have to be trained, of course, but the capital invested in them must be protected. This was a reasonable approach. The law was on my side, and I felt that I could soon get myself reinstated in my job, at all events so long as 'personnel' and 'material' equipment were still there.

11

Law and justice against the 'Black Office': First stage

By the time I had finished transferring equipment and staff, it was already the middle of March. I had deliberately delayed the process, in spite of pressure from above, in order to dispose of the resources of the laboratory as sensibly as possible. There was a great deal of equipment, and to transfer it only to the laboratory of genetics was stupid, most of the instruments were of no value to geneticists. The staff, likewise, were not suitable for work in the genetics laboratory, while over this very laboratory, the head of which was Professor Timofeev-Resovskii, a scientist of world repute, hung a threat of destruction; it was known that the Kaluga provincial committee and the Obninsk Town Committee had strongly recommended the Institute authorities and the Academy of Medical Sciences to dismiss Timofeev-Resovskii on the pension he had 'earned'. To overload the genetics laboratory with my staff was inadvisable. Hence I tried to distribute my staff among several other laboratories of similar type (biophysics, biochemistry, genetics, radio-biology) so that each employee could go on working on his own subject and not interrupt his experimental work. Accordingly the equipment, too, was distributed between these laboratories, and the most compli-cated instruments went into general use by the whole laboratory block. But we had agreed, unofficially, not to break up the very complex system and the well-equipped premises at least for three months. I hoped that in that time I would be reinstated in my job and get the illegal instructions revoked.

But to preserve the laboratory in its immunity for even so short a time proved a difficult task. Three rooms equipped for chemical research were immediately handed over to our neighbours downstairs, although they had no chemical analysts. Seeing that people were going on work-ing in their former working places, the Deputy Director, V. P. Baluda, instructed them to move up at once to the floors of the block where their new bosses were.

Three or four days after the order abolishing my laboratory in the

Institute there was a closed Party meeting. According to the announcements, there was only one item on the agenda: 'The ideological level of
the scientist.' Kopylov was announced as the speaker for this meeting.
It might be supposed that at the meeting he would say a few words
about me.

As I learned later, he said considerably more than a few words about
me in his speech. Kopylov described the history of Medvedev's correspondence with foreigners quite differently from what it was in fact.
He also described the contents of the letters, or rather, he described
what he understood the contents to be, but he refused to read out the
text of the letters when someone who was present asked him about this.
In order to conceal the activity of the 'Black Office', Kopylov explained
that Medvedev was sending stamps in the letters, which was forbidden
by the customs rules, and this gave the customs a reason to open the
letters. But, *as well as stamps*, there were letters enclosed as well. The
customs, of course, did not read the letters, but since these letters *were
written on Institute notepaper*, and were in the form of official business
correspondence, the letters had been returned to the administration of
the Institute and not to the sender. Thus, due to the contraband exchange of stamps, and the illegal use of strictly official notepaper, they
had happened by chance to learn of Medvedev's correspondence. And
what had he been writing about in his 'business' correspondence on the
notepaper of the Institute authorities. Here, of course, everyone listened,
holding their breath. The head of the laboratory, using contraband
official notepaper as a cover was trying to create ideological deviations
under the guise of correspondence with his 'friends'. It was just like a
detective novel.

Having worked up his repertoire, Kopylov gave the selfsame speech
in other institutes and establishments in the town. Moreover he aug-
mented it with other fantastic details. At one place he said that I had
sent the manuscript of my brother's book abroad, and at the meeting of
the workers of the Park of Culture and Rest, together with the workers
from the public services, he accused me of attempts at 'rehabilitating
Stalin' and, describing Medvedev's dismissal, said that the Academic
Council of the Institute had voted him out for 'poor scientific work'.

In order to stop all these rumours and slanders, I decided to send
round to my colleagues an exact copy of my letter to Professor L. The
secrecy of correspondence had been violated anyway, so let everyone
know the exact text, and not the distorted version in Kopylov's public
speeches. From the typewritten copy I had, I retyped, for a start, seven

o*

copies, carefully reproducing even the layout of the letter so that it was clear that this letter could not have been written on Institute paper, where the Institute device occupies the upper part of the sheet. To the copy of the letter to Professor L. I attached an accompanying text in which I explained that this was an exact copy in all respects of my letter which had been intercepted, that it had not been written on official notepaper of the Institute, that the envelope had not contained stamps for exchange and, as could be seen from the text, it was of a strictly private and confidential nature. The aim of all these lies which were being put around about my correspondence at the Party meetings, as I pointed out in the accompanying letter, were fairly clear. Firstly, it was necessary somehow to justify the violation of the secrecy of correspondence which is guaranteed by the Constitution and laws of the USSR, secondly, through regular accusations, especially about 'connections with foreigners', to quieten the conscience of those colleagues who had to find some pretext for not protecting their colleague at work.

(To digress, it must be noted that this 'method of defamation' has evidently been seriously worked out and is taught at special sessions as a very convenient means of at least temporarily 'cooling down' supporters at meetings and sessions. It is used all too often. In 1962, at a large meeting convened to discuss and condemn my work on the genetics discussion, held at the Timiryazev Agricultural Academy, many scientists came prepared to defend this work. However, after hearing the opening address of the Director of the Academy, T. Loz, who said that he had information from *certain* sources that Medvedev was trying secretly to get this work published by an *underground press* in Kiev, the defenders of the work kept silence and some of them even criticized it. Another case of such defamation had a more serious character. In 1963, at the meeting of the State Committee on Lenin Prizes it became apparent that Solzhenitsyn's story, 'One Day in the Life of Ivan Denisovich', had the best chance of the prize for creative literature, but then a member of the Committee, the then secretary of the Central Committee of the Komsomols, Comrade Pavlov, declared that according to his information, Solzhenitsyn had served a sentence and had not been rehabilitated, that he had been in prison, etc. Thus he guaranteed an unfavourable vote. When a short time later, another member of the Committee, Aleksandr T. Tvardovskii put forward exact documents and showed that all this was a *lie*, that Solzhenitsyn had been an officer in the Soviet army until his illegal arrest in 1944, and that he had been completely rehabilitated, then Pavlov readily apologized. But the main purpose of the defamation had been accomplished.)

I sent the first seven copies of my 'refutation' by post to the heads of the laboratories of our Institute, mainly to those whom I considered to be sufficiently objective and honest scientists. There were not, of course, seven such scientists in our Institute, and I proposed, in the immediate future, to continue the distribution of these materials not in the form of typewritten copies but in the more reliable form of a photocopy of the very first original which I had taken back in December, before posting it, and had kept in my library of photocopies. (After cases of attempts to destroy and confiscate the personal files of certain people had become known, I thought it advisable to microfilm the documents of my scientific records so as not to be helpless if in a similar situation.)

But the very next day after sending the first batch of letters, I realized that my plan to combat this misinformation had come to grief. Five out of seven of my letters were at once handed over to the Party Committee or the Director. The Director of the Institute and the Secretary of the Party committee, suspecting that there were more letters, began ringing up all the heads of laboratories and group leaders and demanding that they hand over Medvedev's letters. The majority of them had had no letters from me, but they went on insisting and persuading them to give up the letters 'in your own interests'. At the next Party meeting, there was sharp criticism of one Party member, who, in his own words, had *destroyed* my letter, not handed it over to the Party committee. But another scientist was especially pointed out as a true Party supporter. He had received my letter that evening, and had not waited until he went to work next day, but had rung up the Director of the Institute at his flat and told him about the letter, and then had quickly taken it round to the Director's flat, and from there had rung up Medvedev and scolded him for writing such letters. I remembered that phone call well. He told me in a very threatening monologue that he did not trust me, had no sympathy for me, and had disapproved of my actions from the very beginning. After which he rang off at once so as not to listen to my possible arguments. Since this colleague was planning a long business trip to Austria, I quite understood his swift reaction. For before he had this prospect in view (which did not in fact materialize) he was quite a different person.

It was clear that it was no good counting on the support of the community in Obninsk. All that was left was to count on the support of the law. The law in a just state is the only real and absolute guarantee of justice.

According to the Constitution, the Procurator's Office is in charge of seeing that the law is strictly observed in the USSR. The procurator, in the case of a breach of the laws of the USSR by officials, and in particular of the labour laws, may give the necessary directions to the administration. If the administration does not want to obey the directions issued as 'procuratorial supervision', the Procurator may transfer the matter to the legal organs, and all administrators are bound to obey the decision of the People's Court on labour disputes.

I wrote to the Procurator of Obninsk, senior legal counsellor, F. Ya. Mitrofanov, a very detailed statement, pointing out the illegal character of my unexpected dismissal from my post, although according to the law, I could only be appointed to it or relieved of it by competitive examination. I pointed out the illegal nature of the 'Commission', after the meeting at which I had been so rapidly dismissed. The 'Commission', as I pointed out, sat practically in the absence of the Director, and the head of it was someone who did not work in the Institute and who had no administrative powers. No one had informed me of the purpose and functions of the 'Commission', and it apparently had no legal status at all. My immediate superior was not present at the meeting, the Head of the Section of which my laboratory formed part, and the 'Commission' was not interested in questions of scientific work, the fulfilment of plans, etc. Such a 'Commission' had no right to decide on questions of 'compatibility with the post'. The very instruction on my dismissal had no basis. Since not a single point of the CLL on grounds for dismissal was even cited in the instruction and the procedure of dismissal broke the laws on the engagement and dismissal of staff for posts decided by competitive examinations, I asked the Procurator to give directions reinstating me for scientific work, and, if the administration of the Institute refused to do this, to instigate legal proceedings for illegal dismissal.

A few days later I was called to the Procurator's office. The Procurator's assistant informed me affably that they had made a careful study of my statement, but that, unfortunately, they had no power to interfere in the matter. It seems that in addition to the *Code of Labour Laws*, there is also a *Commentary on the Code of Labour Laws*. This *Commentary* is a systematic explanation by the Supreme Court of the USSR and the Supreme Court of the RSFSR, stating under what conditions and within what limits each article of the law may be applied. This *Commentary*, as I saw from a cursory glance, is a parallel and more detailed code of laws; it is divided up into paragraphs for the articles of the law, and these paragraphs may be used as independent additions to the law, considerably extending their sphere of application where necessary. According to this *Commentary* (section 5, art. 47, para. 90), appeal can be made against dismissal through the Procurator's Office or the Court only in the case of rank-and-file workers. The dismissal of workers in a position of authority is not subject to appeal in the courts, and a protest against it may be made only in administrative orders upward. All 'Heads', 'Chiefs' and 'Leaders' are outside court and procuratorial protection, and this, as I understood, is quite natural in a society with bureaucratic centralization of all systems of control.

When I received this explanation in the Procurator's office, I wrote, without delay, a protest about my illegal dismissal to the President of the Academy of Medical Sciences of the USSR, V. D. Timakov. I had known Timakov personally in the days before he became President of the Academy. He was a microbiologist with leanings towards genetics and biochemistry, and quite recently he had supported my book on the history of the genetic discussion. I thought, therefore, that he would try to help me.

In my statement to the President of the AMS I pointed out my qualifications and my scientific work in Obninsk which gave me the right to consider myself 'compatible with the post' for which I had been chosen in 1965 after three years of work as a Senior Scientist in the laboratory set up under my direction. This choice was confirmed by the Presidium of the AMS and the post would not come up for re-election until May 1970. I pointed out, too, that the destruction of the laboratory which had only just been created would undoubtedly harm the work, and cut short the research which had been started, and that the haste with which it had all been done was quite unjustified. In conclusion, I asked the President of the AMS to take measures to reinstate me in my scientific work, at least as a Senior Scientist, since the breaking up of the laboratory was now an accomplished fact.

About a month later, I received an answer from the Presidium of the AMS. The letter on the notepaper of the Academy of Medical Sciences of the USSR of 22 May 1969 (No. 13–16/17) said (the grammatical mistakes and wrong endings of the words in the letter are errors of the letter-writer):

Dear Comrade Medvdedev,[1]
The Presidium of the Academy of Medical Sciences of the USSR has no grounds for reversing the decision of the administration of the

[1] This, and other inaccuracies, have their equivalents in the original—*Translator*.

Institute of Medical Radiology of the AMS USSR on your dismissal, under paragraph C, art. 47 of the CLL. In considering this question, the Institute has been guided by paragraph 36 of the Commentaries to the Labour Laws (Moscow, 1966) which stating: 'in deciding the question of dismissal due to the unfitness of workers, whose activity is connected with teaching and cultural-educational functions, with work on the selection and training of personnel, one have to take into account not only the qualification and fitness of these workers, but also their moral makeup and their behaviour in the working group and private life.' (Decrees of the Plenum of the Supreme Court of the RSFSR of 29/12/1962.)

Chief Academic Secretary of the Presidium of the AMS USSR. Academician of the AMS USSR, A. SNEZHNEVSKII

The same situation again. I called upon the law, and was slapped down with the *Commentary* on the law. But this *Commentary* in its turn required commentaries. My behaviour in the working group and in private life was not marred by any conflicts. For several years in succession I had been entrusted by the community in the Institute of Medical Radiology with the post of Chairman of the Comrades' Court[1] and had myself examined cases of minor civil disputes in the working group and various petty crimes (theft of alcohol, absenteeism, etc.). As a result, they had dismissed me, according to Snezhnevskii's explanation, on account of my 'moral make-up'. But how did this stand legally? Some Commentary by the Supreme Court was needed here, too. There are many moral principles, they are diverse; so which one must one break in order to be unfit for 'teaching and cultural-educational functions', and for work, connected with the 'selection and training of personnel'? Morality is a subjective concept. There is, for example, Christian religious morality, and it is precisely this, in spite of the universal spread of

---

[1] The 'Comrades' Courts' were founded in 1959 as part of Khrushchev's policy of implementing the 'withering away of the state' (a fundamental tenet of the theory of the development of a fully communist society) by transferring certain functions of the state to the 'organs of society' (which remain, of course, under strict party control). Comrades' Courts are established on a basis of place of residence or place of employment. The members of the court are elected by the 'collective' which they serve, they then elect a chairman, vice-chairman and secretary from among themselves. Comrades' Courts deal with breaches of discipline at work, with civil cases if the amount in question does not exceed 50 roubles and if the parties concerned agree to submit the case to this court, and petty criminal offences (e.g. hooliganism, theft of state, social or personal property) committed for the first time. They may impose 'measures of social influence' (e.g. reprimand, fines of up to 50 roubles, necessity to apologize to victim, recommendation that the offender be transferred to unskilled manual labour for not more than 15 days). The decisions of the Courts are final, but the local Trade Union and Party officials have the right to demand that the Comrades' Court should hear the case again or reconsider their decision, if these officials consider the decision was illegal—*Translator*.

atheism, that still serves as the standard of 'moral level'. If the Supreme Court of the RSFSR had in mind Evangelical and Biblical moral dicta, then my dismissal was clearly illegal. But there are other kinds of morality. There is narrow-minded morality, criminal morality of various kinds, a 'Moral Code of the Builder of Communism', set out in the Programme of the CPSU, which in the main borrows the generally accepted principles of religious morality. Morality, as the dictionaries define it, is something touching on the principles of good and evil and the capacity to distinguish good from evil. The Supreme Court of the RSFSR has decided to dismiss specialists, teachers, professors, chiefs, directors and scientists on account of their 'moral make-up', irrespective of their qualifications and abilities. But they have not laid down at what point between 'low' and 'high' moral make-up one can dismiss a person for 'incompatibility with his duties'. They decided to leave this complicated question to be decided by a 'Commission' headed by Kopylov. But perhaps there were people with a low moral level sitting on the 'Commission', perhaps one of them had a mistress in the laboratory. Perhaps there was an anti-Semite among them, an informer who had energetically and radically fought against 'cosmopolitanism' in 1951-2 and who had been keeping quiet about it for many years after the surviving victims of his denunciations came out of prison in 1953? Perhaps among them, too, was one of the chiefs of the regime in the special camps, who came out of military uniform in 1955. Perhaps one of those in front of me was a cynic who had no moral principles at all. And the huge hundred-square-metre office itself, furnished in oriental luxury at the state's expense, did this correspond to the moral criteria of the Supreme Court of the RSFSR? Behind a curtain a secret door led into yet another 'confidential' office, with a bath, toilet, massage room and the other accommodation for the personal rest of the owner of the office. And all this was decorated fit for the Shah of Persia. Could this also correspond to the 'Moral Code of the Builder of Communism'? To each according to his needs, from each according to his abilities. A bath and massage, of course, improved the spirits of a managerial worker in the middle of his crowded working day.

'He that is without sin among you, let him cast the first stone at her!' Christ once said, according to the Bible story, and no one around him moved. Their morality was not above reproach. But those who had gathered around me in that Persian office were not afraid to cast stones at me. Perhaps they too were not without sin, but they had already been guaranteed absolution, and the Supreme Court of the RSFSR had looked indulgently on their 'moral level'. And the Supreme Council itself, which had issued through its various colleges *millions* of certificates of posthumous rehabilitations 'in the absence of the *corpus delicti*', did not always stand strict guard over the law and was only gradually establishing legal principles in the country—no easy process. In any case, it had not yet reached the stage where I could hope for reinstatement in a job in Obninsk. It was necessary to try another approach to the problem.

I decided to finish off quickly certain surveys which I had already begun, the publication of which would guarantee me a definite payment in the near future. But this plan quickly proved illusory. At the end of May, I received a letter from the 'Meditsina' publishing house. The Editor-in-Chief, G. Ostroverkhov, wrote:

> The Meditsina Publishing House informs you that on reconsideration of the proposal to publish the collection, *Molecular and Functional Principles of Ontogenesis*, it has been judged advisable to abridge it, removing a number of items, including your article, 'Morphogenesis and ageing of haemoglobin-synthesizing systems'.

I went to the publishers to find out what was going on. For the collection was already in production. My article, which was in the nature of a theoretical survey, had been written to the order of the publishing house itself and in answer to an official request from the Editor-in-Chief of the collection. But at the publishers I learned some even more painful news. Another article of mine had also been removed from a Soviet-Polish manual on genetics, which was likewise in the press. This article, entitled 'The Genetics of Ageing', was not an independent unit, but formed the twenty-fifth chapter of the manual, and was linked to the other chapters. Taking it out destroyed the logical structure of the manual and necessitated changes in the remaining part of the book. The chapter had also been written to the order of the publishing house and on the basis of a contract which was now being unilaterally broken.

The reasons for these arbitrary acts remained unknown, but one of the people who worked at the publishers, who was retiring on a pension, having reached seventy years of age, was bolder than the rest. He took me out into the corridor, and told me that although he did not know the details of why my articles were withdrawn, he had heard that it was connected with my correspondence with foreigners.

The 'Black Office' had reached even here.

I went to the Mir Publishing House to get a contract for some scientific translation. A good book would give me a useful occupation

and a breathing space for half a year. The geneticists and biologists who
had been dismissed in 1948 had made ends meet with the help of translations. Professor L. A. Sabinin, who was dismissed from Moscow
University, and had no possibility of getting another job, made translations of two excellent books on plant physiology, before ending his life
by suicide. Although the Managing Editor of biological literature of this
publishing house, which was especially founded to publish translations
from foreign languages, was then the Lysenkoist, I. Glushchenko, he
could maintain the quota for translations only with the aid of specialists
who knew both the subject and foreign languages. In 1948 Professor
A. A. Baev had translated for this press the notable book, *Dynamic
Biochemistry*, which appeared in 1949. However, the translator's name
did not appear on the title-page, but only the name of the editor of the
translation, Academician V. A. Engelhardt. At that time this was understandable; Baev was in prison, but the camp authorities let him do the
translation and have the fee. The publishers also knew that the translator was in prison, and so they did not put his name on the title-page
of the book.

I was received very favourably at the publishing house; the news of
my dismissal had not yet reached them, and I did not stop to tell them
about it. About two years before, I had edited for them a translation of
J. Bonner's book, *The Molecular Biology of Development* and hence there
was no doubt of my ability to translate a new book. I was offered a list
of books from the plans for translations for which there were still no
contracts, and I was delighted to see in it an American book by Professor Markert on the genetics of growth. The subject was one which
fitted in with my interests, and Professor Markert was well known to me.
The publishing house had not yet obtained the original of the book, only
advertisements of it, but I undertook to get hold of the original quickly,
by requesting it from the author, and the people at the publishing house
found this very convenient, as their currency quota for ordinary books
from abroad was extremely restricted. We discussed the whole matter,
and I went home in a cheerful mood. But the following evening an
employee of the publishing house rang me up long-distance and cancelled the order on the grounds that it had already been promised to
someone else. I expressed my willingness to undertake the translation
of any other book they were planning. 'Sorry,' he answered, 'we shall
always be delighted to work with you, but to conclude a contract with
you, according to our new rules, it is necessary to produce a statement
from your place of work, indicating your duties.'

Here again, the 'Black Office' imposed its veto.

At one biological journal, when they learned about my difficulties, they promised, 'Don't worry; we'll provide work for you. We'll send you articles for internal reviewing and freelance editing.' We considered this possibility in detail, decided the scope of what lay within my professional abilities, and agreed everything with the editor of the journal. But not a single article from this journal was sent to me.

I began to make enquiries about the possibility of co-operation with the Institute of Scientific and Technical Information. This institute publishes abstract journals, in particular on biology and biochemistry. For this work they always need freelance abstractors who know foreign languages. In the fifties I had done active work for the Biochemistry Abstract journal. But in 1969 this source, too, was closed to unemployed scientists. To obtain freelance abstracting work, it was necessary here too to produce a statement from one's regular place of work, indicating one's duties.

Just at that time, a well-known employee of the biological section of a popular science journal happened to sit near me in the library. He had already heard of the situation and was thinking how to help me. 'Couldn't you write a series of short articles for us on new discoveries in science? Of course, you understand, they would come out without a signature or under a pseudonym. But you would be paid for them.' I thanked him, but declined this underground popular science work. The conditions were too difficult, since the pseudonym would have to belong to a real person who would receive the payment and would transmit it to me. If the 'Black Office' found out about such an agreement, my kind-hearted 'pseudonym-giver' might also be dismissed from his job.

The hand of the 'Black Office' could be felt everywhere.

But in addition to these purely practical problems of everyday life, another fundamental problem remained unsolved. How to ensure that Professor L. would receive a copy of my letter, No. 34, of 17 December 1968, that was still lost in August 1969. The registered letters, sent in the jubilee envelopes with the VChK–KGB emblems once again did not reach the addressee. It was necessary to think of some other way of getting past the barrier of the 'Black Office'.

How the censorship deals with foreign printed matter coming through the post I already knew. But on what principle they dealt with letters of private correspondence was not entirely clear. Letters of a certain nature are lost whatever the number of copies sent, the addressee, the sender and the means of sending. Objectively this proves the censorship of *all* international letters, and not a selective checking which I had previously thought to be more likely. But why in that case, judging from the experience of philatelists, are not all letters containing stamps for collectors lost, but only a small proportion of them, destroyed? For the sending of stamps in international letters is considered to be contraband, and is actually forbidden by the customs rules. In December 1968, just when I was running into trouble with the 'Black Office', a friend of mine sent a series of envelopes containing stamps as a 'New Year Gift' to his philatelist friends. All these letters got through the system of control quite freely although they went by ordinary mail and even had no return address, so that if they were seized the post would have no worry about claims. Is it possible that these letters were not opened?

The natural assumption to make is that the 'Black Office' deals only with the *censorship* of letters. It does not take on the functions of the customs and is not interested in petty smugglers who do not threaten Soviet ideology, since they do not come under the heading of ideological deviation. The customs control does not have plenipotentiary powers to check all letters: its sphere is printed matter and parcels. It checks letters selectively, those picked out according to special customs criteria. But perhaps the 'Black Office' deliberately pays no attention to stamps, for it could forward such letters to the customs already opened. The 'Black Office' knows the customs rules, of course. But all the same, it does not assist the customs, although they both serve the same state. The fact of the matter is, evidently, that the customs is an open, legal establishment. If they confiscate a letter with stamps, the customs have to issue a statement informing the sender. Otherwise the confiscated letter must be considered to be 'lost' and a high compensation would have to be paid for it. The number of philatelists is very large, and if action was taken against every letter with stamps, then it would be clear to everyone that all the letters were being opened and checked. And this, according to international conventions, does not form part of the functions of the customs. They would then have to stop checking the mail altogether and this would undermine the principles of the 'Black Office', the value of information obtained by reading the mail.

But even after the loss of my eight letters, I was still not absolutely sure that all international letters were checked. Perhaps all three of my addressees were on the same list for selective checking. Perhaps it was really a selective checking, but the list of names to be checked was a long one, and all my regular correspondents were on it.

In many countries, the sorting of mail is now done by special computers. All the British post is being 'computerized' and there have already been several comedy films on the subject. 'Computerized' sorting of letters is based on machines which can read addresses or—which is simpler for a machine—special five- or six-symbol number or letter codes. The United States of America is now divided up into 100,000 postal zones, and each zone has its own code (60208, 21126, etc.) which is written after the name of the state. In Great Britain mixed codes of letters and figures have been introduced, each one for a definite postal district. The sorting of letters by codes is done by automatic machines.

It is well known that the USSR lags behind technical progress in this matter of sorting letters. Judging from a number of items published in the *Communications Journal*, the sorting of letters in the USSR is still in many cases done by hand, but in large sorting offices semi-automatic devices have now been introduced. There was an article on the technical stagnation in the sorting of letters in *Literaturnaya Gazeta*, entitled 'Labelled Atoms' (4 February 1970). Of course the 'Black Office' could acquire an imported postal computer for itself. If a machine can 'read' numbers, its memory can be set to read names as well. It would be possible to introduce into its memory the names of people in whom the 'Black Office' takes an interest. If 'Zh. A. Medvedev' is put into the computer memory, then his regular correspondents could also go into its memory. The mail that has been processed by the International Post Office goes into such a machine, and here the electronic memory sorts it into categories. From the main outlet down the moving belt goes the flow of letters whose addresses and senders arouse no suspicions. A little pulley-cart takes up the smaller number of letters which need checking. It takes them along a special tunnel to the 'Black Office'. This means that it was possible a computer was guilty in the case of my failures, and that I must somehow outwit it. I must prepare my envelope in such a way that it would get into the main flow and not into the 'Black Office'. But even if technical progress in the 'Black Office' had not reached this stage, and the instructions demanded the checking of *all* private international correspondence, even in that case there must be some way of penetrating this dense barrier. For many people work there, and they must have various tastes, various requirements, various outlooks on life and different psychology.

There are, of course, simply very lazy censors, who nevertheless have somehow to fulfil their daily norm. Perhaps a letter might have a chance of getting past one of them. Perhaps not all censors are equally black, perhaps some of them are grey, simply darkish, still young, not yet completely soiled by their illegal, immoral activity which must be concealed even from those close to them. Perhaps in this highly-paid profession there are people who still have some remnants of conscience, who are sick of their daily work?

But perhaps all this is an illusion? For many years the selection of suitable personnel who enjoy their diverse work has been going on. Each time they willingly and delightedly take into their hands the envelope which has already been opened by the technical service, they feel a sadistic delight that they have in their power the unlucky sender, some wayward intellectual, who believes in the Universal Declaration of Human Rights. And perhaps the salary of these secret clerks of the 'Black Office' is negotiated on a progressive bonus basis, depending not only on how many letters they check, but how many they stop. But in any case, it is only possible to score a goal by increasing the number of shots, aiming the ball from different angles, from a different distance, with different force. One of the shots would put the ball in the net. At the end of February, I began to check this hypothesis, starting with the 'easy' letter No. 34, which had previously been lost only twice before. I made seven copies of the letter in Russian and seven copies in English. They were typewritten on thin sheets of postal paper. The letters in Russian were typed on paper of Soviet origin, the letters in English on imported paper. Each copy of the letter was on a single sheet of paper. Then I began to send these letters to colleagues, including in the group of addressees, not only Professors L., C. and J., but also two other English friends, Z. and H. One of them was a physicist, the other a biologist. My correspondence with them had started only recently, and so far no letters to them had been lost. The letters were sent in different versions. I adopted the following means of sending the letters in different ways, to some extent following the advice Friedrich Engels had repeatedly given Karl Marx in order to ensure that they were able to exchange information. I have already quoted some of the methods which these classic figures of scientific communism used. To them may be added some others from a letter of Engels to Marx of 27 October 1852.[1]

But addresses, in particular addresses on letters sent through the post, must be written in different handwriting, turn and turn about, and packages handed in at post office counters must not be handed in by the same person nor at the same place each time.

Bearing in mind Lenin's statement that 'Marxism is not a dogma but

[1] *Works*, vol. 28, pp. 137–8.

a handbook for action' I tried to develop this classic scheme and adopted the following methods:

Firstly, the letters were posted not only from different post offices, but from different towns.

Secondly, at different times throughout the whole of March.

Thirdly, by different classes of the postal service (registered with 'advice of delivery', ordinary registered, ordinary airmail, express airmail). I thought that ordinary air-letters might be looked at more superficially, since they were not registered and there was less responsibility for them.

Fourthly, the letters, as I have noted, were written in two languages, so as to go through different language sections of the censorship.

Fifthly, the addresses on the letters were written in various styles, typewritten, handwritten in different handwritings, and different in character. On some envelopes there was neither the name of the addressee nor the name and the return address of the sender. There was simply a business address: 'Department of Genetics' or 'Physics Laboratory' of some university or other. Sometimes the return address was given, but to Moscow *poste restante*, and the signature in English was completely illegible, some sort of mixture of the letters M and Ж. In the letter itself, which also had a similar illegible signature, there was no official greeting with full title as is customary in English letters. I addressed my correspondents familiarly, like close friends, calling them by name, or rather diminutive, 'Dear Dave' or 'Dear Bob'. I felt that my colleagues, former heads of these laboratories or departments, when they received the letters would doubtless know from the contents who had written them.

Sixthly, one of the letters was sent in a special envelope for international greetings on 8 March with a special greetings insert for women on this day. This insert contained greetings to the wife of Professor L. on this day and was sent to her home address. But I also put in letter No. 34 to her husband.

Seventhly, I adopted still greater cunning. I sent two of the English letters in envelopes of German origin and with German labels '*Mit Luftpost*' (i.e. 'By Airmail'). These were posted at different times from the postal department in the Natsional Hotel. This postal department (No. 600) serves foreign tourists. I assumed that the letters of foreigners would go to some special department of the 'Black Office'.

Eighthly, two of the letters were 'philatelists' letters'. They were sent in envelopes with 'space' stamps and with the 'special postmarks' used in Moscow on Cosmonautics Day, 11 April, each year. An envelope with this postmark is a valuable philatelic souvenir, and on Cosmonautics Day there are long queues of enthusiasts at the post office waiting to get these postmarks. On this day in Moscow alone thousands of such philatelists' envelopes are sent abroad with just a short note for the look of the thing. Every philatelist gets the special postmark on dozens of envelopes. My letters went into this stream.

In similar versions, during March and April, twelve more copies of my previously 'lost' letter to Professor L. of 17 December were sent off to various addressees. In all, over two months, twenty-six copies of these two letters were sent. In addition, of course, I had my other current correspondence which was sent in the normal way, without special refinements.

By May, it became clear that all twenty-six copies of this 'hot' series had been 'lost'. I had had no 'advice of delivery' notes, nor confirmation of receipt, although the 'advice of delivery' notes from other letters had been returned from England and the USA. I made no further attempts to send these two letters to Professor L. by post. To waste money which would only go to the account of the 'Black Office' was senseless.

Finally, I thought, the postal censorship is undoubtedly a department of Glavlit. And if it hinders me from establishing some sort of check on the penetration abroad of information about a work which will cause Glavlit disquiet, if it has no confidence that my reliable friends know all the information they need for this check, then this lack of confidence makes Glavlit and its postal department responsible for all possible consequences. To undertake postal robbery of open legal correspondence is easy, but Glavlit cannot prevent the theft of manuscripts, which is a general calamity for Soviet authors. Nor can Glavlit protect the rights of Soviet authors abroad from piratical presses, and from commercial pillage. For this it is necessary to recognize the international convention on authors' rights, but Glavlit does not want to extend and legally formulate real *author's rights*. Glavlit is not for right, Glavlit is for injustice, Glavlit is not for Law, Glavlit itself, in many of its functions is above the law and outside the law.

But perhaps I was wrong, perhaps after all the USSR is a strictly law-abiding state and the Constitution of the USSR is binding on every state service. This could easily be checked. In my case, the violation of the laws on the preservation of secrecy of correspondence was available —and not only of the violation of *secrecy* of correspondence. As well as disregarding the secrecy of correspondence, the post had resorted to out-and-out blackmail, communicating information about my correspondence not only to the secret organs of surveillance, but to my place of work, to the Town Committee and to the Administration for their public discussion. The post had also done financial damage to the sender by destroying letters which had been *paid for* at the highest rate. All this made it quite possible to make an application to the Procurator's office and the court, to the organs of the *independent* legal system, which according to the Constitution, stand guard over the laws of a socialist country.

My latest plan was simple. Many of the lost letters of the most recent series were registered. I could file an application about them with the Central Claims Bureau of the International Post Office, enclosing the receipts. If an investigation did not show that the addressees had received the letters, the Claims Bureau was bound to send the addressee an official notification of the loss of the letters and pay him monetary compensation at the rate of 7 roubles 35 kopeks for each registered letter, plus the postal charges of the sender. For all the letters lost in the autumn of 1968 they would have to pay me about two hundred roubles. Being out of work, I could not afford to ignore this sum. Furthermore, it would help me to employ a professional lawyer who could then stir up the matter of the violation of the secrecy of correspondence, using the irrefutable evidence which I had on the subject, which the 'Black Office' had fairly easily put at my disposal.

Earlier, at the end of 1968 and the beginning of 1969, I had already sent the International Post Office a number of claims on the subject of searching for lost letters. There had been no answer. In answer to my complaint sent to the Ministry of Communications of the USSR, about the delay in investigations, I received the following letter from the International Post Office (5 February 1969, No. 298/vkh. 118/3):

To Citizen Zh. A. Medvedev
P.O. Box 25
Obninsk
Kaluga Province
   In response to your application, a check is being made. You will be informed more fully of the result.

B. YASTREBOV
(Deputy Head of the International Post Office)

But after this no fuller information followed. At the beginning of May, I prepared applications to the Central Claims Bureau about the fate of the fourteen registered letters, seven of them sent with 'advice of delivery' notes. In the applications I stated the dates and even the times of posting each letter, the number of the post office, the number of the receipt, the address of the recipient and sender. Sometimes they were anonymous addresses—the name of a department or a box number. The post office receipts were attached to the applications. On 14 May I delivered these applications directly to Comrade Litvinova, the representative of the Control Claims Bureau on duty in the International Post Office building. She was extremely surprised at so large a number of claims all at once; it was the first time in her experience. Nevertheless, according to the standard procedure, she checked the receipts with the applications, countersigned the copies of the applications and the receipts and exacted from me the cost of the stamps for each application. The Claims Bureau does not operate gratis, either. For each letter to be searched for, there was an additional 18 kopeks to pay. But to search for a registered letter with an 'advice of delivery' note, the post demands no money, for this investigation, according to the rules, is made free of charge.

After delivering the claims, however, I had to wait a fairly long time before I could begin the next stage in my fight against the violation of Soviet law. The fate of my letters mentioned in the claims was clear to me, and I realized that the Central Claims Bureau would prolong the 'investigation' for as long as possible before officially acknowledging that the letters were 'lost'. After this official acknowledgement of the loss of the letters, the sender has the right to receive compensation. But the maximum possible time which the International Postal Convention of 1964 lays down for searching for correspondence is six months. Of course, the Convention requires that the search for correspondence should be made in as short a time as possible, but since some such limit must be set, if the appeal for a rapid investigation is not taken into account, this limit is six months. If in this time the fate of the letter being searched for is not established, at all events according to the Convention, it is considered to be 'lost', and compensation is due. If in six months the post has not been able to establish the fact that a letter has been delivered to the addressee, they must acknowledge its loss and stop the search. Taking this period into account, I could not expect a final answer about the last main series of claims earlier than the end of November. It was necessary to have patience.

In the meantime, I also had to think about finding a new job, since my efforts to get reinstated in Obninsk had not been crowned with success. The study of the peculiarities of the postal department was, of course, an interesting occupation, but it did not completely satisfy my scientific inclinations as a biochemist, nor did it bring in any salary, a thing very necessary in modern society. It would, of course, have been possible to support my family on an income from the loss of letters, 7 roubles 35 kopeks per lost letter would ensure the basic necessities of life, even if one sent out only one 'losable' letter per day, without abusing the insurance funds of the Ministry of Communications of the USSR. Two letters a day, which is not at all difficult if one has a typewriter, would guarantee me a higher income than my last job. But I did not take this easy path.

According to the existing rules, all posts in scientific establishments, from Junior Scientific Assistant up to Head of Laboratory are filled strictly by competitive examination, on the basis of the voting of the Academic Council of the Institute or Faculty and the recommendations of the special examination commission. But one of the principal documents which must be presented at the examination, together with copies of diplomas and lists of published scientific works is the scientific and general 'character reference'. This character reference is signed by the Director, the Secretary of the Party organization and the Chairman of the Local Trade Union Committee of the establishment where the scientist is working at present or worked before taking part in the competitive examination for the new appointment. In comparatively recent times the character reference was needed not only for scientists but also for many categories of workers and employees. But then the Council of Ministers of the USSR by a special decree abolished the need for a character reference for finding a job in all branches of industry and employment, retaining it only for scientific and educational establishments.

Since it would be impossible to apply for work in a scientific establishment again without a character reference, I went to the personnel department of my former Institute and asked them to prepare and draw up the necessary document as soon as possible. The draft character reference was soon drawn up by the people in charge of the section where I had worked (Section Head, Section Party Organizer and Trade Union Organizer) and sent to the Director's Office for signing. After this, a month went by, but the character reference had still not got past this preliminary stage. I naturally put in a new application asking them to hurry the process along.

Some weeks later, when it was already summer, I was invited to go to the Director's office. The Deputy Director, the Secretary of the Party Committee and the Chairman of the Local Trade Union Committee were awaiting my appearance, together with the Head of the Personnel Department. They took me into the office, and enquired pleasantly to what Institute I was intending to submit my documents for the competitive examination. 'Tell us the address of the Institute, and we will send your character reference there,' said the Deputy Director, 'or else let them write to us for your character reference.' I naturally refused to agree to this old-fashioned procedure, explaining to them that by law they were bound to give me an *open* character reference. 'There is no such law,' interrupted the Secretary of the Party Committee. 'We will not give the character reference into your hands.'

So little respect for the law among the Institute administrators greatly amazed me. From the experiences of several other scientists who had been dismissed previously from other Institutes, I knew that if the administration does not hurry with the issuing of a character reference, one may apply to the Procurator, and after his sanction the character reference is always issued. This is what my friend did, when from being Head of the Laboratory of Radiation Dosimetry he became sanitary engineer in the Housing Department. But one could not envy him his character reference. Its author first of all noted that Comrade V. was a Senior Scientist and a Candidate of Chemical Sciences, that while he was working in the laboratory he had published more than twenty scientific works in the field of radiation, but he then went on to the negative part.

'In the course of the last two years,' he wrote, 'Comrade V. as Head of the laboratory and as a member of the Council of the House of Scientists has committed a number of grave political errors; he has ignored the All-Institute political arrangements, he has praised people with viewpoints contrary to Soviet activity. By his actions he has created a public opinion contrary to the policy of our Party and Government. . . . Taking into account the above-mentioned grave political errors of Comrade V. the governing body and social organizations of the branch of the Physical Chemistry Institute do not recommend that Comrade V. should be allowed to enter the competitive examination for positions in scientific establishments.'

Behind the sinister formula in Comrade V.'s character reference three facts were concealed. He had not attended the meeting of the Institute called to support the entry of the Soviet armies into Czechoslovakian territory. He had written to *Literaturnaya Gazeta* a letter criticizing an article condemning Aleksandr Solzhenitsyn in June 1968. (By some unknown route, a copy of this letter had reached the Obninsk Town Committee of the CPSU.) And he had taken up a collection among his friends for a wreath for his dead friend, the physicist Valerii Pavlinchuk, who had been dismissed from his job shortly before his death.

The concluding formula of Comrade V.'s character reference was, of course, contrary to the Soviet legislation on labour, which forbids denunciation in employment on religious or political grounds. It is also contrary to the International Declaration on the Rights of Scientists, signed by representatives of the Soviet Union.[1] But who cared for the law when writing character references!

Armed with the *Code of Labour Laws* (CLL), and the book *Commentary on the Labour Laws* (Yuridricheskaya Literatura Publishing House, 1966), I drew up a new application to the Institute administration, quoting the relevant articles and paragraphs governing the question of character references. At the same time I wrote protests to the Obninsk Town Procurator and the President of the Academy of Medical Sciences of the USSR requesting that the administration of the Institute should be obliged to observe the law upon this matter. In every case, I quoted in these applications the relevant instructions in the CLL and the commentaries to them. Noting in the 'Commentaries to Article 42' the necessity for character references for scientists and teachers in Institutes of Higher Education, the legislator clearly states that 'the administration is bound to give workers an open character reference. The sending of "closed" [secret] character references from one establishment to another is forbidden' (p. 77).

The law, then, was on my side. This was quickly confirmed by the Academy of Medical Sciences and not so quickly by the Obninsk Procurator's Office. Both authorities sent me replies that the administration of the Institute had received instructions to issue me a character reference for competitive examinations. However, the administration of the Institute, as before, refused to follow the instructions of the CLL. By the time that the search period for my claims at the International Post Office had run out, that is, in November 1969, the administration of the Institute had received three 'instructions' from the Procurator's

[1] This declaration (see *World of Science*, No. 4, 1969) states in the section on 'Issue of character reference for change of employment': 'The organization issuing the reference must first of all discuss it with the scientist personally. . . . This document must not contain anything that might harm the scientist.'— *Author's note.*

office, and two from the Academy of Medical Sciences, but the character reference was still not ready, and this blocked my opportunities of arranging a new job and leaving Obninsk. But it also gave me plenty of free time to investigate the subject of postal problems, which was new to me. And so was born the book which you see before you.

The period for investigating the fate of the 'lost' letters had run out, but the central Claims Bureau kept silence. No letter came from them, nor, moreover, did they send the financial compensation stipulated in the Postal Code of the USSR. It was necessary to go to the International Post Office for an explanation.

I was personally received at the post office by the Head of the Central Claims Bureau, Mrs Kravtsova, and the Head of the Operational Section, Danin. They came out into the main hall of the post office ('outsiders' are not allowed to go into the Claims Bureau itself). In Kravtsova's hands there was a fairly thick file containing correspondence about my letters alone. Leafing through the papers of this file, she affably explained to me that immediately after my applications the Claims Bureau had made enquiries about the fate of my letters to the postal administrations of the USA and Great Britain, but up till now, in spite of reminders neither post office had replied to the enquiries. According to her explanations, it had happened that all my letters the fate of which was being investigated, had been sent abroad together, and there were even registration notes to this effect in the transmission channels of registered postal packets. But it was impossible to pursue their fate further, since the British and American posts completely ignored the efforts of the Claims Bureau. It turned out that the letters had been lost somewhere in England and the USA.

It was clear from all this that Comrade Kravtsova really believed that the letters had been lost somewhere abroad. Before my eyes she leafed through the forms in the 'file', and they were the real postal receipts of the Claims Bureau, coloured forms in two languages, not fakes. There was no mystification, everything had been done accurately in the proper order. Judging from it all, the Claims Bureau had really tried to find my lost letters, but had not found them .

It was obvious that the Postal Department was worried about what had happened. This was shown, too, by a letter which I had received not long beforehand in answer to my complaint to the Ministry of Communications of the USSR that the International Post Office was taking too long over the investigation of the claims I had submitted. This letter, of 6 October 1969, signed by the Head of the Organization

Section of the Postal Administration, Comrade A. Smirnov, informed me that the Chief Postal Administration had 'given instructions to the International Post Office to hasten their search for the letters which you sent abroad'.

According to all the postal notes of the International Post Office, the lost letters were recorded as having been sent abroad. They were, of course, registered letters, and their numbers were entered in the register of postal dispatch of the airport. At the International Post Office, mail is collected from the whole of the Soviet Union and registered letters, for example, from the Moscow post office come in a sack with a register in which the numbers of the letters are indicated. When the international letters are collected into the Moscow mail sack, they are not differentiated by countries. The numbers of the letters are put down in the register of postal packets from the series of registered letters, irrespective of whether they are going to the USA or England. These registers stay at the International Post Office. Sorting by countries takes place at the International Post Office and for the registered letters, for example to England, collected into the post bag between 13.00 and 13.30 a new register list is made which accompanies the sack on its journey. My letters were in these lists of the post office for the sacks with the international mail, ready for loading on to the aeroplane. The International Post Office had ascertained this through the Claims Bureau. But what had happened to the letters afterwards, Kravtsova did not know. According to her assurances, if they were lost , they had been lost somewhere further along the line, in England, or on the way to England. Hence the Claims Bureau had sent enquiries to England about the fate of the lost letters. I knew of a case when a colleague of mine, whose letter to England had not reached its destination, made a claim, like me, and about five months later received a reply from the Claims Bureau. In this reply, this same Kravtsova informed him that 'registered letter No. 292 of 9/xi/68 was lost during transmission to its destination, a fact which we greatly regret'. They even paid my colleague 7 roubles 35 kopeks for the lost letter. But when a second letter of his to the same addressee was lost his application brought neither explanation nor compensation.

What does the formula 'lost during transmission to its destination' mean? It means that it was sent from the USSR but did not arrive in England. At the last checkpoint of the Soviet post in the International Post Office there is a note that the letter was sent, but at the first checkpoint receiving Soviet mail into England the letter was not there. But since there was no question of *force majeure*, compensation was not paid.

'Lost during transmission to its destination', is a convenient formula. At once you think of another convenient formula: 'Shot while attempting to escape.'

The conversation with Kravtsova and Danin convinced me of one thing, that the employees of the International Post Office, who are in direct contact with the customers, play no part in the loss of letters. The sack with the international mail, all ready for dispatch, goes to the 'Black Office' after passing through the post office service. Between the 'Black Office' and the post office there is no direct co-operation, and the post office workers evidently do not know what goes on in the 'Black Office'. The tradition of the old 'Black Office', partitioned off even from the official censorship of newspapers and journals (this was an 'open' censorship) has been preserved.

The entrance to the 'Black Office', according to Maiskii, 'was masked by a large yellow cupboard of the "official" type, through which the "secret clerks" proceeded from the office of the senior censor into the "holy of holies".'

International mail also went to the St Petersburg 'Black Office' after it had been made ready for dispatch and done up in general postal packets. The diplomatic mail, however, when it was ready was enclosed in special sacks with additional embassy locks and seals. But the 'Black Office' could easily deal not only with seals, but with any locks.

One of the Embassies [says Maiskii] sent its mail in a special leather bag with an ingenious lock and with a lead seal, but those precautions did not save its diplomatic correspondence from being read, since, soon after the 'Black Office' received the first bag, they provided themselves with a key to its lock and a pair of pincers for putting in this type of lead seal. They even had spare cords, of a somewhat unusual type, in case they were needed for it.

Of course, the International Post Office in Moscow nowadays does not create such problems for the 'Black Office', but the 'Black Office' creates problems for the post office by not contenting itself with reading letters. The seizure of letters has been a new step in the centuries-old history of 'Black Offices', but the theory and practice of explaining losses has not been sufficiently worked out, and my persistence created a new problem.

Law and justice against the 'Black Office':
Second stage

AT the end of November 1969 I realized that two more of my letters
to Professor L. in the USA which had been sent with 'advice of delivery'
notes in September had been lost. These letters had no connection with
the questions discussed in the letters which were lost previously, and
their loss was unexpected, since from May 1969 onwards all my letters
had reached the addressees very rapidly, and I myself had received
letters from abroad with unusual efficiency and speed. It was beginning
to seem as if the 'Black Office' was sincerely repentant for what had
been happening to my correspondence and was now trying to atone for
its fault by processing my letters ahead of the queue. And now, once
again, two letters were lost at once, and both to the same addressee.
Naturally I at once wrote off a claim, pointing out that I was still waiting
for replies to my previous applications. At the beginning of January 1970
the following answer to these claims came from Kravtsova.

> To Comrade Zh. A. Medvedev,
> In answer to your application of 28/xi, regarding a search for
> registered letters Nos. 716 and 913, please apply in person to the
> Head of the International Post Office, Comrade B. I. Aslanov,
> between 09.00 and 17.00 any day (excluding Saturdays and Sundays)
> at your own convenience.

There was not a word about the old or new claims.

Hence, before entering into conversation with Comrade Aslanov, I
sent him an official application, in which I drew attention to the existing
rules on the material responsibility of the post for the fate of international correspondence and the time-limit for investigation for a given
claim, and asked him to pay me the compensation for the letters lost in
the period December 1968 to April 1969. I attached to my statement a
list of the numbers of the letters and gave the dates of submitting my
claims. In answer to this application, I received a letter from Kravtsova,
in which she said, 'I ask you, once again, for a final decision on your

application to apply in person to the Head of the International Post Office, Comrade V. B. [*sic*] Aslanov . . .'

The expression 'a final decision' put me somewhat on my guard, and I decided not to go and see Aslanov alone, but to take a lawyer, all the more so since my dispute with the post office had reached the stage where the matter was already becoming a question to be referred to the courts. And for this I would need qualified legal help, since I had never taken any case to court before in all my life. However, to find a lawyer who would take on my business was not at all easy. I went to four leading Moscow legal consultants, but none of the advocates who worked there would agree to take on the preparation of a case against the International Post Office, nor to take it to court. Usually they said that they were busy or had no experience or knowledge at all of the postal laws. Judging from first impressions, no one in Moscow had ever brought legal proceedings against the Post Office. As I was unable to obtain qualified legal help, I asked my friend V. to come with me to this discussion of responsibility with Aslanov, at which he had promised me a 'final decision'. I merely wanted at least to have a witness of this conversation.

On 3 February 1970, having fixed a visit by telephone for 16.00 hours, and having told several friends that we were going for a 'final decision', V. and I went to the International Post Office on Komsomol Square. The lady representative of the Claims Bureau wrote out passes for us and took us to the office of the Head of the Post Office, on the topmost floor. Going up the stairs, I noticed that the small modern building of the International Post Office is actually joined on to a longer, hundred-metre block, which penetrates into the prohibited, closed-off part of the territory of the Leningrad terminus. This block was the service part of the International Post Office.

In the office of the Head of the Post Office, five people were waiting for me. Two of them I knew: Kravtsova and Danin. Aslanov himself was a man of Caucasian appearance, aged fifty. He introduced me to his deputy, Malkov, and to another woman. They greeted me cheerfully, like a close friend.

However, Aslanov suddenly turned his attention to the fact that I had not come alone. 'And who are you?' Aslanov demanded of my friend in none too pleasant a manner.

I explained that I had invited a colleague, since he too had a number of questions he would like to put to the International Post Office, and I would like him to take part in the conversation.

'I invited only you, and not your colleague,' snapped Aslanov. 'We've

P

nothing to say to your friend. I'm asking you to leave, Comrade!' Aslanov turned to my friend. 'Go and wait in the waiting room!'

My plan to have a witness had broken down. I remained alone, one against five.

The conversation at first was quite calm. In front of Aslanov lay my thick 'file'. He explained to me, as Kravtsova had done before, that all my letters had been promptly forwarded abroad by the International Post Office, but why they had not reached the addressees remained unknown, since neither the American nor the British post had so far replied to the enquiries of the International Post Office. 'Look, you can see the copies of the enquiries which we sent abroad after you made your claims!' And he handed over a folder of filled-out forms.

The forms, of a yellowish-green colour, judging from them all, really were copies of enquiries for my claims. On the standard forms they had filled in the dates and numbers of my letters and the addresses in English. Everything was in order. But among the forms I was surprised to see enquiries about the letters which Aslanov himself had sent back with the accompanying instructions to the Special Section of the Institute of Medical Radiology. The Claims Bureau had sought these in England and in the USA as well.

I carefully reminded Aslanov of this, pointing out that he had been kind enough then to send me a copy of his covering letter to the Special Section, asking them to explain the rules of correspondence to me. 'So those letters were not sent abroad,' I pointed out. 'I saw with my own eyes that they had been opened. Why then are there international enquiry forms about them? Perhaps this sort of mystification is possible in other directions as well?'

And so the pleasant conversation came to an end. Aslanov began to shout roughly at me, and his subordinates in turn all followed suit.

'Why do you keep talking about censorship? There is no censorship. We are workers in a Soviet establishment, and you are insulting us. You know that the customs has the right to open not only packets and printed papers but letters as well, if there are grounds for suspecting that there is some prohibited article inside, or materials which could harm the state.'

'But what was there in my letters which was breaking the customs rules and could harm the state?' I asked.

This question caused them some embarrassment. They had no answer. It was perfectly obvious that neither Aslanov nor the others knew the contents of my correspondence, although Aslanov himself had sent them back to the First Section. In front of me were the 'public' post office workers, not those of the 'Black Office'. They had not read my letters, for them the secrecy of correspondence existed. But they were covering up the violation of the secrecy of correspondence by some other service, which did not share its secrets with them. They sent enquiries abroad, signed letters to the First Section, but the secrets of the 'Black Office' were secrets from them too. The enquiries abroad from the Claims Bureau doubtless also went through the filter of the 'Black Office', and they sent abroad only those which did not refer to intercepted letters. They did not reveal to their foreign colleagues their actions in destroying certain letters.

Aslanov's deputy, Malkov, now joined in the conversation.

'Why do you keep talking about the loss of letters? Prove to us that your letters have been lost.'

I replied that searching and proof is undertaken by the Claims Bureau, by nature of their functions. 'Advice of delivery' notes had not been returned to me, addressees had informed me that they had not received my letters. This was sufficient for me to put in a claim.

'That's not an objective proof,' stated Malkov. 'Your addressees may simply not want to answer you, and so they write that they have not received your letter. The "advice" note itself may have got lost, for it goes as an ordinary letter, never registered. And even if you did receive it, you could still say that you hadn't, we've no way to prove the contrary. For us, an objective proof of the loss of a letter is information from a foreign post office about it. And so far we have had no such information about your letters.'

(Here Malkov involuntarily explained to me why in the USSR they will not accept for sending abroad registered letters with *registered* 'advice of delivery' notes. By internal post one can send a registered letter with a registered 'advice of delivery'. The International Postal Conventions provide for registered 'advice' notes for international correspondence as well. But the postal rules of the USSR depart from the Conventions on this point, and only allow ordinary mail 'advice' notes.)

I reminded Malkov of Articles 42 and 43 of the World Postal Convention of 1964 which allow one to recognize a letter as lost if the actual fate of the letter is still unknown six months after the sender has notified the Claims Bureau. The posting administration for the letter has the right to pay compensation on behalf of other administrations which take part in the transmission of the letter, and which, after receiving the application in due order have not resolved the question in the course of five months. This reminder was more or less an exact reproduction of the actual text of the Convention. 'Consequently,' I pointed out, 'you can pay me compensation in Soviet currency, and indent for the appropriate sums to the British and American postal services, who have had the allotted time to make a search after receiving your enquiries.'

Here Danin, the Head of the Operational Department suddenly jumped up from his chair. 'You're trying to get rich at the expense of the Soviet state!' he almost shouted. 'You won't get anything out of it! You won't get any money! You see,' he turned to his colleagues, 'it's the same campaign as Tsukerman's. He's using exactly the same expressions as Tsukerman did!'

'Excuse me!' I broke in hotly. 'But I don't know any Tsukerman!'

'Please be quiet!' snapped Aslanov. 'We can all see that you're playing the same game as Tsukerman! But he got nothing out of it either. He bothered us so much that we brought a suit against him, for all the expense that he had put the post office to. He fought us in all the courts, but got no judgement in his favour. We're bringing a case against him now, and after that we'll bring a case against you, and the court will make you pay all the expenses of your claims. You think that all this searching comes cheaply to us. Due to you and Tsukerman, since March we've changed the whole system of dealing with mail sent abroad from the post office. Before that, we sent lists with the bags of registered letters, which gave the numbers of the letters. But that will not do any more. The Americans will accept registered mail from us, only according to the total of letters and not by the numbers on them. A bag with a hundred letters in it, that's all. As for the numbers, they then put them in their register themselves, if they want to.'

The cunning of the new system was at once clear to me. Up till now, the post office, when preparing the mail for, say, the USA, had made a register for each batch. The procedure for filling out this register was laid down in the International Postal Regulations. In the registers, in addition to the directions for delivery, the number of each registered letter was also listed. The registers of registered letters went abroad with each bundle of post and remained in the International Post Office of the USA as a document against which the arrival of a letter could if necessary be checked. But the sacks of post from the International Post Office were not loaded on to the aeroplane straight away, but went to the 'Black Office' for checking. If the matter had ended with checking, then everything would be in order. But the 'Black Office' illegally intercepted certain letters, including registered ones. To rewrite the register because of this was too complicated, and the post office itself had a copy of the original list. Hence they evidently simply crossed off the register the number of a letter which had been taken out and sent the register with the sack of mail in that form. Foreigners with no great wit could see at once that a letter had been removed. And since a search for a letter can be initiated not only by the sender but also by the addressee, the too frequent crossing out of numbers in the register would create an unfavourable impression. If, however, the postbag is accompanied only by a note stating the number of letters in the bag, the traces of the operation of the 'Black Office' are easily masked. If two or three letters are taken out of the bag, they can always be replaced by others, so that the total number shown on the accompanying note corresponds to the number of letters. Moreover, the Americans will not have a basic document from which to initiate a search for a lost letter. If a request is now sent, the Americans will have to search for the letter in their own registers, listing all the registered letters from different countries sent to a given state or large town. When they do not find the number of the 'lost' letter, they can send back the necessary form for the loss of a letter. These answers to requests can be shown to the client, placing the blame for the loss of the letter on the foreign post. And maybe it will be possible to get some dollars from the American post or francs from the French. However, it is hardly likely that the foreign postal administrations will agree to pay in currency for postal theft.

When I saw that Aslanov was explaining to me some specific details of postal operations, I quickly asked him for an explanation of the 'Moscow paradox', that international letters to Moscow addressees are delivered much more slowly than to addressees in other towns.

'That cannot be,' said Aslanov.

I quoted a number of facts, and promised to send him a large batch of envelopes of Moscow and Obninsk deliveries from the USA and other countries.

Here Aslanov's deputy, Malkov, joined in the conversation.

'Why, that's quite possible! Very few letters from abroad come into Kaluga Province each day, and the Kaluga post office can deal with them without delay. But there are tens of thousands of international letters arriving in Moscow each day. Therefore the Moscow post office cannot always manage to sort them and process them quickly. But it's not the International Post Office's fault. We sort letters by destination, and the Moscow letters are sent at once to the Moscow post office. If you want to know, in 1969, the flow of letters from abroad decreased and our people had almost nothing to do. Believe me, the letters were not in our hands for longer than three to four hours.'

If one is really to believe this, then the reading of letters on the 'way out' and 'way in' must be handled by different 'offices'. The Moscow mail on the 'way out' is checked by the 'Black Office' after it has been put in order by the International Post Office, while the post coming from abroad is checked at the Moscow post office, and there is a delay somewhere due to poor work on the part of the 'readers'. This difference may have arisen for many reasons. International letters from the USSR going abroad are initially mixed up with the internal mail, and are filtered out from it not in the Moscow post office but in the local communications departments which sort the mail. The sender may also post such letters directly at the International Post Office. It is unreasonable to check international mail independently at many places. But the checking of the mail has a complex function. To understand the true essence of a letter is possible only if one also understands the personality of its sender or addressee. But the interest in definite personalities and the collection of information on their behaviour and activity is decentralized over the provinces. The file on Zhores Medvedev is kept somewhere in Kaluga, and only the person responsible for this file can really recognize the importance of a particular letter of Zhores Medvedev in reading and intercepting it. Of course there are people, Solzhenitsyn for example, in whom a serious interest is also taken in Moscow; but even in Ryazan they do not leave him without attention. But most ordinary persons are only worthy of attention at the provincial level. In this case, their correspondence ought to be checked in a provincial 'Black Office'; but it is very difficult to carry out this checking. Zhores Medvedev, although he lives in Kaluga province, posts many letters from Moscow. And so do many other citizens of Obninsk. A resident of Tula may send a letter abroad from Leningrad or from Sochi during his summer leave. Hence it has proved necessary to centralize the checking of letters on the 'way out' from the USSR—all the more so since, according to the script they have written, letters are 'lost' only after they have passed through the Moscow International Post Office, and been 'forwarded to their destination'. If the interception of letters being sent abroad were carried out by the provincial post offices, then the Central Claims Bureau at the International Post Office would not have them marked on their list of letters sent abroad, and they would have to pay compensation to the senders of the 'lost' letters.

But with in-coming correspondence the problem is simpler. The International Post Office sorts it by provinces and sends it in separate batches for checking at the provincial post offices leaving only printed matter packages for the centralized censorship. The personal correspondence of citizens, for example, of Kaluga province is, of course, read with great understanding by the employees in Kaluga province. Moreover, the contents of out-going and in-coming international letters are two completely different problems. The information which must not be sent abroad, and the information which must not be received from abroad are very different and are doubtless classified in different instructions. In all these questions the Moscow post occupies a very special position, in Moscow there are the Diplomatic Corps, the Ministries, Academies, and so on, and there are certainly more international letters coming into Moscow than into all the rest of the Soviet Union. And yet the International Post Office in Moscow was opened only in 1962, apparently on account of the growth of provincial international correspondence. Until 1962 there was no International Post Office, and all foreign mail in to and out of the USSR apparently passed through some section of the Moscow post office.

I quickly grasped all this during my conversation with the employees of the International Post Office. But Malkov's explanation did not make the 'Moscow paradox' entirely comprehensible.

'But in that case why is the Moscow mail from abroad delayed so long after it reaches the Moscow post office?' I asked Malkov again. 'Even if there are tens of thousands of international letters per day, that is only a drop in the ocean of the internal mail processed and delivered to addressees in Moscow. Here the count runs into millions, but we all know that a letter posted in the morning in Moscow, to a Moscow addressee, reaches him either by the evening delivery or else next day. But an international letter takes a whole week on the same route, not even to a post office box, but just to reach the post office?'

The Deputy Head would not answer this question.

Towards the end of the conversation, I raised the question of the confiscation of printed matter and other things enclosed in correspondence by the customs. Every confiscation, I said, if it were legal, must be accompanied by a statement notifying the addressee or sender and explaining the reason, so that the breach of the customs rules would not be repeated, and the confiscation would not be considered as the loss or theft of the package. In this connection, I raised the question of the confiscation of *Science* from my personal correspondence.

In discussing this matter, Aslanov was quite categorical. 'Your subscription was not registered with Soyuzpechat, and we do not recognize it as a subscription. Hence we consider each successive number as a separate publication, and the customs has the right to confiscate it, if there are grounds for doing so. As for informing you about confiscations, we are not bound to do so. There is no such law, that we have to notify people about confiscations.'

I was very sorry that I was so poorly prepared for this conversation at the International Post Office, and had not taken with me my copy of the special printed instructions of the Ministry of Communications of the USSR, *Provisions for Financial Responsibility for the Loss of International Mail* (Svyazizdat publishing house).

Point 5 of these *Provisions* states:

The Ministry of Communications of the USSR is free from financial responsibility for international mail in the following cases:
(*a*) when the mail is confiscated by the customs and the fact of the confiscation is notified by a statement made in the appropriate form by the customs and the communications department . . .

Then come points *b*, *c*, *d*, etc., dealing with cases of *force majeure*, the expiry of search time, and so on.

The need to make statement on confiscation and to inform the sender about confiscation is also provided for in the *Customs Code of the USSR*.

I have, of course, described the content of the conversation in the International Post Office very briefly. In reality it took more than an hour, and was much angrier, with frequent digressions from the matter in hand. All of them in turn blamed me for lack of Soviet patriotism, since I insulted the Soviet post with my lack of trust and since my connections with foreigners were suspicious. Aslanov even doubted my scientific competence. I meanwhile tried to explain to him, but with no great success, that the post was a public service and not a branch of the militia or the KGB, that the main principle of the post was its responsibility to the *individual* client, who pays for the services of the post and the guarantees of the post, including the safety and secrecy of correspondence.

That very evening, I started to make enquiries about the mysterious Tsukerman, who had brought a court case against the International Post Office. He was obviously the first person in the Soviet Union to do this. A hundred years ago, when Karl Marx suffered losses and tampering with his letters to Prussia, he intended to bring a case against the Prussian post in a London court. 'If we do not have the means to force the Prussian post to be honest, then at least we can show it up before the London public!' he exclaimed in one of his letters to Engels. Marx was not able to put his idea into practice. But even if he had been able to lift up this stone of international law and reveal to the whole world the hypocrisy of the bourgeois post, the first state in the world to be founded on the principles of Marxism should hardly have decided to retain such detestable relics of monarchical regimes as the reading and interception of personal correspondence.

Was Tsukerman's case successful?

Within two days, I had Tsukerman's telephone number. A week later I was able to have an interview with him and to read through the imposing file of his suit against the International Post Office. The essence of the case was as follows. With Tsukerman's permission, I shall give a very brief account of the course of events.

B. I. Tsukerman works as a scientist in one of the chemical institutes, and his special subject is physical chemistry and mathematics. But he also has a very good knowledge of the history of law, and thanks to his mathematical memory and mathematical logic, he has become not only an excellent expert on law, but is also a capable interpreter of legislative acts. He was therefore often able to give his friends well qualified unofficial legal help. Thanks to this also, according to the testimony of a number of people who knew Tsukerman for many years, he normally would not let any breaches of the law with which fate brought him into contact pass without attention and study. This is what happened in the case of the International Post Office.

At the end of 1968, Tsukerman sent to a colleague at Oxford University in England a letter which undoubtedly was in the nature of private correspondence. The letter, however, was lost and did not reach the addressee. Then, in January 1969, Tsukerman made three copies of this letter and sent them to England registered and with 'advice of delivery' notes, posting them not all at the same time, but at intervals (16, 19 and 21 January). One of them was sent from Postal Department K-9 and the other two from the post office. These tactics were almost exactly the same as I had used a month earlier, but, as in my case, they did not save Tsukerman's letters from being lost. By February, it was clear to Tsukerman from the delay in his colleague's correspondence from England, that all three letters had been lost. Therefore, at the end of February, in accordance with all the rules, Tsukerman put in a claim, which was accepted for investigation in the Central Claims Bureau of the International Post Office.

P*

When the limiting six-month period stipulated by the International Convention for such investigations had elapsed, and, by the same Convention, the letters could now be considered as 'lost', there was still no answer from the Claims Bureau. Tsukerman therefore approached the Head of the International Post Office, B. Aslanov, with an application for compensation: 22 roubles, 5 kopeks. When Tsukerman had made enquiries by telephone, the Claims Bureau had assured him that the letters had been lost in England, and that the British Administration had not answered their enquiries at all, so Tsukerman naturally pointed out in his application to Aslanov, that this irresponsible attitude of the British post to registered letters could not be tolerated, and that the International Post Office of the USSR, which was bound to compensate him for the loss, should demand this sum from the British postal administration in gold currency. To avoid misunderstanding, Tsukerman quoted in his claim for compensation Article 43, Point 2 of the Universal Postal Convention of 1964 (ratified by the USSR) which says that *'payment of compensation must be made at the earliest possible date, and not later than six months from the day following the day of submission of the claim'.*

Tsukerman's application for compensation was dated 22 August 1969, exactly six months after the submission of the claim.

The Head of the International Post Office, Comrade Aslanov, left Tsukerman's application unanswered. A month later, on the basis of the Decree of the Presidium of the Supreme Soviet of the USSR on the rules for consideration of the applications and complaints of citizens by official personnel, Tsukerman wrote a complaint to the Minister of Communications of the USSR, N. D. Psurtsev about the illegal actions of Aslanov, and asked the Minister to put a stop to these breaches of the International Postal Convention and the Postal Code of the USSR. About three months later, the following reply to the complaint was received from the Ministry of Communications of the USSR:

10 October 1969
To Citizen B. I. Tsukerman,
   In accordance with your application to the Minister of Communications of the USSR, a check was made, as a result of which it has been established that your registered letters Nos. 187, 290 and 142 which you addressed to England were forwarded by our service to their destination.
   The International Post Office in accordance with your application have requested the postal service of England to inform them when and to whom they delivered the said letters.

However, at the present time, no definite answer has been received from the English postal service.

The International Post Office has written to England again, requesting that they make haste with the search for your letters.

If an answer is received that your letters have been lost, then you will be paid compensation from the English postal administration.

Deputy Head of the Chief Postal Administration
B. AMENTOV

The formula in Amentov's letter, making the payment of compensation dependent on a long overdue reply from the English post was completely illegal, being a breach of the articles of the Universal Postal Convention recognized by the Postal Code of the USSR. The clear legal mind of Tsukerman could not be content with this, and on 22 November 1969, he sent an application to the Procurator General of the USSR, R. A. Rudenko, asking him to protest against the decision of the Ministry of Communications of the USSR as being contrary to the law. In this application, Tsukerman wrote:

in view of Article 43 of the Universal Postal Convention, I put forward exhaustive arguments of my right to receive compensation *quickly*, without waiting for the results of further investigations. I also explained that the payment should be made at the expense of the postal administration of England, since 'having received the application in due order, it did not settle the question in the course of five months'.

By its decision regarding my complaint, the Ministry of Communications of the USSR has demonstrated its deliberate disregard of the law. It has not even condescended to attempt to answer my arguments. It considered it unnecessary even to allude to the law, by which it ought to be guided in making decisions. The only motive which is immediately perceptible in this decision (since it makes the payment of compensation conditional on receiving an answer from England) is an attempt by any means, scorning the law, to save the English postal administration from making the due payment.

I call upon you to do your duty and protest against this illegal decision.

The Procurator's Office answered Tsukerman's application fairly rapidly, in the following letter (no reference number):

To B. I. Tsukerman,

Your application sent to the Office of the Procurator of the USSR was forwarded on 28 November 1969 as No. 1/1062–68 for consideration by the Head of the Chief Postal Administration of the Ministry

of Communications of the USSR, from whom you will be informed
of the results of the consideration.   Section Procurator
                                                        (illegible signature)

By forwarding the complaint to the Postal Administration the
Administration of the Procurator's Office itself committed a breach of
the legal procedure for considering complaints and applications, laid
down in a special Decree of the Presidium of the Supreme Soviet of the
USSR. Hence Tsukerman once again sent a complaint to the Procurator
General of the USSR, drawing his attention to the improper action of
the Procurator of one of the Sections of the Procurator General's Office.
Tsukerman pointed out that these actions were contrary not only to the
Decree of the Presidium of the Supreme Soviet of the USSR on the
procedure for considering applications and complaints, but also to the
Instructions on Procuratorial Surveillance in the USSR, Article 14 of
which states that:

> The Procurator is bound to receive and consider applications and
> complaints from citizens about breaches of the law, to check these
> applications and complaints and, within the time appointed by the
> law, to take measures to restore the rights that have been violated,
> defending the legal interests of the citizens.

There was no answer to Tsukerman's new complaint to the Procurator's Office, even after the 'time appointed by the law' had elapsed.

In view of the categorical refusal of the International Post Office to
pay compensation for the lost letters, Tsukerman submitted to the
Sokol'nicheskii District People's Court in Moscow (the locality of the
'defendant') a detailed and well-grounded application of suit: 'On seeking compensation for lost registered letters.' The application was drawn
up in accordance with all the legal regulations and rested on the strong
guarantees of the Universal Postal Convention, ratified by the USSR and
of the Postal Code of the USSR confirmed by the Government.

The District Court called both parties to appear on 14 October 1969
(the Post Office was represented by Danin, the Head of the Operational
Section) and after a brief consideration, and without going into the legal
side of the case, decided 'to give the parties until 1 December 1969 to
settle out of court'.

Tsukerman complained against this decision in a detailed and legally
sound application to the Moscow City Court. The Judicial College on
civil cases called both conflicting parties to appear, and, as a result
decreed, 'The decision of the Sokol'nicheskii District People's Court is
to remain unchanged and Tsukerman's complaint unsatisfied.'

Tsukerman quickly made a complaint against this decision in a statement to the Chairman of the Supreme Court of the RSFSR, requesting 'the acceptance of this protest about the supervision procedure'. In this application he pointed out in detail that the decision of the Moscow and district courts was legally unfounded. However, the Supreme Court of the RSFSR would not enter into the details of Tsukerman's legal arguments. The Head of the Complaints Section of the Supreme Court of the RSFSR sent Tsukerman a letter on 24 November 1969 in which he said:

> Your complaint has been sent for consideration to the Chairman of the Moscow City Court, with the request that they inform you of the result of this consideration.

The Moscow court, naturally, confirmed its previous decision, pointing out, however, in a new letter to the 'plaintiff', that 'the defendant has taken the necessary measures to search for the letters which you sent. No answer has been received from the Ministry of Posts and Telecommunications of Great Britain.'

The Moscow court accepted without any doubts the version that it was the English post which was responsible and hoped for the pounds sterling which it expected would be obtained in compensation for Tsukerman's three letters. But Tsukerman did not want to wait for foreign currency, since the Convention guaranteed him compensation from the 'Administration at the posting end'. He once again complained of the decision of the Moscow Court to the Supreme Court of the RSFSR. This time the Supreme Court considered his complaint and informed him in a letter of 25 December that it 'remained without satisfaction'.

Meanwhile the time for 'settlement out of court' had run out, and the two parties had not come to any agreement, nor had the letters been found. Tsukerman therefore applied once again to the Sokol'nicheskii People's Court. On 22 December 1969, this court (case No. 2–2484) fixed an 'open pre-court session', inviting both conflicting parties to it. The phrase 'open, *pre-court* session' was new to the law, and it contravened the existing legal practice. It had several purposes, but the chief point was to avoid a proper *court* session, so as not to create the precedent of court proceedings against the post office. Everything must be done to stop the case going to court, so the session was called a 'pre-court' one. Having heard the statement of the representative of the post office that the search for the lost letters was going on and that all the possibilities had not yet been exhausted, the 'pre-court' session of the court decreed:

> The acceptance of the application of Citizen B. I. Tsukerman for court action is considered to be erroneous, and his case against the International Post Office is closed.

This decree was signed by People's Judge Karpovich and People's Assessors Zamyatin and Pendik.[1]

Tsukerman resolutely complained against this decision of the Sokol'nicheskii People's Court to the Moscow City Court, pointing out that it was illegal and contrary to legal procedure. The protest was exceptionally detailed and argued out on legal grounds. The Moscow court could not ignore the plaintiff's careful arguments. It was perfectly clear that his case was perfectly legal, and to avoid having to satisfy it would require some other more diplomatic means.

On 12 January 1970, the Judicial College of the Moscow City Court of Civil Cases considered Tsukerman's application, and decreed:

> The Decree of the Sokol'nicheskii District People's Court of 22 December 1969 is quashed: the case of B. I. Tsukerman against the International Post Office for the recovery of 22 roubles 5 kopeks remains unheard.

This was already a legal victory for Tsukerman. The case was not closed, but remained unheard, since the post office required additional time to search for the letters. It was still hoping to get a reply from the British Post Office. But one cannot go on searching for ever. According to the same International Convention, claims are accepted for investigation only within twelve months from the posting of the letter. The time for investigating a claim already made and the time for putting in a possible claim are two entirely different things. According to the Convention, the time for investigation cannot exceed six months, after which the letter must be assumed lost if it has not been found. Twelve months is the time within which the sender can put in a claim for a search to be made. If more than fifteen months has gone by since the posting of the

---

[1] In any Soviet court (including the Supreme Court of the USSR) sitting as a court of first instance, the bench consists of one professional Judge and two People's Assessors.

Professional Judges of People's Courts are elected by the citizens of the district over which the territorial jurisdiction of the court extends. People's Assessors are elected by special general assemblies of collectives of workers or citizens either at their place of work or at their place of residence. The Judge (who need have no previous legal training) once elected works full-time in the court; the People's Assessors are essentially laymen and perform their duty as Assessors for not more than two weeks per year—*Translator*.

letter, then investigation is impossible, since the post office cannot keep its records for any longer than that. Hence by fifteen months from the posting of the letters the post office will have already completely exhausted all means of searching for them and they should be declared lost once and for all. This fifteen months is the limit for the British post as well, if it really did receive the request and make searches for the lost letters. The fifteen months from the date of posting of the last of the three letters expired on 21 April 1970, and on 22 April all searches must have been called off. On 22 April, Tsukerman could renew his case against the Post Office if by that time he had still not been paid his compensation or his letters had not been found.

But Tsukerman decided not to wait until then, but to solve the argument sooner in a more equitable manner. Since all the official data stated that it was the British post which was responsible for the loss of the letters, Tsukerman came to the only legal way out; he decided to transfer his right to compensation to the British addressee. The British post, which was responsible for the loss, would have to pay compensation to a citizen of England and not to Tsukerman. The Universal Postal Convention equitably stipulates that the right to compensation belongs equally to the sender and the addressee, since it is not known who suffers to the greater extent from the loss of the correspondence. They can divide the compensation between them in some proportion or other, by mutual agreement. Thus Tsukerman set the International Post Office free of all bother and expense and proposed a solution which was most reasonable in the situation which had arisen. It was to be hoped that such a traditionally law-abiding country as Great Britain would provide the addressee with all means to compel the British post by law to pay the compensation for the registered letters they had lost.

Tsukerman, in strict accordance with Point 3, Article 39 of the Universal Postal Convention drew up a statement renouncing his right to compensation in favour of the English addressee and applied to the First Moscow Notary's Office to have his signature to this statement witnessed. This type of action by the Notary is laid down in the instructions of the 'Duties of the Notary' in the USSR.

However, the Notary's Office refused to carry out its notarial duty. Tsukerman tried to protest and to show that this refusal was illegal, but the Deputy Senior State Notary, A. Yakovlev, informed him in a written 'Decree' that this kind of statement can be witnessed only with the permission of the Foreign Currency Control of the Ministry of Finance of the USSR.

Tsukerman at once made a complaint about the refusal of the Notary's Office to witness his signature to the Baumanovskii District People's Court, and, in his statement, after setting out in detail the reasons why this refusal was illegal, he asked the court to compel the Notary to carry out his due notarial duty. Even by common sense it was clear that the Foreign Currency Control could not forbid a British citizen to seek compensation from the British post. The court, however, having received the complaint and called the parties to a session, decreed: 'The petition of the claimant is rejected.'

Then Tsukerman, as the Notary required, sent an application to the Head of the Foreign Currency Control of the Ministry of Finance of the USSR, Comrade V. Moshkin, asking him to give permission for the transfer of the right of compensation for the loss of the letters to the British addressee, since the official organs had informed him that it was the British post which was responsible for the loss. The Foreign Currency Control quickly replied that concerning this question, Tsukerman must apply to the Ministry of Communications of the USSR. Things had now come full circle. Trying to break out of this deadlock, Tsukerman made a protest against the reply of the Foreign Currency Control in a complaint addressed to the Minister of Finance. However, the Deputy Minister of Finance sent Tsukerman a letter, informing him that the 'explanation given you by the Foreign Currency Control is legal and based on the relevant decisions of the Government of the USSR'.

There was no way out, the only thing left to do was to apply once again to the Sokol'nicheskii District People's Court.

I too awaited the outcome of this court with great impatience. For if Tsukerman was able with his three lost letters to force the legal defences and capture a small bridgehead, then I could throw into this breach my heavy artillery of twenty lost registered letters and strike at the 'Black Office'. But there were no great hopes of capturing a bridgehead. No one had yet said that the court would really stand up for the law. The laws of the USSR were against the 'Black Office', but the servants of the law acted in concert with the 'Black Office', and, sacrificing their sacred professional duty, they tried in every way possible to conceal and protect from public scrutiny its criminal activity.

POSTSCRIPT APRIL 1970

On 23 April 1970 Tsukerman once again filed an application of suit against the International Post Office in the Sokol'nicheskii People's

Court. The session of the court to hear this suit was fixed for 7 May. Since sessions on civil cases are open, I too went to Moscow, to be present at the hearing of this case.

In the small courtroom, as the beginning of the court examination approached, all places were filled, but there was no representative of the defendant. I had begun to think that he would not appear and so would frustrate the consideration of the case. But this supposition, happily, was false. Exactly at 13.05 Danin, the Head of the Operational Section of the International Post Office, appeared in the courtroom, entering for some reason not from the corridor but from the Justices' 'consulting room'. After him came the Justices—the People's Judge and two People's Assessors. The Judge announced who the Justices were: People's Judge Aleinikova and Assessors Petrov and Kovalenko. After this, everyone sat down, and the court cases began.

First there came a case on a claim for alimony. This was quickly settled, and the court went on to consider Tsukerman's suit. The Judge allowed the plaintiff to speak, to explain the essence of his claims. Tsukerman explained in detail the history of his case and the legal basis of his suit. He also produced all the arguments which testified to the fact that the letters under discussion really had been lost.

After this it was open to the Court to put questions to the plaintiff. Both Assessors remained silent until the very end of the session, and Aleinikova put all the questions. The People's Judge's tone of voice, expression and whole attitude were full of disdain. Almost all her questions to Tsukerman were of the same nature:

'Where do you work? . . .

'Who told you to correspond with foreigners? . . .

'Do they know at your work about this correspondence? . . .

'What is the nature of your correspondence? . . .

'Could it possibly cause damage to the state? . . .

'Perhaps the addressee simply wants nothing to do with you and throws your precious letters away? . . .

'We know something else about your activity, Comrade Tsukerman. We know that you have an illegal underground practice as a lawyer. . . .

'And what are you writing down over there?' Aleinikova suddenly turned to a bearded man sitting next to Tsukerman. 'This is not an international case! I forbid you to make notes!'

Tsukerman quietly answered all these questions, hanging his head only in reply to the accusation of carrying on an underground practice as a lawyer: 'That assertion is a slander,' he said.

After the plaintiff's answers, the Section Head of the International Post Office spoke. He at once denied the suit, saying that there was no proof that the letters were lost. The English post, he said, had for some reason not replied to eight enquiries sent to them about Tsukerman's letters. However, England always replied quickly and precisely to all other enquiries from our post office. The reasons for this silence in the matter of Tsukerman's letters was completely incomprehensible. (Danin was hinting that perhaps Tsukerman had some special understanding with the English Postal Administration.) In this case, said Danin, there is evidence that the letters were sent abroad by the International Post Office, and hence all responsibility for their fate rests on the English postal authorities.

Then the plaintiff had the opportunity to put a number of questions to the defendant. There were two main questions, on arbitration and on action against the British post. Tsukerman quoted excerpts from the Postal Convention, according to which the Soviet post should bring a case against the British post, since the administration, by not replying to the enquiries within the appointed time, bears the financial responsibility. If it refuses to do this, then the question is transferred to a special arbitration authority in the Bureau of the Universal Postal Union.

Danin replied that the USSR was not going to trouble an international organization and bring such a case against the British post for a matter of 22 roubles.

The People's Judge in her questions to Danin first of all asked what all the work of checking Tsukerman's claims was costing the post office. Brandishing his folder, Danin declared that to check and elucidate all Tsukerman's claims in the post office had been a full time job for a year for a special worker who was paid 85 roubles per month. 'For you see, all the correspondence has to be translated into French, which is the official language of the Universal Postal Union.'

Then the Bench withdrew for a consultation. After ten minutes, the Bench came back again. Everyone stood up. 'In the name of the Union of Soviet Socialist Republics,' Aleinikova pronounced solemnly, 'the suit of Tsukerman against the International Post Office, claiming compensation for the loss of mail, is denied.'

The plaintiff had lost the case at the first level. But the law granted him the right to complain against this decision within ten days.[1]

---

[1] The 'Postscript April 1970', which is an interpolation in the original, breaks off here—*Translator*.

13

Preservation of the secrecy of correspondence in the internal post

ALMOST every adult on earth sends and receives letters, but by no means all of them engage in international correspondence. Hence people's chief concern may be about questions of internal correspondence. And there are not a few people who are concerned in various ways that international and internal civil rights should be respected. Moreover it is obvious that an Administration that does not honour the international conventions which it has signed will also be incapable of honouring its internal laws. As it does not honour the principles of secrecy of personal international correspondence, the system of 'Black Offices', those leeches of the postal department, cannot honour the secrecy of internal correspondence, and in this it is true to a two-hundred-year-old tradition. There remains only the question of quality and quantity; to check all the seven thousand million letters sent annually in the USSR would not only be impossible—it would also be uninteresting. Only rarely in the reading of the internal mail does it become necessary to destroy letters, and this leads to the comparative rarity of disputes between the post and its clients similar to those described above. Personally, I have never come into conflict with the postal department over internal correspondence; I have always received mine promptly. But certain facts on the partial checking of internal correspondence, with which I inevitably came into contact, have caused me to think about this side of the problem too. I shall describe them in order.

Thoughts about the possible violation of secrecy of correspondence in the internal mail first occurred to me at the beginning of 1968. In January and February 1968 there came to Obninsk a special sociological and Party Commission, appointed by the highest authorities, to check the attitude of mind and ideological and political level of the scientific and technological intelligentsia of the town. The question had arisen somewhere: were these 'science towns' a good thing from the ideological point of view, and ought scientists to be separated into such isolated scientific communities? The commission distributed about two thousand special 'anonymous' questionnaires to the scientists and specialists of the town, with various questions, some of an 'investigatory' nature. ('Do you listen to foreign broadcasts? What political literature do you read? What is your opinion of Soviet literature? Who is your favourite Soviet writer? etc.) In the vestibules of the institutes there were ballot boxes into which these questionnaires had to be dropped when they had been filled in. The report of the Commission was then considered by the highest authorities, and what results came out of this 'anonymous' survey of public opinion I do not know. But the intelligent secretary of the Town Committee of the CPSU, Comrade Fedorov, was dismissed after this for 'spinelessness', and we had transferred to the town from a country District Committee a tougher and more resolute secretary who began to 'normalize' the situation. During the time this sociological commission was at work I received from Moscow an invitation to an interesting session of the Scientific Council on the biology of growth, and I saw with surprise that they had invited me to a meeting which had occurred two days previously. Judging from the postmark on the envelope and the cancellation postmark, the letter had taken eight days to get from Moscow to Obninsk! Previously, letters had almost always reached Obninsk in two days, on rare occasions in three. A hundred kilometres by railway, not more than two hours' travelling time. Such a hold-up could, of course, occur by accident. But in the days immediately following, other letters from Moscow and Leningrad were also arriving at my flat seven or eight days after posting. I thought uneasily of the possibility that the letters of my internal correspondence were being read. But when I asked my colleagues at my own Institute and some acquaintances at other institutes, I learned with surprise that their letters, too, were being considerably delayed. By all accounts, this had caused a certain amount of trouble, since scientists had been unable to attend important meetings to which they had been invited. After the sociological commission had finished its work, the post once more began to operate normally. I had no grounds, of course, for connecting the work of the commission with the troubles in the delivery of correspondence in Obninsk (newspapers, naturally, continued to arrive on time) but I did not exclude the possibility that certain missing information about attitudes of mind in the town could at that time have been clarified with the aid of the 'Black Office'.

The second time I turned my attention to the problem of the internal post was also by chance and comparatively recently. An American colleague from the National Cancer Institute with whom I had been corresponding previously on the possibility of obtaining a special enzyme preparation for the treatment of acute leucosis which was threatening the life of the daughter of some friends of mine, and who had come to the Congress on Blood Transfusion in Moscow in 1969, told me by letter that he was willing to do anything he could to help treat the sick girl. After the Congress, my colleague sent his letter to my Obninsk address from Moscow in an envelope of the US embassy. On this long envelope my address at the Institute was typed in Russian, and the return address, (Embassy of the United States of America, Tchaikovsky Street 19–21, Moscow, USSR) was also in Russian. The return address was printed in the top left-hand corner of the envelope. There were no foreign words requiring translation on the envelope, and it should have reached me by internal post in not more than two to three days. The letter was sent by ordinary mail from Moscow on 15 September 1969. The stamp was cancelled by the postmark of Moscow postal division G-9, not far from the Embassy. The cancellation postmark bore the date '15/9/69' and the figure '12' signifying the time of cancellation, twelve o'clock noon. But the letter for some reason did not come straight to Obninsk, as usually happens with ordinary letters posted in Moscow. On the back of the letter was the red postmark of International Post Office 1. In the centre of this postmark was 25/9/69. For ten days the letter had been who knows where, and then it had ended up at the International Post Office which ought not to handle internal mail at all. The letter reached Obninsk on 28 September, as the Obninsk postmark testified. By that time I was no longer working at the Institute. But instead of them forwarding the letter to me, or returning the letter to the post office requesting that it be readdressed, the Administration of the Institute was interested in an envelope from the US Embassy. It was lying about somewhere in the Institute for a considerable time, and I received it from the Director's secretary only on 3 February 1970, and, moreover, it had been roughly opened and damaged—the latter fact without doubt due to the initiative of the Administration of the Institute. When I received the letter, my colleague had, of course, long since gone home, and the preparation about which we had been corresponding was no longer required. After so long a delay, I naturally wrote to thank him for his kindness, and excused my slowness in replying, which was due, I said, to his letter going astray, owing to my having changed my job. My colleague answered the letter, but once again through the Embassy. However, this time, he sent a letter with my own address (box number) in an ordinary American envelope to the Embassy, and the Embassy only had to stick on a Soviet stamp and drop it in the postbox. The address on the envelope was typed in English, but at the Embassy they had added in Russian, Dr Zh. A. Medvedev, Obninsk. And once again, the letter followed the same route, only quicker. The G-9 postmark was dated 2/4/70. On the back was the red stamp of the International Post Office, dated 6 April. The letter reached Obninsk on 9 April.

Thinking over this case, I remembered several stories of people who had received invitations to receptions at embassies, which had arrived after the receptions had taken place. Evidently, knowing this peculiarity of the post, the various creative unions (Union of Writers, Union of Composers, etc.), Academies of Science and other organizations always ask embassies not to send invitations to official receptions to the home or business address of the intended guests but to give the whole bundle of them to the Secretariat or Presidium. There the foreign envelopes are sealed up in Soviet envelopes of business type, and in this form they are then handed over to the postal service, evidently after some filtering. It is not to be ruled out that this slowness of the Moscow post is no secret to the embassies, and therefore, in the case of small receptions, they send out the invitations by messenger, and do not trust them to the post.

The adventures of the embassy envelopes led me to think that foreign-type envelopes are picked out of the internal post for checking, and that they come under the heading of 'international correspondence'. This assumption I quickly and easily checked, with positive results. I sent two envelopes from Moscow to my box number in Obninsk. One was an ordinary Soviet envelope; the other was a foreign one with the trade-mark of a firm, but addressed in Russian. The letter in the Soviet envelope arrived on the second day, without any signs of having been opened. The letter in the foreign envelope, which had been posted in the same letter box, arrived on the ninth day, with clear signs of having been opened. This letter had been sealed up with a water-resistant synthetic glue called 'Supercement', and the 'Black Office' must have had to do a great deal of experimenting to get it open. The same scheme was repeated a second time, posting a letter from Moscow to Moscow. The delay of the foreign envelope was less (three days), but it too had been opened, with consequent damage to the flaps.

The ordinary internal post coming to me until most recently was not read, but the 'Black Office' is more seriously interested in the correspondence of other citizens. Aleksandr Solzhenitsyn, the author, in the last few years has very frequently had letters of his lost, even registered ones. Some of his correspondents told him afterwards that they had been sent for and reprimanded because they had sent letters to him; these had not reached him. Once Academician Vinogradov invited Solzhenitsyn to the phonetics office to record on magnetic tape certain of his works for the phonetic library of the Institute. The date of the recording was agreed by letter. Academician Vinogradov was then unexpectedly summoned to the Frunzenovsko District Committee of the Party and told to cancel this recording. But unfortunately he could not do this, as the recording had been made the day before. However, Solzhenitsyn's repeated statements that this internal correspondence had not only been read but had been intercepted was met by certain of my acquaintances with obvious scepticism. Sometimes even I had had my doubts, since my letters to Solzhenitsyn always reached him. However, to test these doubts, I recently made a small experiment. Some relatives of Solzhenitsyn's wife live in Moscow, and when he was in Moscow, he often stayed with them for the night or even for two or three days. As I proposed, it would be possible to keep a watch on this flat for postal checking. At the beginning of April 1970 I sent two registered letters from Obninsk addressed to the flat in Moscow. One letter was to the owner of the flat. The other letter was also addressed to him, but bore the inscription in brackets '(for A. I. Solzhenitsyn)'. But before posting the letters I unsealed the lower flap of the envelopes and then sealed down both lower and upper flaps firmly with 'Supercement', which is impervious to steaming. (The ordinary postal glues can be steamed open very easily and lose their adhesive properties in a moist chamber even at room temperature.) I warned the addressees, so that they would not open the letters before I arrived.

Both letters were posted from Obninsk on 3 April, and reached the addressee on 6 April, i.e. without any appreciable delay. However, the letter with the inscription '(for A. I. Solzhenitsyn)', unlike the other, showed rough signs of having been opened. The reader had first tried to open the upper flap of the letter by inserting some sharp object in the usual gap at the top of the flap. (The layer of glue on standard envelopes does not extend to the top of the flap, and there is always a gap left for the 'ventilation' of the letter.) But I had glued the upper flap right to the end and it would not yield. Then, having damaged the top left-hand corner of the flap somewhat, the reader started to open the lower flap of the letter in the same way. But this would not yield either. Then, losing patience, he roughly opened the bottom flap, tearing it in several places, and tried to take out the letter. But the letter would not budge, since it had been lightly glued to the lower flap of the envelope. Then he tore out the letter with part of the flap, read it, apparently swore with vexation, since this brief little note contained nothing of interest, and put it back, paying no attention to the fact that he had put it in back to front. To seal the letter up again he carelessly smeared some ordinary post office glue along the edges of the flap, stuck the letter to the lower flap again, but on the other side than before. Afterwards, I carefully cut up the side of the envelope, and took out the letter with the piece of flap glued on to the side which had been turned round to the front, clean side of the envelope. On the other side of the folded letter a piece was torn off, which was glued to the flap of the envelope.

Solzhenitsyn, however, was not alone in attracting the attention of the 'Black Office'. We have already mentioned B. I. Tsukerman. With the help of the same method of water-resistant glue, he established that part of his internal correspondence was being read. If everyone who wants to protect his mail against the curiosity of the secret censorship would start to use synthetic glues and to fix both flaps of the envelope firmly, then there would be confusion in the ranks of the employees of the 'Black Offices'. The productivity of labour would fall off sharply. To open an ordinary envelope, as Maiskii pointed out in his pamphlet, presents no difficulty. It can often be opened easily without any steam, since the layer of glue, especially on the lower flap, is very insignificant and does not reach the edge of the flap. This phenomenon has, of course, already been described in fiction. Few of those who read Solzhenitsyn's *Cancer Ward* pay attention to the brief episode at the end of the story, when the hero of the novel, hurrying for a train, sends a letter.

> Oleg read it through, folded it, put it in and wanted to seal it up (from childhood he remembered a detective novel, where everything started from a confusion of envelopes), but no such luck! Only a shadow on the diagonals of the envelope indicated the place where the State Standard Specifications said glue should be, but there was none, of course. . . .
>
> It was the same with the second envelope; a shadowy strip, not sticky at all. Oleg for some reason always thought that this was not accidental. . . .

I have already mentioned an article in *Literaturnaya Gazeta* of 4 February 1970, entitled 'Labelled Atoms'. In this article the operation of the post was criticized on account of poor and slow delivery of letters on an All-Union scale. According to the results of experiments carried out by the newspaper, the letters of correspondents within the Union now take two to three days longer to reach the addressees than they did seventy years ago.

The newspaper put two fundamental questions to the Ministry of Communications: 'Why do letters take so long?' and 'Why do letters travel at different speeds?'

The Ministry tried to explain this by the theory of 'congestion' due to the great bulk of correspondence. And the *Literaturnaya Gazeta* seemed to accept this theory, seeing the solution in the mechanization and automation of sorting. Now the theory of 'congestion', that is of a 'queue' arising in the processing of letters, does not stand up to criticism. It is absolutely erroneous from a mathematical point of view. If a processing channel is insufficient to let the whole flow of letters pass at a given speed, then naturally a queue will be formed. But this queue should then progressively grow, and the delivery time should progressively increase. In a short time, in a dynamic system of circulation of mail, a state of critical overloading will arise, which can cause total disorganization of delivery. But this does not occur. Moreover, newspapers, for example, are delivered faster than letters, although in volume and weight the newspaper mail is much bigger than personal letters. This means that it is not a matter of jamming, but of some additional stage of processing, which normally might have been avoided. What contribution to the general slowing down of the flow of correspondence is introduced by the 'Black Office' is difficult to say, but it is perfectly evident that in the former tsarist times the 'Black Offices' dealt with their task quicker and better. 'Letters read by the censor in Russia,' affirms Maiskii in his pamphlet *The Black Office*, 'however cunningly they were fastened, did not bear even the slightest trace of having been opened, even to the most searching eye, even the experienced eye of the censor often could not tell that the letter had already been opened once. . . .'

As for the speed of operation of the 'Black Offices' in the olden days, it is unnecessary to remark that they were much faster than at present.

14

Instructive episodes, postal puzzles, notes and comments

WHILE working on the main theme of this investigation, and discussing it with colleagues and various people, and simply from my own memories and experience some interesting cases have come to light, puzzling occurrences, additional aspects of phenomena which do not quite fit into the general logical scheme of the book subject by subject. I was unable to follow up these digressions from the main theme in detail, and they are sometimes left hanging in the air, without being substantiated by other facts. Nevertheless I would still like at this point to describe some of these cases, in the hope that readers may be interested in some of them and may co-operate in working on them further. In the present study any fact, even a fragmentary one, is important, and may prove useful to other investigations of this problem or of associated ones.

(A) DIFFICULTIES OF A RARE LANGUAGE

It is easy, of course, to check letters written in Russian. It is not difficult to impose a control on letters in English, French, German, Spanish and other widely-known languages. But what is to be done if a letter is written in the language of an African tribe or in the language of one of the peoples of the island of Ceylon? Of course, such letters occur very rarely, and even printed matter in these languages comes into the USSR in very limited quantities.

We have already quoted Maiskii's evidence on how the Old Russian censorship coped with this problem. The following account will throw some light on how they cope with this problem today.

There is on this earth a small island republic which has less than a million inhabitants. However, the people of this land, although not very numerous, have their own unique language, and this language is carefully protected from foreign and 'international' words. For words which are common to most languages, such as 'motor', 'automobile', 'liner', 'bomb', 'intellect', 'silhouette', 'army', etc., new words are carefully formed in this language from original roots. And since the proportion of such words, due to technical and scientific progress, is increasing, the study of this language becomes more and more complicated. In Moscow there are several citizens of this country studying in various Institutes. From various pieces of evidence, certain students of this association of compatriots began to suspect that their correspondence was being read. Perhaps some letters were lost or were too long delayed, perhaps someone noticed signs that they had been opened. When they discussed this question, however, they rejected any real possibility of their correspondence being read, because of the difficulty of the language barrier. The postal censorship, in their opinion, could not have an employee who knew so rare a language sufficiently well, for to learn it without having spent at least a short time in the country would be very difficult. And, from a practical point of view, it seemed unreasonable to the students to have in the censorship an employee with such a rare linguistic experience just to check an extremely small number of letters. All the more so, since their country was friendly.

In Moscow there were not more than two or three such scholars and journalists who knew the language of this country. One of them was very friendly with the compatriots' association; he had visited the country many times, he had written articles about it, he had made lasting friendships there. One of the students suddenly got the idea that this Soviet friend might possibly be the expert who in case of necessity was brought in to read their letters. The students decided to check this theory. During the summer vacation, when they went back home, the following plan matured. In their country there was a certain activist, Miss S., who was very well known to the Soviet linguist and who had played a lively part in the work of the Committee for Friendship with the USSR. She was a relative of one of the students. They came to the following agreement with her. She was alive and well, but she would pay no attention to news about her death and expressions of sympathy in the correspondence between the students in Moscow and their friends back home. Such a correspondence was quickly got under way. From their country to Moscow and back again went letters with expressions of deep sorrow at the untimely death of poor Miss S. A little while later there was a reception at the Consulate to which the Soviet linguist was also invited. He went up to a group of his student friends and with great sorrow said to the relative of Miss S., 'We have heard that Miss S. is dead. What a loss for her country and for all of us. I should like to offer my sincere condolences.'

(B) COMPLICATIONS DUE TO ABSENTMINDEDNESS

In 1968 Mrs R., who lived in Moscow, received a printed matter package from a relative in the USA. In the packet, as well as the parcel addressed to her she was surprised to find a letter without an envelope. The letter was addressed to someone in the Soviet Union and had been posted in France. Mrs R. sent this letter back to the International Post Office with an appropriate explanation.

A well-known Soviet scientist once told me that on one occasion he received a sealed letter from an English colleague in England, but in the envelope as well as the letter, he was surprised to find a manuscript abstract of this letter, written in Russian. It was quite out of the question that this abstract had been put in by the sender. The sender did not know Russian, and he was well aware that his Russian colleague, who had been to England on several occasions, had an excellent command of English. The addressee naturally decided that this was the trace of the censor, who had made a summary of the letter and had absentmindedly forgotten it and had sealed it up with the letter itself. The scientist, greatly alarmed, wrote a protest to the highest authorities, attaching the letter and the Russian summary. The censorship was not, of course, abolished after this, but the person responsible for the mistakes was no doubt reprimanded and criticized at the Trade Union Meeting of the 'Black Office'.

But in this absentmindedness the modern 'Black Office' only repeated the mistakes of the old St Petersburg one. We have already recalled the case described by S. Maiskii, of how Spanish and Dutch letters were mixed up while being read by the censor. More interesting was the case of the censor's cufflink.

When one of the bags with the diplomatic mail was opened [states Maiskii], an amusing thing happened; the 'reader' dropped into it, by accident, of course, the gold link off his cuff. The Consulate in Petrograd, finding the cufflink in the bag, sent it back by the next post with a letter to the Ministry. The 'reader' who had thought his cufflink irretrievably lost, was delighted when he found it next day in the bag he had just opened. He took it back, and simply destroyed the accompanying letters, and thus the incident was closed. These cufflinks had a monogram on them but the letters of the monogram were 'O.B.', which are the same in both Russian and foreign alphabets. If, on the other hand, it had been some Russian letter, 'Ш' or 'Ф', it would, of course, have led the foreign consulate to undesirable conclusions. (*The Black Office*, pp. 17–18, 1922.)

(C) 'PROBLEMS OF PEACE AND SOCIALISM'

The international communist journal, *Problems of Peace and Socialism*, which has its editorial office in Prague, in 1962, after a certain provocative article on the contradictions of present-day capitalism, asked its readers to send in their comments on the points discussed. One such comment was sent by a responsible employee of a Moscow publishing house, a member of the Communist Party. This was a three-page, typewritten note. The employee of the publishing house sent his note by post directly to Prague. He knew that articles from the USSR were dealt with by the Soviet Group in the editorial office and that there was a representative of Glavlit there. Sending material to the journal ranks therefore with sending articles to any Soviet journal within the territory of the USSR. After some time the Comrade who had answered the appeal by *Problems of Peace and Socialism* was summoned by the Director of the publishing house. On the Director's table lay unsealed the envelope he had sent to Czechoslovakia. High-ranking employees of publishing houses are presumed to know all the secret instructions of Glavlit, and hence the Director did not mince matters in giving his subordinate an official reprimand for sending abroad 'unlicensed' material meant for publication. The letter was returned to the Director of Glavlit. The author of the article, however, rang up the Press Section of the Central Committee of the Communist Party and received the explanation that *Problems of Peace and Socialism* is an exception to the general rules, and correspondence addressed to that journal ranks as correspondence within the Soviet Union.

As was shown by the persistence of the outraged employee of the publishing house, the 'Black Office' did not know the instructions on the special status of *Problems of Peace and Socialism* and, apparently, prevented this journal from receiving any mail from readers who did not send it by business channels. After this case Glavlit made the necessary arrangements with the postal censorship.

(D) PROFESSIONAL REPUTATION

We have already pointed out several times that the Old Russian 'Black Office' was very proud of its professional reputation, and tried to carry out the reading of correspondence in such a way that no traces of it were evident. The present-day censorship, however, by adding to reading the piratical practice of impounding and destroying letters has definitely departed from this noble and humane tradition. But I was interested whether professional reputation had been preserved in the technical service of the 'Black Office'. In order to check this I made the following simple experiment.

I sent to England two registered letters with 'advice of delivery' notes, a short interval apart. One letter was sent on 10 February from Moscow and had as return address my Moscow post office box. The second was sent on 13 February from Obninsk and had an Obninsk return address. The contents of each envelope were harmless—an offprint of a brief article of mine from the journal *Tsitologiya* (Cytology). Printed offprints of articles are forwarded without any trouble. But in spite of the harmless contents, both envelopes were firmly sealed by a synthetic, water-resistant glue, both on the upper and the lower flap. It was impossible to open these envelopes without damage. But since there was nothing forbidden to be found in them, then, so I thought, they would be sent on, after being damaged, since the 'Black Office' already knew that Zh. A. Medvedev always put in a claim for every lost letter and had already prepared a court action on the question of compensation. To increase the amount of this compensation by 15 roubles would be senseless for the post. But the main cunning of the experiment was as follows. Both letters were sent to non-existent addressees, the British post would have to return them to me 'not known at this address'. I had had some rare cases of returned mail, and I knew that this was so.

In preparing the experiment, I assumed that the post would decide not to send abroad envelopes that had been greatly damaged by the censorship, but would transfer the contents of the letters into new envelopes. So I photographed the letters when they were ready for posting, to have pictures for comparison. The Obninsk letter came back first. Judging from the postmarks it had reached England in seven days, i.e. on 20 February. On 23 February, the British post, being unable to find the addressee at the given address, sent the letter back, and it reached Obninsk on 6 March. When I saw it I was astounded. All along the top and side folds, the envelope was stuck together with strips of brown paper, clearly not of British origin. Careful examination of the letter revealed the following. The censor, being unable to get the flaps open, simply opened the letter along the top fold with a blunt instrument, so as to give the impression of accidental damage, and had then stuck it up with a strip of paper. But on the return journey the letter was opened again, since the strips of paper down the sides were stuck over the British postmark, hiding the edge of it. The Moscow letter reached England in ten days and was sent back on 24 February. Its return journey, however, was a very long one. I found it in my post office box with two postmarks on the back. One postmark belonged to the 'International Post Office No. 1' and bore the date of 20 March. The second postmark belonged to Postal Department G-19 and had the date '25 March 70'. The letter had also been opened twice, at the top and at the sides, but the cuts had been stuck together with transparent sticky tape. Some years ago, such tape would have proved that the British post was responsible for opening the letter, but nowadays transparent sticky tape is also available in the USSR and so the question of where the letter was opened remains open.

Of course, the post will always justify itself and assert that the letter was worn through on the folds due to its long journey and shaking in the sacks, and the appearance of the letter actually was bedraggled, especially at the edges. But I took into consideration the possibility of such justifications. So I sent to England yet a third letter, hardly sealing it up at all, only lightly moistening the edge of the top flap. This letter, sent on 15 February, returned on 7 March in excellent condition.

(E) THE PRIVILEGES OF CERTAIN CORRESPONDENTS

In *Izvestiya* of 7 May 1969 (No. 107) a long article was published entitled: 'Mr Sionskii's Lost Bet'. In the article there was a detailed description of how Aleksandr Khrabrovitskii, who lived in Moscow, corresponded freely with Mr Sionskii, an employee of the anti-Soviet émigré organization, the National Labour Union (NTS), who also worked for a number of spying centres. Co-operation with the NTS, the headquarters of which is located in West Germany, is a criminal offence under Soviet law, and several cases of this type have been known and publicized in the press. However, Khrabrovitskii (whose life as a spy was described in detail in the article) not only freely received *through the post* numerous letters from Sionskii over the course of a number of years (more than 200 letters) but also a large amount of anti-Soviet literature. According to the article, the literature went and *was received* through post office boxes. Moreover Khrabrovitskii involved other citizens in various towns in his correspondence, and anti-Soviet literature in Russian started coming through the post to these citizens too. It was only possible to put a stop to the matter as a result of a complaint from certain unnamed employees of one of the university libraries, who protested that great quantities of the most double-dyed anti-Soviet literature in Russian kept arriving in the mail for their library from the NTS.

We see in this case completely free correspondence. No confiscations by the customs, no lost letters. Maybe this was an experiment which was allowed to flourish especially for the article. Why did the 'Black Office' grant Sionskii and Khrabrovitskii these privileges? Maybe Khrabrovitskii's correspondence was of a business nature and was posted with a form 103M. Khrabrovitskii's name, so I ascertained, was well known to a number of Moscow writers. Khrabrovitskii had written bold letters to them, offering his services to establish contacts with the 'free' world. Khrabrovitskii even treated his correspondence with Ilya Ehrenburg, whom he had boldly denounced for compromise, to the honour of publication in 'samizdat'.

I thought at first that 'Khrabrovitskii' was not a real person, but a pseudonym, but I was told that a man of that name really exists and seems to be going on working and has not been dismissed for 'incompatibility with his duties'. Since I do not know him personally, I cannot discuss the reasons why he is able successfully to negotiate all the reefs of the 'Black Office'. Returning once again to Maiskii's pamphlet on the 'Black Office', one could put forward the hypothesis that Sionskii must have known a special sign which is put on letters that are not to be subject to reading. Maiskii writes that, after the reading of letters, a special sign, unnoticed by the addressee, was put on them to indicate that the letter had been checked. This excused the letter from being read a second time in some other 'Black Office', say in Moscow or Tiflis, whither it was travelling from abroad via St Petersburg. Moreover the letters of certain people, even private ones, were not subject to being read (for example, the letters of the Minister of Internal Affairs, the Chief of Police, and so on—all those who were initiated into the secret of the 'Black Office' and received its reports).

But another case of correspondence with Sionskii which I know of can be treated with greater certainty. Some time ago, I learned that a certain worker in Moscow, a member of the Communist Party and an employee of a responsible establishment was carrying on an active correspondence with Mr Sionskii in private life, and was receiving books from him published abroad in Russian, including some of a sexual and erotic nature. Furthermore, when he was abroad on a tourist trip, this person went to see Mr Sionskii and talked to him as a representative of certain 'liberal circles'. When he was reproached for this eccentric behaviour quite recently, he replied that some one had to know about these things. But personally I had had no doubts about this, even some years back. I had come to know of this man through his friend Valerii Pavlinchuk, who has already been mentioned. And he aroused my suspicion that a 'double game' was being played; but Pavlinchuk would not listen to my advice, and this cost him dear.

To be as brief as possible, the matter was as follows. Back in 1963, a group of progressive physicists, who were fired with enthusiasm at that time by the course of democratization and the denunciation of the 'personality cult' proposed at the Twentieth and Twenty-Third Party Congresses, formed an active group in Obninsk. These physicists, who worked at the High Energy Physics Institute around which the town of Obninsk had been built, organized a weekly 'Scientists' Day' in the House of Culture. This was in the nature of a discussion club and was enormòusly popular in the town. They invited literary critics, composers, theatrical producers and social activists from Moscow to the 'Scientists' Day'. The writers V. Dudintsev, K. Simonov, V. Tendrya-kov, V. Kavernin and others, the littérateur V. Lashkin, the theatrical producer M. Romm, the poet Rozhdestvenskii, and many others well-known exponents of Soviet culture met with great success in this club. Even Marshal G. K. Zhukov, whose home was close to our town, came. Among the group of physicists who took and developed this valuable initiative, the central figure was Valerii Pavlinchuk, who was at that time still a research student and Party Organizer of the Theoretical Section.

On one occasion, an old communist came to visit us. He had actually seen Lenin and was an orator and historian, who was well known for his speeches against the 'personality cult' and in favour of restoring Lenin's standards in Party life. On the evening of the 'Scientists' Day', he made an excellent speech. After the speech the most active members of the 'Scientists' Day' held a supper party in his honour. At this supper it turned out that the old communist had not come from Moscow alone. He had brought a friend with him, an elderly man, who soon found a common language with the young physicists. This 'friend' then invited Valerii Pavlinchuk to visit him in Moscow, he made friends with him and began to supply him 'for friends in Obninsk' with various 'samizdat' publications, and sometimes with books in Russian printed abroad. Pavlinchuk and I had a mutual friend, a Laboratory Head in another Institute, an excellent man and a noted connoisseur of literature. This friend was not interested in political questions which did not relate to creative literature. One day, when Pavlinchuk had received some manuscript or other from this new Moscow 'liberal' 'just for two days', he found he could not take it back to Moscow himself on account of illness, and he asked this literature lover to do it for him. The latter had no great wish to get mixed up in the affair, but Valerii persuaded him, saying that he need not give his name, but just present himself as 'Comrade Pavlinchuk's friend'. The literature lover went to the elderly Party 'liberal' saying that he was Comrade Pavlinchuk's friend, and gave him back the parcel with the manuscript. After a pleasant chat with this new acquaintance, our Obninsk colleague started to say goodbye. Grasping his hand, the Moscow 'liberal' suddenly said, 'You know, "Comrade Pavlinchuk's friend" is really very vague. Can't you tell me who you are, your name and surname. It's not really satisfactory, is it? We've been talking together, but I don't know who you are.' Our Obninsk colleague formally introduced himself. 'Now we really know each other,' said the Moscow man with satisfaction, and taking out his notebook, he wrote down the name of his new acquaintance and his Obninsk telephone number.

Our colleague told me about this episode, and it alarmed me for some reason, so I questioned Pavlinchuk about his acquaintance in greater detail. Valerii's account did not cause me any doubt, although I did not then know about the 'liberal's' correspondence with Sionskii. He was always interested in *who* had read this or that work which he gave to Pavlinchuk, and if Valerii himself got something new and took it to him, then he was bound to ask *from whom* Pavlinchuk had received this manuscript. For the sake of scenic effect he always told Valerii to meet him in some unusual place, although they always arranged these meetings by a telephone call from the Moscow man's home. Among these rendezvous, for example, was a meeting at ten o'clock at night in the vestibule of the Moskva Hotel. Pavlinchuk, unsuspecting, told him everything about affairs in Obninsk. When the affair had matured, the dénouement was simple. Valerii had obtained a 'criminal' book by Djilas to read; it was found in the Section in his possession. A search was made in the desks in the Theoretical Section, and a number of other works came to light. Valerii Pavlinchuk was expelled from the Communist Party, he was dismissed from his job, because he had lost his 'pass'. Party proceedings were brought against other employees in the Theoretical Section, and some of them were dismissed, others were downgraded, reprimanded, and so on. Shortly afterwards, in the other Institute 'Pavlinchuk's friend' was deprived of his 'pass' and dismissed. The organizing committee for the 'Scientists' Day' was reconstructed. They stopped inviting literary men and people active in other fields to these 'Days', and what they talk about now I do not know, as I no longer attend.

After this, I met the Moscow 'liberal', who was corresponding with Mr Sionskii once more, at the funeral of Valerii Pavlinchuk, who died in summer 1968 from inflammation of the lungs. Although he was ill, he would not go into hospital for a long time, and when he was taken there in an almost unconscious state it was already too late. The chronic nephritis from which Pavlinchuk suffered made active chemotherapy impossible, and his kidneys could not cope with the increased burden.

(F) 'MEETING OUR LISTENERS'

In the broadcasts of foreign radio stations in Russian, there is a special programme called 'Meeting Our Listeners'. Besides the state radio services like the BBC and 'The Voice of America', there is also the special anti-Soviet 'Radio Liberty' which always says in every broadcast to the USSR: 'We look forward to your letters; write to us at this address', and they spell out the address, letter by letter. Now 'Radio Liberty', day after day and several times a day puts out a special announcement. In that announcement, the radio station expresses its doubts as to the possibility of building a communist society and asks listeners in the USSR to write in to it, saying what they understand by the word 'communism' and whether they believe or not in the possibility of building a communist society. And then they spell out their postal address in West Berlin. 'Write to us at this address!' appeals 'Radio Liberty'. 'We look forward to your letters!' This announcement is repeated after every anti-Soviet broadcast, sometimes conspiratorially changing the number of the post office box (*Lagerkarte*) in West Berlin. The old box number, they say, will not do now, we will spell out the number of the new one for your correspondence. And sometimes all these stations broadcast letters they have received, but, to preserve confidentiality, they do not give the names of the senders but say simply 'A student from Gor'kii' or 'A worker from Smolensk'. What letters can reach these radio stations through the post I do not know, and whether Soviet citizens write to the addresses given I do not know either, but I can compare all these appeals to write letters to the West Berlin or French addresses of 'Radio Liberty' to a savoury-smelling bait in the net stretched across the paths of international correspondence by the 'Black Office'. Sometimes, of course, it lets one such 'opposition' letter go through to West Berlin, so as not to dry up the broadcasters' source of inspiration. But, in the main, the 'Black Office' undoubtedly feels most grateful to these radio announcements, which help them to ascertain those people who still believe that the secrecy of correspondence is observed. But do the experts on Russian affairs at these radio stations really believe that it is?

(G) Is it possible to read a letter without taking it out of the envelope?

We have already noted that in the St Petersburg 'Black Office' many letters were opened simply with a bone knife or with the additional aid of a thin jet of steam from a special apparatus. The postal glue of Soviet envelopes contains a large percentage of starch (iodine turns it blue), and it comes unstuck very easily, not only at a high temperature, but even in a moist chamber. It is sufficient to hold such envelopes over water in a closed box at room temperature and they open easily.

But sometimes letters are stuck with synthetic water-resistant glue or special sticky tape which does not yield to steaming. What is to be done with them, if owing to the nature of the letter, the censor does not want the envelope to show obvious traces of having been opened? I have heard three hypotheses concerning this case.

According to the first hypothesis, the letter can be read, without being opened, in infra-red light using a special screen. But in the case of letters which are folded several times, this is of course not at all easy.

According to the second hypothesis, the censor can draw out the letter through a tear at the side or bottom of the envelope, or through the clearance of the flap, by rolling it in a special device on to a thin rod. Such tears at the side or on top (as if from jostling *en route*) are very often encountered on foreign envelopes.

The third hypothesis is that through such a tear or through the clearance in the flap, it is possible to introduce a thin optical device into the letter; this device is fixed into a flexible tube, and by turning it to the various sides of a folded letter it is easy to read the text (this is especially easy to do with long envelopes of foreign manufacture in which the letter is put folded in only one plane). These optical systems are similar to the 'peep-holes' which are nowadays recommended for installing in doors. They give a wide field of view even when they are brought right up close to an object. These devices are almost identical with optical gastroscopes and cystoscopes. Nowadays a doctor, by introducing a thin flexible tube through the urinary canal, can illuminate and observe ('read') the walls of the bladder. The Japanese cystoscopes are said to be especially good. It is not impossible that the employees of the 'Black Office', who on account of their profession must possess exceptional erudition, actually use the most modern techniques in their work.

(H) YOUR NAME IS ON OUR CHECK-LIST

At the end of June 1969 I was worried about the long time a parcel of books sent by Professor J. was taking to reach me from the USA. This was creative literature, about ten 'pocket' novels, which would make good reading matter in the train. I decided on this occasion to telephone directly to the department of the International Post Office which dealt with printed matter. But, of course, you cannot ask over the telephone: 'Where is your censorship office for journals and books?' I began to study the postmarks of the International Post Office. On the receipts which are issued when registered letters are handed in in the main hall there is a postmark which reads 'International Post Office-6'. This means that the Section of the International Post Office which is open to everyone is called Section 6. In the main Moscow Post Office in Kirov Street, the business hall, according to the postmarks, is Department 8. Then I noticed that when registered letters are handed in at Postal Department K-9, in the Main Telegraph building on Gor'kii Street, the number of the letter is entered in a register bearing the legend 'International Post Office-2'. Evidently, Section 2 collects outgoing international mail from the other post offices. But on the envelope from the US Embassy and on the copy of Aslanov's letter to the First Section of the Institute was the postmark: 'International Post Office-1'. The same postmark 'International Post Office-1' was on all the envelopes of printed matter given to me in a certain Moscow editorial office, and these were covers from printed matter which, evidently, would bear a hexagon and not a double angle. I had also found the postmark 'International Post Office-1' on a medical abstract journal, a very thin one which arrived without an envelope with the address written directly on the cover of the journal. In the Central Medical Library this journal had 'International Post Office-1' postmarks, but in our Institute in Obninsk it had only the Obninsk postmark.

But on issues of this journal of the same date, in spite of the different circular postmarks, there was generally the same personal check number of the large type (for example, 62 or 10). This means that the Obninsk issues also pass through Section 1, but it does not put its postmark on them. From all this I concluded that Section 1 is the first to come into contact with printed matter arriving from abroad, and the censorship department evidently forms part of it. It would not be profitable to keep moving them from place to place.

Having come to this conclusion, I rang up the official number of the International Post Office, which is quoted on all their forms (22-8-69-56) and asked them to give me the telephone number of International Post Office-1, that is, Section No. 1. When they asked why I needed that number, I firmly explained that several issues of a journal which I had on international subscription had not arrived. They gave me the telephone number (29-4-62-72), from which I judged Section 1 must be in another building. The figures 29-4 also come at the beginning of the telephone number of the Head of the Station Post Office at the Kazan terminus in Moscow, a gigantic building, over a hundred metres long and with two broad twelve-storey wings. In this building, which has a volume of not less than 400,000 cubic metres, it is possible, of course, to put International Post Office-1 with all its services, otherwise why should a railway station post office have twelve storeys? (Though I may be wrong about the site of the Sections which interest me.) I telephoned the number I had been given. Someone picked up the receiver. In an authoritative tone I started to inform Section 1 about the loss of the copies of *Science* which I had on subscription and the loss of the parcel of books. The person listening was at first taken aback, and then started to ask whom they were dealing with. I gave my name and surname. The voice at the other end changed at once. With a faint note of respect, he categorically denied any possibility of anything being lost in my mail. 'Your name, Comrade Medvedev, is on our *check-list*.' (He gave this word a special emphasis.) 'Everything which comes for you is sorted at once and sent on to its destination. No losses are possible, we can answer for that!'

To what destination it is sent he did not say. But, in 1970, international letters started coming to me more slowly. Not so slowly as to Moscow, but all the same noticeably more slowly than in 1968 and 1969. The average time taken by air-letters from the USA has increased from 7.2 to 11 days. Evidently this is what one pays for the high honour of having one's name *on the check-list*.

Conclusion

I do not know what to say in conclusion to this work. I can tell my readers only one thing. If, dear readers, you have some comment, additional material or opinions on this manuscript, please do not send them to me by post, neither to my Obninsk address nor to my Moscow one. Please give them to me in person.

ZH. A. MEDVEDEV

Obninsk
September 1969–April 1970